Unity 2018 By Example

Second Edition

Learn about game and virtual reality development by creating five engaging projects

Alan Thorn

BIRMINGHAM - MUMBAI

Unity 2018 By Example
Second Edition

Copyright © 2018 Packt Publishing

All rights reserved. No part of this book may be reproduced, stored in a retrieval system, or transmitted in any form or by any means, without the prior written permission of the publisher, except in the case of brief quotations embedded in critical articles or reviews.

Every effort has been made in the preparation of this book to ensure the accuracy of the information presented. However, the information contained in this book is sold without warranty, either express or implied. Neither the authors, nor Packt Publishing or its dealers and distributors, will be held liable for any damages caused or alleged to have been caused directly or indirectly by this book.

Packt Publishing has endeavored to provide trademark information about all of the companies and products mentioned in this book by the appropriate use of capitals. However, Packt Publishing cannot guarantee the accuracy of this information.

Commissioning Editor: Kunal Chaudhari
Acquisition Editor: Larissa Pinto
Content Development Editor: Onkar Wani
Technical Editor: Ralph Rosario
Copy Editor: Safis Editing
Project Coordinator: Devanshi Doshi
Proofreader: Safis Editing
Indexer: Rekha Nair
Graphics: Jason Monteiro
Production Coordinator: Aparna Bhagat

First published: March 2016

Second edition: July 2018

Production reference: 1300718

Published by Packt Publishing Ltd.
Livery Place
35 Livery Street
Birmingham B3 2PB, UK.

ISBN 978-1-78839-870-1

www.packtpub.com

mapt.io

Mapt is an online digital library that gives you full access to over 5,000 books and videos, as well as industry leading tools to help you plan your personal development and advance your career. For more information, please visit our website.

Why subscribe?

- Spend less time learning and more time coding with practical eBooks and Videos from over 4,000 industry professionals
- Learn better with Skill Plans built especially for you
- Get a free eBook or video every month
- Mapt is fully searchable
- Copy and paste, print, and bookmark content

PacktPub.com

Did you know that Packt offers eBook versions of every book published, with PDF and ePub files available? You can upgrade to the eBook version at www.PacktPub.com and as a print book customer, you are entitled to a discount on the eBook copy. Get in touch with us at service@packtpub.com for more details.

At www.PacktPub.com, you can also read a collection of free technical articles, sign up for a range of free newsletters, and receive exclusive discounts and offers on Packt books and eBooks.

Contributors

About the author

Alan Thorn is an educator, author, and multidisciplinary games-developer with 18 years of tech-industry experience. He is currently Head of Department for the Games Design and Development MA degree at the BAFTA-winning National Film and Television School, London. He has written 27 technical books on game development and presented 29 online training courses. He founded the game-studio Wax Lyrical Games and created the award-winning game Baron Wittard: Nemesis of Ragnarok.

About the reviewer

Adam Larson started programming professionally in 2005. He has shipped 14 console games, 2 PC titles, and 8 mobile games. In 2012, he founded a company that focused on using Unity for business applications. He spent the following 5 years building a million dollar agency that built high-end software. Recently, he moved to another start-up that focuses on revolutionizing the banking industry. When he isn't doing something with technology, you will find him spending time with his wife and three kids.

Packt is Searching for Authors Like You

If you're interested in becoming an author for Packt, please visit `authors.packtpub.com` and apply today. We have worked with thousands of developers and tech professionals, just like you, to help them share their insight with the global tech community. You can make a general application, apply for a specific hot topic that we are recruiting an author for, or submit your own idea.

Table of Contents

Preface	**vii**
Chapter 1: Unity Fundamentals	**1**
Game design	1
Getting started – Unity and projects	2
Projects and project folders	4
Importing assets	9
Starting a level	15
Transformations and navigation	20
Scene building	30
Lighting and sky	35
Play testing and the Game tab	41
Adding a water plane	50
Adding a coin to collect	57
Summary	59
Test your knowledge	60
Further Reading	61
Chapter 2: Creating a Collection Game	**63**
Creating a coin material	64
C# scripting in Unity	74
Counting coins	78
Code Sample 2.3	79
Collecting coins	79
Code Sample 2.5	87
Coins and prefabs	87
Timers and countdowns	91
Code Sample 2.6	94

Table of Contents

Celebrations and fireworks!	**96**
Code Sample 2.7	100
Play testing	**101**
Building	**104**
Summary	**115**
Test your knowledge	**116**
Further reading	**117**
Chapter 3: Creating a Space Shooter	**119**
Looking ahead – the completed project	**120**
Getting started with a space shooter	**121**
Creating a player object	**127**
Player input	**133**
Code Sample 3.1	135
Configuring the game camera	**136**
Bounds locking	**143**
Code Sample 3.2	144
Health	**145**
Code Sample 3.3	147
Death and particles	**148**
Code Sample 3.4	151
Enemies	**156**
Code Sample 3.6	161
Code Sample 3.7	163
Code Sample 3.8	166
Enemy spawning	**168**
Code Sample 3.9	169
Summary	**172**
Test your knowledge	**172**
Further reading	**173**
Chapter 4: Continuing the Space Shooter	**175**
Guns and gun turrets	**176**
Ammo prefabs	**178**
Code Sample 4-1	184
Ammo spawning	**185**
Code Sample 4.2	188
Code Sample 4.3	192
User controls	**198**
Scores and scoring – UI and text objects	**202**

Working with scores – scripting with text	**210**
Code Sample 4.4	212
Polishing	**214**
Testing and diagnosis	**219**
Building	**223**
Summary	**224**
Test your knowledge	**225**
Further Reading	**226**
Chapter 5: Creating a 2D Adventure Game	**227**
A 2D Adventure – getting started	**228**
Importing assets	**229**
Creating an environment – getting started	**234**
Environment Physics	**242**
Creating a player	**249**
Scripting the player movement	**262**
Code Sample 5.1	266
Optimization	**270**
Summary	**276**
Test your knowledge	**277**
Further reading	**277**
Chapter 6: Continuing the 2D Adventure	**279**
Moving platforms	**280**
Code Sample 6.1	283
Creating other scenes – levels 2 and 3	**284**
Kill zones	**286**
Code Sample 6.2	287
The UI health bar	**289**
Code Sample 6.3	301
Ammo and hazards	**302**
Gun turrets and ammo	**312**
NPCs and quests	**314**
Code Sample 6.8	319
Summary	**325**
Test your knowledge	**325**
Further Reading	**326**
Chapter 7: Creating Artificial Intelligence	**327**
An overview of the project	**328**
Getting started	**329**
Terrain construction	**334**

Navigation and navigation meshes	**343**
Building an NPC	**350**
Code Sample 7.1	354
Creating patrolling NPCs	**355**
Summary	**362**
Test your knowledge	**363**
Further Reading	**364**
Chapter 8: Continuing with Intelligent Enemies	**365**
Enemy AI – range of sight	**365**
Code Sample 8.1	368
An overview of Finite State Machines	**373**
Code Sample 8.2	376
The Patrol state	**377**
Code Sample 8.3	378
The Chase state	**380**
Code Sample 8.4	382
The Attack state	**382**
Code Sample 8.5	387
Summary	**389**
Test your knowledge	**390**
Further Reading	**391**
Chapter 9: Entering Virtual Reality	**393**
Project Overview – Getting Started	**393**
Setting Scene Lighting	**396**
Post-Processing Stack 2	**407**
Preparing for VR	**414**
Summary	**422**
Test your knowledge	**423**
Chapter 10: Completing the VR Game	**425**
Object Pool and Spawning	**426**
Code Sample 10.1	428
Code Sample 10.2	429
Creating Intelligent Enemies – Navigation	**431**
Creating Intelligent Enemies – FSMs	**437**
Code Sample 10.3	440
Code Sample 10.4	442
Attack and Damage	**443**
Code Sample 10.5	448
Summary	**450**
Test your knowledge	**450**

Appendix: Test Your Knowledge Answers	**451**
Chapter 1- Unity Fundamentals	**451**
Chapter 2- Creating a Collection Game	**452**
Chapter 3- Creating a Space Shooter	**452**
Chapter 4- Continuing the Space Shooter	**453**
Chapter 5- Creating a 2D Adventure	**453**
Chapter 6- Continuing the 2D Adventure	**454**
Chapter 7- Creating Artificial Intelligence	**454**
Chapter 8- Continuing with Intelligent Enemies	**455**
Chapter 9- Entering Virtual Reality	**455**
Chapter 10- Completing the VR Game	**456**
Other Books You May Enjoy	**457**
Leave a review - let other readers know what you think	459
Index	**461**

Preface

Video games are a cultural phenomenon that has captivated, entertained, and moved billions of people worldwide over the past 50 years. As an industry and movement, video games are an exciting place to be, both for the developer and the artist. In these roles, your vision, ideas, and work can influence wide audiences, shaping and changing generation after generation in an unprecedented way. In more recent times, there's been a general movement toward democratizing game development, making the development process simpler, smoother, and more accessible to a wider audience, including developers perhaps working from home on a very limited budget. Instrumental in this movement is the Unity engine, which forms the main subject of this book. The Unity engine is a computer program that works with your existing asset pipeline (such as 3D modeling software) and is intended for compiling video games that work seamlessly across multiple platforms and devices, including Windows, Mac, Linux, Android, iOS, and Windows Phone. Using Unity, developers import ready-made assets (such as music, textures, and 3D models), and assemble them into a coherent whole, forming a game world that works by a unified logic. Unity is an amazing program. The latest version is free for most people to download and use, and it works well with many other programs, including free software such as GIMP and Blender. This book focuses on the Unity engine and how it can be used in a practical context for making playable and fun games. No prior knowledge of Unity is expected, although some knowledge of programming and scripting (such as JavaScript, ActionScript, C, C++, Java, or C#) would be beneficial. Let's now take a look at what this book covers, on a chapter-by-chapter basis.

Preface

Who this book is for

You don't need to have any previous experience with Unity to enjoy Unity 2018 by Example, although you need to have basic knowledge of C#.

What this book covers

This book explores how to use the Unity engine in a hands-on, practical way by looking at concrete examples that result in real-world playable games. Specifically, it focuses on the implementation of 5 distinct projects divided across 10 chapters, 2 chapters per project. Let's take a look at what these projects are:

Chapter 1, *Unity Fundamentals*, begins our journey into Unity by creating a first-person collection game. This is a great starting point if you're totally new to Unity and are ready to create your first game.

Chapter 2, *Creating a Collection Game*, continues from the previous chapter and completes the first project. It assumes that you have completed the first chapter and brings a closure to our project, leading neatly to the next chapter.

Chapter 3, *Creating A Space Shooter*, marks the beginning of our second project, focusing on the creation of a space shooter game. Here, we'll create a project in which the player must shoot the oncoming enemies.

Chapter 4, *Continuing the Space Shooter*, completes the space shooter project, taking the project from its state in the previous chapter and adding final touches to it.

Chapter 5, *Creating a 2D Adventure Game*, enters the world of 2D and UI functionality. Here, we'll explore Unity's wide range of 2D features in making a side-view platformer game that relies on 2D physics.

Chapter 6, *Continuing the 2D Adventure*, completes the 2D adventure game project that was started in the previous chapter, adding the final touches and linking it together with the overarching game logic. This is a great place to see how multiple parts and facets of a game come together to form a whole.

Chapter 7, *Creating Artificial Intelligence*, focuses on artificial intelligence and creating enemies that can patrol, chase, and attack the player's character at relevant times, while cleverly navigating their way around the level.

Chapter 8, *Continuing with Intelligent Enemies*, brings closure to the AI project started in the previous chapter. Here, we'll see how to use finite-state machines to achieve powerful intelligence functionality that'll help us in a variety of scenarios.

Chapter 9, Entering Virtual Reality, explores how to create a first-person shooter in VR where the player must tackle waves on oncoming enemies. In this chapter, we'll lay the foundations for creating a VR game.

Chapter 10, Completing the VR Game, completes the VR project by adding gameplay elements, core functionality, and by creating a build.

Appendix, Test Your Knowledge Answers, the answers to the Test Your Knowledge section of each chapter.

To get the most out of the book

This book contains almost everything you need to follow along. Each chapter considers practical, real-world projects for learning Unity and includes companion files that can be downloaded and used. The only thing you need, apart from this book and your concentration, is a copy of the latest version of Unity. At the time of writing, this is Unity 5.3.1. This software is available for free as a personal edition, and it can be downloaded from the Unity website at https://unity3d.com/. In addition to Unity, if you want to create props, character models, and other 3D assets, you'll also need 3D modeling and animation software, such as 3DS Max, Maya, or Blender; you'll also need image editing software, such as Photoshop or GIMP. Blender can be downloaded and used for free from http://www.blender.org/. Also, GIMP can be downloaded and used for free from https://www.gimp.org/.

Download the example code files

You can download the example code files for this book from your account at http://www.packtpub.com. If you purchased this book elsewhere, you can visit http://www.packtpub.com/support and register to have the files emailed directly to you.

You can download the code files by following these steps:

1. Log in or register at http://www.packtpub.com.
2. Select the SUPPORT tab.
3. Click on Code Downloads & Errata.
4. Enter the name of the book in the Search box and follow the on-screen instructions.

Preface

Once the file is downloaded, please make sure that you unzip or extract the folder using the latest version of:

- WinRAR / 7-Zip for Windows
- Zipeg / iZip / UnRarX for Mac
- 7-Zip / PeaZip for Linux

The code bundle for the book is also hosted on GitHub at https://github.com/PacktPublishing/Unity-2018-By-Example-Second-Edition. In case there's an update to the code, it will be updated on the existing GitHub repository.

We also have other code bundles from our rich catalog of books and videos available at https://github.com/PacktPublishing/. Check them out!

Download the color images

We also provide a PDF file that has color images of the screenshots/diagrams used in this book. You can download it here:https://www.packtpub.com/sites/default/files/downloads/Unity2018ByExampleSecondEdition_ColorImages.pdf.

Conventions used

There are a number of text conventions used throughout this book.

`CodeInText`: Indicates code words in text, database table names, folder names, filenames, file extensions, pathnames, dummy URLs, user input, and Twitter handles. For example; "Mount the downloaded `WebStorm-10*.dmg` disk image file as another disk in your system."

A block of code is set as follows:

```
[default]
exten => s,1,Dial(Zap/1|30)
exten => s,2,Voicemail(u100)
exten => s,102,Voicemail(b100)
exten => i,1,Voicemail(s0)
```

When we wish to draw your attention to a particular part of a code block, the relevant lines or items are set in bold:

```
[default]
exten => s,1,Dial(Zap/1|30)
exten => s,2,Voicemail(u100)
exten => s,102,Voicemail(b100)
exten => i,1,Voicemail(s0)
```

Any command-line input or output is written as follows:

```
# cp /usr/src/asterisk-addons/configs/cdr_mysql.conf.sample
    /etc/asterisk/cdr_mysql.conf
```

Bold: Indicates a new term, an important word, or words that you see on the screen, for example, in menus or dialog boxes, also appear in the text like this. For example: "Select **System info** from the **Administration** panel."

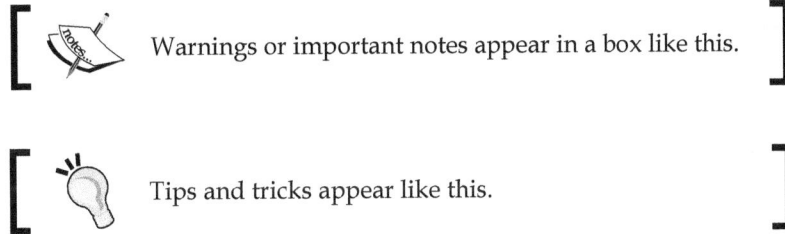

Get in touch

Feedback from our readers is always welcome.

General feedback: Email `feedback@packtpub.com`, and mention the book's title in the subject of your message. If you have questions about any aspect of this book, please email us at `questions@packtpub.com`.

Errata: Although we have taken every care to ensure the accuracy of our content, mistakes do happen. If you have found a mistake in this book we would be grateful if you would report this to us. Please visit, `http://www.packtpub.com/submit-errata`, selecting your book, clicking on the Errata Submission Form link, and entering the details.

Piracy: If you come across any illegal copies of our works in any form on the Internet, we would be grateful if you would provide us with the location address or website name. Please contact us at `copyright@packtpub.com` with a link to the material.

If you are interested in becoming an author: If there is a topic that you have expertise in and you are interested in either writing or contributing to a book, please visit `http://authors.packtpub.com`.

Reviews

Please leave a review. Once you have read and used this book, why not leave a review on the site that you purchased it from? Potential readers can then see and use your unbiased opinion to make purchase decisions, we at Packt can understand what you think about our products, and our authors can see your feedback on their book. Thank you!

For more information about Packt, please visit `packtpub.com`.

1
Unity Fundamentals

This chapter starts the first project on our list, which will be a fun collection game. Remember, it doesn't matter if you've never used Unity before. We'll go through everything necessary step by step. By the end of the next chapter, you'll have pieced together a simple, but complete and functional, game. This is an important thing to achieve because you'll get familiar with a start-to-end game development workflow. This chapter will demonstrate the following topics:

- Game design
- Projects and folders
- Asset importing and configuration
- Level design
- Game objects
- Hierarchies

Game design

Let's make a coin collection game. Here, the player should control a character in the first-person mode, and he must wander the level, collecting all coins before a time limit runs out. If the timer runs out, the game is lost. On the other hand, if all coins are collected before the timer expires, the game is won. The first-person controls will use the default WASD keyboard setup, where *W* moves forward, *A* and *S* move left and right, and *D* walks backward. Head movement is controlled using the mouse, and coins are collected by simply walking into them. See *Figure 1.1*, featuring the coin collection game in action in the Unity Editor.

The great benefit in making this game is that it demonstrates all the core Unity features together and we don't need to rely on any external software to make assets, such as textures, meshes, and materials:

Figure 1.1: Preparing for a coin collection game (the completed game)

 The completed CollectionGame project, as discussed in this chapter and the next, can be found in the book companion files in the Chapter01/CollectionGame folder.

Getting started – Unity and projects

Every time you want to make a new Unity game, including coin collection games, you'll need to create **New Project**. Generally speaking, Unity uses the term **Project** to mean a **Game**. There are two main ways to make a new project, and it really doesn't matter which one you choose because both end up in the same place. If you're already in the Unity interface, looking at an existing scene or level, you can select **File | New Project** from the application menu. See *Figure 1.2*. It may ask if you want to save changes to the currently opened project and you should choose either **Yes** or **No**, depending on what you need.

After selecting the **New Project** option, Unity leads you to the project creation wizard:

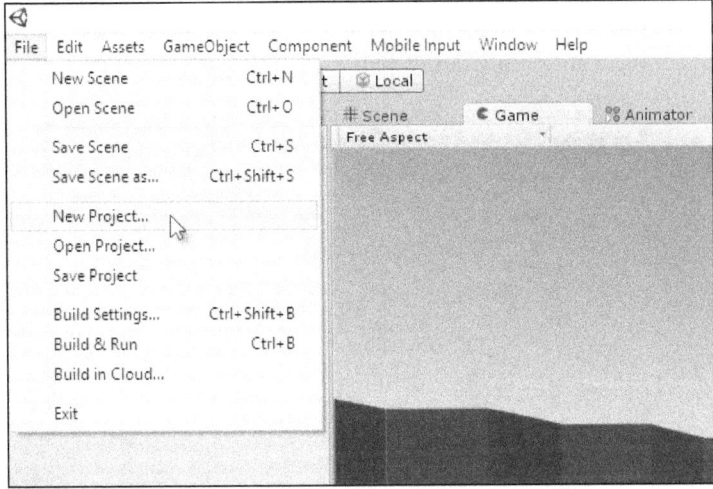

Figure 1.2: Creating a new project via the main menu

Alternatively, if you've just started Unity for the first time, you'll probably begin at the welcome dialog. See *Figure 1.3*. From here, you can access the new project creation wizard by choosing the **NEW PROJECT** button:

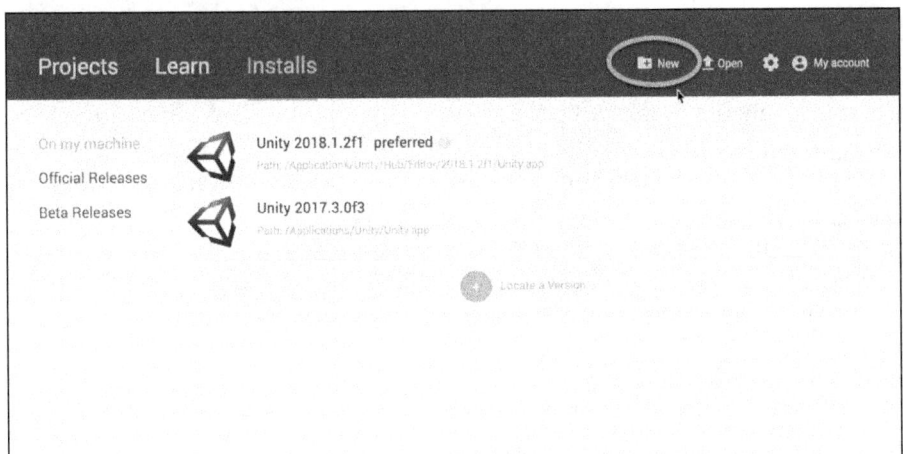

Figure 1.3: The Unity welcome screen

Unity Fundamentals

On reaching the **NEW PROJECT** creation wizard, Unity can generate a new project for you on the basis of some basic settings. Simply fill in the name of your project (such as `CollectionGame`), and select a folder on your computer to contain the project files that will be generated automatically. Finally, select the **3D** option from the template dropdown to create a 3D game, as opposed to **2D**, and then click on the **Create project** button to complete the project generation process. See *Figure 1.4*:

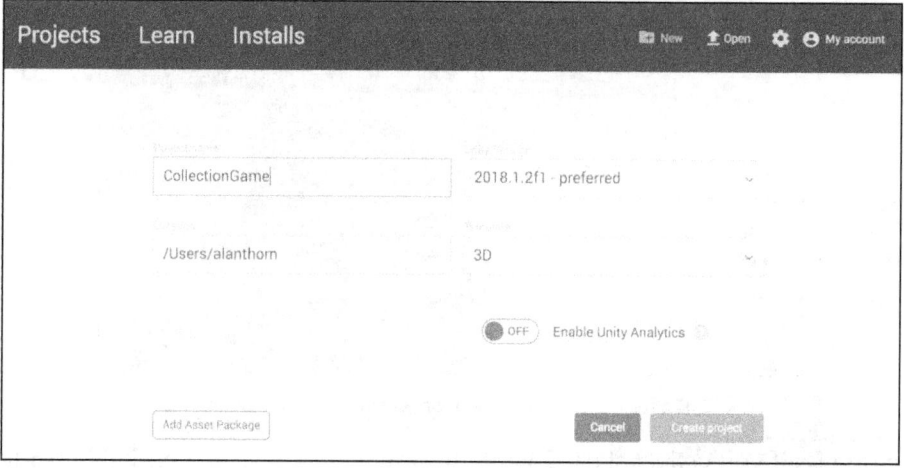

Figure 1.4: Creating a new project

Projects and project folders

Unity has now created a blank, new, and empty project. This represents the starting point for any game development project and is the place where development begins. The newly created project contains nothing initially: no meshes, textures, or any other **Assets**. You can confirm this by simply checking the **Project** panel area at the bottom of the editor interface. This panel displays the complete contents of the project folder, which corresponds to an actual folder on your local drive created earlier by the project wizard. This folder should be empty. See *Figure 1.5*.

This panel will later be populated with more items, all of which we can use to build a game:

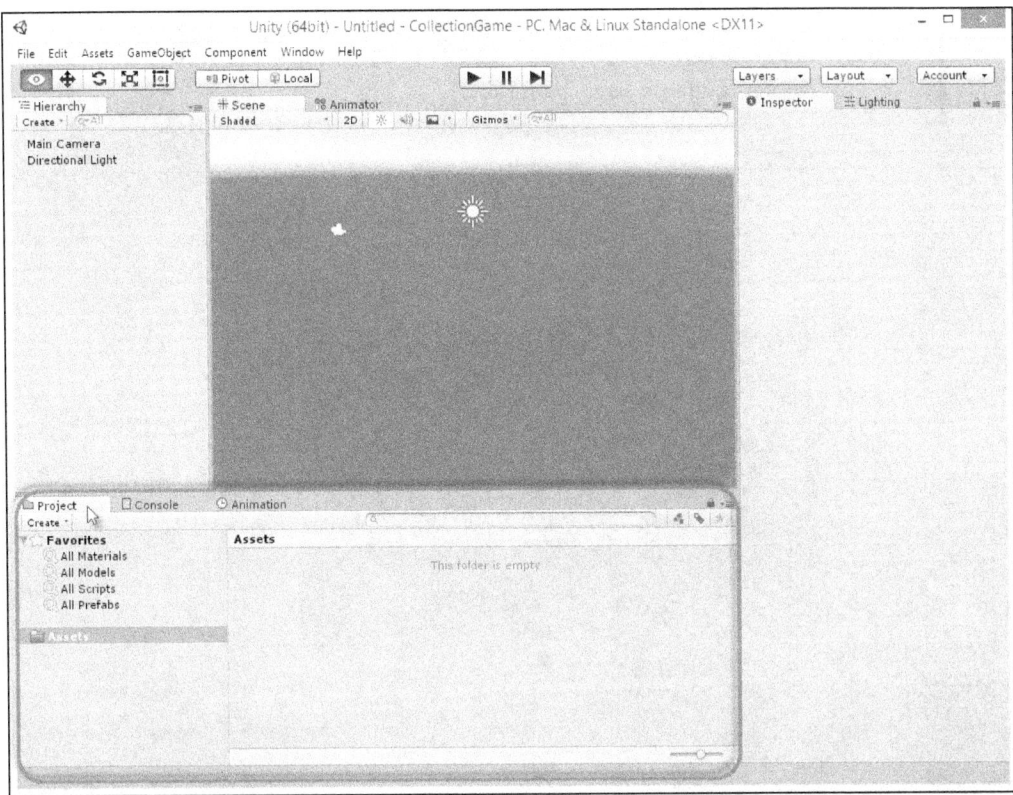

Figure 1.5: The Unity project panel docked at the bottom of the interface

Unity Fundamentals

> If your interface looks radically different from *Figure 1.5*, in terms of its layout and arrangement, then you can reset the UI layout to its defaults. To do this, click on the **Layout** drop-down menu from the top-right corner of the editor interface, and choose **Default**. See *Figure 1.6*:

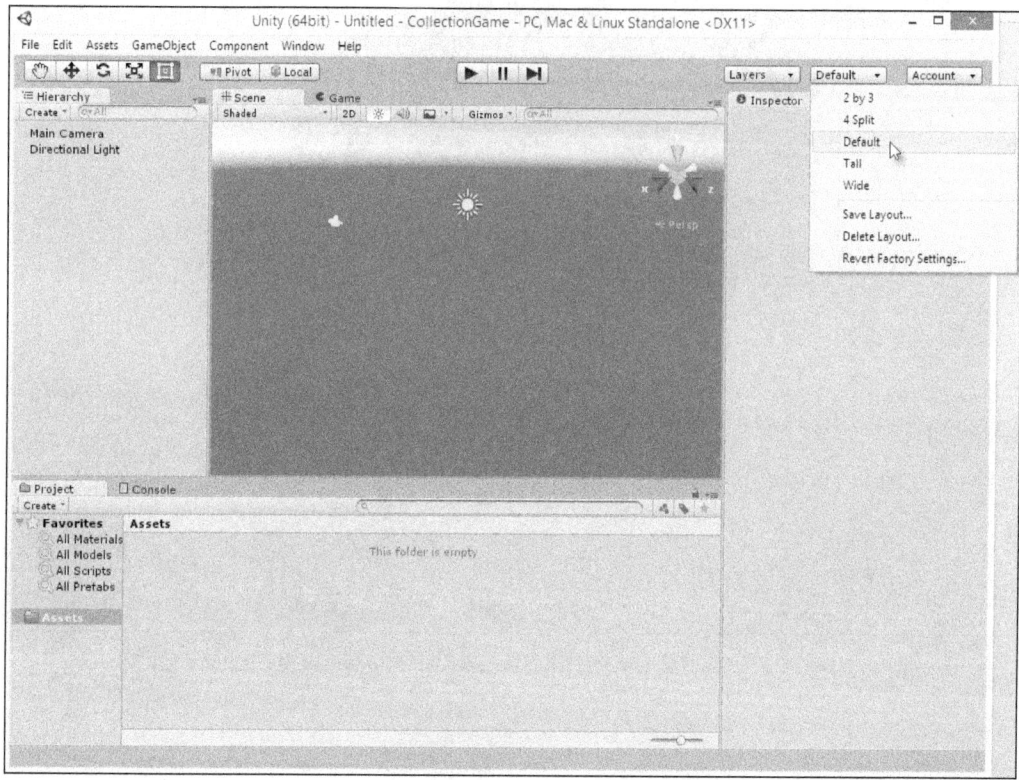

Figure 1.6: Switching to the default interface layout

Chapter 1

You can view the contents of your project folder directly via either Windows Explorer or Mac Finder, by right-clicking the mouse in the **Project** panel from the **Unity Editor** to reveal a context menu, and from there, choose the **Show in Explorer** (Windows) or **Reveal in Finder** (Mac) option. See *Figure 1.7*:

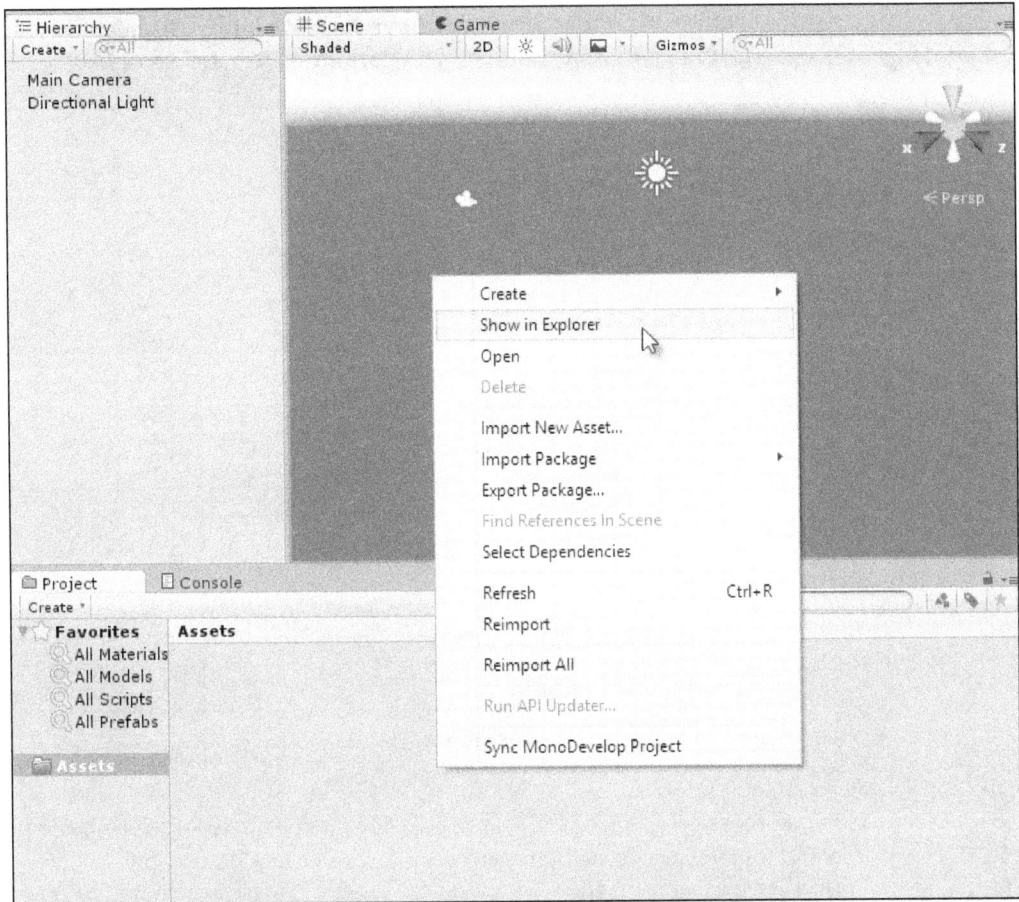

Figure 1.7: Displaying the project folder via the Project panel

[7]

Unity Fundamentals

Clicking on **Show in Explorer** displays the folder contents in the default system file browser. See *Figure 1.8*. This view is useful to inspect files, count them, or back them up. However, don't change the folder contents manually this way via Explorer or Finder. Specifically, don't move, rename, or delete files from here, because doing so can corrupt your Unity project irretrievably. Instead, delete and move files where needed within the **Project** panel in the **Unity Editor**. This way, Unity updates its metadata as appropriate, ensuring that your project continues to work properly:

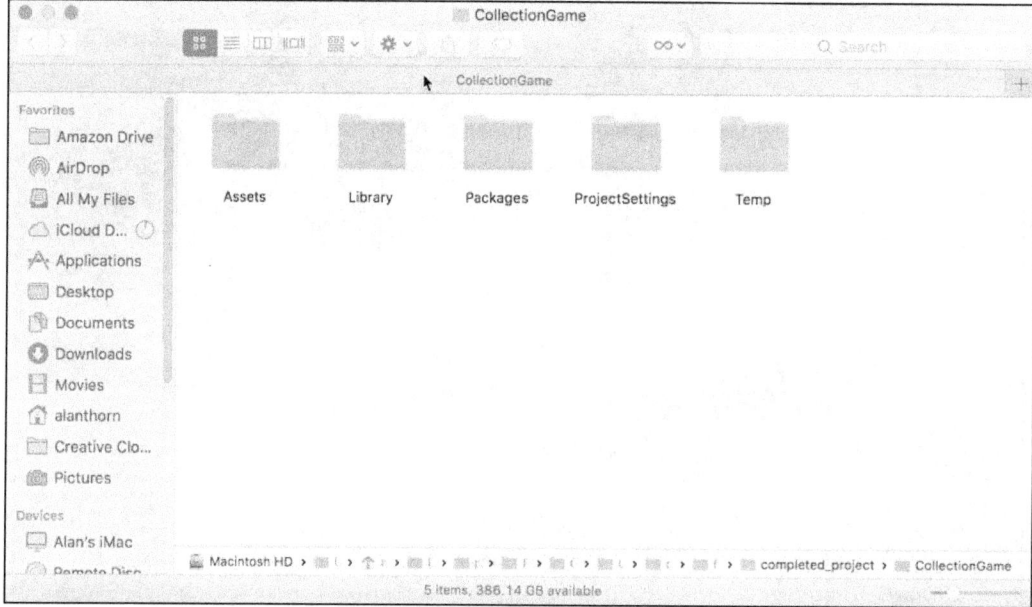

Figure 1.8: Viewing the Project panel from the OS file browser

 Viewing the project folder in the OS file browser will display additional files and folders not visible in the **Project** panel, such as **Library** and **ProjectSettings**, and maybe a Temp folder. Together, these are known as the project metadata. This is not directly a part of your project per se, but contains additional settings and preferences that Unity needs to work properly. These folders and their files should not be edited or changed.

Importing assets

Assets are the ingredients or building blocks for games—the building blocks from which they're made. `Assets` include meshes (or 3D models), such as characters, props, trees, houses, and more: textures, which are image files such as JPEGs and PNGs (these determine how the surface of a mesh should look); music and sound effects to enhance the realism and atmosphere of your game, and finally, scenes, which are 3D spaces or worlds where meshes, textures, sounds, and music live, exist, and work together holistically as part of a single system. Thus, games cannot exist without assets—they would otherwise look completely empty and lifeless. For this reason, we'll need assets to make the coin collection game we're working toward. After all, we'll need an environment to walk around in and coins to collect!

Unity, however, is a *game engine* and not primarily an *asset creation* program, like Blender or Photoshop (though it can create assets). This means that assets, such as characters and props, are typically made first by artists in external, third-party software. From here, they are exported and transferred ready-made to Unity, and Unity is responsible only for bringing these assets to life in a coherent game that can be played. Third-party asset creation programs include **Blender** (which is free of charge), **Maya** or **3DS Max** to make 3D models, **Photoshop** or **GIMP** (which is free of charge) to create textures, and **Audacity** (which is free of cost) to generate audio. There are plenty of other options too. The details of these programs are beyond the scope of this book. In any case, Unity assumes that you already have assets ready to import to build a game. For the coin collection game, we'll use assets that ship with Unity. So, let's import these to our project.

Unity Fundamentals

To do this, select **Assets | Import Package** from the application menu. Then select **Characters, ParticleSystems, Environment**, and **Prototyping**. See *Figure 1.9*:

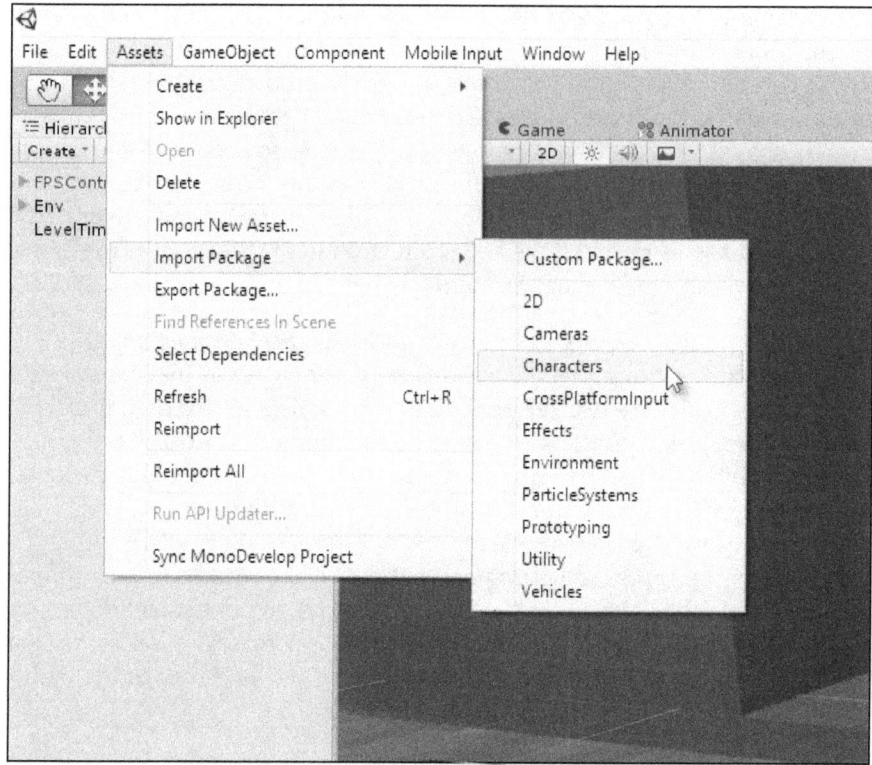

Figure 1.9: Importing assets via the Import Package menu

Each time you import a package from the menu, you'll be presented with an **Import** dialog. Simply leave all settings at their defaults, and click on **Import**. See *Figure 1.10*:

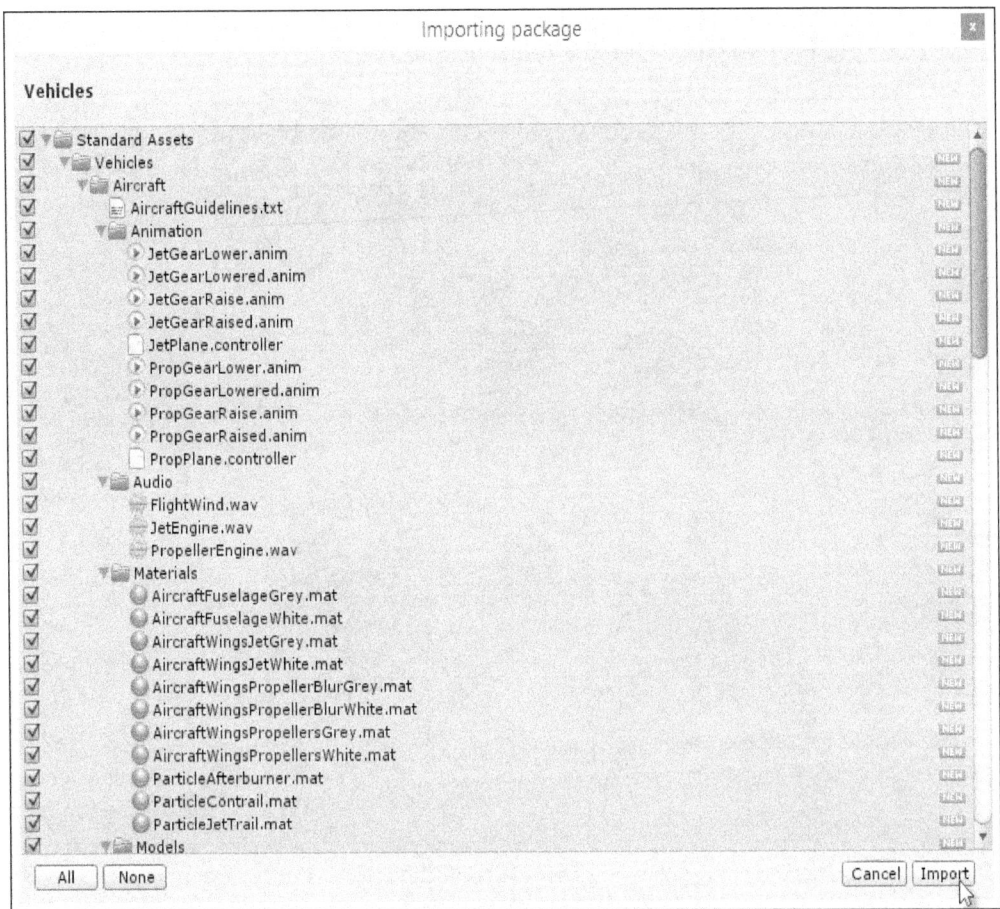

Figure 1.10: Choosing Assets to import

By default, Unity decompresses all files from the package (a library of assets) into the current project. After importing, lots of different assets and data will have been added to the **Project**, ready for use. These files are copies of the originals. So, any changes made to the imported files will not affect or invalidate the originals, which Unity maintains internally.

Unity Fundamentals

The files include models, sounds, textures, and more. These are listed in the **Unity Editor** from the **Project** panel. See the following screenshot:

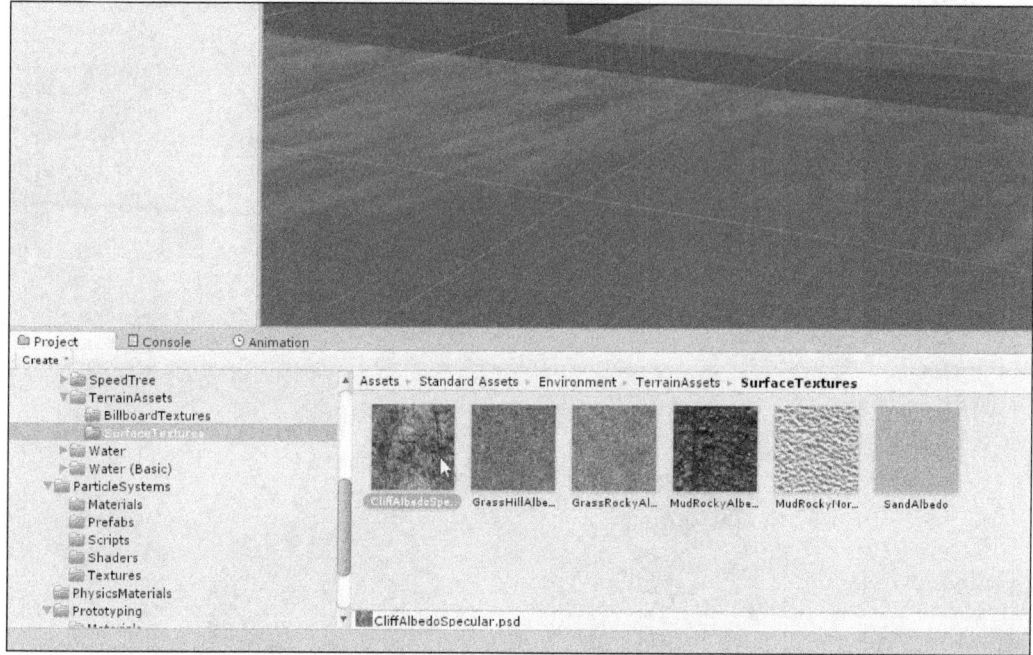

Figure 1.11: Browsing imported assets from the Project panel

 When selecting **Assets | Import** from the application menu, if you don't see all, or any, asset packages listed, you can download and install them separately from the Unity website at https://unity3d.com/. From the downloads page, choose the **Additional Downloads** option, and then select the Standard Assets package. See *Figure 1.12*.

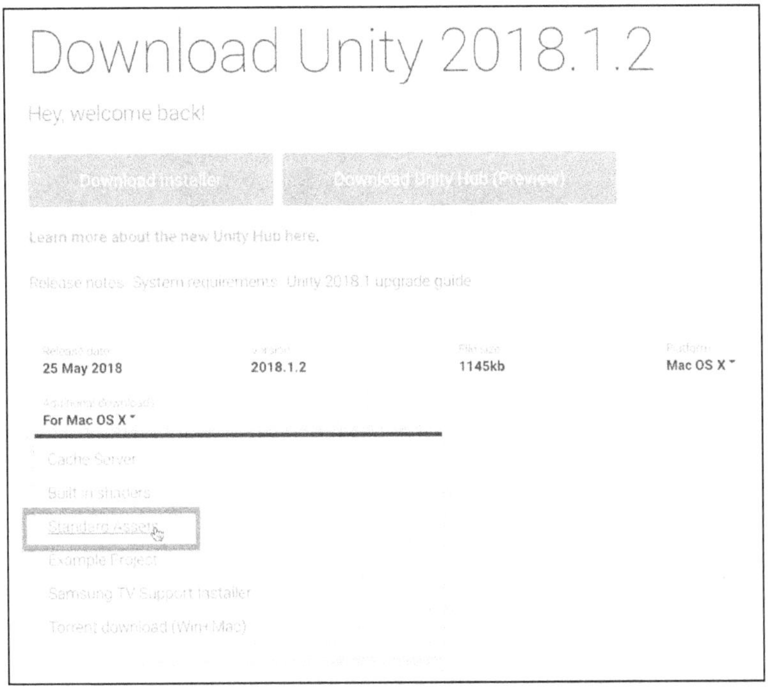

Figure 1.12: Downloading the Standard Assets package

The imported assets don't exist yet in our game scene or level. They don't appear in the game, and they won't do anything when the level begins! Rather, they're simply added to the **Project** panel, which behaves as a library or repository of assets, from which we can pick and choose to build up a game when needed. The assets imported thus far are built-in into Unity and we'll continually using them in subsequent sections to make a functional coin collection game. To get more information about each asset, you can select the asset by clicking on it with the mouse, and asset-specific details will be shown on the right-hand side of the **Unity Editor** in the **Inspector**. The **Inspector** is a property sheet editor that appears on the right-hand side of the interface.

Unity Fundamentals

It is context-sensitive and always changes to display properties for the selected object. See *Figure 1.13*:

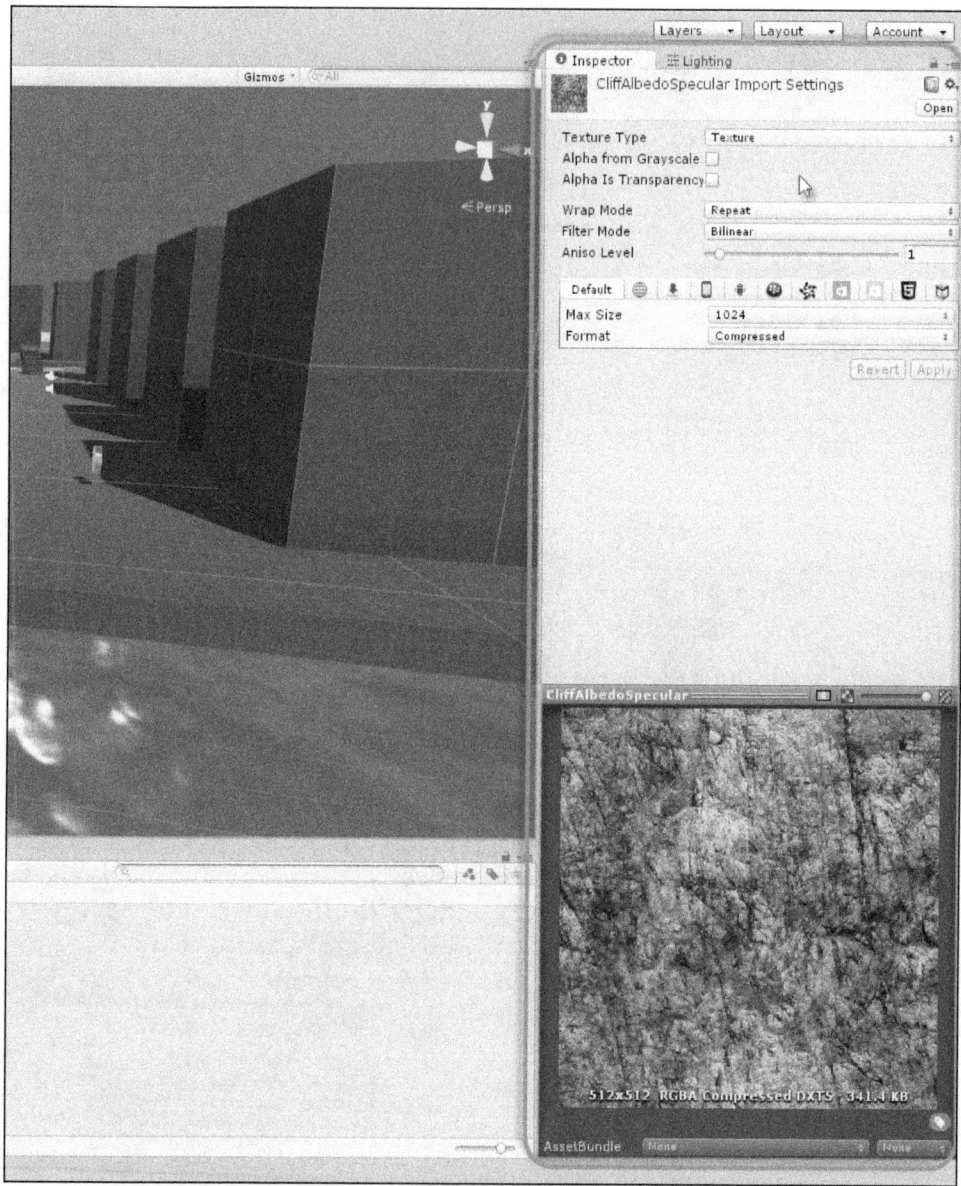

Figure 1.13: The Inspector displays all the properties for the currently selected object

Starting a level

We've now created a Unity project and imported a large library of assets via the **Unity Standard Asset** package, including architectural meshes for walls, floors, ceilings, and stairs. This means that we're now ready to build our first level using these assets! Remember, in Unity, a scene means a level. The word scene and level can be used interchangeably here. They refer simply to a 3D space, that is, the space-time of the game world—the place where things exist. Since all games happen in space and time, we'll need a scene for the coin collection game. To create a new scene, select **File | New Scene** from the application menu or press *Ctrl + N* on the keyboard. When you do this, a new and empty scene is created. You can see a visualization or preview of the scene via the **Scene** tab, which occupies the largest part of the Unity interface. See *Figure 1.14*:

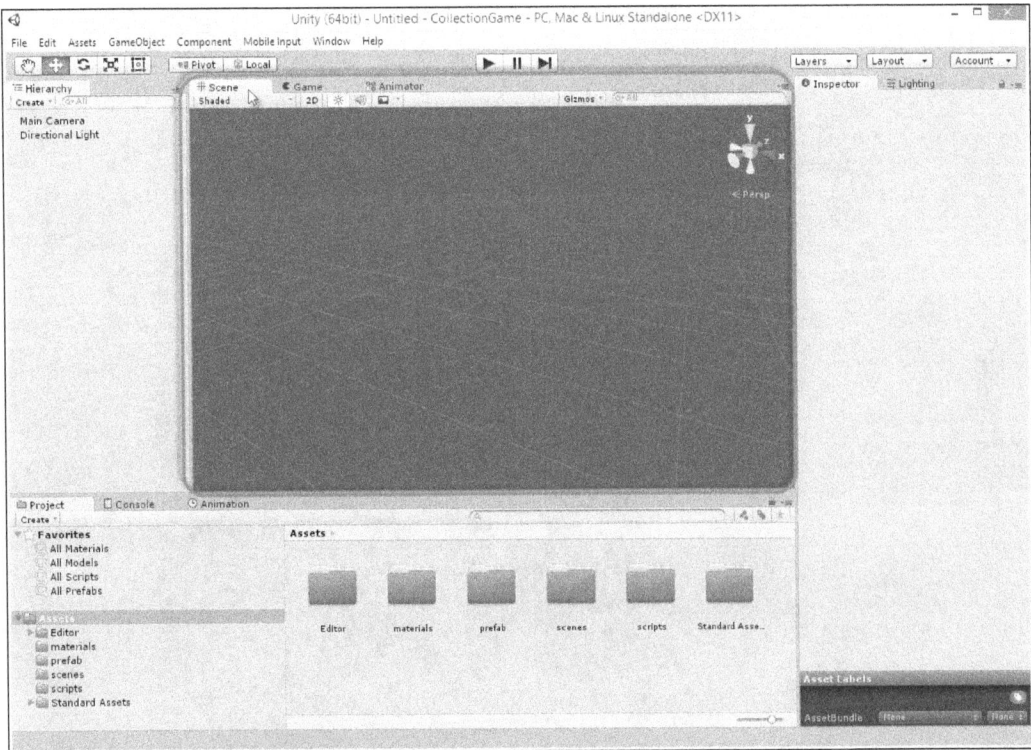

Figure 1.14: The Scene tab displays a preview of a 3D world

Unity Fundamentals

 As shown in *Figure 1.14*, other tabs besides the scene are visible and available in Unity. These include a **Game** tab and an **Animator** tab; in some cases, there could be more as well. For now, we can ignore all the tabs except **Scene**. The Scene tab is designed for quick and easy previewing of a level during its construction.

Each new scene begins empty; well, almost empty. By default, each new scene begins with two objects; specifically, a **Light** to illuminate any other objects that are added and a **Camera** to display and render the contents of the scene from a specific vantage point. You can view a complete list of all the objects existing in the scene using the **Hierarchy** panel, which is docked to the left-hand side of the Unity interface. See *Figure 1.15*. This panel displays the name of every **GameObject** in the scene. In Unity, the word **GameObject** simply refers to a single, independent, and unique thing that lives within the scene, whether visible or not: meshes, lights, cameras, props, and more. Hence, the **Hierarchy** panel tells us about everything in the **Scene**:

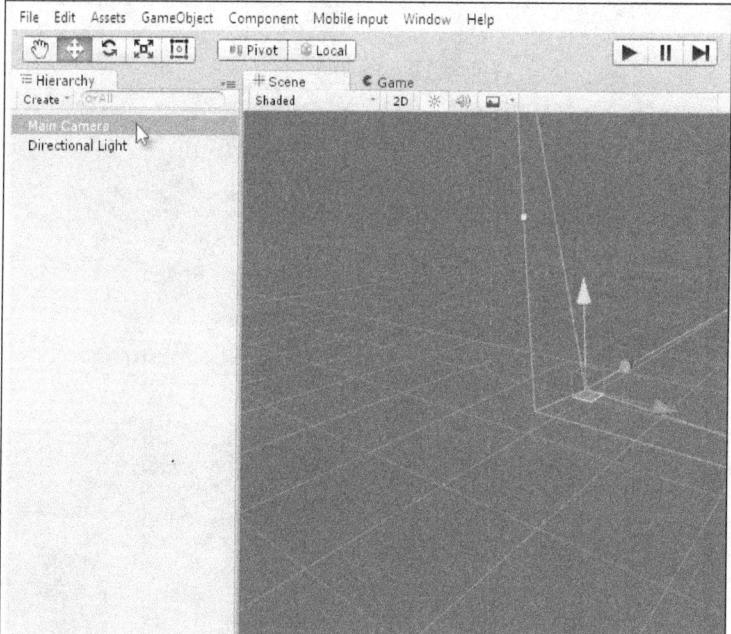

Figure 1.15: The Hierarchy panel

 You can even select objects in the scene by clicking on their name in the **Hierarchy** panel.

Chapter 1

Next, let's add a floor to the scene. After all, the player needs something to stand on! We could build a floor mesh from scratch using third-party modeling software, such as Maya, 3DS Max, or Blender. However, the Unity Standard Asset package, which was imported earlier, contains floor meshes that we can use. This is very convenient. These meshes are part of the `Prototyping` package. To access them via the **Project** panel, open the `Standard Assets` folder by double-clicking it and then access the `Prototyping | Prefabs` folder. From here, you can select objects and preview them from the **Inspector**. See *Figure 1.16*:

You could also quickly add a floor to the scene by choosing **GameObject | 3D Object | Plane** from the application menu. However, this just adds a dull, grey floor, which isn't very interesting. Of course, you could change its appearance. As we'll see later, Unity lets you do this. However, for this tutorial, we'll use a specifically modeled floor mesh via the Standard Assets package from the Project panel.

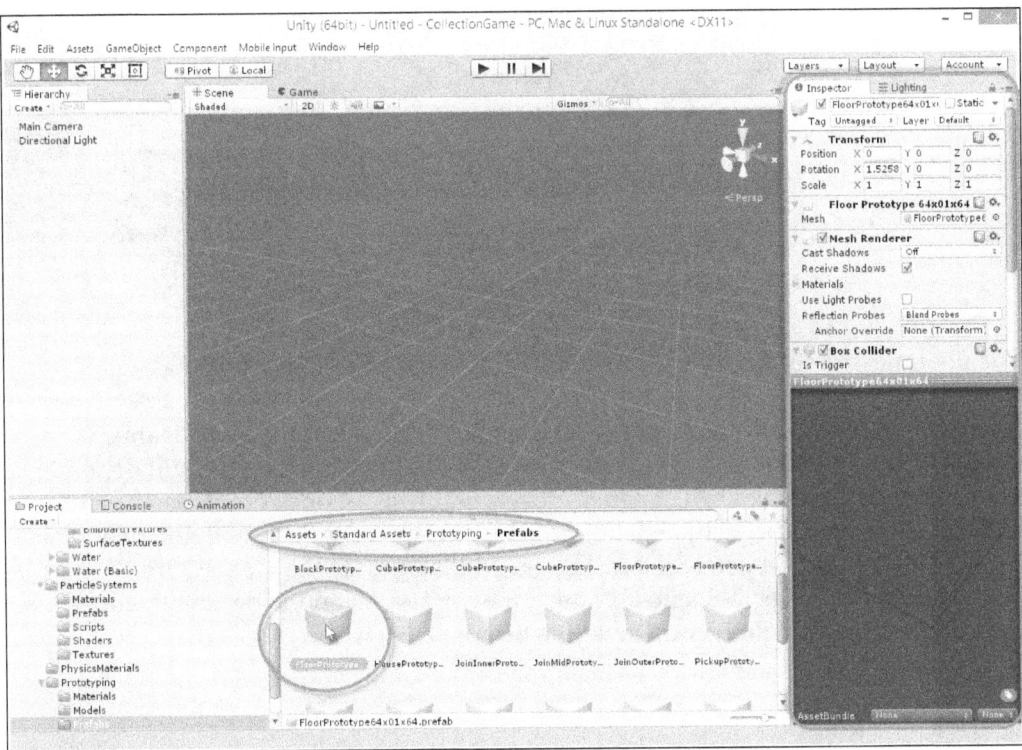

Figure 1.16: The Standard Assets/Prototyping package contains many meshes for quick scene building

[17]

Unity Fundamentals

The mesh named `FloorPrototype64x01x64` (as shown in *Figure 1.16*) is suitable as a floor. To add this mesh to the scene, simply drag and drop the object from the **Project** panel to the **Scene** view and then release the mouse. See *Figure 1.17*. When you do this, notice how the **Scene** view changes to display the newly added mesh within the 3D space, and the mesh name also appears as a listing in the **Hierarchy** panel:

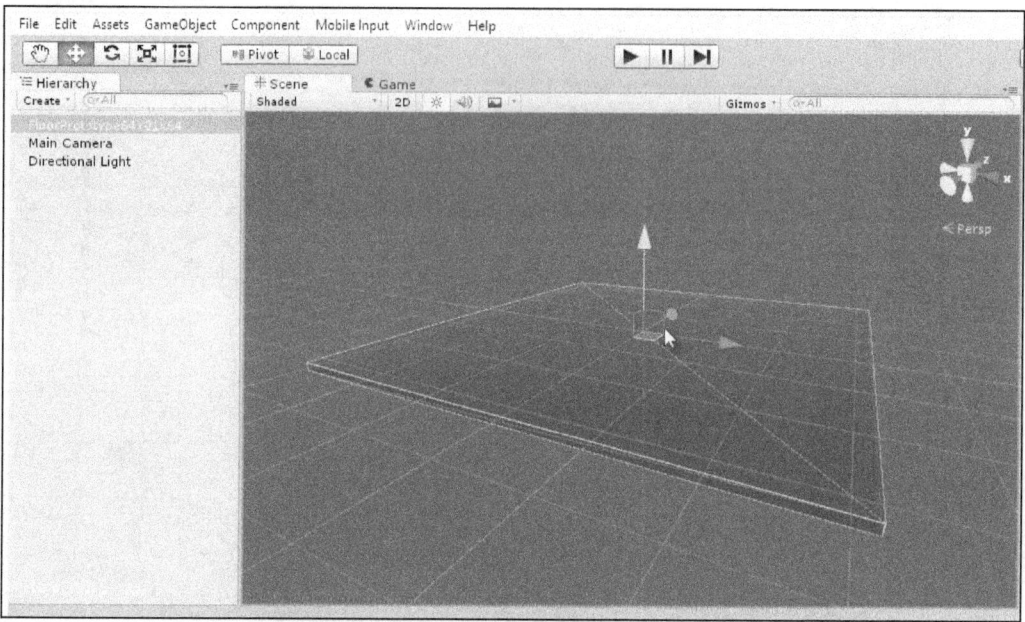

Figure 1.17: Dragging and dropping mesh assets from the Project panel to the Scene view will add them to the scene

The floor mesh asset from the **Project** panel has now been instantiated as a **GameObject** in the scene. This means that a copy or clone of the mesh asset, based on the original in the **Project** panel, has been added to the scene as a separate **GameObject**. The **Instance** (or **GameObject**) of the floor in the scene still depends on the floor asset in the **Project** panel. However, the asset does not depend on the instance. This means that, by deleting the floor in the scene, you will not delete the asset. However, if you delete the asset, you will invalidate the **GameObject**. You can also create more floors in **Scene** if you want by dragging and dropping the floor asset many times from the **Project** panel to the **Scene** view.

Each time, a new instance of the floor is created in the **Scene** as a separate and unique **GameObject**, although all the added instances will still depend on the single floor asset in the **Project** panel. See *Figure 1.18*:

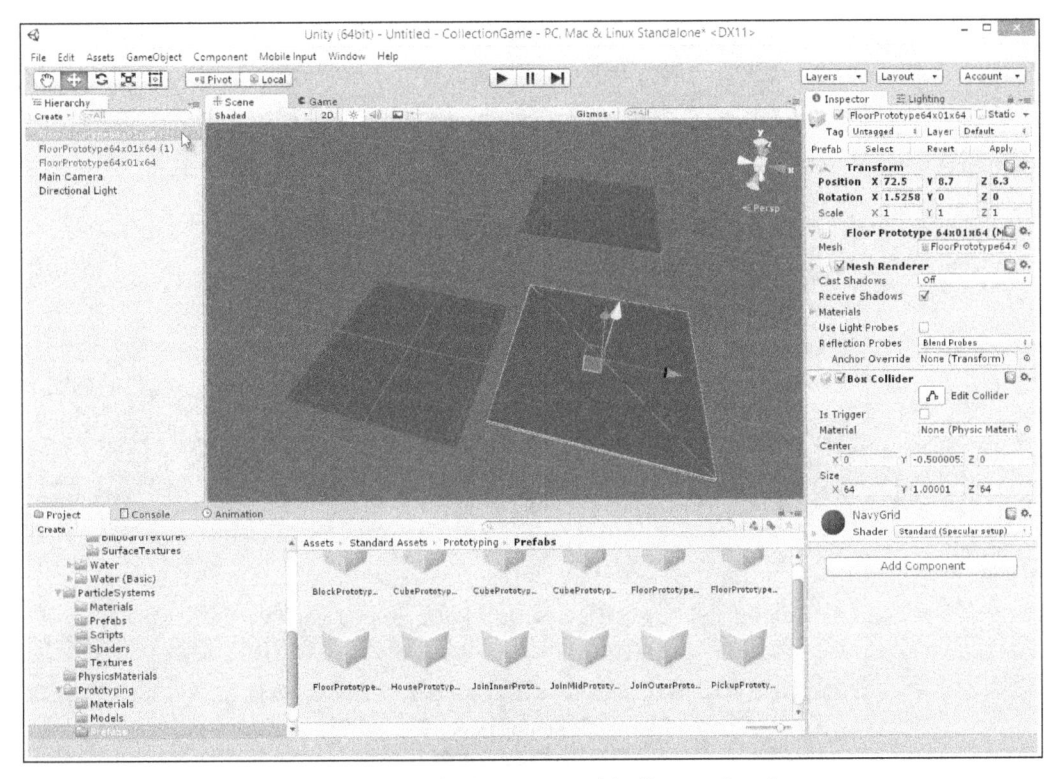

Figure 1.18: Adding multiple instances of the floor mesh to the scene

We don't actually need the duplicate floor pieces. So, let's delete them. Just click on the duplicates in the **Scene** view and then press *Delete* on the keyboard to remove them. Remember, you can also select and delete objects by clicking on their name in the **Hierarchy** panel and pressing *Delete*. Either way, this leaves us with a single floor piece and a solid start to building our scene. One remaining problem, though, concerns the floor and its name. By looking carefully in the **Hierarchy** panel, we can see that the floor name is `FloorPrototype64x01x64`. This name is long, obtuse, and unwieldy. We should change it to something more manageable and meaningful. This is not technically essential but is good practice to keep our work clean and organized. There are many ways to rename an object.

Unity Fundamentals

One way is to first select it and then enter a new name in the name field in the **Object Inspector**. I'll rename it `WorldFloor`. See *Figure 1.19*:

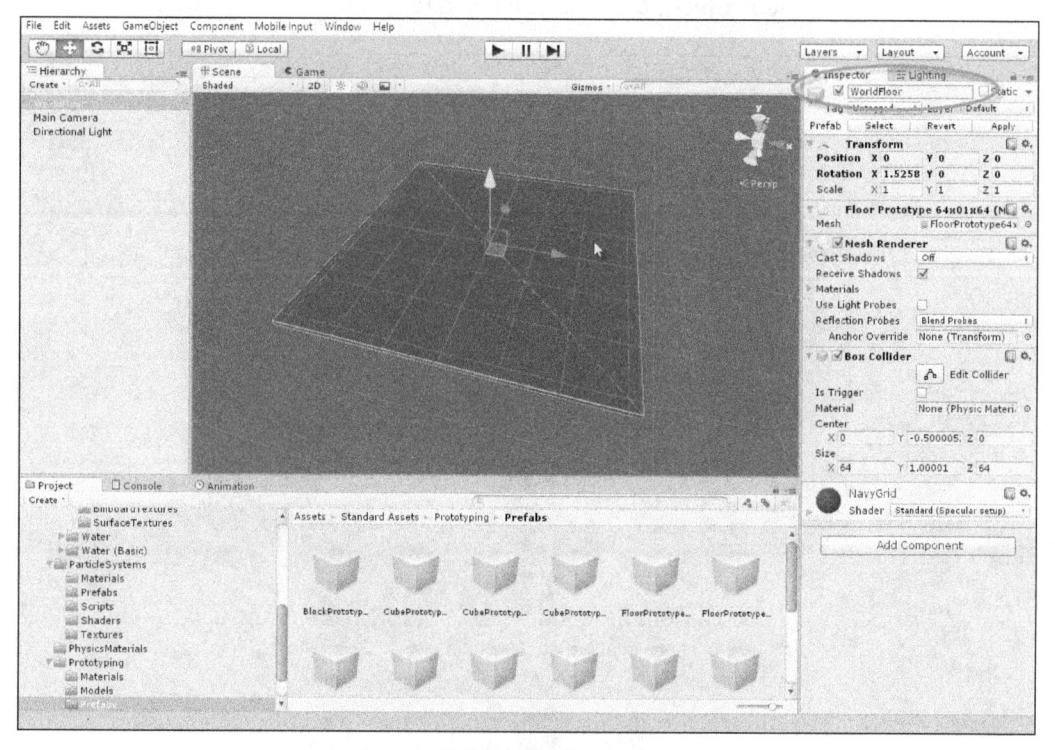

Figure 1.19: Renaming the floor mesh

Transformations and navigation

A scene with a floor mesh has been established, but this alone is uninteresting. We need to add more, such as buildings, stairs, columns, and perhaps more floor pieces. Otherwise, there would be no world for the player to explore. Before building on what we've got, however, let's make sure that the existing floor piece is centered at the world origin. Every point and location within a scene is uniquely identified by a coordinate, measured as an (X, Y, Z) offset from the world center (**origin**).

The current position for the selected object is always visible from the **Object Inspector**. In fact, the **Position**, **Rotation**, and **Scale** of an object are grouped together under a category (**component**) called **Transform**. **Position** indicates how far an object should be moved in three axes from the world center. **Rotation** indicates how much an object should be turned or rotated around its central axes. **Scale** indicates how much an object should be shrunk or expanded to smaller or larger sizes. A default **Scale** of one means that an object should appear at normal size, two means twice the size, and 0.5 means half the size, and so on. Together, the **Position**, **Rotation** and **Scale** of an object constitute its transformation. To change the position of the selected object, you can simply type new values in the **X**, **Y**, and **Z** fields for **Position**. To move an object to the world center, simply enter (0, 0, and 0), as shown in *Figure 1.20*:

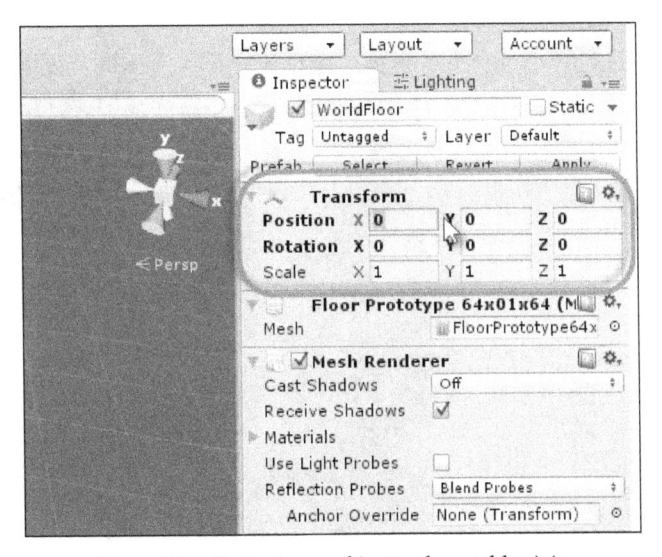

Figure 1.20: Centering an object to the world origin

Unity Fundamentals

Setting the position of an object, as we've done here, by typing numerical values is acceptable and appropriate for the specifying of exact positions. However, it's often more intuitive to move objects using mouse-based controls. To do this, let's add a second floor piece and position it away from the first instance. Drag and drop a floor piece from the **Project** panel in **Scene** to create a second floor **GameObject**. Then click on the new floor piece to select it and switch to the **Translate** tool. To do this, press *W* on the keyboard or click on the translate tool icon from the toolbar at the top of the editor interface. The translate tool allows you to reposition objects in **Scene**. See *Figure 1.21*:

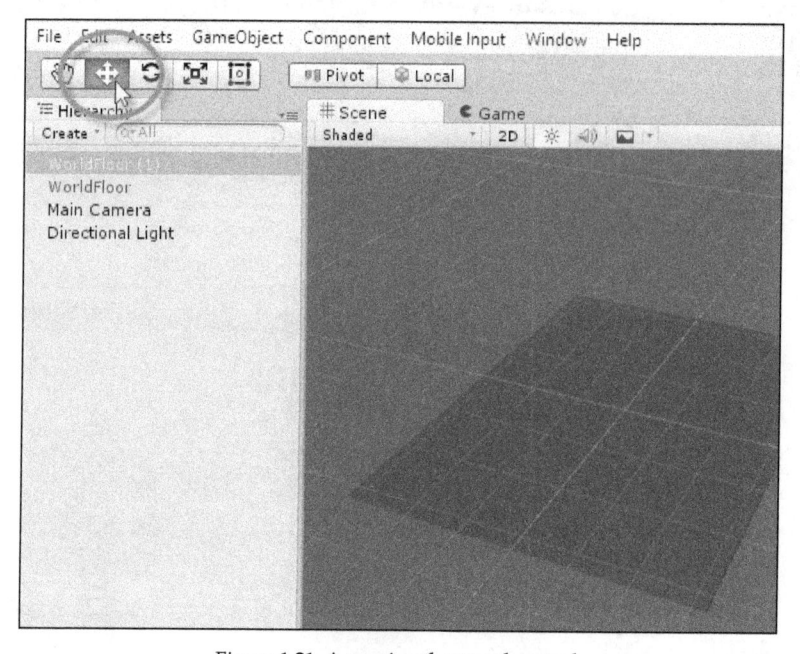

Figure 1.21: Accessing the translate tool

When the translate tool is active and an object is selected, a **Gizmo** appears centered on the object (three colored axes visible in the **Scene** tab). The translate Gizmo appears as three colored perpendicular axes: red, green, and blue corresponding to *X*, *Y*, and *Z* respectively.

To move an object, hover your cursor over one of the three axes (or planes between axes), and then click and hold the mouse while moving it to slide the object in that direction. You can repeat this process as often as needed to ensure that your objects are positioned where you need them to be. Use the translate tool to move the second floor piece away from the first. See *Figure 1.22*:

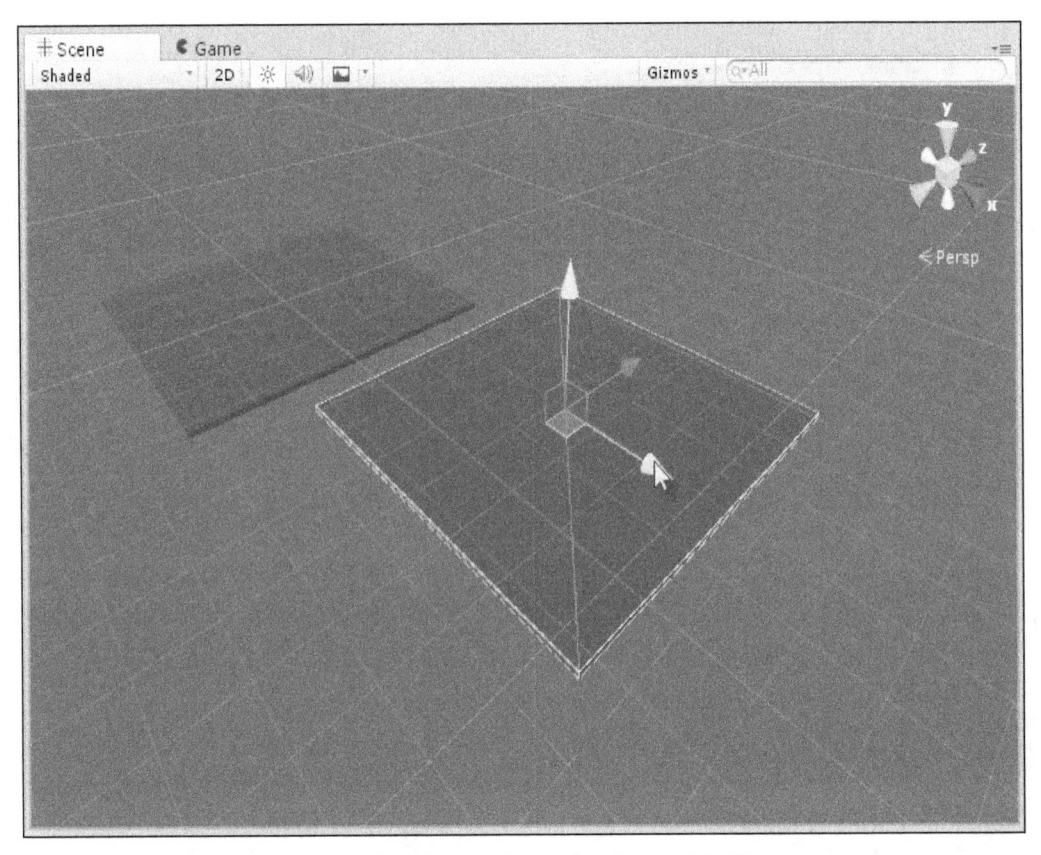

Figure 1.22: Translate an object using the translate Gizmo

Unity Fundamentals

You can also rotate and scale objects using the mouse, as with translate. Press *E* to access the rotate tool or *R* to access the scale tool, or you can activate these tools using their respective toolbar icons from the top of the editor. When these tools are activated, a Gizmo appears centered on the object, and you can click and drag the mouse over each specific axis to rotate or scale objects as needed. See *Figure 1.23*:

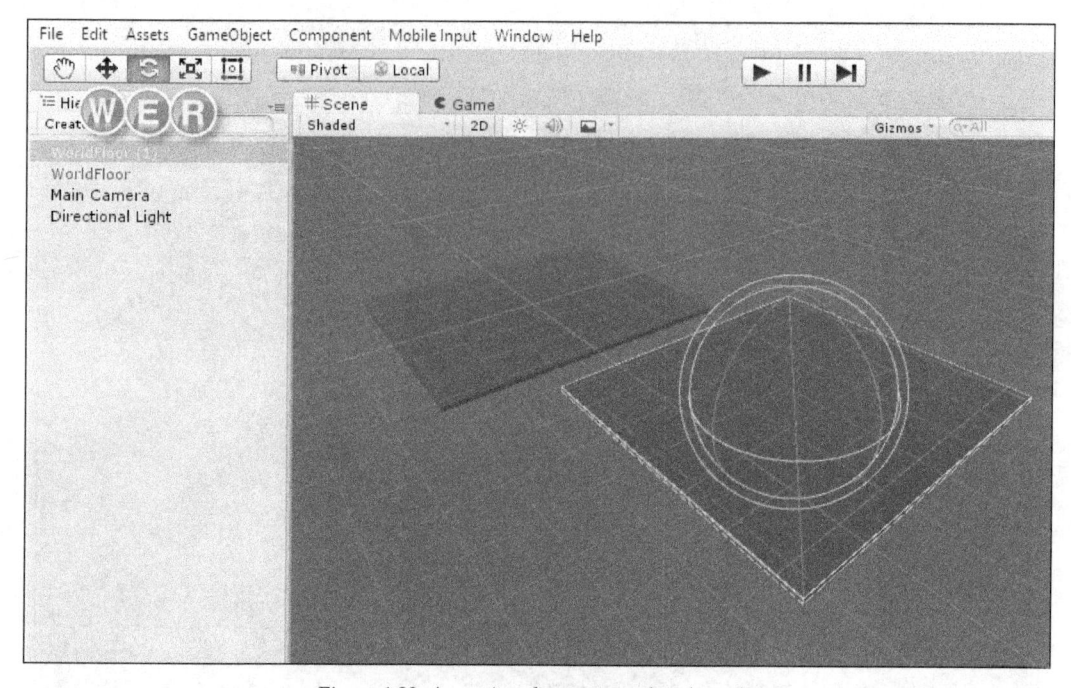

Figure 1.23: Accessing the rotate and scale tools

Being able to translate, rotate, and scale objects quickly through mouse and keyboard combinations is very important when working in Unity. For this reason, make using the keyboard shortcuts a habit, as opposed to accessing the tools continually from the toolbar.

However, in addition to moving, rotating, and scaling objects, you'll frequently need to move around yourself in the **Scene** view in order to see the world from different positions, angles, and perspectives. This means that you'll frequently need to reposition the scene preview camera in the world. You'll want to zoom in and zoom out of the world to get a better view of objects and change your viewing angle to see how objects align and fit together properly. To do this, you'll need to make extensive use of both the keyboard and mouse together.

To zoom closer or further from the object you're looking at, simply scroll the mouse wheel up or down—up zooms in and down zooms out. See *Figure 1.24*:

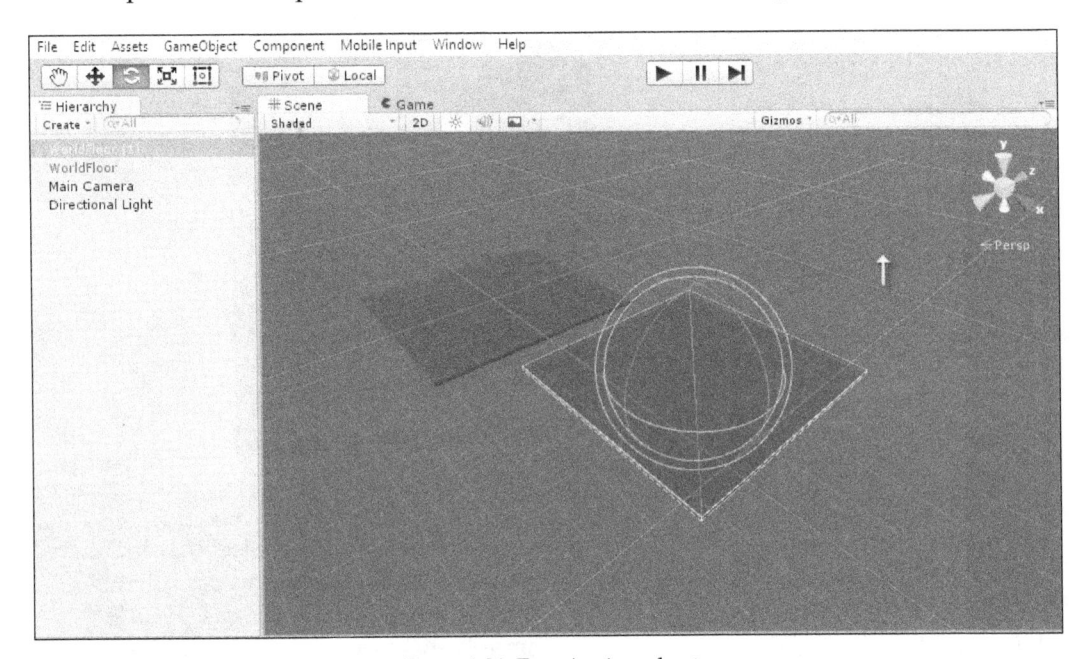

Figure 1.24: Zooming in and out

Unity Fundamentals

To pan the **Scene** view left or right, or up or down, hold down the middle mouse button while moving the mouse in the appropriate direction. Alternatively, you can access the pan tool from the application toolbar (or press *Q* on the keyboard) and then simply click and drag in the **Scene** view while the tool is active. Pan does not zoom in or out; it simply slides the camera left and right, or up and down:

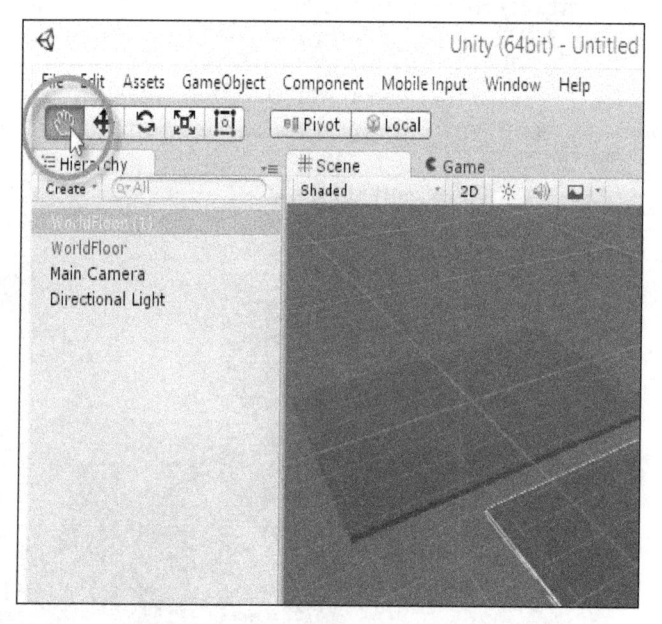

Figure 1.25: Accessing the Pan tool

Sometimes, while building levels, you'll lose sight entirely of the object that you need. For example, your viewport camera could be focusing on a completely different place from the object you really want to click or see. In this case, you'll often want to shift the viewport camera automatically in order to focus on that specific object.

Specifically, you'll want to reposition and rotate the viewport as necessary to bring a desired object to the center of the view. To do this automatically, select the object to focus on (or frame) by clicking on its name from the **Hierarchy** panel. Then, press the F key on the keyboard. Alternatively, you can double-click its name in the **Hierarchy** panel. See *Figure 1.26*:

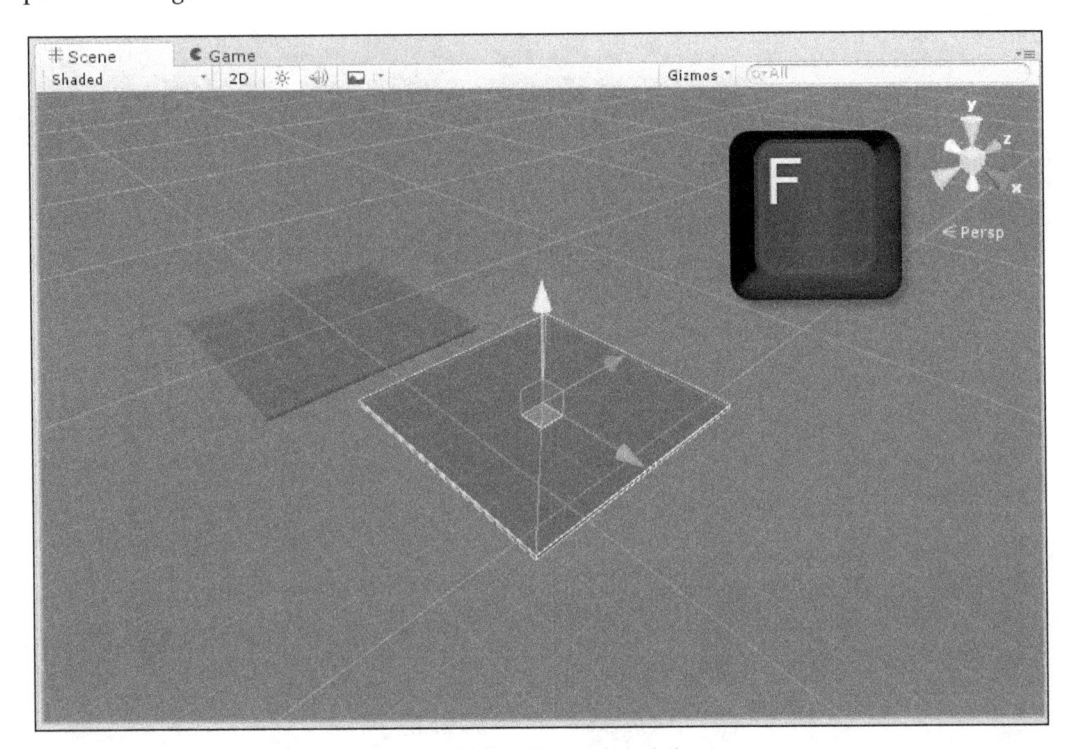

Figure 1.26: Framing a selected object

Unity Fundamentals

After framing an object, you'll often want to *rotate around* it in order to quickly and easily view it from all important angles. To achieve this, hold down the *Alt* key on the keyboard while clicking and dragging the mouse to rotate the view. See *Figure 1.27*:

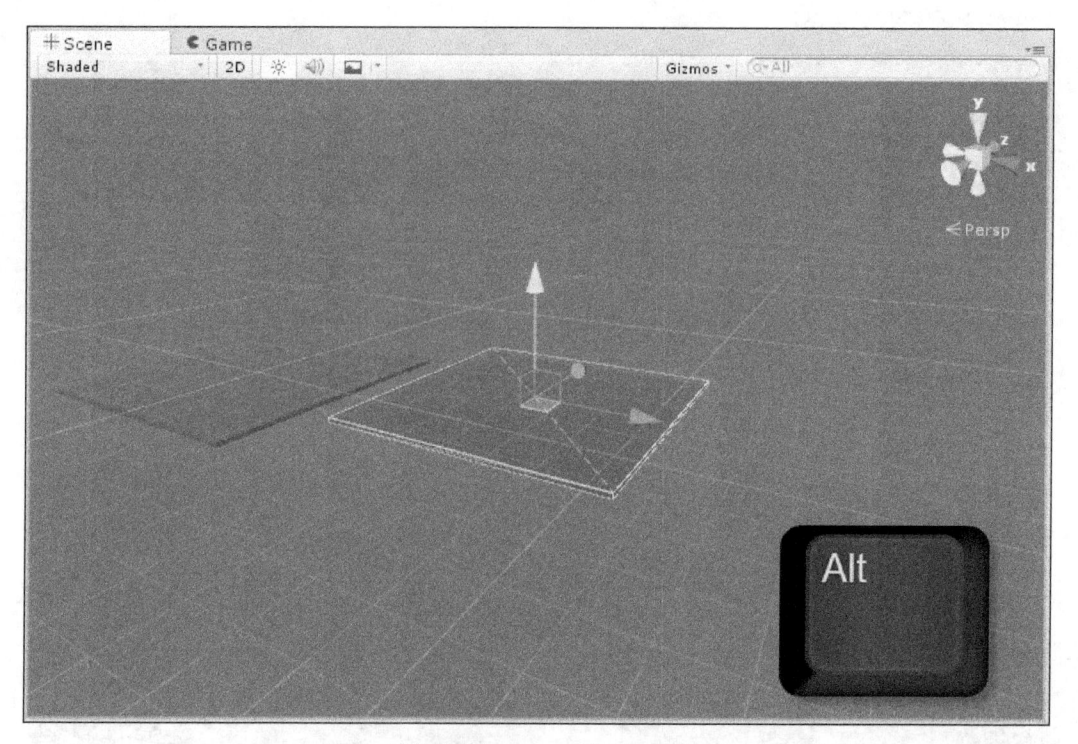

Figure 1.27: Rotating around the framed object

Lastly, it's helpful to navigate a level in the **Scene** view using first-person controls, that is, controls that mimic how first-person games are played. This helps you experience the scene at a more personal and immersive level.

To do this, hold down the right mouse button and (with the button depressed) use the WASD keys on the keyboard to control forward, backward, and strafing movement. Movement of the mouse controls head orientation. You can also hold down the *Shift* key while moving to increase movement speed. See *Figure 1.28*:

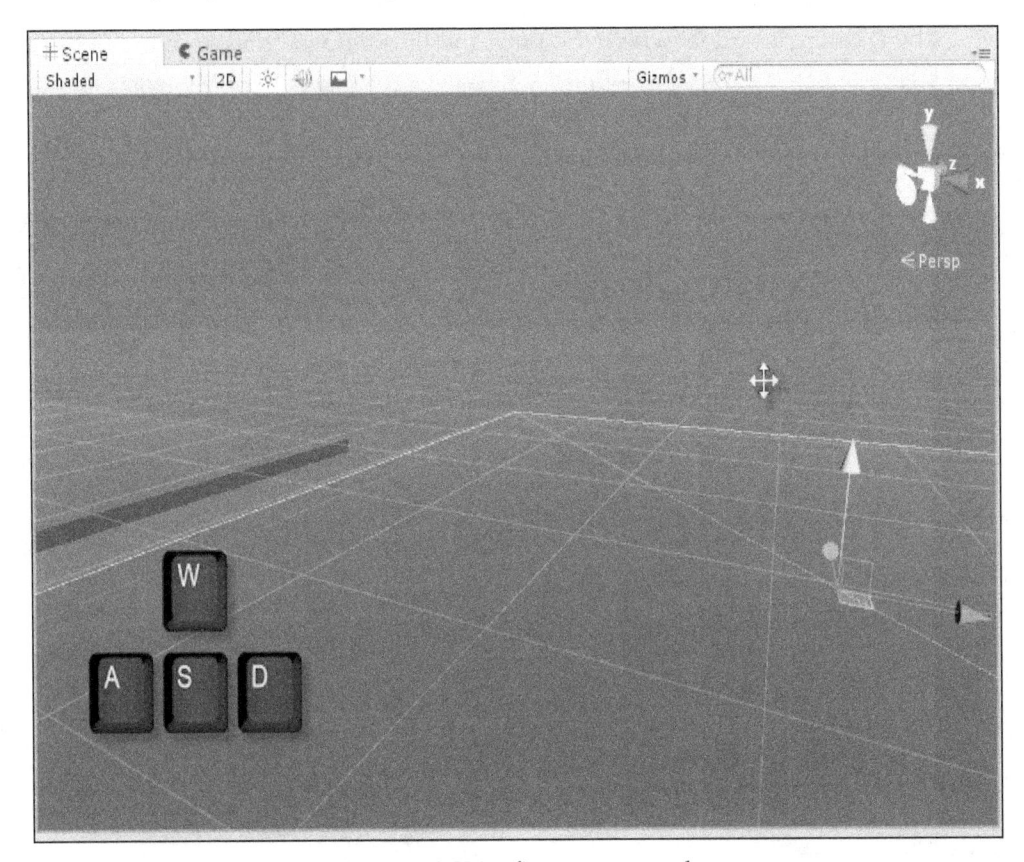

Figure 1.28: Using first-person controls

The great thing about learning the versatile transformation and navigation controls is that, on understanding them, you can move and orient practically any object in any way, and you can move and view the world from almost any position and angle. Being able to do this is critically important to build quality levels quickly. All of these controls, along with some others that we'll soon see, will be used frequently throughout this book to create scenes and work in Unity generally.

Scene building

Now that we've seen how to transform objects and navigate the scene viewport successfully, let's proceed to complete our first level for the coin collection game. Let's separate the two floor meshes apart in space, leaving a gap between them that we'll fix by creating a bridge, which the player will be able to cross, moving between the floor spaces like islands. We can use the translate tool (W) to move objects around. See *Figure 1.29*:

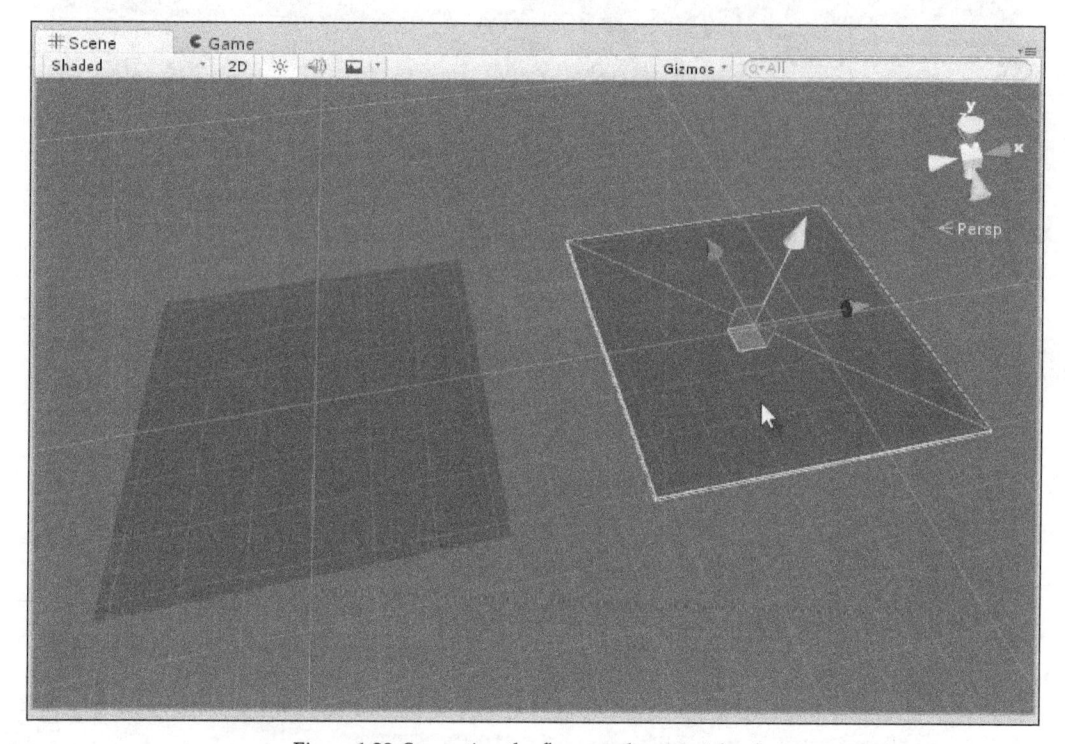

Figure 1.29: Separating the floor meshes into islands

> If you want to create more floor objects, you can use the method that we've seen already by dragging and dropping the mesh asset in the Project panel in the Scene viewport. Alternatively, you can duplicate the selected object in the viewport by pressing *Ctrl + D* on the keyboard. Both methods produce the same result.

Next, we'll add some props and obstacles to the scene. Drag and drop some house objects onto the floor. The house object (`HousePrototype16x16x24`) is found in the `Assets | Standard Assets | Prototyping | Prefabs` folder. See *Figure 1.30*:

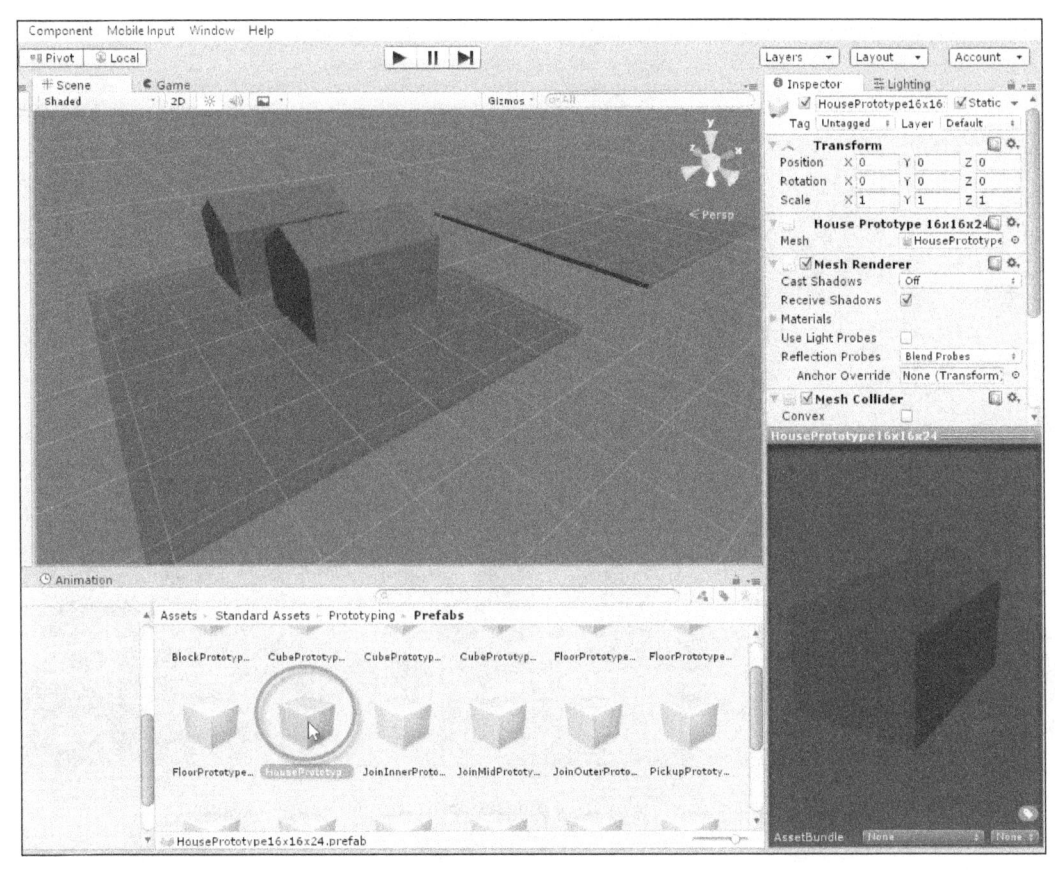

Figure 1.30: Adding house props to the scene

On dragging and dropping the house in the scene, it may align to the floor nicely with the bottom against the floor, or it may not align like that. If it does, that's splendid and great luck! However, we shouldn't rely on luck every time because we're professional game developers! Thankfully, we can make any two mesh objects align easily in Unity using vertex snapping. This feature works by forcing two objects into positional alignment within the scene by overlapping their vertices at a specific and common point.

Unity Fundamentals

For example, consider *Figure 1.31*. Here, a house object hovers awkwardly above the floor and we naturally want it to align level with the floor and perhaps over to the floor corner. To achieve this, start by selecting the house object (click on it or select it from the **Hierarchy** panel). The object to be selected is the one that *should move* to align and not the destination (which is the floor), which should remain in place:

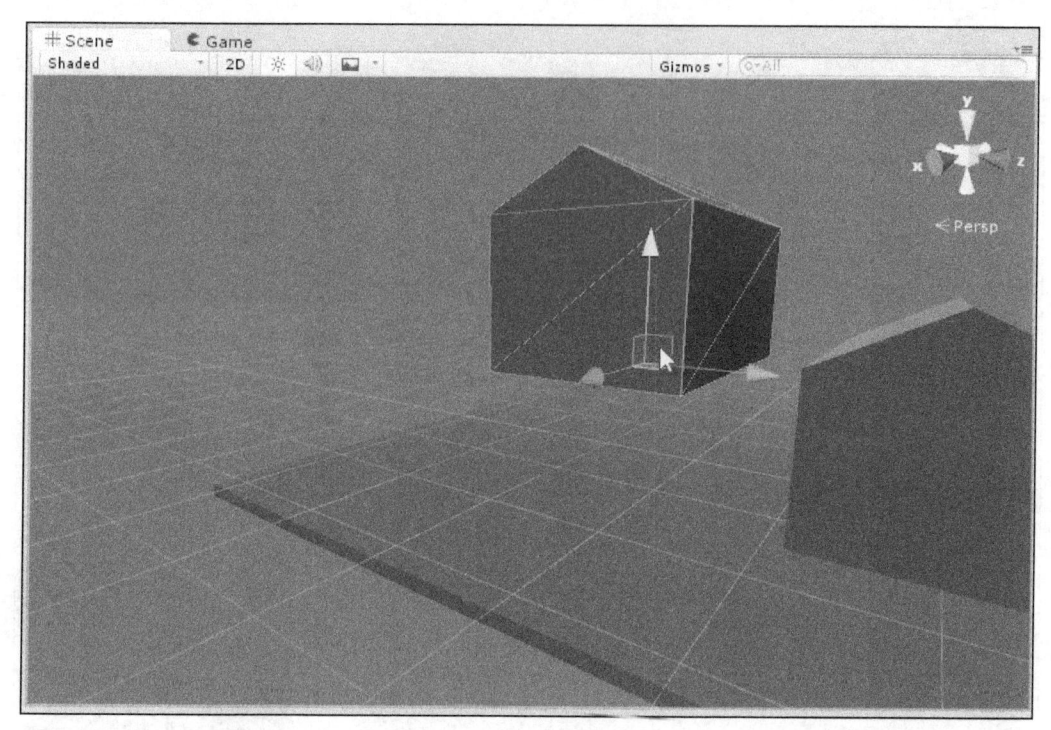

Figure 1.31: Misaligned objects can be snapped into place with Vertex Snapping

Next, activate the translate tool (*W*) and hold down the *V* key for vertex snapping. With *V* held down, move the cursor around and see how the Gizmo cursor sticks to the nearest vertex of the selected mesh. See *Figure 1.32*. Unity is asking you to pick a source vertex for the snapping:

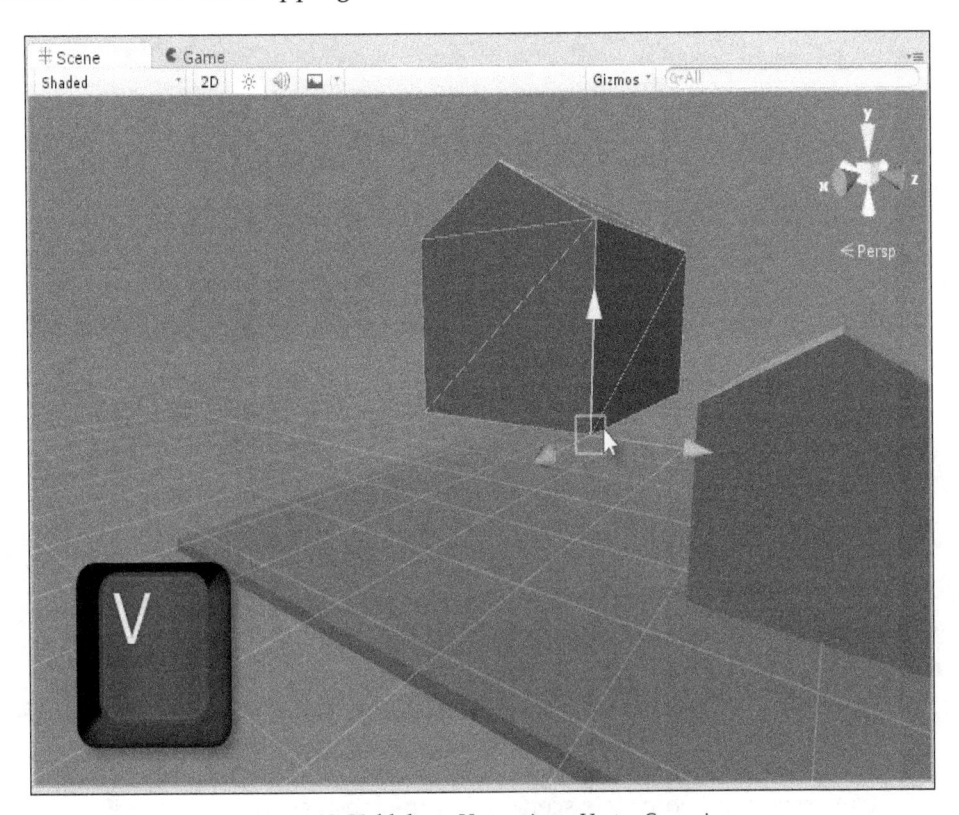

Figure 1.32: Hold down V to activate Vertex Snapping

Unity Fundamentals

With *V* held down, move the cursor to the bottom corner of the house, and then click and drag from the corner to the floor mesh corner. The house will then snap align to the floor, corner to corner. When aligned this way, it releases the *V* key, and the two meshes get aligned exactly at the vertices. See *Figure 1.33*:

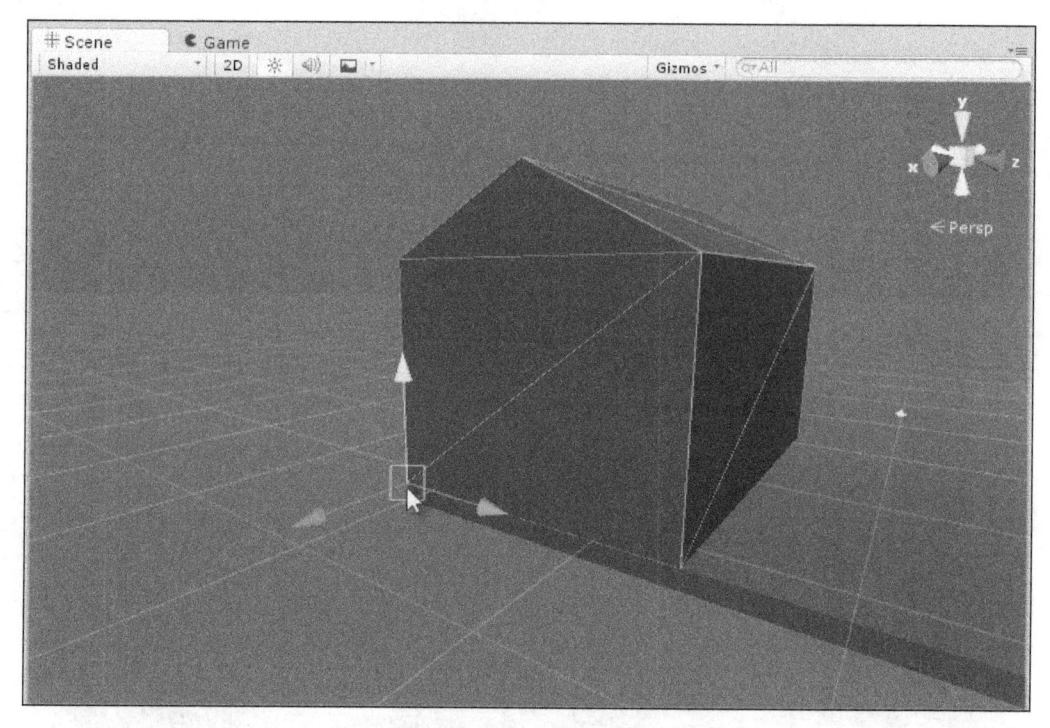

Figure 1.33: Align two meshes by vertices

Now you can assemble a complete scene using the mesh assets included in the `Prototyping` package. Drag and drop props in the scene, and using translate, rotate, and scale, you can reposition, realign, and rotate these objects; using vertex snapping, you can align them wherever you need. Give this some practice.

See *Figure 1.34* for the scene arrangement that I made using only these tools and assets:

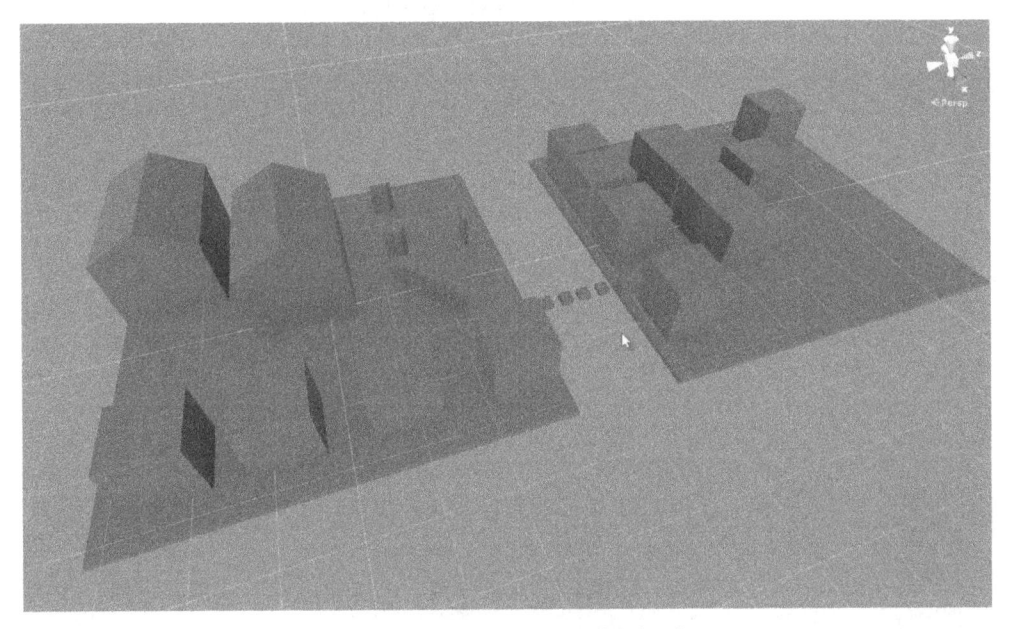

Figure 1.34: Building a complete level

Lighting and sky

The basic level has been created in terms of architectural models and layout; this was achieved using only a few mesh assets and some basic tools. Nevertheless, these tools are powerful and offer us a multitude of combinations and options to create great variety and believability in game worlds. One important ingredient is missing for us, however. This ingredient is lighting. You'll notice from *Figure 1.34* that everything looks relatively flat, with no highlights, shadows, or light or dark areas. This is because scene lighting is not properly configured for best results, even though we already have a light in the scene, which was created initially by default.

Unity Fundamentals

Let's start setting the scene for the coin collection game by enabling the sky, if it's not already enabled. To do this, click on the **Extras** drop-down menu from the top toolbar in the **Scene** viewport. From the context menu, select **Skybox** to enable **Skybox** viewing. A **Skybox** simply refers to a large cube that surrounds the whole scene. Each interior side has a continuous texture (image) applied to simulate the appearance of a surrounding sky. For this reason, clicking the **Skybox** option displays a default sky in the **Scene** viewport. See *Figure 1.35*:

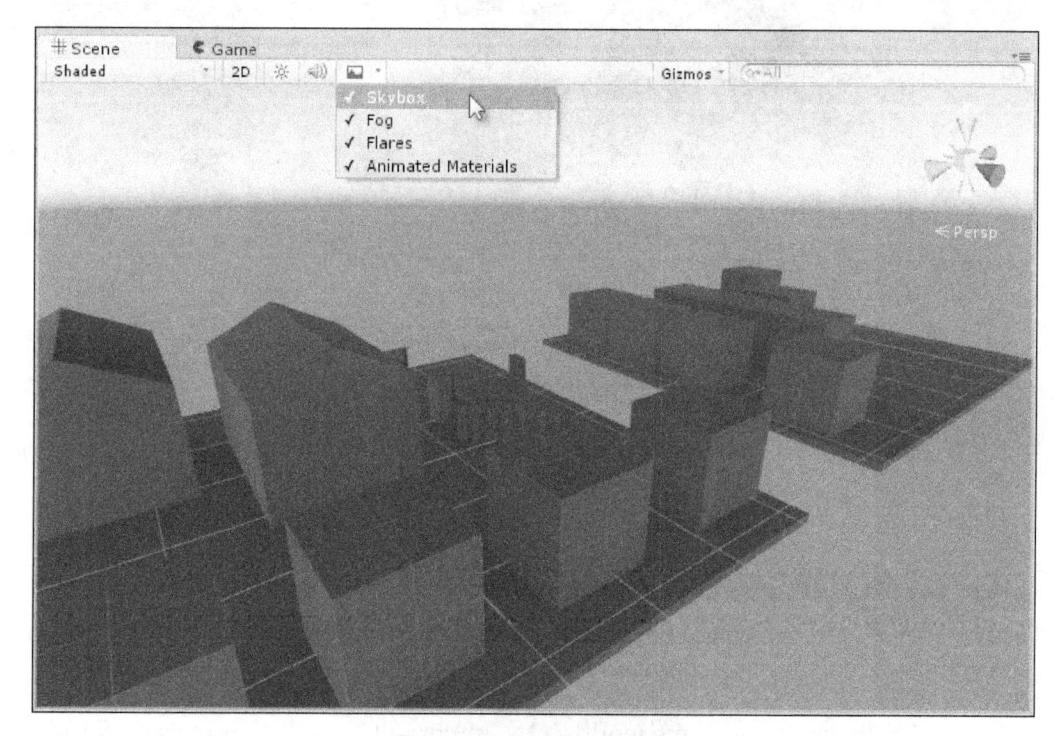

Figure 1.35: Enabling the sky

Now, although the **Skybox** is now enabled and the scene looks better than before, it's still not being illuminated properly—the objects lack shadows and highlights. To fix this, be sure that lighting is enabled for the scene by toggling on the lighting icon at the top of the **Scene** viewport. See *Figure 1.36*. This setting is for display purposes only. It only affects whether lighting effects are shown in the **Scene** viewport and not whether lighting is truly enabled for the final game:

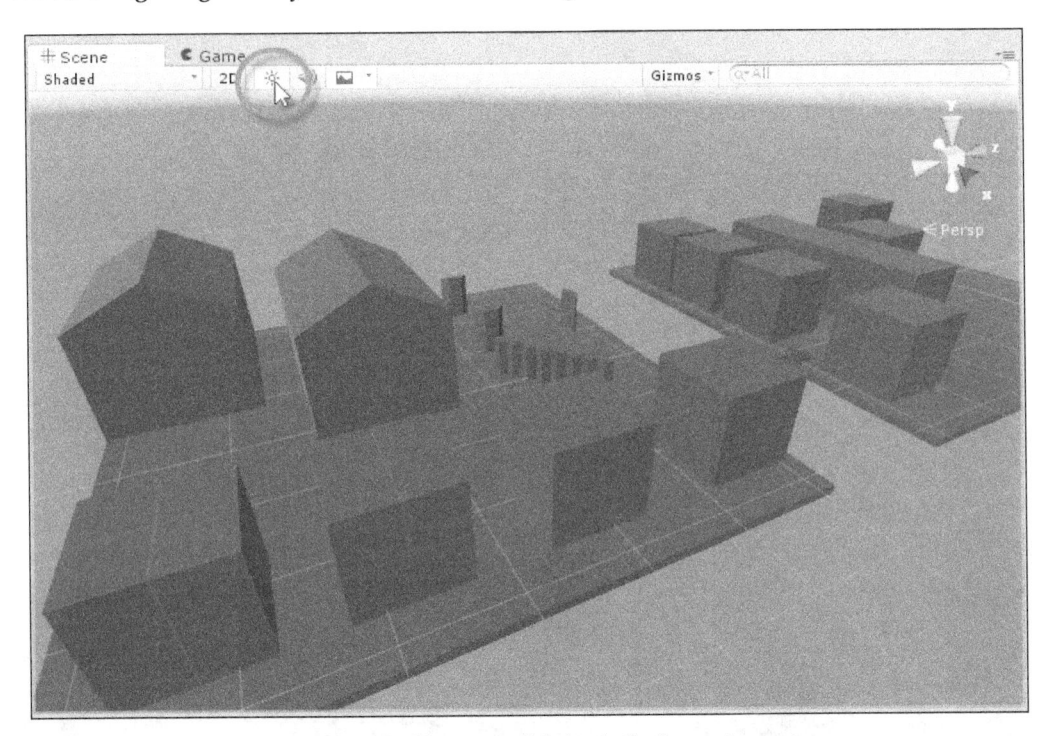

Figure 1.36: Enabling scene lighting in the Scene viewport

Unity Fundamentals

Enabling lighting display for the viewport will result in some differences to the scene appearance and, again, the scene should look better than before. You can confirm that scene lighting is taking effect by selecting **Directional Light** from the **Hierarchy** panel and rotating it. Doing this controls the time of day, rotating the light cycles between day and night and changing the light intensity and mood. This changes how the scene is rendered. See *Figure 1.37*:

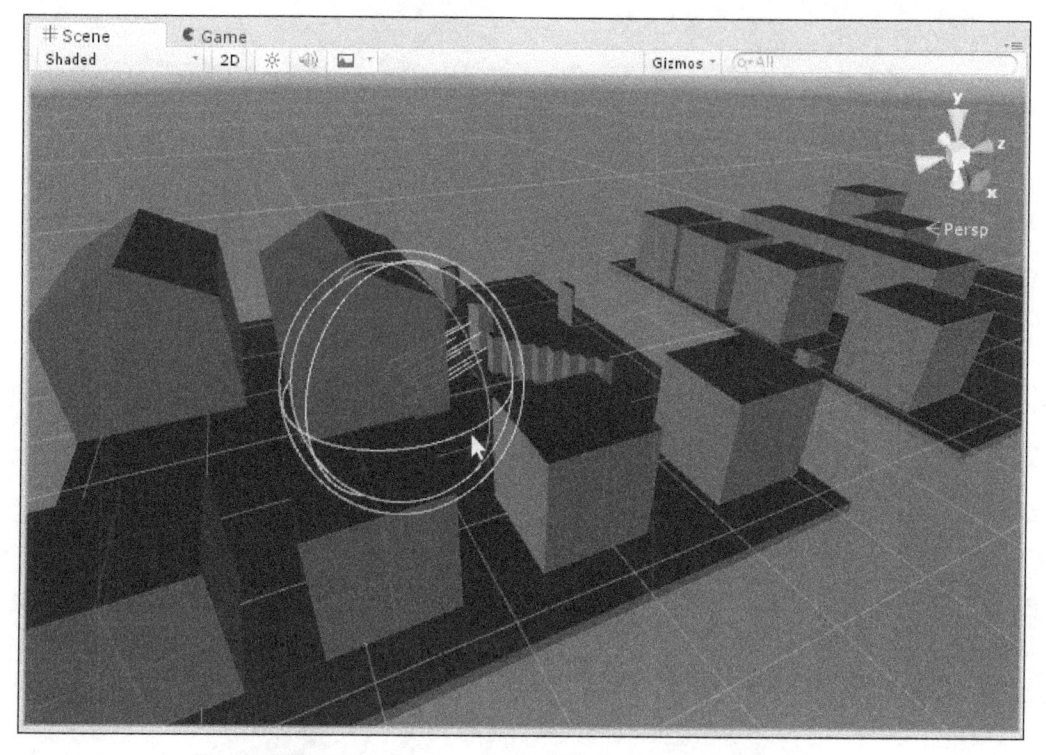

Figure 1.37: Rotating the scene directional light changes the time of day

Let's undo any rotations to the **Directional Light** by pressing *Ctrl + Z* on the keyboard. To prepare for final and optimal lighting, all non-movable objects in the scene (such as walls, floors, chairs, tables, ceilings, grass, hills, towers, and more) should be marked as **Static**. This signifies to Unity that the objects will never move, no matter what happens during gameplay. By marking non-movable objects ahead of time, you can help Unity optimize the way it renders and lights a scene. To mark objects as **Static**, simply select all non-movable objects (which includes practically the entire level so far), and then enable the **Static** checkbox via the **Object Inspector**. Note that you don't need to enable the **Static** setting for each object separately. By holding down the *Shift* key while selecting objects, you can select multiple objects together, allowing you to adjust their properties as a batch through the **Object Inspector**. See *Figure 1.38*:

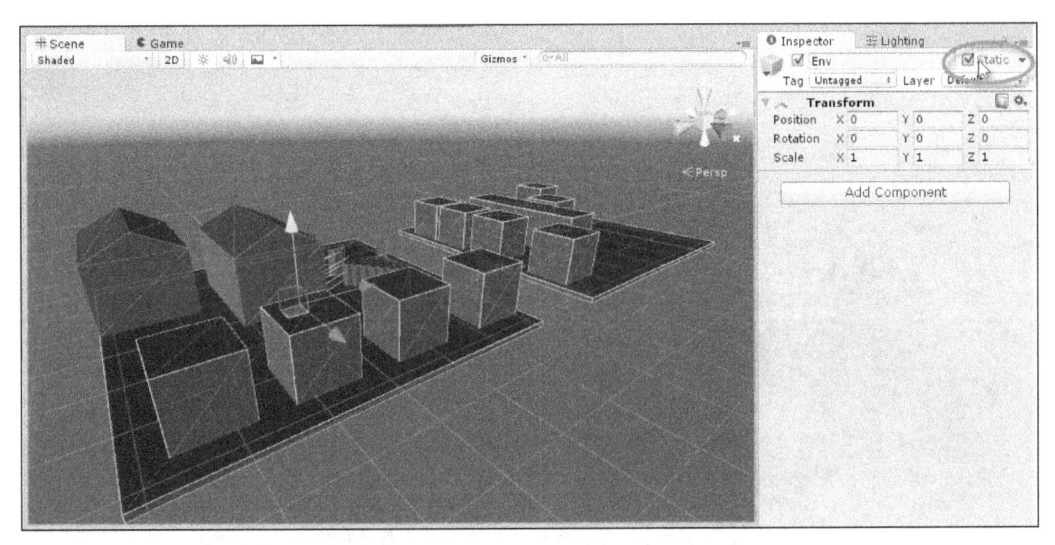

Figure 1.38: Enabling the Static option for multiple non-movable objects improves lighting and performance

Unity Fundamentals

When you enable the **Static** checkbox for geometry, Unity auto-calculates scene lighting in the background—effects such as shadows, indirect illumination, and more. It generates a batch of data called the **GI Cache**, featuring **Light Propagation Paths**, which instructs Unity how light rays should bounce and move around the scene to achieve greater realism. Even so, enabling the **Static** checkbox as we've done still won't produce cast shadows for objects, and this seriously detracts from realism. This happens because most mesh objects have the **Cast Shadows** option disabled. To fix this, select all meshes in the scene. Then, from the **Object Inspector**, click on the **Cast Shadows** checkbox from the **Mesh Renderer** component, and choose the **On** option from the context menu. When you do this, all mesh objects should cast shadows. See *Figure 1.39*:

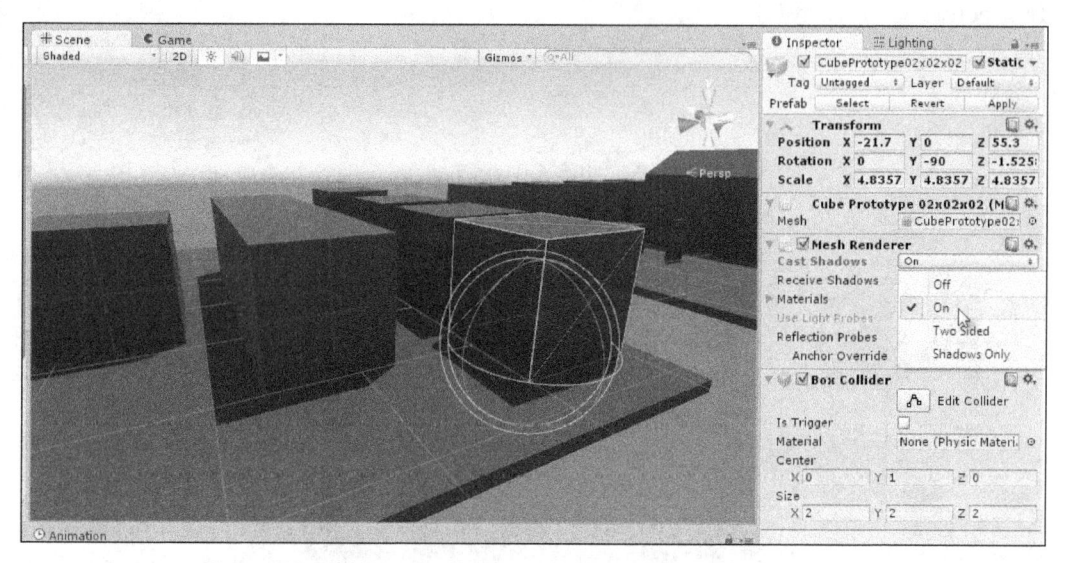

Figure 1.39: Enabling cast shadows from the Mesh Renderer component

Voila! Your meshes now cast shadows. Splendid work: in reaching this far, you've created a new project, populated a scene with meshes, and successfully illuminated them with directional lighting. That's excellent. However, it'd be even better if we could explore our environment in the first-person mode. We'll see how next.

Play testing and the Game tab

The environment created thus far for the coin collection game has been assembled using only the mesh assets included with the native `Prototyping` package. My environment, as shown in *Figure 1.40*, features two main floor islands with houses, and the islands themselves are connected together by a stepping-stone bridge. Your version may be slightly different, and that's fine:

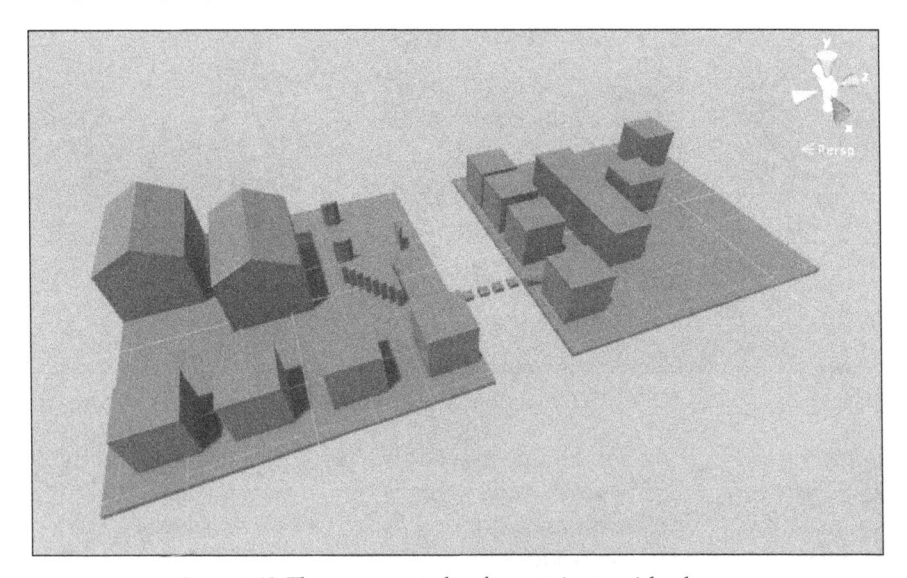

Figure 1.40: The scene created so far contains two island areas

Overall, the scene is good work. It's well worth saving (remember to save regularly!). To save the scene, press *Ctrl + S* on the keyboard or else choose **File | Save Scene** from the application menu. See *Figure 1.41*.

Unity Fundamentals

If you're saving the scene for the first time, Unity displays a pop-up **Save** dialog, prompting you to name the scene descriptively (I called it Level_01):

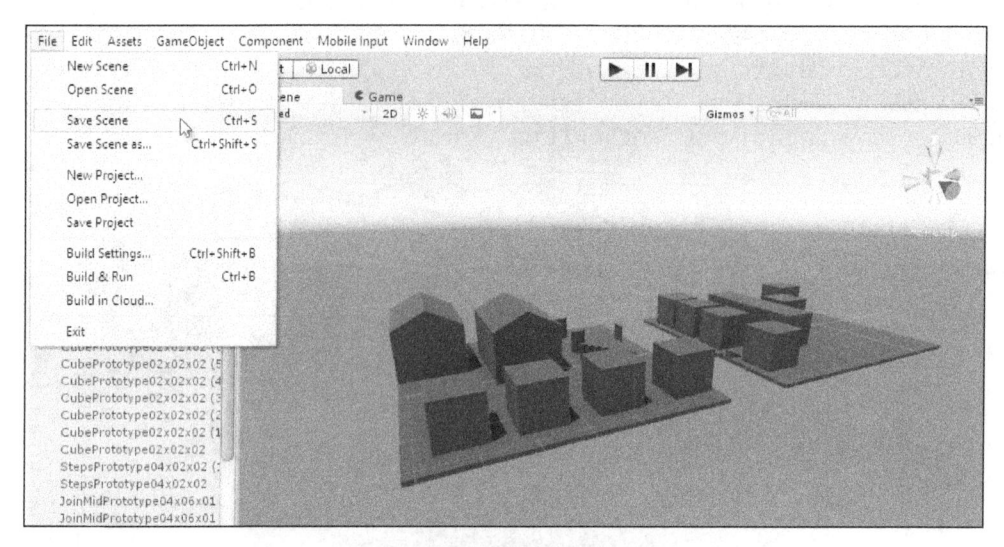

Figure 1.41: Saving a scene

After saving the scene, it becomes scene asset of the project and appears in the **Project** panel. See *Figure 1.42*. This means that the scene is now a genuine and integral part of the project and not just a temporary work-in-progress as it was before. *Notice* also that saving a scene is conceptually *different* from saving a project. For example, the application menu has entries for **Save Scene** and **Save Project**. Remember, a **Project** is a collection of files and folders, including assets and scenes. A scene, by contrast, is one asset within the project and represents a complete 3D map that may be populated by other assets, such as meshes, textures, and sounds. Thus, saving a project saves the configuration between files and assets, including scenes. Saving a scene, in contrast, just retains the level changes within that specified scene.

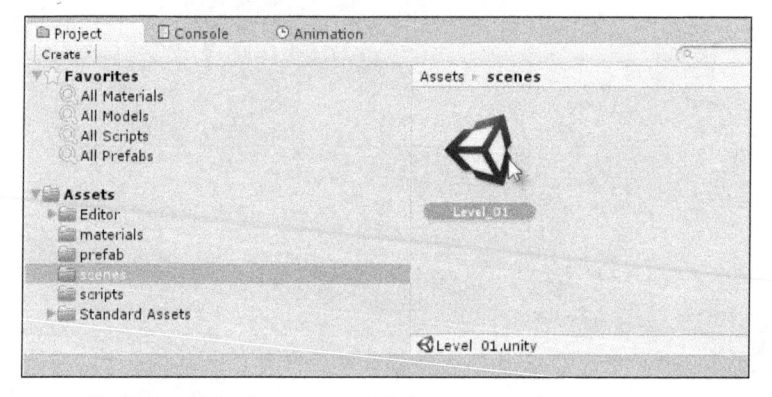

Figure 1.42: Saved scenes are added as assets within your project

> You can see from *Figure 1.42* that I've saved my scene in a folder named `Scenes`. `Folders` can be created in your project by right-clicking on any empty area in the Project panel and choosing **New Folder** from the context menu, or else choose **Assets | Create | Folder** from the application menu. You can easily move and rearrange assets among folders by simply dragging and dropping them.

Now, the level, as it stands, contains nothing really *playable*. It's simply a static, lifeless, and non-interactive 3D environment made using the **Editor** tools. Let's correct this by making our scene playable, allowing the player to wander around and explore the world in first-person mode, controlled using the standard WASD keys on the keyboard. To achieve this, we'll add a first-person character controller to the scene. This is a ready-made asset included with Unity, which contains everything necessary to create quick and effective first-person controls. Open the `Standard Assets | Characters | FirstPersonCharacter | Prefabs` folder. Then drag and drop the **FPSController** asset from the **Project** panel in the scene. See *Figure 1.43*:

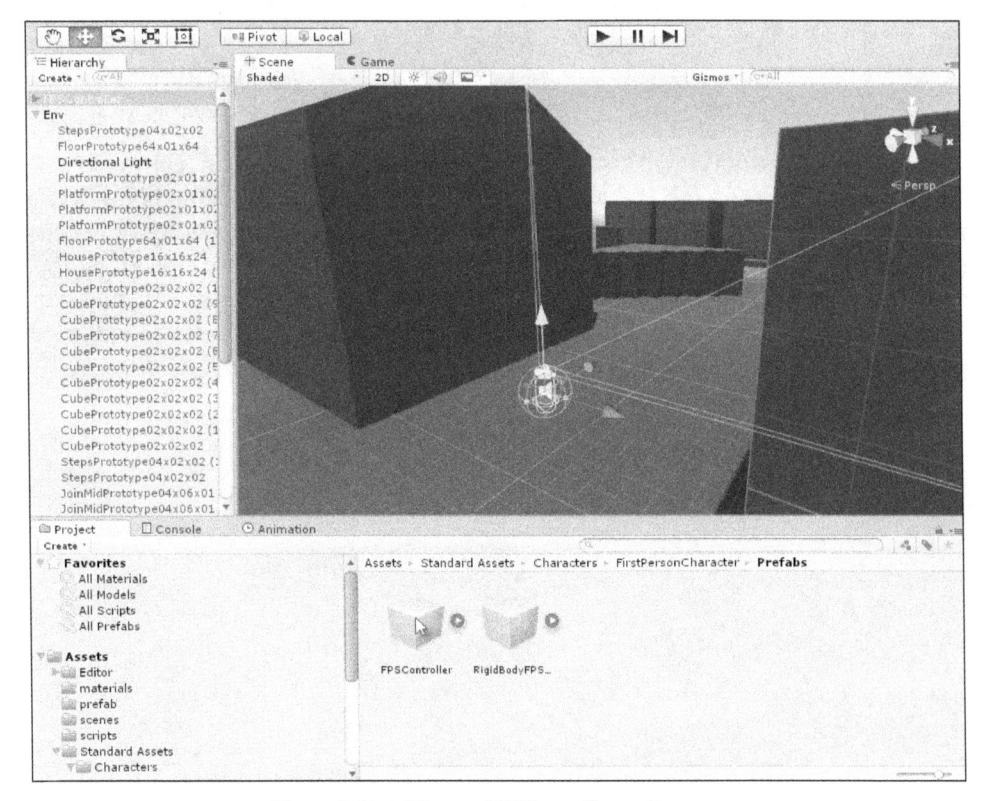

Figure 1.43: Adding an FPSController to the scene

[43]

Unity Fundamentals

After adding the first-person controller, click on the play button from the Unity toolbar to play test the game in first-person mode. See *Figure 1.44*:

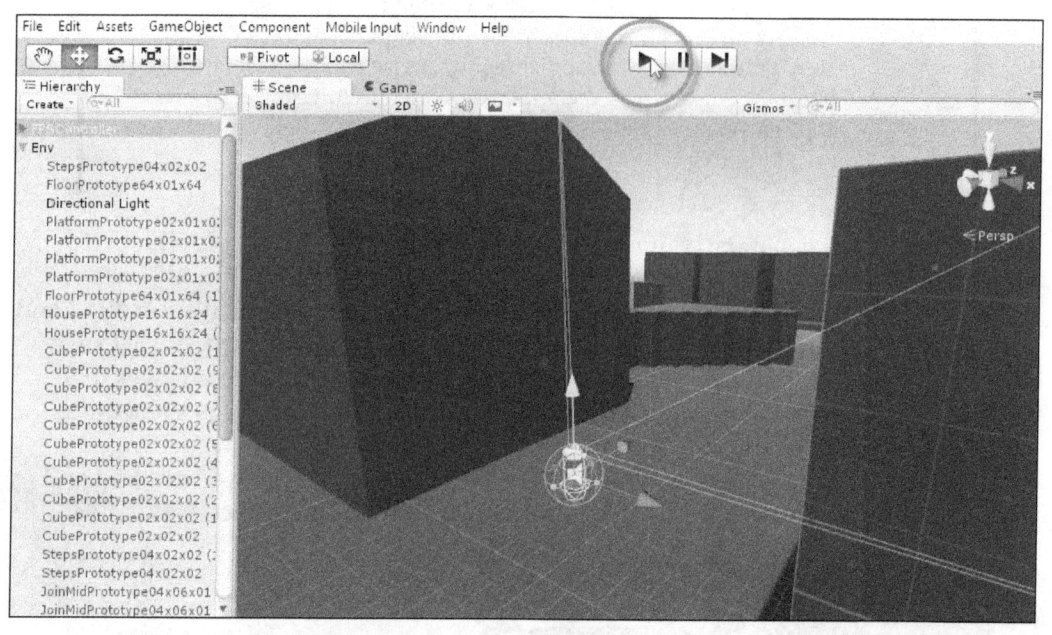

Figure 1.44: Unity scenes can be play tested by clicking on the play button from the toolbar

On clicking play, Unity typically switches from the **Scene** tab to the **Game** tab. As we've seen, the **Scene** tab is a *director's-eye view* of the active scene; it's where a scene is edited, crafted, and designed. In contrast, the **Game** tab is where the active scene is played and tested from the perspective of the gamer. From this view, the scene is displayed through the main game camera. While play mode is active, you can play test your game using the default game controls, provided that the **Game** tab is *in focus*.

The first-person controller uses the WASD keys on the keyboard and mouse movement controls head orientation. See *Figure 1.45*:

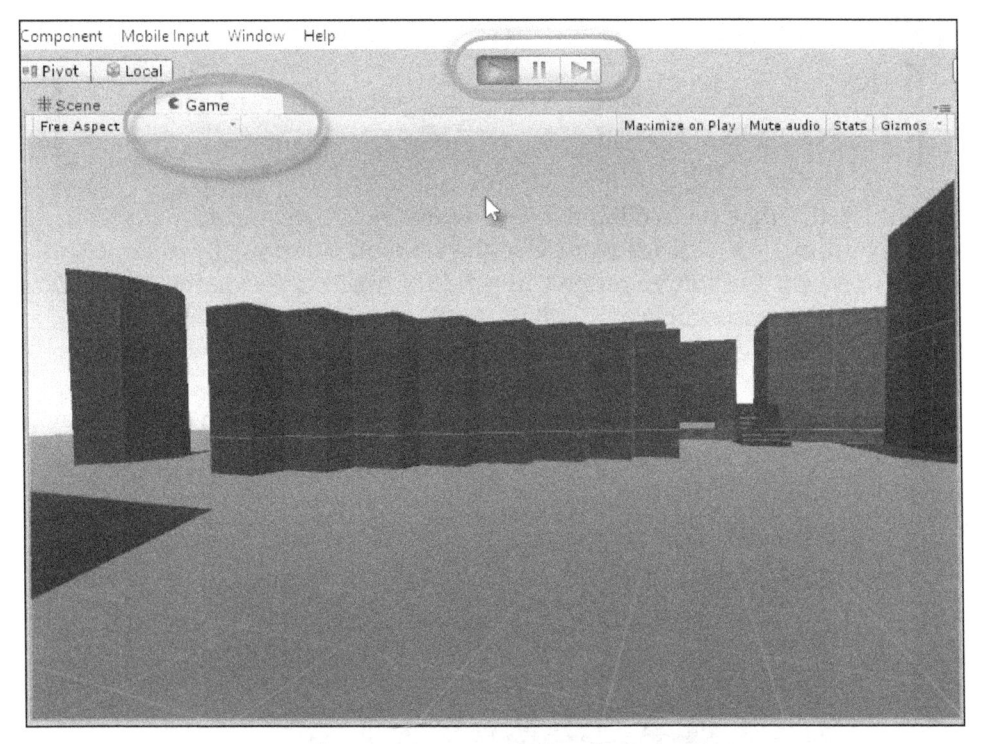

Figure 1.45: Play testing levels in the Game tab

> You can switch back to the Scene tab while in play mode. You can even edit the scene and change, move, and delete objects there too! However, any and all scene changes made during play mode will automatically revert back to their original settings when play mode ends. This behavior is intentional. It lets you edit properties during gameplay to observe their effects and debug any issues without permanently changing the scene.

Unity Fundamentals

Congratulations! Your level should now be walkable in first-person mode. When completed, you can easily stop playback by clicking on the play button again or by pressing *Ctrl + P* on the keyboard. Doing this will return you to the **Scene** tab.

> Unity also features a *Toggle-Pause* button to suspend and resume gameplay.

You should notice that, on playing the level with a first-person controller, you receive an information message printed to the **Console** window. By default, this window appears at the bottom of the **Unity Editor**, docked beside the **Project** panel. This window is also accessible manually from the application menu, **Window | Console**. The **Console** window is where all encountered errors or warnings are displayed for your review as well as information messages. Errors are printed in red and warnings in yellow, and information messages appear as a default grey. Sometimes, a message appears just once, or sometimes it appears many times repeatedly. See *Figure 1.46*:

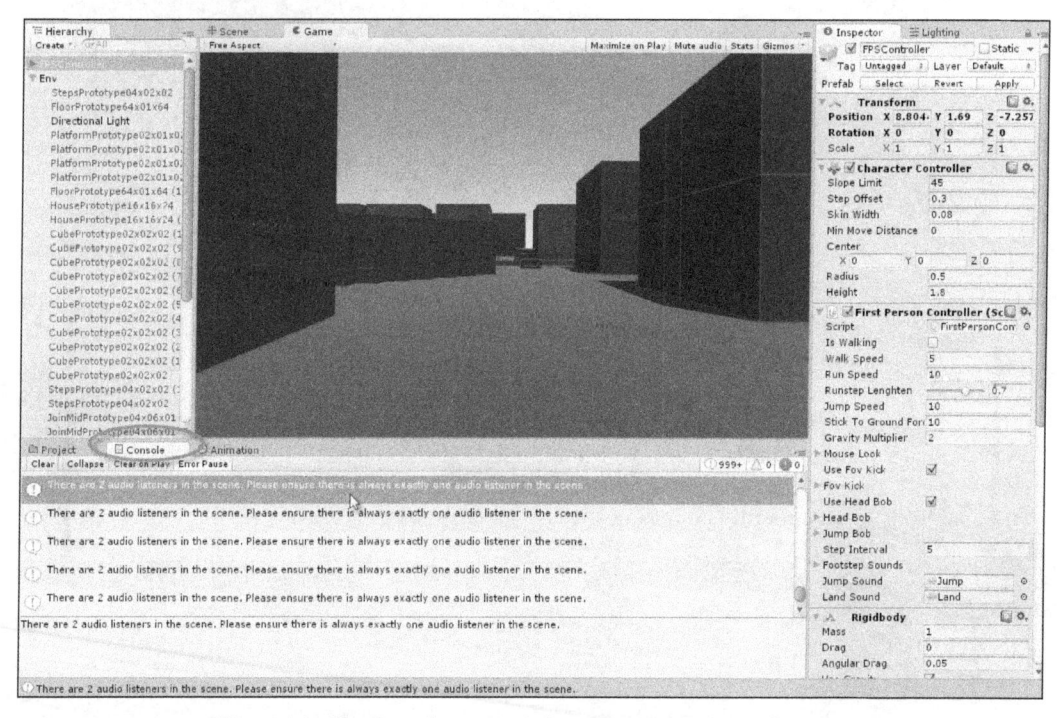

Figure 1.46: The Console outputs information, warnings, and errors

[46]

As mentioned, the **Console** window outputs three distinct types of message: information, warnings, and errors. Information messages are typically Unity's way of making best practice recommendations or suggestions based on how your project is currently working. Warnings are slightly more serious and represent problems either in your code or scene, which (if not corrected) could result in unexpected behaviors and suboptimal performance. Finally, errors describe areas in your scene or code that require careful and immediate attention. Sometimes, errors will prevent your game from working altogether and sometimes errors happen at runtime and can result in game crashes or freezes. The **Console** window, therefore, is helpful because it helps us debug and address issues with our games. *Figure 1.46* has identified an issue concerning duplicated *audio listeners*.

An audio listener is a component attached to a camera object. Specifically, each and every camera, by default, has an audio listener component attached. This represents an *ear point*, that is, the ability to hear sound within the scene from the position of the camera. Unfortunately, Unity doesn't support multiple active audio listeners in the same scene, which means that you can only hear audio from one place at any one time. This problem happens because our scene now contains two cameras, one that was added automatically when the scene was created, and the other that is included in the first-person controller. To confirm this, select the first-person controller object in the **Hierarchy** panel and click on the triangle icon beside its name to reveal more objects underneath, which are part of the first-person controller. See *Figure 1.47*:

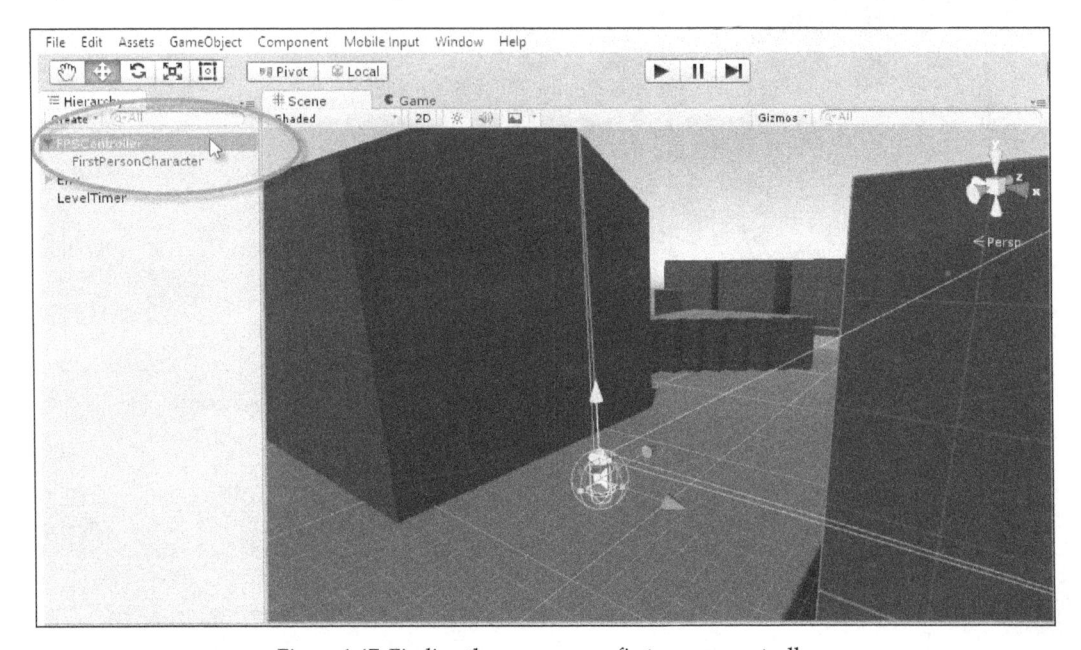

Figure 1.47: Finding the camera on a first-person controller

Unity Fundamentals

Select the `FirstPersonCharacter` object, which is underneath the `FPSController` object (as shown in *Figure 1.47*). The `FirstPersonCharacter` object is a child of the `FPSController`, which is the parent. This is because `FPSController` contains or encloses the `FirstPersonCharacter` object in the **Hierarchy** panel. Child objects inherit the transformations of their parents. This means that as parent objects move and rotate, all transformations will cascade downwards to all children. From the **Object Inspector**, you can see that the object has an **Audio Listener** component. See *Figure 1.48*:

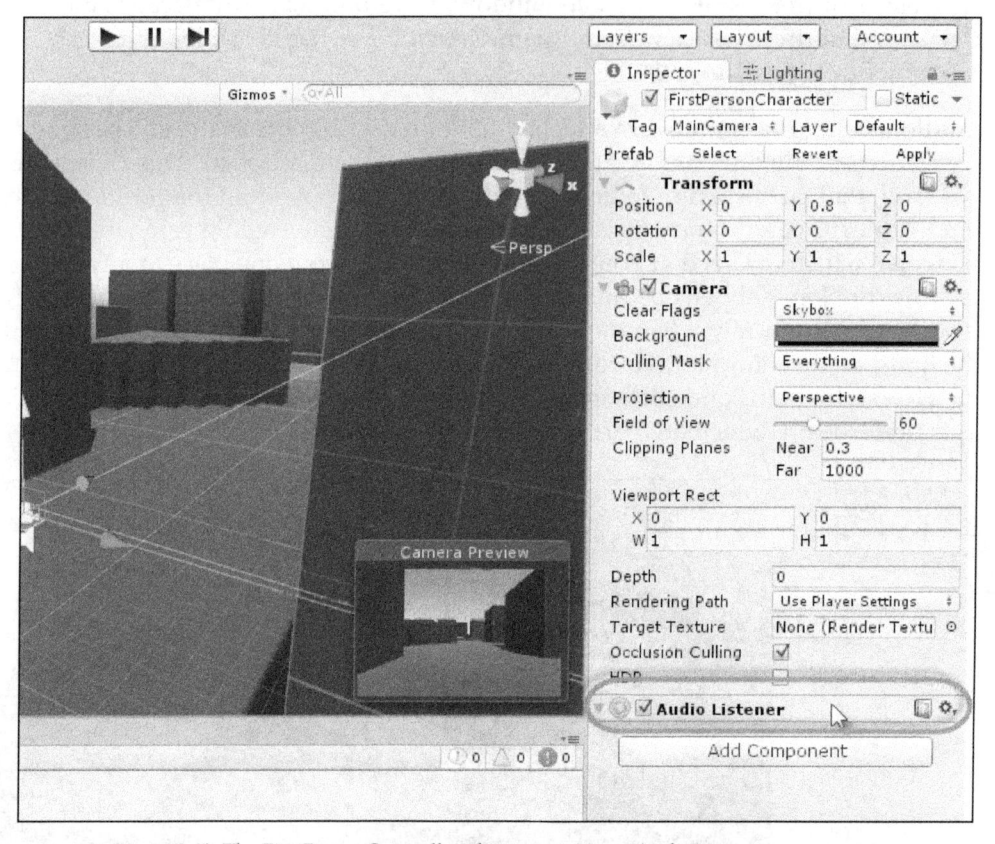

Figure 1.48: The FirstPersonController object contains an AudioListener component

[48]

Chapter 1

We could remove the **Audio Listener** component from the `FPSController`, but this would prevent the player hearing sound in first-person perspective. So, instead, we'll delete the original camera created by default in the scene. To do this, select the original camera object in the hierarchy and press *Delete* on the keyboard. See *Figure 1.49*. This removes the **Audio Listener** warning in the **Console** during gameplay. Now, give the game a play test!

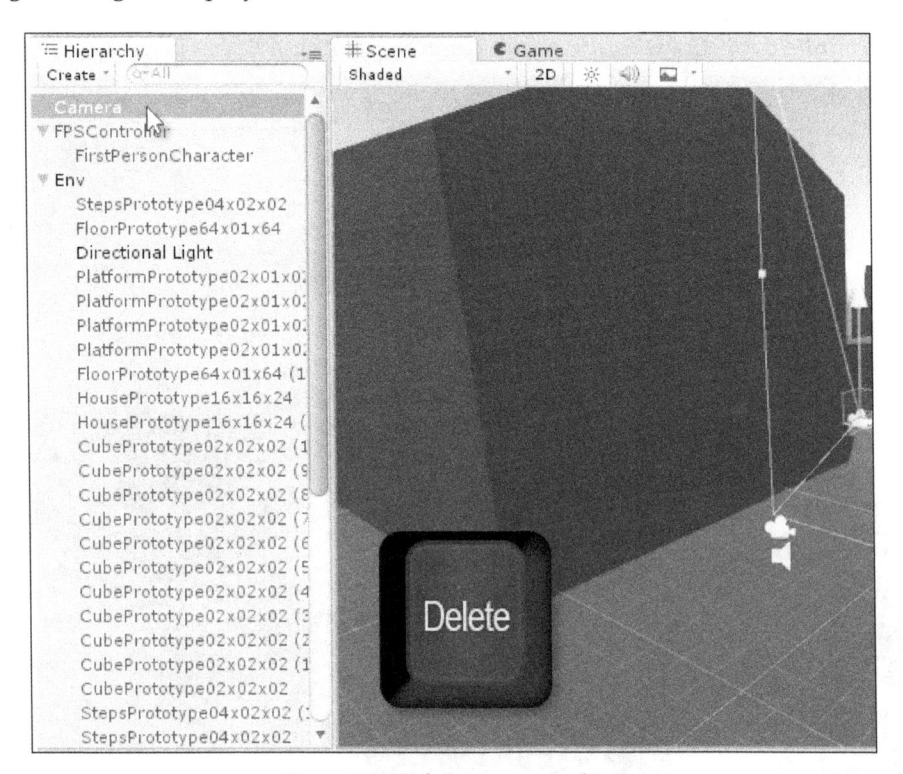

Figure 1.49: Deleting a camera object

Adding a water plane

The collection game is making excellent progress. We now have something playable insofar as we can run around and explore the environment in first-person mode. However, the environment could benefit from additional polish. Right now, for example, the floor meshes appear suspended in mid-air with nothing beneath them to offer support. See *Figure 1.50*. Further, it's possible to walk over the edge and fall into an infinite drop. So, let's add some water beneath the floors to complement the scene as a complete environment:

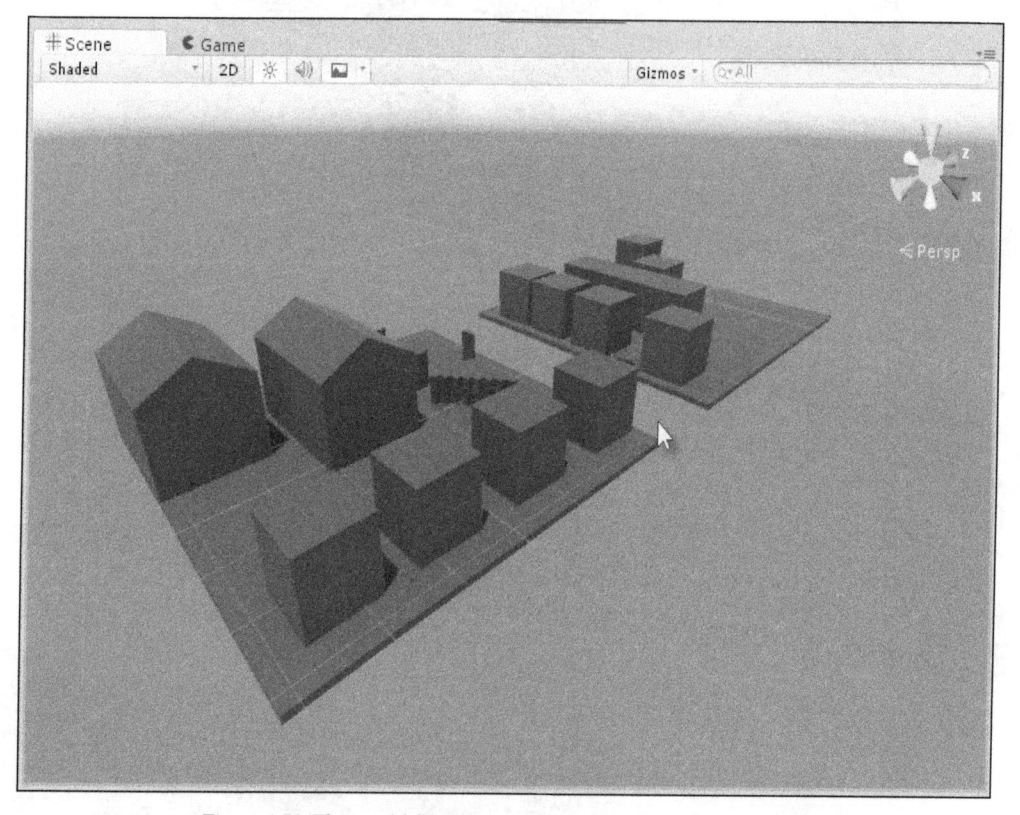

Figure 1.50: The world floor appears to float and have no support

To add water, we can use another ready-made Unity asset included in the **Project** panel. Open the `Standard Assets | Environment | Water | Water | Prefabs` folder. Then drag and drop the `WaterProDaytime` asset from the **Project** panel in the scene. See *Figure 1.51*. This appears as a circular object, which is initially smaller than needed:

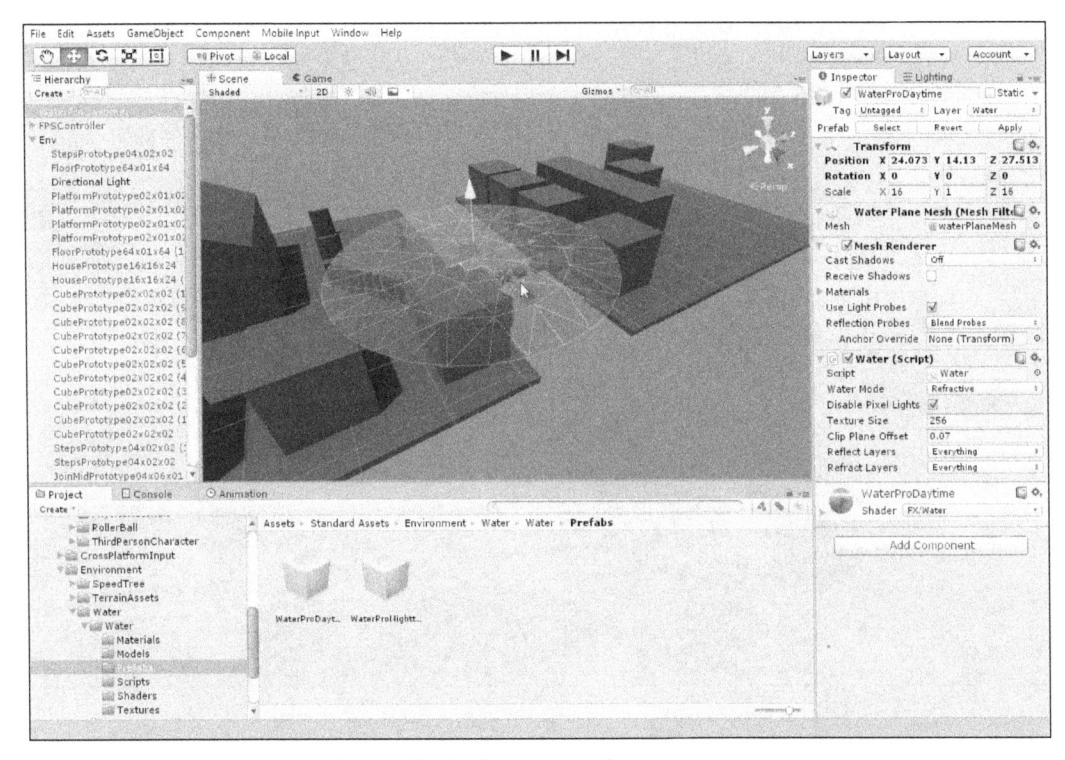

Figure 1.51: Adding water to the environment

After adding the `Water` prefab, position it below the floor level and use the scale tool (R) to increase its planar size (X, Z) to fill the environment outward into the distant horizon. This creates the feel that the floor meshes are smaller islands within an expansive world of water. See *Figure 1.52*:

Figure 1.52: Scaling and sizing water for the environment

Now, let's take another test run in the **Game** tab. Press play on the toolbar and navigate the character around in first-person mode. See *Figure 1.53*. You should see the water in the level. Of course, you can't walk on the water! Neither can you swim or dive beneath it. If you try walking on it, you'll simply fall through it, descending into infinity as though the water had never been there. Right now, the water is an entirely cosmetic feature, but it makes the scene look much better:

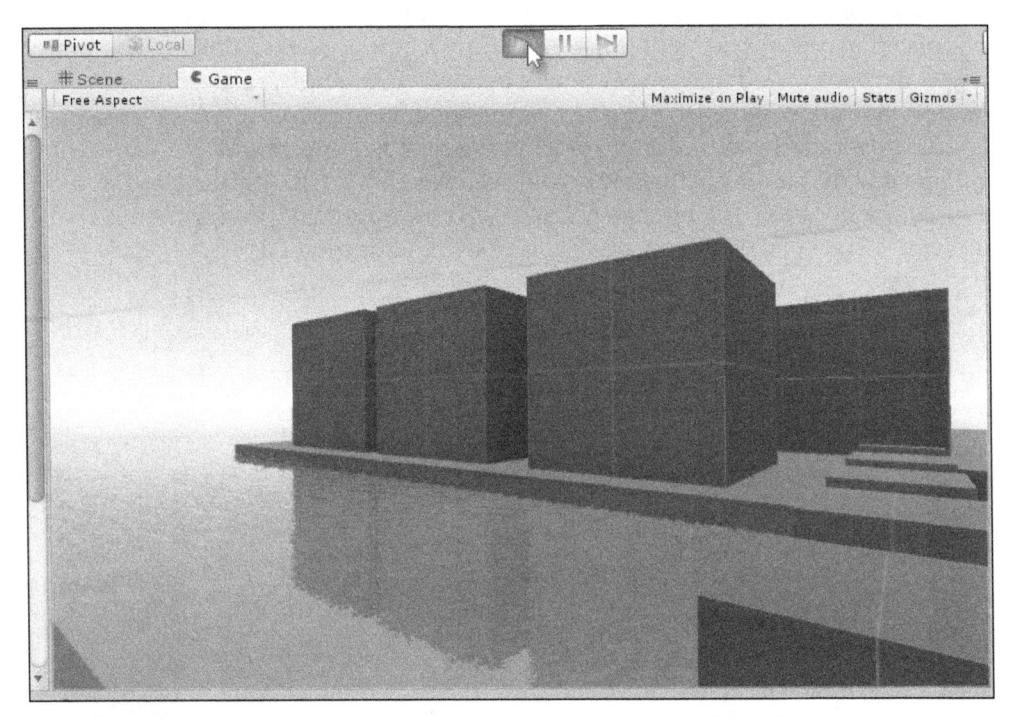

Figure 1.53: Testing the environment with water in FPS mode

Unity Fundamentals

The water is really a substanceless, ethereal object through which the player can pass easily. Unity doesn't recognize it as a solid or even a semi-solid object. As we'll see in more detail later, you can make an object solid very quickly by attaching a **Box Collider** component to it. Colliders and physics is covered in more depth from *Chapter 3, Creating a Space Shooter*, onward. For now, however, we can add solidity to the water by first selecting the `Water` object from the **Hierarchy** panel (or in the **Scene** viewport) and then by choosing **Component | Physics | Box Collider** from the application menu. See *Figure 1.54*. Attaching a component to the selected object changes the object itself; it changes how it behaves. Essentially, components add behavior and functionality to objects, making them behave in different ways. Even so, resist the temptation to add lots of components to an object without reason and with the view that it makes them more versatile or powerful. It's better to have as few components on an object as necessary. This strategy of preferring relevant simplicity keeps your workflow neater, simpler, and optimized:

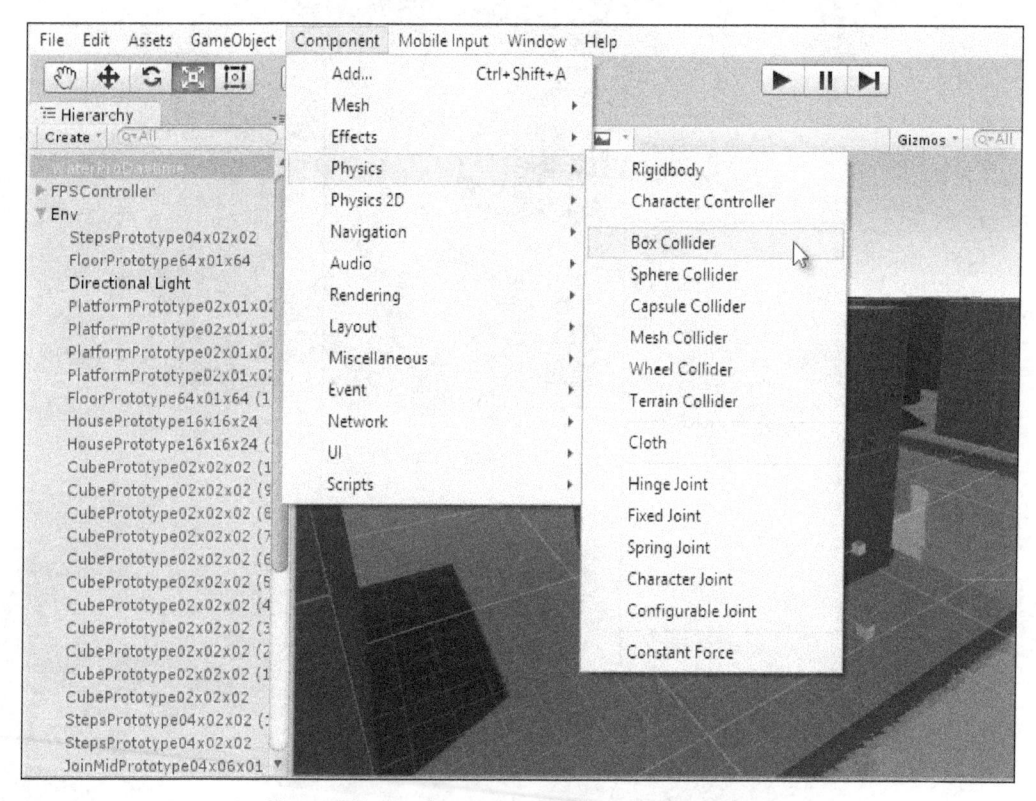

Figure 1.54: Attaching a Box Collider to a Water object

[54]

Chapter 1

When a **Box Collider** is added to the water, a surrounding green cage or mesh appears. This approximates the volume and shape of the Water object and represents its physical volume, namely, the volume of the object that Unity recognizes as solid. See *Figure 1.55*:

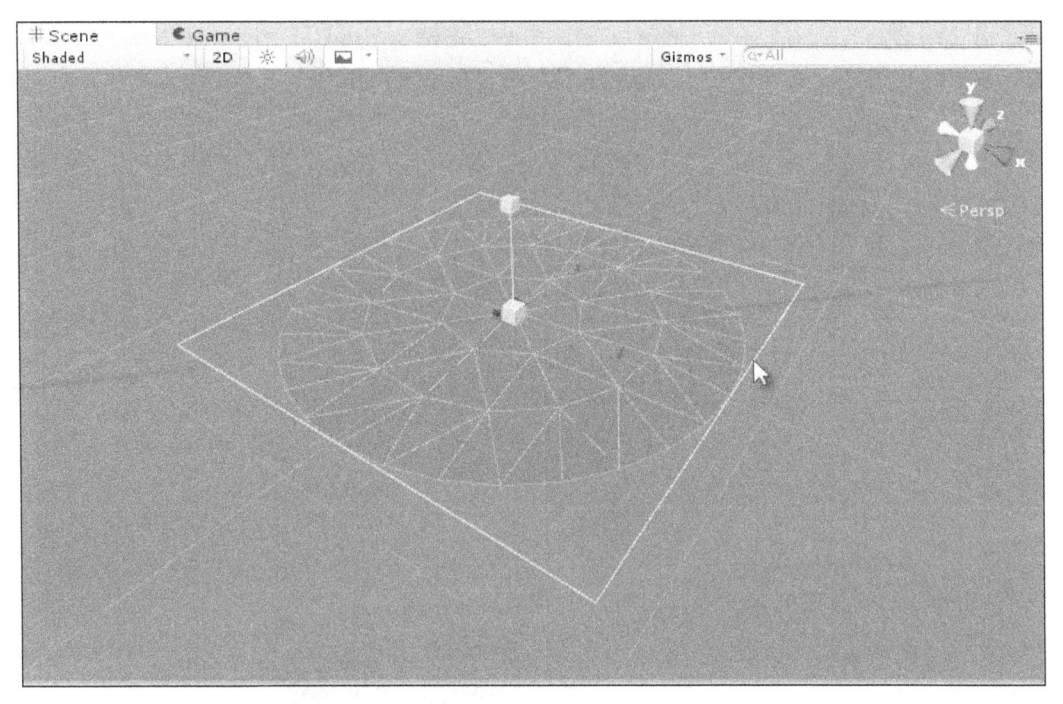

Figure 1.55: Box Colliders approximate physical volume

Unity Fundamentals

If you play the game now, your character will walk on water as opposed to falling through. True, the character should be able to swim properly, but walking might be better than falling. To achieve full swimming behavior would require significantly more work and is not covered here. If you want to remove the **Box Collider** functionality and return the water back to its original, ethereal state, then select the `Water` object, click on the cog icon on the **Box Collider** component, and then choose **Remove Component** from the context menu. See *Figure 1.56*:

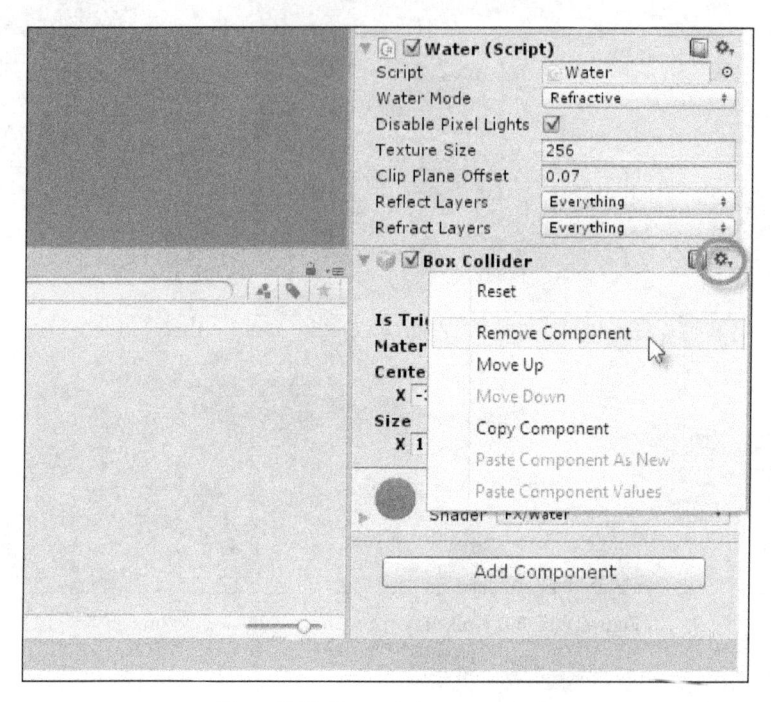

Figure 1.56: Removing a component

Adding a coin to collect

On reaching this far, our game has many features, namely, a complete environment, first-person controller, and water. However, we're supposed to be making a coin collection game and there aren't any coins for the player to collect yet. Now, to achieve fully collectible coins, we'll need to write some C# script, which will happen in the next chapter of this book. However, we can at least get started here at creating the coin object itself. To do this, we'll use a **Cylinder** primitive that's scaled to form a coin-looking shape. To create a cylinder, select **GameObject | 3D Object | Cylinder** from the application menu:

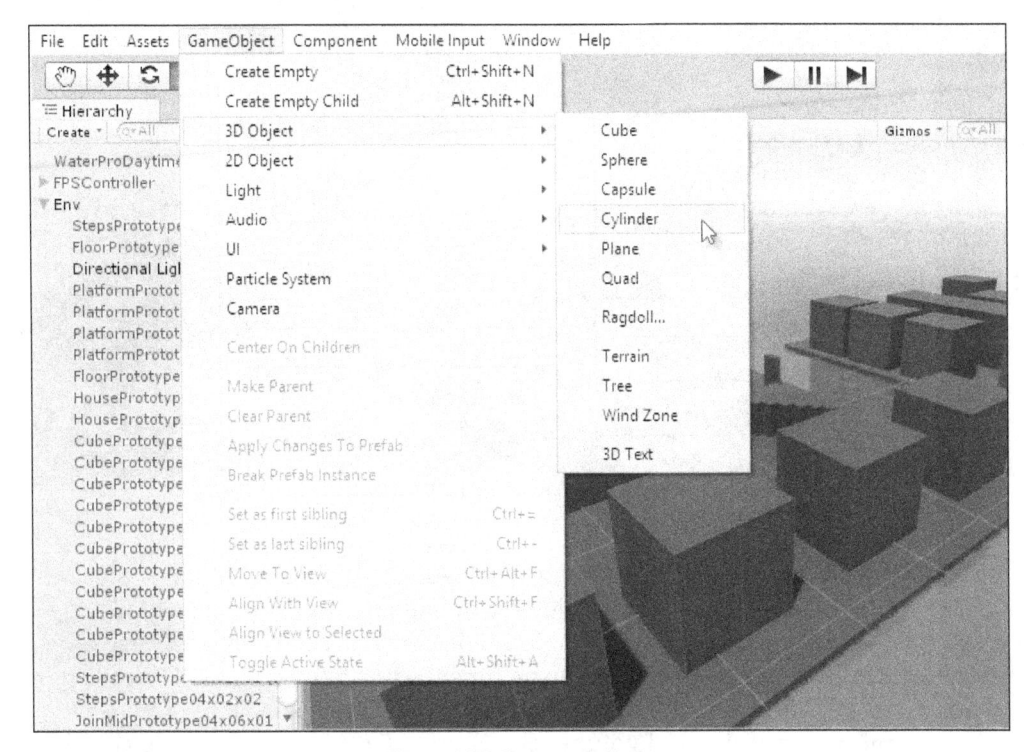

Figure 1.57: Create a Cylinder

Initially, the cylinder looks nothing like a coin. However, this is easily changed by scaling non-uniformly in the Z axis to make the cylinder thinner. Switch to the scale tool (R) and then scale the **Cylinder** inward. See *Figure 1.58*:

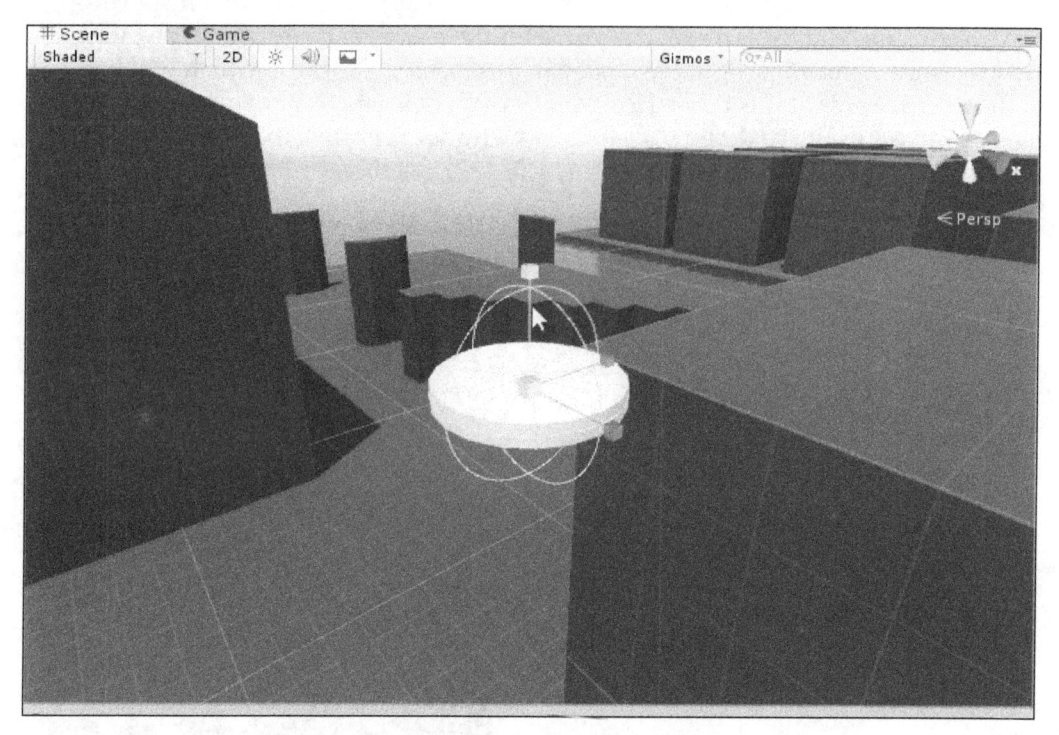

Figure 1.58: Scaling the cylinder to make a collectible coin

After rescaling the coin, its collider no longer represents its volume. It appears much larger than it should (see *Figure 1.58*). By default, the **Cylinder** is created with a **Capsule Collider** as opposed to a **Box Collider**. You can change the size of the **Capsule Collider** component by adjusting the **Radius** field from the **Object Inspector** when the coin is selected. Lower the **Radius** field to shrink the collider to a more representative size and volume. See *Figure 1.59*. Alternatively, you could remove **Capsule Collider** altogether and add **Box Collider** instead. Either way is fine; generally choose the simpler shape where possible. The colliders will be used in script in the next chapter to detect when the player collides with the coin to collect them:

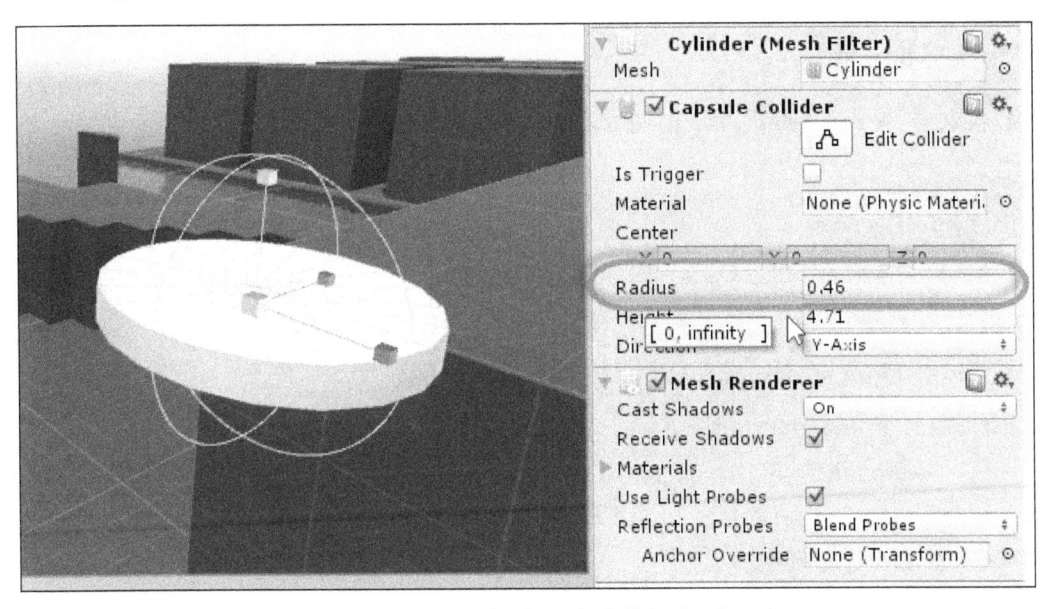

Figure 1.59: Adjusting the Capsule Collider for the coin

Here we are! We now have the basic shape and structure for a coin. We will, of course, improve it carefully and critically in many ways in the next chapter. For example, we'll make it collectible and assign it a material to make it look shiny. However, here, using only a basic Unity primitive and scale tool, we're able to generate a shape that truly resembles a coin.

Summary

Congratulations! On reaching this point, you have laid the foundations for a coin collection game that will be complete and functional in the next chapter. Here, we've seen how to create a Unity project from scratch and populate it with assets, such as meshes, textures, and scenes. In addition, we've seen how to create a scene for our game and use a range of assets to populate it with useful functionality that ships out of the box with the Unity engine, such as water, first-person controllers, and environment prototyping assets. In the next chapter, we'll resume work from where we ended here by making a coin that is collectible, and establishing a set of rules and logic for the game, making it possible to win and lose.

Test your knowledge

Q1. Assets are imported directly into the...

- A. Object Inspector
- B. Hierarchy
- C. Scene
- D. Project Panel

Q2. You can quickly create first person controls using

- A. Camera objects
- B. Capsules
- C. First Person Controllers
- D. Box Colliders

Q3. The Prototyping Package is most useful for...

- A. Building Levels
- B. Prototyping Code
- C. Animating Objects
- D. Creating Camera Effects

Q4. When pressed in the scene tab, the F key will...

- A. Center the view on the selected object
- B. Remove the selected object
- C. Hide the selected object
- D. Freeze the selected object

Q5. You can access the Snapping Feature by pressing...

- A. C
- B. V
- C. D
- D. E

Further Reading

Check out the below-mentioned links for more information:

- https://unity3d.com/learn/tutorials/s/interactive-tutorials
- https://docs.unity3d.com/Manual/CreatingScenes.html
- https://docs.unity3d.com/Manual/GameObjects.html
- **Mastering Unity 2017 Game Development with C# - Second Edition**, Alan Thorn, 9781788479837 (https://www.packtpub.com/web-development/mastering-unity-2017-game-development-c-second-edition)

2
Creating a Collection Game

This chapter continues from the previous one by building a collection game with Unity. In this game, the player wanders an environment in first-person mode, searching for and collecting all the coins in a scene before a global timer expires. If all coins are collected before timer expiry, the game is won. However, if the timer expires before all coins are collected, the game is lost. The project created so far features a complete environment, with a floor, props, and water, and it also features a first-person controller along with a basic coin object, which looks correct in shape and form but still cannot be collected.

This chapter completes the project by creating a coin object to collect and adding a timer system to determine whether the total game time has elapsed. In essence, this chapter is about defining a system of logic and rules governing the game. To achieve this, we'll need to code in C# and so this chapter requires a basic understanding of programming. This book is about Unity and developing games with that engine. The basic of programming as a subject is, however, beyond the scope of this book. So, I'll assume that you already have a working knowledge of coding generally but have simply not coded in Unity before. Overall, this chapter will demonstrate the following topics:

- Material creation
- Prefabs
- Coding with C#
- Writing script files
- Using particle systems
- Building and compiling games

Creating a coin material

The previous chapter closed by creating a basic coin object from a non-uniformly scaled cylinder primitive. This object was created by selecting **GameObject | 3D Object | Cylinder** from the application menu. See *Figure 2.1*. The coin object, as a concept, represents a basic or fundamental unit in our game logic because the player character should be actively searching the level looking for coins to collect before a timer runs out. This means that the coin is more than mere *appearance*; its purpose in the game is not simply eye candy, but is functional. It makes an immense difference to the game outcome whether the coin is collected by the player or not. Therefore, the coin object, as it stands, is lacking in two important respects. Firstly, it looks dull and grey—it doesn't really stand out and grab the player's attention. Secondly, the coin cannot actually be collected yet. Certainly, the player can walk into the coin, but nothing appropriate happens in response:

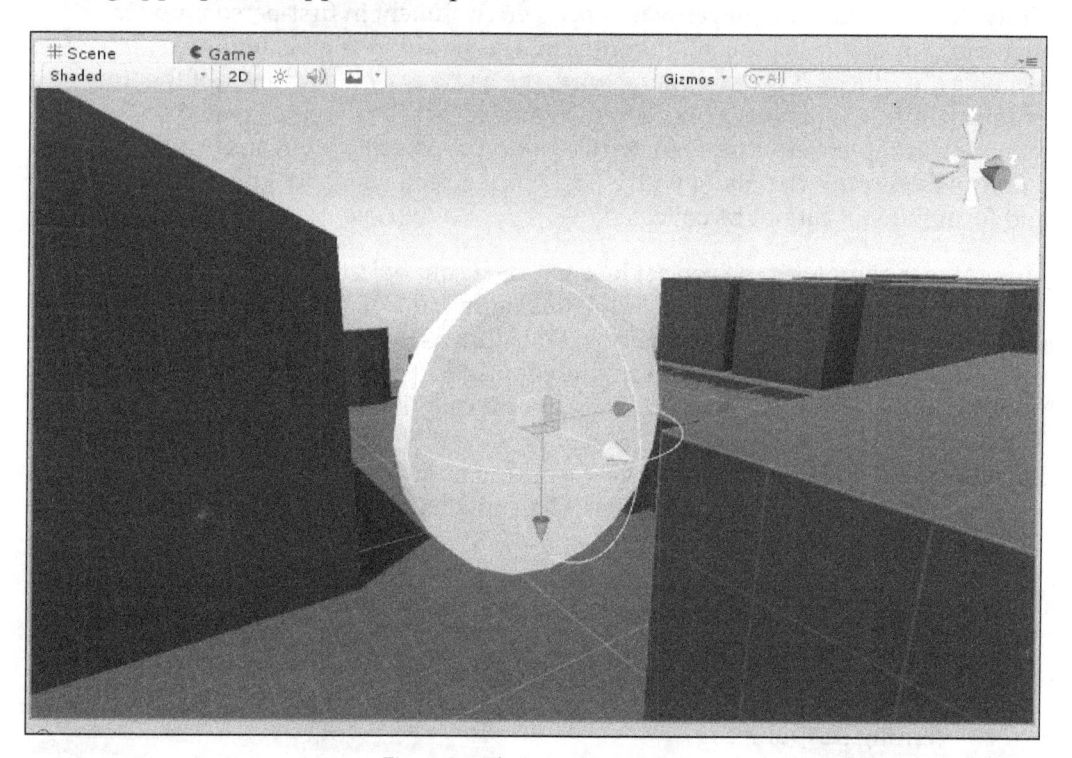

Figure 2.1: The coin object so far

> The completed CollectionGame project, as discussed in this chapter and the next, can be found in the book companion files in the `Chapter02/CollectionGame` folder.

In this section, we'll focus on improving the coin appearance using a **material**. A material defines an algorithm (or instruction set) specifying how the coin should be rendered. A material doesn't just say what the coin should look like in terms of color; it defines how shiny or smooth a surface is, as opposed to rough and diffuse. This is important to recognize and is why a texture and material refer to different things. A texture is simply an image file loaded in memory, which can be wrapped around a 3D object via its UV mapping. In contrast, a material defines how one or more textures can be combined together and applied to an object to shape its appearance. To create a new material asset in Unity, right-click on an empty area in the Project panel, and from the context menu, choose **Create | Material**. See *Figure 2.2*. You can also choose **Assets | Create | Material** from the application menu:

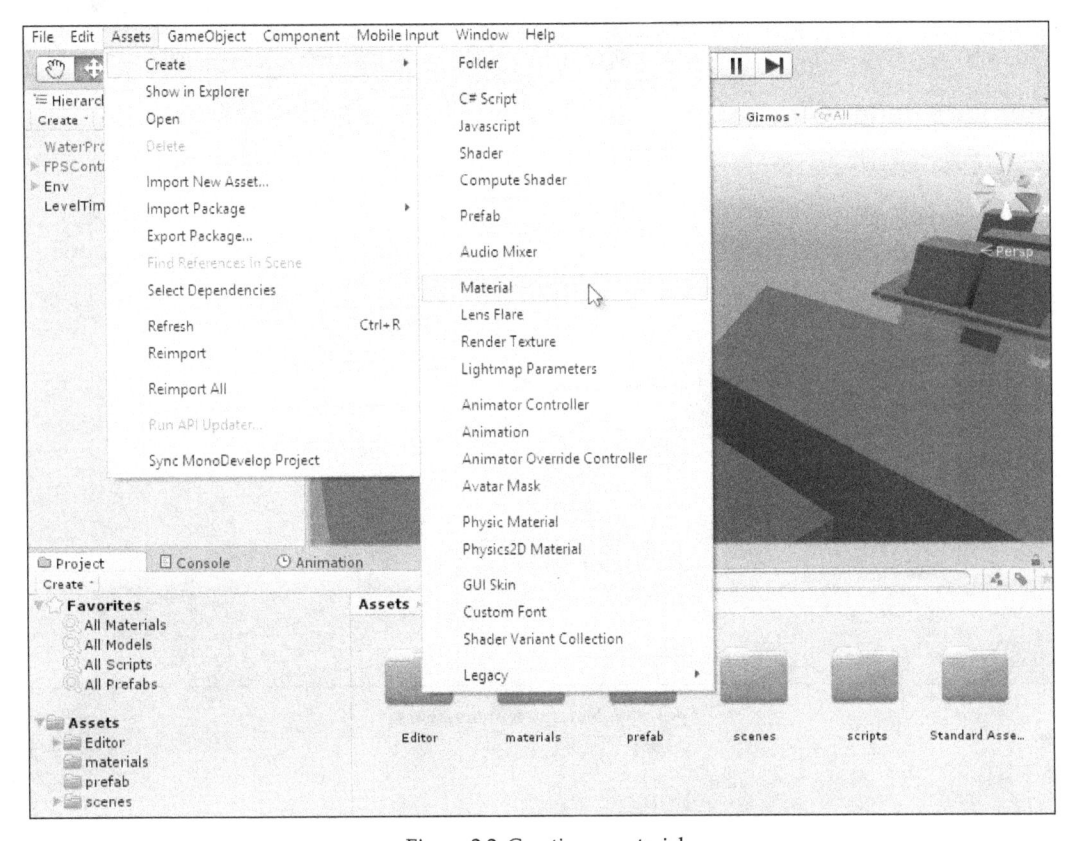

Figure 2.2: Creating a material

> A material is sometimes called a Shader. If needed, you can create custom materials using a Shader language or you can use a Unity add-on, such as Shader Forge.

Creating a Collection Game

After creating a new material, assign it an appropriate name from the **Project** panel. As I'm aiming for a gold look, I'll name the material `mat_GoldCoin`. Prefixing the asset name with mat helps me know, just from the asset name, that it's a material asset. Simply type a new name in the text edit field to name the material. You can also click on the material name twice to edit the name at any time later. See *Figure 2.3*:

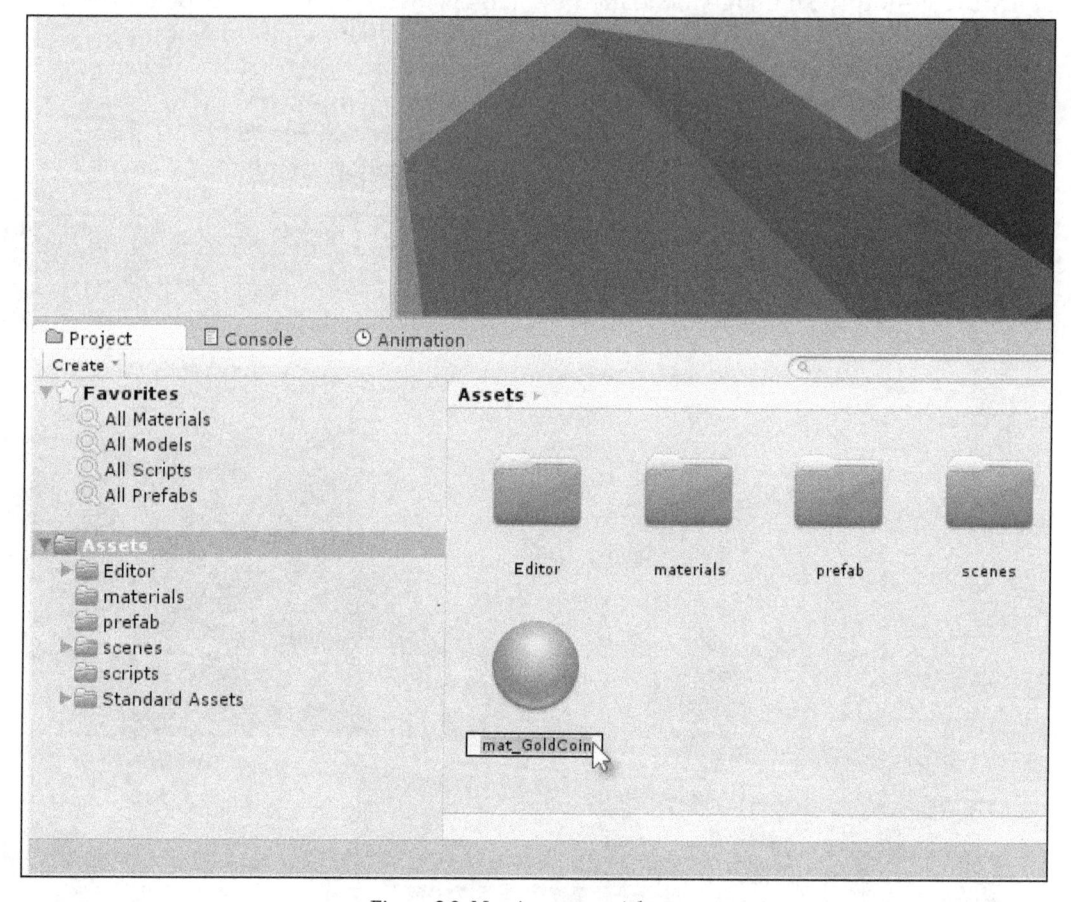

Figure 2.3: Naming a material asset

Next, select the material asset in the **Project** panel, if it's not already selected, and its properties display immediately in the **Object Inspector**. There are lots of properties listed! In addition, a material preview displays at the bottom of the **Object Inspector**, showing you how the material would look, based on its current settings, if it were applied to a 3D object, such as a sphere. As you change material settings from the Inspector, the preview panel updates automatically to reflect your changes, offering instant feedback on how the material would look. See the following screenshot:

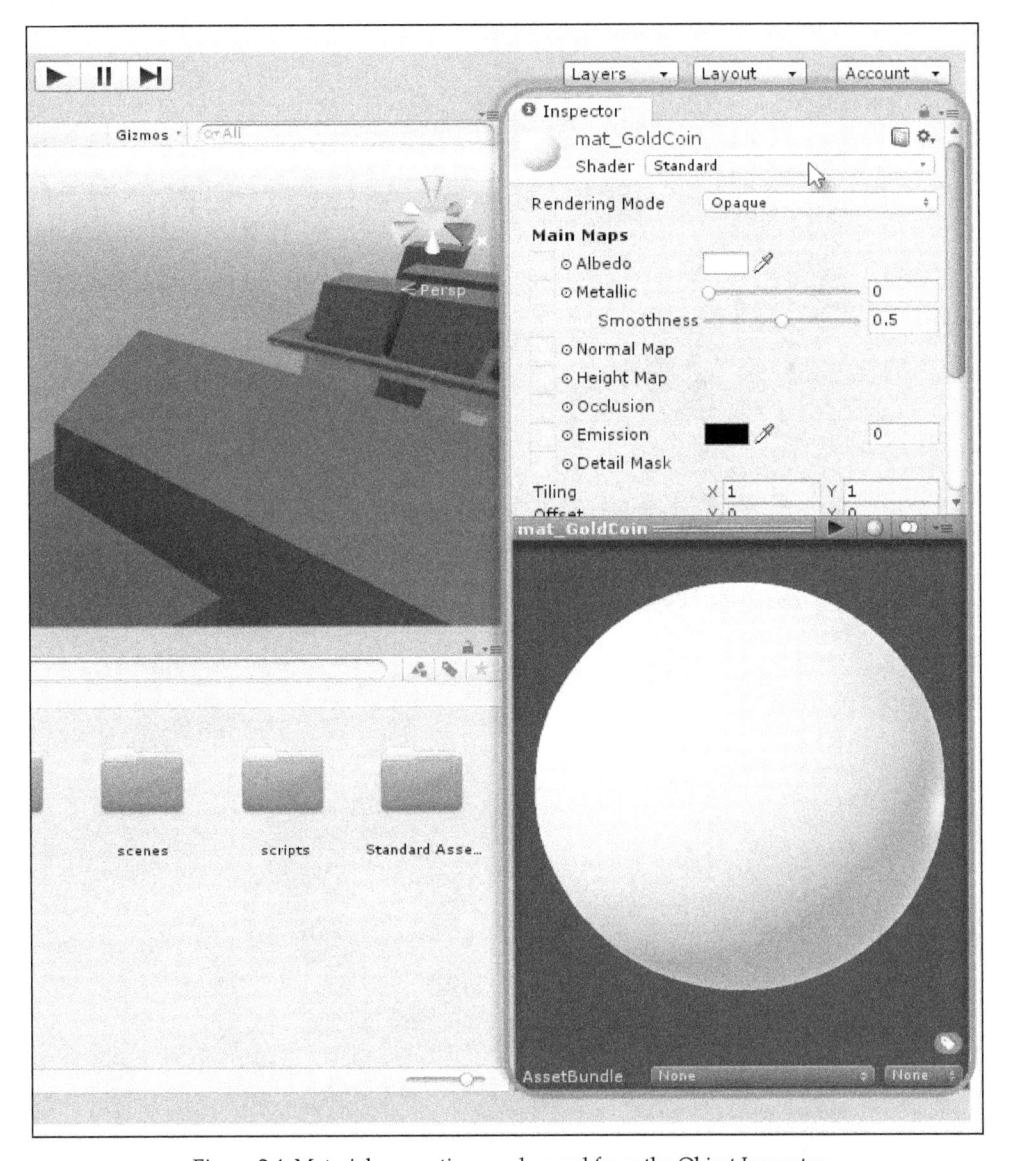

Figure 2.4: Material properties are changed from the Object Inspector

Creating a Collection Game

Let's now create a gold material for the coin. When creating any material, the first setting to choose is the **Shader** type because this setting affects all other parameters available to you. The **Shader** type determines which algorithm will be used to shade your object. There are many different choices, but most material types can be approximated using either **Standard** or **Standard (Specular setup)**. For the gold coin, we can leave the **Shader** as **Standard**. See the following screenshot:

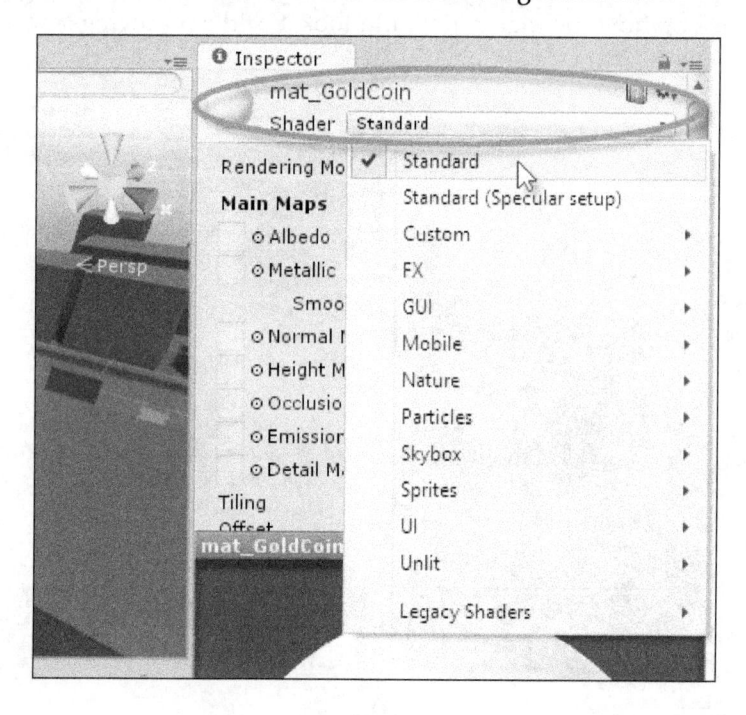

Figure 2.5: Setting the material Shader type

Chapter 2

Right now, the preview panel displays the material as a dull grey, which is far from what we need. To define a gold color, we must specify the Albedo. To do this, click on the Albedo color slot to display a Color picker, and from the Color picker dialog, select a gold color. The material preview updates in response to reflect the changes. Refer to the following screenshot:

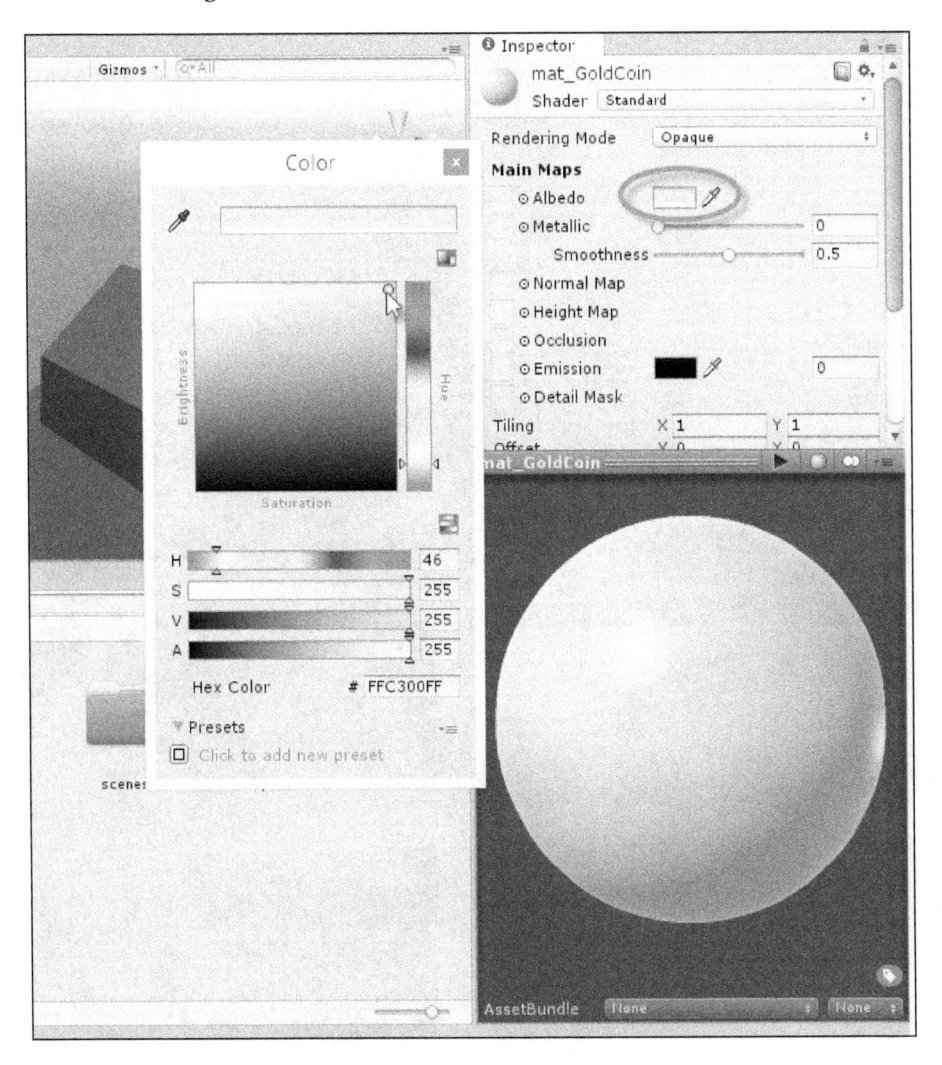

Figure 2.6: Selecting a gold color for the Albedo channel

Creating a Collection Game

The coin material is looking better than it did, but it's still supposed to represent a metallic surface, which tends to be shiny and reflective. To add this quality to our material, click and drag the Metallic slider in the Object Inspector to the right-hand side, setting its value to 1. This indicates that the material represents a fully metal surface as opposed to a diffuse surface such as cloth or hair. Again, the preview panel will update to reflect the change. See *Figure 2.7*:

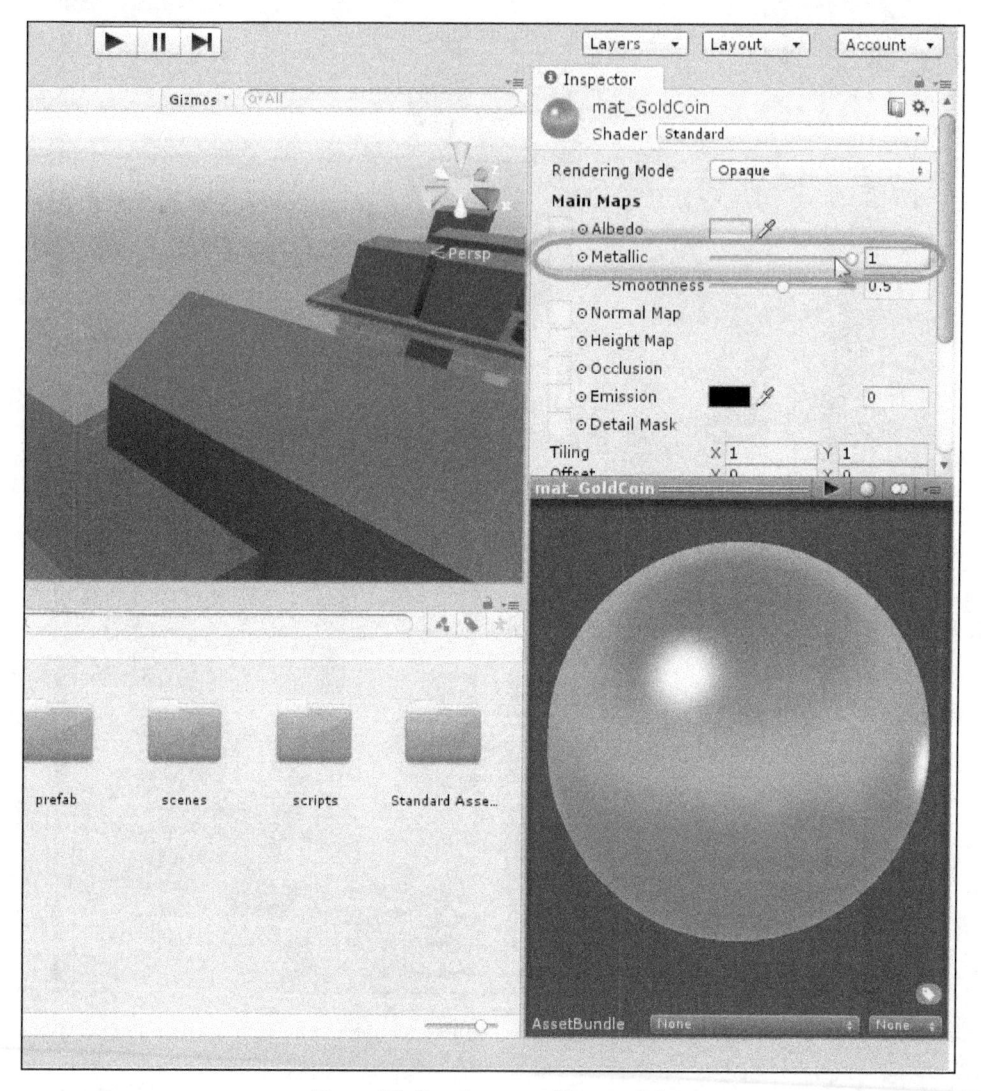

Figure 2.7: Creating a metallic material

[70]

We now have a gold material created, and it's looking good in the preview panel. If needed, you can change the kind of object used for a preview. By default, Unity assigns the created material to a sphere, but other primitive objects are allowed, including cubes, cylinders, and torus. This helps you preview materials under different conditions. You can change objects by clicking on the geometry button directly above the preview panel to cycle through them. See *Figure 2.8*:

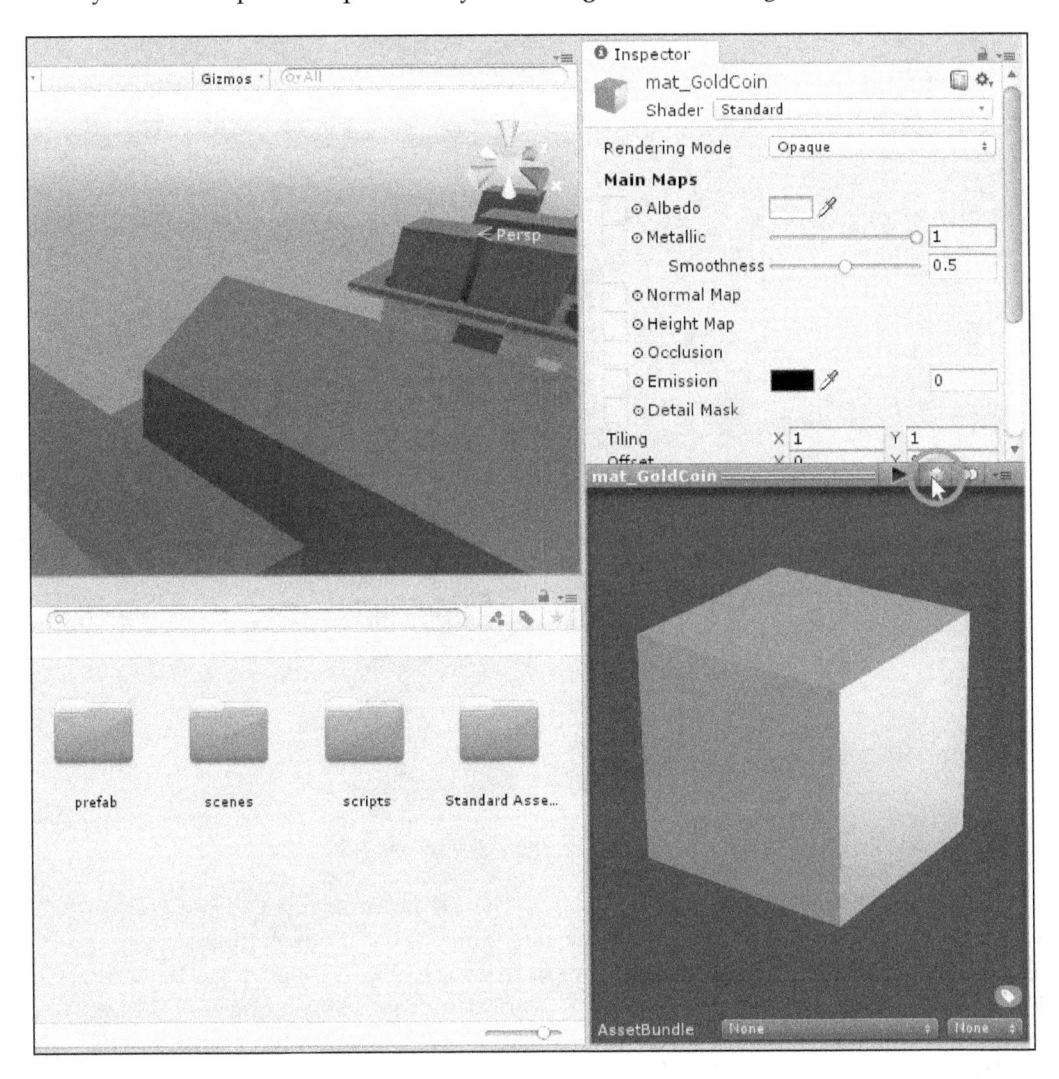

Figure 2.8: Previewing a material on an object

Creating a Collection Game

When your material is ready, you can assign it directly to meshes in your scene just by dragging and dropping. Let's assign the coin material to the coin. Click and drag the material from the Project panel to the coin object in the scene. On dropping the material, the coin will change appearance. See *Figure 2.9*:

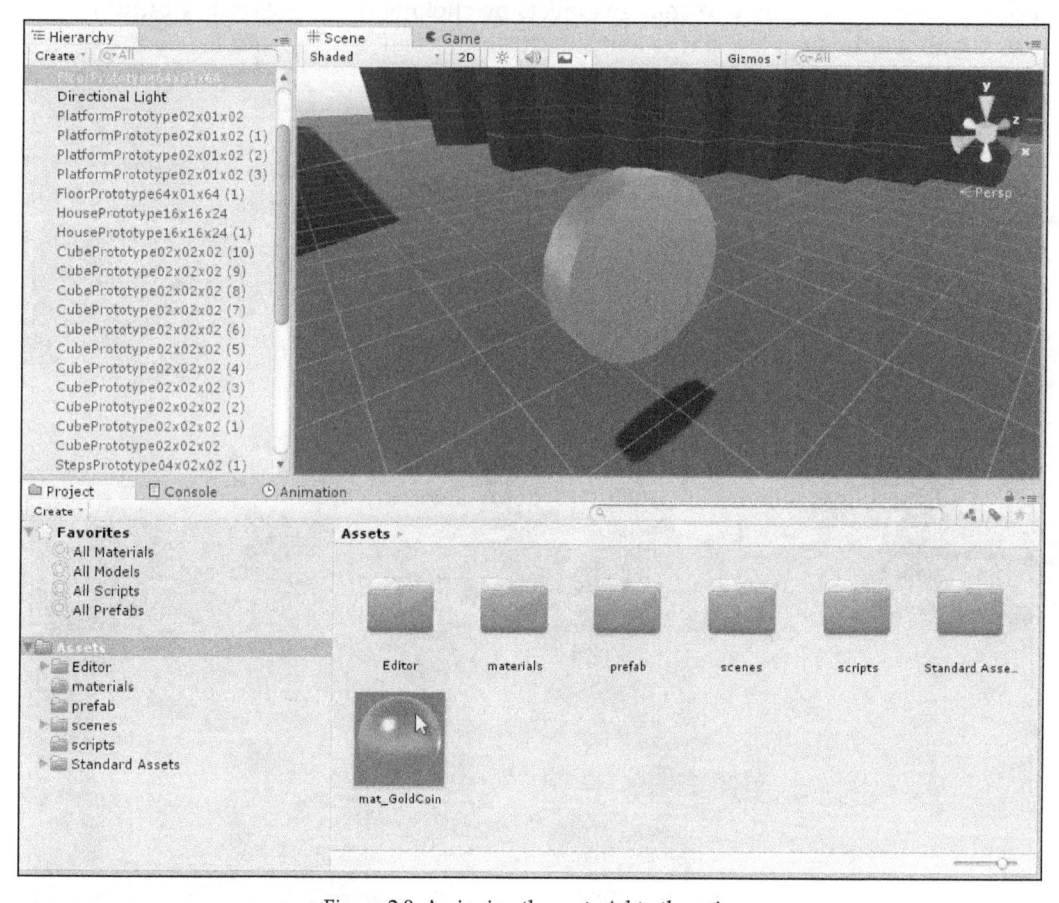

Figure 2.9: Assigning the material to the coin

You can confirm that material assignment occurred successfully and can even identify which material was assigned by selecting the Coin object in the Scene and viewing its Mesh Renderer component from the Object Inspector. The Mesh Renderer component is responsible for making sure that a mesh object is actually visible in the scene when the camera is looking. The Mesh Renderer component contains a Materials field. This lists all materials currently assigned to the object. By clicking on the material name from the Materials field, Unity automatically selects the material in the Project panel, making it quick and simple to locate materials. See *Figure 2.10*.

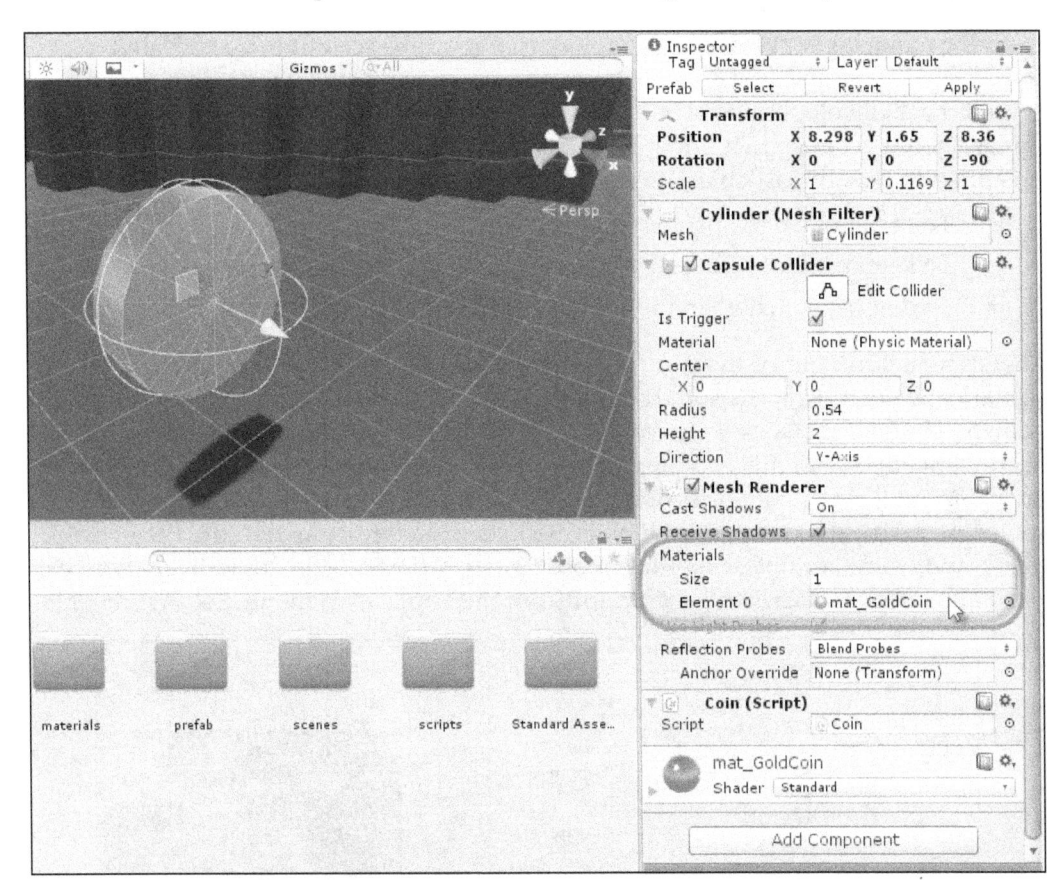

The Mesh Renderer component lists all materials assigned to an object:

Figure 2.10: The Mesh Renderer component lists all materials assigned to an object

> Mesh objects may have multiple materials, with different materials assigned to different faces. For the best in-game performance, use as few unique materials on an object as necessary. Make the extra effort to share materials across multiple objects, if possible. Doing so can significantly enhance the performance of your game. For more information on optimizing rendering performance, see the online documentation at http://docs.unity3d.com/Manual/OptimizingGraphicsPerformance.html.

That's it! You now have a complete and functional gold material for the collectible coin. It's looking good. However, we're still not finished with the coin. The coin looks right, but it doesn't behave right. Specifically, it doesn't disappear when touched, and we don't yet keep track of how many coins the player has collected overall. To address this, then, we'll need to script.

C# scripting in Unity

Defining game logic, rules, and behavior often requires scripting. Specifically, to transform a static and lifeless scene with objects into an environment that does something, a developer needs to code behaviors. It requires someone to define how things should act and react under specific conditions. The coin collection game is no exception to this. In particular, it requires three main features:

- To know when the player collects a coin
- To keep track of how many coins are collected during gameplay
- To determine whether a timer has expired

There's no default out-of-the-box functionality included with Unity to handle this scenario. So we must write some code to achieve it. Unity supports two languages, namely, UnityScript (sometimes called JavaScript) and C#. Both are capable and useful languages, but this book uses C# because, going forward, support for JavaScript will eventually be dropped. Let's start coding these three features in sequence. To create a new script file, right-click on an empty area in the Project panel, and from the context menu, choose **Create | C# Script**. Alternatively, you can navigate to **Assets | Create | C# Script** from the application menu. See *Figure 2.11*:

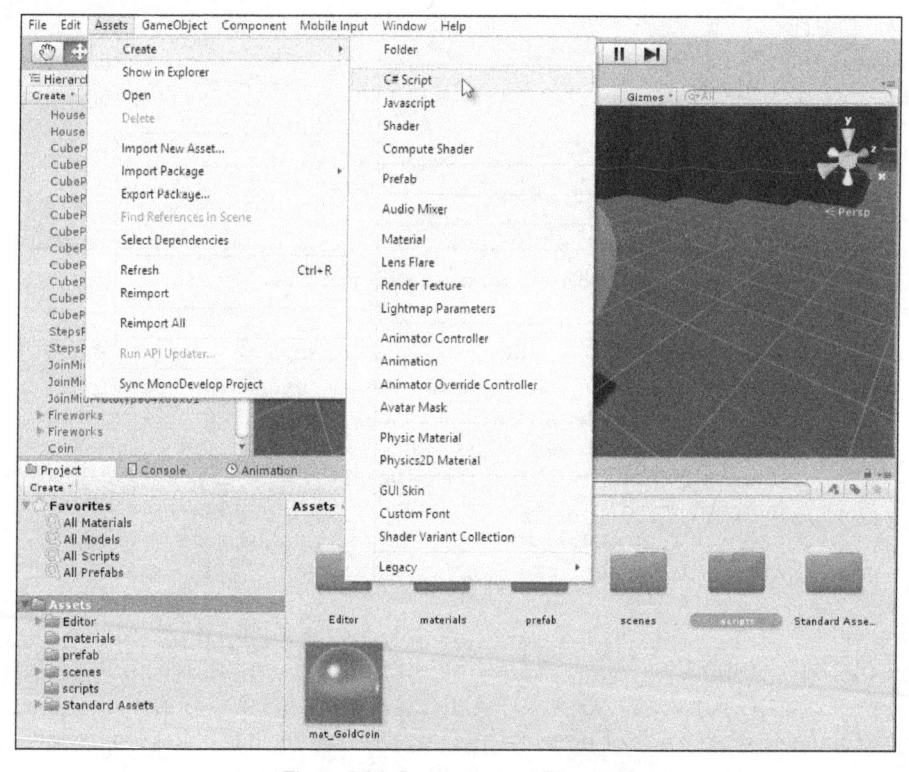

Figure 2.11: Creating a new C# script

After the file is created, you'll need to assign a descriptive name to it. I'll call it Coin.cs. In Unity, each script file represents a single, discrete class of matching names. Hence, the Coin.cs file encodes the Coin class. The Coin class will encapsulate the behavior of a Coin object and will, eventually, be attached to the Coin object in the scene. See *Figure 2.12*:

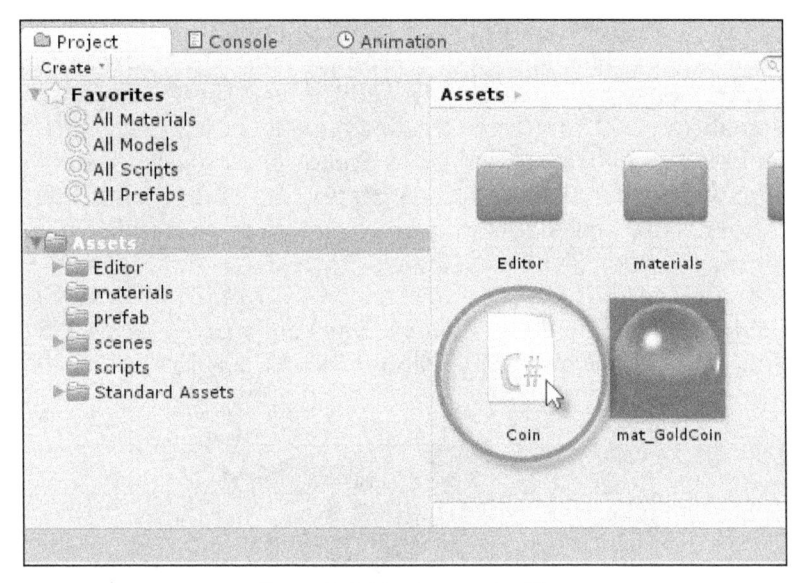

Figure 2.12: Naming a script file

Double-click on the Coin.cs file from the Object Inspector to open it to edit in Visual Studio, a third-party IDE application that ships with Unity. This program lets you edit and write code for your games. Once opened in Visual Studio, the source file will appear, as shown in *Code Sample 2.1*:

```
using UnityEngine;
using System.Collections;

public class Coin : MonoBehaviour
{

  // Use this for initialization
  void Start () {}

  // Update is called once per frame
  void Update () {}
}
```

> **Downloading the example code**
> You can download the example code files for this book from GitHub: `https://github.com/PacktPublishing/Unity-2018-By-Example-Second-Edition`

By default, all newly created classes derive from MonoBehavior, which defines a common set of functionality shared by all components. The Coin class features two autogenerated functions, namely Start and Update. These functions are events invoked automatically by Unity. Start is called once as soon as the GameObject (to which the script is attached) is created in the Scene. Update is called once per frame on the object to which the script is attached. Start is useful for initialization code and Update is useful to create behaviors over time, such as motion and change. Now, before moving any further, let's attach the newly created script file to the Coin object in the Scene. To do this, drag and drop the `Coin.cs` script file from the Project panel on the Coin object. When you do this, a new Coin component is added to the object. This means that the script is instantiated and lives on the object. See *Figure 2.13*, attaching a script file to an object:

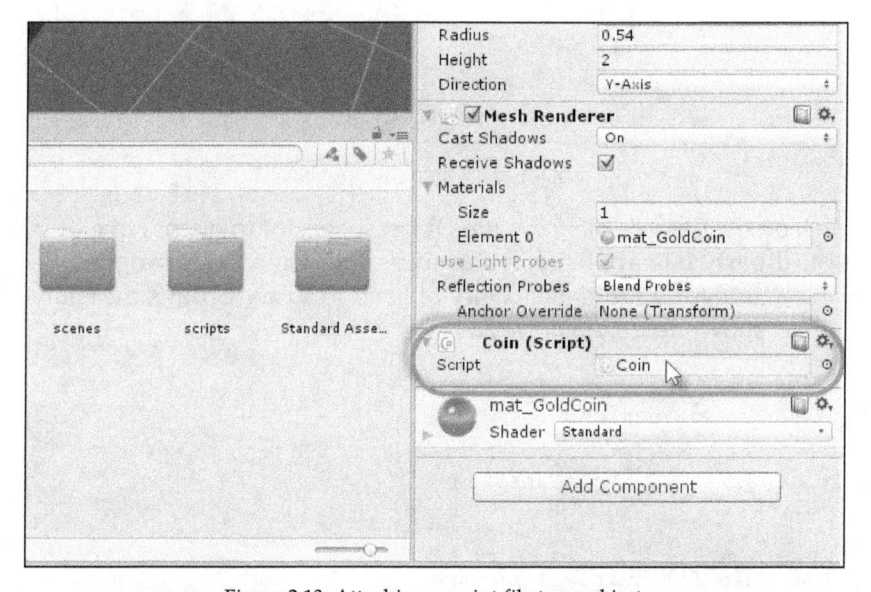

Figure 2.13: Attaching a script file to an object

When a script is attached to an object, it exists on the object as a component. A script file can normally be added to multiple objects and even to the same object multiple times. Each component represents a separate and unique instantiation of the class. When a script is attached in this way, Unity automatically invokes its events, such as Start and Update. You can confirm that your script is working normally by including a Debug.Log statement in the Start function.

[76]

This prints a debug message to the Console window when the GameObject is created in the Scene. Consider *Code Sample 2.2*, which achieves this:

```
using UnityEngine;
using System.Collections;

public class Coin : MonoBehaviour
  {
    // Use this for initialization
    void Start () {
      Debug.Log ("Object Created");
    }

    // Update is called once per frame
    void Update () {


    }
  }
```

If you press play (Ctrl + P) on the toolbar to run your game with the preceding script attached to an object, you will see the message, Object Created, printed to the Console window — once for each instantiation of the class. See *Figure 2.14*:

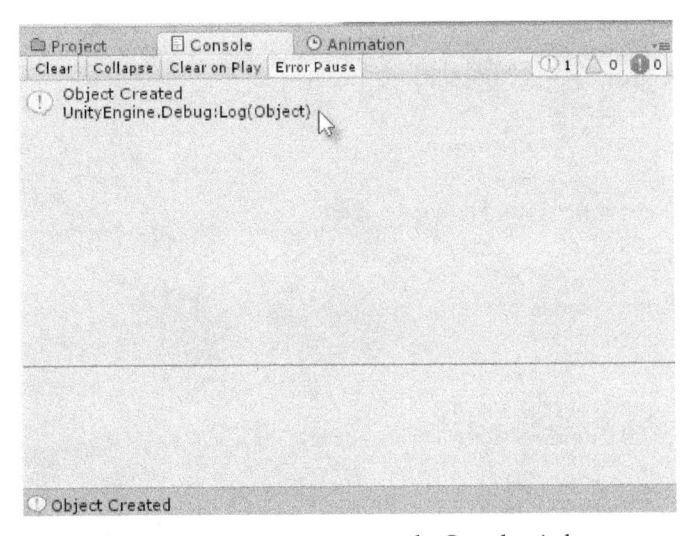

Figure 2.14: Printing messages to the Console window

Good work! We've now created a basic script for the Coin class and attached it to the coin. Next, let's define its functionality to keep track of coins as they are collected.

Counting coins

The coin collection game wouldn't really be much of a game if there were only one coin. The central idea is that a level should feature many coins, all of which the player should collect before a timer expires. Now, to know whether all coins have been collected, we'll need to know how many coins there are in total in the scene. After all, if we don't know how many coins there are, then we can't know if we've collected them all. So, our first task in scripting is to configure the Coin class so that we can know the total number of coins in the scene at any moment easily. Consider *Code Sample 2.3*, which adapts the Coin class to achieve this:

```
//------------------------
using UnityEngine;
using System.Collections;
//------------------------
public class Coin : MonoBehaviour
{
    //------------------------
    //Keeps track of total coin count in scene
    public static int CoinCount = 0;
    //------------------------
    // Use this for initialization
    void Start ()
    {

        //Object created, increment coin count
        ++Coin.CoinCount;
    }
    //------------------------
    //Called when object is destroyed
    void OnDestroy()
    {
        //Decrement coin count
        --Coin.CoinCount;

        //Check remaining coins
        if(Coin.CoinCount <= 0)
        {
            //We have won
        }
    }
    //------------------------
}
//------------------------
```

[78]

Code Sample 2.3

The following points summarize the code sample:

- The Coin class maintains a static member variable, CoinCount, which, being static, is shared across all instances of the class. This variable keeps count of the total number of coins in the scene and each instance has access to it.
- The Start function is called once per Coin instance when the object is created in the Scene. For coins that are present when the scene begins, the Start event is called at scene startup. This function increments the CoinCount variable by one per instance, thus keeping count of all coins.
- The OnDestroy function is called once per instance when the object is destroyed. This decrements the CoinCount variable, reducing the count for each coin destroyed.

Altogether, *Code Sample 2.3* maintains a CoinCount variable. In short, this variable allows us to always keep track of the total coin count. We can query it easily to determine how many coins remain. This is good, but is only the first step towards completing the coin collection functionality.

Collecting coins

Previously, we developed a coin counting variable telling us how many coins are in the scene. However, regardless of the count, the player still can't collect the coins during gameplay. Let's fix this now. To start, we need to think about collisions. Thinking carefully, we know that a coin is considered collected whenever the player walks into it, that is, a coin is collected when the player and the coin intersect or collide.

To determine when a collision happens like that, we must approximate the volume of both the player and coin in order to determine when the two volumes overlap in space. This is achieved in Unity through colliders. Colliders are special physics objects attached to meshes. They tell us when two meshes intersect. The FPSController object (First-person controller) already has a collider on it, through its Character Controller component. This approximates the physical body of a generic person. This can be confirmed by selecting FPSController in the Scene and examining the green wireframe cage surrounding the main camera. It is capsule-shaped. See *Figure 2.15*.

Creating a Collection Game

The Character Controller features a Collider to approximate the player body:

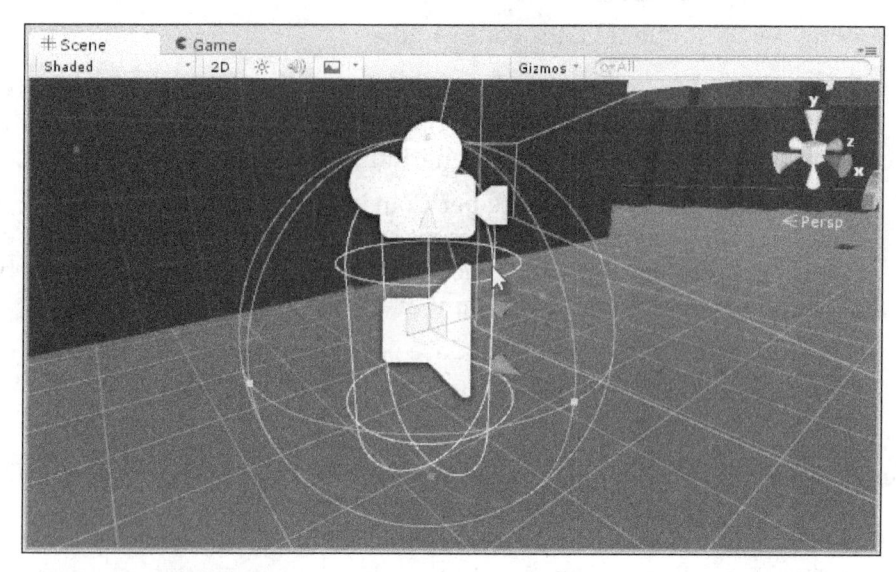

Figure 2.15: The Character Controller features a collider to approximate the player body

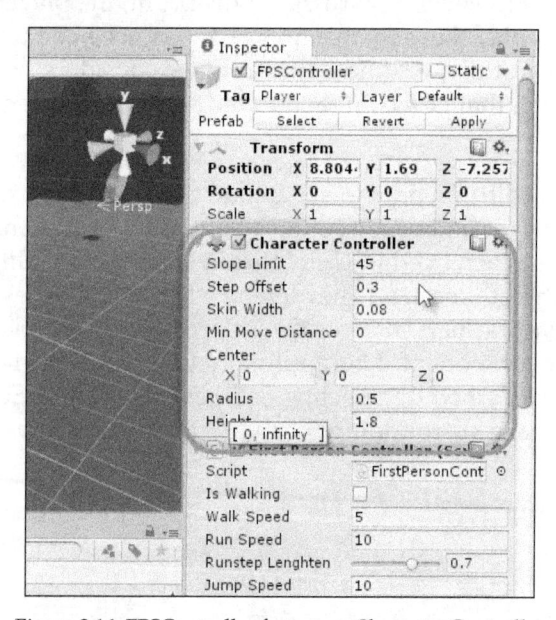

FPSController features a Character Controller component attached, which is configured by default with Radius, Height, and Center settings, defining the physical extents of the character in the scene. See *Figure 2.16*, FPSController features Character Controller. These settings can be left unchanged for our game:

Figure 2.16: FPSController features a Character Controller

[80]

The Coin object, in contrast, features only a Capsule Collider component, which was added automatically when we created the Cylinder primitive earlier to resemble a coin. This approximates the coin's physical volume in the scene without adding any additional features specific to characters and motion as found in the Character Controller component. This is fine, because the coin is a Static object as opposed to a moving and dynamic object like the FPSController. See *Figure 2.17*, Cylinder primitives feature a Capsule Collider component:

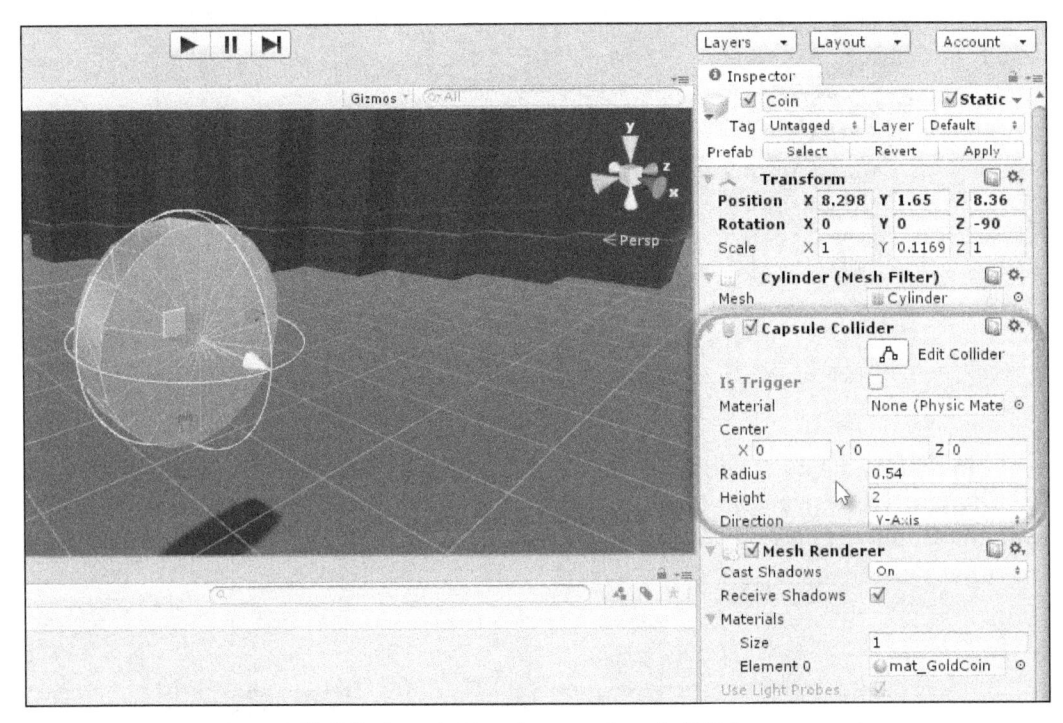

Figure 2.17: Cylinder primitives feature a Capsule Collider component

For this project, I'll stick to using a Capsule Collider component for the Coin object. However, if you want to change the attached collider to a different shape instead, such as a box or sphere, you can do this by first removing any existing collider components on the coin—click on the cog icon of the component in the Object Inspector and then select Remove Component from the context menu.

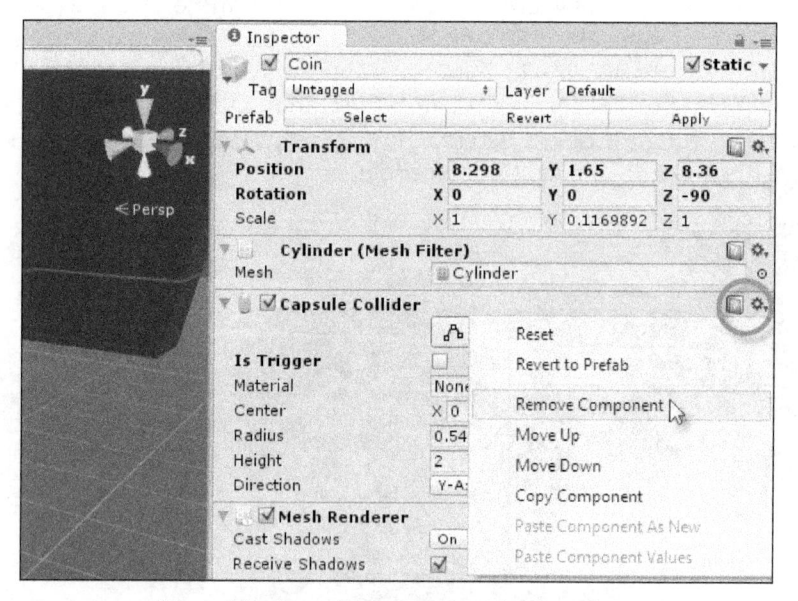

See *Figure 2.18*:

Figure 2.18: Removing a component from an object

You can then add a new collider component to the selected object by choosing **Component | Physics** from the application menu and then choosing a suitably shaped collider. See *Figure 2.19*:

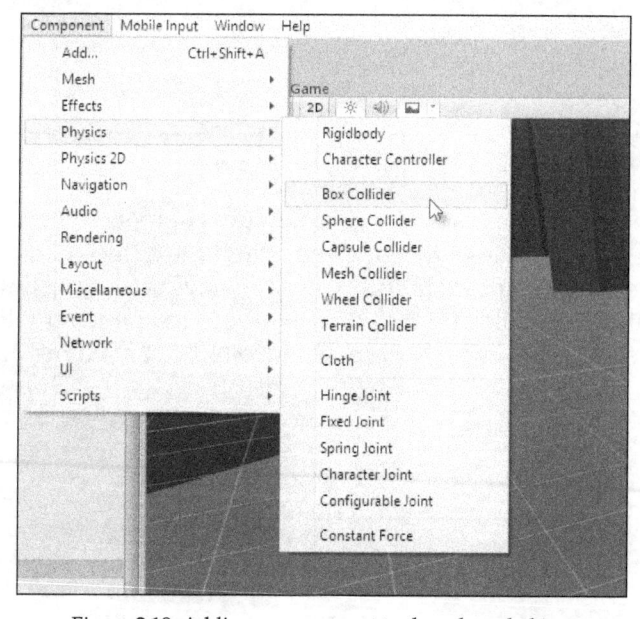

Figure 2.19: Adding a component to the selected object

Regardless of the collider type used, there's a minor problem. If you play the game now and try to run through the coin, it'll block your path. The coin acts as a solid, physical object through which FPSController cannot pass. However, for our purposes, this isn't how the coin should behave. It's supposed to be a collectible object. The idea is that when we walk through it, the coin is collected and disappears. We can fix this easily by selecting the Coin object and enabling the Is Trigger checkbox in the Capsule Collider component, in the Object Inspector. The Is Trigger setting appears for almost all collider types. It lets us detect collisions and intersections with other colliders while allowing them to pass through. See *Figure 2.20*:

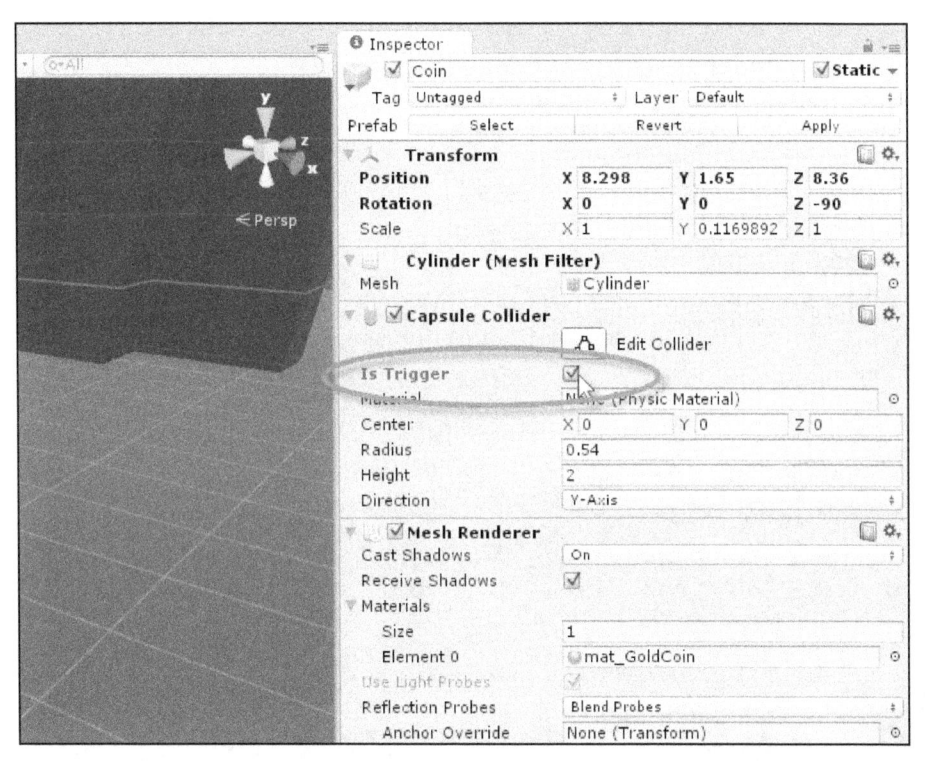

Figure 2.20: The Is Trigger setting allows objects to pass through colliders

If you play the game now, FPSController will easily walk through all coin objects in the scene. This is a good start. However, the coins don't actually disappear when touched; they still don't get collected. To achieve this, we'll need to add more script to the `Coin.cs` file. Specifically, we'll add an OnTriggerEnter function. This function is called automatically when an object, like the player, enters a collider. For now, we'll add a Debug.Log statement to print a debug message when the player enters the collider, just for test purposes. See *Code Sample 2.4*:

```
//------------------------
using UnityEngine;
```

Creating a Collection Game

```csharp
using System.Collections;
//------------------------
public class Coin : MonoBehaviour
{
  //------------------------
  public static int CoinCount = 0;
  //------------------------
  // Use this for initialization
  void Start () {
    //Object created, increment coin count
    ++Coin.CoinCount;
  }
  //------------------------
  void OnTriggerEnter(Collider Col)
  {
    Debug.Log ("Entered Collider");
  }
  //------------------------
  //Called when object is destroyed
  void OnDestroy()
  {
    //Decrement coin count
    --Coin.CoinCount;

    //Check remaining coins
    if(Coin.CoinCount <= 0)
    {
      //We have won
    }
  }
  //------------------------
}
//------------------------
```

> More information on the OnTriggerEnter function can be found at the online Unity documentation here:
> http://docs.unity3d.com/ScriptReference/MonoBehaviour.OnTriggerEnter.html

Test the *Code Sample 2.4* by pressing play on the toolbar. When you run into a coin, the OnTriggerEnter function will be executed and the message displayed. However, the question remains as to what object initiated this function in the first place. It's true that something collided with the coin, but what exactly? Was it the player, an enemy, a falling brick, or something else? To check this, we'll use Tag. The Tag feature lets you mark specific objects in the scene with specific tags or labels, allowing these objects to be easily identified in code so that we can check quickly that the player, rather than other objects, are colliding with the coins. After all, it should only be the player that can collect coins. So, firstly, we'll tag the player object with a tag called Player. To do this, select the FPSController object in the scene and then click on the Tag drop-down box in the Object Inspector. From here, select the Player tag. This marks FPSController as the Player object. See Figure 2.21:

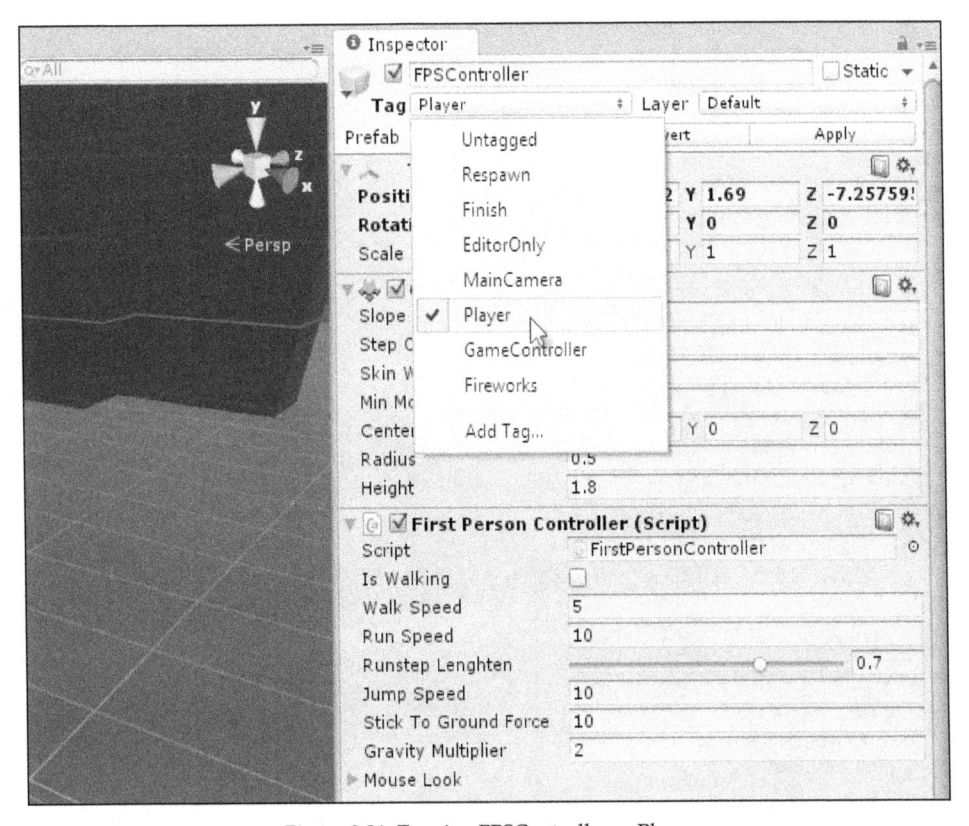

Figure 2.21: Tagging FPSController as Player

Creating a Collection Game

With FPSController now tagged as Player, we can refine the Coin.cs file, as shown in *Code Sample 2.5*. This handles coin collection, making the coin disappear on touch and decreasing the coin count:

```
//-------------------------
using UnityEngine;
using System.Collections;
//-------------------------
public class Coin : MonoBehaviour
{
  //-------------------------
  public static int CoinCount = 0;
  //-------------------------
  // Use this for initialization
  void Start () {
    //Object created, increment coin count
    ++Coin.CoinCount;
  }
  //-------------------------
  void OnTriggerEnter(Collider Col)
  {
    //If player collected coin, then destroy object
    if(Col.CompareTag("Player"))
      Destroy(gameObject);
  }
  //-------------------------
  //Called when object is destroyed
  void OnDestroy()
  {
    //Decrement coin count
    --Coin.CoinCount;

    //Check remaining coins
    if(Coin.CoinCount <= 0)
    {
      //We have won
    }
  }
  //-------------------------
}
//-------------------------
```

Code Sample 2.5

The following points summarize the code sample:

- OnTriggerEnter is called once automatically by Unity each time FPSController intersects the Coin collider
- When OnTriggerEnter is called, the Col argument contains information about the object that entered the collider on this occasion
- The CompareTag function is used to determine if the colliding object is the Player as opposed to a different object
- The Destroy function is called to destroy the Coin object itself, represented internally by the inherited member variable, gameObject

    When the Destroy function is called, the OnDestroy event is invoked automatically, which decrements the Coin count

Excellent work! You've just created your first working coin. The player can now run into the coin, collect it, and remove it from the scene. This is a great beginning, but the scene should contain more than one coin. We could solve this by duplicating the existing coin many times and repositioning each duplicate to a different place. However, there's a better way, as we'll see next.

Coins and prefabs

The basic coin functionality is now created, but the scene needs more than one coin. The problem with simply duplicating a coin and scattering the duplicates is that if we make a change later to one coin and need to propagate that change to all other coins, we'd need to delete the former duplicates and manually replace those with newer and amended duplicates. To avoid this tedious repetition, we can use prefabs. Prefabs let you convert an object in the scene to Assets in the Project panel. This can be instantiated in the scene as frequently as needed, as though it were a mesh asset. The advantage is that changes made to the asset are automatically applied to all instances automatically, even across multiple scenes.

Creating a Collection Game

This makes it easier to work with custom assets, so let's prefab the coin right now. To do this, select the Coin object in the scene and then drag and drop it in the Project panel. When this happens, a new prefab is created. The object in the scene is automatically updated to be an instance of prefab. This means that if the asset is deleted from the Project panel, the instance will become invalidated. See *Figure 2.22*:

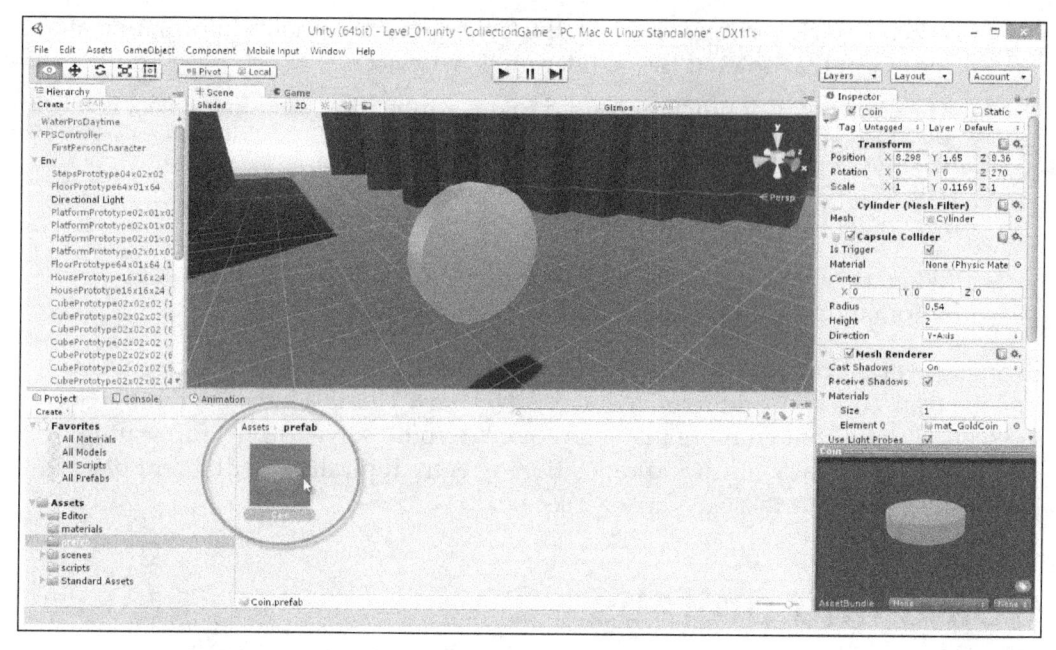

Figure 2.22: Creating a coin prefab

After prefab is created, you can add more instances of the coin easily to the level by dragging and dropping prefab from the Project panel to the Scene. Each instance is linked to the original prefab asset, which means that all changes made to the asset will immediately be made to all instances.

With this in mind, go ahead now and add as many Coin prefabs to the level as suitable for your coin collection game. Refer to the following figure for my arrangement:

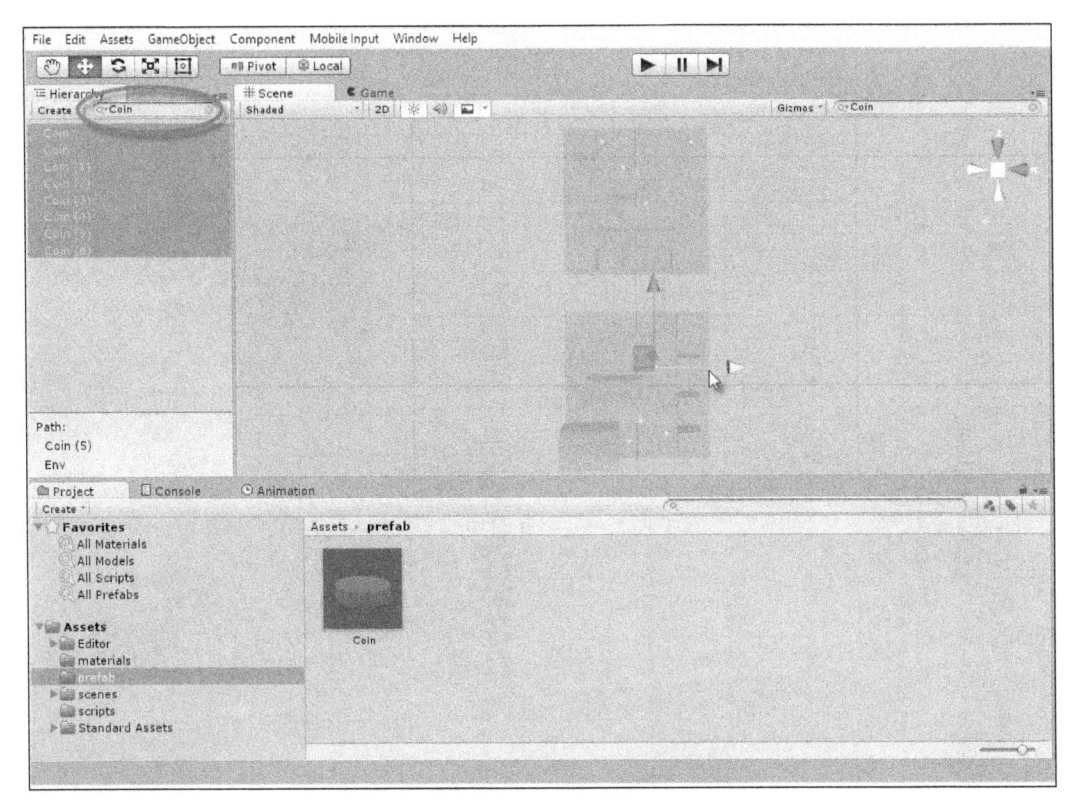

Figure 2.23: Adding coin prefabs to the level

Creating a Collection Game

One question that naturally arises is how you can transform prefab back into an independent GameObject that is no longer connected to the prefab asset. This is useful to do if you want some objects to be based on prefab but deviate from it slightly. To achieve this, select a prefab instance in the Scene, and then navigate to **GameObject | Break Prefab Instance** from the application menu. See *Figure 2.24*:

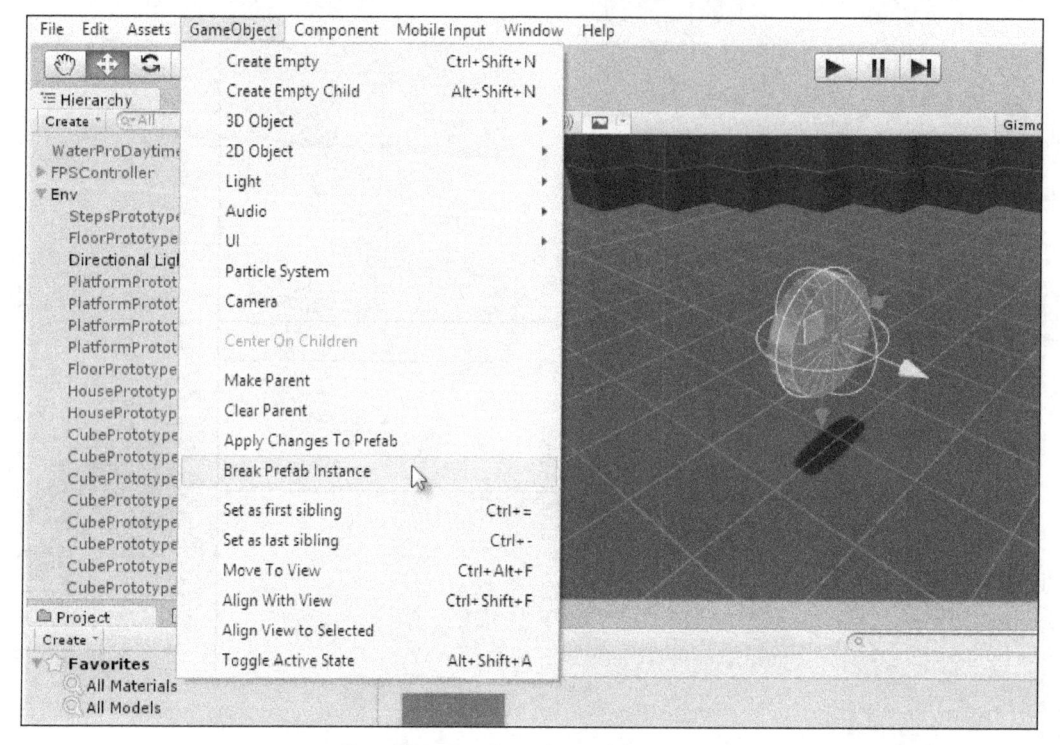

Figure 2.24: Breaking the prefab instance

> If you add a prefab instance to Scene and make changes to it that you like and want to distribute upstream back to the prefab asset, then select the object and choose GameObject | Apply Changes to Prefab.

Timers and countdowns

You should now have a level complete with geometry and coin objects. Thanks to our newly added Coin.cs script, the coins are both countable and collectible. Even so, the level still poses little or no challenge to the player because there's no way the level can be won or lost. Specifically, there's nothing for the player to achieve. This is why a time limit is important for the game: it defines a win and loss condition. Namely, collecting all coins before the timer expires results in a win condition and failing to achieve this results in a loss condition. Let's get started at creating a timer countdown for the level. To do this, create a new and empty game object by selecting **GameObject | Create Empty** and rename this LevelTimer. See *Figure 2.25*:

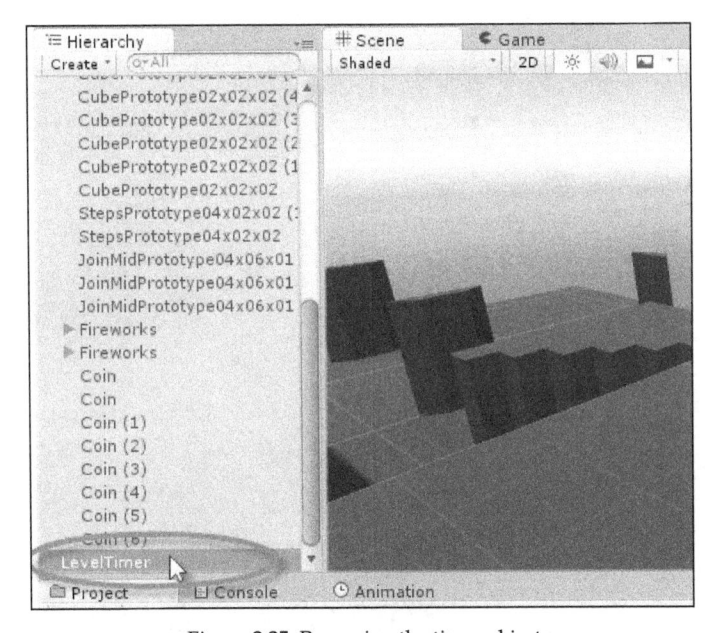

Figure 2.25: Renaming the timer object

> Remember that empty game objects cannot be seen by the player because they have no mesh renderer component. They are especially useful to create functionality and behaviors that don't correspond directly to physical and visible entities, such as timers, managers, and game logic controllers.

Creating a Collection Game

Next, create a new script file named Timer.cs and add it to the LevelTimer object in Scene. By doing this, the timer functionality will exist in the scene. Make sure, however, that the timer script is added to one object, and no more than one. Otherwise, there will effectively be multiple, competing timers in the same scene. You can always search a scene to find all components of a specified type by using the Hierarchy panel. To do this, click in the Hierarchy search box and type t:Timer. Then press Enter on the keyboard to confirm the search. This search the scene for all objects with a component attached of the timer type, and the results are displayed in the Hierarchy panel. Specifically, the Hierarchy panel is filtered to show only the matching objects. The t prefix in the search string indicates a search by type operation. See *Figure 2.26*:

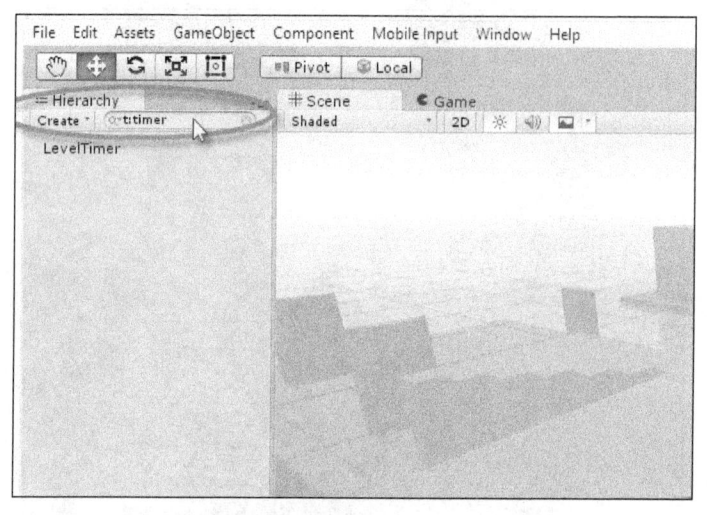

Figure 2.26: Searching for objects with a component of matching type

You can easily cancel a search and return the Hierarchy panel back to its original state by clicking on the small cross icon aligned to the right-hand side of the search field. This button can be tricky to spot. See *Figure 2.27*:

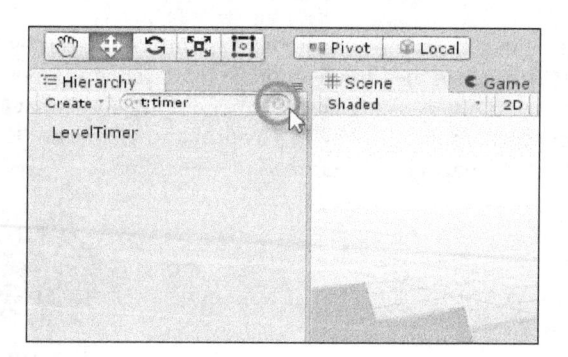

Figure 2.27: Canceling a type search

Chapter 2

The timer script itself must be coded if it's to be useful. The full source code for the Timer.cs file is given in the following *Code Sample 2.6*. This source code is highly important if you've never scripted in Unity before. It demonstrates so many critical features. See the comments for a fuller explanation.

```csharp
//------------------------
using UnityEngine;
using System.Collections;
//------------------------
public class Timer : MonoBehaviour
{
  //------------------------
  //Maximum time to complete level (in seconds)
  public float MaxTime = 60f;
  //------------------------
  //Countdown
  [SerializeField]
  private float CountDown = 0;
  //------------------------
  // Use this for initialization
  void Start ()
  {
    CountDown = MaxTime;
  }
  //------------------------
  // Update is called once per frame
  void Update ()
  {
    //Reduce time
    CountDown -= Time.deltaTime;

    //Restart level if time runs out
    if(CountDown <= 0)
    {
      //Reset coin count
      Coin.CoinCount=0;
      Application.LoadLevel(Application.loadedLevel);
    }
  }
  //------------------------
}
//------------------------
```

Code Sample 2.6

The following points summarize the code sample:

- In Unity, class variables declared as public (such as public float MaxTime) are displayed as editable fields in the Object Inspector of the editor. However, this applies to a range of supported data types only, but it's a highly useful feature. It means that developers can monitor and set public variables for classes directly from the Inspector as opposed to changing and recompiling code every time a change is needed. The private variables, in contrast, are hidden from the Inspector by default. However, you can force them to be visible, if needed, using the SerializeField attribute. The private variables prefixed with this attribute, such as the CountDown variable, will be displayed in the Object Inspector just like a public variable, even though the variable's scope still remains private.

- The Update function is a Unity native event supported for all classes derived from MonoBehaviour. Update is invoked automatically once per frame for all active GameObjects in the scene. This means that all active game objects are notified about frame change events. In short, Update is therefore called many times per second; the game FPS is a general indicator as to how many times each second. The actual number of calls will vary in practice from second to second. In any case, Update is especially useful to animate, update, and change objects over time. In the case of a CountDown class, it'll be useful to keep track of time as it passes, second by second. More information on the Update function can be found at the online Unity documentation at http://docs.unity3d.com/ScriptReference/MonoBehaviour.Update.html.

> In addition to the Update function called on each frame, Unity also supports two other related functions, namely, FixedUpdate and LateUpdate. FixedUpdate is used when coding with Physics, as we'll see later, and is called a fixed number of times per frame. LateUpdate is called once per frame for each active object, but the LateUpdate call will always happen after every object has received an Update event. Thus, it happens after the Update cycle, making it a late update. There are reasons for this late update and we'll see them later in the book.
>
> More information on FixedUpdate can be found in the online Unity documentation at http://docs.unity3d.com/ScriptReference/MonoBehaviour.FixedUpdate.html
> More information on the LateUpdate function can be found in the online Unity documentation at http://docs.unity3d.com/ScriptReference/MonoBehaviour.LateUpdate.html.

- When scripting, the static Time.deltaTime variable is constantly available and updated automatically by Unity. It always describes the amount of time (in seconds) that has passed since the previous frame ended. For example, if your game has a frame rate of 2 FPS (a very low frame rate!) then deltaTime will be 0.5. This is because, in each second, there would be two frames, and thus each frame would be half a second. The deltaTime is useful because, if added over time, it tells you how much time in total has elapsed or passed since the game began. For this reason, deltaTime floating point variable is used heavily in the Update function for the timer to subtract the elapsed time from the countdown total. More information can be found on deltaTime at the online documentation at http://docs.unity3d.com/ScriptReference/Time-deltaTime.html.

- The static Application.LoadLevel function can be called anywhere in code to change the active scene at runtime. Thus, this function is useful to move the gamer from one level to another. It causes Unity to terminate the active scene, destroying all its contents, and load a new scene. It can also be used to restart the active scene, simply by loading the active level again. Application.LoadLevel is most appropriate for games with clearly defined levels that are separate from each other and have clearly defined beginnings and endings. It is not, however, suitable for large open-world games in which large sprawling environments stretch on, seemingly without any breakage or disconnection. More information on Application.LoadLevel can be found in the online Unity documentation at http://docs.unity3d.com/ScriptReference/Application.LoadLevel.html.

After the timer script is created, select the LevelTimer object in the scene. From the Object Inspector, you can set the maximum time (in seconds) that the player is allowed in order to complete the level. See *Figure 2.28*. I've set the total time to 60 seconds. This means that all coins must be completed within 60 seconds from the level start.

If the timer expires, the level is restarted.

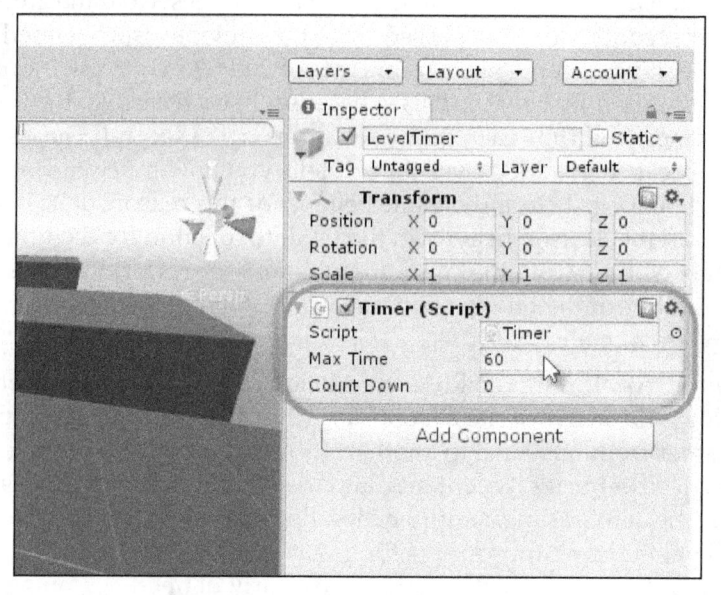

Figure 2.28: Setting the level total time

Great work! You should now have a completed level with a countdown that works. You can collect coins and the timer can expire. Overall, the game is taking shape. There is a further problem, however, which we'll address next.

Celebrations and fireworks!

The coin collection game is nearly finished. Coins can be collected and a timer expires, but the win condition itself is not truly handled. That is, when all coins are collected before time expiry, nothing actually happens to show the player that they've won. The countdown still proceeds and even restarts the level as though the win condition hadn't been satisfied at all. Let's fix this now. Specifically, when the win scenario happens, we should delete the timer object to prevent further countdown and show visual feedback to signify that the level has been completed. In this case, I'll add some fireworks! So, let's start by creating the fireworks. You can add these easily from the Unity Particle System packages. Navigate to the Standard Assets | ParticleSystems | Prefabs folder. Then, drag and drop the Fireworks particle system in Scene.

Add a second or even a third one if you want:

Figure 2.29: Adding two Fireworks prefabs

By default, all firework particle systems will play when the level begins. You can test this by pressing play on the toolbar. This is not the behavior that we want. We only want the fireworks to play when the win condition has been satisfied. To disable playback on level startup, select the Particle System object in the Scene and, from the Object Inspector, disable the Play On Awake checkbox, which can be found in the Particle System component.

Creating a Collection Game

See Figure 2.30, Disabling Play On Awake:

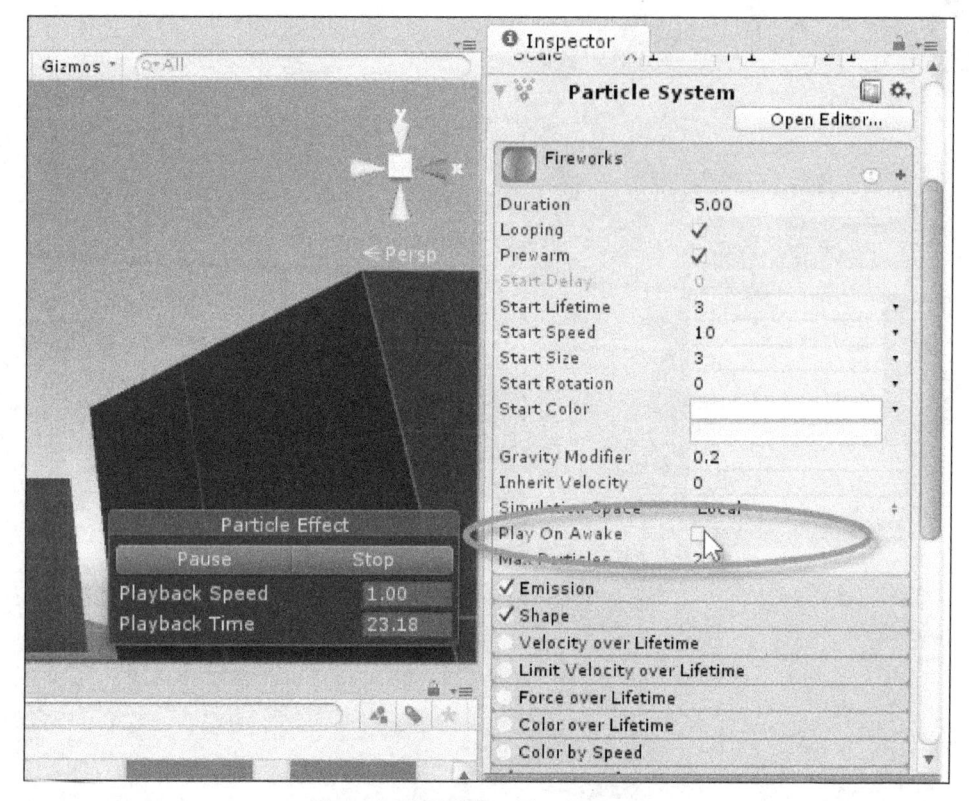

Figure 2.30: Disabling Play On Awake

Disabling Play On Awake prevents particle systems playing automatically at level startup. This is fine, but if they are ever to play at all, something must manually start them at the right time. We can achieve this through code. Before resorting to a coding solution, however, we'll first mark all firework objects with an appropriate tag. The reason for this is that, in code, we'll want to search for all firework objects in the scene and trigger them to play when needed. To isolate the firework objects from all other objects, we'll use tags. So, let's create a new Fireworks tag and assign them to the firework objects only in the Scene.

Tags were created earlier in this chapter when configuring the player character for coin collisions. See *Figure 2.31*:

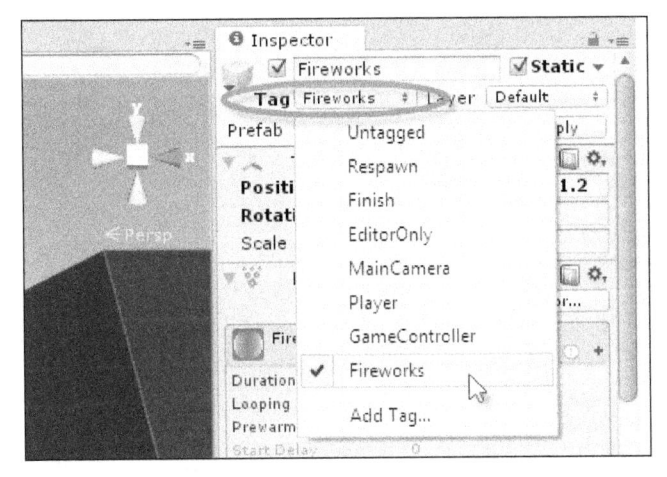

Figure 2.31: Tagging firework objects

With the firework objects now tagged, we can refine the Coin.cs script class to handle a win condition for the scene, as shown in *Code Sample 2.7*. Comments follow:

```
//------------------------
using UnityEngine;
using System.Collections;
//------------------------
public class Coin : MonoBehaviour
{
  //------------------------
  public static int CoinCount = 0;
  //------------------------
  // Use this for initialization
  void Awake ()
  {
    //Object created, increment coin count
    ++Coin.CoinCount;
  }
  //------------------------
  void OnTriggerEnter(Collider Col)
  {
    //If player collected coin, then destroy object
    if(Col.CompareTag("Player"))
```

```
      Destroy(gameObject);
  }
  //-----------------------
  void OnDestroy()
  {
    --Coin.CoinCount;

    //Check remaining coins
    if(Coin.CoinCount <= 0)
    {
      //Game is won. Collected all coins
      //Destroy Timer and launch fireworks
      GameObject Timer = GameObject.Find("LevelTimer");
      Destroy(Timer);

      GameObject[] FireworkSystems =
        GameObject.FindGameObjectsWithTag("Fireworks");
      foreach(GameObject GO in FireworkSystems)
      GO.GetComponent<ParticleSystem>().Play();
    }
  }
  //-----------------------
}
//-----------------------
```

Code Sample 2.7

The following points summarize the code sample:

- The OnDestroy function is critical. It occurs when a coin is collected and features an if statement to determine when all coins are collected (the win scenario).

- When a win scenario happens, the GameObject.Find function is called to search the complete scene hierarchy for any active object named LevelTimer. If found, the object is deleted. This happens to delete the timer and prevent any further countdown when the level is won. If the scene contains multiple objects of a matching name, then only the first object is returned. This is one reason why the scene should contain one and only one timer.

> Avoid using the GameObject.Find function wherever possible. It's slow for performance. Instead, use FindGameObjectsWithTag. It's been used here only to demonstrate its existence and purpose. Sometimes, you'll need to use it to find a single, miscellaneous object that has no specific tag.

- In addition to deleting the LevelTimer object, the OnDestroy function finds all firework objects in the scene and initiates them. It finds all objects of a matching tag using the GameObject.FindGameObjectsWithTag function. This function returns an array of all objects with the Fireworks tag and the ParticleSystem is initiated for each object by calling the Play function.

> As mentioned, each GameObject in Unity is really made from a collection of attached and related components. An object is the sum of its components. For example, a standard cube (created using **GameObject | 3D Object | Cube**) is made from a Transform component, Mesh Filter component, Mesh Renderer component, and Box Collider component. These components together make the cube what it is and behave how it does.
>
> The GetComponent function can be called in script to retrieve a reference to any specified component, giving you direct access to its public properties. The OnDestroy function in the preceding code uses GetComponent to retrieve a reference to the ParticleSystem component attached to the object. GetComponent is a highly useful and important function. More information on GetComponent can be found at the online Unity documentation at http://docs.unity3d.com/ScriptReference/GameObject.GetComponent.html.

Play testing

You've now completed your first game in Unity! It's time to take it for a test run and then finally build it. Testing in Unity firstly consists of pressing play on the toolbar and simply playing your game to see that it works as intended from the perspective of a gamer. In addition to playing, you can also enable debugging mode from the Object Inspector to keep a watchful eye on all public and private variables during runtime, making sure that no variable is assigned an unexpected value.

Creating a Collection Game

To activate the Debug mode, click on the menu icon at the top right corner of the Object Inspector and, from the context menu that appears, select the Debug option. See Figure 2.32:

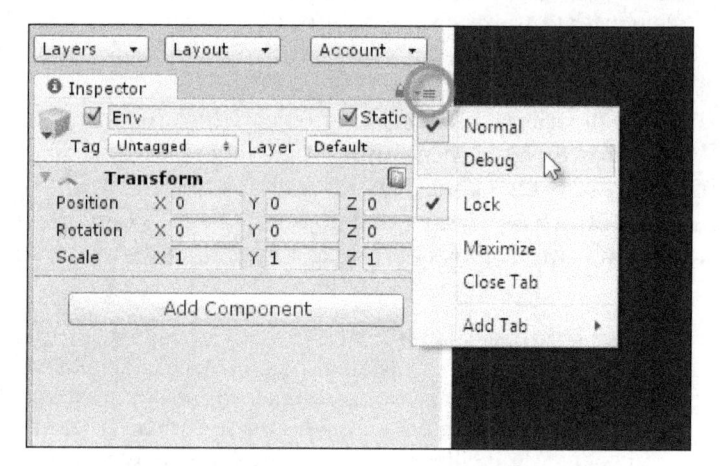

Figure 2.32: Activating Debug mode from the Object Inspector

After activating the Debug mode, the appearance of some variables and components in the Object Inspector may change. Typically, you'll get a more detailed and accurate view of your variables, and you'll also be able to see most private variables. See *Figure 2.33* for the Transform component in Debug mode:

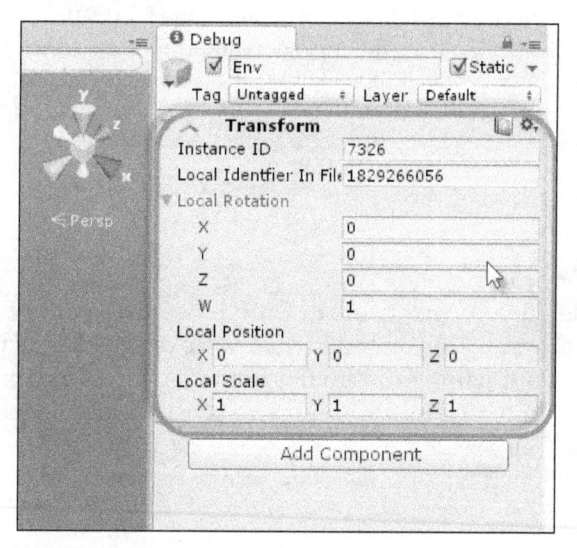

Figure 2.33: Viewing the Transform component in Debug mode

Another useful debugging tool at runtime is the Stats panel. This can be accessed from the Game tab by clicking on the Stats button from the toolbar. See *Figure 2.34*:

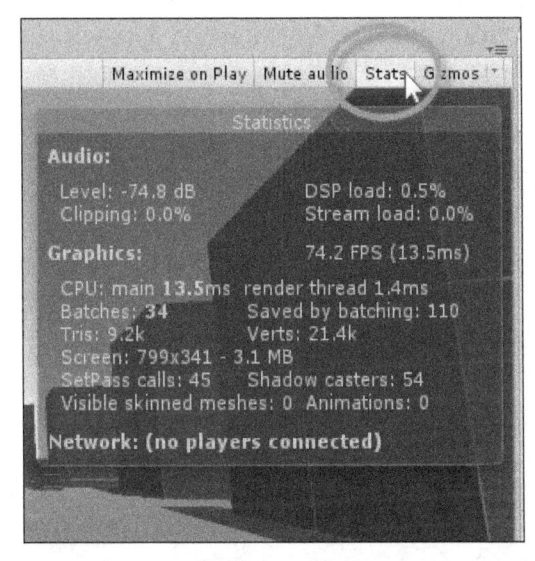

Figure 2.34: Accessing the Stats panel from the Game tab

The Stats panel is only useful during the play mode. In this mode, it details the critical performance statistics for your game, such as Frame Rate (FPS) and memory usage. This lets you diagnose or determine whether any problems may be affecting your game. The FPS represents the total number of frames (ticks or cycles) per second that your game can sustain on average. There is no right, wrong, or magical FPS, but higher values are better than lower ones. Higher values represent better performance because it means that your game can sustain more cycles in one second. If your FPS falls below 20 or 15, it's likely that your game will appear choppy or laggy as the performance weight of each cycle means it takes longer to process. Many variables can affect FPS, some internal and some external to your game. Internal factors include the number of lights in a scene, vertex density of meshes, number of instructions, and complexity of the code. Some external factors include the quality of your computer's hardware, number of other applications and processes running at the same time, and amount of hard drive space, among others.

Creating a Collection Game

In short, if your FPS is low, then it indicates a problem that needs attention. The solution to that problem varies depending on the context and you'll need to use judgement, for example, are your meshes too complex? Do they have too many vertices? Are your textures too large? Are there too many sounds playing? See *Figure 2.35* for the coin collection game up and running. The completed game can be found in the book companion files in the Chapter02/End folder:

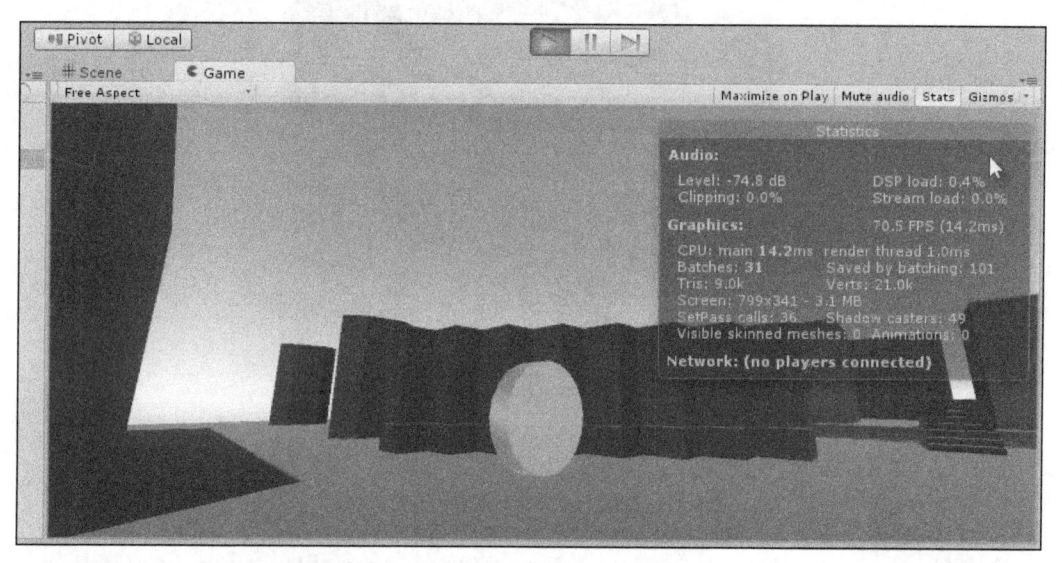

Figure 2.35: Testing the coin collection game

Building

So, now it's time to build the game! That is, to compile and package the game into a standalone and self-executing form, which the gamer can run and play without needing to use the Unity Editor. Typically, when developing games, you'll reach a decision about your target platform (such as Windows, iOS, Android, and others) during the design phase and not at the end of development. It's often said that Unity is a 'develop once, deploy everywhere tool. This slogan can conjure up the unfortunate image that, after a game is made, it'll work just as effortlessly on every platform supported by Unity as it does on the desktop.

Chapter 2

Unfortunately, things are not so simple; games that work well on desktop systems don't necessarily perform equally well on mobiles and vice versa. This is largely due to the great differences in target hardware and industry standards that hold between them. Due to these differences, I'll focus our attention here to the Windows and Mac desktop platforms, ignoring mobiles and consoles and other platforms. To create a build for desktop platform, select **File | Build Settings** from the File menu:

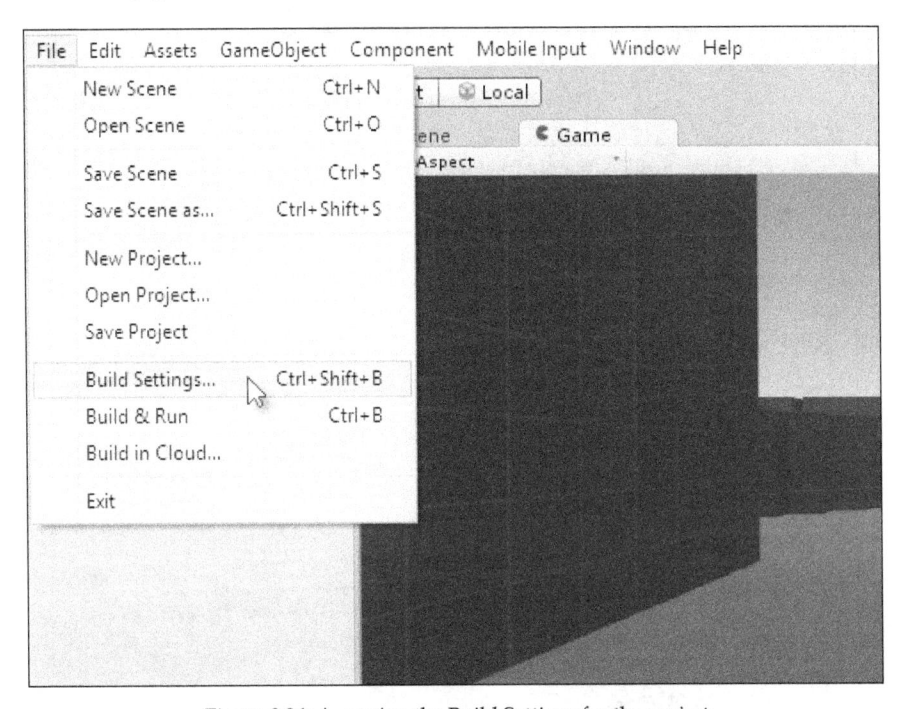

Figure 2.36: Accessing the Build Settings for the project

The Build Settings dialog is displayed and its interface consists of three main areas. The Scenes In Build list is a complete list of all scenes to be included in the build, regardless of whether the gamer will actually visit them in the game. It represents the totality of all scenes that could ever be visited in the game.

[105]

In short, if you want or need a scene in your game, then it needs to be in this list. Initially, the list is empty. See *Figure 2.37*:

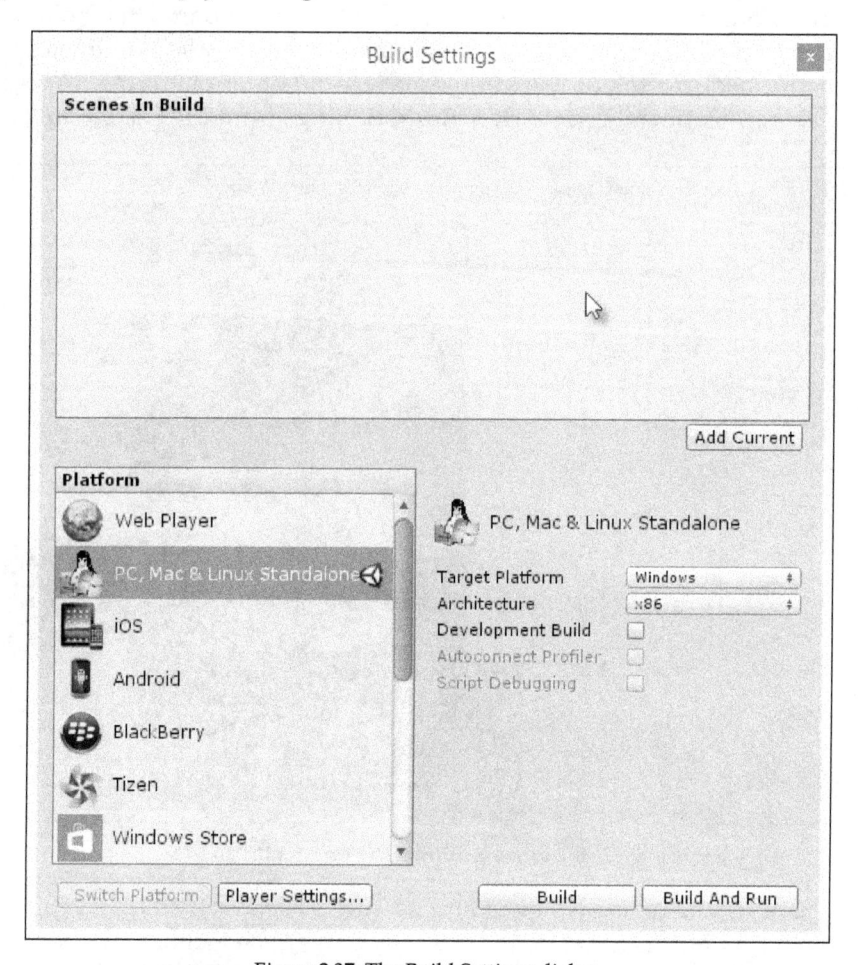

Figure 2.37: The Build Settings dialog

Chapter 2

You can easily add scenes to the list by simply dragging and dropping the scene asset from the Project panel to the Scenes In Build list. For the coin collection game, I'll drag and drop the Level_01 scene to the list. As scenes are added, Unity automatically assigns them a number, depending on their order in the list. 0 represents the topmost item, 1 the next item, and so on. This number is important insofar as the 0 item is concerned. The topmost scene (scene 0) will always be the starting scene. That is, when the build runs, Unity automatically begins execution from scene 0. Thus, scene 0 will typically be your splash or intro scene. See *Figure 2.38*, Adding a level to the Build Settings dialog:

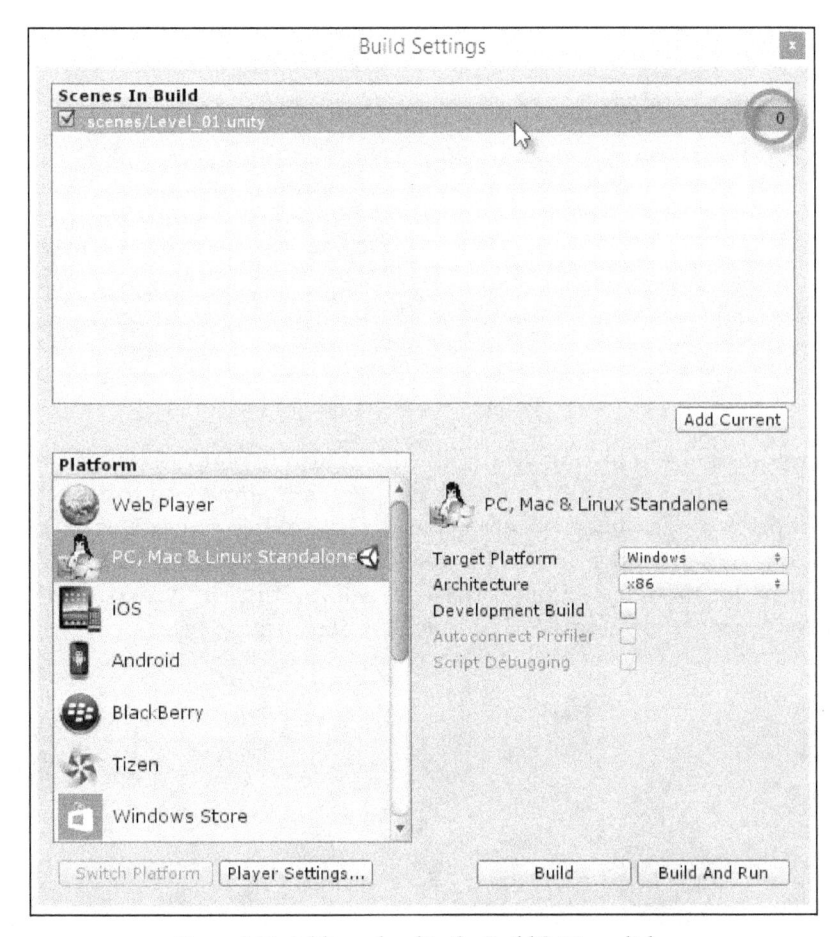

Figure 2.38: Adding a level to the Build Settings dialog

Creating a Collection Game

Next, be sure to select your target platform from the Platform list at the bottom left-hand side of the Build Settings dialog. For desktop platforms, choose PC, Mac & Linux Standalone, which should be selected by default. Then, from the options, set the Target Platform drop-down list to either Windows, Linux, or Mac OS X, depending on your system. See *Figure 2.39*:

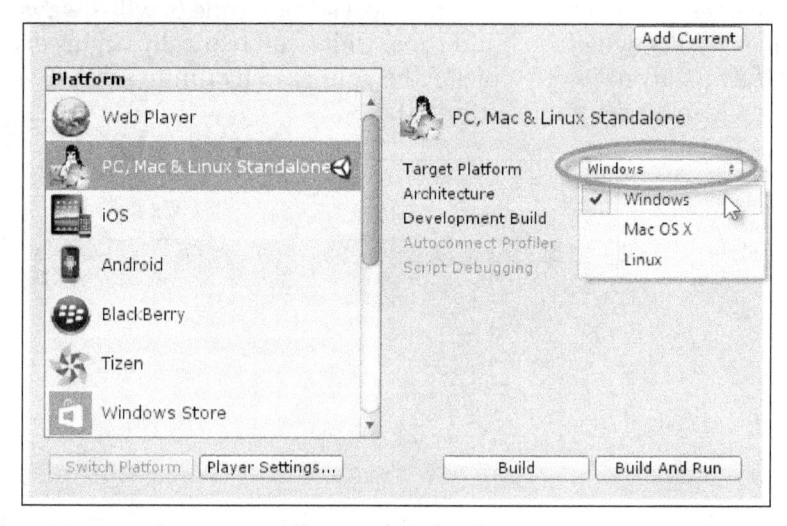

Figure 2.39: Choosing a target build platform

If you've previously been testing your game for multiple platforms or trying out other platforms such as Android and iOS, the Switch Platform button (at the bottom left of the Build Settings dialog) might become active when you select the Standalone option. If it does, click on the Switch Platform button to confirm to Unity that you intend building for the selected platform. On clicking this, Unity may spend a few minutes configuring your assets for the selected platform:

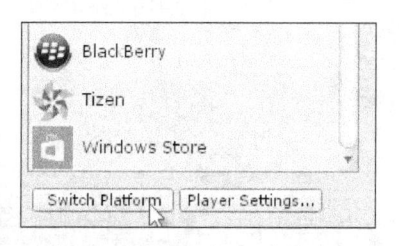

Figure 2.40: Switching platforms

Chapter 2

Before building for the first time, you'll probably want to view the Player Settings options to fine-tune important build parameters, such as game resolution, quality settings, executable icon, and information, among other settings. To access the Player Settings, you can simply click on the Player Settings button from the Build dialog. This displays the Player Settings in the Object Inspector. The same settings can also be accessed via the application menu by navigating to **Edit | Project Settings | Player**. See *Figure 2.4*:

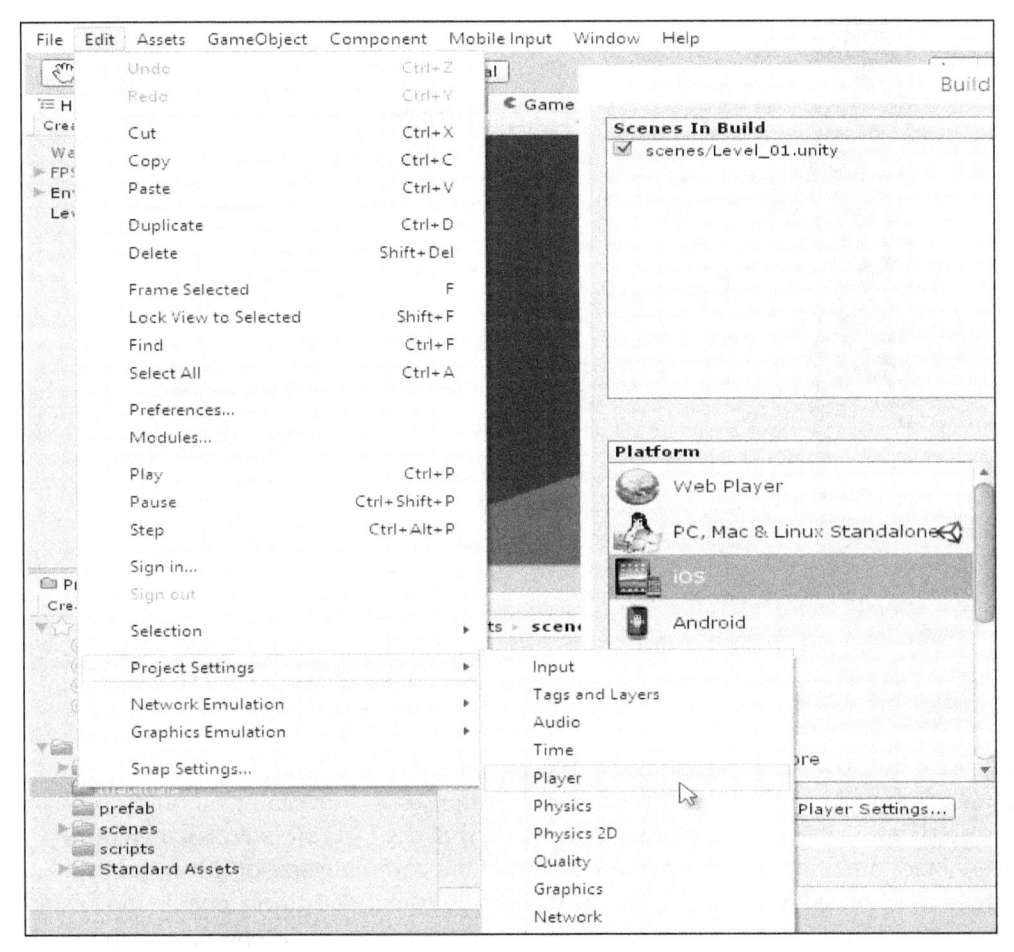

Figure 2.41: Accessing the Player Settings options

[109]

Creating a Collection Game

From the Player Settings options, set Company Name and Product Name as this information is baked and stored within the built executable. You can also specify an icon image for the executable as well as a default mouse cursor, if one is required. For the collection game, however, these latter two settings will be left empty. See *Figure 2.42*:

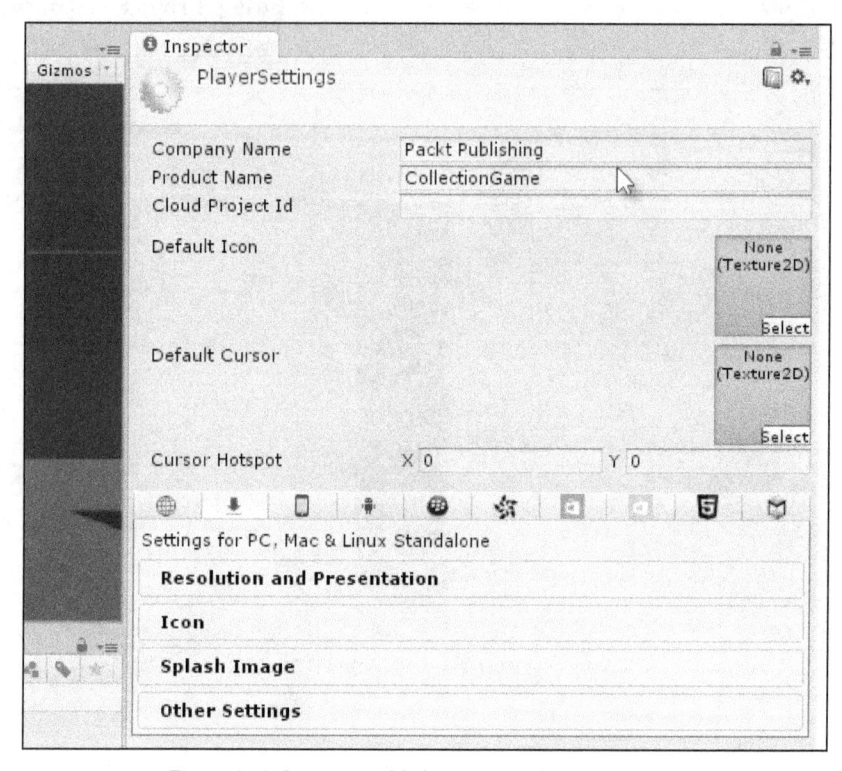

Figure 2.42: Setting a publisher name and product name

The Resolution and Presentation tab is especially important as it specifies the game screen size and whether a default splash screen (Resolution dialog) should appear at the application startup. From this tab, ensure that the Default Is Full Screen option is enabled, meaning that the game will run at the complete size of the system's screen as opposed to a smaller and movable window. In addition, enable the Display Resolution Dialog drop-down list. See *Figure 2.43*. When this is enabled, your application will display an options screen at startup, allowing the user to select a target resolution and screen size and customize controls.

For a final build, you'll probably want to disable this option, presenting the same settings through your own customized options screen in-game instead. However, for test builds, the Resolution dialog can be a great help. It lets you test your build easily at different sizes:

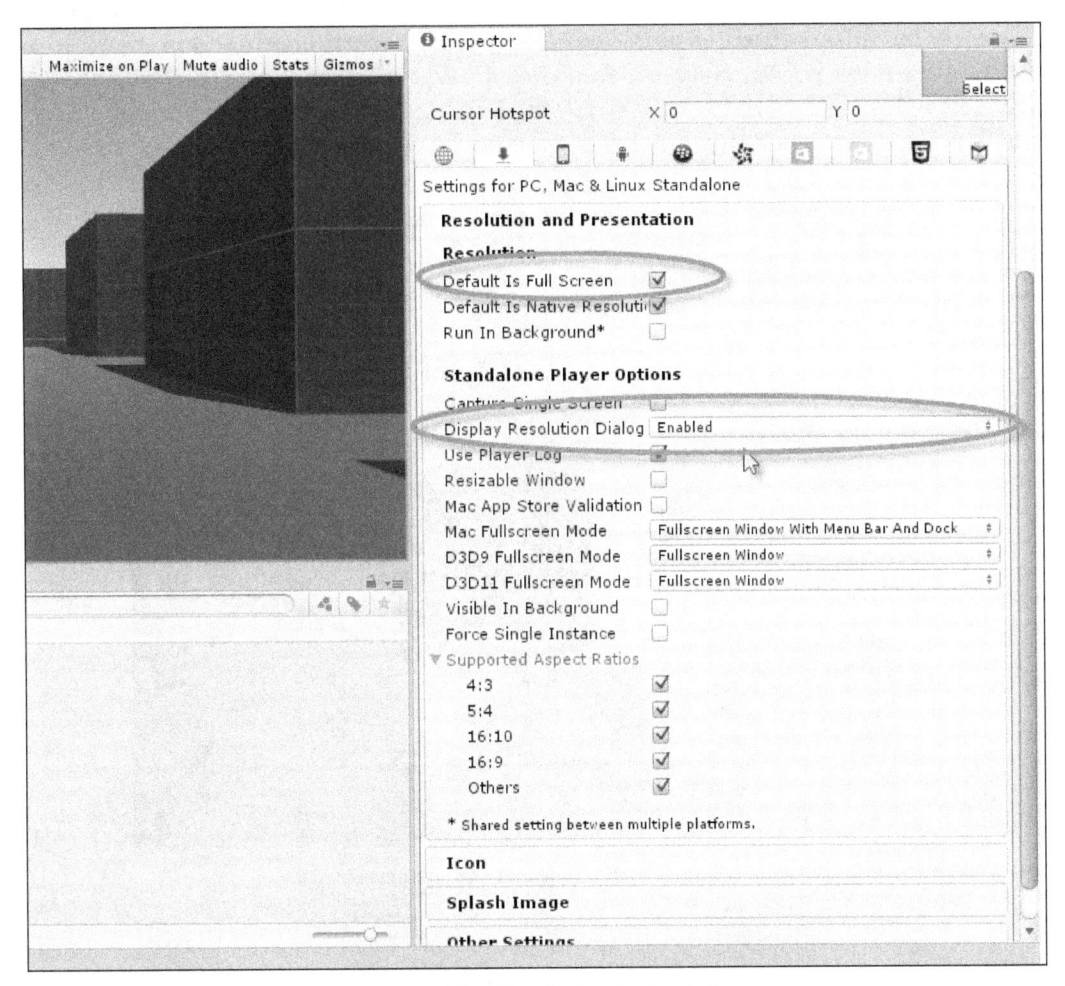

Figure 2.43: Enabling the Resolution dialog

Creating a Collection Game

Now you're ready to make your first compiled build. So, click on the **Build** button from the **Build Settings** dialog or else, choose **File** | **Build & Run** from the application menu. When you do this, Unity presents you with a **Save** dialog, asking you to specify a target location on your computer where the build should be made. Select a location and choose **Save**, and the build process will be completed. Occasionally, this process can generate errors, which are printed in red in the Console window. This can happen, for example, when you save to a read-only drive, have insufficient hard drive space, or don't have the necessary administration privileges on your computer. However, generally, the build process succeeds if your game runs properly in the editor. See *Figure 2.44*:

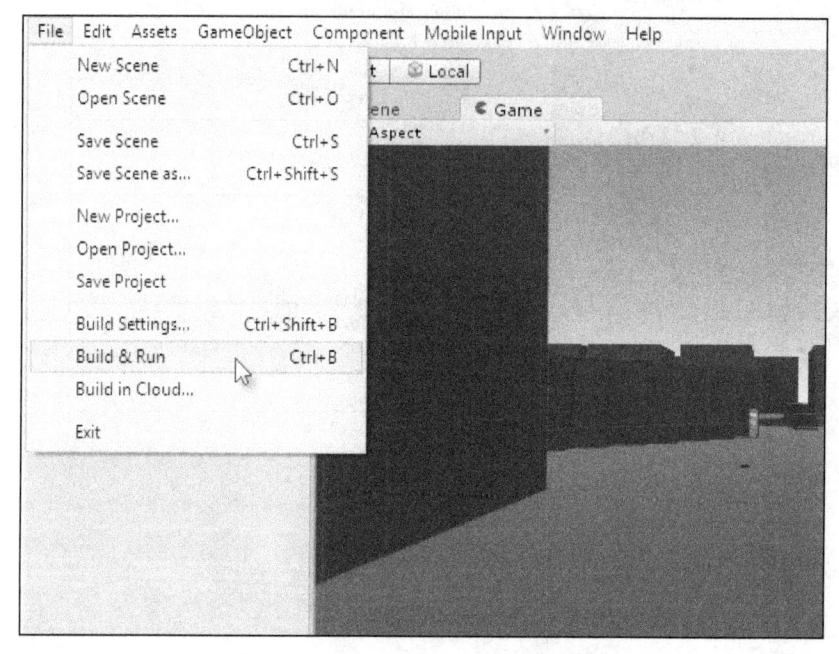

Figure 2.44: Building and running a game

After the Build is completed, Unity generates new files at your destination location. For Windows, it generates an executable file and data folder. See *Figure 2.45*. Both are essential and interdependent. That is, if you want to distribute your game and have other people play it without needing to install Unity, then you'll need to send users both the executable file and associated data folder and all its contents.

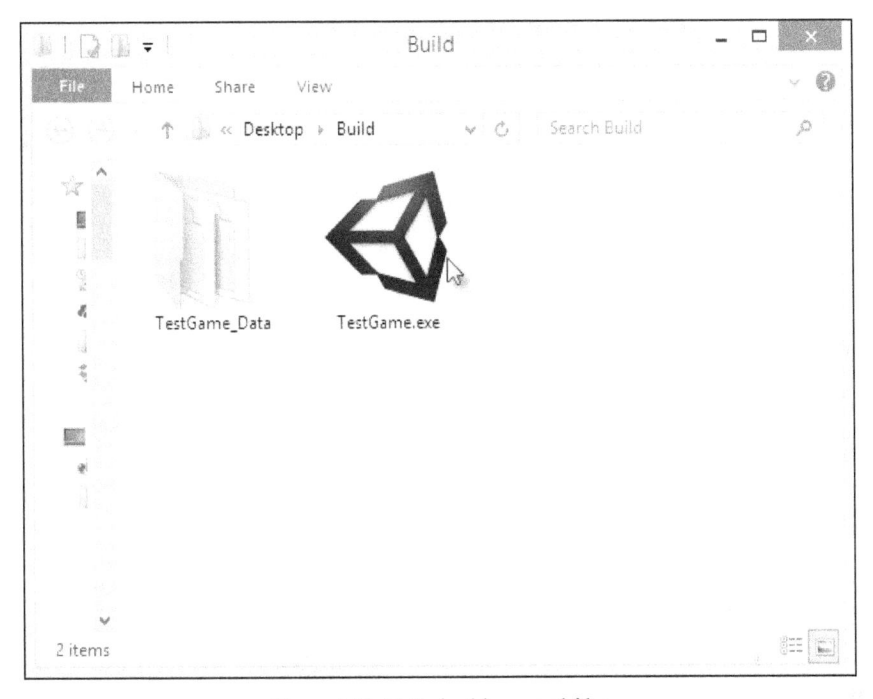

Figure 2.45: Unity builds several files

Creating a Collection Game

On running your game, the Resolution dialog will show, assuming that you Enabled the Display Resolution Dialog option from the Player Settings. From here, users can select the game resolution, quality, and output monitor and configure player controls:

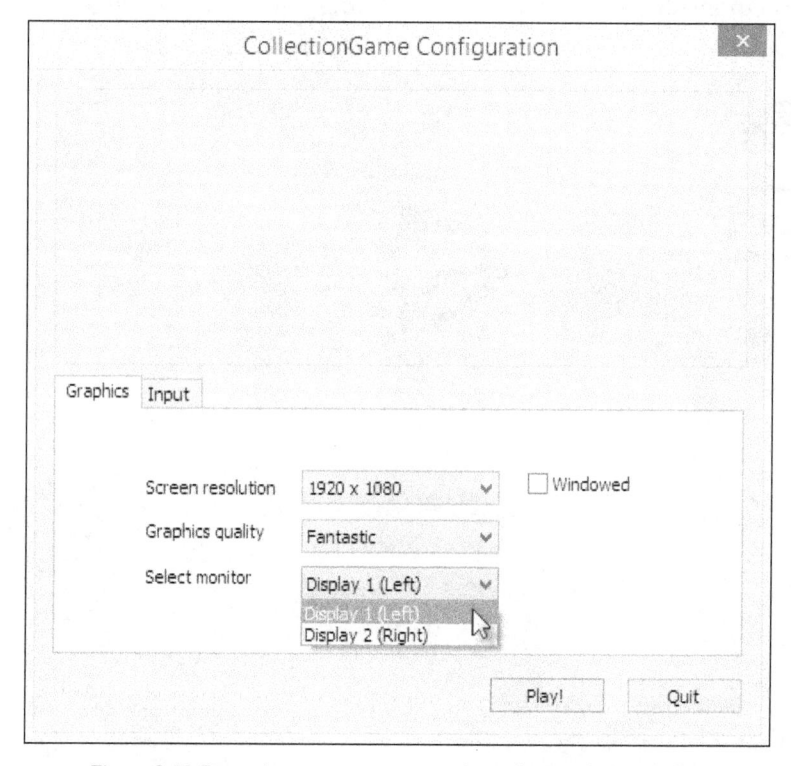

Figure 2.46: Preparing to run your game from the Resolution dialog

On clicking the play button, your game will run by default in fullscreen mode. Congratulations! Your game is now completed and built and you can send it to your friends and family for play testing! See *Figure 2.47*:

Figure 2.47: Running the coin collection game in fullscreen mode

But wait! How do you exit your game when you're finished playing? There's no quit button or main menu option in the game. For Windows, you just need to press Alt + F4 on the keyboard. For Mac, you press cmd + Q and for Ubuntu, it's Ctrl + Q.

Summary

Excellent work! On reaching this point, you've completed the coin collection game, as well as your first game in Unity. On achieving this, you've seen a wide range of Unity features including level editing and design, prefabs, particle systems, meshes, components, script files, and build settings. That's a lot! Of course, there's a lot more to be said and explored for all these areas, but nevertheless, we've pulled them together to make a game. Next, we'll get stuck in with a different game altogether and, in doing this, we'll see a creative reuse of the same features as well as the introduction of completely new features. In short, we're going to move from the world of beginner-level Unity development to intermediate.

Test your knowledge

Q1. You can easily find `GameObjects` in code by using...

- A. Layers
- B. Tags
- C. Components
- D. Integers

Q2. You can search the hierarchy for objects that contain specific component types by using a prefix of...

- A. C
- B. T
- C. W
- D. D

Q3. Static variables are always...

- A. Shared across all instances of a class
- B. Public
- C. Reset on every new frame
- D. The same

Q4. The main color for a material is defined by the...

- A. Normal Channel
- B. Detail Channel
- C. Albedo Channel
- D. Specular Channel

Q5. By default, when you run a Unity game, you will first see...

- A. The First Scene
- B. A Happy Face
- C. A Splash Screen
- D. The Resolution Config Dialog

Further reading

You can check out the below-mentioned links for more information:

- `https://unity3d.com/learn/tutorials/s/scripting`
- `https://www.packtpub.com/game-development/unity-5-scripting-and-gameplay-mechanics-video`
- `https://www.packtpub.com/game-development/mastering-unity-5x-scripting`

3
Creating a Space Shooter

This chapter enters new territory now as we begin development work on our second game, which is a twin-stick space shooter. The twin-stick genre simply refers to any game in which the player input for motion spans two dimensions or axes, typically one axis for movement and one for rotation. Example twin-stick games include *Zombies Ate My Neighbors* and *Geometry Wars*. Our game will rely heavily on coding in C#, as we'll see. The primary purpose of this is to demonstrate by example just how much can be achieved with Unity procedurally (that is, via script), even without using the editor and level-building tools. We'll still use these tools to some extent but not as much here, and that's a deliberate and not an accidental move. Consequently, this chapter assumes that you have not only completed the game project created in the previous two chapters, but also have a good, basic knowledge of C# scripting generally, though not necessarily in Unity. So, let's roll up our sleeves, if we have any, and get stuck in making a twin-stick shooter. This chapter covers the following important topics as well as others:

- Spawning and prefabs
- Twin-stick controls and axial movement
- Player controllers and shooting mechanics
- Basic enemy movement and AI

> Remember to see the game created here, and its related work, in abstract terms, that is, as general tools and concepts with multiple applications. For your own projects, you may not want to make a twin-stick shooter, and that's fine. I cannot possibly know every kind of game that you want to make. However, it's important to see the ideas and tools used here as being transferrable, as being the kind of things you can creatively use for your own games. Being able to see this is very important when working with Unity or any engine.

Creating a Space Shooter

Looking ahead – the completed project

Before getting stuck in with the twin-stick shooter game, let's see what the completed project looks like and how it works. See *Figure 3.1*. The game to be created will contain one scene only. In this scene, the player controls a spaceship that can shoot oncoming enemies. The directional keyboard arrows, and WASD, move the spaceship around the level, and it will always turn to face the mouse pointer. Clicking the left mouse button will fire ammo:

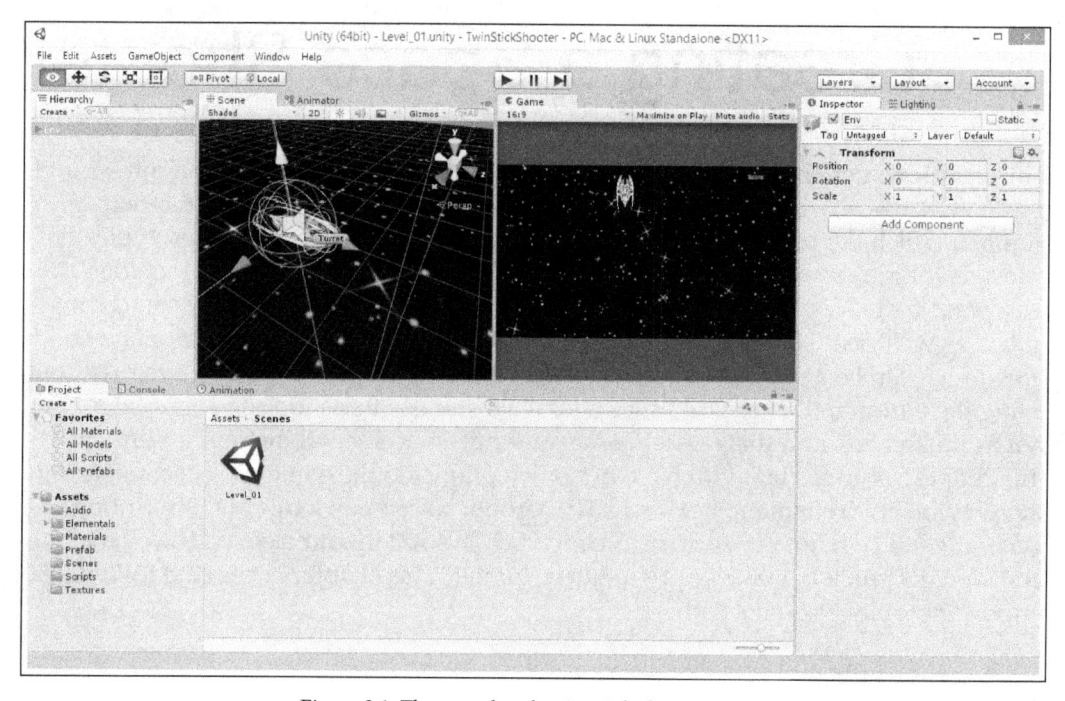

Figure 3.1: The completed twin-stick shooter game

> The completed TwinStickShooter project, as discussed in this chapter and the next, can be found in the book companion files in the Chapter03/TwinStickShooter folder.
>
> Most assets for this game (including sound and textures) were sourced from the freely accessible site, OpenGameArt.org. Here, you can find many game assets available through the public domain or creative common licenses or other licenses.

Getting started with a space shooter

To get started, create a blank Unity 3D project without any packages or specific assets. Details about creating new projects can be found in *Chapter 1, Unity Fundamentals*. We'll be coding everything from scratch this time around. Once a project is generated, create some basic folders to structure and organize the project assets from the outset. This is very important to keep track of your files as you work. Create folders for Textures, Scenes, Materials, Audio, Prefabs, and Scripts. See *Figure 3.2*:

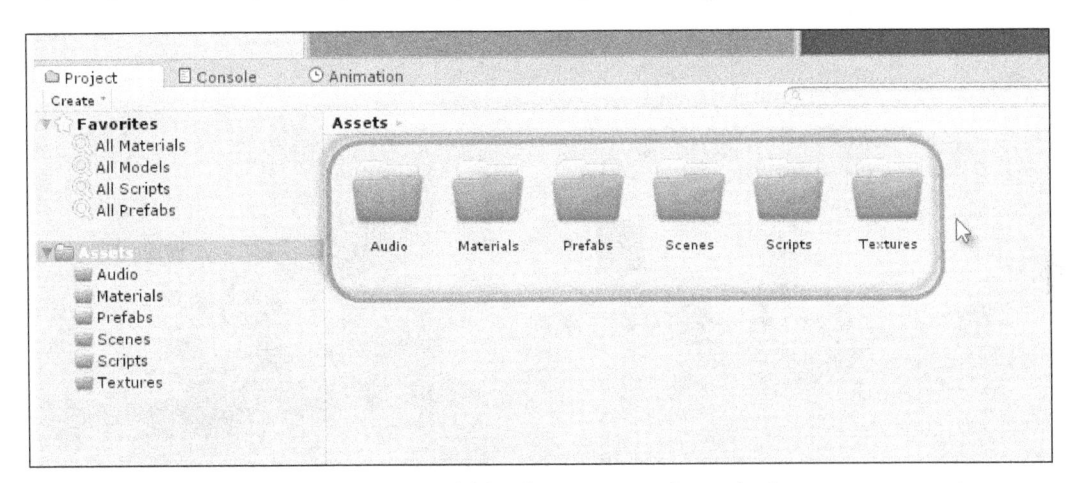

Figure 3.2: Create folders for structure and organization

Next, our game will depend on some graphical and audio assets. These are included in the book companion files in the Chapter03/Assets folder, but can also be downloaded online from OpenGameArt.org. Let's start with textures for the player spaceship, enemy spaceships, and star-field background. Drag and drop Textures from Windows Explorer or Finder to the Unity **Project** panel in the Textures folder.

Creating a Space Shooter

Unity imports and configures the textures automatically. *See Figure 3.3:*

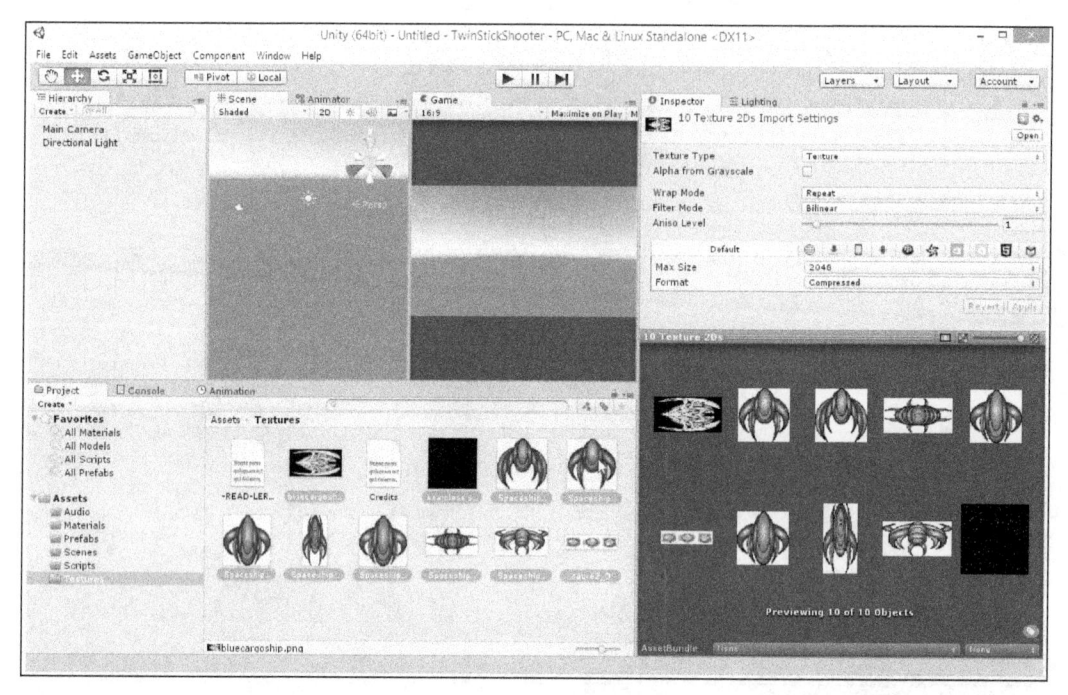

Figure 3.3: Importing Texture assets for the spaceship, enemies, star background, and ammo

> Use of the provided assets is optional. You can create your own if you prefer. Just drag and drop your own textures in place of the included assets, and you can still follow along with the tutorial just fine.

By default, Unity imports image files as regular textures for use on 3D objects, and it assumes that their pixel dimensions are a power-2 size (4, 8, 16, 32, 64, 128, 256, and so on). If the size is not actually one of these, then Unity will up-scale or down-scale the texture to the nearest valid size. This is not appropriate behavior, however, for a 2D top-down space shooter game in which imported textures should appear at their native (imported) size without any scaling or automatic adjustment. To fix this, select all the imported textures and, from the **Object Inspector**, change their **Texture Type** from **Texture** to **Sprite (2D and UI)**. Once changed, click on the **Apply** button to update the settings and the textures will retain their imported dimensions. See *Figure 3.4:*

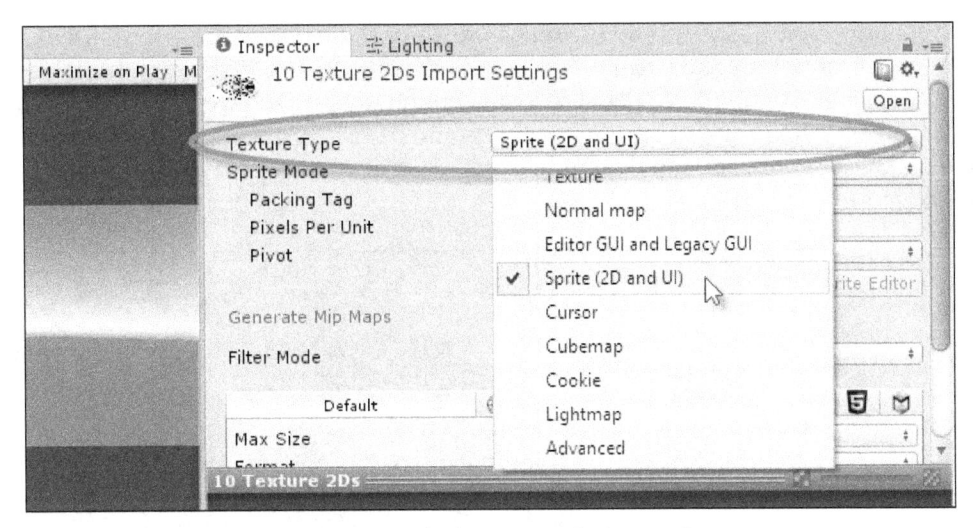

Figure 3.4: Changing the Texture type for imported textures

After changing the **Texture Type** setting to **Sprite (2D and UI)**, also remove the check mark from the **Generate Mip Maps** box, in case this box is enabled. This will prevent Unity from automatically downgrading the quality of textures based on their distance from the camera in the scene. This ensures that your textures retain their highest quality. More information on 2D texture settings and Mip Maps can be found at the online Unity documentationat http://docs.unity3d.com/Manual/class-TextureImporter.html. *See Figure 3.5*:

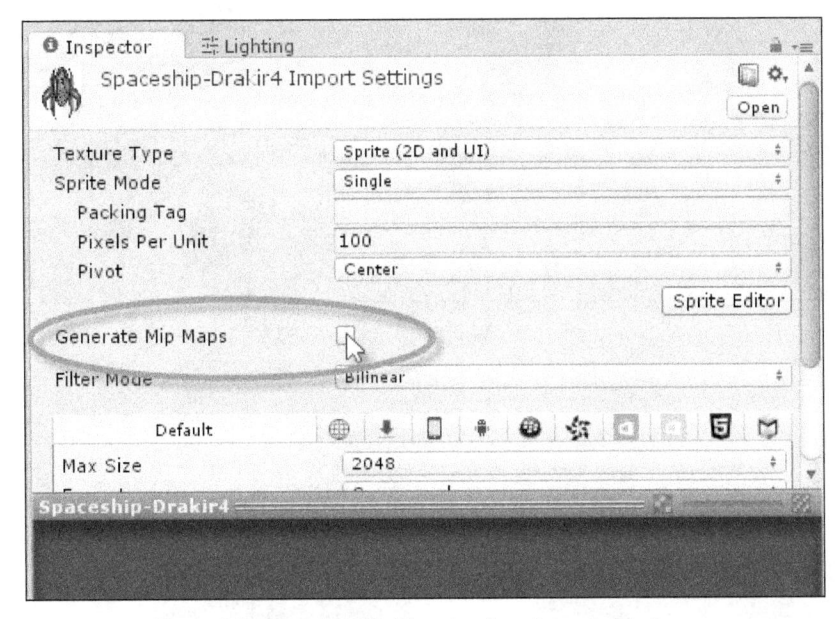

Figure 3.5: Removing MipMapping from imported textures

[123]

Creating a Space Shooter

Now you can easily drag and drop your textures to the scene adding them as sprite objects. You can't drag and drop them from the **Project** panel to the viewport, but you can drag and drop them from the **Project** panel to the **Hierarchy** panel. When you do this, the texture will automatically be added as a sprite object in the **Scene**. We'll make frequent use of this feature as we work at creating spaceship objects. See *Figure 3.6*:

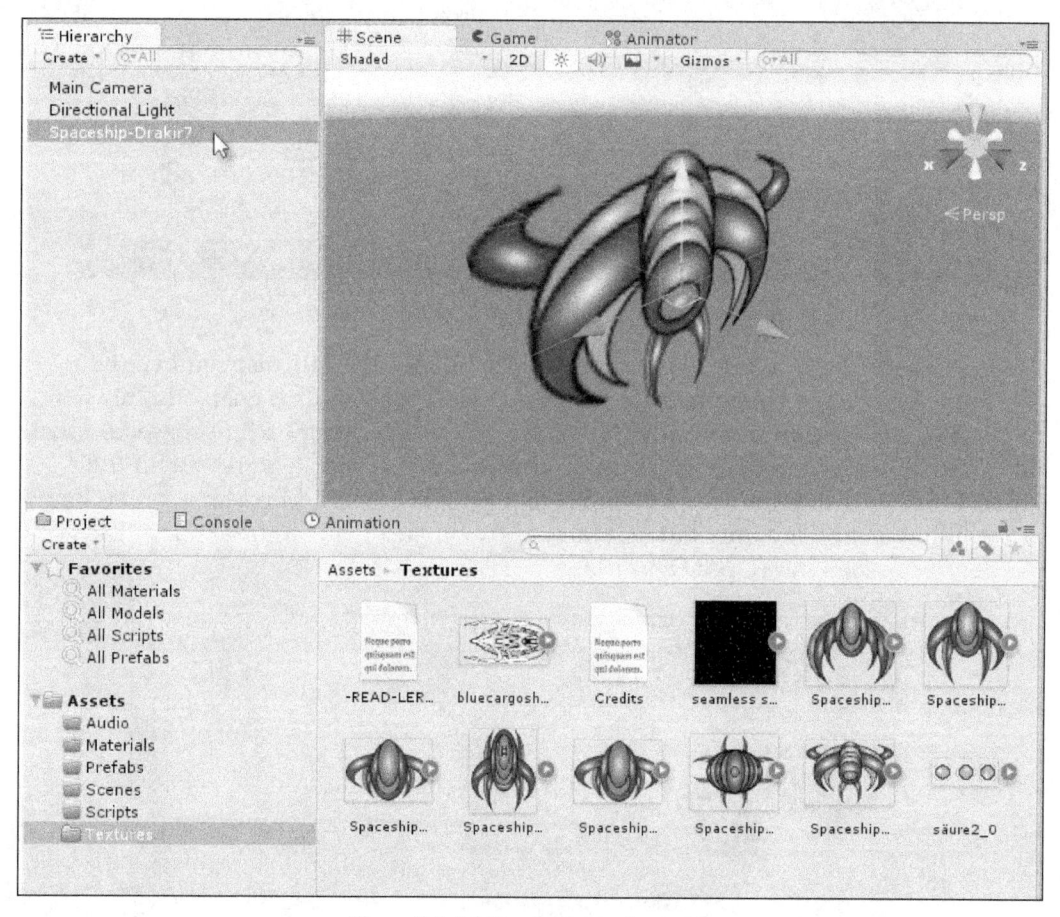

Figure 3.6: Adding sprites to the scene

Next, let's import music and sound effects, which are also included in the book companion files in the `Chapter03/Assets/Audio` folder. These assets were downloaded from `OpenGameArt.org`. To import the audio, simply drag and drop the files from Windows Explorer or Mac Finder to the **Project** panel. When you do this, Unity automatically imports and configures the assets. You can give the audio a test from within the Unity Editor by pressing play on the preview toolbar from the **Object Inspector**. See *Figure 3.7*:

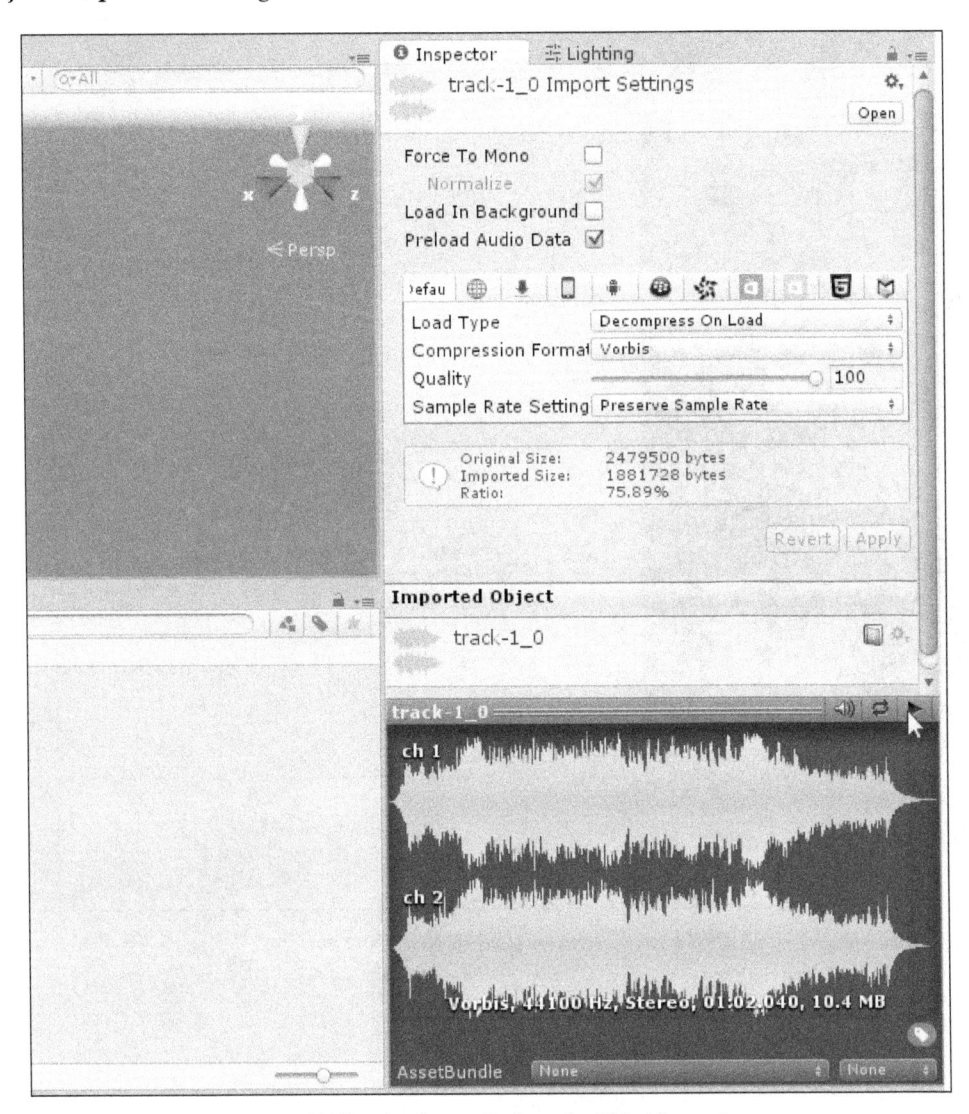

Figure 3.7: Previewing audio from the Object Inspector

Creating a Space Shooter

As with texture files, Unity imports audio files using a set of default parameters. These parameters are typically suitable for short sound effects such as footsteps, gunshots, and explosions, but for longer tracks such as music, they can be problematic, causing long level-loading times. To fix this, select the music track in the **Project** panel, and from the **Load Type** drop-down box, select the **Streaming** option. This ensures that the music track is streamed as opposed to loaded wholly in memory at level startup. See *Figure 3.8*:

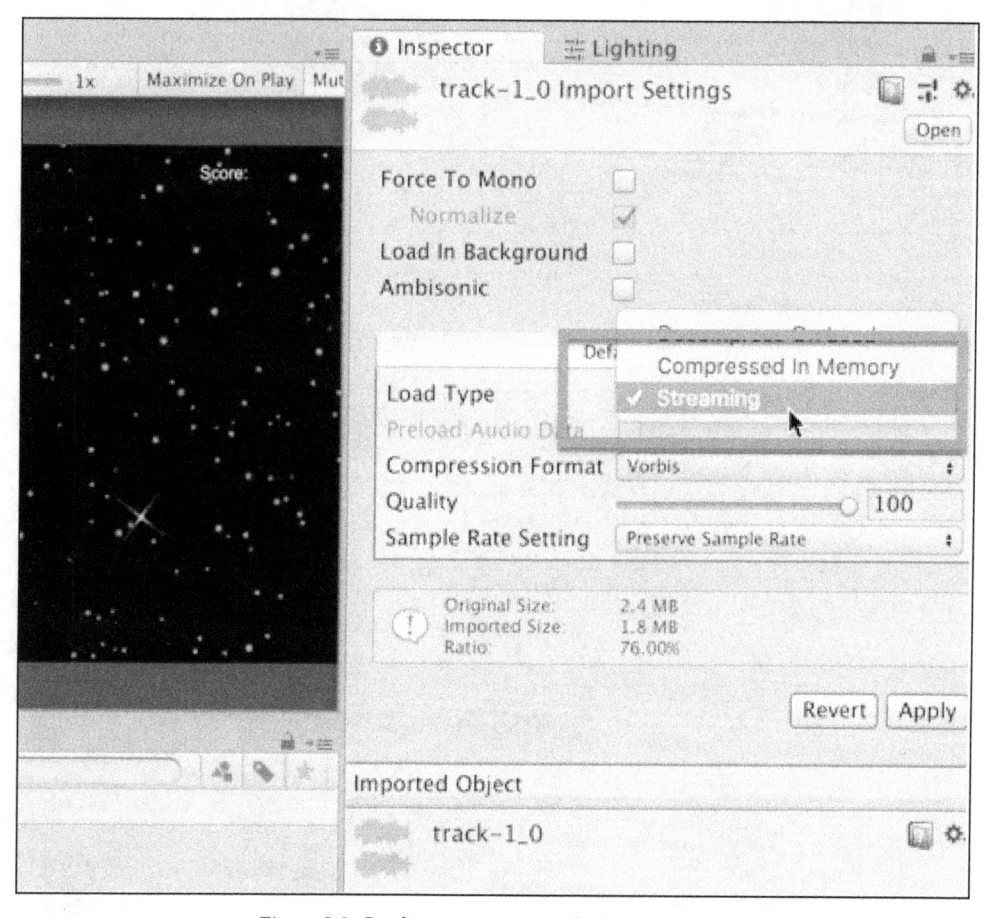

Figure 3.8: Configuring music tracks for streaming

Creating a player object

We've now imported most assets for the twin-stick shooter and we're ready to create a player spaceship object, that is, the object that the player will control and move around. Creating this might seem a trivial matter of simply dragging and dropping the relevant player sprite from the **Project** panel to the scene, but things are not so simple. The player is a complex object with many different behaviors, as we'll see. For this reason, more care needs to be taken about creating the player. To get started, create an empty game object in the scene by navigating to **GameObject | Create Empty** from the application menu and name the object, Player. See *Figure 3.9*:

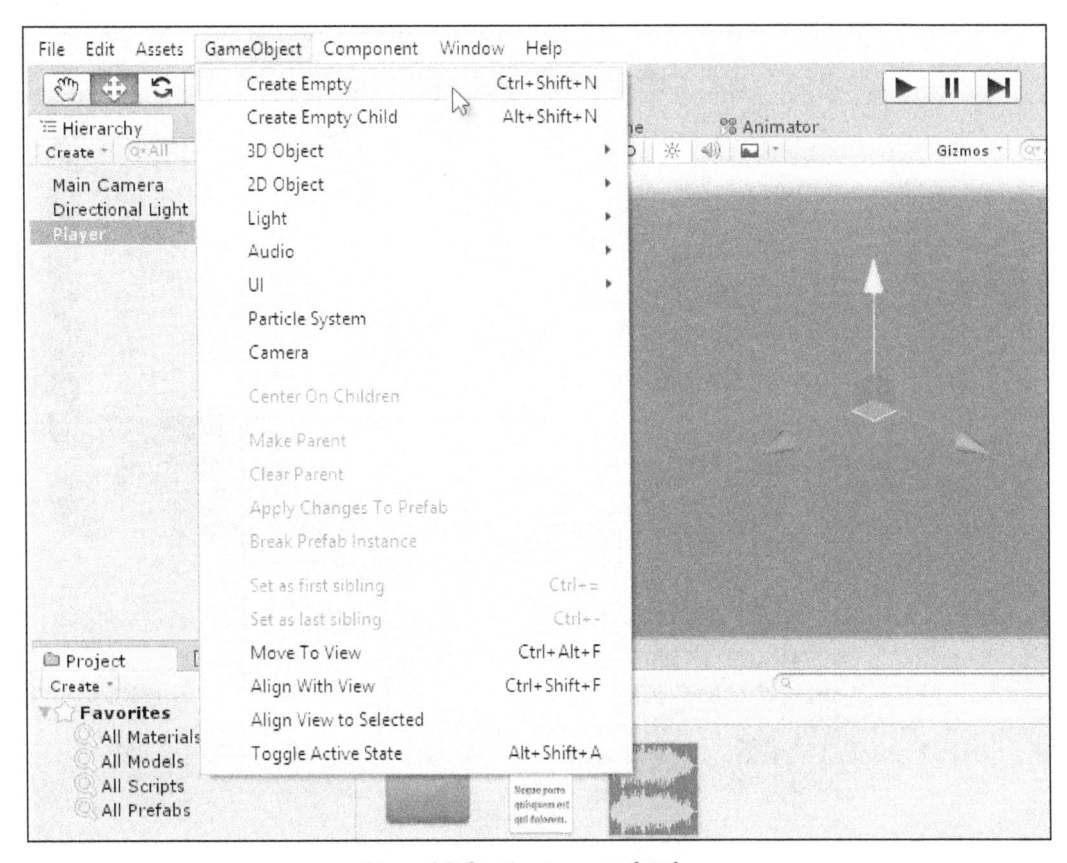

Figure 3.9: Starting to create the player

Creating a Space Shooter

The newly created object may or may not be centered at the world origin of *(0, 0, 0)* and its rotation properties may not be consistently 0 across **X**, **Y**, and **Z**. To ensure a completely zeroed transform, you could manually set the values to 0 by entering them directly in the **Transform** component for the object in the **Object Inspector**. However, you can set them all to 0 automatically by clicking on the cog icon at the top left corner of the **Transform** component and selecting **Reset** from the context menu. See *Figure 3.10*:

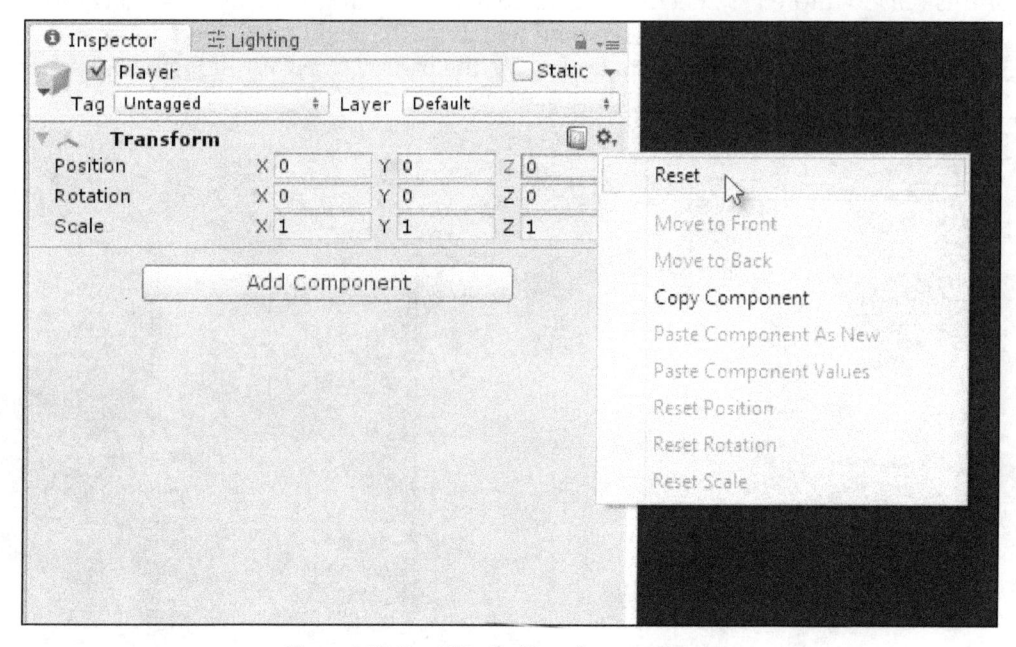

Figure 3.10: Resetting the Transform component

Next, drag and drop the `Player` drop ship sprite (in the `Textures` folder) from the **Project** panel to the **Hierarchy** panel, making it a child of the empty player object. Then, rotate the drop ship sprite by 90 degrees in **X** and -90 degrees in **Y**. This makes the sprite oriented in the direction of its parent's forward vector and also flattened on the ground plane. The game camera will take a top-down view. See *Figure 3.11*:

Chapter 3

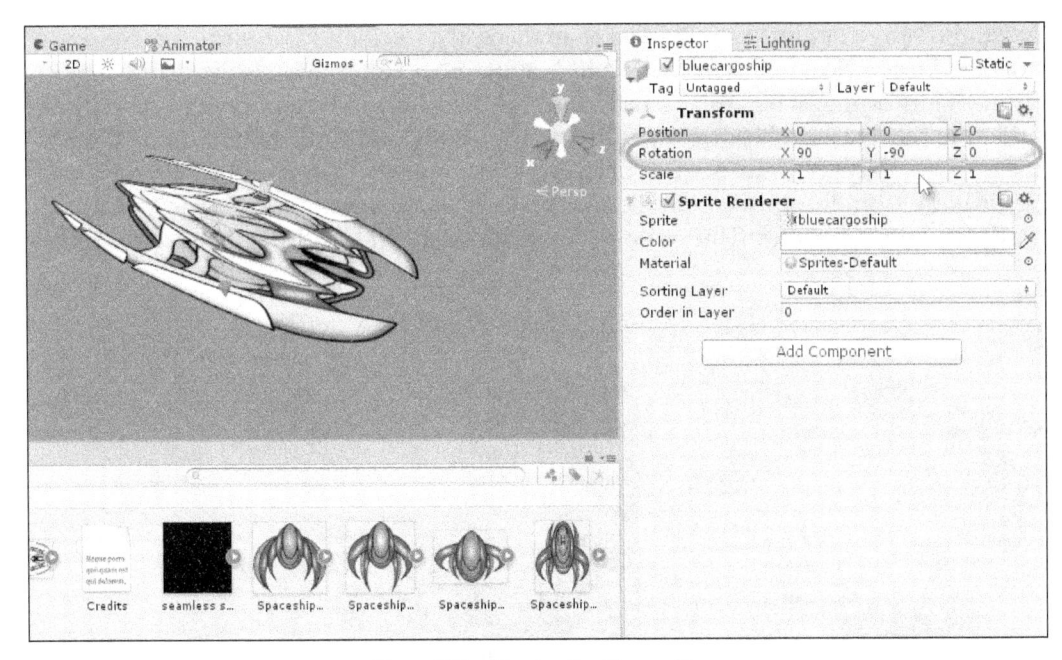

Figure 3.11: Aligning the Player ship

You can confirm that the ship sprite has been aligned correctly in relation to its parent by selecting the `Player` object and viewing the blue forward vector arrow. The front of the ship sprite and the blue forward vector should be pointing in the same direction. If they're not, then continue to rotate the sprite by 90 degrees until they're in alignment. This will be important later when coding player movement to make the ship travel in the direction it's looking. See *Figure 3.12*:

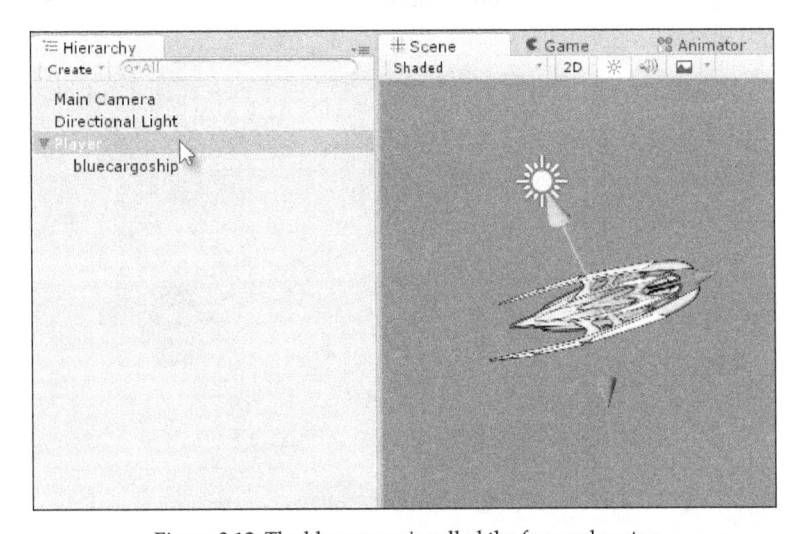

Figure 3.12: The blue arrow is called the forward vector

[129]

Creating a Space Shooter

Next, the `Player` object should react to physics, that is, the `Player` object is solid and affected by physical forces. It must collide with other solids and also take damage from enemy ammo when hit. To facilitate this, two additional components should be added to the `Player` object, specifically, a **Rigidbody** and **Collider**. To do this, select the `Player` object (not the `Sprite` object) and navigate to **Component | Physics | Rigidbody** from the application menu. Then, choose `Component` | **Physics** | **Capsule Collider** from the menu. This adds both a **Rigidbody** and **Collider**. See *Figure 3.13*:

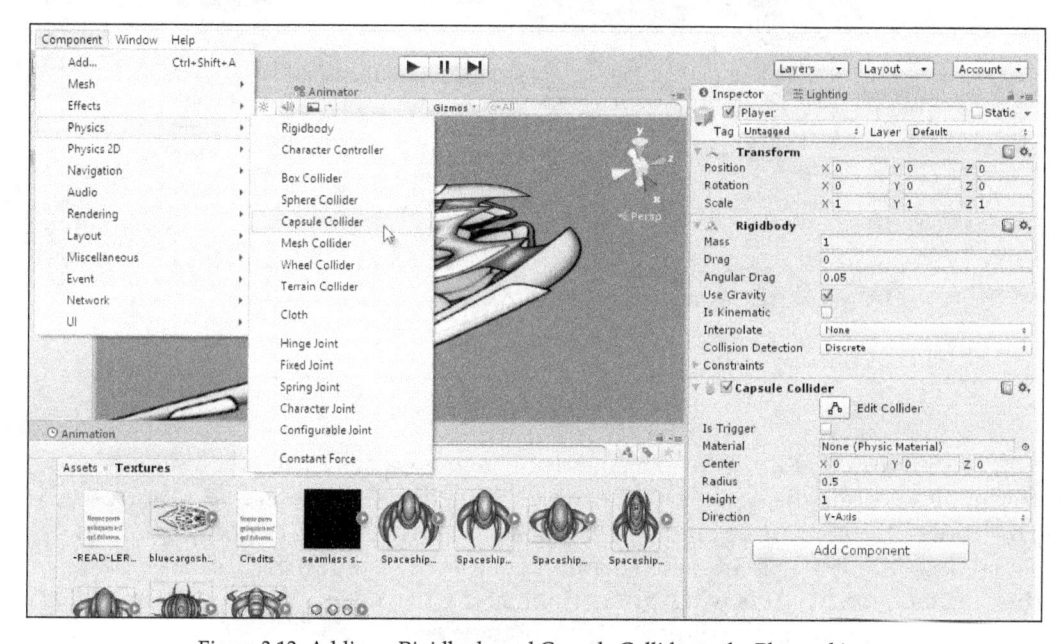

Figure 3.13: Adding a Rigidbody and Capsule Collider to the Player object

Chapter 3

The **Collider** component is used to approximate the volume of the object and the **Rigibody** component uses the **Collider** to determine how physical forces should be applied realistically. Let's adjust **Capsule Collider** a little because the default settings typically do not match up with the `Player` sprite as intended. Specifically, adjust the **Direction**, **Radius**, and **Height** values until **Capsule** encompasses the `Player` sprite and represents the volume of the player. See *Figure 3.14*:

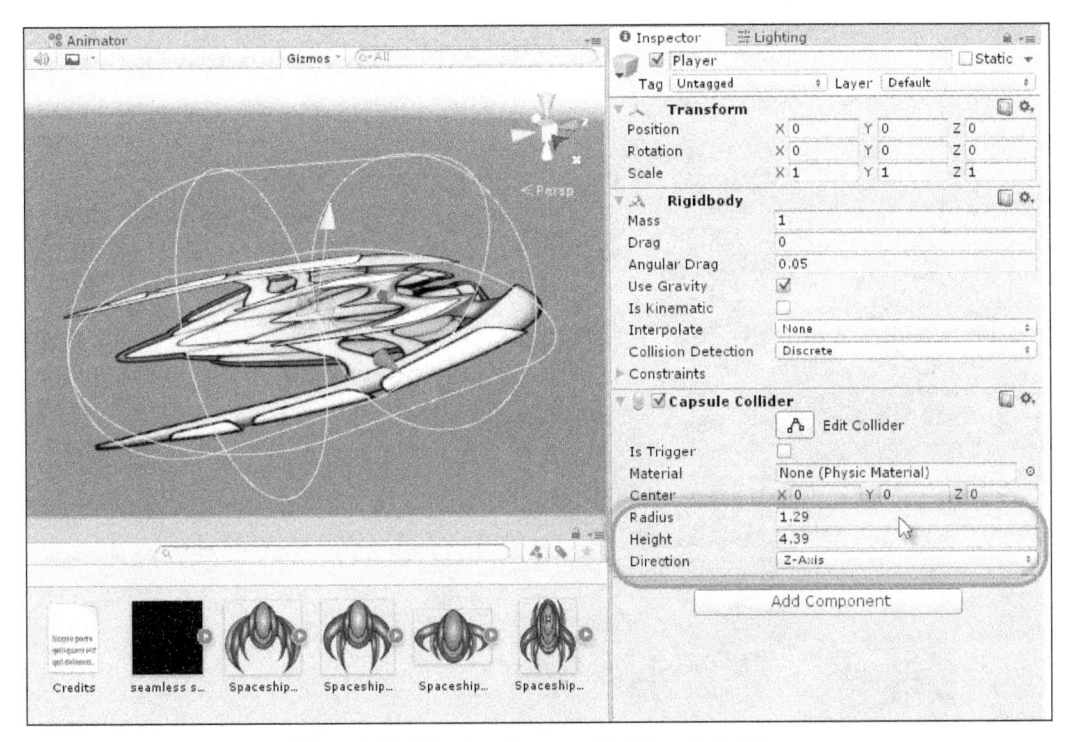

Figure 3.14: Adjusting the spaceship Capsule Collider

Creating a Space Shooter

By default, the `Rigidbody` component is configured to approximate objects that are affected by gravity and fall to the ground, bumping into and reacting to other solids in the scene. This is not appropriate for a spaceship that flies around. Consequently, the `Rigidbody` should be adjusted. Specifically, remove the **Use Gravity** check mark to prevent the object from falling to the ground. Additionally, enable the **Freeze Position Y** checkbox and the **Freeze Rotation Z** checkbox to prevent the spaceship moving and rotating around axes that are undesirable in a 2D top-down game. See *Figure 3.15*:

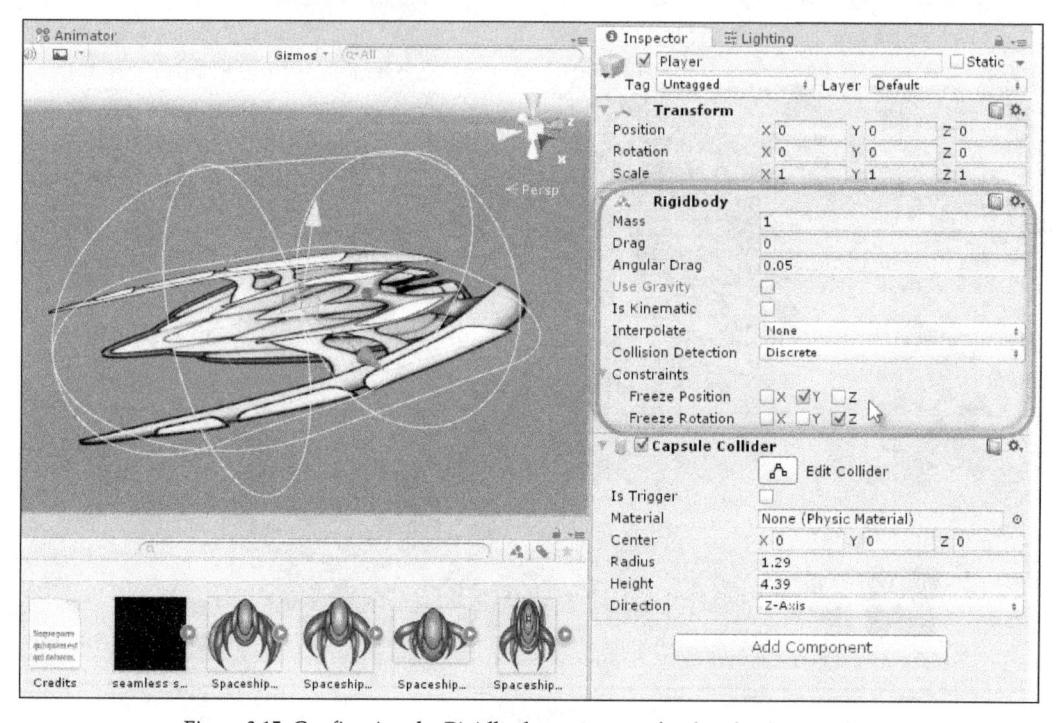

Figure 3.15: Configuring the Rigidbody component for the player spaceship

Excellent work! We've now configured the player spaceship object successfully. Of course, it still doesn't move or do anything specific in the game. This is simply because we haven't added any code yet. That's something we'll turn to next—making the player object respond to user input.

[132]

Player input

The `Player` object is now created in the scene, configured with both **Rigidbody** and **Collider** components. However, this object doesn't respond to player controls. In a twin-stick shooter, the player provides input on two axes and can typically shoot a weapon. This often means that keyboard WASD buttons guide player movements up, down, left, and right. In addition, mouse movement controls the direction in which the player is looking and aiming and the left mouse button typically fires a weapon. This is the control scheme required for our game. To implement this, we'll need to create a `PlayerController` script file. Right-click on the `Scripts` folder of the **Project** panel and create a new C# script file named `PlayerController.cs`. See *Figure 3.16*:

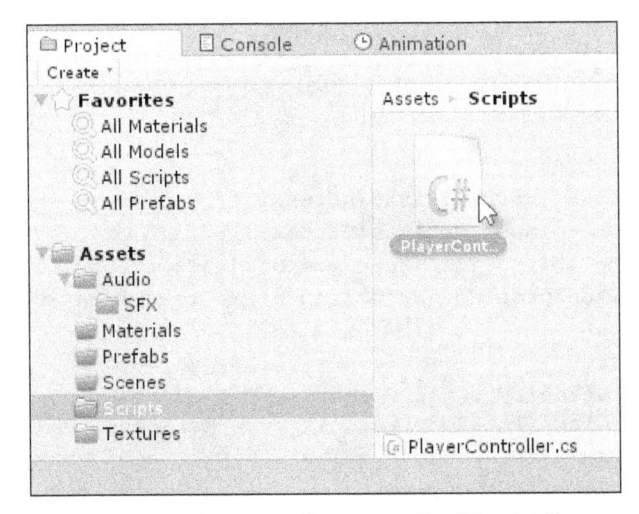

Figure 3.16: Creating a player controller C# script file

In the `PlayerController.cs` script file, the following code (as shown in *Code Sample 3.1*) should be featured. Comments follow this sample:

```
//------------------------------
using UnityEngine;
using System.Collections;
//------------------------------
public class PlayerController : MonoBehaviour
{
    //------------------------------
    private Rigidbody ThisBody = null;
    private Transform ThisTransform = null;
```

Creating a Space Shooter

```csharp
public bool MouseLook = true;
public string HorzAxis = "Horizontal";
public string VertAxis = "Vertical";
public string FireAxis = "Fire1";
public float MaxSpeed = 5f;

//------------------------------
// Use this for initialization
void Awake ()
{
  ThisBody = GetComponent<Rigidbody>();
  ThisTransform = GetComponent<Transform>();
}
//------------------------------
// Update is called once per frame
void FixedUpdate ()
{
  //Update movement
  float Horz = Input.GetAxis(HorzAxis);
  float Vert = Input.GetAxis(VertAxis);
  Vector3 MoveDirection = new Vector3(Horz, 0.0f, Vert);
  ThisBody.AddForce(MoveDirection.normalized * MaxSpeed);

  //Clamp speed
  ThisBody.velocity = new Vector3
    (Mathf.Clamp(ThisBody.velocity.x, -MaxSpeed, MaxSpeed),
    Mathf.Clamp(ThisBody.velocity.y, -MaxSpeed, MaxSpeed),
    Mathf.Clamp(ThisBody.velocity.z, -MaxSpeed, MaxSpeed));

  //Should look with mouse?
  if(MouseLook)
  {
    //Update rotation - turn to face mouse pointer
    Vector3 MousePosWorld = Camera.main.ScreenToWorldPoint(new
      Vector3(Input.mousePosition.x,
      Input.mousePosition.y, 0.0f));
    MousePosWorld = new Vector3(MousePosWorld.x, 0.0f,
      MousePosWorld.z);
    //Get direction to cursor
    Vector3 LookDirection = MousePosWorld -
      ThisTransform.position;

    //FixedUpdate rotation
```

```
        ThisTransform.localRotation = Quaternion.LookRotation
            (LookDirection.normalized,Vector3.up);
    }

  }
 }
//------------------------------
```

Code Sample 3.1

The following points summarize the code sample:

- The `PlayerController` class should be attached to the `Player` object in the scene. Overall, it accepts input from the player and will control the movement of the spaceship.

- The `Awake` function is called once when the object is created at the level start, for each object. You cannot rely on the order in which objects receie an Awake call. During this function, two components are retrieved, namely, the **Transform** component for controller player rotation and the **Rigidbody** component for controller player movement. The **Transform** component can be used to control player movement through the **Position** property, but this ignores collisions and solid objects. The **Rigidbody** component, in contrast, prevents the player object from passing through other solids.

- The `FixedUpdate` function is called once on each update of the physics system, which is a fixed number of times per second. `FixedUpdate` differs from `Update`, which is called once per frame and can vary on a per second basis as the frame rate fluctuates. If you ever need to control an object through the physics system, using components such as **Rigidbody**, then you should always do so in `FixedUpdate` and not `Update`. This is a Unity convention that you should remember for best results.

- The `Input.GetAxis` function is called on each `FixedUpdate` to read the axial input data from an input device, such as the keyboard or gamepad. This function reads from two named axes, `Horizontal` (left-right) and `Vertical` (up-down). These work in a normalized space of -1 to 1. This means that when the left key is pressed and held down, the `Horizontal` axis returns -1 and, when the right key is being pressed and held down, the `Horizontal` axis returns 1. A value of 0 indicates that either no relevant key is being pressed or both left and right are being pressed together, canceling each other out. A similar principle applies for the `Vertical` axis. Up refers to 1, down to -1, and no keypress relates to 0. More information on the `GetAxis` function can be found online in the Unity documentation at http://docs.unity3d.com/ScriptReference/Input.GetAxis.html.

Creating a Space Shooter

- The `Rigidbody.AddForce` function is used to apply a physical force to the `Player` object, moving it in a specific direction. `AddForce` represents a velocity, moving the object in a specific direction by a specific strength. The direction is encoded in the `MoveDirection` vector, which is based on player input from both the `Horizontal` and `Vertical` axes. This direction is multiplied by our maximum speed to ensure that the object travels as fast as needed. For more information on `AddForce`, see the online Unity documentation at `http://docs.unity3d.com/ScriptReference/Rigidbody.AddForce.html`.

- The `Camera.ScreenToWorldPoint` function is used to convert the screen position of the mouse cursor in the game window into a position in the game world, giving the player a target destination to look at. This code is responsible for making the player look at the mouse cursor always. However, as we'll see soon, some further tweaking is required to make this code work properly. For more information on `ScreenToWorldPoint`, see the Unity online documentation at `http://docs.unity3d.com/ScriptReference/Camera.ScreenToWorldPoint.html`.

Configuring the game camera

The preceding code allows you to control the `Player` object, but there are some problems. One of them is that the player doesn't seem to face the position of the mouse cursor, even though our code is designed to achieve this behavior. The reason is that the camera, by default, is not configured as it needs to be for a top-down 2D game. We'll fix this in this section. To get started, the scene camera should have a top-down view of the scene.

Chapter 3

To achieve this, switch the **Scene** viewport to a top-down 2D view by clicking on the **ViewCube**, the up arrow in the top right corner of the **Scene** viewport. This switches your viewport to a top view. See *Figure 3.17*:

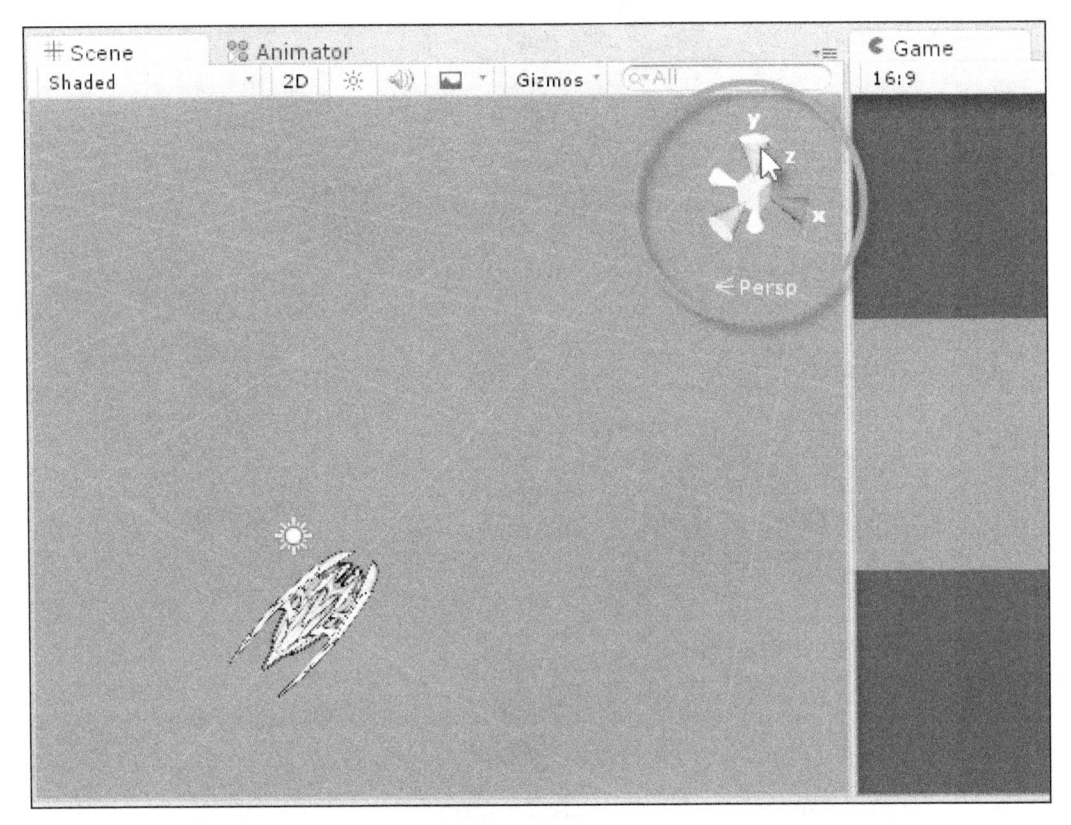

Figure 3.17: The viewcube can change the viewport perspective

Creating a Space Shooter

You can see that the viewport is in a top view because the viewcube will list **Top** as the current view. See *Figure 3.18*:

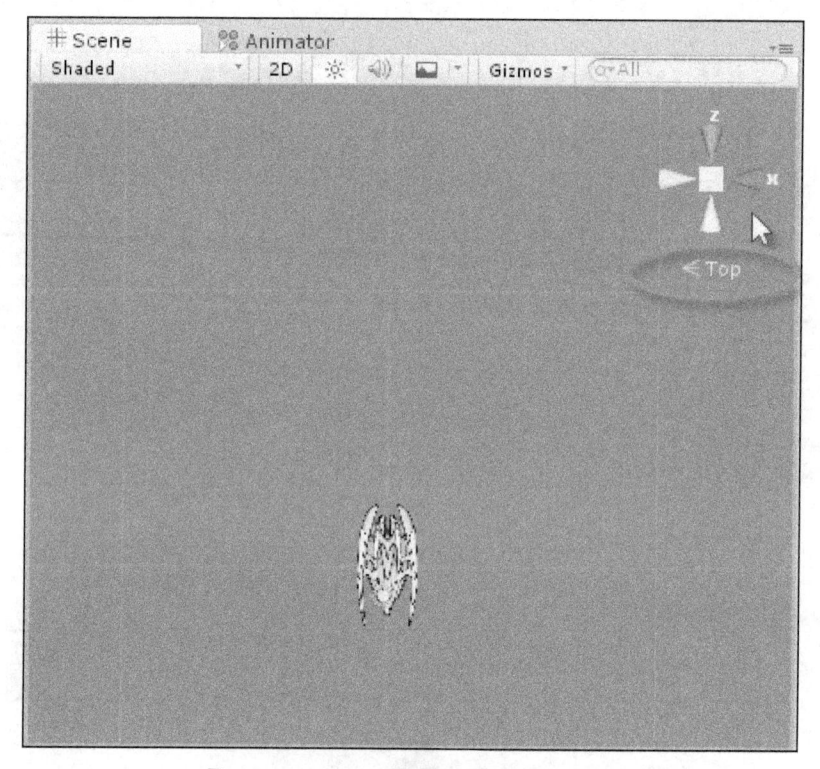

Figure 3.18: Top view in the Scene viewport

From here, you can have the scene camera conform to the viewport camera exactly, giving you an instant top-down view for your game.

To do this, select the **Camera** in the **Scene** (or from the **Hierarchy** panel) and then choose **GameObject | Align With View** from the application menu. See *Figure 3.19*:

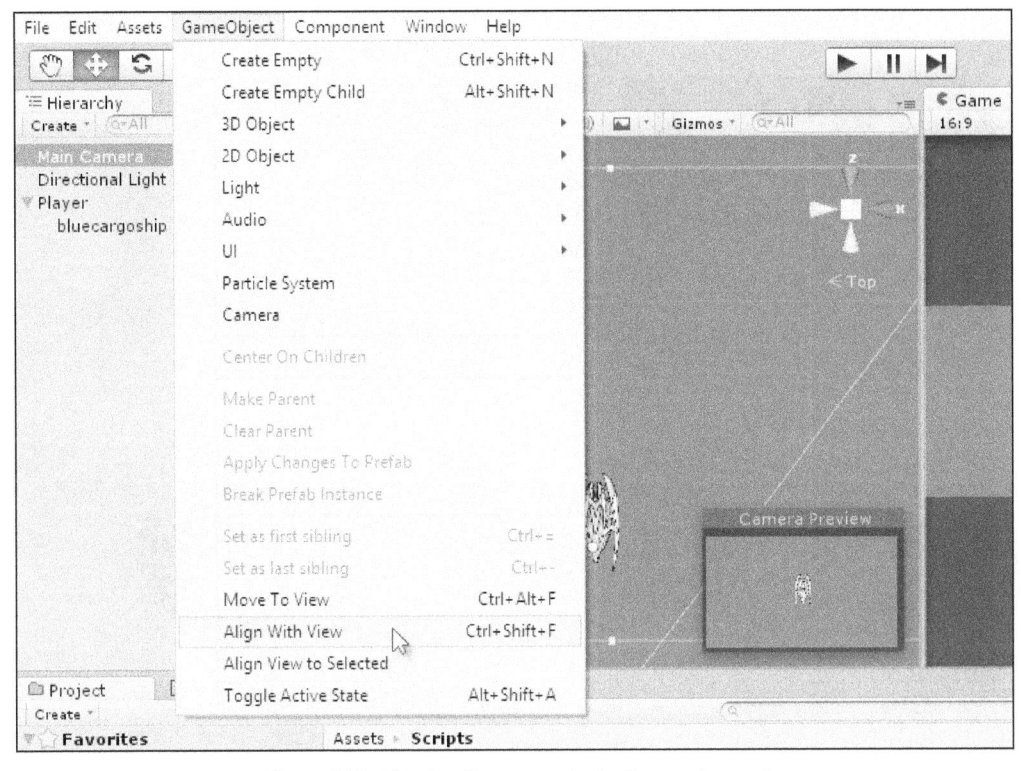

Figure 3.19: Aligning the camera to the Scene viewport

This makes your game look much better than before, but there's still a problem. When the game is running, the spaceship still doesn't look at the mouse cursor as intended. This is because the camera is a **Perspective** camera and the conversion between a screen point and world point is leading to unexpected results. We can fix this by changing the camera to an **Orthographic** camera, which is a truly 2D camera that allows no perspective distortion.

To do this, select the **Camera** in the scene, and from the **Object Inspector**, change the **Projection** setting from **Perspective** to **Orthographic**:

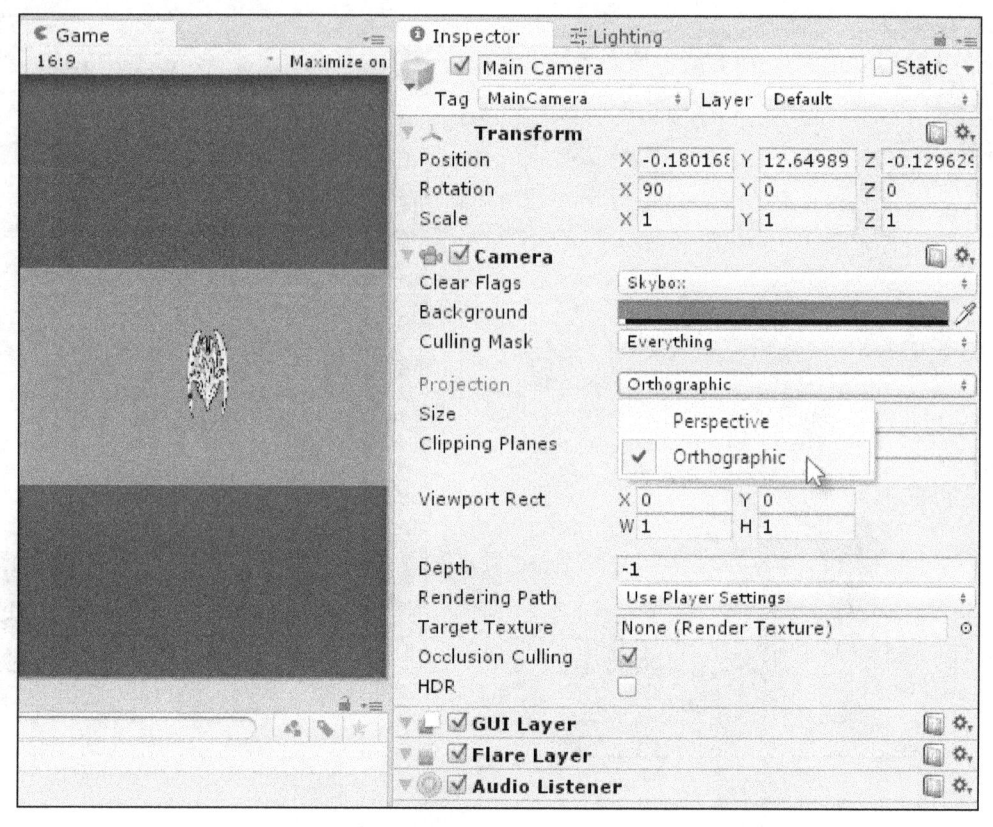

Figure 3.20: Changing the Camera to Orthographic mode

Every orthographic camera has a **Size** field in the **Object Inspector**, which is not present for perspective cameras. This field controls how many units in the world view correspond to pixels on the screen. We want a 1:1 ratio or relationship between world units to pixels in order to ensure that our textures appear at the correct size and cursor movement has the intended effect. The target resolution for our game will be Full HD, which is 1920 x 1080, and this has an aspect ratio of 16:9. For this resolution, the orthographic **Size** should be 5.4.

The reasons for this value are beyond the scope of this book, but the formula to arrive at it is *screen height (in pixels) / 2 / 100*. Therefore, *1080 / 2 / 100 = 5.4*. See *Figure 3.21*:

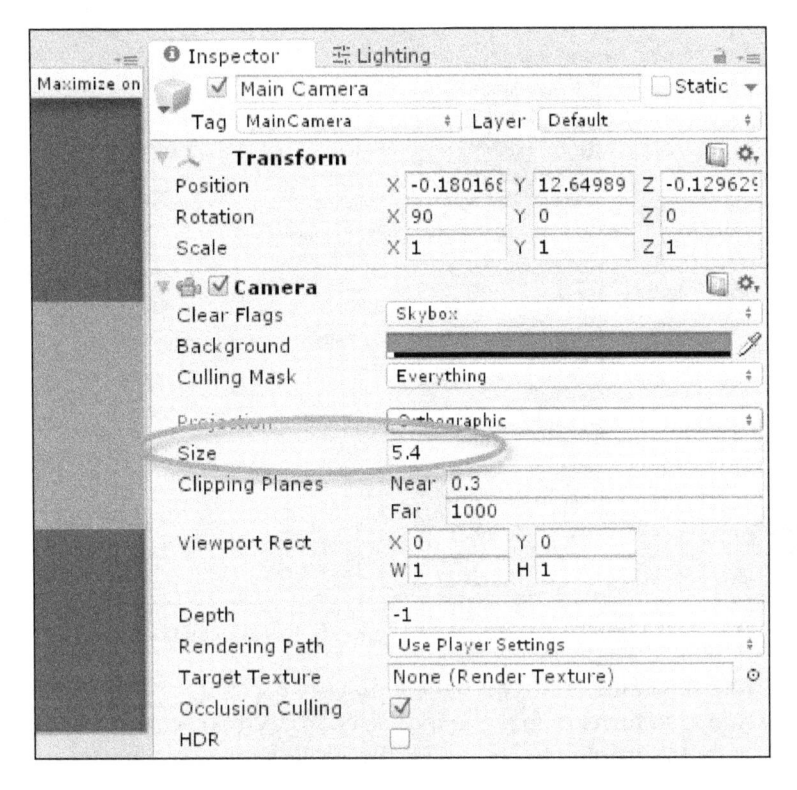

Figure 3.21: Changing orthographic size for a 1:1 pixel-to-screen ratio

Finally, make sure that your **Game** tab view is configured to display the game at a **16:9** aspect ratio. If it isn't, click on the aspect drop-down list at the top left corner of the **Game** view and choose the **16:9** option. See *Figure 3.22*:

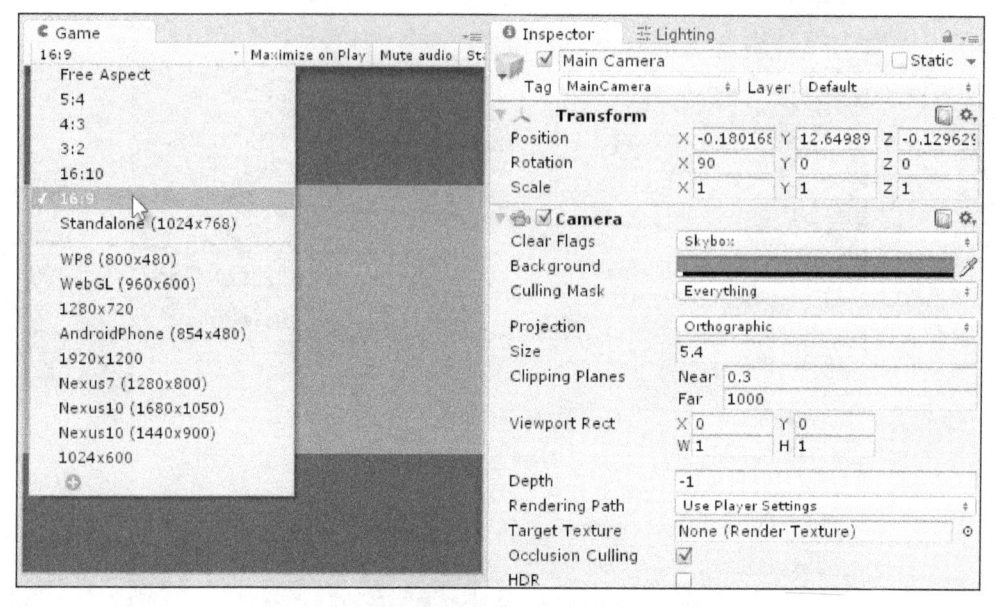

Figure 3.22: Displaying the game at a 16:9 aspect ratio

Now try running the game, and you have a player spaceship that moves based on WASD input and also turns to face the mouse cursor. Great work! See *Figure 3.23*. The game is really taking shape. However, there's lots more work to do.

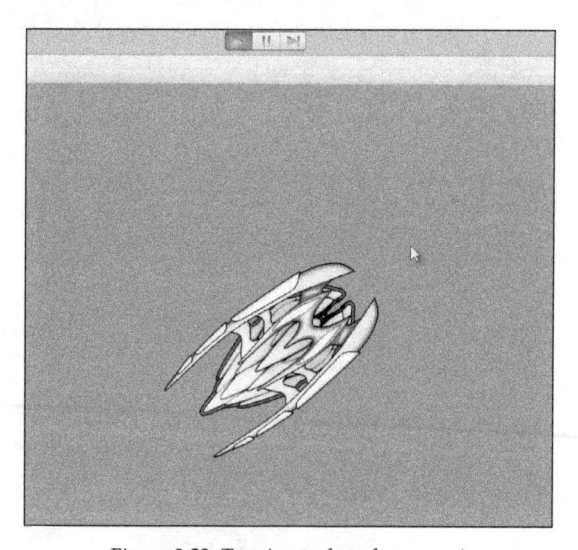

Figure 3.23: Turning to face the cursor!

Bounds locking

On previewing the game thus far, the spaceship probably looks too large. We can fix this easily by changing the scale of the `Player` object. I've used a value of 0.5 for the **X**, **Y**, and **Z** axes. See *Figure 3.24*. However, even with a more sensible scale, a problem remains. Specifically, it's possible to move the player outside the boundaries of the screen without limit. This means that the player can fly off into the distance, out of view, and never be seen again. Instead, the camera should remain still and the player movement should be limited to the camera view or bounds so that it never exits the view.

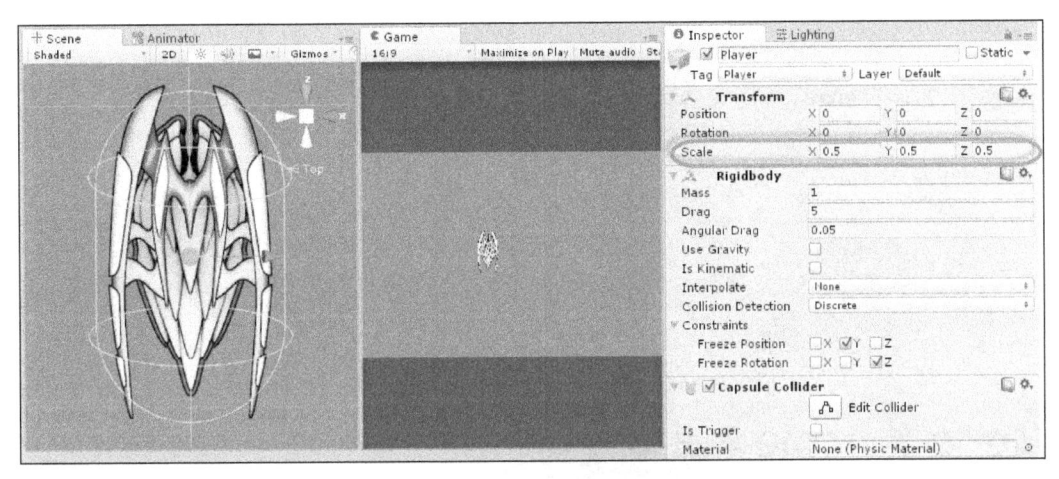

Figure 3.24: Rescaling the player

There are different ways to achieve bounds locking, most of which involve scripting. One way is to simply clamp the positional values of the `Player` object between a specified range, a minimum and maximum. Consider *Code Sample 3.2* for a new C# class called `BoundsLock`. This script file should be attached to the player:

```
//-----------------------------
using UnityEngine;
using System.Collections;
//-----------------------------
public class BoundsLock : MonoBehaviour
{
    //-----------------------------
    private Transform ThisTransform = null;
    //Can be changed from inspector
```

Creating a Space Shooter

```csharp
    public Vector2 HorzRange = Vector2.zero;
    public Vector2 VertRange = Vector2.zero;
    //------------------------------
    // Use this for initialization
    void Awake ()
    {
      ThisTransform = GetComponent<Transform>();
    }
    //------------------------------
    // Update is called once per frame
    void LateUpdate ()
    {
      //Clamp position
      ThisTransform.position = new Vector3(Mathf.Clamp
        (ThisTransform.position.x, HorzRange.x, HorzRange.y),
      ThisTransform.position.y,
        Mathf.Clamp(ThisTransform.position.z, VertRange.x,
          VertRange.y));
    }
    //------------------------------
}
//------------------------------
```

Code Sample 3.2

The following points summarize the code sample:

- The `LateUpdate` function is always called after all the `FixedUpdate` and `Update` calls, allowing an object to modify its position before it's rendered to the screen. More information on `LateUpdate` can be found at http://docs.unity3d.com/ScriptReference/MonoBehaviour.LateUpdate.html.
- The `Mathf.Clamp` function ensures that a specified value is capped between a minimum and maximum range.
- To use the `BoundsLock` script, simply drag and drop the file to the `Player` object and specify minimum and maximum values for its position. These values are specified in world position coordinates and can be determined by temporarily moving the `Player` object to the camera extremes and recording its position from the **Transform** component:

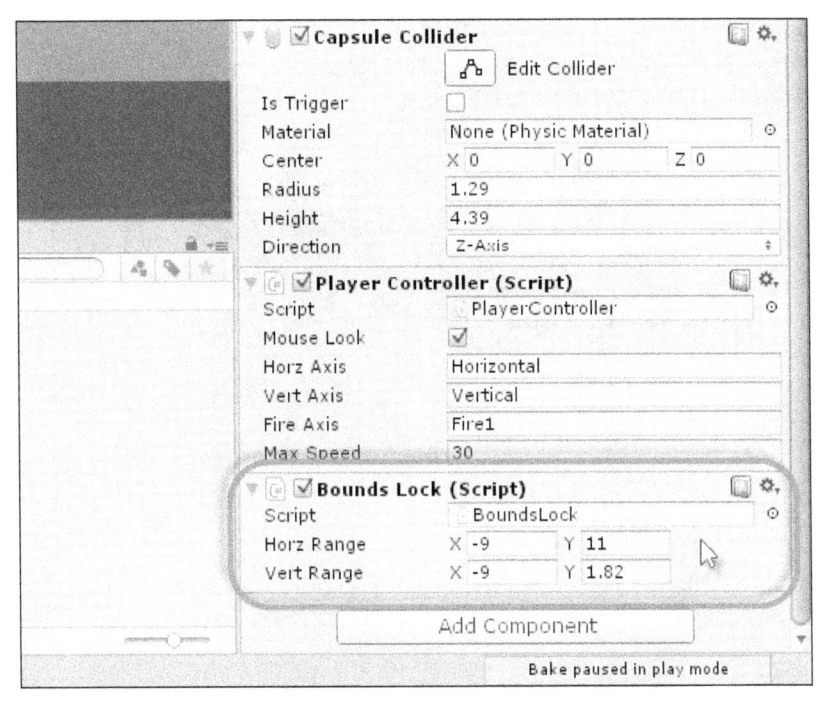

Figure 3.25: Setting Bounds Lock

Now take the game for a test run by pressing play on the toolbar. The player spaceship should remain in view and be unable to move offscreen. Splendid!

Health

Both the player spaceship and enemies need health. Health is a measure of a character's presence and legitimacy in the scene, typically scored as a value between 0-100. 0 means death and 100 means full health. Now, although health is, in many respects, specific to each instance, (The player has a unique health bar and each enemy has theirs.) there are nevertheless so many things in common, in terms of behavior, between player and enemy health that it makes sense to code health as a separate component and class that can be attached to all objects that need health. Consider *Code Sample 3.3*, which should be attached to the player and all enemies or objects that need health. Comments follow:

```
using UnityEngine;
using System.Collections;
//-----------------------------
public class Health : MonoBehaviour
{
```

```csharp
    public GameObject DeathParticlesPrefab = null;
    private Transform ThisTransform = null;
    public bool ShouldDestroyOnDeath = true;
    //------------------------------
    void Start()
    {
      ThisTransform = GetComponent<Transform>();
    }
    //------------------------------
    public float HealthPoints
    {
      get
      {
        return _HealthPoints;
      }

      set
      {
        _HealthPoints = value;

        if(_HealthPoints <= 0)
        {        SendMessage("Die",
           SendMessageOptions.DontRequireReceiver);

          if(DeathParticlesPrefab != null)
            Instantiate(DeathParticlesPrefab,
              ThisTransform.position, ThisTransform.rotation);

          if(ShouldDestroyOnDeath)
            Destroy(gameObject);
        }
      }
    }
    //------------------------------
    [SerializeField]
    private float _HealthPoints = 100f;
  }
  //------------------------------
```

Code Sample 3.3

The following points summarize the code sample:

- The `Health` class maintains object health through a `private` variable, `_HealthPoints`, which is accessed through a C# property, `HealthPoints`. This property features both `get` and `set` accessors to return and set the `Health` variable.

- The `_HealthPoints` variable is declared as `SerializedField`, allowing its value to be visible in the **Inspector**. This helps us see the value of the player's health during runtime and debug and test the effects of our code. The prefab variable was left as public, allowing its value to be both seen in the inspector and changeable from elsewhere in code if needed.

- The `Health` class is an example of event-driven programming. This is because the class could have continually checked the status of object health during an `Update` function; checking to see whether the object had died by its health falling below 0. Instead, the check for death is made during the C# property `set` method. This makes sense because `set` is the only place where health will ever change. This means that Unity is saved from a lot of work in each frame. That's great performance saving!

- `Health` class uses the `SendMessage` function. This function lets you call any other public function on any component attached to the object by specifying the function name as a string. In this case, a function called `Die` will be executed on every component attached to the object (if such a function exists). If no function of a matching name exists, then nothing happens for that component. This is a quick and easy way to run customized behavior on an object in a type-agnostic way without using any polymorphism. The disadvantage is that `SendMessage` internally uses a process called `Reflection`, which is slow and performance-prohibitive. For this reason, `SendMessage` should be used infrequently only for death events and similar events, but not frequently, such as every frame. More information on `SendMessage` can be found at the online Unity documentation at http://docs.unity3d.com/ScriptReference/GameObject.SendMessage.html.

- When health falls below 0, triggering a death condition, the code will instantiate a death particle system to show an effect on death if a particle system is specified (more on this shortly).

Creating a Space Shooter

When the `Health` script is attached to the player spaceship, it appears as a component in the **Inspector**. It contains a field for a **Death Particles Prefab**. This is an optional field (it can be null), specifying a particle system to be spawned when the object dies. This lets you create explosions or blood splatter effects easily when objects die. See *Figure 3.26*:

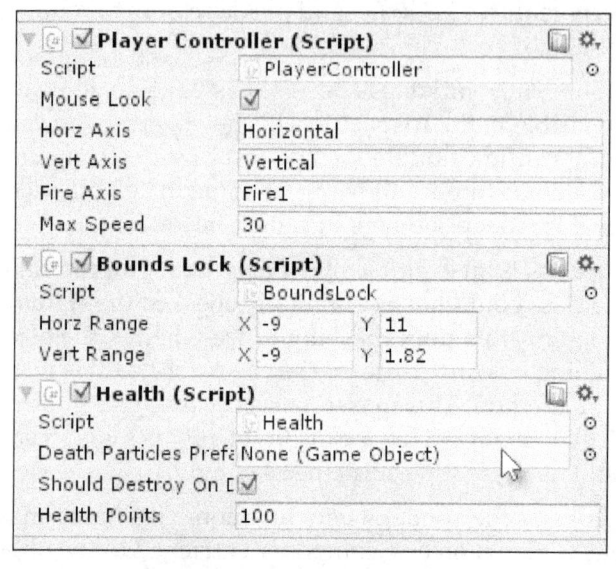

Figure 3.26: Attaching the Health script

Death and particles

In this twin-stick shooter game, both the player and enemies are spaceships. When they're destroyed, they should explode in a fiery ball. This is really the only kind of effect that would be believable. To achieve explosions, we can use a particle system. This simply refers to a special kind of object that features two main parts, namely, a **Hose** (or **Emitter**) and **Particles**. The emitter refers to the part that spawns or generates new particles into the world and the particles are many small objects or pieces that, once spawned, move and travel along their own trajectories. In short, particle systems are ideal to create rain, snow, fog, sparkles, and explosions. We can create our own Particle Systems from scratch using the menu option, **GameObject | Particle System**, or we can use any premade particle system included with Unity. Let's use some of the premade particle systems. To do this, import the `ParticleSystems` package to the project by navigating to **Assets | Import Package | ParticleSystems** from the application menu. See *Figure 3.27*:

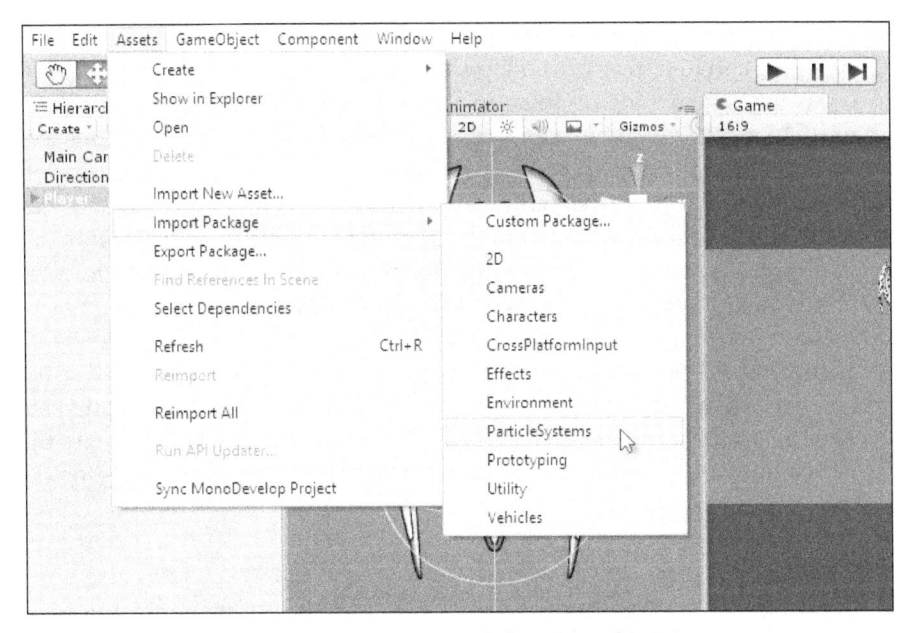

Figure 3.27: Importing Particle Systems to the project

After the **Import** dialog appears, leave all settings at their defaults, and simply click on **Import** to import the complete package, including all particle systems. The `ParticleSystems` will be added to the **Project** panel in the `Standard Assets | ParticleSystems | Prefabs` folder. See *Figure 3.28*. You can test each of the particle systems by simply dragging and dropping each prefab to the scene. Note that you can only preview a particle system in the **Scene** viewport while it is selected.

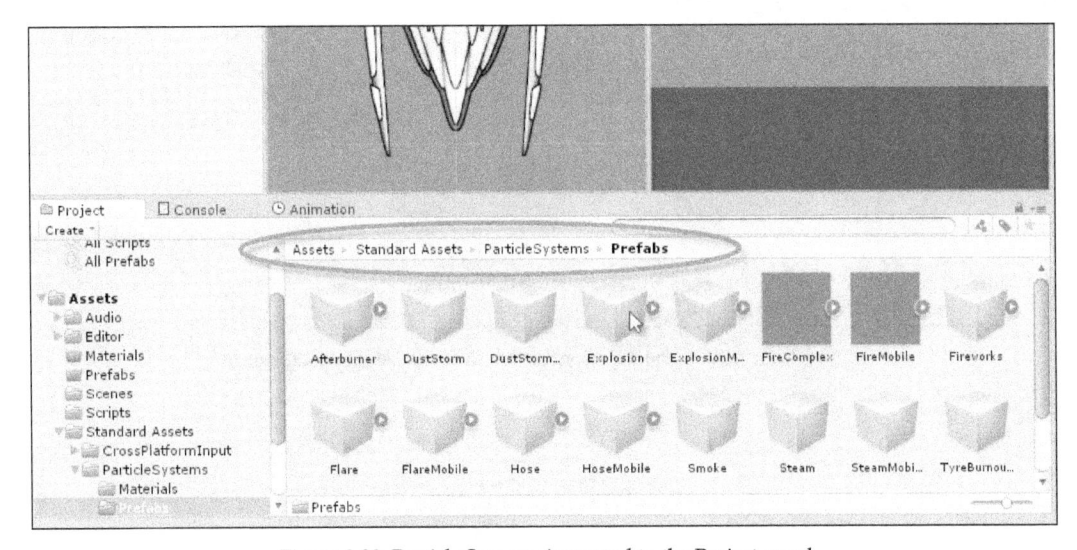

Figure 3.28: Particle Systems imported to the Project panel

[149]

Creating a Space Shooter

Notice from *Figure 3.28* that an **Explosion** system is included among the default assets. To test, we can just drag and drop the explosion to the scene, press play on the toolbar, and see the explosion in action. Good! We're almost done, but there's still a bit more work. We've now seen that an appropriate particle system is available and we could just drag and drop this system to the **Death Particles Prefab** slot in the **Health** component in the **Inspector**. This will work technically: when a player or enemy dies, the explosion system will be spawned, creating an explosion effect. However, the particle system will never be destroyed! This is problematic because, on each enemy death, a new particle system will be spawned. This raises the possibility that, after many deaths, the scene will be full of disused particle systems. We don't want this; it's bad for performance and memory usage to have a scene full of unused objects lingering around. To fix this, we'll modify the explosion system slightly, creating a new and modified prefab that'll suit our needs. To create this, drag and drop the existing explosion system anywhere to the scene and position it at the world origin. See *Figure 3.29*:

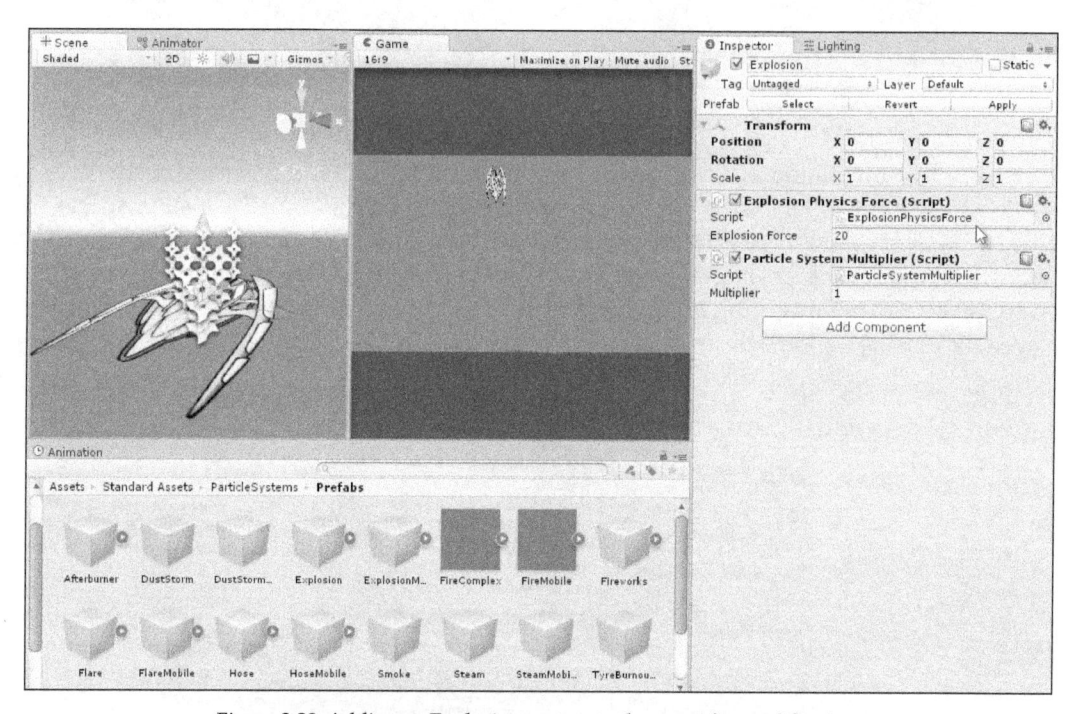

Figure 3.29: Adding an Explosion system to the scene for modification

Next, we must refine the particle system to destroy itself soon after instantiation. By making a prefab from this arrangement, each and every generated explosion will eventually destroy itself. To make an object destroy itself after a specified interval, we'll create a new C# script. I'll name this script `TimeDestroy.cs`. Refer the following code in *Code Sample 3.4*:

```
//-----------------------------
using UnityEngine;
using System.Collections;
//-----------------------------
public class TimedDestroy : MonoBehaviour
{
  public float DestroyTime = 2f;

  //-----------------------------
  // Use this for initialization
  void Start ()
  {
    Invoke("Die", DestroyTime);
  }


  void Die ()
  {
    Destroy(gameObject);
  }
  //-----------------------------
}
//-----------------------------
```

Code Sample 3.4

The following points summarize the code sample:

- The `TimeDestroy` class simply destroys the object to which it's attached after a specified interval (`DestroyTime`) has elapsed.
- The `Invoke` function is called in the `Start` event. Invoke will execute a function of the specified name once, and only once, after a specified interval has elapsed. The interval is measured in seconds.

Creating a Space Shooter

- Like `SendMessage`, the `Invoke` function relies on `Reflection`. For this reason, it should be used sparingly for best performance.
- The `Die` function will be executed by `Invoke` after a specified interval to destroy the `gameobject` (such as a particle system).

Now, drag and drop the `TimedDestroy` script file to the explosion particle system in the scene and then press play on the toolbar to test that the code works and the object is destroyed after the specified interval, which can be adjusted from the **Inspector**. See *Figure 3.30*:

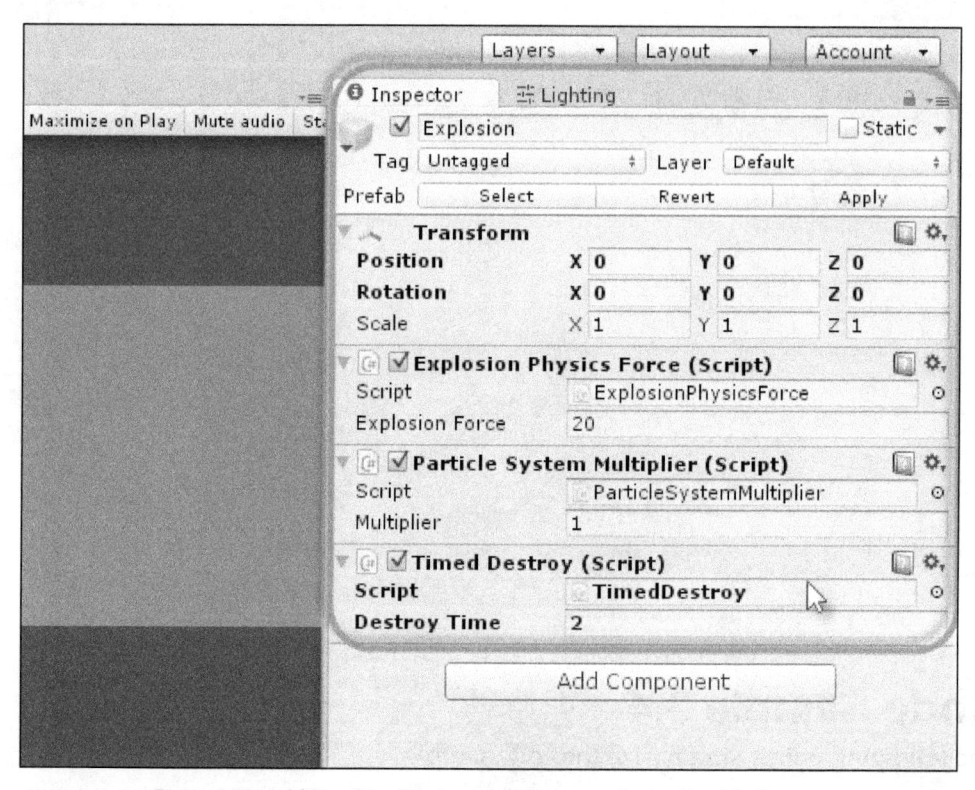

Figure 3.30: Adding a TimeDestroy script to an explosion Particle System

Chapter 3

The `TimeDestroy` script should remove the explosion particle system after the delay expires. So let's create a new and separate prefab from this modified version. To do this, rename the explosion system in the **Hierarchy** panel to `ExplosionDestroy`, and then drag and drop the system from the **Hierarchy** to the **Project** panel in the `Prefabs` folder. Unity automatically creates a new prefab, representing the modified particle system. See *Figure 3.31*:

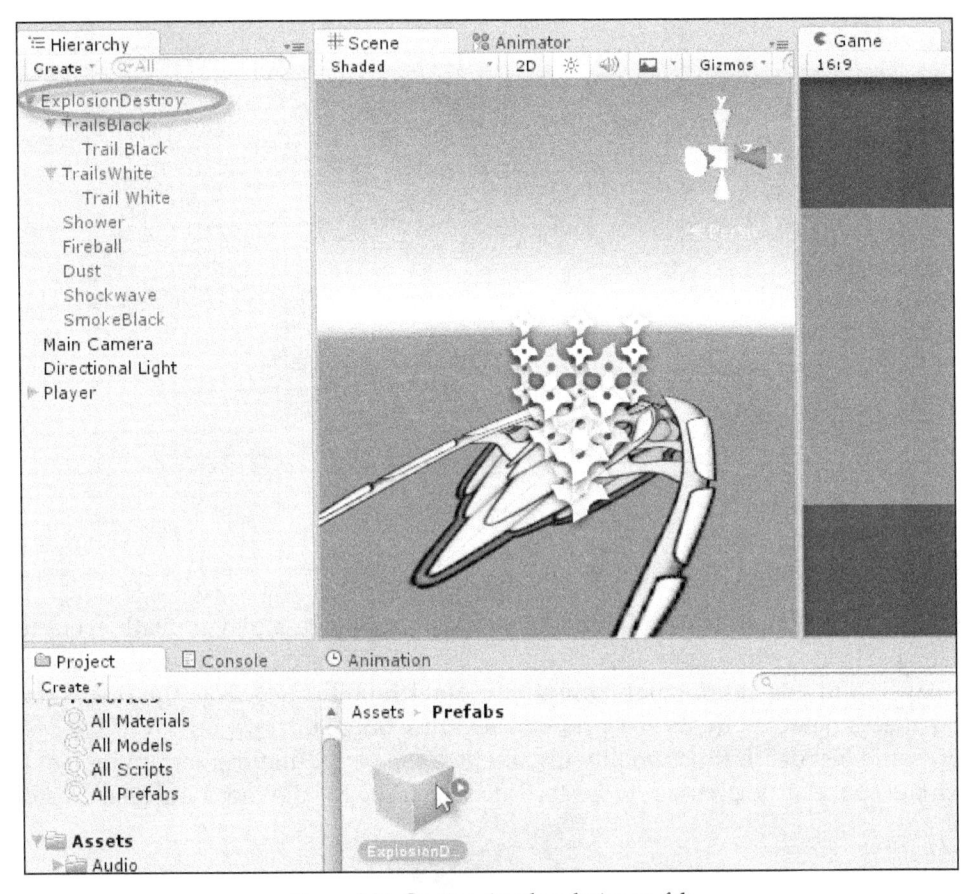

Figure 3.31: Create a timed explosion prefab

[153]

Creating a Space Shooter

Now, drag and drop the newly created prefab from the **Project** panel to the **Death Particle System** slot on the **Health** component for the **Player** in the **Object Inspector**. This ensures that the prefab is instantiated when the player dies. See *Figure 3.32*:

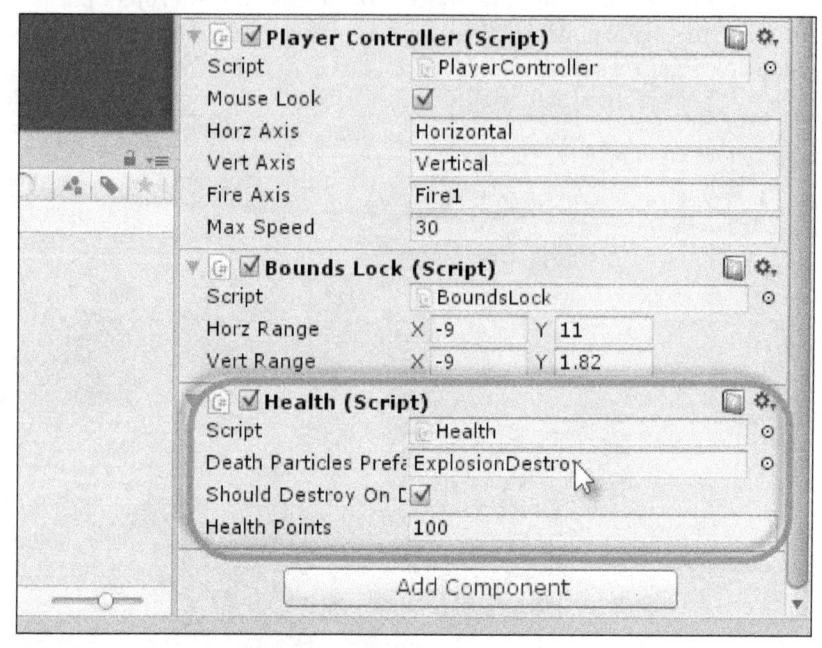

Figure 3.32: Configuring the health script

If you run the game now, you'll see that you cannot initiate a player death event to test the particle system generation. Nothing exists in the scene to destroy or damage the player, and you cannot manually set the **Health** points to 0 from the **Inspector** in a way that is detected by the C# property set function. For now, however, we can insert some test death functionality into the Health script that triggers an instant kill when the spacebar is pressed. Refer to *Code Sample 3.5* for the modified Health script:

```
//-----------------------------
using UnityEngine;
using System.Collections;
//-----------------------------
public class Health : MonoBehaviour
{
    public GameObject DeathParticlesPrefab = null;
    private Transform ThisTransform = null;
```

```csharp
    public bool ShouldDestroyOnDeath = true;
    //------------------------------
    void Start()
    {
      ThisTransform = GetComponent<Transform>();
    }
    //------------------------------
    public float HealthPoints
    {
      get
      {
        return _HealthPoints;
      }

      set
      {
        _HealthPoints = value;

        if(_HealthPoints <= 0)
        {
          SendMessage("Die",
            SendMessageOptions.DontRequireReceiver);

          if(DeathParticlesPrefab != null)
            Instantiate(DeathParticlesPrefab,
              ThisTransform.position, ThisTransform.rotation);

          if(ShouldDestroyOnDeath)Destroy(gameObject);
        }
      }
    }
    //------------------------------
    void Update()
    {
      if(Input.GetKeyDown(KeyCode.Space))
        HealthPoints = 0;
    }
    //------------------------------
    [SerializeField]
    private float _HealthPoints = 100f;
}
//------------------------------
```

On running the game now, with the modified `Health` script, you can trigger an instant player death by pressing the spacebar key on the keyboard. When you do this, the player object is destroyed and the particle system is generated until the timer destroys that too. Excellent work! We now have a playable, controllable player character that supports health and death functionality. Things are looking good. See *Figure 3.33*:

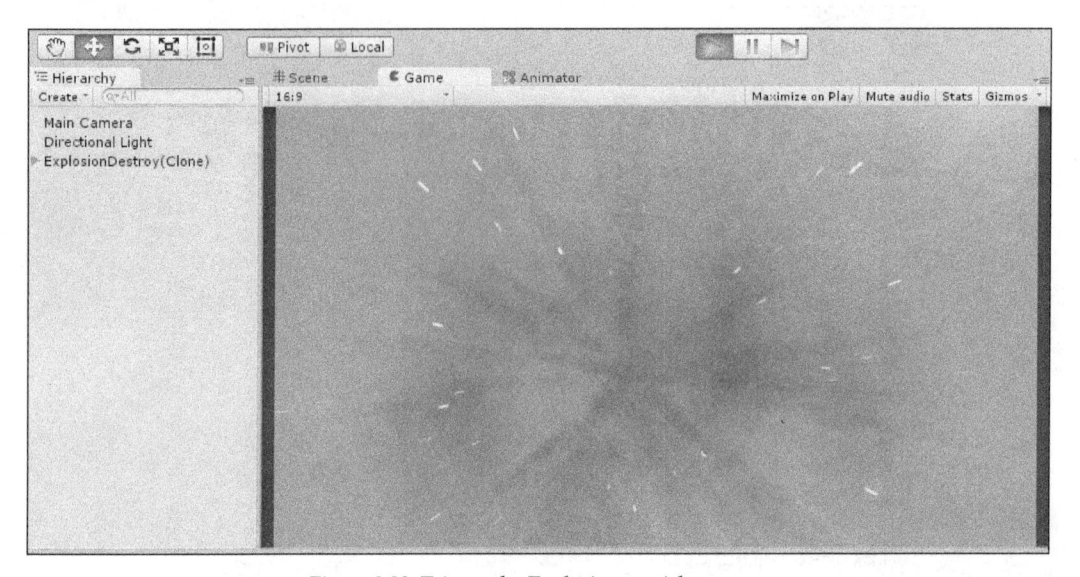

Figure 3.33: Trigger the Explosion particle system

Enemies

The next step is to create something for the player to shoot and destroy, which can also destroy us, namely, enemy characters. These take the form of roaming spaceships that will be spawned into the scene at regular intervals and will follow the player, drawing nearer and nearer. Essentially, each enemy represents a complex or combination of multiple behaviors working together and these should be implemented as separate scripts. Let's consider them in turn:

- **Health**: Each enemy supports health functionality. They begin the scene with a specified amount of health and will be destroyed when that health falls below 0. We already have a `Health` script created to handle this behavior.
- **Movement**: Each enemy will constantly be in motion, traveling in a straight line along a forward trajectory. That is, each enemy will continually travel forward in the direction it is looking.

- **Turning**: Each enemy will rotate and turn toward the player even when the player moves. This ensures that the enemy always faces the player and, in combination with the movement functionality, will always be traveling toward the player.
- **Scoring**: Each enemy rewards the player with a score value when destroyed. Thus, the death of an enemy will increase the player score.
- **Damage**: Each enemy causes damage to the player on collision. Enemies cannot shoot but will harm the player on proximity.

Now that we've identified the range of behaviors applicable to an enemy, let's create an enemy in the scene. We'll make one specific enemy, create a prefab from that, and use it as the basis to instantiate many enemies. Start by selecting the player character in the scene and duplicate the object with *Ctrl + D* or select **Edit | Duplicate** from the application menu. This initially creates a second player. See *Figure 3.34*:

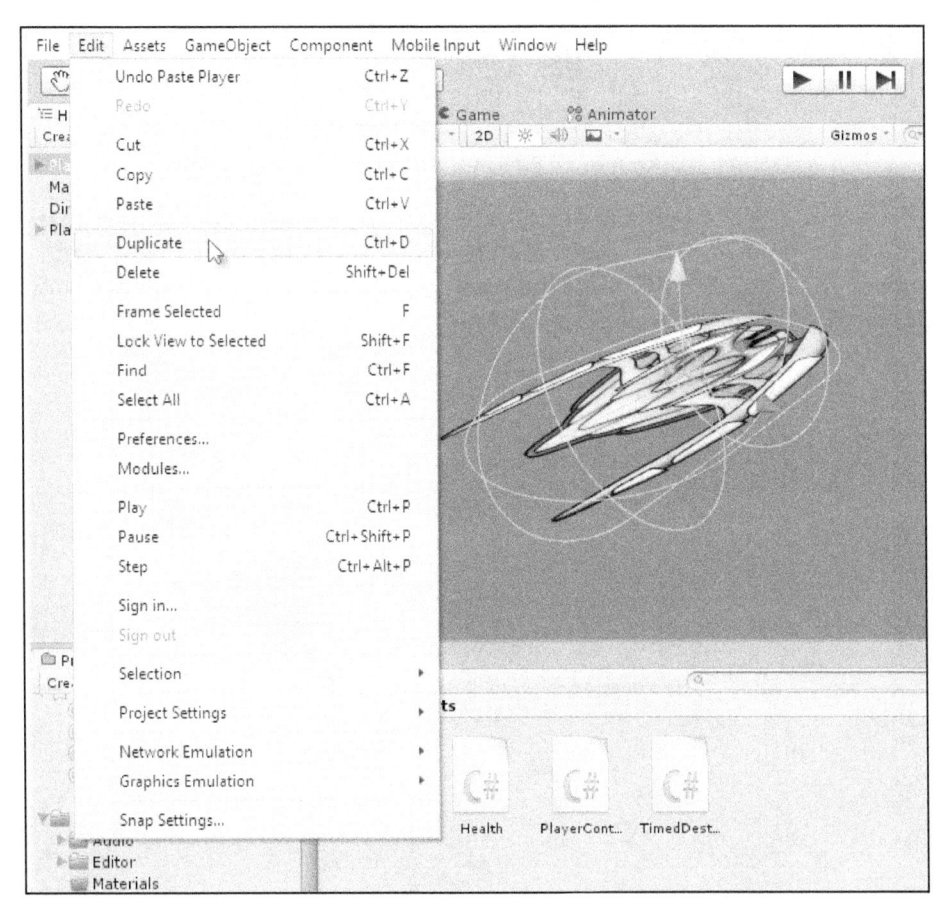

Figure 3.34: Duplicating the Player object

Creating a Space Shooter

Rename the object to `Enemy` and ensure that it is not tagged as `Player`, as there should be one and only one object in the scene with the `Player` tag, namely, the real player. In addition, temporarily disable the `Player` game object, allowing us to focus more clearly on the `Enemy` object in the **Scene** tab. See *Figure 3.35*:

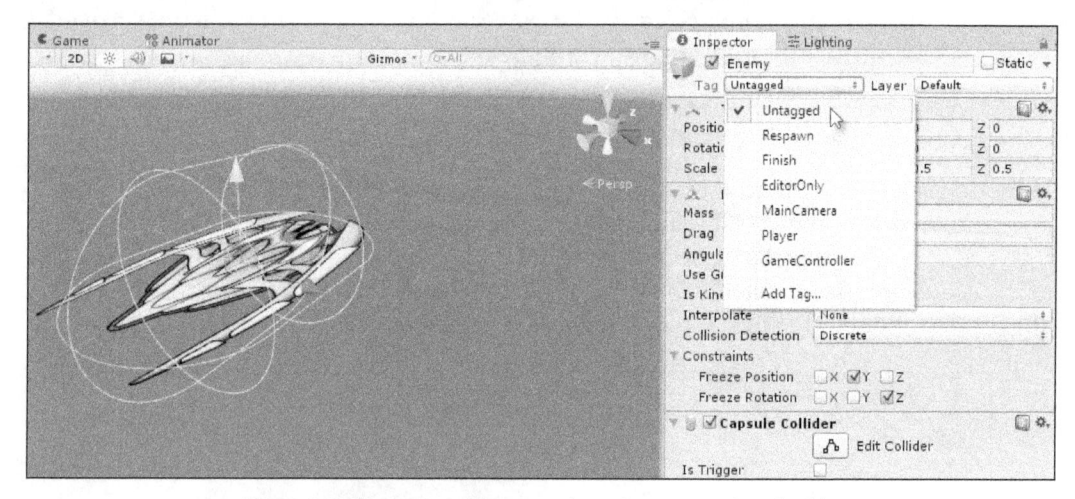

Figure 3.35: Removing a Player tag from the enemy, if applicable

Select the sprite child object of the duplicated enemy, and from the **Object Inspector**, click on the **Sprite** field of the **Sprite Renderer** component to pick a new sprite. Pick one of the darker imperial ships for the enemy character, and the sprite will update for the object in the viewport. See *Figure 3.36*:

Chapter 3

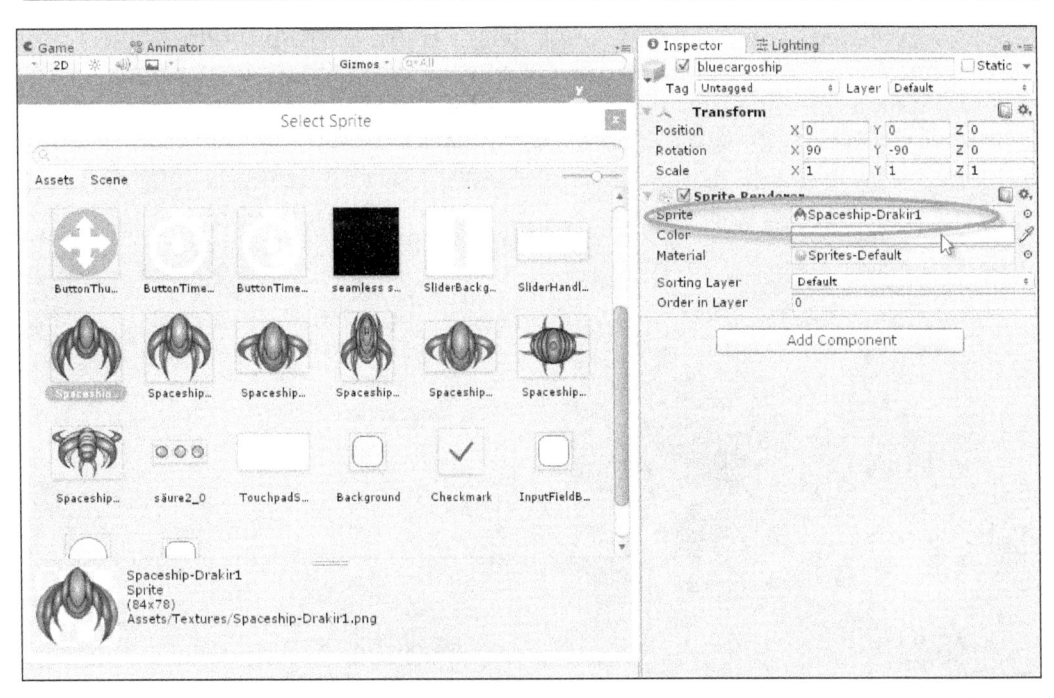

Figure 3.36: Selecting a sprite for the Sprite Renderer component

After changing the sprite to an enemy character, you may need to adjust the rotation values to align the sprite to the parent forward vector, ensuring that the sprite is looking in the same direction as the forward vector. See *Figure 3.37*:

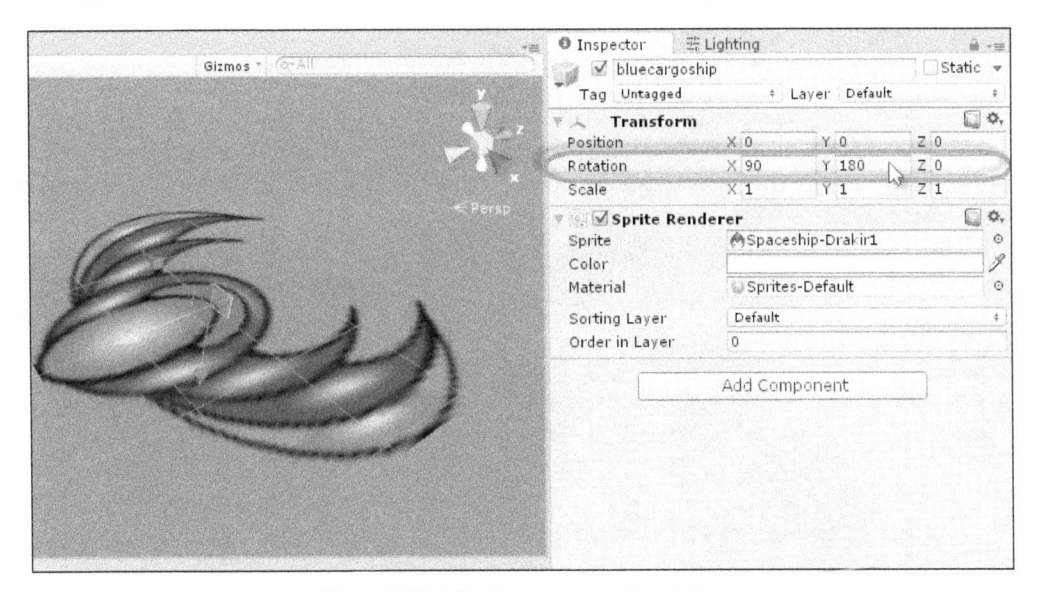

Figure 3.37: Adjusting enemy sprite rotation

Creating a Space Shooter

Now, select the parent object for the enemy and remove the **Rigidbody**, **PlayerController**, and `BoundsLock` components, but keep the **Health** component as the enemy should support health. See *Figure 3.38*. In addition, feel free to resize the **Capsule Collider** component to better approximate the `Enemy` object:

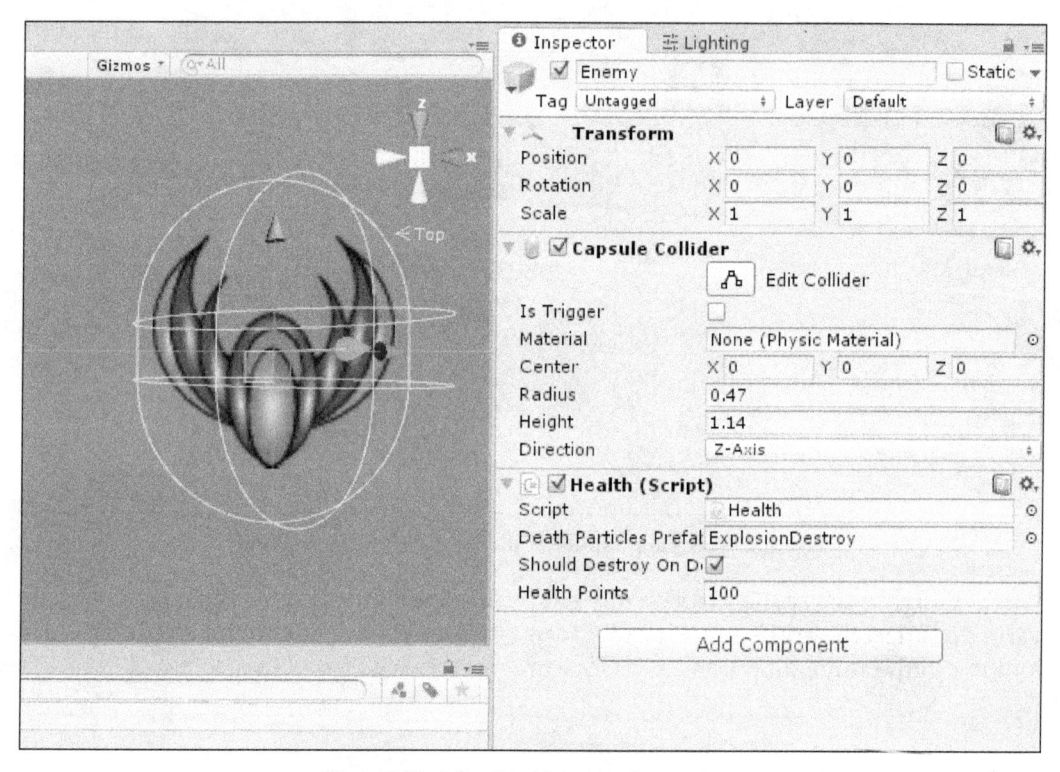

Figure 3.38: Adjusting enemy sprite rotation

Let's start coding the enemy, focusing on movement. Specifically, the enemy should continually move in the forward direction at a specified speed. To achieve this, create a new script file named `Mover.cs`. This should be attached to the `Enemy` object. The code for this class is included in *Code Sample 3.6*:

```csharp
//------------------------------
using UnityEngine;
using System.Collections;
//------------------------------
public class Mover : MonoBehaviour
{
    //------------------------------
    private Transform ThisTransform = null;
```

```
      public float MaxSpeed = 10f;
      //-----------------------------
      // Use this for initialization
      void Awake ()
      {
        ThisTransform = GetComponent<Transform>();
      }
      //-----------------------------
      // Update is called once per frame
      void Update ()
      {
        ThisTransform.position += ThisTransform.forward * MaxSpeed *
          Time.deltaTime;
      }
      //-----------------------------
    }
    //-----------------------------
```

Code Sample 3.6

The following points summarize the code sample:

- The `Mover` script moves an object at a specified speed (`MaxSpeed` per second) along its forward vector. To do this, it uses the **Transform** component.

- The `Update` function is responsible for updating the position of the object. In short, it multiplies the forward vector by the object speed and adds this to its existing position to move the object further along its line of sight. The `Time.deltaTime` value is used to make the motion frame rate independent—moving the object per second as opposed to per frame. More information on `deltaTime` can be found in the online Unity documentation at http://docs.unity3d.com/ScriptReference/Time-deltaTime.html.

Press play on the toolbar to test run your code. It's always good practice to frequently test code like this. Your enemy may move too slow or too fast. If so, stop playback to exit game mode, and select the enemy in the scene.

Creating a Space Shooter

From the **Object Inspector**, adjust the **Max Speed** value of the **Mover** component. See *Figure 3.39*:

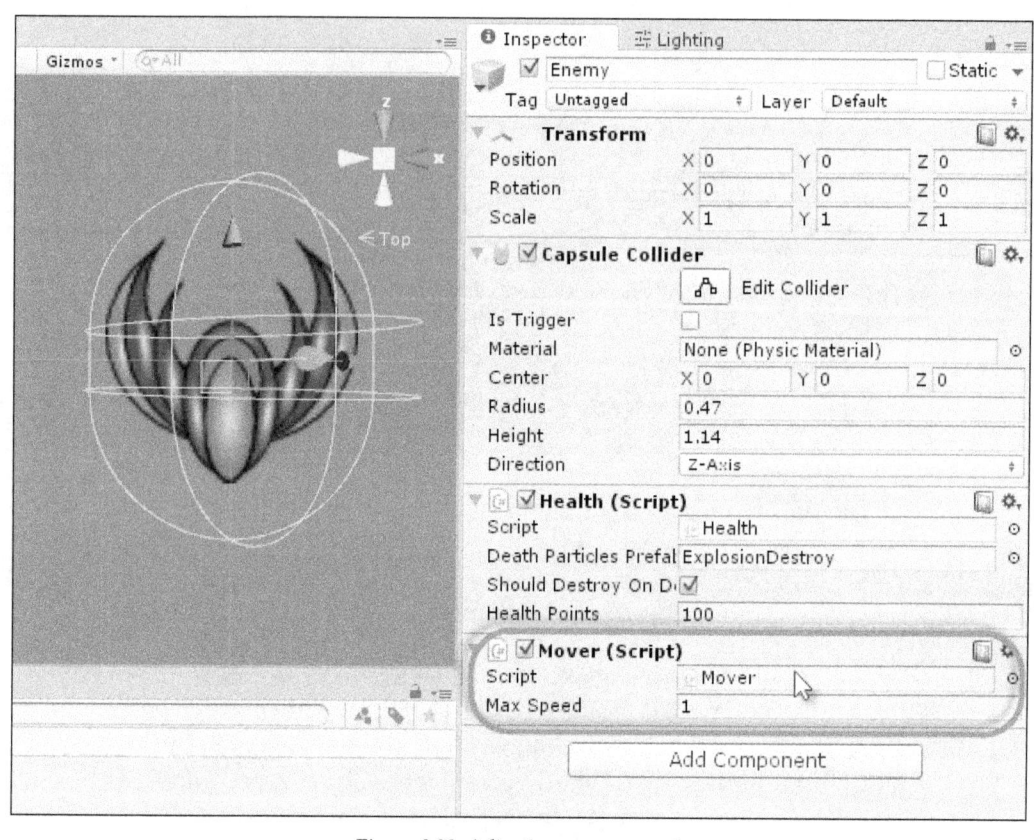

Figure 3.39: Adjusting enemy speed

In addition to moving in a straight line, the enemy should also continually turn to face the player wherever they move. To achieve this, we'll need another script file that works similarly to the player controller script. While the player turns to face the cursor, the enemy turns to face the player. This functionality should be encoded in a new script file called `ObjFace.cs`. This script should be attached to the enemy. See *Code Sample 3.7*:

```
//-------------------------------
using UnityEngine;
using System.Collections;
//-------------------------------
public class ObjFace : MonoBehaviour
{
    //-------------------------------
    public Transform ObjToFollow = null;
    public bool FollowPlayer = false;
```

```
  private Transform ThisTransform = null;
//------------------------------
// Use this for initialization
void Awake ()
{
  //Get local transform
  ThisTransform = GetComponent<Transform>();

  //Should face player?
  if(!FollowPlayer)return;

  //Get player transform
  GameObject PlayerObj =
    GameObject.FindGameObjectWithTag("Player");
  if(PlayerObj != null)
    ObjToFollow = PlayerObj.GetComponent<Transform>();
}
//------------------------------
// Update is called once per frame
void Update ()
{
  //Follow destination object
  if(ObjToFollow==null)return;

  //Get direction to follow object
  Vector3 DirToObject = ObjToFollow.position -
    ThisTransform.position;

  if(DirToObject != Vector3.zero)
    ThisTransform.localRotation = Quaternion.LookRotation
      (DirToObject.normalized,Vector3.up);
}
//------------------------------
}
//------------------------------
```

Code Sample 3.7

The following points summarize the code sample:

- The `ObjFace` script will always rotate an object so that its forward vector points towards a destination point in the scene.
- In the `Awake` event, the `FindGameObjectWithTag` function is called to retrieve a reference to the one and only object in the scene tagged as a player, which should be the player spaceship. The player represents the default look-at destination for an enemy object.

Creating a Space Shooter

- The `Update` function is called automatically once per frame and will generate a displacement vector from the object location to the destination location, and this represents the direction in which the object should be looking. The `Quaternion.LookRotation` function accepts a direction vector and will rotate an object to align the forward vector with the supplied direction. This keeps the object looking towards the destination. More information on `LookRotation` can be found at the online Unity documentation at http://docs.unity3d.com/ScriptReference/Quaternion.LookRotation.html.

This is looking excellent! However, before testing this code, make sure that the `Player` object in the scene is tagged as **Player**, is enabled, and the enemy is offset away from the player. Be sure to enable the **Follow Player** checkbox from the **Obj Face** component in the **Object Inspector**. When you do this, the enemy will always turn to face the player. See *Figure 3.40*:

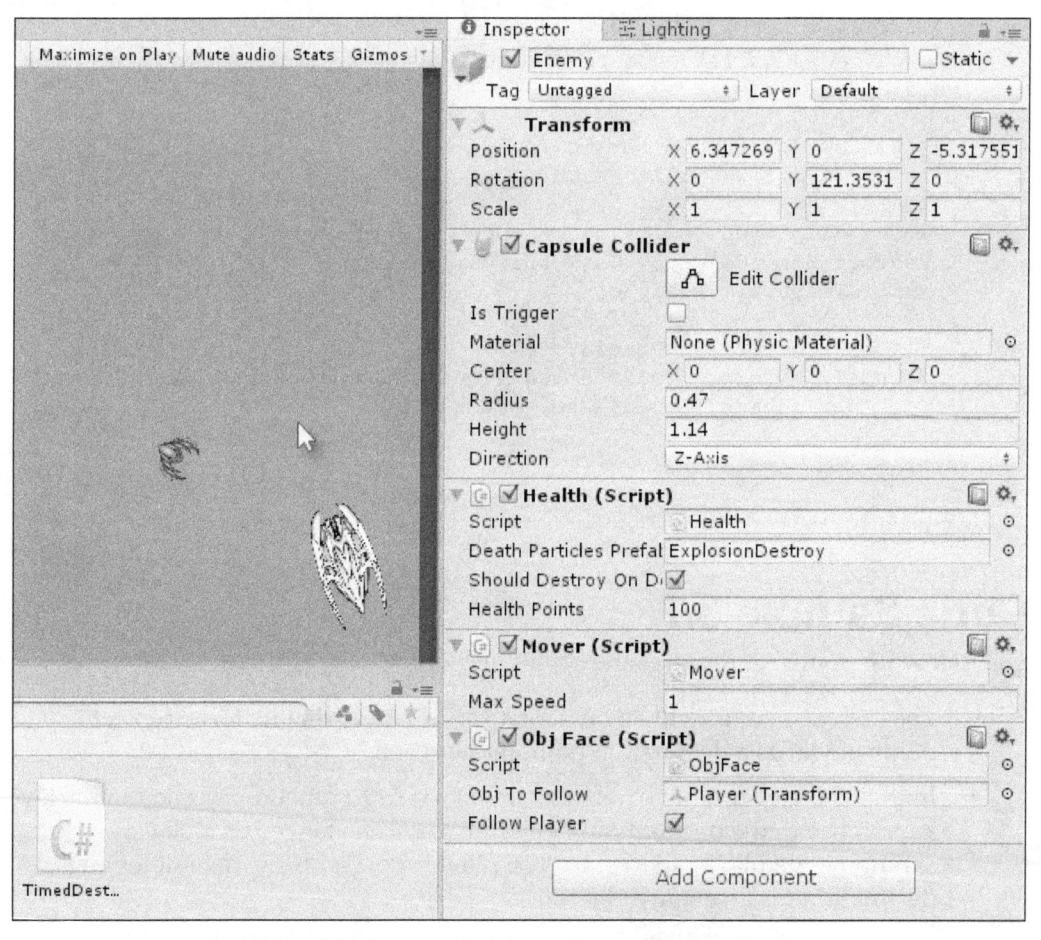

Figure 3.40: Enemy spaceship moving towards the player

[164]

Now, if and when the enemy finally collides with the player, it should deal out damage and potentially kill the player. To achieve this, a collision between the enemy and player must be detected. Let's start by configuring the enemy. Select the **Enemy** object, and from the **Object Inspector**, enable the **Is Trigger** checkbox in the **Capsule Collider** component. This changes the **Capsule Collider** component to allow a true intersection between the player and enemy and prevent Unity from blocking the collision. See *Figure 3.41*:

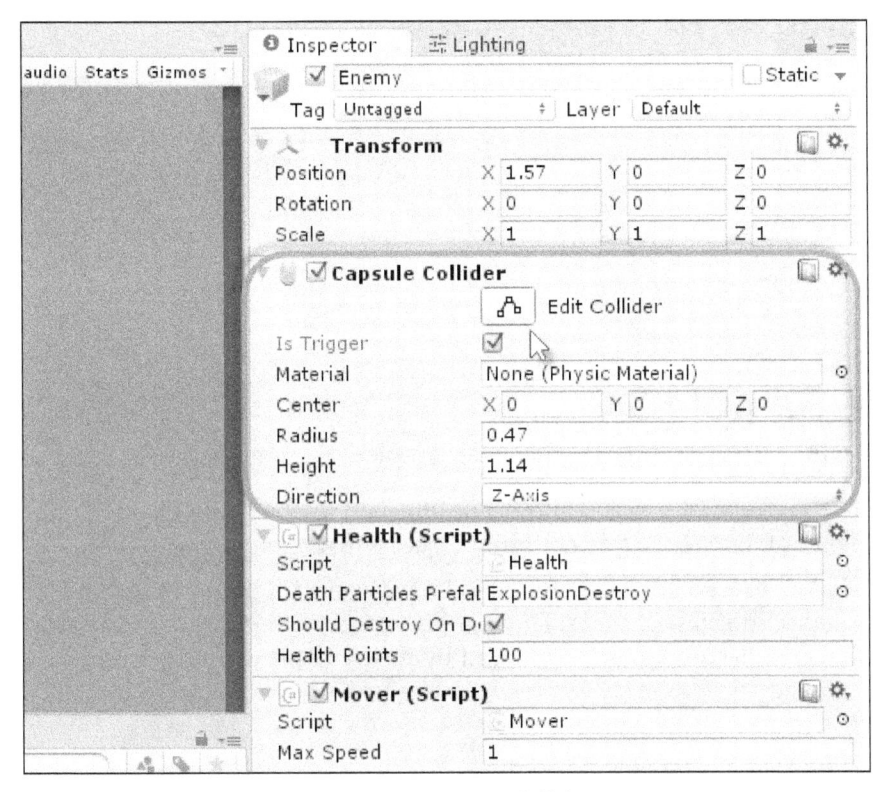

Figure 3.41: Changing the Enemy Collider to a trigger

Next, we'll create a script that detects collisions and will continually deal out damage to the player as and when they occur and for as long as the collision state remains. Refer to the following code (`ProxyDamage.cs`), which should be attached to the enemy character:

```
//------------------------------
using UnityEngine;
using System.Collections;
//------------------------------
```

```
public class ProxyDamage : MonoBehaviour
{
  //------------------------------
  //Damage per second
  public float DamageRate = 10f;
  //------------------------------
  void OnTriggerStay(Collider Col)
  {
    Health H = Col.gameObject.GetComponent<Health>();

    if(H == null) return;

    H.HealthPoints -= DamageRate * Time.deltaTime;
  }
  //------------------------------
}
//------------------------------
```

Code Sample 3.8

The following points summarize the code sample:

- The `ProxyDamage` script should be attached to an enemy character and it will deal out damage to any colliding object with a `Health` component.
- The `OnTriggerStay` event is called once every frame for as long as an intersection state persists. During this function, the `HealthPoints` value of the `Health` component is reduced by the `DamageRate` (which is measured as damage per second).

After attaching the `ProxyDamage` script to an enemy, use the **Object Inspector** to set the **Damage Rate** of the **Proxy Damage** component. This represents how much health should be reduced on the player, per second, during a collision. For a challenge, I've set the value to `100` health points. See *Figure 3.42*:

Figure 3.42: Setting the Damage Rate for a Proxy Damage component

Now, let's give things a test run. Press play on the toolbar and attempt a collision between the player and enemy. After one second, the player should be destroyed. Things are coming along well. However, we'll need more than one enemy to make things challenging.

Enemy spawning

To make the level fun and challenging, we'll need more than simply one enemy. In fact, for a game that's essentially endless, we'll need to continually add enemies. These should be added gradually over time. Essentially, we'll need either regular or intermittent spawning of enemies, and this section will add that functionality. Before we can do this, however, we'll need to make a prefab from the enemy object. This can be achieved easily. Select the enemy in the **Hierarchy** panel and then drag and drop it to the **Project** panel in the Prefabs folder. This creates an Enemy prefab. See *Figure 3.43*:

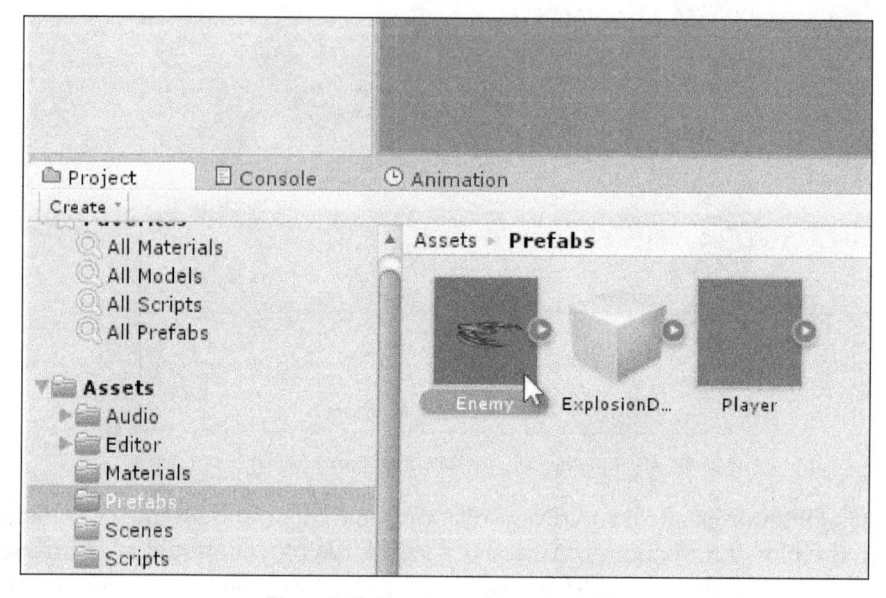

Figure 3.43: Creating an Enemy prefab

Now, we'll make a new script (Spawner.cs) that spawns new enemies in the scene over time within a specified radius from the player spaceship. This script should be attached to a new, empty game object in the scene. See *Code Sample 3.9*:

```
//-------------------------------
using UnityEngine;
using System.Collections;
//-------------------------------
public class Spawner : MonoBehaviour
{
  public float MaxRadius = 1f;
  public float Interval = 5f;
```

```
    public GameObject ObjToSpawn = null;
    private Transform Origin = null;
    //------------------------------
    void Awake()
    {
    Origin = GameObject.FindGameObjectWithTag
      ("Player").GetComponent<Transform>();
    }
    //------------------------------
    // Use this for initialization
    void Start ()
    {
       InvokeRepeating("Spawn", 0f, Interval);
    }
    //------------------------------
    void Spawn ()
    {
       if(Origin == null)return;

       Vector3 SpawnPos = Origin.position + Random.onUnitSphere *
         MaxRadius;
       SpawnPos = new Vector3(SpawnPos.x, 0f, SpawnPos.z);
       Instantiate(ObjToSpawn, SpawnPos, Quaternion.identity);
    }
    //------------------------------
}
//------------------------------
```

Code Sample 3.9

The following points summarize the code sample:

- The Spawner class will spawn instances of ObjToSpawn (a prefab) on each interval of Interval. The interval is measured in seconds. The spawned objects will be created within a random radius from a center point, Origin.
- During the Start event, the InvokeRepeating function is called to continually execute the Spawn function on every interval to spawn a new enemy.
- The Spawn function will create instances of the enemy in the scene at a random radius from an origin point. Once spawned, the enemy will behave as normal, heading toward the player for an attack.

Creating a Space Shooter

The Spawner class is a global behavior that applies scene-wide. It does not depend on the player specifically, nor on any specific enemy. For this reason, it should be **attached** to **an empty gam**e object. Create one of these by selecting `GameObject | Create Empty` from the application menu. Name this Spawner and attach the Spawner script to it. See Figure 3.44:

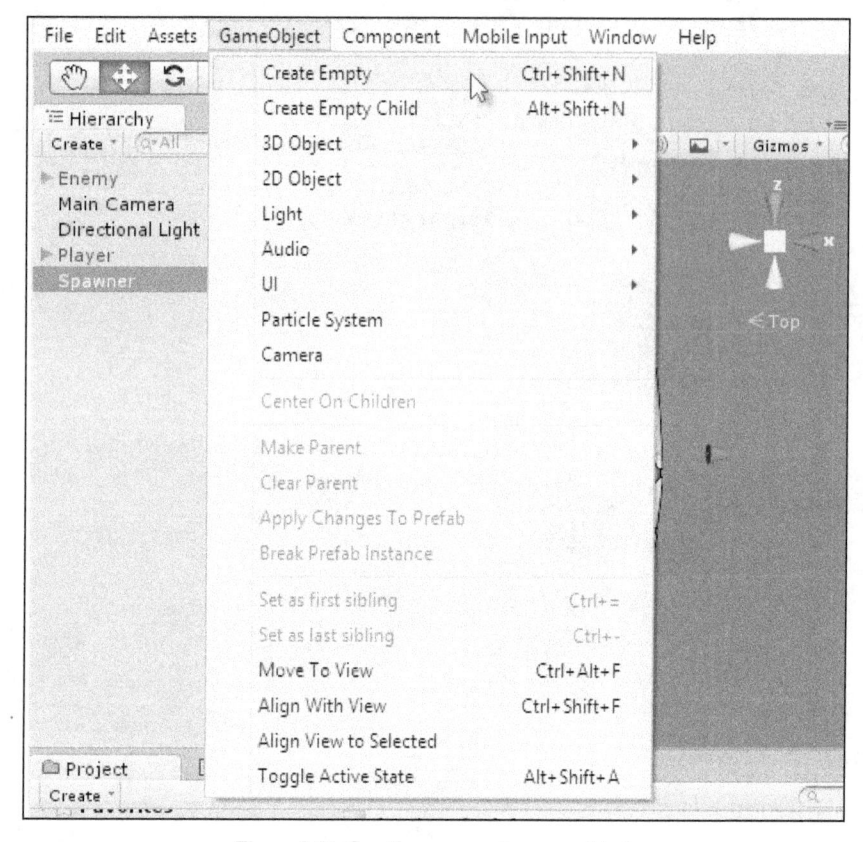

Figure 3.44: Creating an empty game object

Once added to the scene, **from the** Object Inspector, **drag** and drop the Enemy **prefab** to the Obj To Spawn field in the **Spawner** component. *Set the Int*erval to 2 seconds and increase the Max Radius to 5. See Figure 3.45:

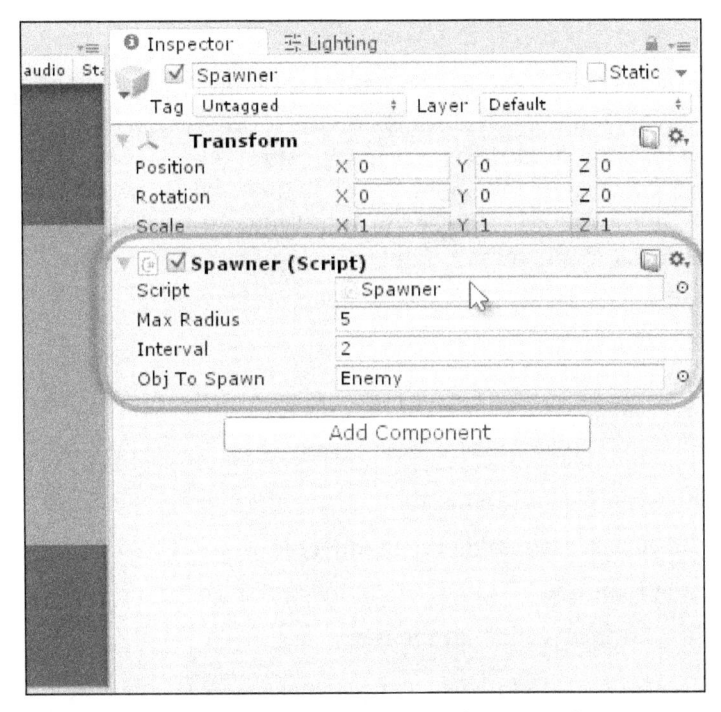

Figure 3.45: Configuring the Spawner for Enemy objects

Now (drum roll), let's try the level. Press play on the toolbar and take the game for a test run. You should now have a level with a fully controllable player character surrounded by a growing army of tracking enemy ships! Excellent work! See Figure 3.46:

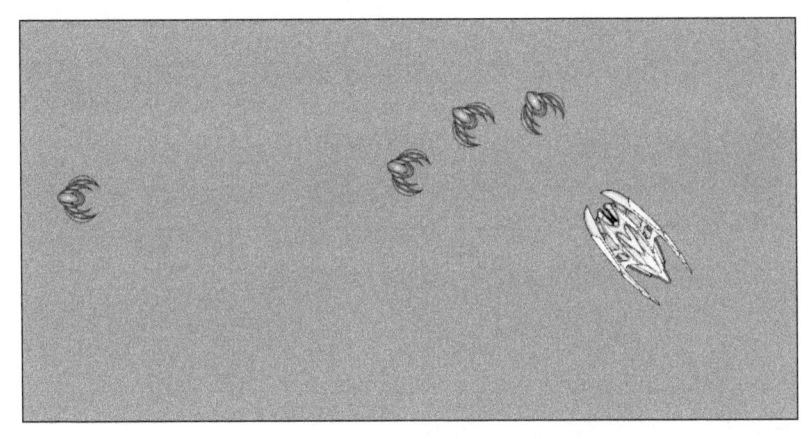

Figure 3.46: Spawned enemy objects moving toward the player

Creating a Space Shooter

Summary

Good job on getting this far! The space shooter is really taking shape now, featuring a controllable player character that relies on native physics, twin-stick mechanics, enemy ships, and a scene-wide spawner for enemies. All these ingredients together still don't make a game: we can't shoot, we can't increase the score, and we can't destroy enemies. These issues will need to be addressed, along with other technical issues that we'll certainly encounter. Nevertheless, we now have a solid foundation for moving further, and in the `next chapter,` we'll complete the shooter.

Test your knowledge

Q1. SerializableField makes...

- A. Public variables hidden in the inspector
- B. Private variables visible in the inspector
- C. Protected variables hidden in the inspector
- D. Public variables visible in the inspector

Q2. Importing audio with the Streaming Load Type means...

- A. The Audio will be loaded whole at startup
- B. The Audio will be loaded in segments
- C. The Audio will be muted
- D. The Audio will be deleted

Q3. Orthographic Cameras Remove...

- A. Perspective `effects`
- B. `Distant` objects
- C. Post-Processing
- D. MeshRenderers

Q4. The Input.GetAxis function lets you read input from...

- A. Horizontal and Vertical Axes
- B. VR Touch Controllers
- C. Mobile Touches
- D. Mouse `Clicks`

Further reading

Visit following links for more information:

- https://unity3d.com/learn/tutorials/s/scripting
- https://www.packtpub.com/game-development/unity-5-scripting-and-gameplay-mechanics-video
- https://www.packtpub.com/game-development/mastering-unity-5x-scripting

4
Continuing the Space Shooter

This chapter continues from the previous one in creating a twin-stick space shooter game. At this stage, we have a working game. At least, the gamer can control a spaceship using two axes: movement and rotation. WASD keys on the keyboard control movement (up, down, left, and right) and the mouse cursor controls rotation—the spaceship always rotates to face the cursor. In addition to player controls, the level features enemy characters that spawn at regular intervals, fly around the level, and move toward the player with hostile intent. Finally, both the player and enemies support a `Health` component, which means both are susceptible to damage and can be destroyed. Right now, however, the player lacks two important features: it cannot fire a weapon and it cannot increase the score. This chapter tackles these issues and more. Firing weapons, as we'll see, represents a particularly interesting problem. Overall, this chapter covers the following topics:

- Weapons
- Spawning ammo
- Memory management and pooling
- Sound and audio
- Scoring
- Debugging and testing
- Building and distribution

Continuing the Space Shooter

> The completed project so far can be found in the book's companion files in the `Chapter04/Start` folder. You can start here and follow along with this chapter if you don't have your own project already.

Guns and gun turrets

Let's start tackling weapons in detail. Specifically, the level contains a player and enemy ships, which the player must shoot. See *Figure 4.1*. On thinking carefully about weapons, we identify three main concepts or things that need development. First, there's the spawner or generator—the object that actually fires ammo in the scene when the fire button is pressed. Second, there's the ammo itself that, once generated, travels through the level on its own. Third, there's the ability for ammo to collide with other objects and damage them.

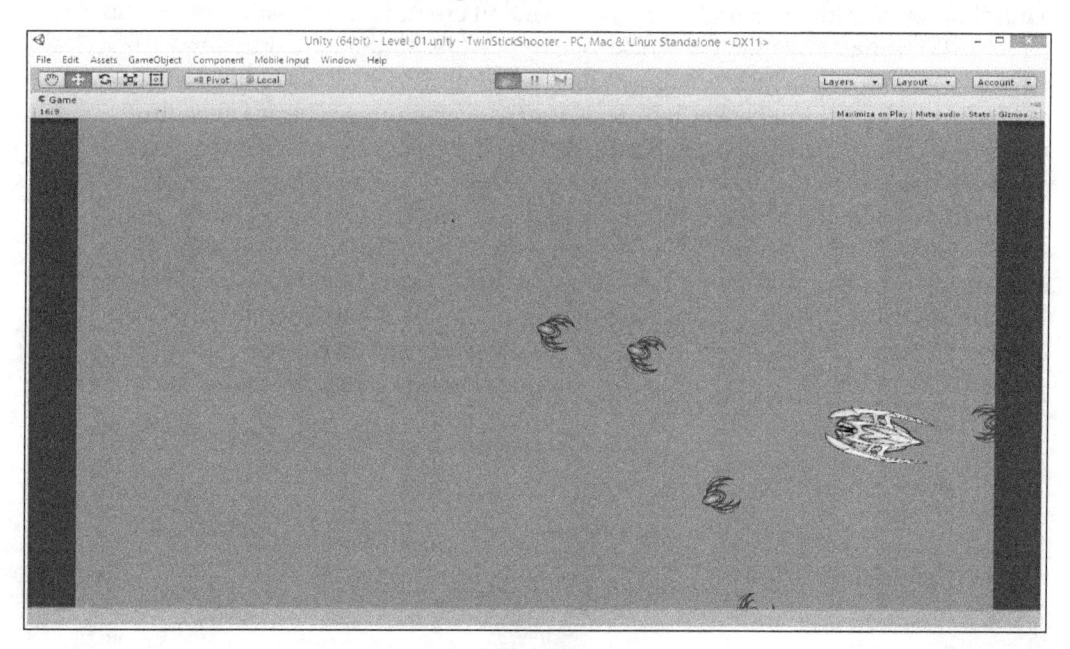

Figure 4.1: The game so far

Tackling each area in order, we begin with turrets—the points where bullets are spawned and fired. For this game, the player will have only one turret, but ideally, the game should support the addition of more, if desired, allowing the player to dual-fire or more! To create the first turret, add a new empty game object to the scene by selecting **GameObject | Create Empty** from the application menu. Name this `Turret`. Then, position the `Turret` object to the front of the spaceship, making sure that the blue forward vector arrow is pointing ahead in the direction that ammo will be fired. Finally, make the turret a child of the spaceship by dragging and dropping it in the **Hierarchy** panel. See *Figure 4.2*:

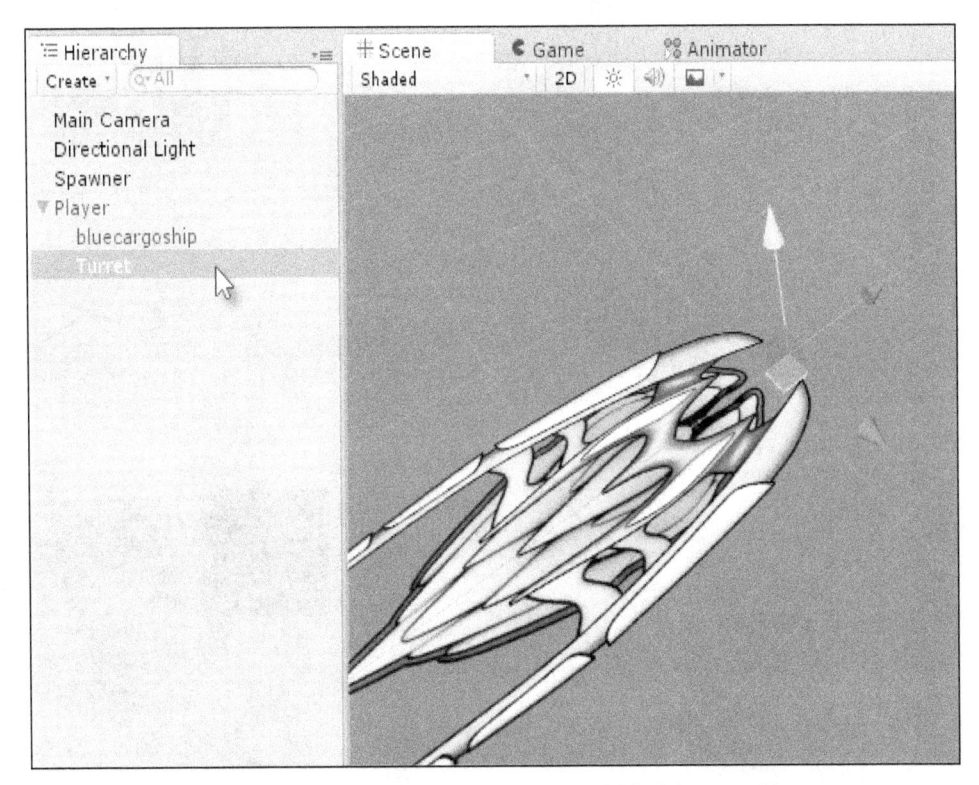

Figure 4.2: Positioning a Turret object as a child of the spaceship

Creating a `Turret` object for the ammo as a spawn location is a splendid beginning, but for ammo to actually be fired, we'll need an ammo object. Specifically, we'll create an `Ammo` prefab that can be instantiated as ammo, when needed. We'll do this next.

Ammo prefabs

When the player presses the fire button, the spaceship should shoot ammo objects in the scene. These objects will be based on an Ammo prefab. Let's create this prefab now. To start, we'll configure the texture to be used as an ammo graphic. Open the Textures folder in the **Project** panel, and select the Ammo texture. This texture features several different versions of an ammo sprite, aligned in a row side by side. See *Figure 4.3*. When ammo is fired, we don't want to show the complete texture; instead, we want to show either just one of the images or the images played as an animation sequence, frame by frame:

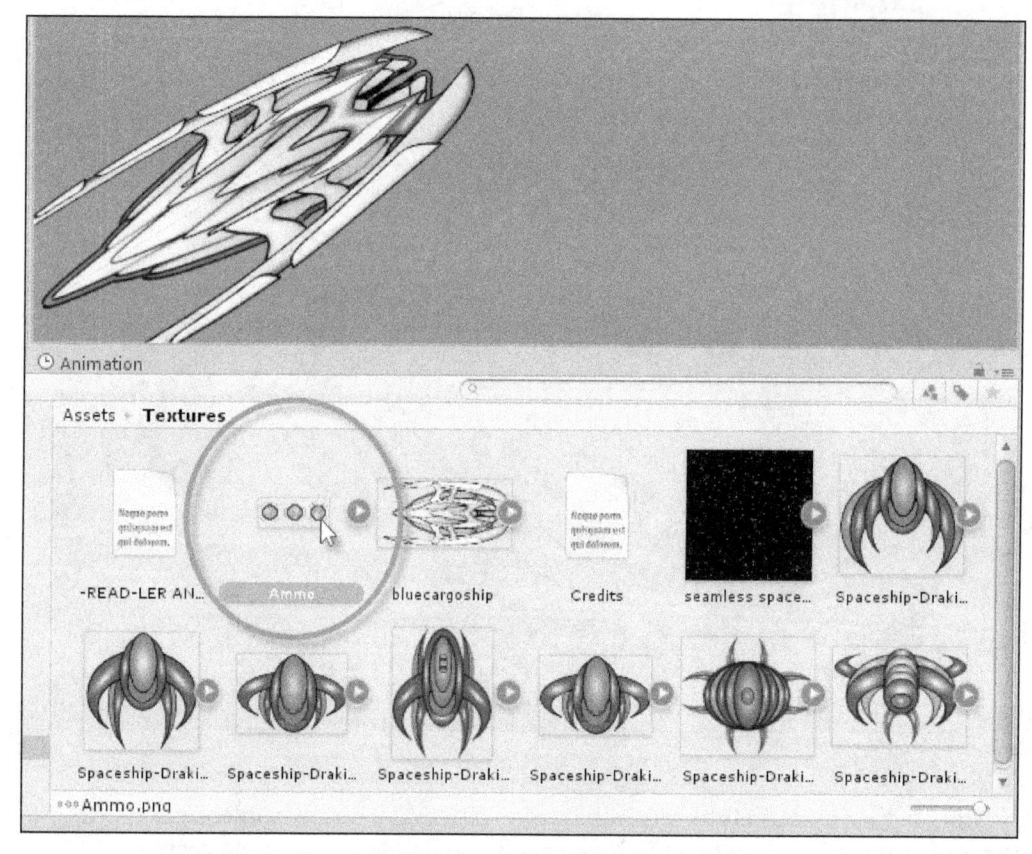

Figure 4.3: Preparing to create an Ammo prefab

Presently, Unity recognizes the texture (and each ammo element) as a complete unit. We can use Sprite Editor, however, to separate each part. To do this, select the **Texture** in the project (if it's not already selected), and then (from the **Object Inspector**) change the **Sprite Mode** drop-down from **Single** to **Multiple**. This signifies that more than one sprite is contained within the texture space. See *Figure 4.4*:

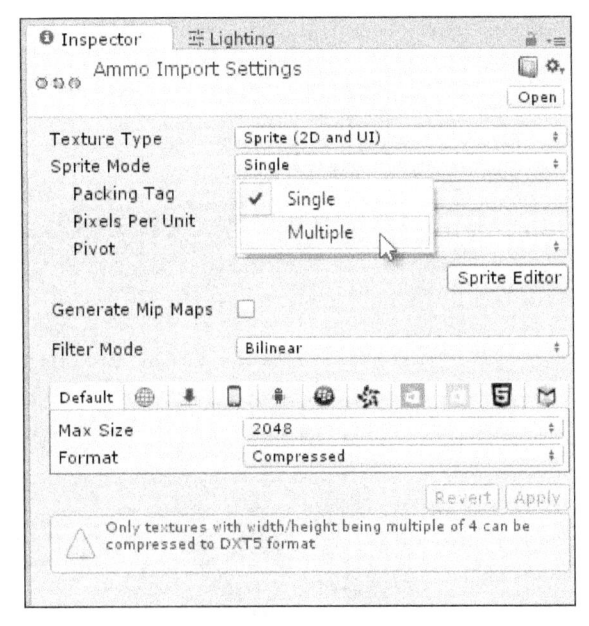

Figure 4.4: Select multiple sprites for textures featuring more than one sprite

Click on the **Apply** button, and then click on the **Sprite Editor** button from the **Object Inspector**. This opens the Sprite Editor, allowing you to separate each sprite. To do this, click and drag your mouse to select each sprite, making sure that the **Pivot** is aligned to the object **Center**. See *Figure 4.5*. Then, click on **Apply** to accept the changes.

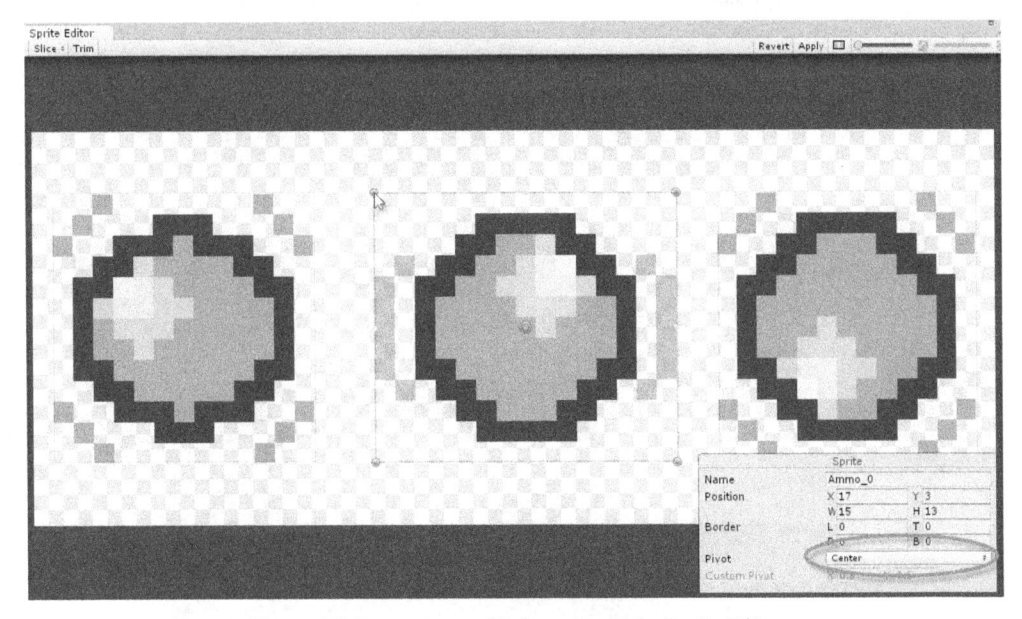

Figure 4.5: Separating multiple sprites in the Sprite Editor

Continuing the Space Shooter

After accepting the changes in the Sprite Editor, Unity automatically cuts the relevant sprites into separate units, each of which can now be selected as a separate object in the **Project** panel. Click on the right arrow at the side of the texture, and all sprites within will expand outwards. See *Figure 4.6*:

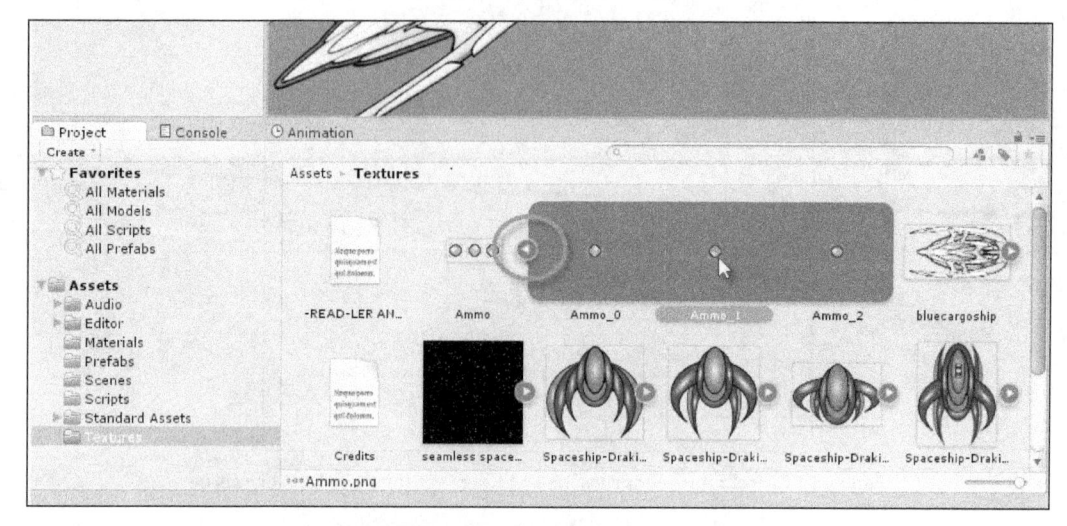

Figure 4.6: Expand all sprites within a texture

Now, drag and drop one of the sprites from the **Project** panel to the **Scene** via the **Hierarchy** panel. On doing this, it will be added as a sprite object. This represents the beginning of our Ammo prefab. The sprite itself may not initially be oriented to face upward at the game camera. If so, rotate the sprite by **90** degrees until it looks correct. See *Figure 4.7*:

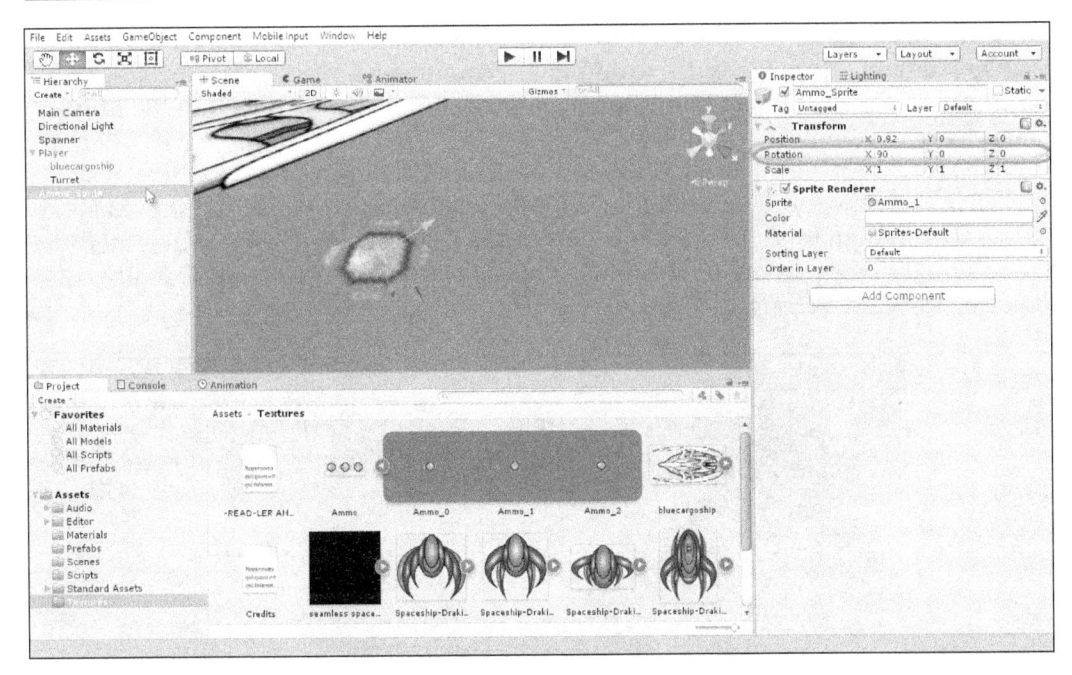

Figure 4.7: Aligning the ammo sprite

Now create a new, empty game object in the scene (**GameObject | Create Empty** from the application menu) and rename it `Ammo`. Make this new object a parent of `Ammo_Sprite` and ensure that its local forward vector is pointing in the direction that the ammo should travel. We'll soon reuse the `Mover` script (created in the previous chapter) on the ammo to make it move.

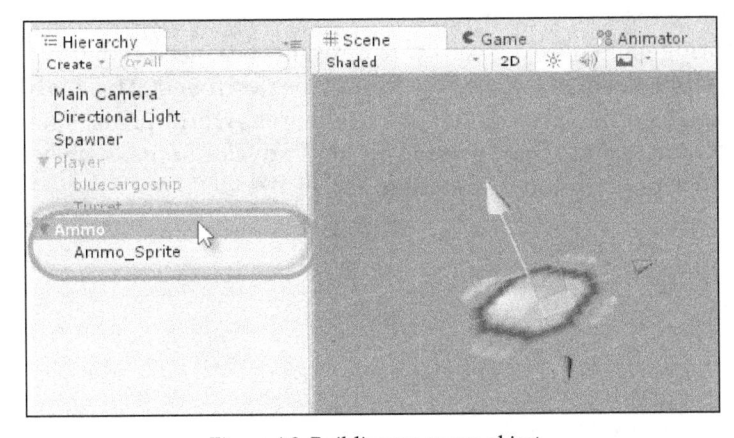

Figure 4.8: Building an ammo object

Continuing the Space Shooter

Drag and drop the Mover.cs script from the **Project** panel to the Ammo parent object via the **Hierarchy** panel in order to add it as a component. Then, select the Ammo object and, from the **Object Inspector**, change the ammo's **Max Speed** in the **Mover** component to 7. Finally, add a **Box Collider** to the object to approximate its volume (**Component | Physics | Box Collider** from the application menu), and then test this all in the viewport by pressing play on the toolbar. The Ammo object should shoot forward as though fired from a weapon. If it moves up or down incorrectly, then make sure that the parent object is rotated so that its blue forward vector really is pointing forward. See *Figure 4.9*:

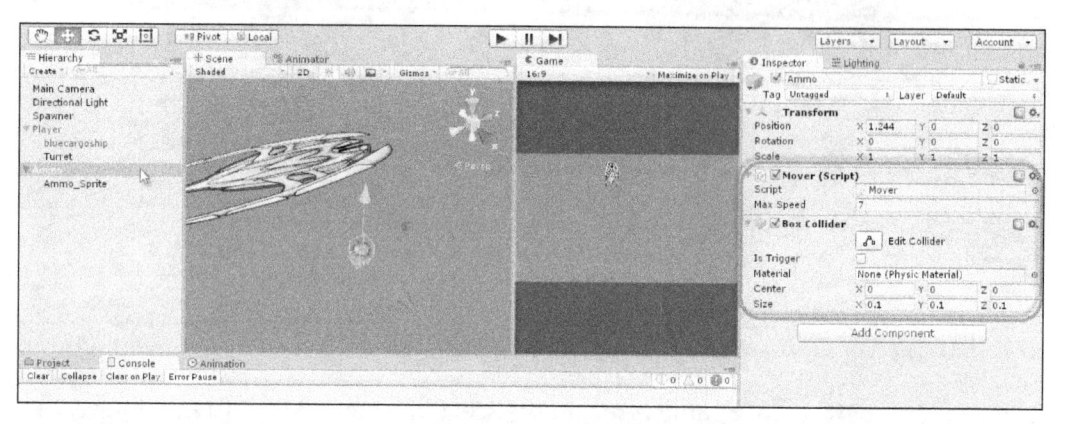

Figure 4.9: Moving forward with an Ammo prefab (Mover and Collider)

Next, add a **Rigidbody** component to the ammo to make it part of the Unity Physics system. To do this, select the Ammo object and navigate to **Component | Physics | Rigidbody** from the application menu. Then, from the **Rigidbody** component in the **Inspector**, disable the **Use Gravity** checkbox to prevent the ammo from falling to the ground during gameplay. For our purposes, gravity need not apply to the ammo as it should simply travel along and eventually be destroyed. This highlights an important point in game development generally: real-world physics need not apply to every object accurately. We only need enough physics to make objects appear correct to the player when they're looking. See *Figure 4.10*:

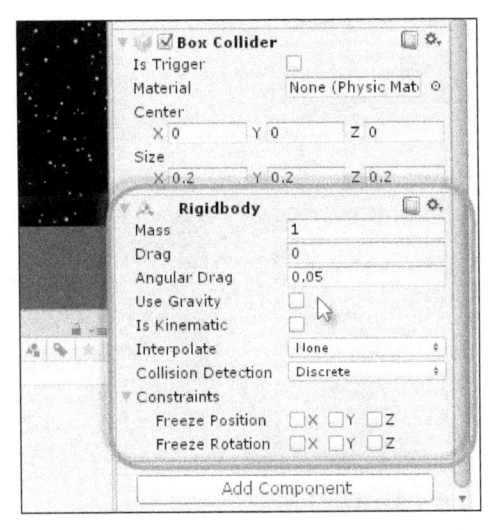

Figure 4.10: Removing gravity from the Ammo object

In addition to adding a `Mover` script and physics components, we also need the ammo to behave distinctly. Specifically, it should damage the objects with which it collides, and it should also destroy or disable itself on collision. To achieve this, a new script file must be created, `Ammo.cs`. The entire code for this is included in *Code Sample 4.1* as follows:

```
//-------------------------------
using UnityEngine;
using System.Collections;
//-------------------------------
public class Ammo : MonoBehaviour
{
  public float Damage = 100f;
  public float LifeTime = 2f;
  //-----------------------------
  void OnEnable()
  {
    CancelInvoke();
    Invoke("Die", LifeTime);
  }
  //-----------------------------
  // Update is called once per frame
  void OnTriggerEnter(Collider Col)
  {
    //Get health component
    Health H = Col.gameObject.GetComponent<Health>();
```

```
        if(H == null)return;

        H.HealthPoints -= Damage;
    }
    //-----------------------------
    void Die()
    {
        gameObject.SetActive(false);
    }

    //-----------------------------
}
//-----------------------------
```

Code Sample 4-1

The following points summarize the code sample:

- The `Ammo` class should be attached to the `Ammo` prefab object and will be instantiated for all ammo objects created. Its main purpose is to damage any objects with which it collides.

- The `OnTriggerEnter` function is invoked for the ammo when it enters a trigger attached to a movable unit, such as the player or enemies. Specifically, it retrieves the `Health` component attached to the object, if it has one, and reduces its health by the `Damage` amount. The `Health` component was created in the previous chapter.

- Notice that each ammo object will have a lifetime. This represents the amount of time in seconds for which the ammo should remain alive and active after it is fired and generated in the scene. After the lifetime expires, the ammo should either be destroyed entirely or deactivated (more on this shortly).

- The `Invoke` function is used to deactivate the ammo object after the `LifeTime` interval. This happens during the `OnEnable` event. This is called automatically by Unity each time an object is activated (that is, changed from being disabled to enabled).

Now, drag and drop the `Ammo` script file from the `Scripts` folder in the **Project** panel to the `Ammo` object, and then finally, drag and drop the whole `Ammo` object in the **Scene** back to the **Project** panel in the `Prefabs` folder in order to create a new `Ammo` prefab. See *Figure 4.11*:

Chapter 4

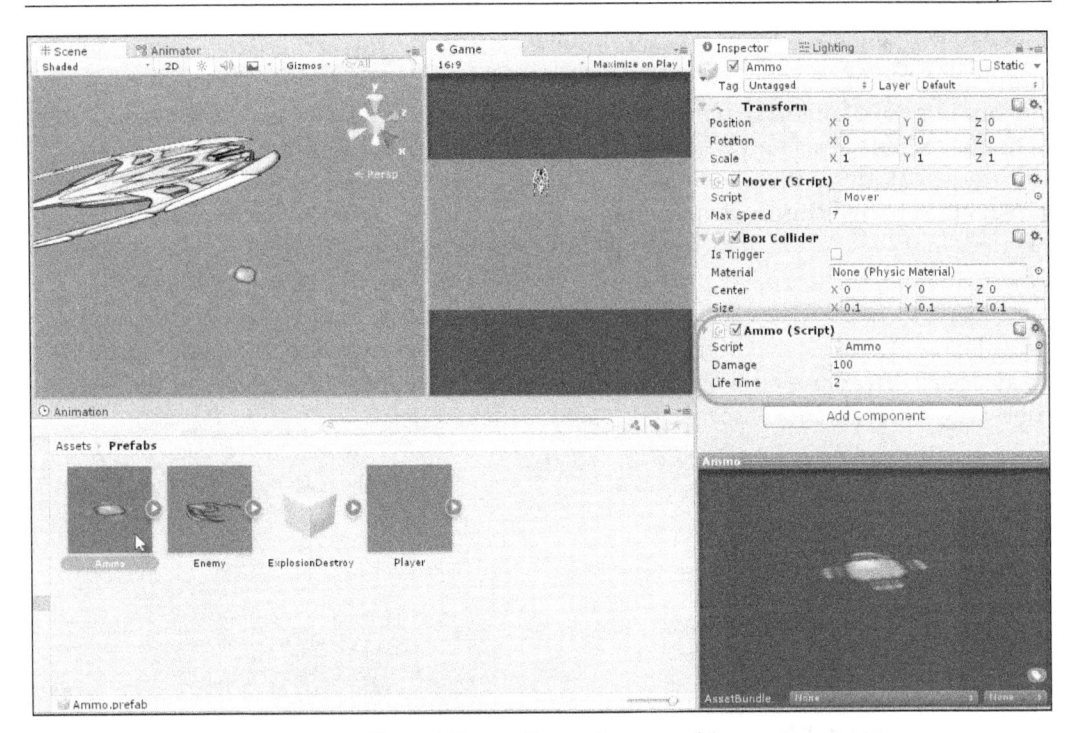

Figure 4.11: Creating an Ammo prefab

Congratulations! You've now created an `Ammo` prefab, which can be spawned from weapon points to attack enemies directly. This is good, but we've still not handled the spawning process itself and we'll address this next.

Ammo spawning

The `Ammo` prefab created so far presents us with a technical problem that, if not taken seriously, has the potential to cause some serious performance penalties for our game. Specifically, when the spaceship weapon is fired, we'll need to generate ammo that launches into the scene and destroys the enemies on collision. This is fine in general, but the problem is that the player could potentially press the fire button many times in quick succession and could even hold down the fire button for long periods of time, and thereby spawn potentially hundreds of ammo prefabs. We could, of course, use the `Instantiate` function seen already to generate these prefabs dynamically, but this is problematic because instantiate is computationally expensive. When used to generate many items in succession, it will typically cause a nightmarish slowdown that'll reduce the FPS to unacceptable levels. We need to avoid this!

[185]

Continuing the Space Shooter

The solution is known as **Pooling**, **Object Pooling**, or **Object Caching**. In essence, it means that we must spawn a large and recyclable batch of ammo objects at the level startup (a pool of objects) that initially, begin hidden or deactivated, and we simply activate the objects as and when needed (when the player fires a weapon). When the ammo collides with an enemy or when its lifetime expires, we don't destroy the object entirely, we simply deactivate it again, returning it to the pool for reuse later if needed. In this way, we avoid all calls to Instantiate and simply recycle all ammo objects that we have. To get started with coding this functionality, we'll make an AmmoManager class. This class will be responsible for two features: first, generating a pool of ammo objects at scene startup, and second, giving us a valid and available ammo object from the pool on demand, such as on weapon-fire. Consider the following AmmoManager *Code Sample 4.2* to achieve this:

```
//------------------------------
using UnityEngine;
using System.Collections;
using System.Collections.Generic;
//------------------------------
public class AmmoManager : MonoBehaviour
{
  //------------------------------
  //Reference to ammo prefab
  public GameObject AmmoPrefab = null;

  //Ammo pool count
  public int PoolSize = 100;

  public Queue<Transform> AmmoQueue = new Queue<Transform>();

  //Array of ammo objects to generate
  private GameObject[] AmmoArray;

  public static AmmoManager AmmoManagerSingleton = null;
  //------------------------------
  // Use this for initialization
  void Awake ()
  {
    if(AmmoManagerSingleton != null)
    {
```

```
      Destroy(GetComponent<AmmoManager>());
      return;
    }

    AmmoManagerSingleton = this;
    AmmoArray = new GameObject[PoolSize];

    for(int i=0; i<PoolSize; i++)
    {
      AmmoArray[i] = Instantiate(AmmoPrefab, Vector3.zero,
        Quaternion.identity) as GameObject;
      Transform ObjTransform =
        AmmoArray[i].GetComponent<Transform>();
      ObjTransform.parent = GetComponent<Transform>();
      AmmoQueue.Enqueue(ObjTransform);
      AmmoArray[i].SetActive(false);
    }
  }
  //-----------------------------
  public static Transform SpawnAmmo
    (Vector3 Position, Quaternion Rotation)
  {
    //Get ammo
    Transform SpawnedAmmo =
      AmmoManagerSingleton.AmmoQueue.Dequeue();

    SpawnedAmmo.gameObject.SetActive(true);
    SpawnedAmmo.position = Position;
    SpawnedAmmo.localRotation = Rotation;

    //Add to queue end
    AmmoManagerSingleton.AmmoQueue.Enqueue(SpawnedAmmo);

    //Return ammo
    return SpawnedAmmo;
  }
  //-----------------------------
}
//-----------------------------
```

Code Sample 4.2

The following points summarize the code sample:

- `AmmoManager` features an `AmmoArray` member variable, which holds a complete list (sequential array of references) of all ammo objects to be generated at startup (during the `Awake` event).

- `AmmoArray` will be sized to `PoolSize`. This refers to the total number of ammo objects to be generated. The `Awake` function generates the ammo objects at the beginning of the level, and these are added to the queue with `Enqueue`.

- Once generated, each ammo object is deactivated with `SetActive(false)` and is held in the pool until needed.

- `AmmoManager` uses the `Queue` class from the `Mono` library to manage how specific ammo objects are selected from the pool to be activated when fire is pressed. The queue works as a **First-In-First-Out** (**FIFO**) object. That is, ammo objects are added to the queue one at a time and can be removed when selected to be activated. The object removed from the queue is always the object at the front. More information on the `Queue` class can be found online at https://msdn.microsoft.com/en-us/library/7977ey2c%28v=vs.110%29.aspx.

- The `Enqueue` function of the `Queue` object is called during `Awake` to add objects initially to the queue, one by one, as they are generated.

- The `SpawnAmmo` function should be called to generate a new item of ammo in the scene. This function does not rely on the `Instantiate` function but uses the `Queue` object instead. It removes the first ammo object from the queue, activates it, and then adds it to the end of the queue again behind all the other ammo objects. In this way, a cycle of generation and regeneration happens, allowing all ammo objects to be recycled.

- `AmmoManager` is coded as a singleton object, meaning that one, and only one, instance of the object should exist in the scene at any one time. This functionality is achieved through the static member, `AmmoManagerSingleton`.

> For more information on singleton objects, refer to *Mastering Unity Scripting* by *Packt Publishing* at https://www.packtpub.com/game-development/mastering-unity-5x-scripting.

Chapter 4

To use this class, create a new `GameObject` in the scene called `AmmoManager` by selecting **GameObject | Create Empty** from the application menu. Then, drag and drop the `AmmoManager` script from the **Project** panel to select the object in the scene. Once created, drag and drop the `Ammo` prefab from the `Prefabs` folder to the **Ammo Prefab** slot for the **Ammo Manager** component in the **Object Inspector**. See *Figure 4.12*:

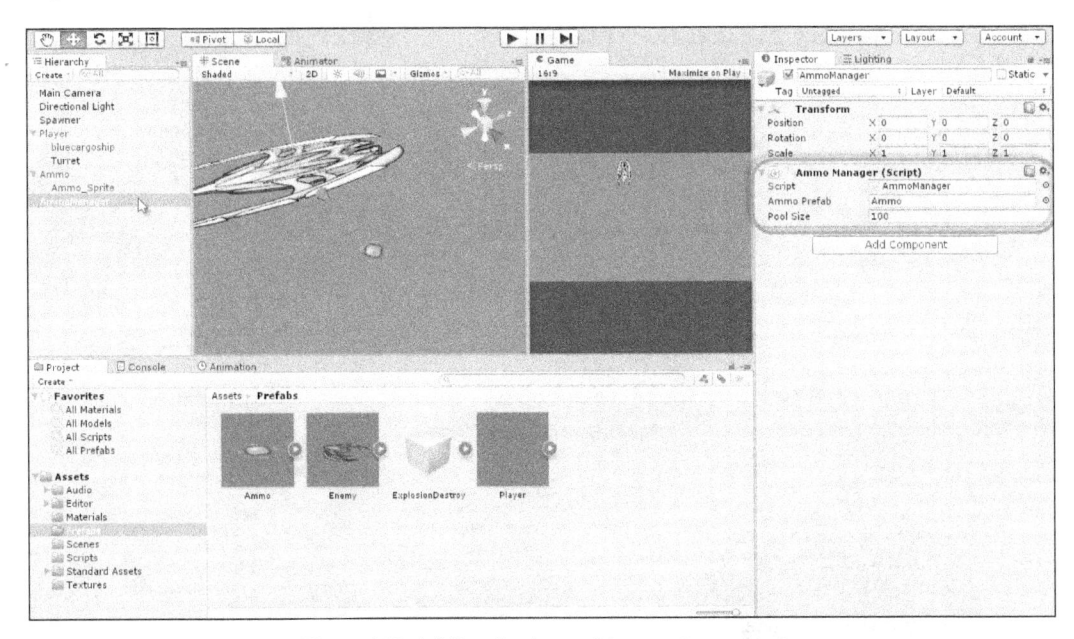

Figure 4.12: Adding the Ammo Manager to an object

Now, the scene features an `AmmoManager` object to hold an ammo pool, offscreen and hidden. However, still nothing about our existing functionality actually connects a fire button press from the gamer with the generation of ammo in the scene. That is, we have no code to actually make the ammo visible and working! This connection should now be made via the `PlayerController` script that we started in the previous chapter. This class should now be amended to handle ammo generation. The recoded `PlayerController` class is included in the following *Code Sample 4.3*. The amendments are highlighted:

```
//-----------------------------
using UnityEngine;
using System.Collections;
//-----------------------------
public class PlayerController : MonoBehaviour
{
```

```csharp
//------------------------------
private Rigidbody ThisBody = null;
private Transform ThisTransform = null;

public bool MouseLook = true;
public string HorzAxis = "Horizontal";
public string VertAxis = "Vertical";
public string FireAxis = "Fire1";

public float MaxSpeed = 5f;
public float ReloadDelay = 0.3f;
public bool CanFire = true;

public Transform[] TurretTransforms;
//------------------------------
// Use this for initialization
void Awake ()
{
  ThisBody = GetComponent<Rigidbody>();
  ThisTransform = GetComponent<Transform>();
}
//------------------------------
// Update is called once per frame
void FixedUpdate ()
{
  //Update movement
  float Horz = Input.GetAxis(HorzAxis);
  float Vert = Input.GetAxis(VertAxis);
  Vector3 MoveDirection = new Vector3(Horz, 0.0f, Vert);
  ThisBody.AddForce(MoveDirection.normalized * MaxSpeed);

  //Clamp speed
  ThisBody.velocity = new Vector3
    (Mathf.Clamp(ThisBody.velocity.x, -MaxSpeed, MaxSpeed),
  Mathf.Clamp(ThisBody.velocity.y, -MaxSpeed, MaxSpeed),
  Mathf.Clamp(ThisBody.velocity.z, -MaxSpeed, MaxSpeed));

  //Should look with mouse?
  if(MouseLook)
```

```csharp
    {
      //Update rotation - turn to face mouse pointer
      Vector3 MousePosWorld = Camera.main.ScreenToWorldPoint(new
        Vector3(Input.mousePosition.x, Input.mousePosition.y,
        0.0f));
      MousePosWorld = new Vector3(MousePosWorld.x, 0.0f,
        MousePosWorld.z);

      //Get direction to cursor
      Vector3 LookDirection = MousePosWorld -
        ThisTransform.position;

      //FixedUpdate rotation
      ThisTransform.localRotation = Quaternion.LookRotation
        (LookDirection.normalized,Vector3.up);
    }

    //Check fire control
    if(Input.GetButtonDown(FireAxis) && CanFire)
    {
      foreach(Transform T in TurretTransforms)
        AmmoManager.SpawnAmmo(T.position, T.rotation);

      CanFire = false;
      Invoke ("EnableFire", ReloadDelay);
    }
  }
  //------------------------------
  void EnableFire()
  {
    CanFire = true;
  }
  //------------------------------
  public void Die()
  {
    Destroy(gameObject);
  }
}
//------------------------------
```

[191]

Continuing the Space Shooter

Code Sample 4.3

The following points summarize the code sample:

- `PlayerController` now features a `TurretTransform` array variable, listing all child empties being used as turret spawn locations.
- During the `Update` function, `PlayerController` checks for fire button presses. If detected, the code cycles through all turrets and spawns one ammo object at each turret location.
- Once ammo is fired, `ReloadDelay` is engaged (set to `true`). This means that the delay must first expire before new ammo can be fired again later.

After adding this code to `PlayerController`, select the `Player` object in the scene and then drag and drop the `Turret` empty object on to the `TurretTransform` slot. This example uses only one turret, but you could add more if desired. See *Figure 4.13*:

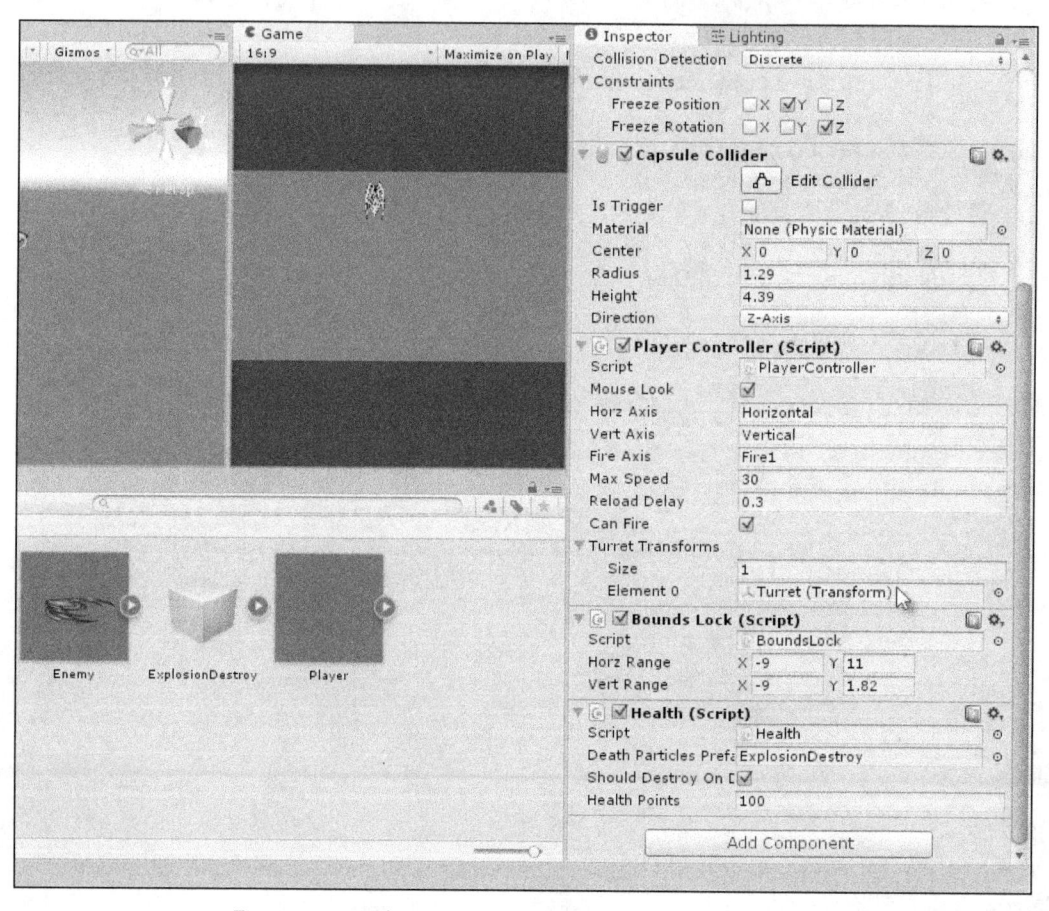

Figure 4.13: Configuring TurretTransform for spawning ammo

Chapter 4

Now you're ready to play test and fire ammo. By playing the scene and pressing fire on the keyboard or mouse (left-click), ammo will be generated. Excellent! However, on testing this, you may notice two main problems. First, the ammo appears too big or too small. Second, the ammo sometimes bounces, flips, or reacts to the player spaceship. Let's fix these in turn.

If the ammo appears wrongly-sized, you can simply change the scale of the prefab. Select the Ammo prefab in the **Project** panel, and from the **Object Inspector**, enter a new scale in the **Transform** component. See *Figure 4.14*:

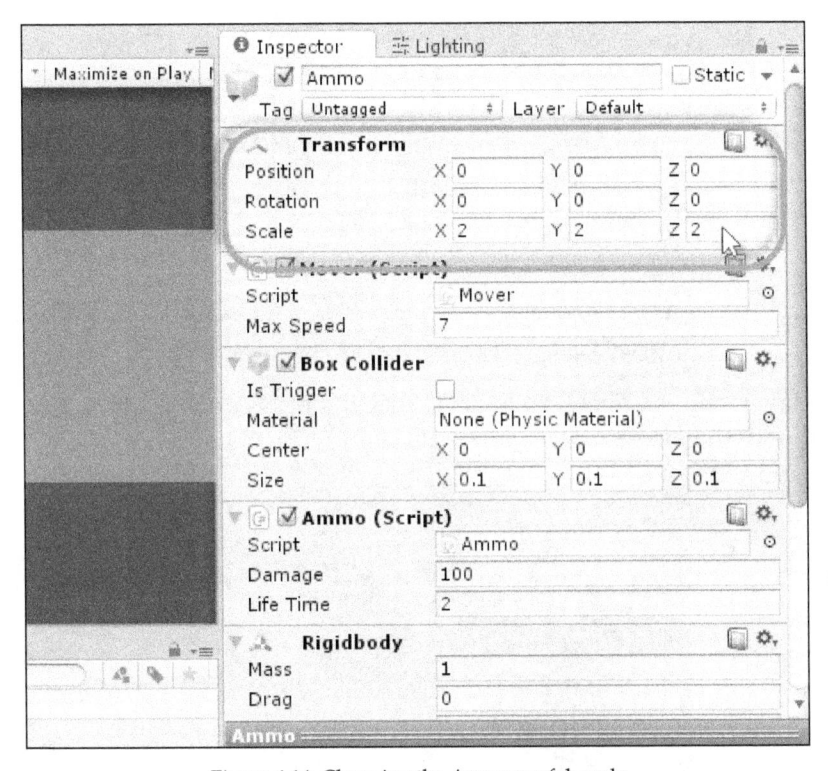

Figure 4.14: Changing the Ammo prefab scale

If the ammo appears to bounce or react to the player spaceship, then we'll need to make the ammo immune or unresponsive to the player. To achieve this, we can use physics layers. In short, both the player spaceship and ammo should be added to a single layer, and all objects on this layer should be defined as immune to each other in terms of physical reactions.

[193]

Continuing the Space Shooter

First, select the `Player` object in the scene. Then, from the **Object Inspector**, click on the **Layer** drop-down, and choose **Add Layer** from the context menu. See *Figure 4.15*:

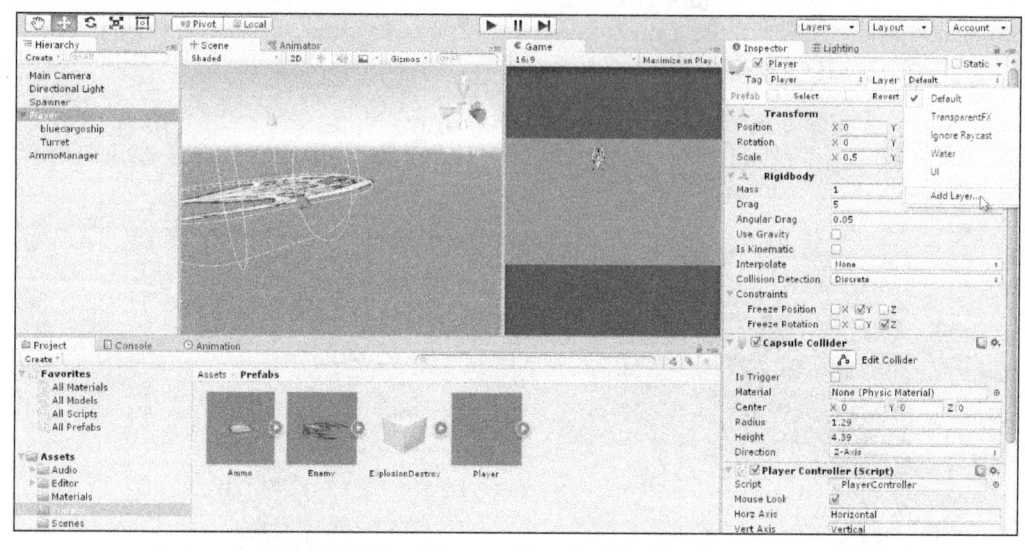

Figure 4.15: Creating a new layer for Physics exclusions

Name the layer `Player`. This is to indicate that all objects attached to the layer are associated with the `Player`. See *Figure 4.16*:

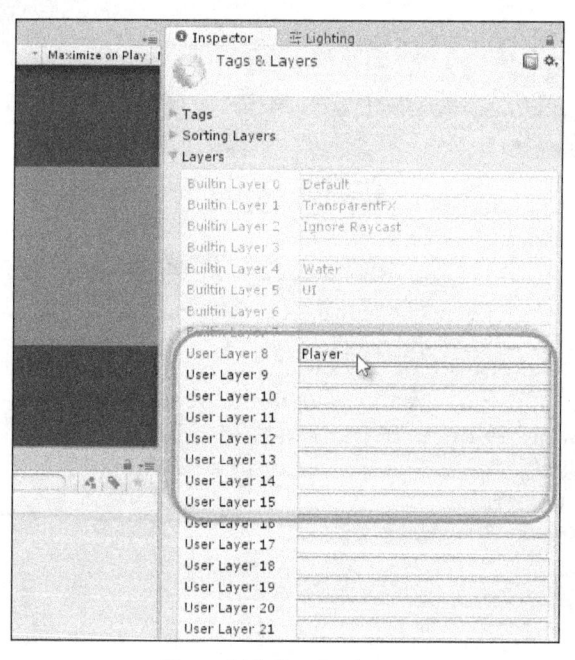

Figure 4.16: Creating layers

Now, assign both the `Player` object in the scene and `Ammo` prefab in the **Project** panel to the newly created **Player** layer. Select each, and simply click on the **Layer** drop-down, selecting the **Player** option. See *Figure 4.17*. If prompted with a pop-up dialog, choose to change children also. This makes sure that all child objects are also associated with the same **Layer** as the parent:

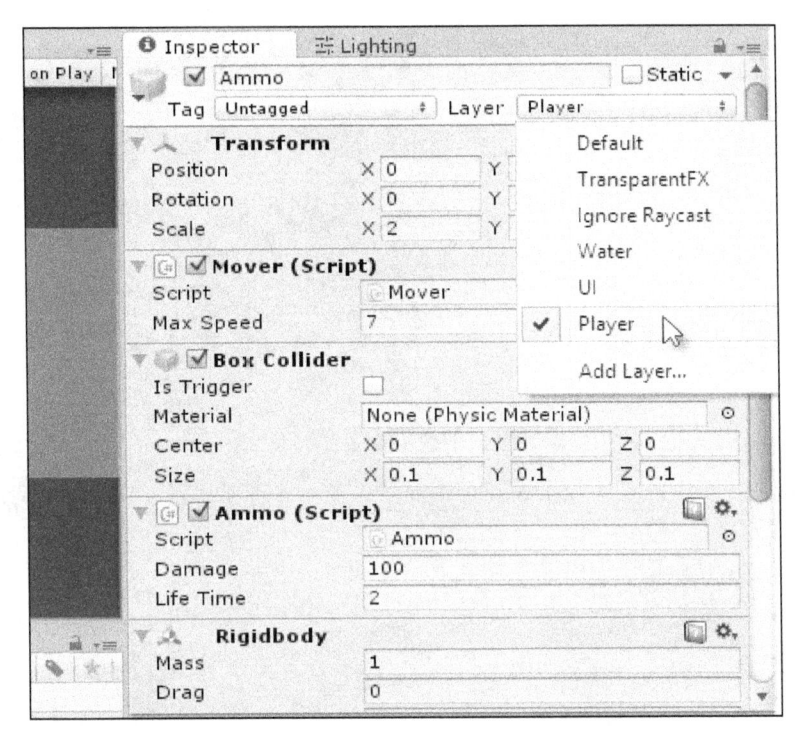

Figure 4.17: Assigning Player and Ammo to the Player layer

Both **Player** and **Ammo** have now been assigned to the same layer. From here, we can make all objects in the same layer immune from each other insofar as **Physics** applies.

Continuing the Space Shooter

To do this, navigate to **Edit | Project Settings | Physics** from the application menu. See *Figure 4.18*:

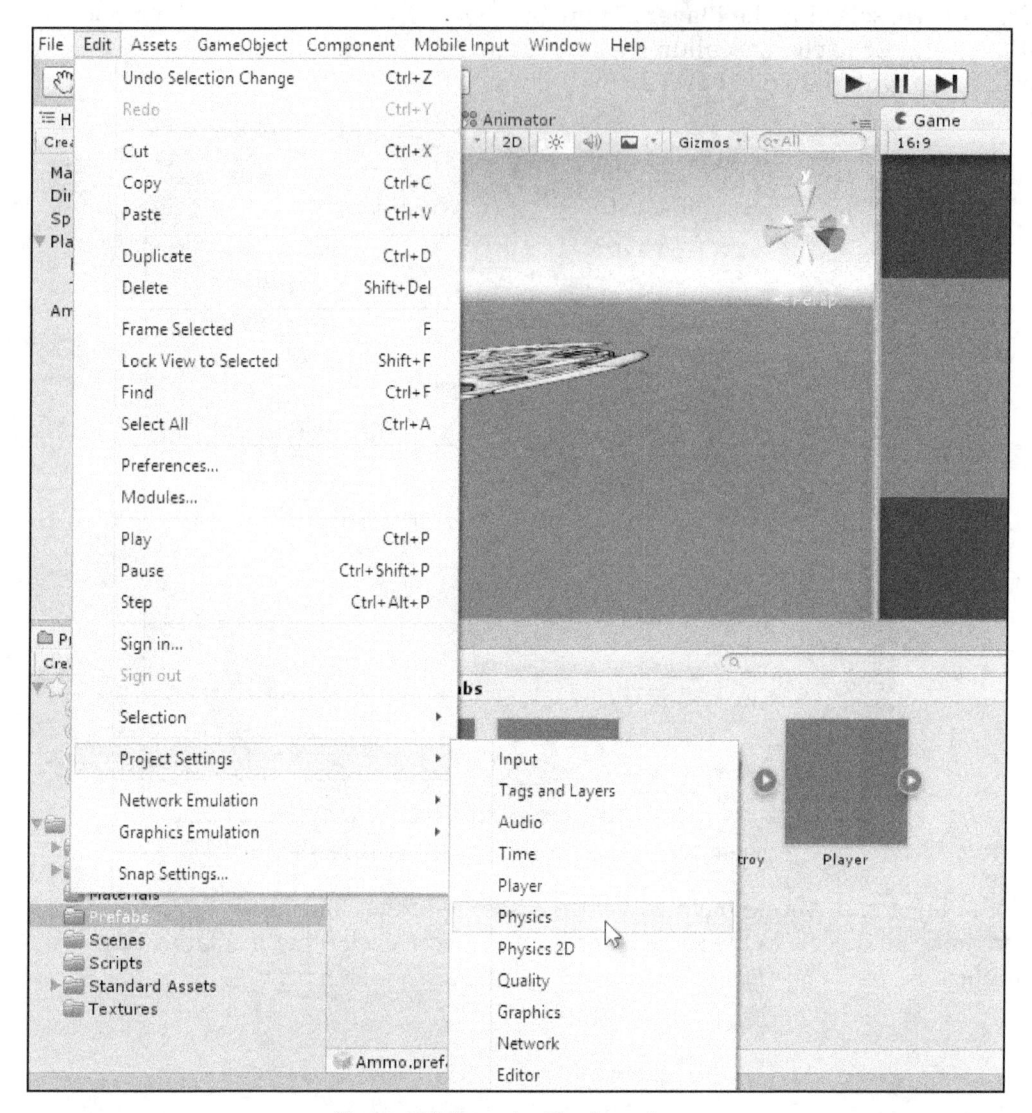

Figure 4.18: Accessing Physics options

The global **Physics** settings appear in the **Object Inspector**. At the bottom of the **Inspector**, the **Layer Collision Matrix** displays how layers affect each other. Intersecting layers with a check mark can and will affect each other. For this reason, remove the check mark for the **Player** layer to prevent collisions occurring between objects on this layer. See *Figure 4.19*:

[196]

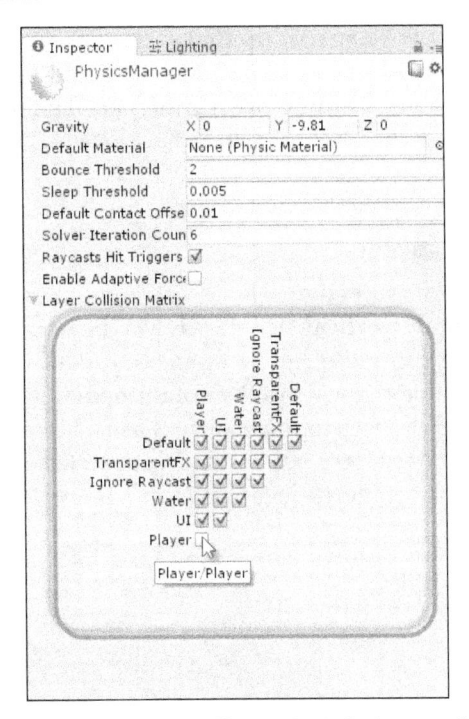

Figure 4.19: Setting the Layer Collision Matrix for improved collisions

With the **Layer Collision Matrix** set from the **Object Inspector**, test run the game so far by pressing play on the toolbar. When you do this and press fire, ammo will issue from the turrets and no longer react to the player spaceship. The ammo should, however, collide with, and destroy, the enemies. See *Figure 4.20*:

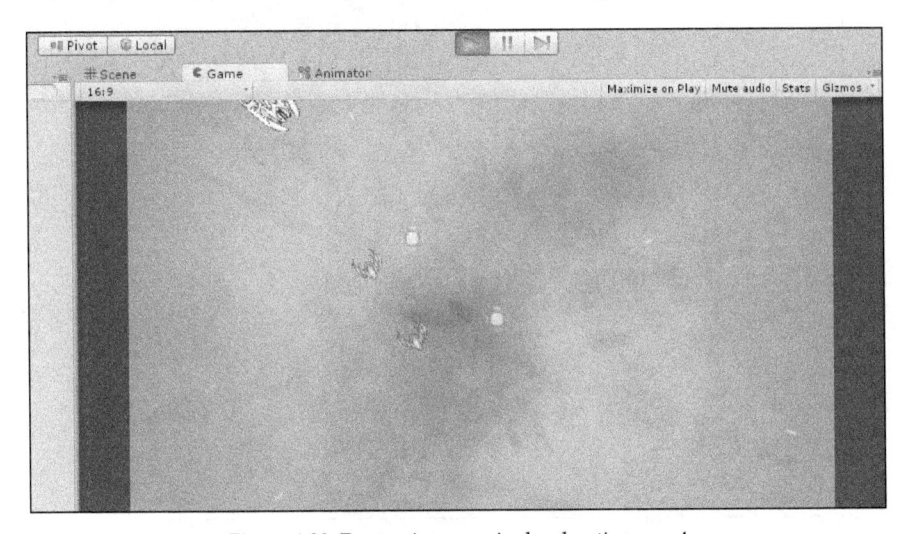

Figure 4.20: Destroying enemies by shooting guns!

Continuing the Space Shooter

Excellent work! We now have a spaceship that can fire weapons and destroy enemies, and the physics works as expected. Maybe you'd like to customize player controls a little or perhaps you want to use a gamepad. The next section will explore this issue further.

User controls

Maybe you don't like the default controls and key combinations associated with the input axes—**Horizontal**, **Vertical**, and **Fire1**. Maybe you want to change them. These input axes are read using the Input.GetAxis function (shown earlier) and are specified by human readable names, but it's not immediately clear how Unity maps specific input buttons and devices to these virtual axes. Here, we'll see briefly how to customize these. To get started, let's access the **Input** settings by navigating to **Edit | Project Settings | Input** from the application menu. See *Figure 4.21*:

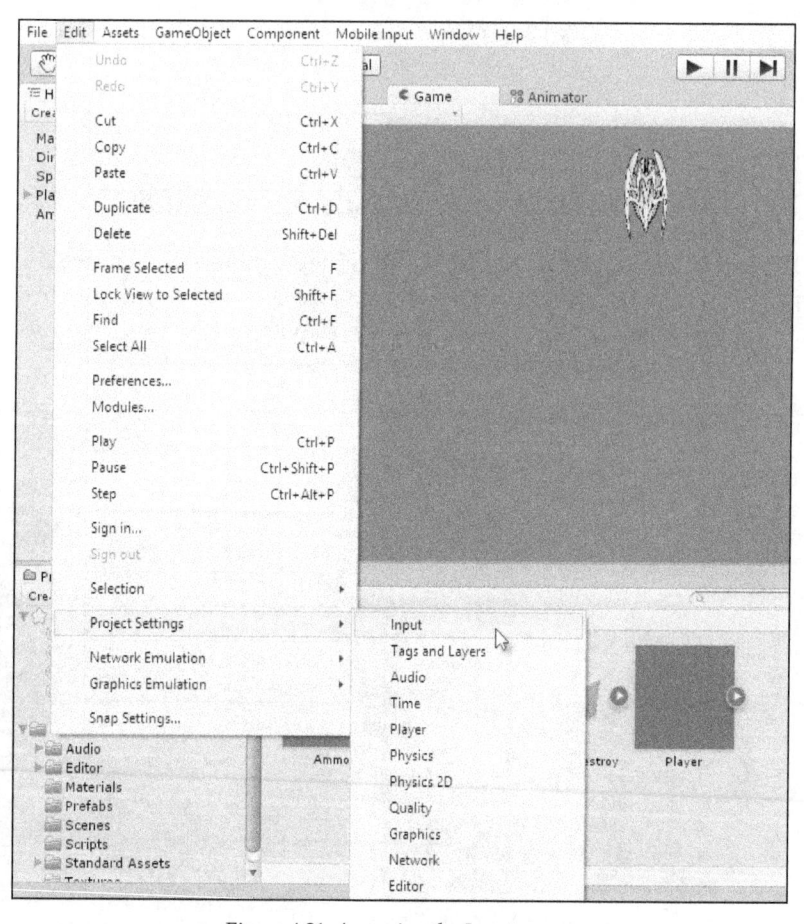

Figure 4.21: Accessing the Input menu

On selecting this option, a collection of custom-defined input axes appear as a list in the **Object Inspector**. See *Figure 4.22*. This defines all axes used by the input system. The **Horizontal** and **Vertical** axes should be listed here:

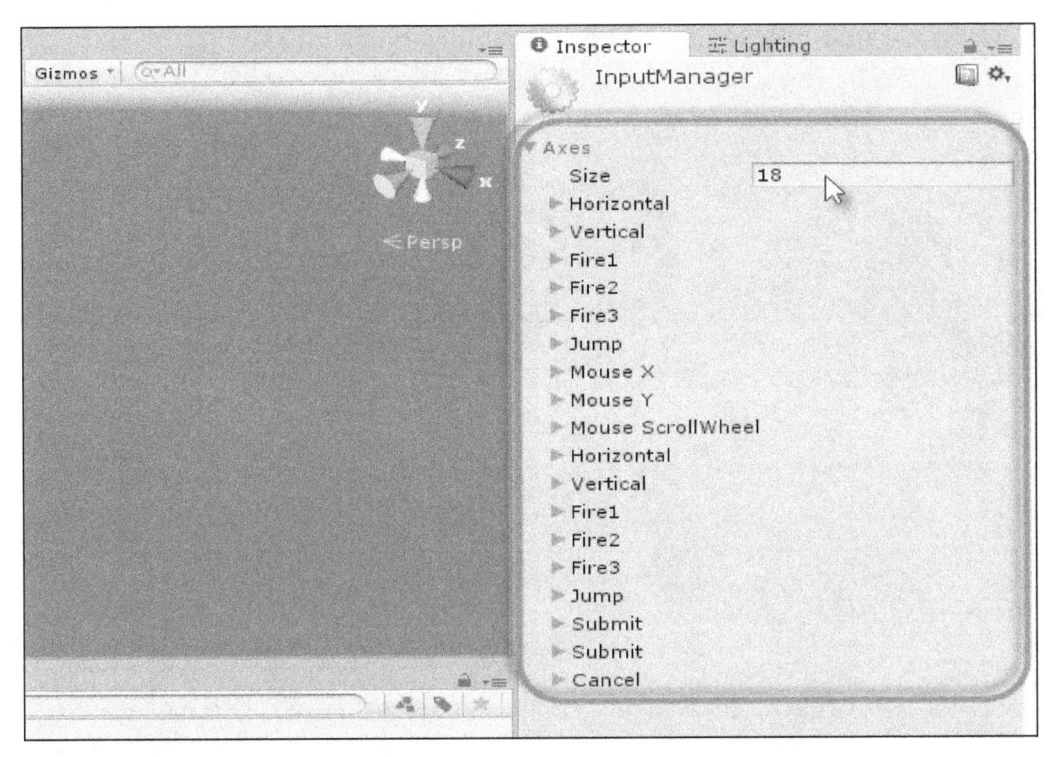

Figure 4.22: Exploring the input axes

By expanding each axis in the **Object Inspector**, you can easily customize how user input is mapped, that is, how specific keys and controls on hardware devices, such as a keyboard and mouse, will map to an axis. The **Horizontal** axis, for example, is defined twice. For the first definition, **Horizontal** is mapped to the left, right, and A and D keys on the keyboard. Right and D are mapped as **Positive Button** because, when pressed, they produce positive floating-point values from the Input.GetAxis function (0-1). Left and A are mapped as **Negative Button** because, when pressed, they result in negative floating-points values for Input.GetAxis.

This makes it easy to move objects left and right using negative and positive numbers. See *Figure 4.23*:

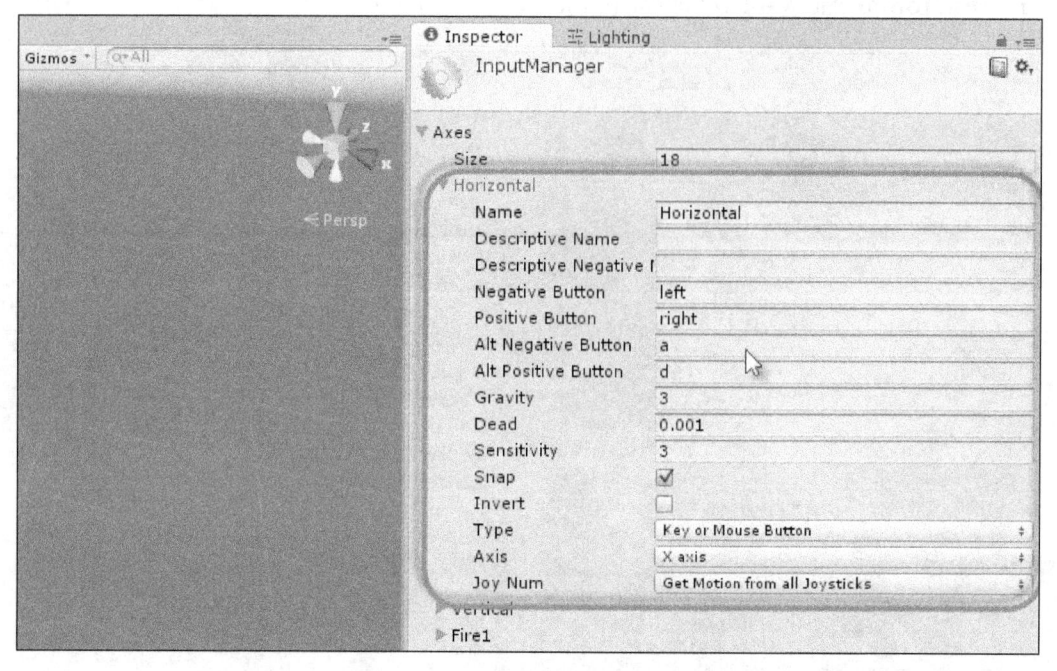

Figure 4.23: Configuring an Input axis

Notice that **Horizontal** is defined twice in the **Object Inspector**—once near the top of the list and once near the bottom. These two definitions are accumulative and not contradictory—they stack atop one another. They allow you to map multiple devices to the same axis, giving you cross-platform and multidevice control over your games. By default, **Horizontal** is mapped in the first definition to the `left`, `right`, *A*, and *D* keys on the keyboard, and in the second definition, to joystick motion. Both definitions are valid and work together.

You can have as many definitions for the same axis as you need, depending on the controls you need to support. See *Figure 4.24*:

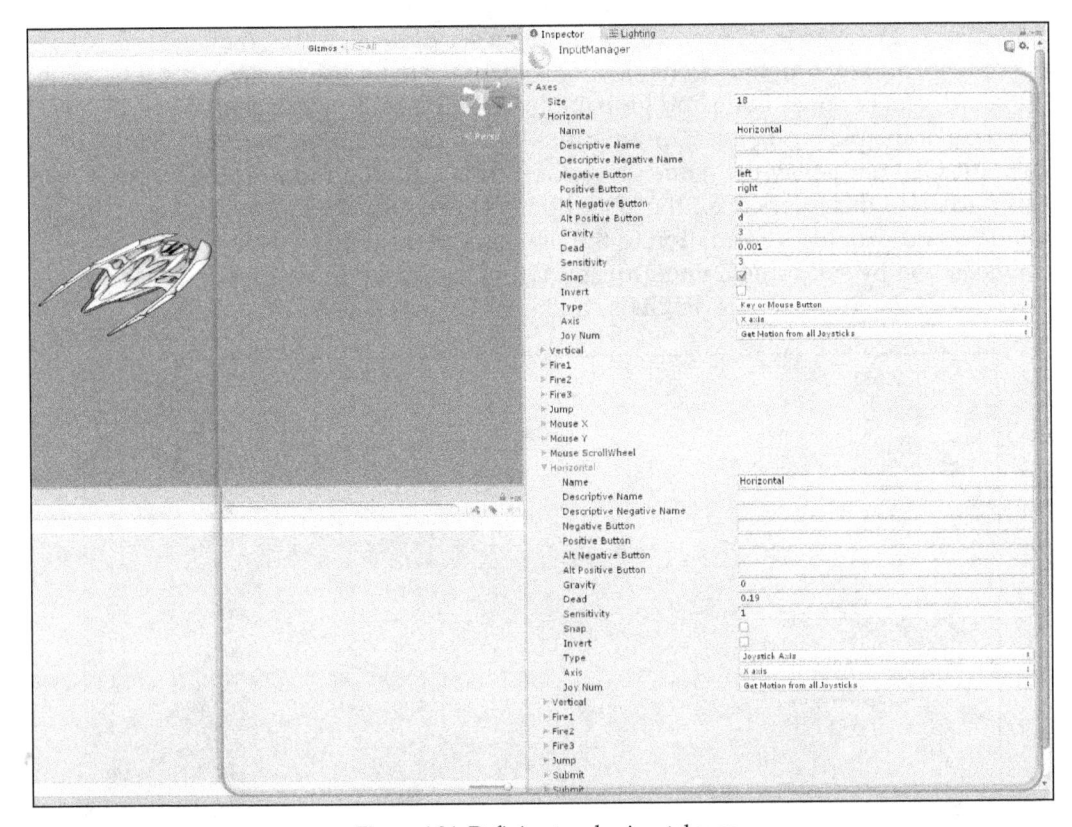

Figure 4.24: Defining two horizontal axes

For this project, the controls will remain at their defaults, but go ahead and change or add additional controls if you want to support different configurations.

> More information on player input and customizing controls can be found in the online Unity documentation at http://docs.unity3d.com/Manual/class-InputManager.html.

Continuing the Space Shooter

Scores and scoring – UI and text objects

Let's move on to the scoring system and, in creating this, we'll create `GameController`. `GameController` is simply a script or class that manages all game-wide and overarching behavior. This includes the score because, for this game, the score refers to one single and global number representing the achievements and progress of the player. Before jumping into the implementation, start by creating a simple GUI to display the game score. GUI is an acronym for **Graphic User Interface**, and this refers to all the 2D graphical elements that sit atop the game window and provide information to the player. To create this, create a new GUI canvas object by selecting **GameObject | UI | Canvas** from the application menu. See *Figure 4.25*. More details on GUIs can be found in the next two chapters:

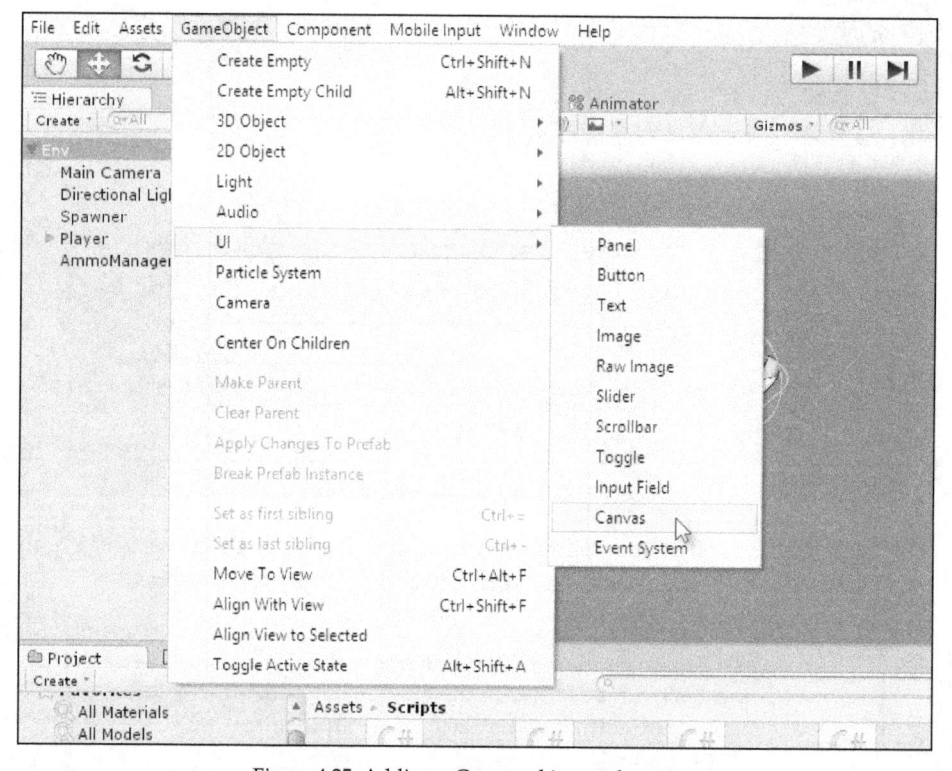

Figure 4.25: Adding a Canvas object to the scene

The `Canvas` object defines the total surface or area in which the GUI lives, including all buttons, text, and other widgets. On being generated in the scene, `Canvas` also features in the **Hierarchy** panel. Initially, the `Canvas` object may be too large or too small to be seen clearly in the viewport, so select the `Canvas` object in the **Hierarchy** panel and press the *F* key on the keyboard to focus the object. It should appear as a large vertically-aligned rectangle. See *Figure 4.26*:

[202]

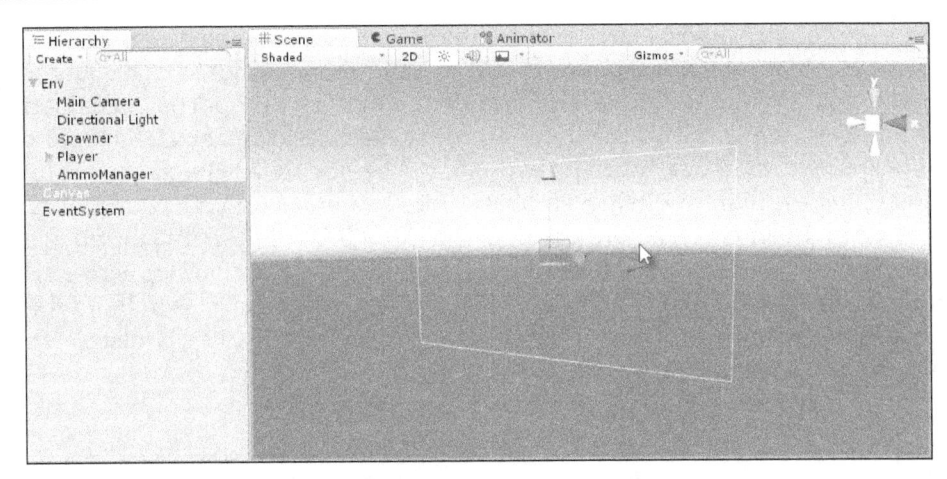

Figure 4.26: Examining the Canvas object in the viewport

The `Canvas` object is not visible itself in the **Game** tab. Rather, it acts simply as a container. Even so, it strongly influences how contained objects appear on the screen in terms of size, position, and scale. For this reason, before adding objects and refining the design of an interface, it's helpful to configure your `Canvas` object first. To do this, select the `Canvas` object in the scene, and from the **Object Inspector**, click on the **UI Scale Mode** drop-down option from the **Canvas Scaler** component. From the drop-down list, choose the **Scale With Screen Size** option and enter an HD resolution in the **Reference Resolution** field, that is, specify 1920 for the **X** field and 1080 for the **Y** field. See *Figure 4.27*:

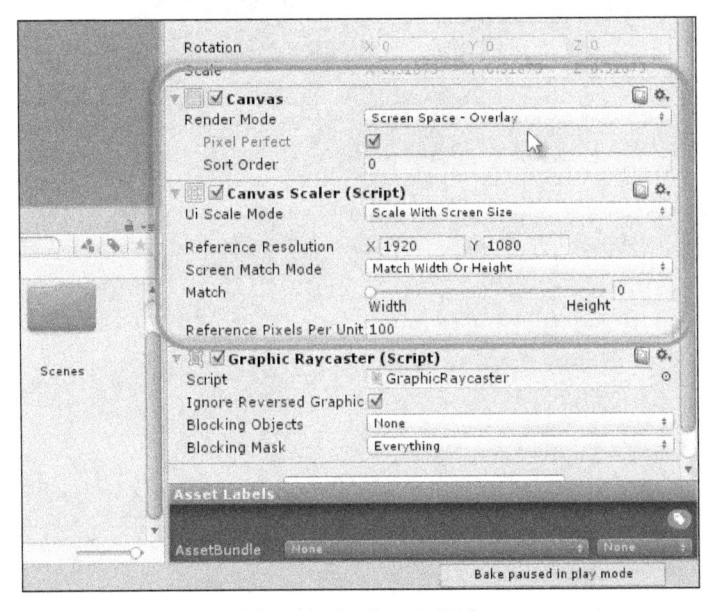

Figure 4.27: Adjusting the Canvas Scaler component

Continuing the Space Shooter

By adjusting the **Canvas Scaler** to **Scale With Screen Size**, the user interface for the game will automatically stretch and shrink (up- and down-scale) to fit the target resolution, ensuring that each element is scaled to the same proportions, maintaining the overall look and feel. This is a quick and easy method to create a UI once and have it adjust size to fit nearly any resolution. It may not always be the best solution to maintaining the highest quality graphical fidelity, but it's functional and suitable in many cases. In any case, before proceeding with the UI design, it's helpful to see both the **Scene** viewport and **Game** tab side by side in the interface (or across two monitors, if you have a multi-monitor configuration). This allows us to build the interface in the **Scene** viewport, and then preview its effects in the **Game** tab. You can rearrange the **Scene** and **Game** tabs simply by dragging and dropping the **Game** tab beside the **Scene** tab in the **Unity Editor**. See *Figure 4.28*:

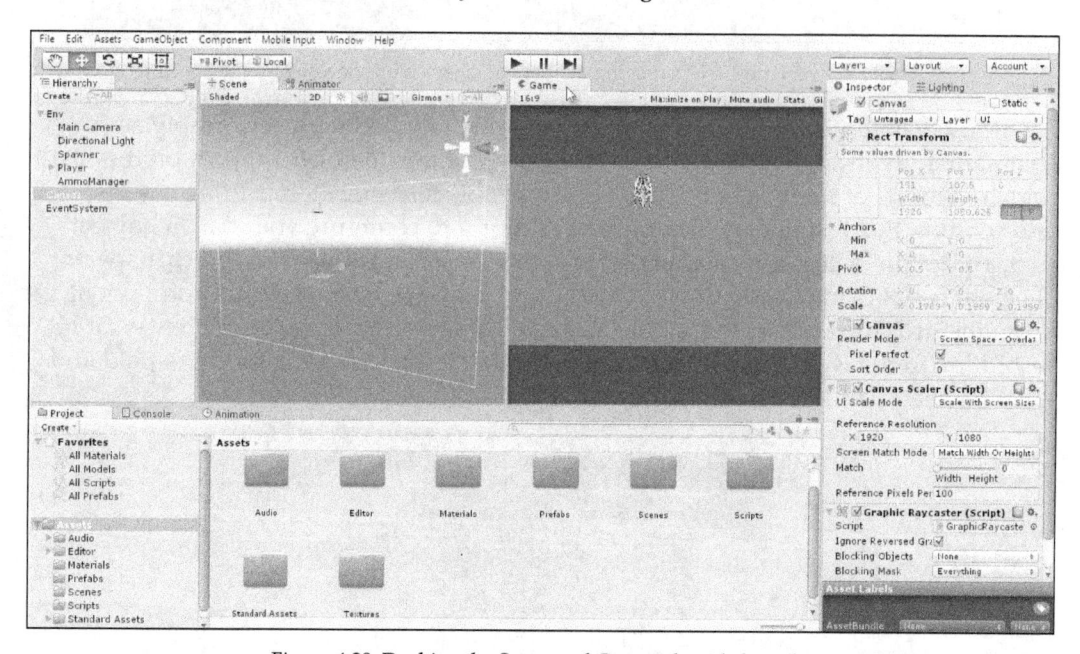

Figure 4.28: Docking the Scene and Game tabs side by side

Next, let's add the text widget to the GUI to display the game score. To do this, select the `Canvas` object in the **Hierarchy** panel, and then right-click on that object (in the **Hierarchy** panel) to display a context menu. From here, select **UI** | **Text**. This creates a new text object as a child of the `Canvas` object as opposed to a top-level object with no parent. See *Figure 4.29*. The `Text` object is useful to draw text onscreen with a specific color, size, and font setting:

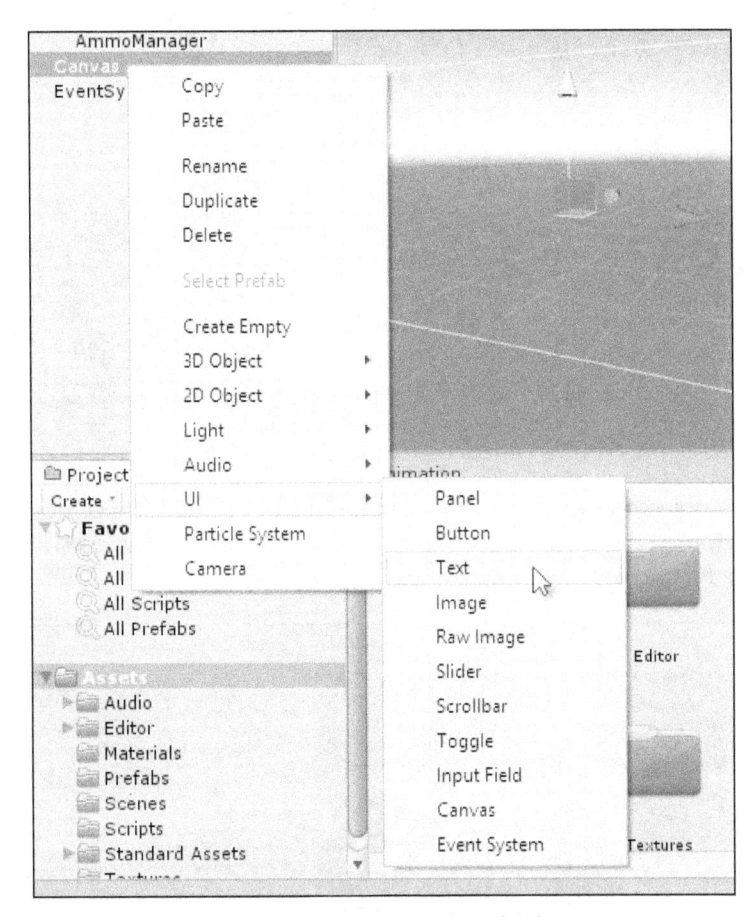

Figure 4.29: Creating a text object for the UI

By default, the `Text` object may not initially appear visible in either the scene or viewport, even though it's listed as an object in the **Hierarchy** panel. However, look more closely in the **Scene** and you're likely to see very small and dark text, which appears both in the **Canvas** and **Game** tab. See *Figure 4.30*.

Continuing the Space Shooter

By default, new text objects feature black text at a small font size. For this project, these settings will need to be changed:

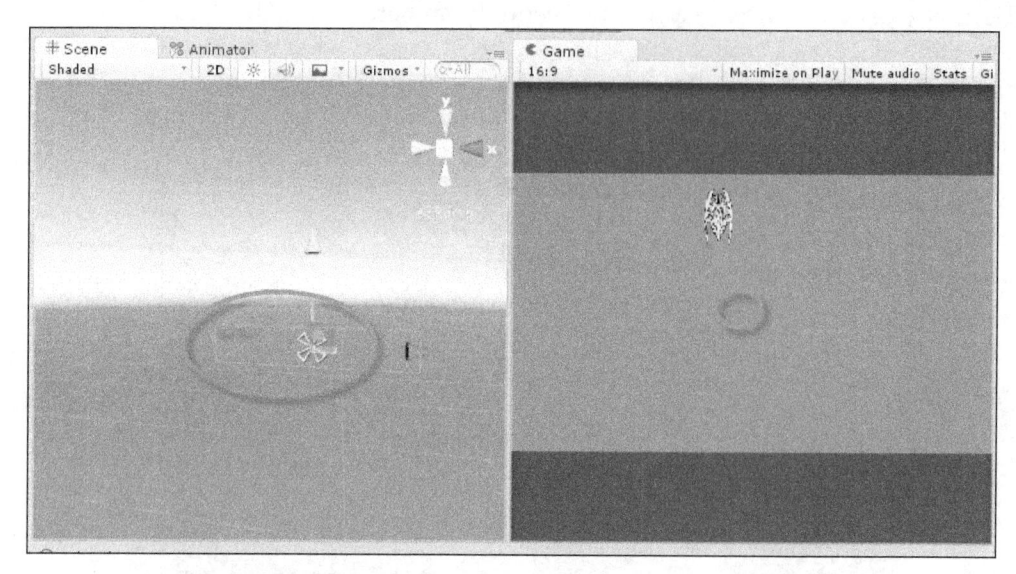

Figure 4.30: Newly created text objects can sometimes be difficult to see

Select the Text object in the **Hierarchy** panel, if it's not already selected, and from the **Object Inspector** (in the **Text** component), change the text **Color** to white and **Font Size** to 20. See *Figure 4.31*:

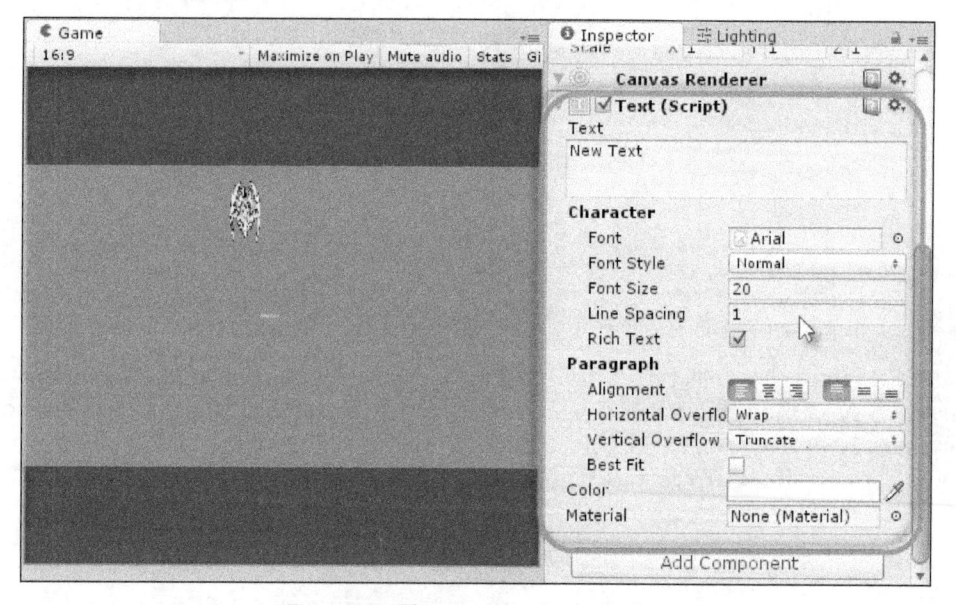

Figure 4.31: Changing text size and color

Chapter 4

The text, however, still appears too small even after changing its size. If you increase the size further, however, the text may disappear from view. This happens because each Text object has a rectangular boundary defining its limits, and when the font size increases beyond what can fit in the boundary, the text is automatically hidden altogether. To fix this, we'll increase the text boundary. To do this, switch to the **Rect Transform** tool with *T* or select the tool from the toolbar. See *Figure 4.32*:

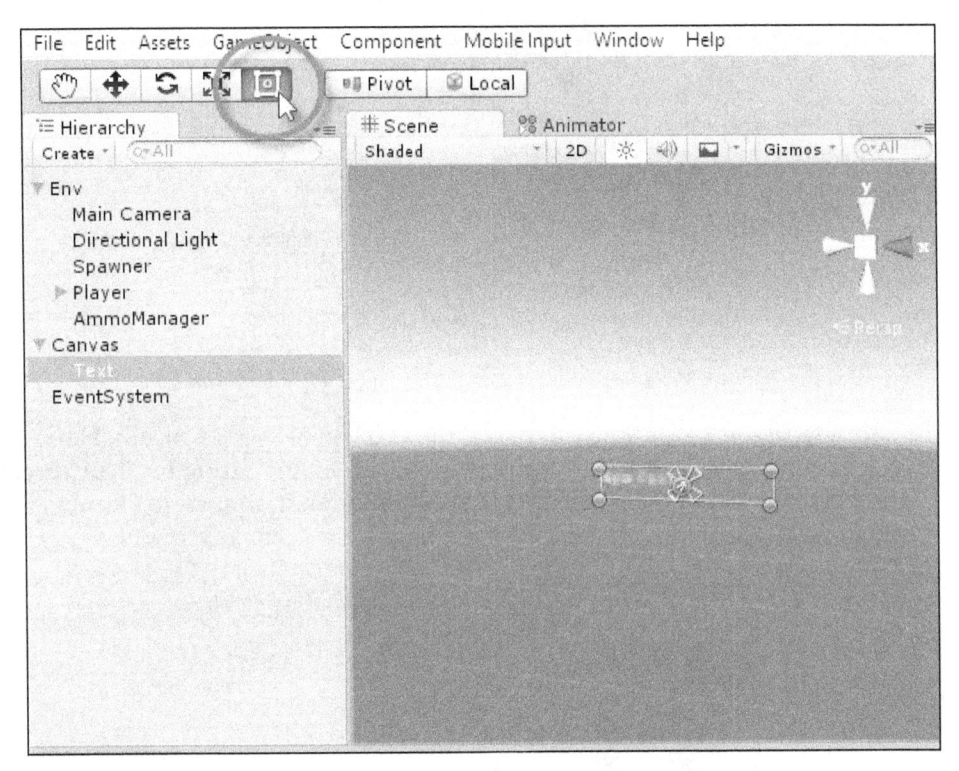

Figure 4.32: Selecting the Rect Transform tool

On activating the **Rect Transform** tool, a clearly defined boundary will be drawn around the selected Text object in the **Scene** viewport, indicating its rectangular extents. Let's increase the boundary size to accommodate larger text. To do this, simply click and drag on the boundary edges with the mouse to extend them as needed. See *Figure 4.33*.

This will increase the boundary size and now you can increase **Font Size** to improve text readability:

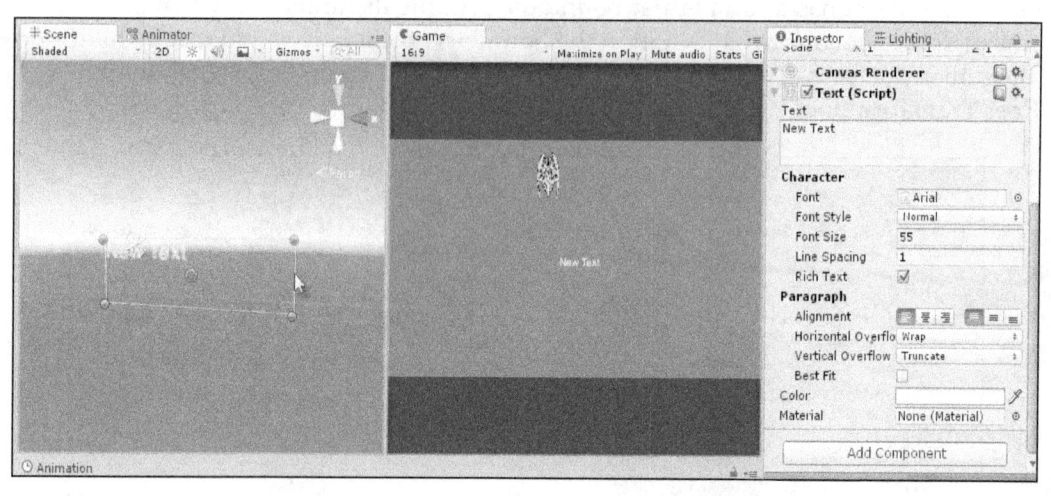

Figure 4.33: Adjust the text rectangle to support larger font sizes

In addition to setting the text boundary size, the text can also be vertically aligned to the boundary center. Simply click on the center alignment button for the vertical group. For horizontal alignment, the text should remain left-aligned to allow for the score display. See *Figure 4.34*:

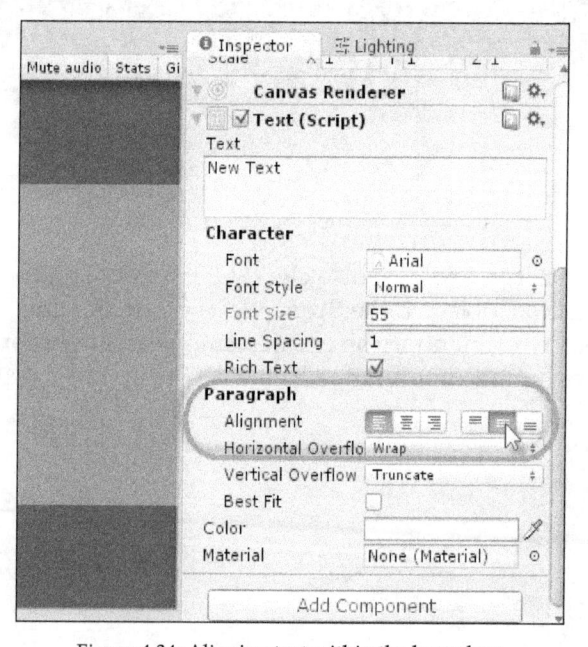

Figure 4.34: Aligning text within the boundary

Chapter 4

Although the text is now aligned vertically within its containing boundary, we'll still need to align it as a whole to the canvas container to ensure that it remains on screen at the same position and orientation, even if the **Game** window is resized and realigned. To do this, we'll use **Anchors**. To start, use the transform tool (*W*) to reposition the Text object to the top-right corner of the screen at the location where the **Score** should appear. The object will automatically move within a 2D plane as opposed to 3D space. As you move the Text object in the **Scene** viewport, check its appearance in the **Game** tab to ensure that it looks correct and appropriate. See *Figure 4.35*:

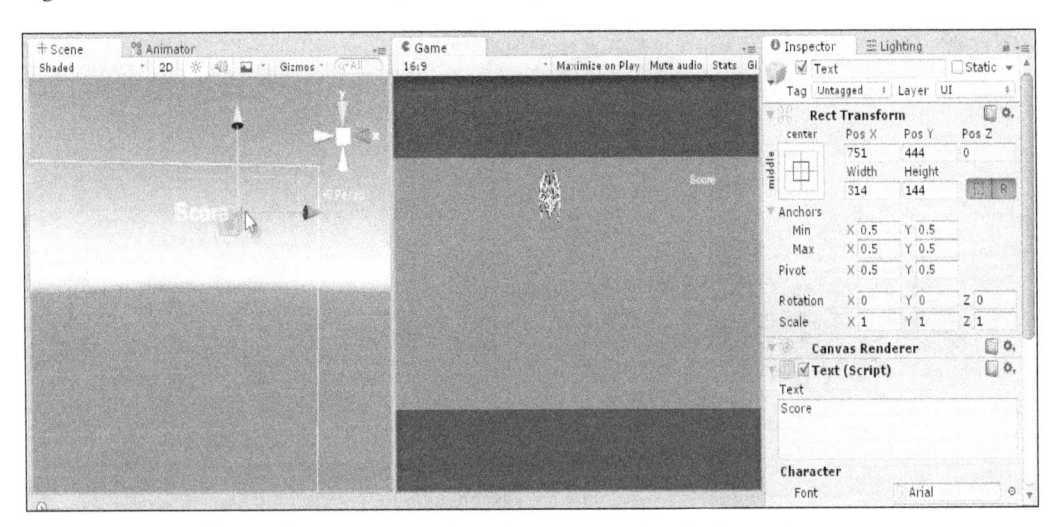

Figure 4.35: Positioning the Score text within the Game tab

To secure the position of the Text object on screen (preventing it from sliding or moving), even if the **Game** tab is resized by the user, we can set the object's anchor position to the top right corner of the screen. This ensures that the text is always positioned as a constant, proportional offset from its anchor. To do this, click on the **Anchor Presets** button in the **Rect Transform** component in the **Object Inspector**. When you do this, a preset menu appears from which you can choose a range of alignment locations. Each preset is graphically presented as a small diagram, including a red dot at the location of anchor alignment.

Select the top-right preset. See *Figure 4.36*:

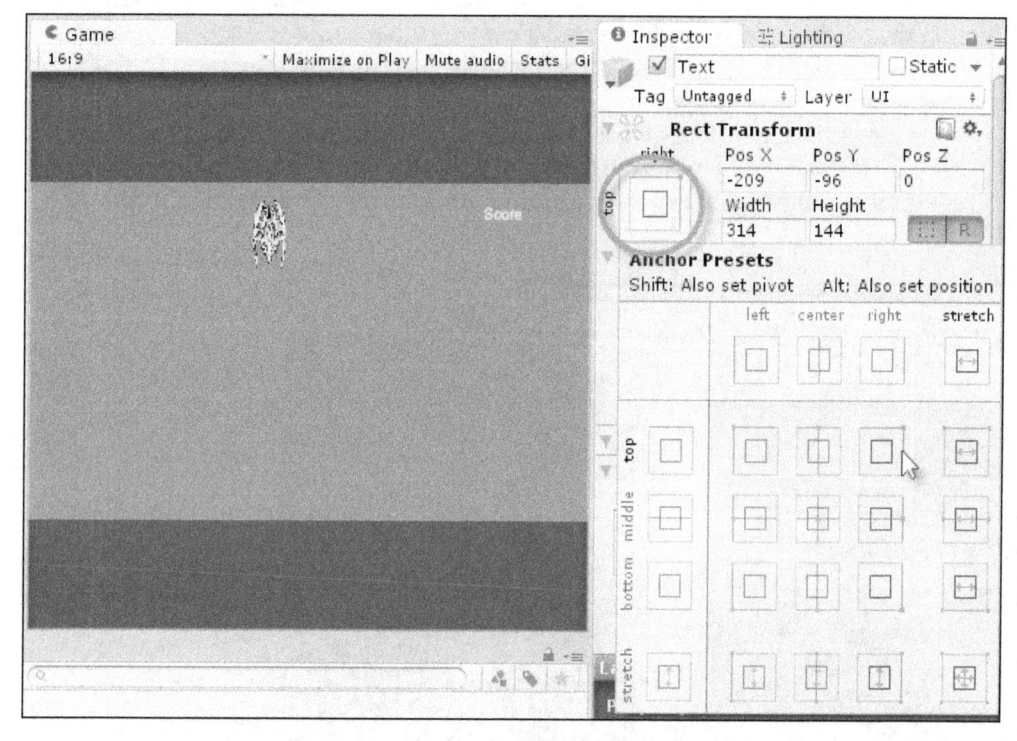

Figure 4.36: Aligning the Text object to the screen

Excellent work! The Text object is now created and ready to use. Of course, in play mode, the text remains unchanged and doesn't display a real score. That's because we need to add some code. However, overall, the Text object is in place and we can move on.

Working with scores – scripting with text

To display a score in the GUI, we'll first need score functionality, that is, code to create a score system. Essentially, the score functionality will be added to a general, overarching GameController class, responsible for all game-wide logic and features. The code for GameController and its score feature set is included in *Code Sample 4.4*, as follows. This file should be added to the Scripts folder of the project:

```
using UnityEngine;
using System.Collections;
using UnityEngine.UI;
```

```csharp
//------------------------------
public class GameController : MonoBehaviour
{
  //Game score
  public static int Score;

  //Prefix
  public string ScorePrefix = string.Empty;ic

  //Score text object
  public Text ScoreText = null;

  //Game over text
  public Text GameOverText = null;

  public static GameController ThisInstance = null;
  //------------------------------
  void Awake()
  {
    ThisInstance = this;
  }
  //------------------------------
  void Update()
  {
    //Update score text
    if(ScoreText!=null)
      ScoreText.text = ScorePrefix + Score.ToString();
  }
  //------------------------------
  public static void GameOver()
  {
    if(ThisInstance.GameOverText!=null)
    ThisInstance.GameOverText.gameObject.SetActive(true);
  }
  //------------------------------
}
```

Continuing the Space Shooter

Code Sample 4.4

The following points summarize the code sample:

- The `GameController` class uses the `UnityEngine.ui` namespace. This is important because it includes access to all the UI classes and objects in Unity. If you don't include this namespace in your source files, then you cannot use UI objects from that script.
- The `GameController` class features two text public members, namely, `ScoreText` and `GameOverText`. These refer to two text objects, both of which are optional insofar as the `GameController` code will work just fine, even if the members are null. `ScoreText` is a reference to a text GUI object to display score text, and `GameOverText` is to display any message when a game-over condition occurs.

To use the `GameController` code, create a new, empty object in the scene named `GameController`. Then, drag and drop the `GameController` script file to that object. Once added, drag and drop the `ScoreText` object to the **Score Text** field for `GameController` in the **Object Inspector**. See *Figure 4.37*. In the **Score Prefix** field, enter the text that should prefix the `Score` itself. The score, on its own, is simply a number (such as 1,000). The prefix allows you to add text to the front of this score, indicating to the player what the numbers mean:

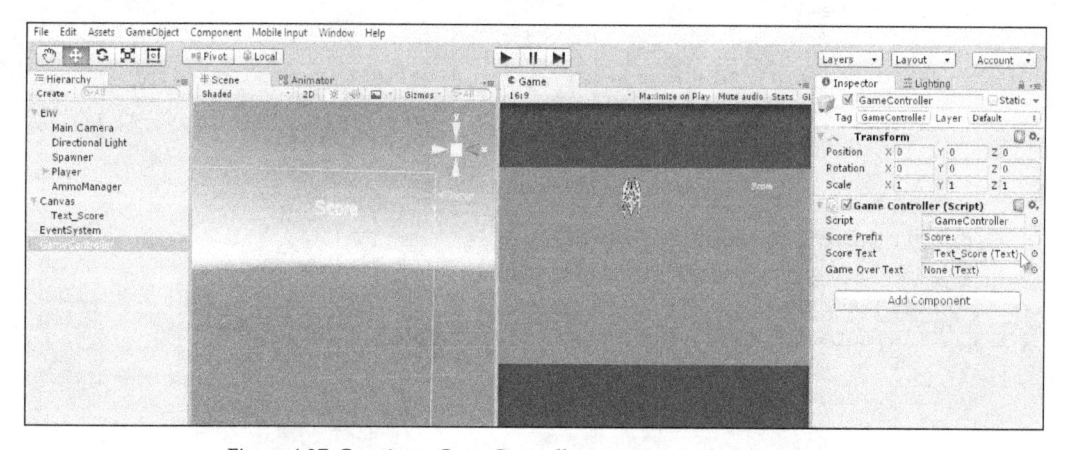

Figure 4.37: Creating a GameController to maintain the game score

Now, take the game for a test run and you'll see the score display at the top right corner of the `Game` tab using the GUI text object. This is fine, but the score always remains at 0 right now. This is because we have no code, yet, to increase the score. For our game, the score should increase when an `Enemy` object is destroyed. To achieve this, we'll create a new script file, `ScoreOnDestroy`. This is included in *Code Sample 4.5*, as follows:

```
using UnityEngine;
using System.Collections;
//-----------------------------
public class ScoreOnDestroy : MonoBehaviour
{
    //-----------------------------
    public int ScoreValue = 50;
    //-----------------------------
    void OnDestroy()
    {
       GameController.Score += ScoreValue;
    }
    //-----------------------------
}
//-----------------------------
```

The script should be attached to any object that assigns you points when it's destroyed, such as the enemies. The total number of points assigned is specified by `ScoreValue`. To attach the script to the enemy prefab, select the `Prefabs` in the **Project** panel, and from the **Object Inspector**, click on the **Add Component** button. Then type `ScoreOnDestroy` in the search field to add the component to the prefab. Once added, specify the total number of points to be allocated for destroying an enemy. For this game, a value of 50 points is assigned. See *Figure 4.38*:

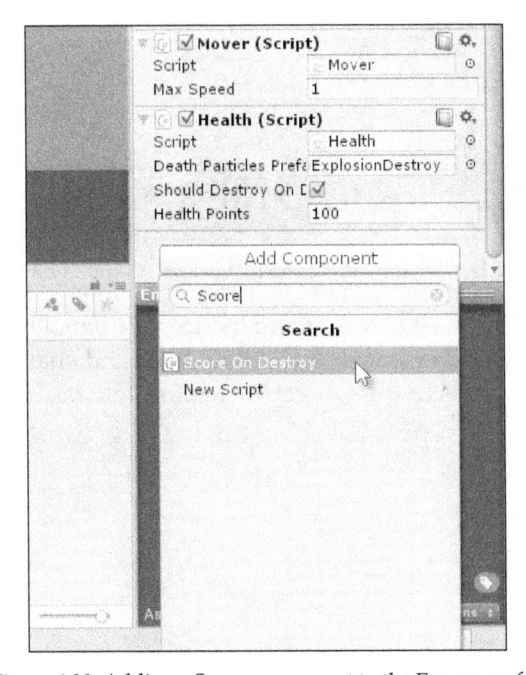

Figure 4.38: Adding a Score component to the Enemy prefab

Great work! You now have destroyable enemies that assign you points on destruction. This means that you can finally have an in-game score and could even extend gameplay to include high-score features and leaderboards. This also means that our game is almost finished and ready to build. Next, we'll add some final touches.

Polishing

In this section, we'll add the final touches to the game. First on the agenda is to fix the game background! Until now, the background has simply displayed the default background color associated with the game camera. However, as the game is set in space, we should display a space background. To do this, create a new **Quad** object in the **Scene** that'll display a space image. Navigate to **GameObject | 3D Object | Quad** from the menu. Then rotate the object and move it downward so that it displays a flat, vertically-aligned backdrop. You may need to scale the object to look correct. See *Figure 4.39*:

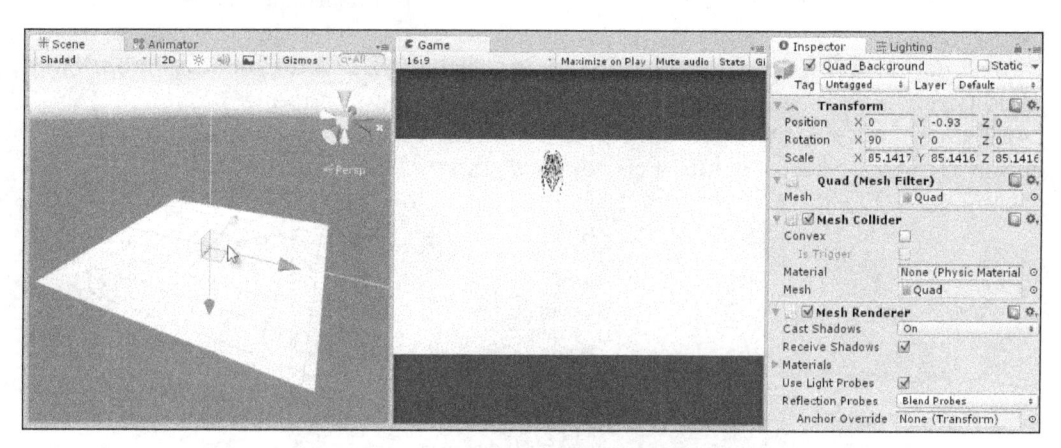

Figure 4.39: Creating a backdrop for the level and building a Quad

Now, drag and drop the space texture from the **Project** panel to **Quad** in the **Scene** to apply it as a material. Once assigned, select the **Quad** and change the **Tiling** settings from the material properties in the **Object Inspector**. Increase the **X** and **Y** tiling to 3. See *Figure 4.40*:

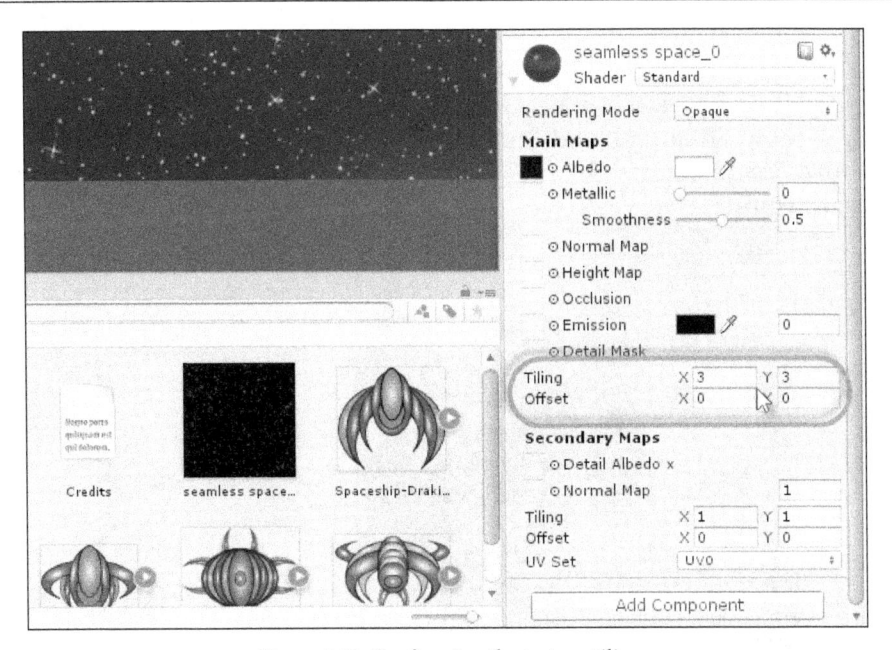

Figure 4.40: Configuring the texture tiling

If texture tiling seems broken for you, then be sure to check the **Texture Importing** settings. To do this, select the texture in the **Project** panel, and from the **Object Inspector**, ensure that **Texture Type** is set to **Texture** and the **Wrap Mode** is set to **Repeat**. See *Figure 4.41*:

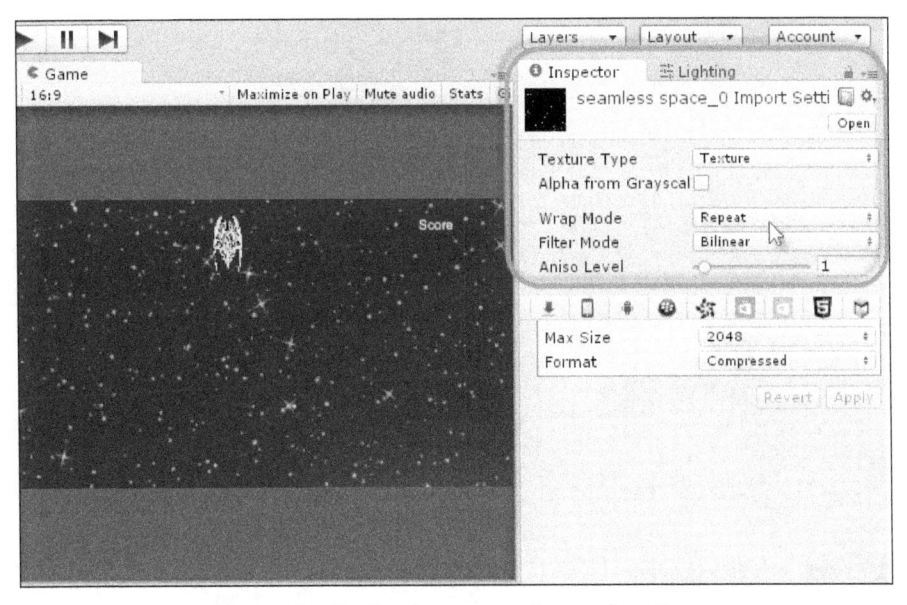

Figure 4.41: Configuring a texture for seamless tiling

Continuing the Space Shooter

Now the level has a suitable background. Let's add some background music, which will play on a loop. To do this, first select the music track in the **Project** panel in the `Audio` folder. When selected, make sure that the music **Load Type**, from the **Object Inspector**, is set to **Streaming** and **Preload Audio Data** is disabled. See *Figure 4.42*. This improves loading times as Unity will not need to load all music data to memory as the scene begins:

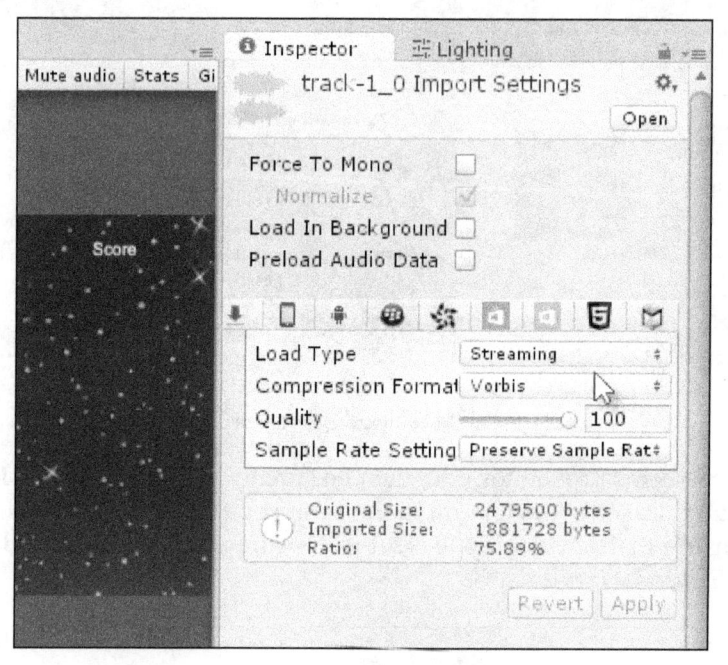

Figure 4.42: Configuring audio data ready for playback

Next, create a new, empty **GameObject** in the scene named `Music`, and then drag and drop the `Music` track from the **Project** panel to the `Music` object, adding it as an **Audio Source** component. **Audio Source** components play sound effects and music. See *Figure 4.43*:

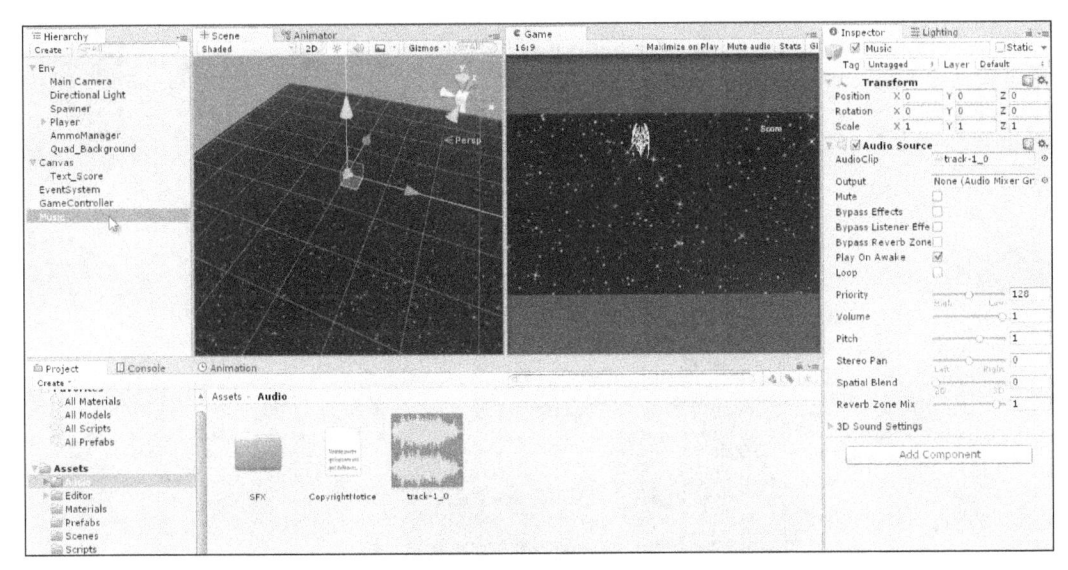

Figure 4.43: Creating a GameObject with an AudioSource component

From the **Audio Source** component in the **Object Inspector**, enable the **Play On Awake** and **Loop** checkboxes to ensure that the music is played from the level beginning and loops endlessly for as long as the game is running. The **Spatial Blend** field should be set to 0, meaning 2D. In short, 2D sounds have a consistent volume throughout the level regardless of the player's position.

This is because 2D sounds are not spatially located. 3D sounds, in contrast, are used for gunshots, footsteps, explosions, and other sounds that exist in 3D space and whose volume should change based on how close the player is standing to them when they play. See *Figure 4.44*:

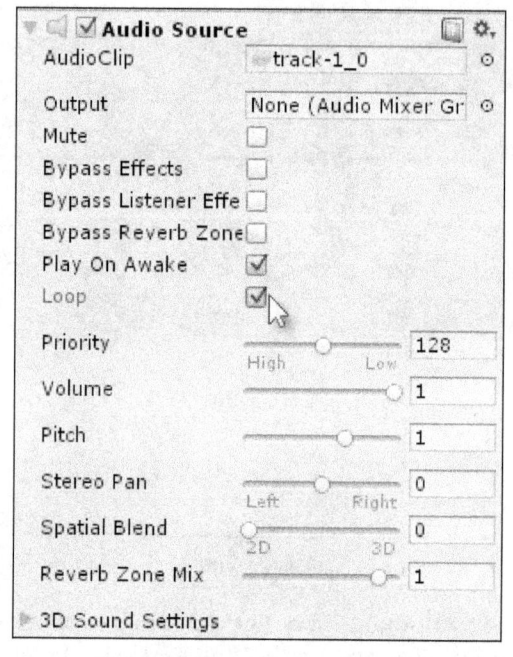

Figure 4.44: Looping a music track

Now, let's take the game for a test run! Click on the play button on the toolbar and test it out. If the music doesn't play, check that the **Mute Audio** button is not enabled from the **Game** tab. See *Figure 4.45*:

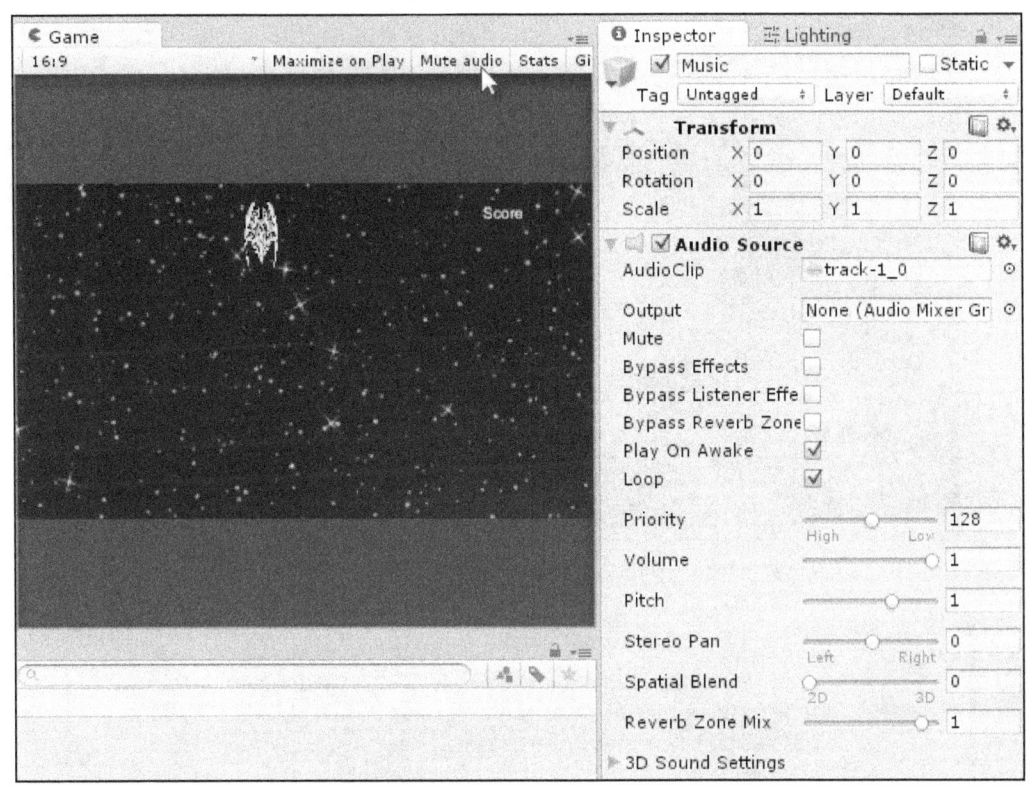

Figure 4.45: Playing a game – disabling Mute Audio, if necessary

Testing and diagnosis

With practically all games, you'll need to spend considerable time testing and debugging heavily to reduce bugs and errors as much as humanly possible. With this sample program, very little debugging and testing has been required by you, but that's not because the game is simple. It's because I've already prechecked and pretested most of the code and functionality before presenting the material to you in this book, ensuring that you get a smooth learning experience. For your own projects, however, you'll need to do lots of testing. One way to get started is using the **Stats** panel.

Continuing the Space Shooter

To open this, click on the **Stats** button on the **Game** tab. See *Figure 4.46*:

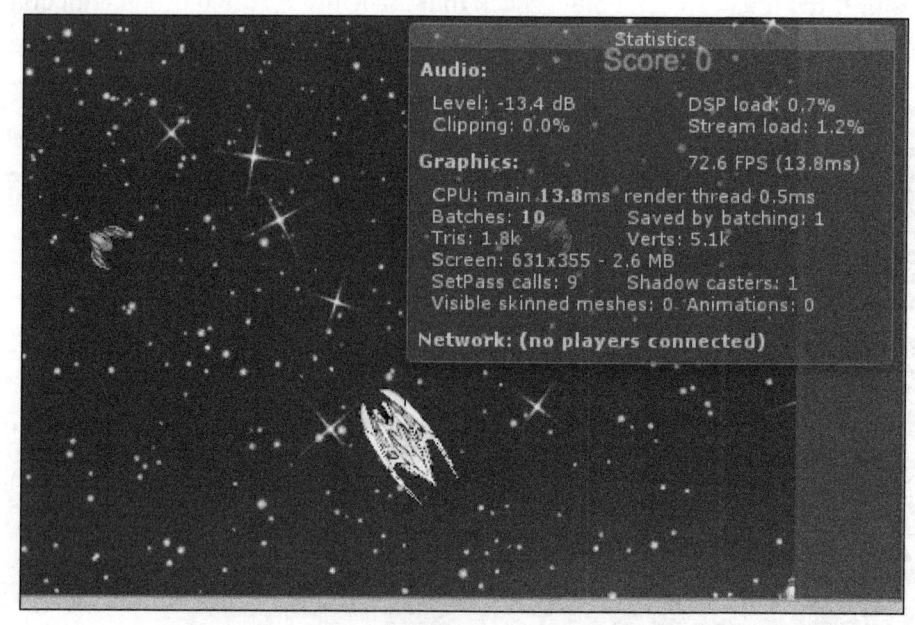

Figure 4.46: Viewing game performance information via the Stats panel

> More details on the **Stats** panel are included in *Chapter 2, Creating a Collection Game* of this book, and more information can be found online in the Unity documentation at http://docs.unity3d.com/Manual/RenderingStatistics.html.

Another debugging tool is the **Profiler**. This is useful when the **Stats** panel has already helped you identify a general problem, such as a low FPS, and you want to dig deeper to find where the problem might be located. More details on **Profiler** are included later in *Chapter 6, Continuing the 2D Adventure* but a short introduction is worth including here. To access the **Profiler** tool, select **Window | Profiler** from the application menu. This displays the **Profiler** window. See *Figure 4.47*:

Chapter 4

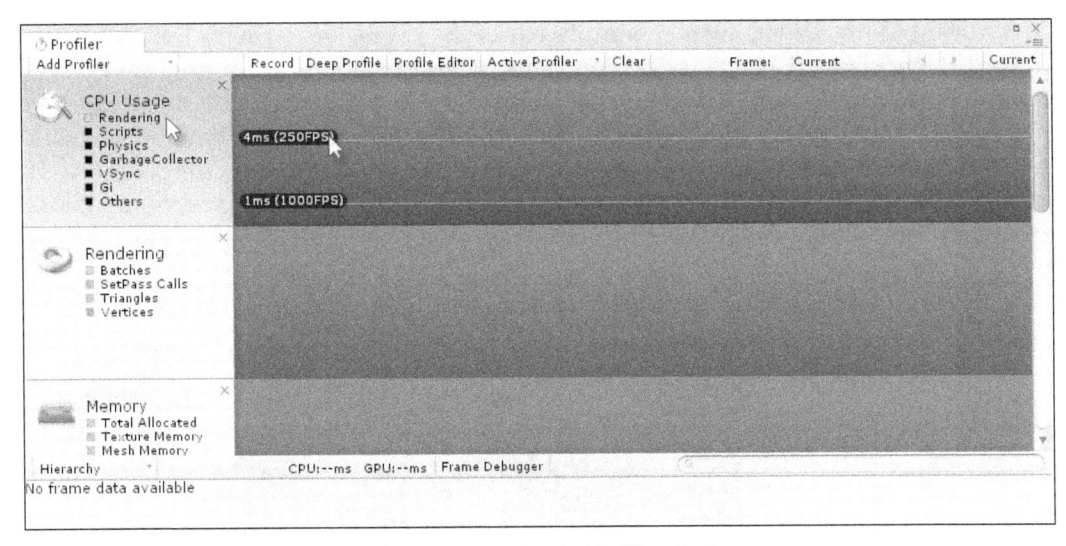

Figure 4.47: Accessing the Profiler window

With the **Profiler** window open, click on play on the toolbar to play test your game. When you do this, the **Profiler** window fills with color-coded performance data in a graph. See *Figure 4.48*. Green represents the performance of rendering (graphical) data. Reading and understanding the graph requires some experience, but as a general rule, watch out for mountains and peaks, that is, watch out for sharp fluctuations in the graph (sharp ups and downs) as this could indicate a problem, especially when it roughly coincides with frame rate drops:

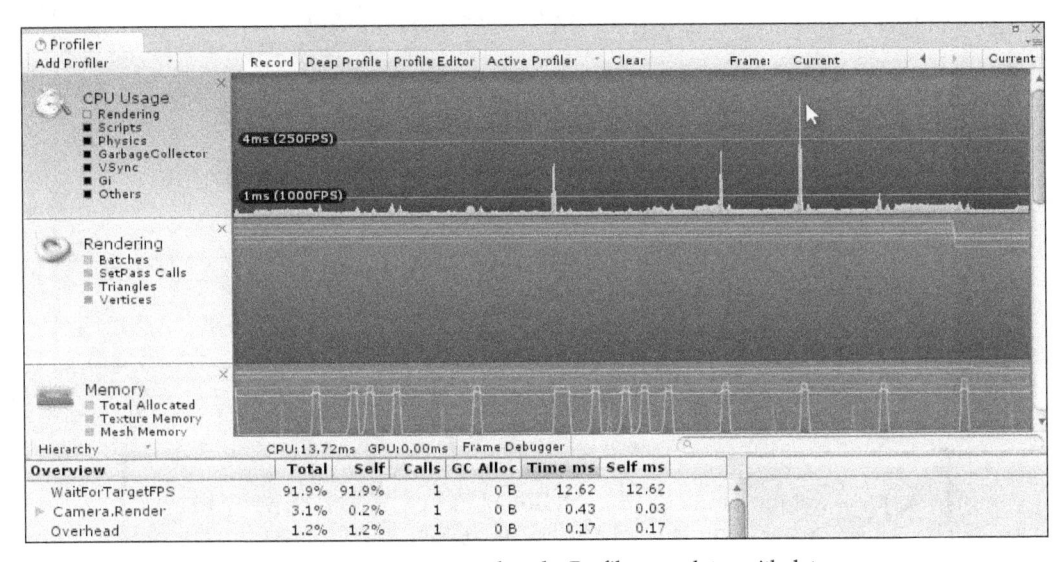

Figure 4.48: During gameplay, the Profiler populates with data

[221]

Continuing the Space Shooter

If you want to investigate further, simply pause the game, and then click in the graph. The horizontal axis (X axis) represents the most recent frames, and the vertical axis represents workload. When you click in the graph, a line marker is added to indicate the frame under investigation. Beneath the graph, a list of all main processes for that frame are presented, typically ordered from top to bottom by the heaviness of their workload and proportion of frame time for which the process accounted. Heavier processes are listed at the top. See *Figure 4.49*:

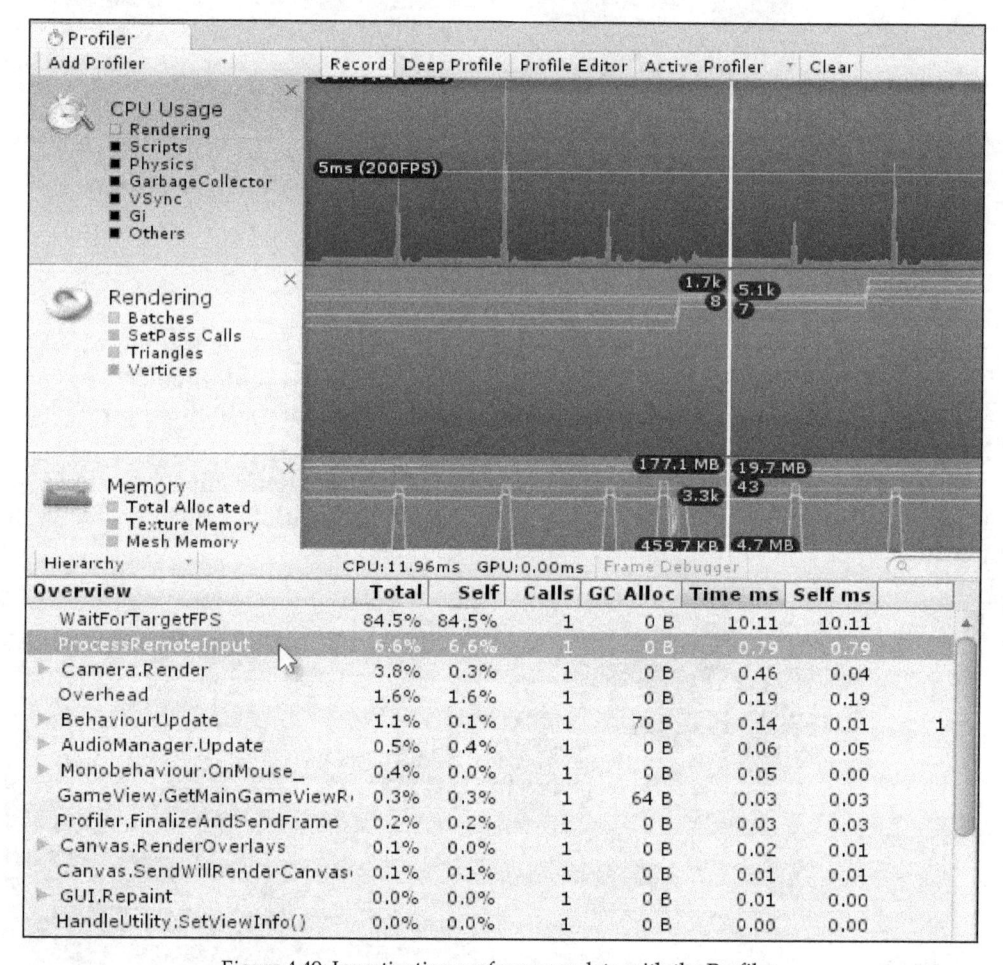

Figure 4.49: Investigating performance data with the Profiler

> More information on the **Profiler** can be found in the online Unity documentation at http://docs.unity3d.com/Manual/Profiler.html.

Building

Now, finally, we're ready to build our game to a standalone form ready to send o ff to friends, family, and testers! The process to do this is the same as detailed in *Chapter 2, Creating a Collection Game*, to build the coin collection game. From the application menu, choose **File | Build Settings**. From the build dialog, add our level to the level list by simply clicking on the **Add Current** button. Otherwise, drag and drop the level from the **Project** panel to the level list. See *Figure 4.50*:

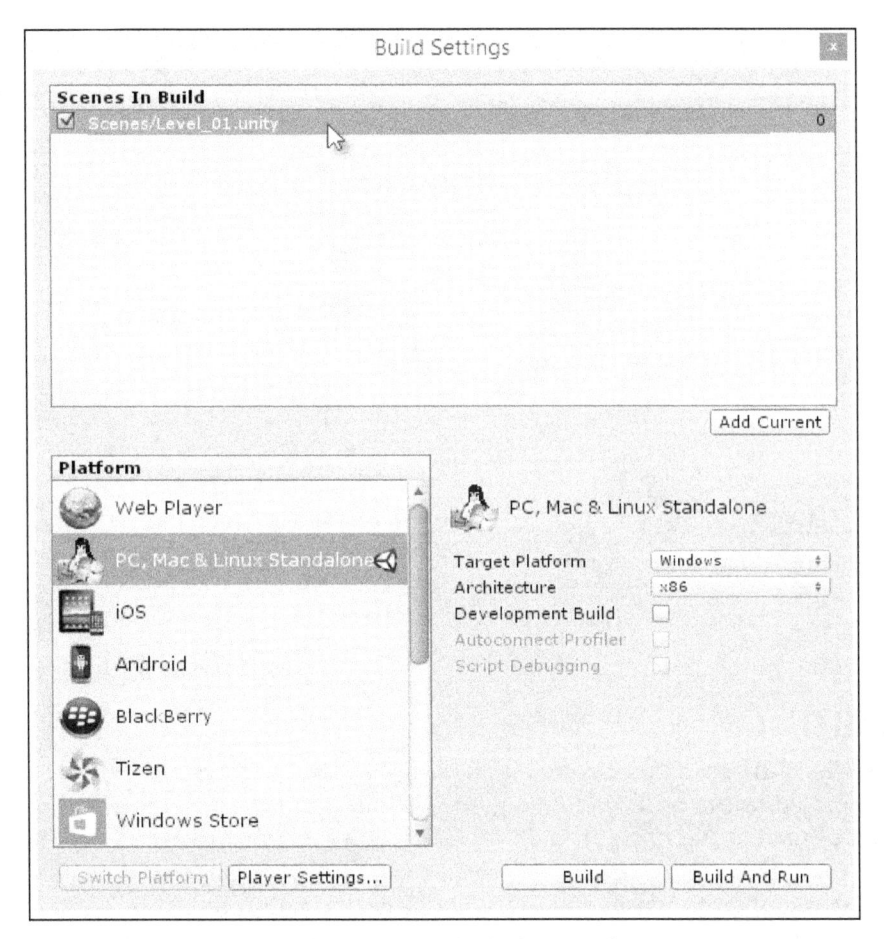

Figure 4.50: Preparing to build the space shooter

For this game, the target platform will be Windows. Consequently, select the **PC, Mac & Linux Standalone** option from the **Platform** list, if it's not selected already. If the **Switch Platform** button (at the bottom-left) is not disabled, then you will need to press this button, confirming to Unity that it should build for the selected platform as opposed to a different platform.

Then, click on the **Build And Run** button. On clicking this, Unity prompts you to select a folder on your computer where the built file will be output and saved. Once generated, double-click the executable to run it and test. See *Figure 4.51*:

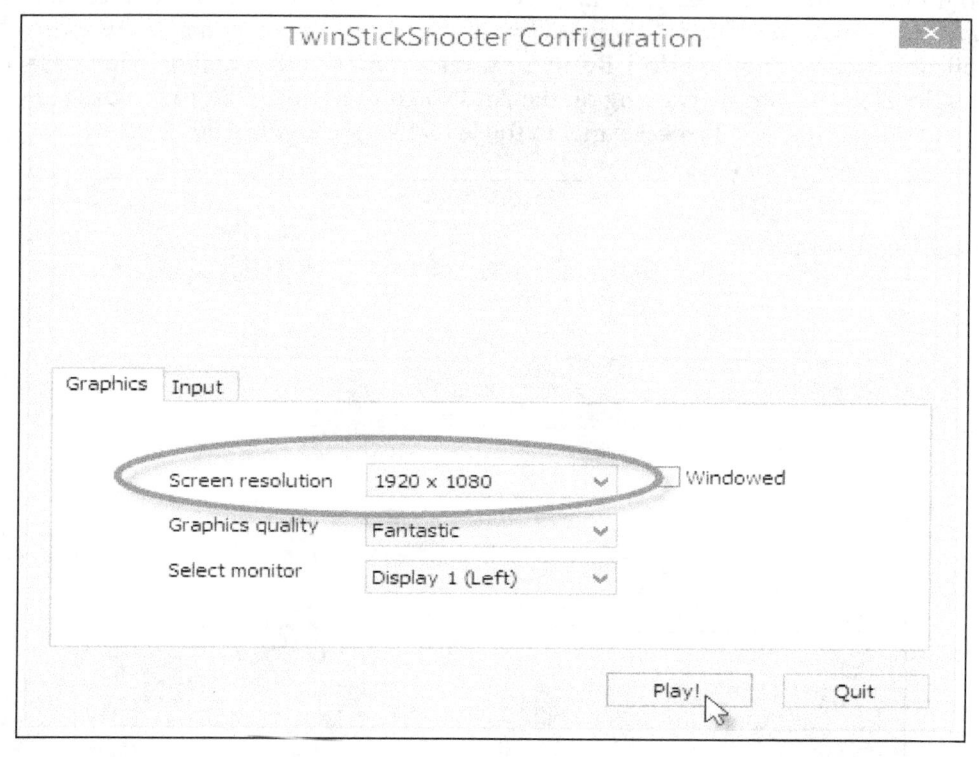

Figure 4.51: Test running the game as a standard Windows executable

Summary

Great work! We're really on a roll now, having completed two solid Unity projects. The first project was a coin collection game and the second was a twin-stick shooter. Both are, ultimately, simple games in that they don't rely on advanced mechanics or display sophisticated features. However, even very sophisticated games, when boiled down to their fundamental ingredients, can be found to rest on a similar foundation of essential concepts such as the ones that we've covered so far. That's why our projects are so critical to understanding Unity in a deep way. Next, we'll move on to creating a more 2D-focused game, considering interfaces, sprites, and physics, and lots more!

Test your knowledge

Q1. Static Variables are...

- A. Hidden variables for static objects
- B. Shared variables across all instances of a class
- C. Protected variables
- D. Constants

Q2. The profiler is useful for...

- A. Pausing gameplay
- B. Identifying performance issues
- C. Removing Objects
- D. Checking audio levels

Q3. UI Objects are useful for...

- A. Creating interface elements
- B. Making animations
- C. Sorting objects by name
- D. Editing mesh objects

Q4. The Collision Matrix lets you

- A. Prevent groups of objects colliding
- B. Make objects collide
- C. Removes all collisions
- D. Activates low quality collisions

Further Reading

For more information take look at the following links:

- `https://unity3d.com/learn/tutorials/s/scripting`
- `https://www.packtpub.com/game-development/unity-5-scripting-and-gameplay-mechanics-video`
- `https://www.packtpub.com/game-development/mastering-unity-5x-scripting`

5
Creating a 2D Adventure Game

In this chapter, we will begin a completely new project; specifically, a 2D adventure game in which the player controls an alien character, exploring and navigating a dangerous world complete with quests and interactive elements. This project will incorporate elements and ideas from previous chapters, as well as focus on new techniques, such as Complex Collisions, 2D Physics, Singletons and Statics, and more. In short, we will cover the following topics:

- 2D characters and player movement
- Assembling complex and multipart characters
- Level design
- 2D Physics and collision detection

> The starting project and assets can be found in the book companion files in the Chapter05/Start folder. You can start here and follow along with this chapter if you don't have your own project already.

A 2D Adventure – getting started

Adventure games require the player to use their cunning, dexterity, mental sharpness, and acumen to make progress. Such games feature dangerous obstacles, challenging missions, and character interaction, as opposed to *all-out* action like many first-person shooter games. Our adventure game will be no exception. See *Figure 5.1* for a glimpse of the game that we'll create. In this game, the player moves around using the keyboard arrows or *W*, *A*, *S*, *D* keys. Furthermore, they can jump with the spacebar and interact with characters simply by approaching them. During the game, the player will be tasked with a mission from an NPC character to collect an ancient gem hidden somewhere within a level. The player must then navigate dangerous obstacles in search of the gem, and then finally collect it before returning to the NPC, completing the game.

Figure 5.1: The 2D adventure game to create

To get started with creating the adventure, create a completely new and empty Unity project, and then import the `Particles`, `Effects`, `Characters`, `2D`, `ParticleSystems`, and `CrossPlatformInput` packages. You can import these from the **Project Creation Wizard** or from the application menu via the **Assets | Import Packages** option. See *Figure 5.2*. Details on how to import standard assets are included in *Chapter 1*, *Unity Fundamentals*.

Chapter 5

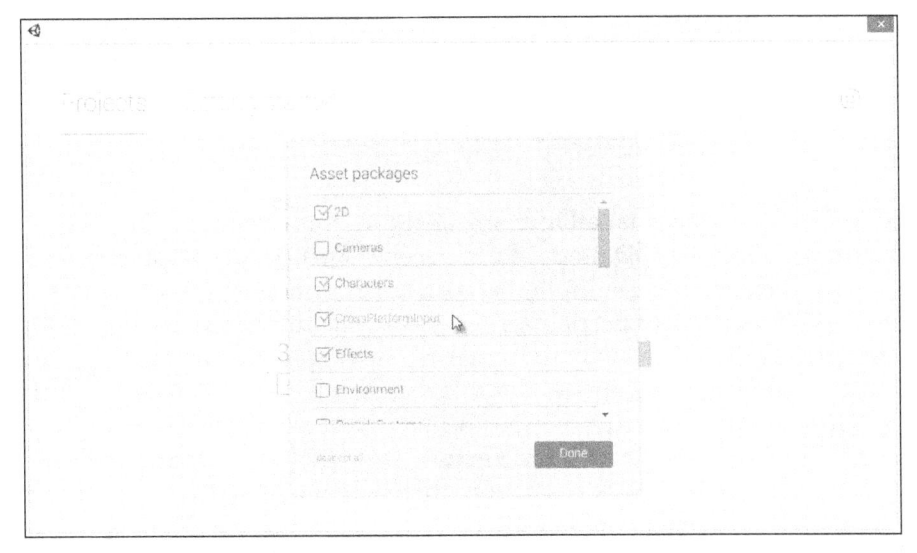

Figure 5.2: Importing packages to a new project from the Project Creation screen

Importing assets

Starting from an empty project created in the previous section, let's now import the texture assets we'll be using, both for the player character and environment. The assets to import are included in the book companion files in the `Chapter05/Assets` folder. From here, select all textures together in Windows Explorer or Mac Finder, and drag and drop them to the Unity Project panel in a designated `Textures` folder. (Create one if you haven't already!). This imports all relevant textures to the active Project. See *Figure 5.3*:

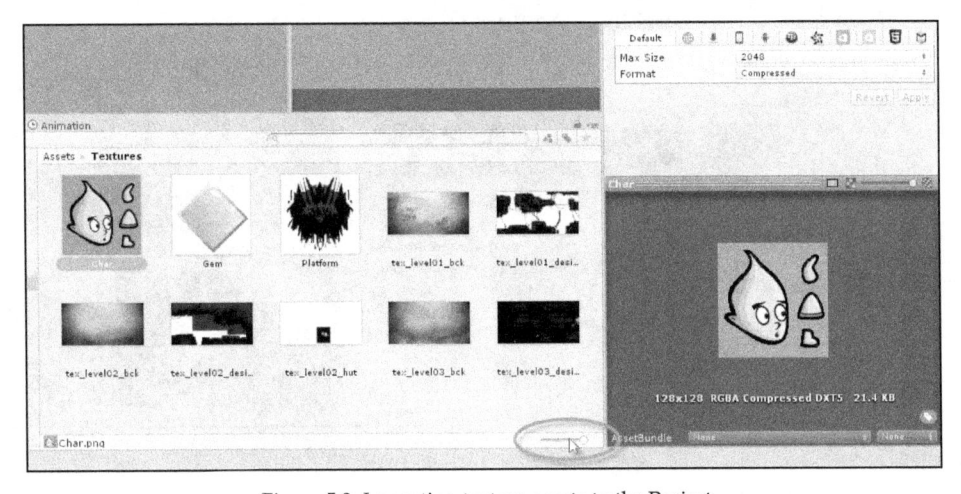

Figure 5.3: Importing texture assets to the Project

[229]

Creating a 2D Adventure Game

> Remember that you can always use the Thumbnail Size Slider (at the bottom right corner of the Project panel) to adjust the size of thumbnail previews in order to get an easier view of your texture assets.

By default, Unity assumes that all imported textures will eventually be used as regular textures applied to 3D models in the scene, such as cubes, spheres, and meshes. In most cases, this assumption is correct because most games are 3D. However, for 2D games like the one we're making, the settings should be different. In our case, objects don't recede in the distance, moving further away, but just remain at a constant offset from the camera. For this reason, we must adjust some crucial properties for all imported textures. Specifically, select all imported textures, and, from the **Object Inspector**, change the **Texture Type** field from **Texture** to **Sprite 2D and UI**. Then, remove the check mark from the **Generate Mip Maps** box. Then, click on the **Apply** button. When you do this, Unity flags the assets as having a *2D usage* internally. It allows transparent backgrounds to be applied where applicable (such as for PNG sprites) and also has important performance implications for graphics rendering, as we'll see. See *Figure 5.4*:

Figure 5.4: Configuring imported textures

[230]

Now that we've imported all essential textures for the project, let's configure our main scene, game camera, and target resolution. Switch to the **Game** tab and set the resolution to **1024 x 600**; which works well across many devices. To do this, click on the **Free Aspect** button from the **Game** tab toolbar and pick **1024 x 600** from the drop-down menu, if it appears as an option. If not, click on the **+** button from the bottom of the list to add the new resolution. See *Figure 5.5*:

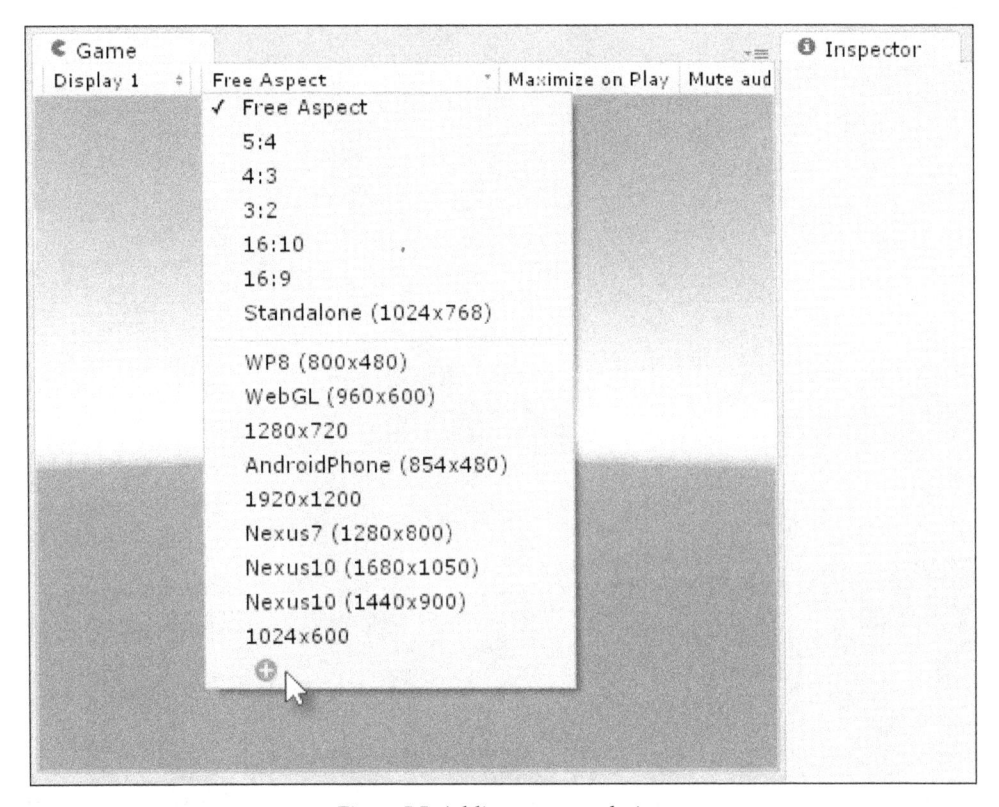

Figure 5.5: Adding game resolutions

Creating a 2D Adventure Game

To add a new resolution, enter a custom name in the **Name** field, select **Fixed Resolution** from the **Type** drop-down, and then type your resolution dimensions in the **Width & Height** fields. Once completed, click on **OK**. Your target resolution should then be added as a selectable option from the **Game** tab. See *Figure 5.6*:

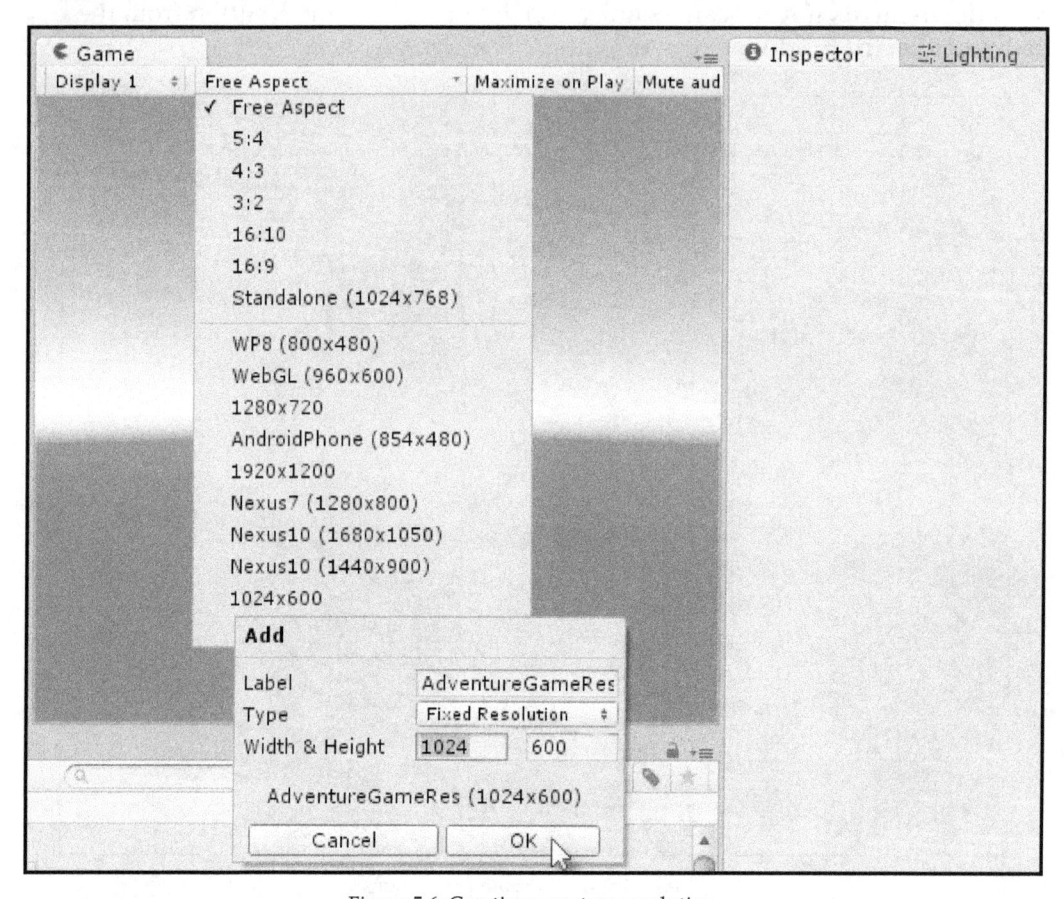

Figure 5.6: Creating a custom resolution

Next, we'll configure the scene camera for a 2D setup so that our textures, when added as sprites, will display onscreen at a 1:1 ratio, texel for pixel. To achieve this, select the **MainCamera** in the scene, either by clicking on it in the **Scene viewport** or selecting it in the **Scene Hierarchy**. Then, from the **Object Inspector**, change **Projection** to **Orthographic**. This ensures that the camera displays objects in true 2D with perspective and foreshortening effects removed. Then, change the camera Size to 3. The formula for this field is *Screen Height / 2 / Pixel to World*. In this case, the *Screen Height* is *600*. Thus, *600 / 2 = 300*. Then, *300 / 100 = 3. 100* refers to the pixel to world ratio applied to sprite textures; this details how many pixels in the texture will be mapped to a square meter in the world. A value of 1 means *1 pixel = 1 meter*. This value can be viewed and changed by selecting a sprite in the **Project** panel and changing the **Pixel to World ratio** field in the **Object Inspector**. See *Figure 5.7*:

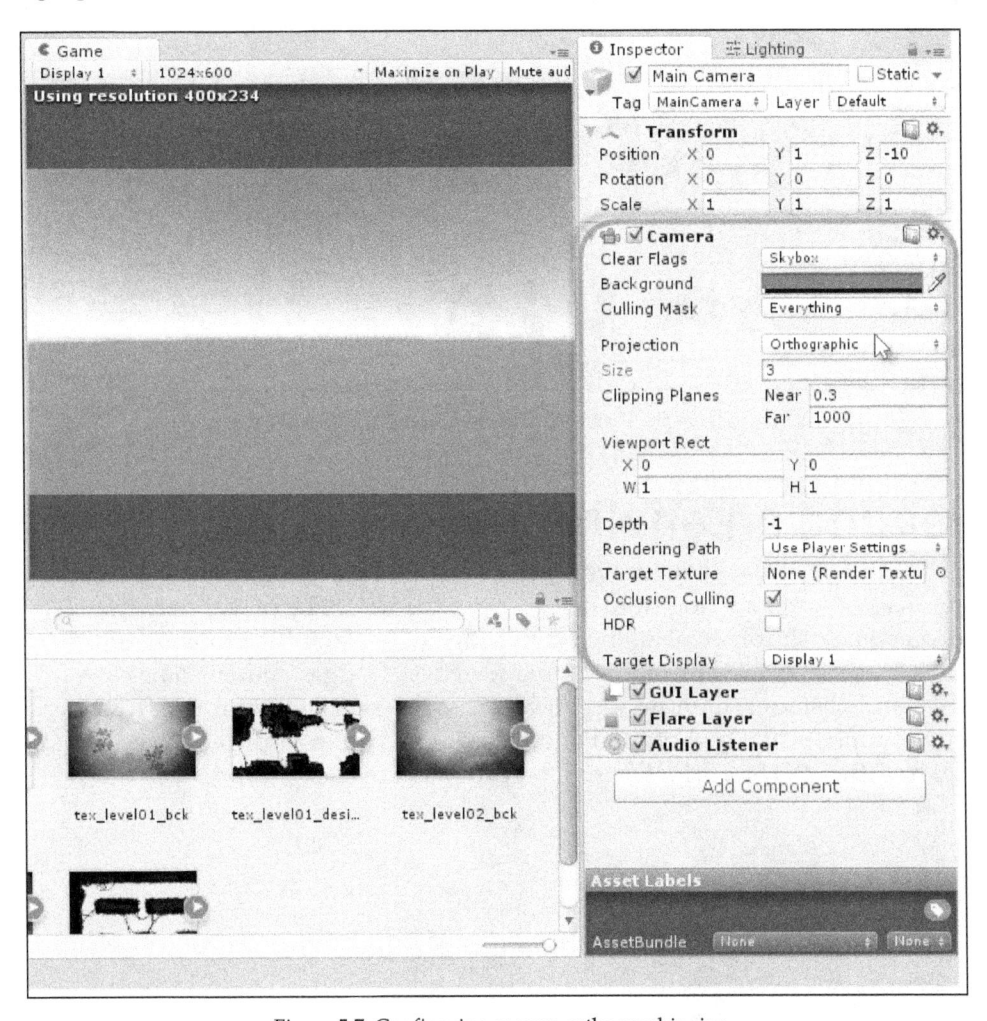

Figure 5.7: Configuring camera orthographic size

Creating a 2D Adventure Game

To test the camera and scene settings, simply drag and drop a background texture from the **Project** panel to the scene. The **Background** textures are sized at exactly 1024 x 600 to fit the scene background. Therefore, when added to a scene and when the camera is configured correctly, the background textures should fill the screen. See *Figure 5.8*:

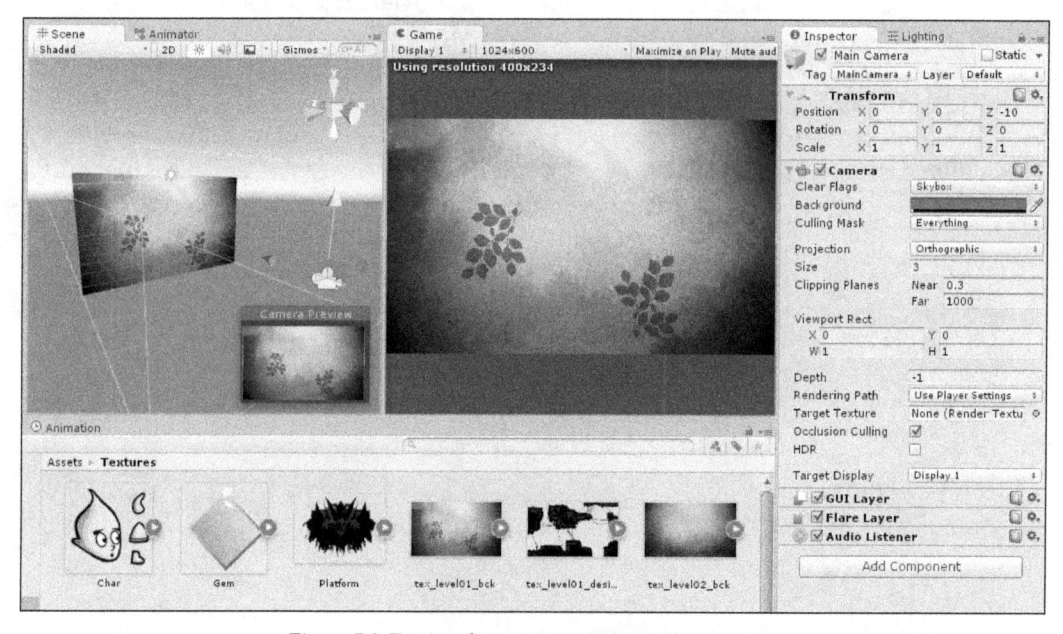

Figure 5.8: Testing the camera settings with a texture

Creating an environment – getting started

Our adventure game will feature three separate but connected scenes, which the player may explore, moving from one scene to the next. The player may travel between scenes, simply by walking off the edge of one and then moving into the next. Each scene consists primarily of platforms and ledges and, in some cases, dangers and obstacles. In terms of graphical assets, each scene is made from two textures or sprites: the background and foreground. An example for Scene 1 is shown in *Figures 5.9* and *Figure 5.10*. *Figure 5.9* represents the background scene:

Figure 5.9: Scene background

and *Figure 5.10* represents the foreground, which includes a complete layout of all the platforms and ledges that the player must traverse:

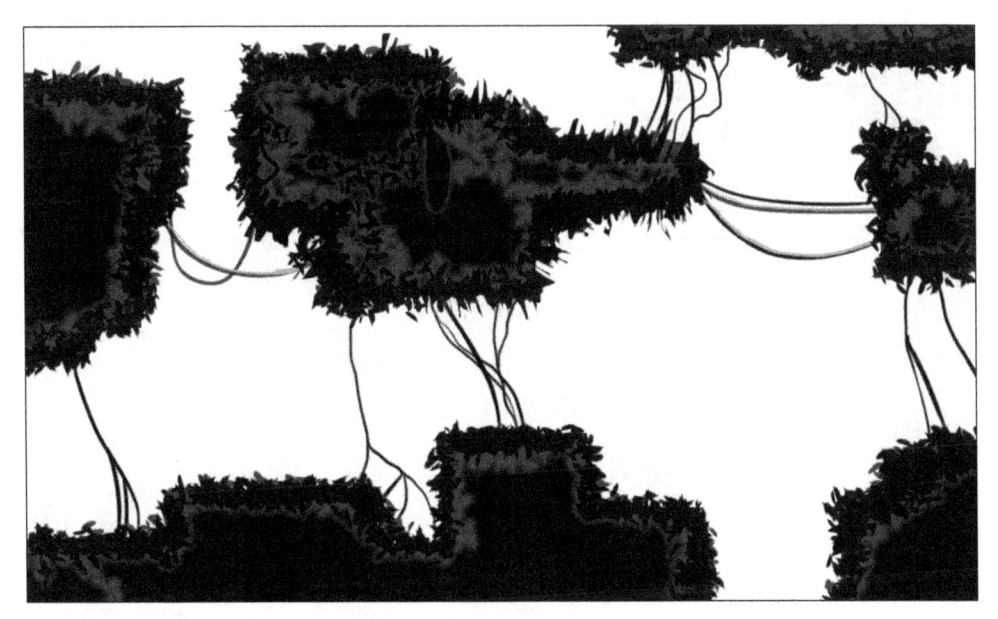

Figure 5.10: Scene foreground

Creating a 2D Adventure Game

These files are included in the book companion files in the `Chapter05/Assets` folder

Let's create the first level now, based on the sprites in *Figure 5.9* and *Figure 5.10*. To do this, use the existing empty scene, or create a new scene, ensuring that the scene camera is configured to display textures at their native size. Then, drag and drop both the background and foreground sprites from the **Project** panel to the scene. Both will be added to the scene as separate sprite objects. Then, position them both to the World Origin at (0,0,0). See *Figure 5.11*:

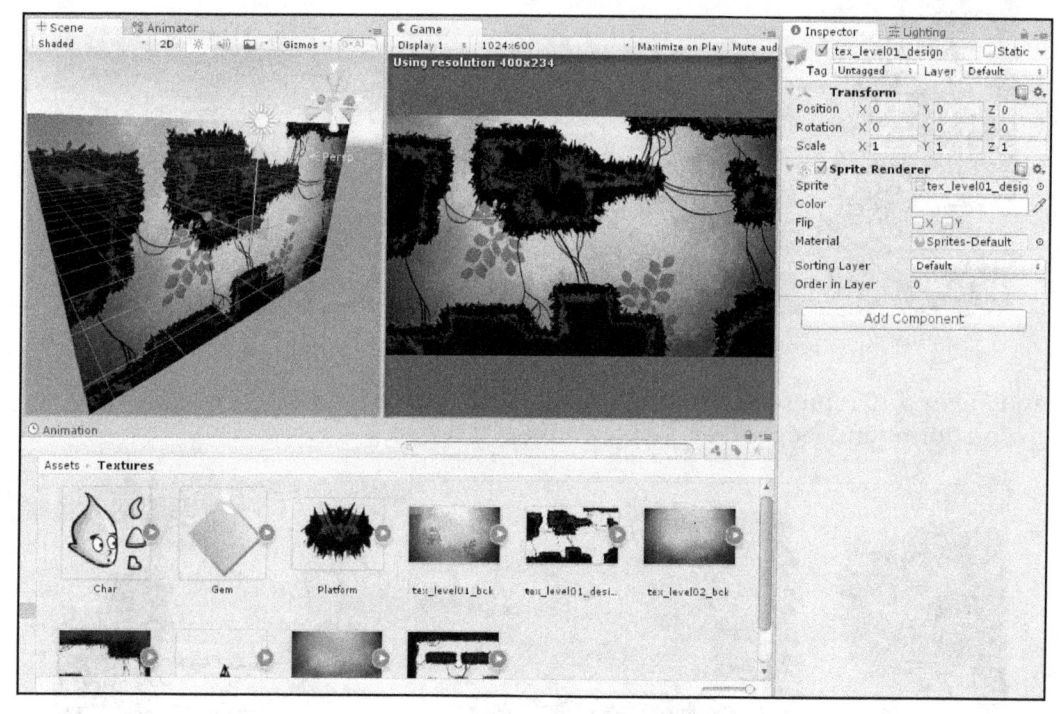

Figure 5.11: Adding a scene background and foreground

> If you drag and drop both the background and foreground textures together as one selection from the Project panel to the scene, Unity may ask you to create an Animation when you release your mouse. In such cases, Unity assumes that you want to create an animated sprite in which each selected texture becomes a frame of animation played in a sequence. You don't want to do this; instead, drag and drop each sprite to a separate Hierarchy panel, allowing both the foreground and background to be seen at the same time.

Both sprite objects are now added to the scene at the same world position (0,0,0). The question arises now as to which sprite Unity should display on top, given that both sprites overlap one another. Left as it is right now, there is a conflict and ambiguity about depth order, and we cannot rely on Unity consistently showing the correct sprite on top. We can solve this problem with two methods: one is to move the sprite forward in the Z axis, closer to the Orthographic camera; and the other is to change its **Order** setting from the **Object Inspector**. High values for **Order** result in the sprite appearing atop lower-order sprites. Here, I'll use both methods and that's fine too! See *Figure 5.12*. Note, however, that **Order** always takes precedence over **Position**. This means that higher-order objects will always appear on top of lower-order objects, even if higher-order objects are positioned behind lower-order objects.

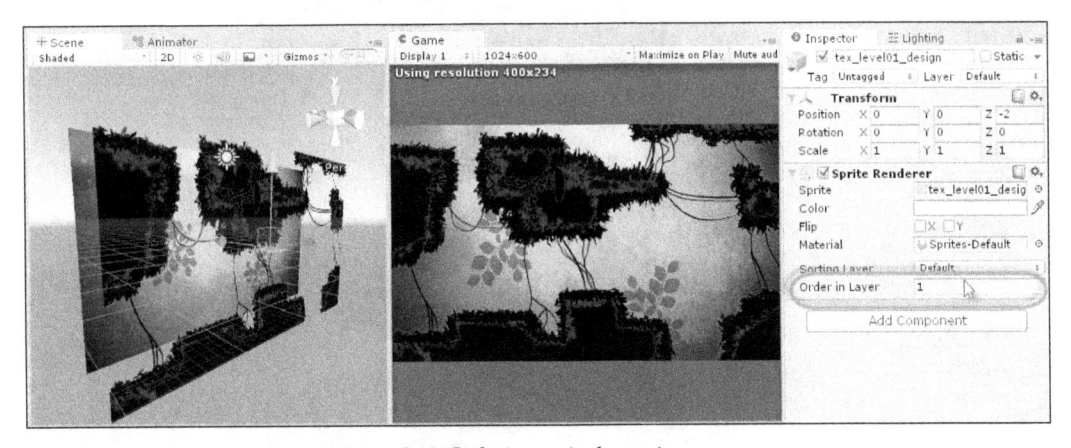

Figure 5.12: Ordering sprite layers in a scene

[237]

Creating a 2D Adventure Game

Before moving further, let's get organized in terms of scene hierarchy to prevent overcomplication and confusion happening later. Select each environment object and name them appropriately. I named the background `scene_background` and the foreground `scene_foreground`. Having done this, create a new, empty **GameObject** named `Env` (for Environment), which will be the ultimate parent or ancestor of all static (non-movable) objects in the environment. This lets us group together all related objects easily. To do this, choose **GameObject | Create Empty** from the application menu, position the created empty object to the world origin, and drag and drop both the background and foreground objects as its children. See *Figure 5.13*:

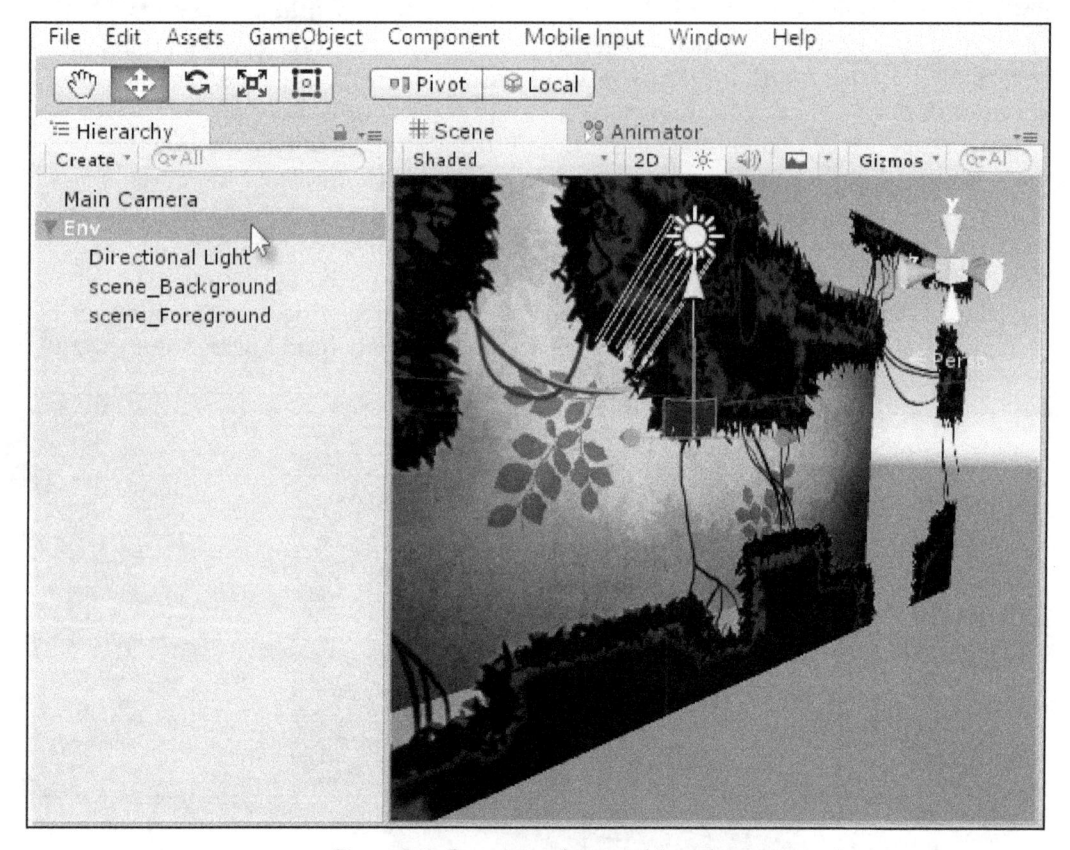

Figure 5.13: Organizing the scene hierarchy

By switching to the **Game** tab, we can get an early preview of the level as it will appear to the gamer in terms of mood and emotional resonance. This feel can be enhanced further by adding some Camera Post-process Effects with the post-processing stack. These refer to pixel-based effects that can be applied to the camera in order to enhance the atmosphere of the final, rendered image on each frame. The **Image Effects** can be downloaded and imported from the Unity Asset Store (just search for Post-Processing Stack). Once imported, you can add Image Effects to the selected camera using a Post-Processing Profile. To do this, right-click in the **Project Panel**, and select **Create | Post-Processing Profile** to generate a new asset for saving all post-processing data.

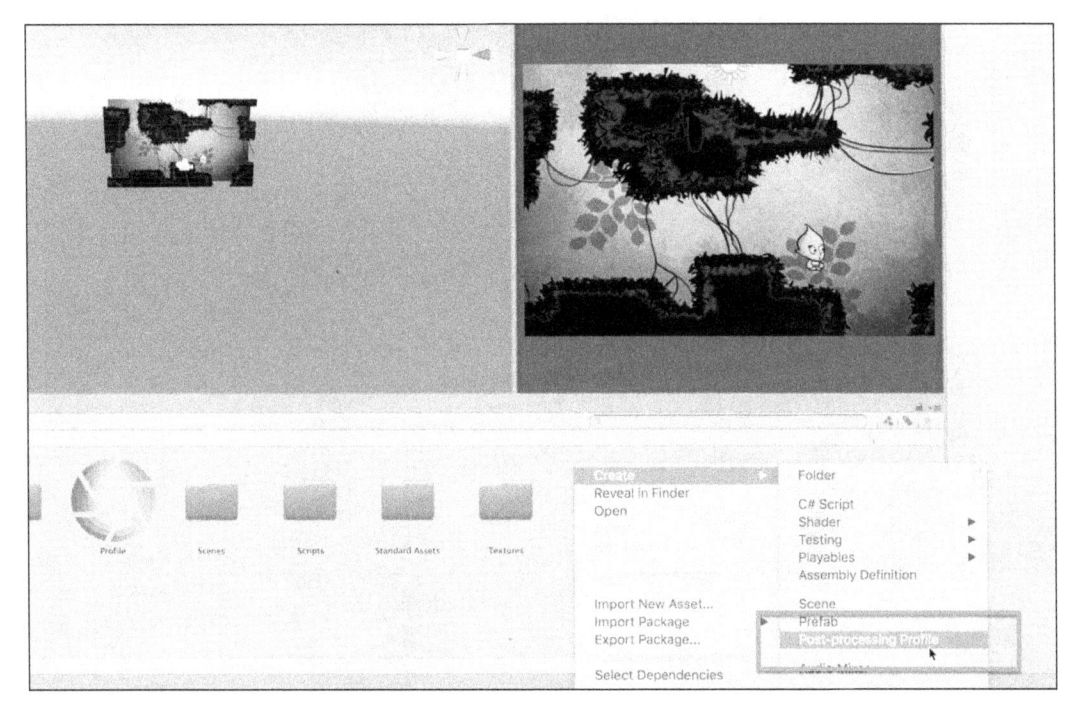

See *Figure 5.14*:

Figure 5.14: Adding Image Effects to the selected camera

Creating a 2D Adventure Game

Next, let's create a new Post-Process Volume in the scene to define a volume inside which the effect will apply whenever the camera enters. To do this, choose **GameObject |3D Object | Post-Process Volume** from the main menu to create a new post-process volume object in the scene. Then, use the Size field of the Box Collider to enclose the entire scene, as we want the effects to apply throughout the game. See *Figure 5.15*.

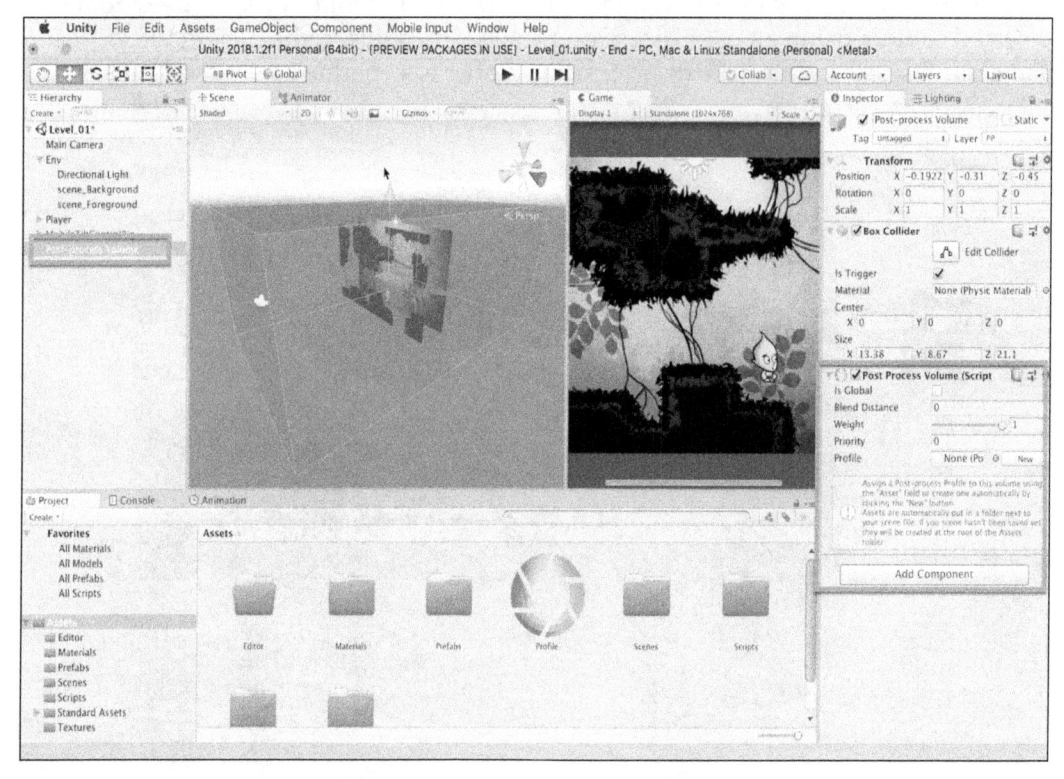

Figure 5.15: Defining a post-process volume

Be sure to drag and drop the Post-Processing Profile from the project panel into the Profile slot of the Post-Processing Volume component. This associates the profile, and its effects, with the volume. Next, you'll need to add a Post-Processing Layer component to the main camera for the effects to work as intended. To do this, select the camera, and choose **Component | Rendering | Post-Process Layer** from the application menu. Once added, you'll need to define post-process effects using the profile. I'll configure two: Bloom and Grain. To add these; just select the profile asset in the Project Panel, and then choose Add. Add both Bloom and Grain: their settings are shown in *Figure 5.16*:

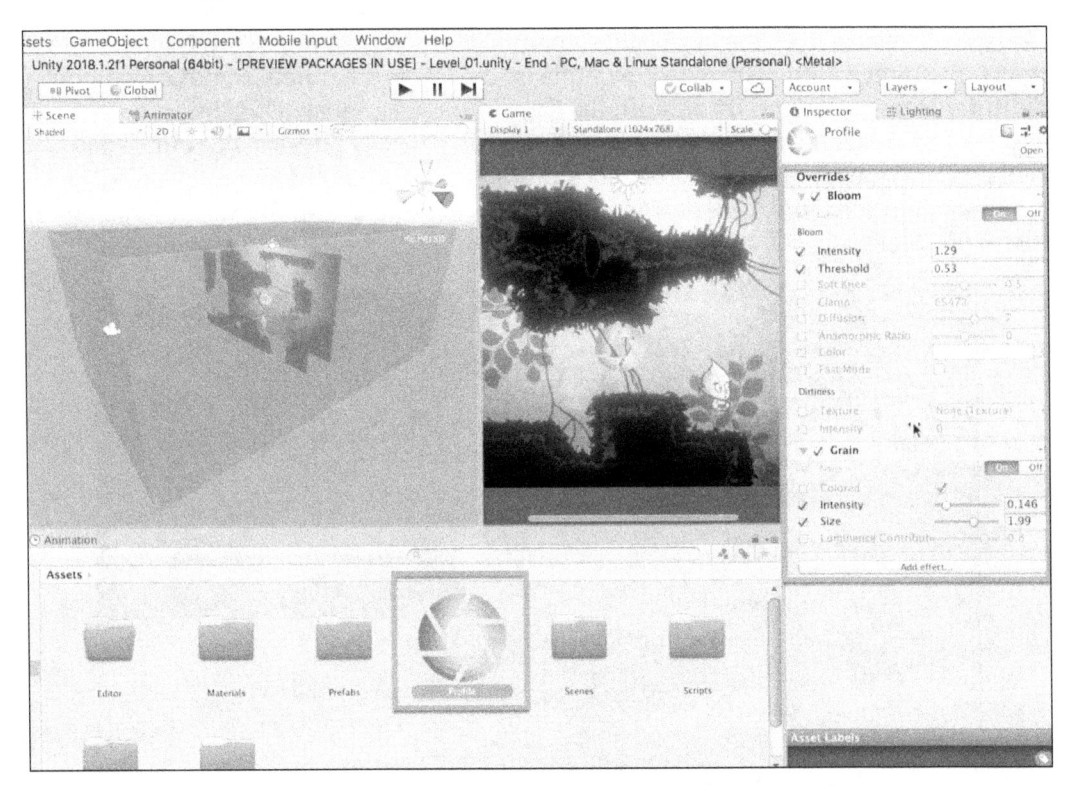

Figure 5.16: Image Effects applied to the game camera

Good work. The scene so far features a background and foreground taken from texture files and enhancing special effects using the Post-Processing Stack assets package. This is a great start, but there's still much to do so let's move on!

Creating a 2D Adventure Game

Environment Physics

The main problem with our level as it stands is that it lacks interactivity. Specifically, if we dragged and dropped a player object to the level and pressed play on the toolbar, the player would drop through the floor and walls because the foreground texture isn't recognized by Unity as a solid object. It's just a texture and exists only in appearance and not in substance. In this section, we'll correct this using Physics and Colliders. To get started, we'll create a temporary player object (not the final version but just a temporary *White Box* version used only for testing purposes). To create this, generate a capsule object in the scene by navigating to **GameObject | 3D Object | Capsule** from the application menu. Set the *Z* position of the transform to match the foreground texture (for me, this is -2). Once generated, remove **Capsule Collider** from the object. By default, the Capsule is assigned a 3D collider (such as the **Capsule Collider**), which is useful primarily for 3D physics, but our game will be 2D. To remove the Collider, click on the Cog icon on the **Capsule Collider** component in the **Object Inspector** and choose **Remove Component** from the menu. See *Figure 5.17*:

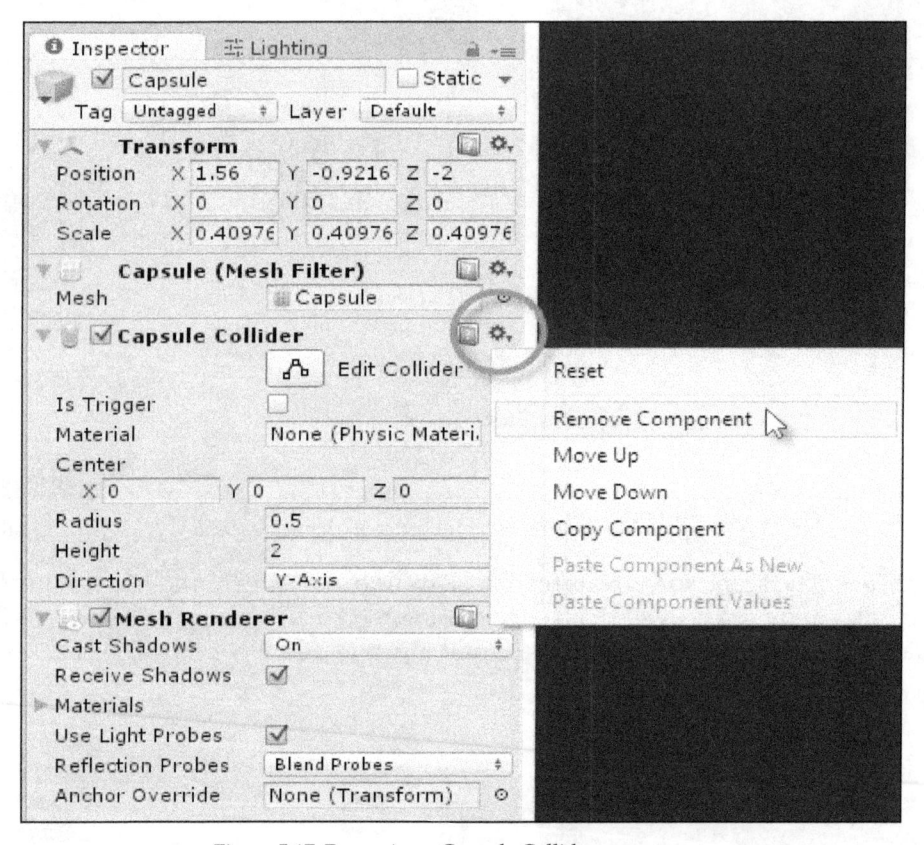

Figure 5.17: Removing a Capsule Collider component

Chapter 5

To make the object compatible with 2D Physics, add a Circle Collider component by choosing **Component | Physics 2D | Circle Collider** from the application menu. Once added, use the **Offset** and **Radius** settings on the Circle Collider component in the Inspector to adjust the size and position of the circle in relation to the capsule object in order to approximate the feet of a player character. To aid you in positioning the **Circle Collider** more easily, you can switch the **Scene** viewport mode to **Wireframe** and **2D**, if needed. To do this, use the **2D Toggle** button and the **Scene Render** mode drop-down button in the viewport toolbar. See *Figure 5.18*:

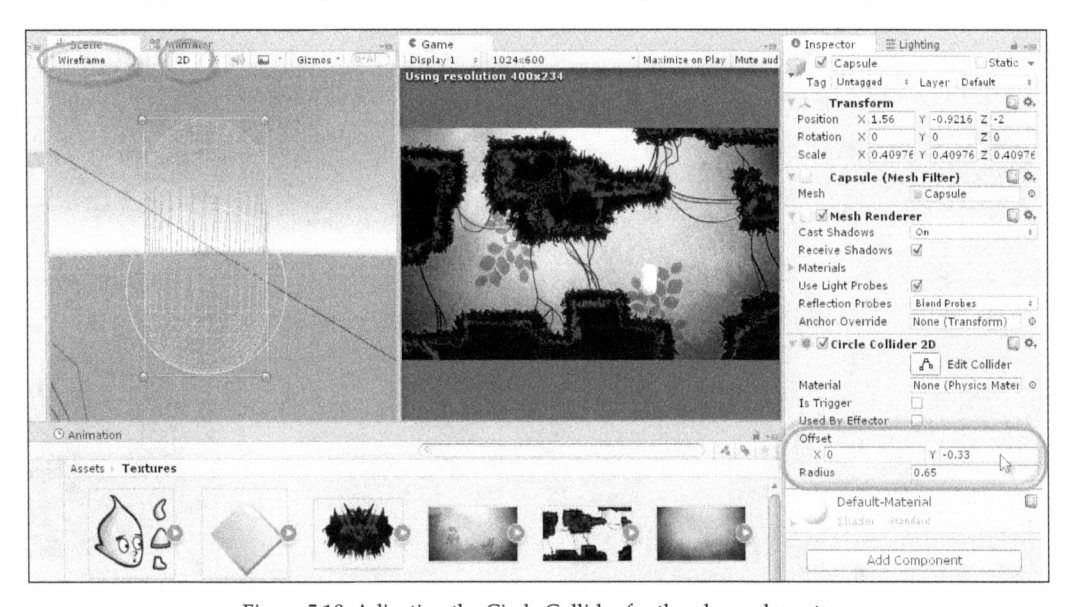

Figure 5.18: Adjusting the Circle Collider for the player character

Creating a 2D Adventure Game

Next, to make the **Circle Collider** work with 2D Physics, add a RigidBody2D component to the Capsule. To do this, select **Component | Physics 2D | RigidBody2D** from the application menu. You can confirm that this has worked by previewing the game in Play mode. When you click on the play icon, the Capsule object should fall down and through the foreground floor under the effect of gravity. See *Figure 5.19*:

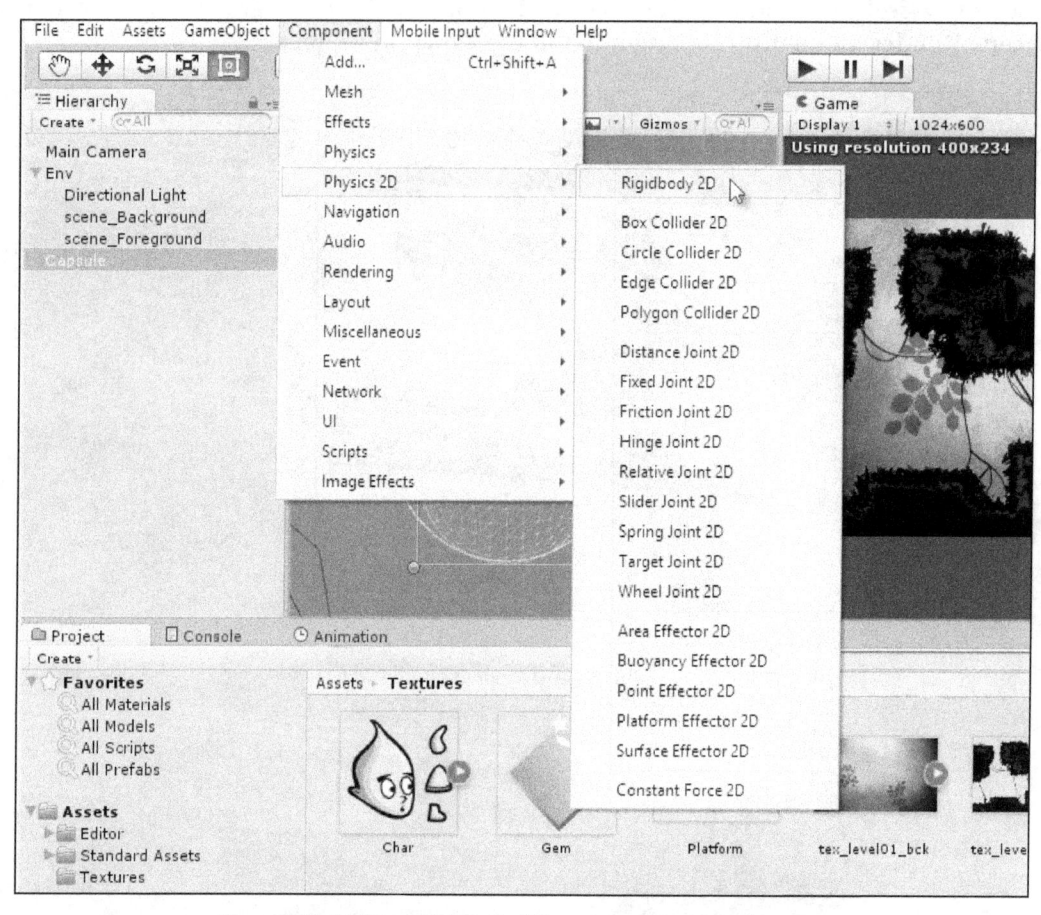

Figure 5.19: Adding a Rigidbody 2D component to a test character

Now, it's time to configure the foreground texture to work as a unified whole with physics. Right now, our test player character falls through the floor and this is not what we want. To fix this, we'll need to add a collider to the foreground environment. One method for this is to use Edge Collider 2D. This lets you draw out a low polygon mesh collider around your ground image manually, approximating the terrain. To get started, select the foreground in the scene and then choose **Component | Physics 2D | Edge Collider 2D** from the application menu. Doing this will add an Edge Collider 2D component to the foreground object. See *Figure 5.20*:

[244]

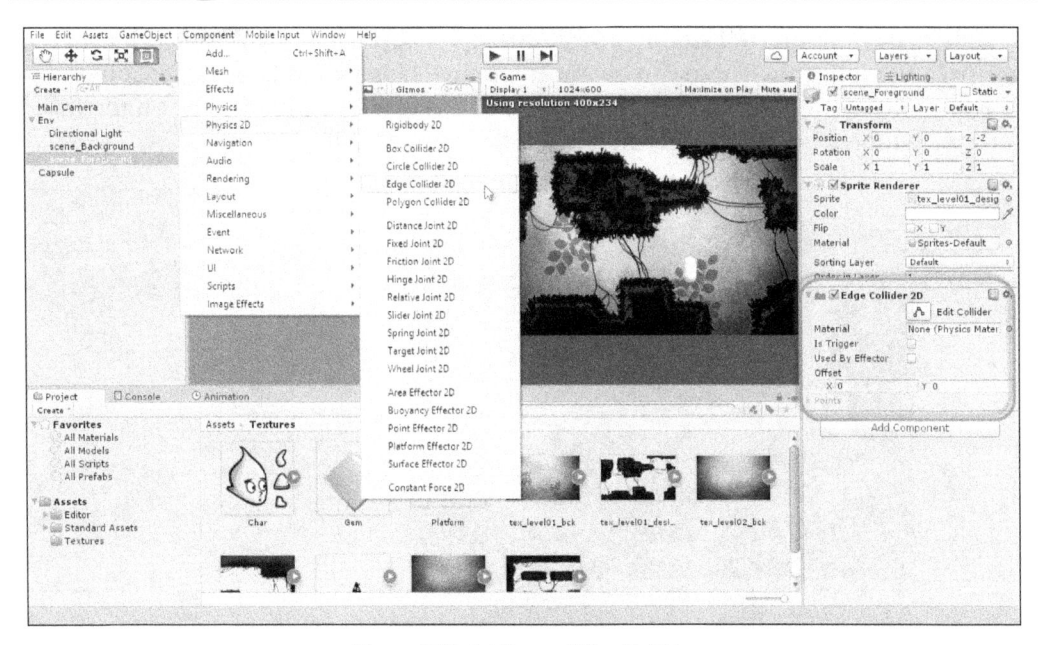

Figure 5.20: Adding an Edge Collider

By default, adding an Edge Collider 2D appears to have little effect on the selected object or any other objects, except for a single horizontal line drawn across the width of the scene. This can be seen in the **Scene** tab when the **Foreground** object is selected and in the **Game** tab if the **Gizmos** tool button is enabled. If the player is positioned above the horizontal line and you press Play on the toolbar, the player character will fall downward and treat the horizontal edge as a solid platform. See *Figure 5.21*:

Figure 5.21: The Edge Collider is useful to approximate platforms and solid surfaces

Creating a 2D Adventure Game

Of course, our terrain isn't simply a straight-edged surface. Rather, it has elevations, bumps, and platforms. These can be approximated closely with the Edge Collider 2D component using the **Collider Edit** mode. To access this mode, click on the **Edit Collider** button from the **Object Inspector**. See *Figure 5.22*:

Figure 5.22: The Edit Collider mode lets you change the shape of an Edge Collider 2D

With the **Edit Collider** mode active, you can reshape the collider to conform to the terrain. Let's focus on one area such as the bottom right-hand side of the terrain. By moving your mouse cursor over the edge points of the **Edge Collider** (the green line), you can click and drag to reposition it. To approximate the bottom right island of the terrain, click and drag the rightmost edge point to the right-hand side of the scene. See *Figure 5.23*:

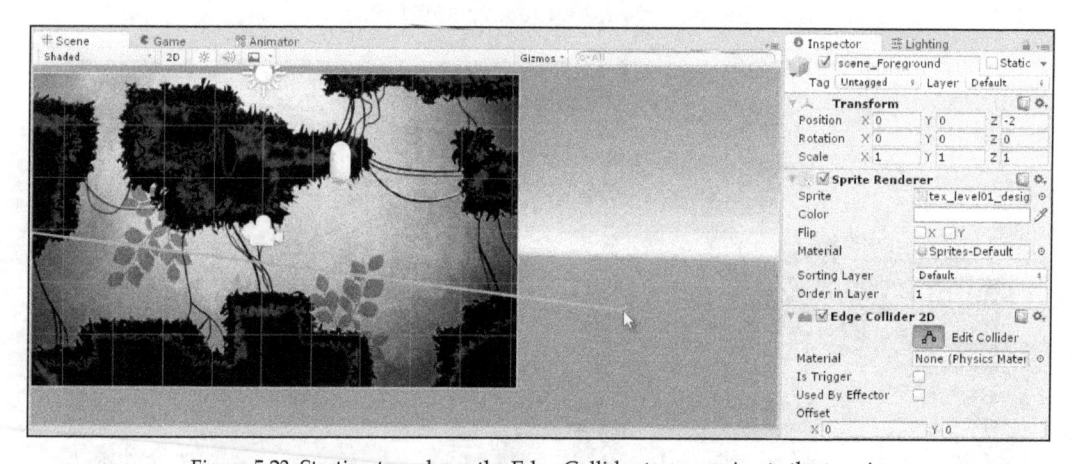

Figure 5.23: Starting to reshape the Edge Collider to approximate the terrain

Next, click and drag the left point of the collider to match with the leftmost edge of the right-hand island. See *Figure 5.24*:

[246]

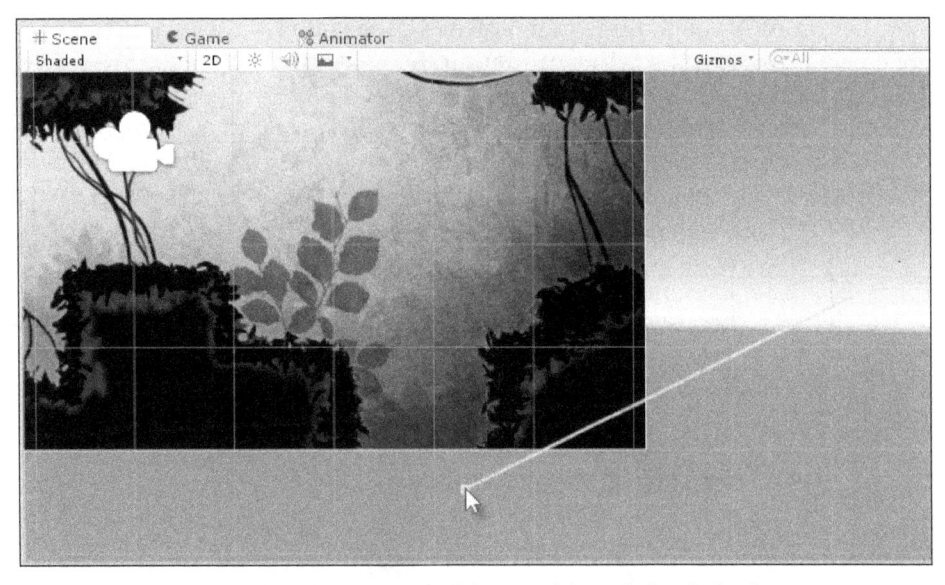

Figure 5.24: Positioning the left-most of the right-hand island

Now that the left and right edge points are positioned, let's add some additional points on the line between to reshape it, conforming to the right-hand island. Move your cursor anywhere on the line, click and drag to insert a new point, and reposition it to match the island. Repeat this process, adding additional points to reshape the line as needed. See *Figure 5.25*:

Figure 5.25: Shaping the Edge Collider to the right-most island

Creating a 2D Adventure Game

You now have a fully shaped line that matches the terrain's right-most island. Having created this, exit the **Edit Collider** mode by simply clicking on the **Edit Collider** button again from the **Object Inspector**. To create colliders for the remaining islands of the terrain, add a new **Edge Collider** to the same object. You can then add any number of **Edge Colliders** to a single object, and each collider should be used to approximate the topology of a single, isolated island in the complete terrain. See *Figure 5.26*:

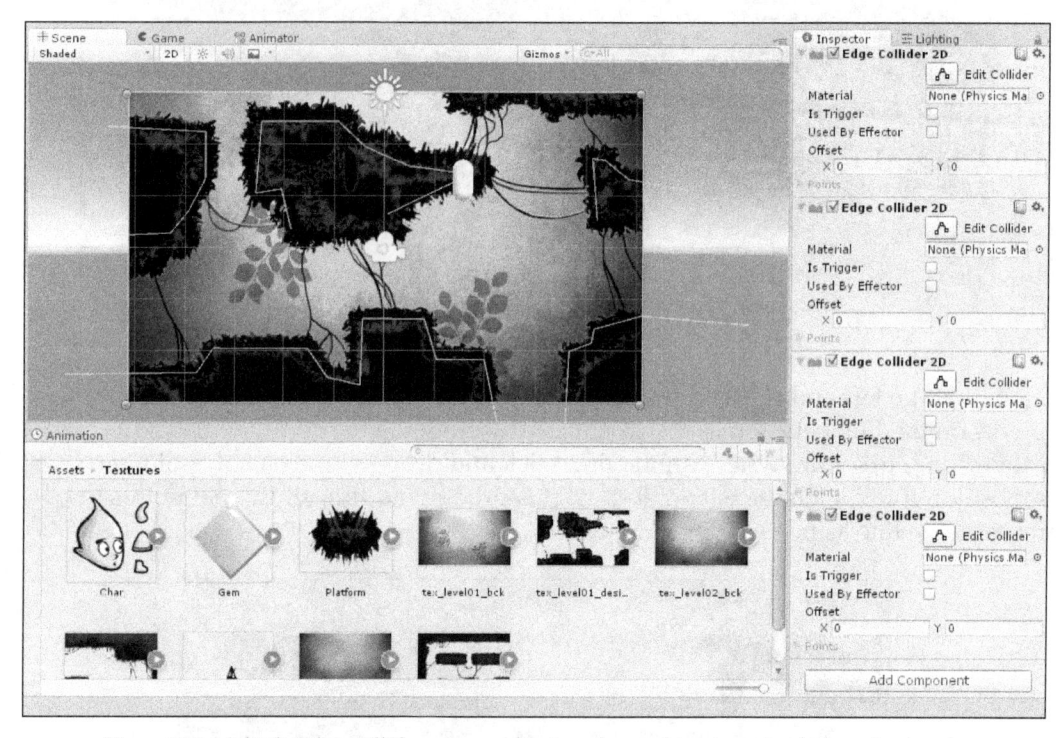

Figure 5.26: Multiple Edge Colliders on one object can be used to approximate complex terrain

Multiple Edge Collider components are now added together to a single foreground object, approximating the complete terrain for the scene. We can now test play collisions against the **Player Capsule** object by pressing the play icon on the toolbar and seeing how the capsule reacts against the terrain. This time, the capsule will collide and interact with the ground as opposed to passing through. This confirms that the terrain is configured appropriately with the physics system. See *Figure 5.27*:

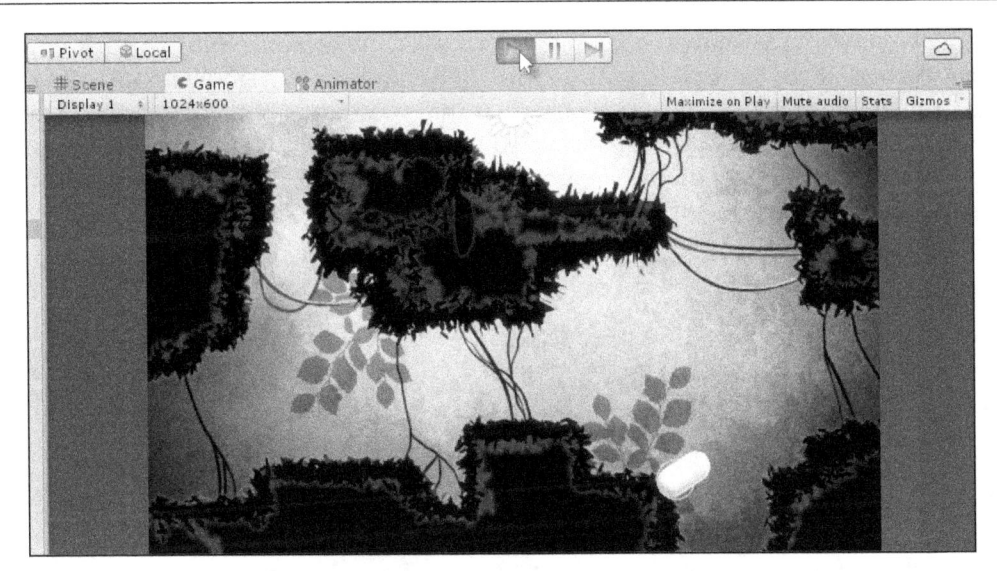

Figure 5.27: Capsule Object interacting with a terrain made from Edge Colliders

Congratulations! In this section, we've created a complete terrain for a single scene using Edge Collider components. This terrain not only fits the screen and appears as intended, but acts as a physical obstacle for the player character and other physics-based objects. Of course, so far, we've been using a rough approximation for the player and now it's time to expand upon this.

Creating a player

The player character is a small, green alien-looking creature that can be controlled and guided by the gamer through a level using many conventional platform-game mechanics, such as walking, jumping, and interacting. In the previous section, we built a *White Box* (prototype) character to test physical interactions with the environment, but here, we'll develop the player character in more depth. *Figure 5.28* illustrates our character texture imported earlier in the chapter, representing all limbs and parts for the player:

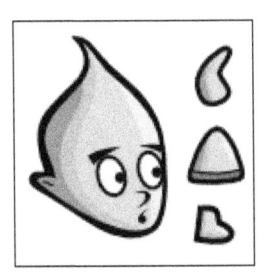

Figure 5.28: Character and his limbs in a consolidated texture

Creating a 2D Adventure Game

The player texture, as shown in *Figure 5.28*, is called an **Atlas Texture** or **Sprite Sheet** because it contains all frames or parts of a character in a single texture space. The problem with this texture, as it stands, is that when dragged and dropped from the **Project** panel to the scene, it'll be added as a single, self-contained sprite. This is because Unity recognizes all the separate parts as a single sprite. Rather, these should be separated into distinct units. See *Figure 5.29*:

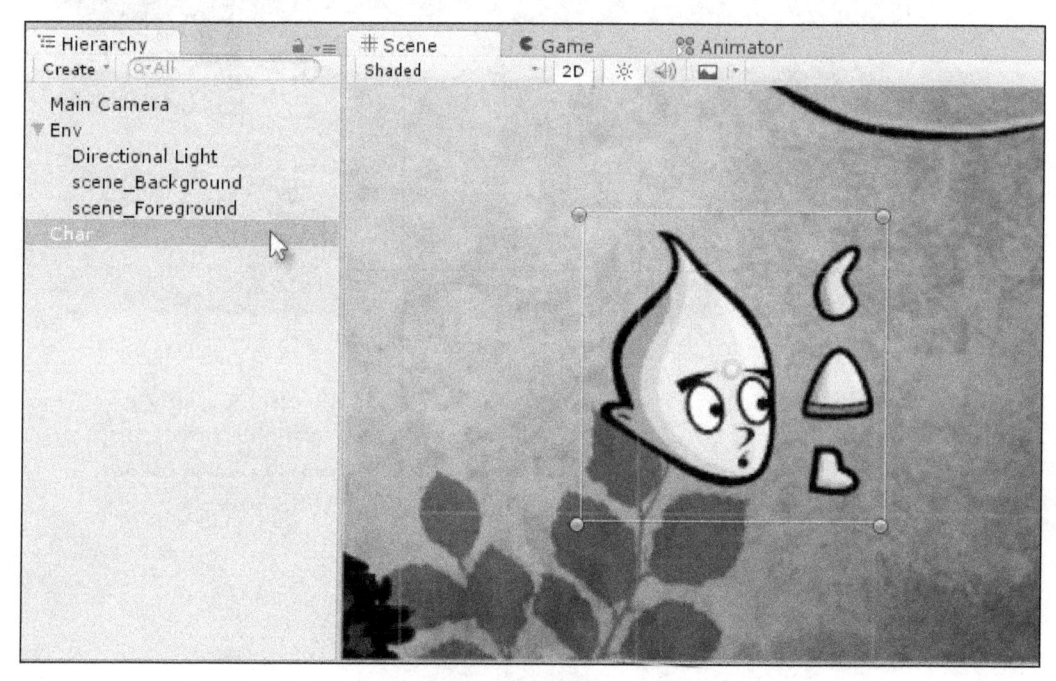

Figure 5.29: The player sprite texture needs to be divided into separate parts

To divide the character texture into separate parts on a per-limb basis, we'll use **Sprite Editor**. To access this tool, select the character texture in the **Project** panel. Then, from the **Object Inspector**, change **Sprite Mode** from **Single** to **Multiple**. Then, click on **Apply**. Next, click on the **Sprite Editor** button to open the **Sprite Editor** tool, allowing you cut apart the whole texture into specific slices. See *Figure 5.30*:

Figure 5.30: Specifying a sprite as Multiple

With the **Sprite Editor** tool, you can separate different parts of a texture into discrete and separate units. One method to achieve this is by drawing a rectangle around each image area that should be separate, and simply clicking and dragging your mouse to draw a texture region. See *Figure 5.31*:

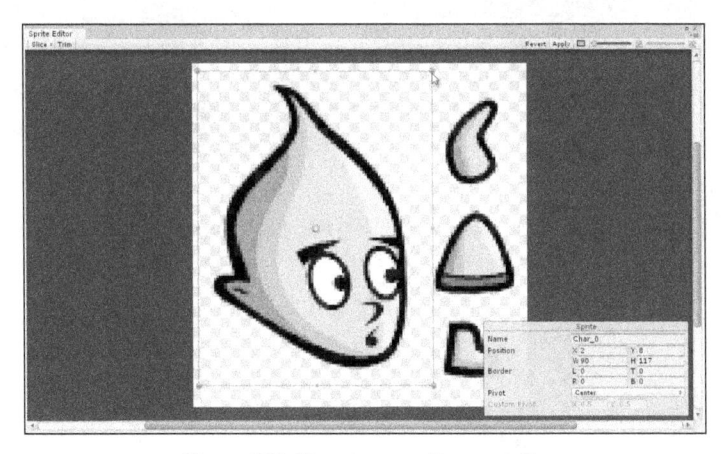

Figure 5.31: Drawing a sprite manually

Creating a 2D Adventure Game

Now, although a sprite can be separated manually, as we've just seen, Unity can often cut apart the texture automatically, identifying isolated areas of pixels and saving us a lot of time. We'll do that here for the player character. To do this, click on the **Slice** button listed at the top left corner of the **Sprite Editor** window. See *Figure 5.32*:

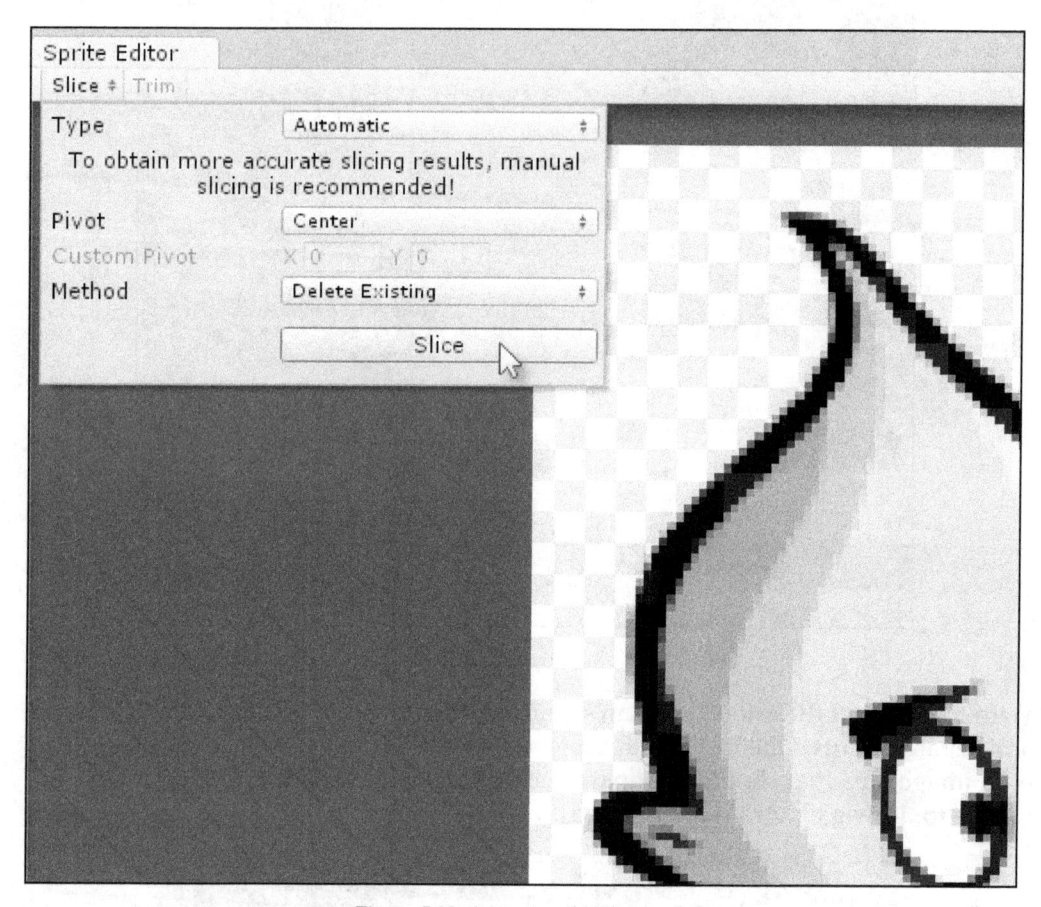

Figure 5.32: Accessing the Slice tool

From the **Slice** tool window, ensure that **Type** is set to **Automatic**, which means that Unity will auto-detect the location of separate sprites. **Pivot** can be left at **Center**, determining the pivot point for each sprite. **Method** should be **Delete Existing**, meaning that any existing sprites or slices in the texture space will be erased and replaced entirely by the newly autogenerated slices. Then, click on the **Slice** button to confirm the operation and the texture will be sliced into separate sprites with a clear border drawn around each sprite. See *Figure 5.33*:

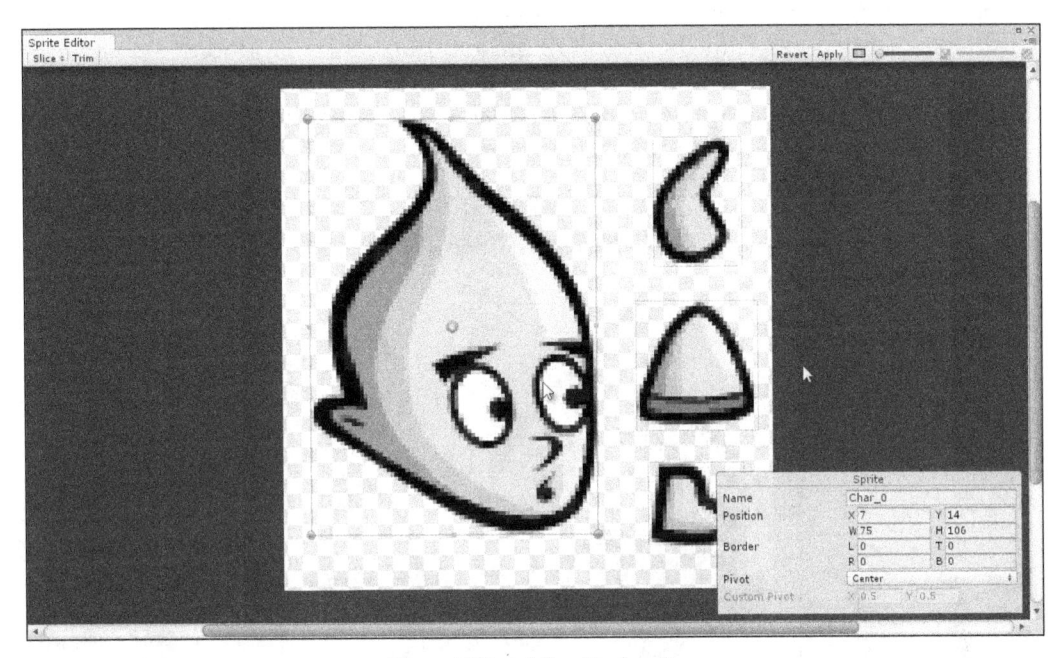

Figure 5.33: A fully sliced sprite

Creating a 2D Adventure Game

The texture is now divided into several sprites: head, body, arm, and leg. The final character in-scene will obviously have two arms and two legs but these will be formed from duplicated sprites. The final process now is to set the pivot point for each sprite – the point around which the sprite will rotate. This will be important later to animate the character correctly, as we'll see. Let's start by setting the pivot for the head. Select the head sprite in the editor and then click and drag the pivot handle (blue circle) to reposition the sprite's center of rotation. Click and drag the handle to the bottom middle of the head, roughly where the head would connect to the neck. This makes sense because the head will rotate and hinge from around this point.

As you move the pivot around, you should see the **X** and **Y** values change from the **Custom Pivot** field in the **Sprite Properties** dialog, shown in the bottom right-hand corner of the **Sprite Editor** window. See *Figure 5.34*:

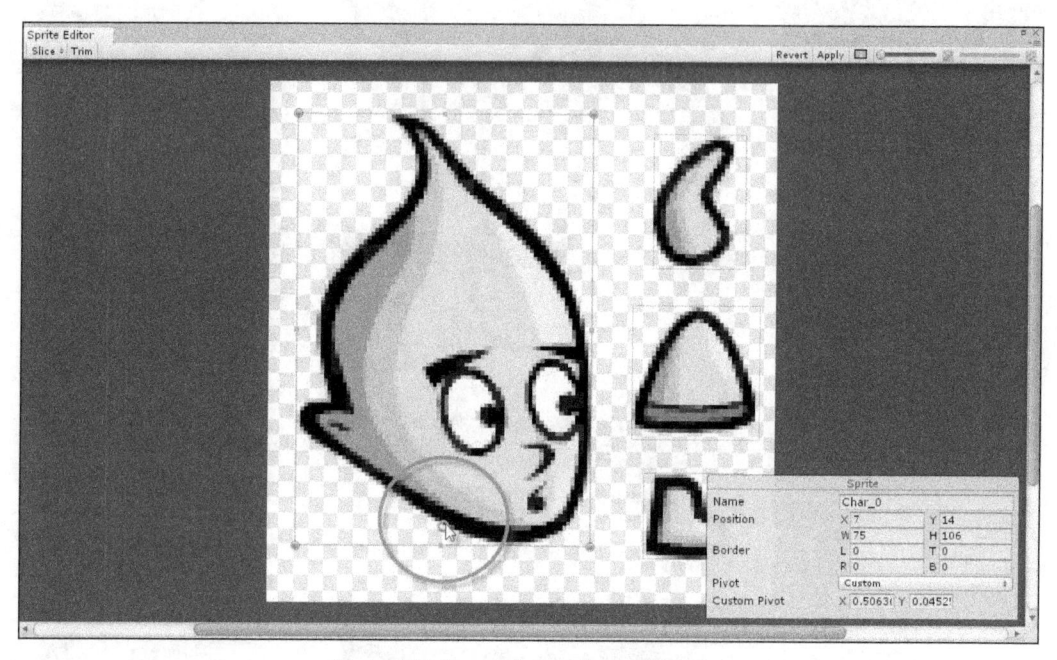

Figure 5.34: Repositioning the sprite pivot

Next, position the pivot for the arm, which should be at the shoulder joint where the arm connects to a torso; then for the leg, which should be near the hip where the leg connects to a torso, and finally, the torso itself, whose pivot should be at the hip joint. See *Figure 5.35*:

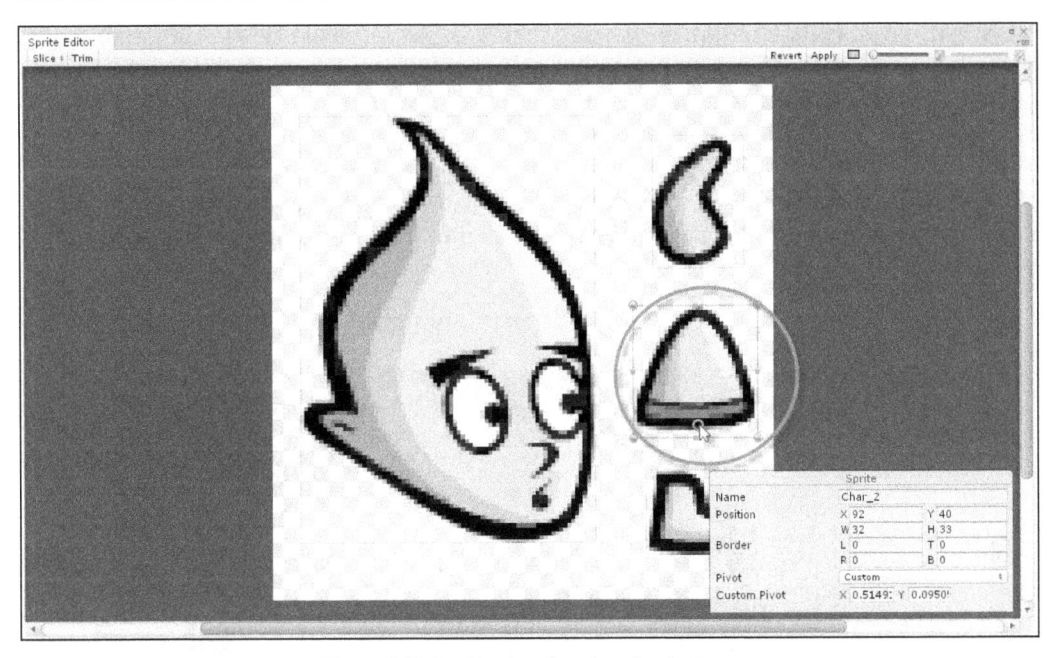

Figure 5.35: Positioning the pivot for the torso

When completed, click on the **Apply** button to confirm changes and then close the **Sprite Editor**. On returning to the main Unity interface, the appearance of the character texture will have changed in the **Project** panel. Specifically, the character texture features a small arrow icon attached to the right-hand side. When you click this, the texture expands to review all the separate sprites in a row, which can be dragged and dropped individually to the scene. See *Figure 5.36*:

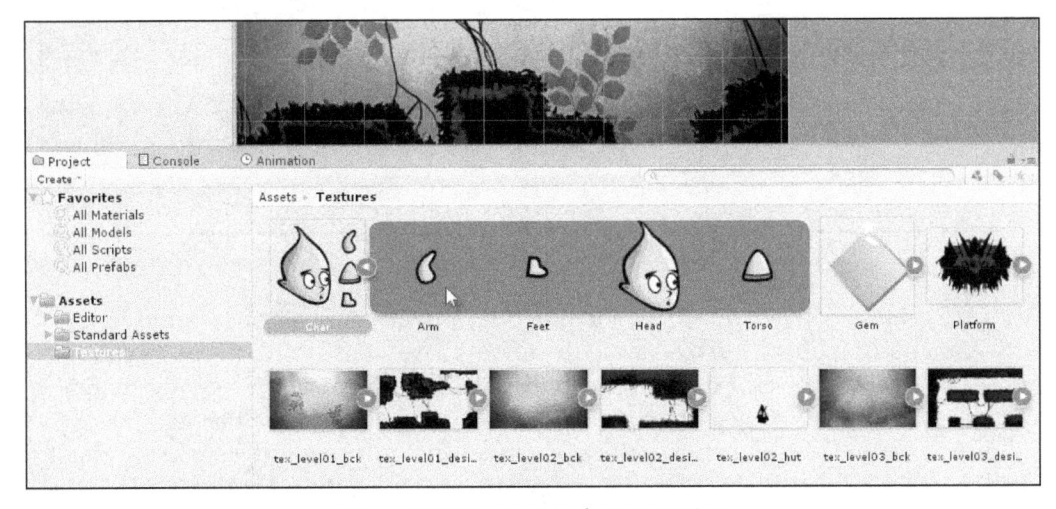

Figure: 5.36: Previewing character sprites

[255]

Creating a 2D Adventure Game

Now that we've isolated all player sprite textures, we can start to build a game character in the scene. Start by creating an empty game object with the **GameObject | Create Empty** command from the application menu. Name the object `Player` and assign it a Player Tag from the Inspector. This object will act as the ultimate or topmost parent object for the player character. Existing beneath this object as children will be the character's constituent parts: torso, arms, and legs. So, let's drag and drop the Torso sprite from the **Project** panel to the **Hierarchy** panel as a child of the **Player** object. See *Figure 5.37*:

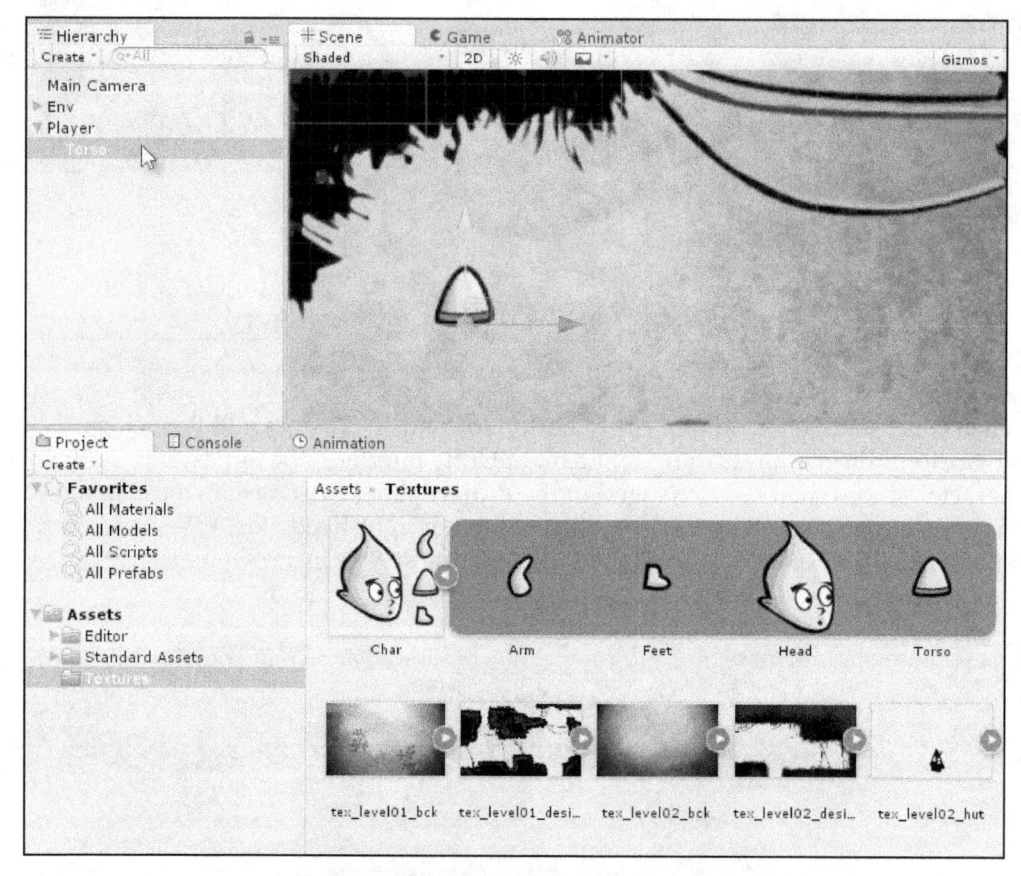

Figure 5.37: Starting the player character

After the torso has been added, we can add legs and arms. The arms should be added as children of the torso because the torso determines where the arms will be. However, the legs should be added as children of the **Player** object and are therefore siblings of the torso, because the torso can rotate independently of the legs. See *Figure 5.38* for the complete hierarchical arrangement. As you add each limb, you'll want to offset its position so that it appears correctly in relation to other limbs—the head should appear above the feet and so on.

[256]

Figure 5.38: Building a character

The rendering order of body parts is probably not correct by default insofar as each item will have an identical order in the Sprite Renderer component. This means that Unity could potentially render each limb in any order, allowing arms to appear in front of the head, legs to appear in front of the body, and so on. To correct this, we'll select each limb in turn and assign it an appropriate order value, taking care that it's higher than the world background order and less than the world foreground order. I've assigned the body an order of `103`, the head `105`, left arm `102`, right arm `104`, left leg `100`, and right leg `101`. See *Figure 5.39*:

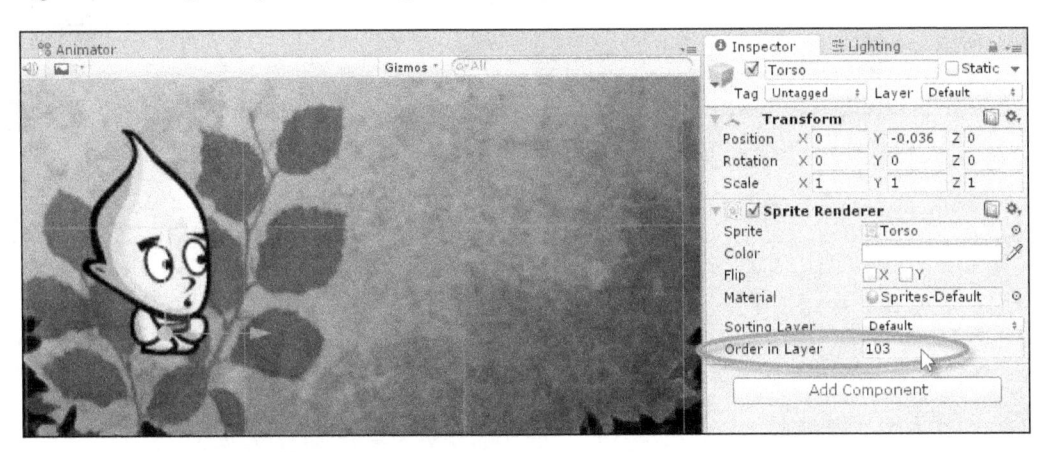

Figure 5.39: Ordering body parts

Creating a 2D Adventure Game

The rendering order for limbs is now configured successfully. Let's set up collisions and physics for the player. To do this, add two colliders—a Circle Collider to approximate the character feet, allowing us to determine when the character is in contact with the ground, and a Box Collider that approximates most of the body including the head. These colliders can be added by selecting the **Player** object (the topmost object) and then navigating to **Component | Physics 2D | Circle Collider 2D** and **Component | Physics 2D | Box Collider 2D**. See *Figure 5.40*:

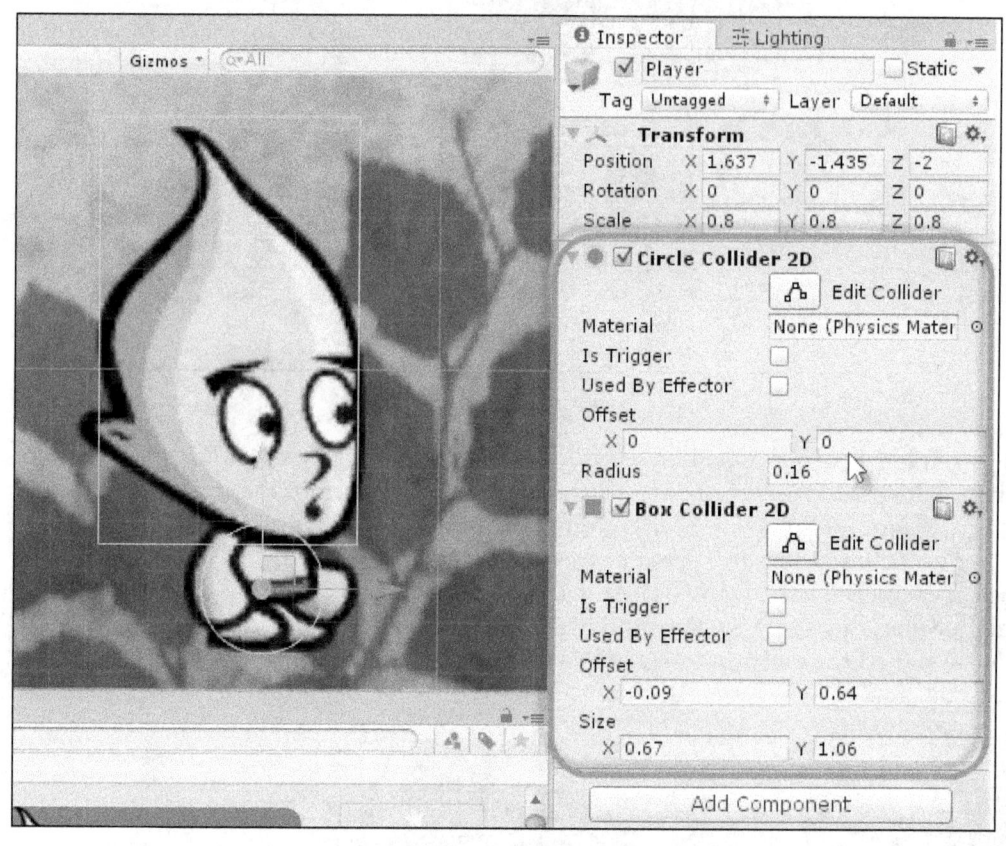

Figure 5.40: Adding two colliders to the Player Object: Circle Collider and Box Collider

[258]

The Circle Collider is of special importance because it's the primary means to determine whether the character is touching the ground, and it'll also be in contact with the ground as the character moves. For this reason, a Physics Material should be assigned to this collider to prevent friction effects from stopping or corrupting character motion as it moves around the scene. To achieve this, create a new Physics Material by right-clicking in the empty space in the **Project** panel and choose **Create | Physics2D Material** from the context menu. Name the material `Low Friction`. See *Figure 5.41*:

Figure 5.41: Creating a new Physics Material

Creating a 2D Adventure Game

Select the Physics2D material in the **Project** panel, and from the **Inspector**, change the Friction setting to 0.1. Then, drag and drop the Physics2D material from the **Project** panel to the **Material** slot for the CircleCollider2D component on the **Player** object. See *Figure 5.42*. Using these settings, the character will behave more realistically.

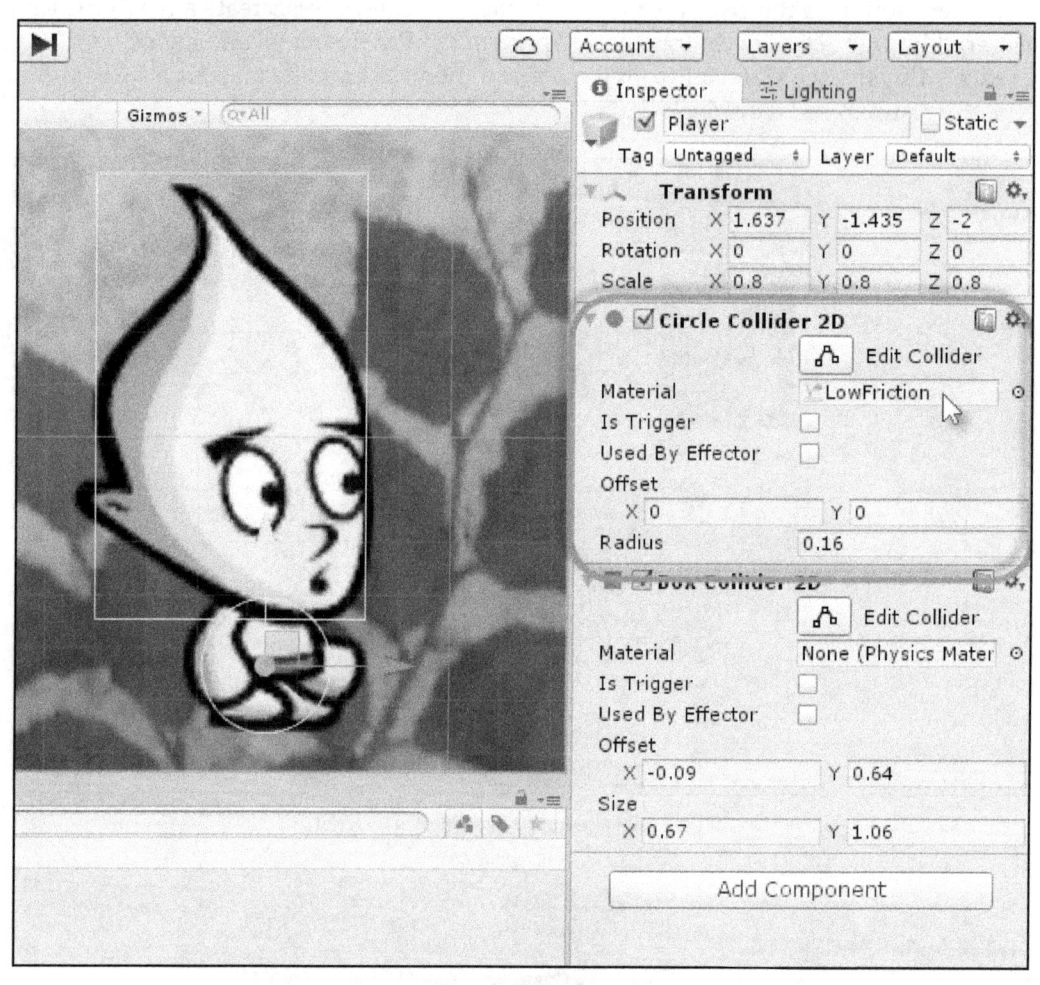

Figure 5.42: Assigning a Physics material to the player character

Chapter 5

Then, finally assign RigidBody2D to the **Player** object and set both **Linear Drag** and **Gravity Scale** to 3. In addition, set **Collison Detection** to **Continuous** for the most accurate collision detection and **Freeze Rotation** of the object on the Z axis because the player character should never rotate. Now, you have a fully completed physical object representing the player. See *Figure 5.43*. Good work!

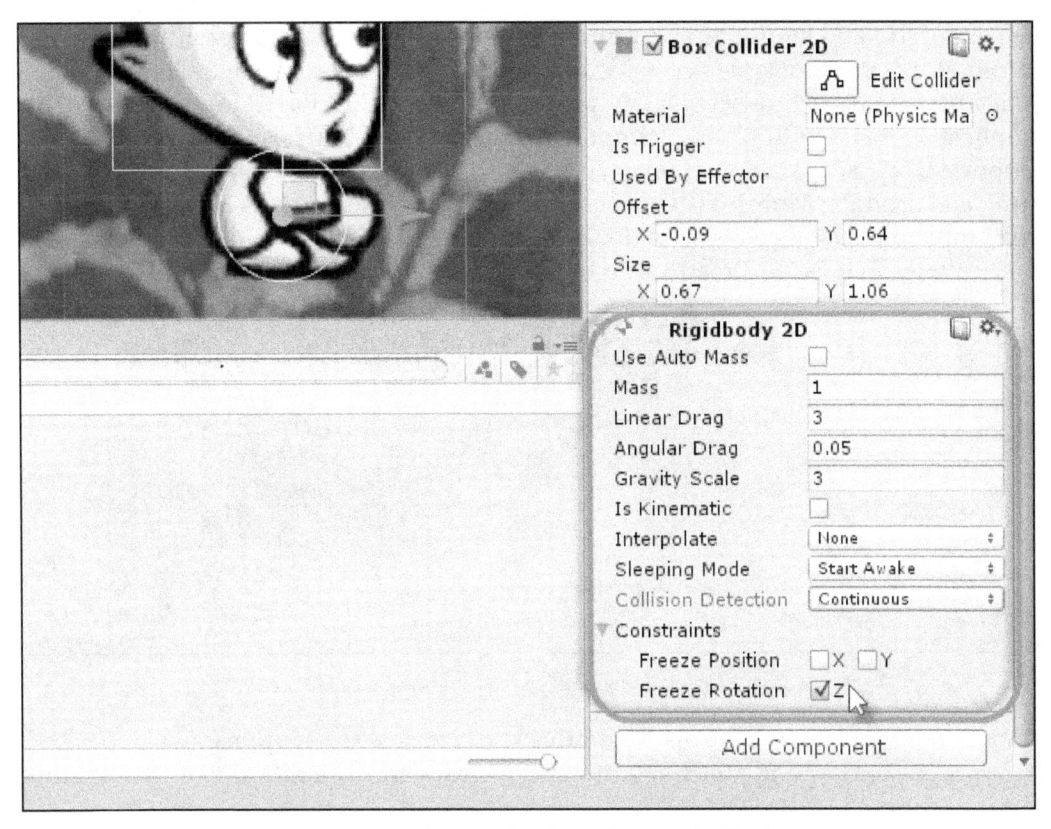

Figure 5.43: Configuring the player character for Physics

Scripting the player movement

The game so far features an environment with collision data and a multipart player object that interacts and responds to this environment. The player, however, cannot yet be controlled, and this section explores controller functionality further. The user will have two main input mechanics, namely, movement (walking left and right) and jumping. This input can be read seamlessly and easily using `CrossPlatformInputManager`, which is a native Unity asset package. This package was imported at the project creation phase, but it can be imported now via the application menu with **Assets | Import Package | CrossPlatformInput**. Once imported, open the `Standard Assets | CrossPlatformInput | Prefabs` folder and drag and drop the **MobileTiltControlRig** prefab to the scene. This prefab lets you read input data across a range of devices, mapping directly to the horizontal and vertical axes that we've already seen in previous chapters. See *Figure 5.44*:

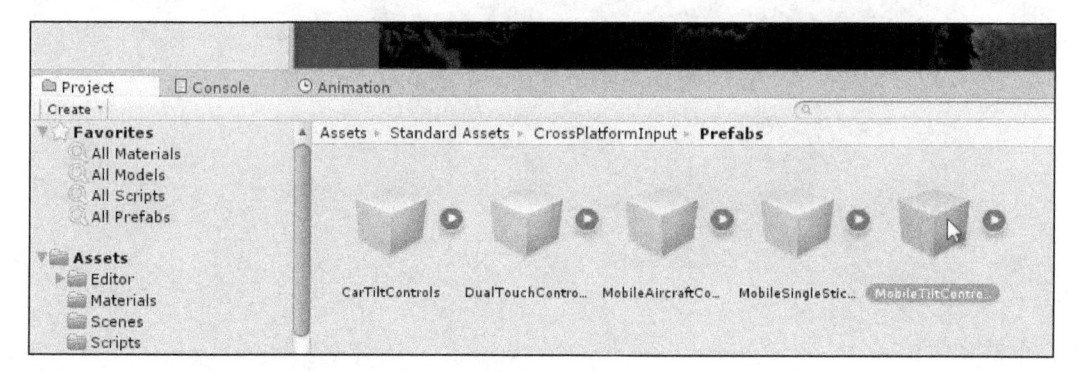

Figure 5.44: Cross-platform input prefabs offer easy multidevice control

Let's now script player controls. To do this, create a new C# script named `PlayerControl.cs` and attach it to the Player character. The full source code for this file is given in the *Code Sample 5.1*:

```
//--------------------------------
using UnityEngine;
using System.Collections;
using UnityStandardAssets.CrossPlatformInput;
//--------------------------------
public class PlayerControl : MonoBehaviour
{
    //--------------------------------
    public enum FACEDIRECTION {FACELEFT = -1, FACERIGHT = 1};
    //Which direction is the player facing - left or right?
    public FACEDIRECTION Facing = FACEDIRECTION.FACERIGHT;
    //Which objects are tagged as ground
    public LayerMask GroundLayer;
```

```csharp
//Reference to rigidbody
private Rigidbody2D ThisBody = null;
//Reference to transform
private Transform ThisTransform = null;
//Reference to feet collider
public CircleCollider2D FeetCollider = null;
//Are we touching the ground?
public bool isGrounded = false;
//What are the main input axes
public string HorzAxis = "Horizontal";
public string JumpButton = "Jump";
//Speed variables
public float MaxSpeed = 50f;
public float JumpPower = 600;
public float JumpTimeOut = 1f;
//Can we jump right now?
private bool CanJump = true;
//Can we control player?
public bool CanControl = true;
public static PlayerControl PlayerInstance = null;
//-------------------------------
public static float Health
{
  get
  {
    return _Health;
  }

  set
  {
    _Health = value;

    //If we are dead, then end game
    if(_Health <= 0)
    {
      Die();
    }
  }
}

[SerializeField]
private static float _Health = 100f;
//-------------------------------
// Use this for initialization
```

```csharp
void Awake ()
{
    //Get transform and rigid body
    ThisBody = GetComponent<Rigidbody2D>();
    ThisTransform = GetComponent<Transform>();

    //Set static instance
    PlayerInstance = this;
}
//---------------------------------
//Returns bool - is player on ground?
private bool GetGrounded()
{
    //Check ground
    Vector2 CircleCenter = new Vector2(ThisTransform.position.x,
        ThisTransform.position.y) + FeetCollider.offset;
    Collider2D[] HitColliders =
        Physics2D.OverlapCircleAll(CircleCenter,
            FeetCollider.radius, GroundLayer);
    if(HitColliders.Length > 0) return true;
    return false;
}
//---------------------------------
//Flips character direction
private void FlipDirection()
{
    Facing = (FACEDIRECTION) ((int)Facing * -1f);
    Vector3 LocalScale = ThisTransform.localScale;
    LocalScale.x *= -1f;
    ThisTransform.localScale = LocalScale;
}
//---------------------------------
//Engage jump
private void Jump()
{
    //If we are grounded, then jump
    if(!isGrounded || !CanJump) return;

    //Jump
    ThisBody.AddForce(Vector2.up * JumpPower);
    CanJump = false;
    Invoke ("ActivateJump", JumpTimeOut);
}
//---------------------------------
```

```csharp
//Activates can jump variable after jump timeout
//Prevents double-jumps
private void ActivateJump()
{
  CanJump = true;
}
//---------------------------------
// Update is called once per frame
void FixedUpdate ()
{
  //If we cannot control character, then exit
  if(!CanControl || Health <= 0f)
  {
    return;
  }

  //Update grounded status
  isGrounded = GetGrounded();
  float Horz = CrossPlatformInputManager.GetAxis(HorzAxis);
  ThisBody.AddForce(Vector2.right * Horz * MaxSpeed);

  if(CrossPlatformInputManager.GetButton(JumpButton))
    Jump();

  //Clamp velocity
  ThisBody.velocity = new
    Vector2(Mathf.Clamp(ThisBody.velocity.x, -MaxSpeed,
      MaxSpeed),
    Mathf.Clamp(ThisBody.velocity.y, -Mathf.Infinity,
      JumpPower));

  //Flip direction if required
  if((Horz < 0f && Facing != FACEDIRECTION.FACELEFT) ||
    (Horz > 0f && Facing != FACEDIRECTION.FACERIGHT))
    FlipDirection();
}
//---------------------------------
void OnDestroy()
{
  PlayerInstance = null;
}
//---------------------------------
//Function to kill player
static void Die()
{
```

Creating a 2D Adventure Game

```
      Destroy(PlayerControl.PlayerInstance.gameObject);
   }
   //-------------------------------
   //Resets player back to defaults
   public static void Reset()
   {
      Health = 100f;
   }
   //-------------------------------
}
//-------------------------------
```

Code Sample 5.1

The following points summarize the code sample:

- The `PlayerControl` class is responsible for handling all player input, making the character move left and right and jump.

- To achieve player movement, a reference to the RigidBody2D component is retained in the `ThisBody` variable, which is retrieved in the `Awake` function. The movement and motion of the player is set using the `RigidBody2D.Velocity` variable.

> More information on this variable can be found online at http://docs.unity3d.com/ScriptReference/Rigidbody2D-velocity.html.

- The `FlipDirection` function is used to invert the horizontal scale of the sprite, turning it to face left or right as needed (reversing the image direction, for example, 1 and -1). From Unity 5.3 onward, the `Flip` property of the `SpriteRenderer` component can be used instead.

- The `FixedUpdate` function is used instead of Update to update the movement of the player character because we're working with `RigidBody2D`—a physics-based component. All physics functionality should be updated in `FixedUpdate` that is invoked at a fixed interval each second as opposed to every frame.

> More information can be found at the Unity online documentation at `http://docs.unity3d.com/ScriptReference/MonoBehaviour.FixedUpdate.html`.

- The `GetGrounded` function detects where any `CircleCollider` intersects and overlaps with any other collider in the scene on a specific layer. In short, this function indicates whether the player character is touching the ground at the position of the feet. If so, the player is able to jump; otherwise, the player cannot jump as they are already airborne. Double-jumping is not allowed in this game!

For the preceding code to work correctly, a few tweaks must be made to both the scene and player character. Specifically, the `GetGrounded` function requires that the floor area of the level is grouped together on a single layer. This simply means that the level foreground should be on a distinctive layer from other objects. To achieve this, create a new layer named `Ground`, and then assign the foreground object to this layer. To create a new layer, select the foreground object and, from the **Object Inspector**, click on the drop-down named **Layer**. Then, select Add Layer from the context menu. See *Figure 5.45*:

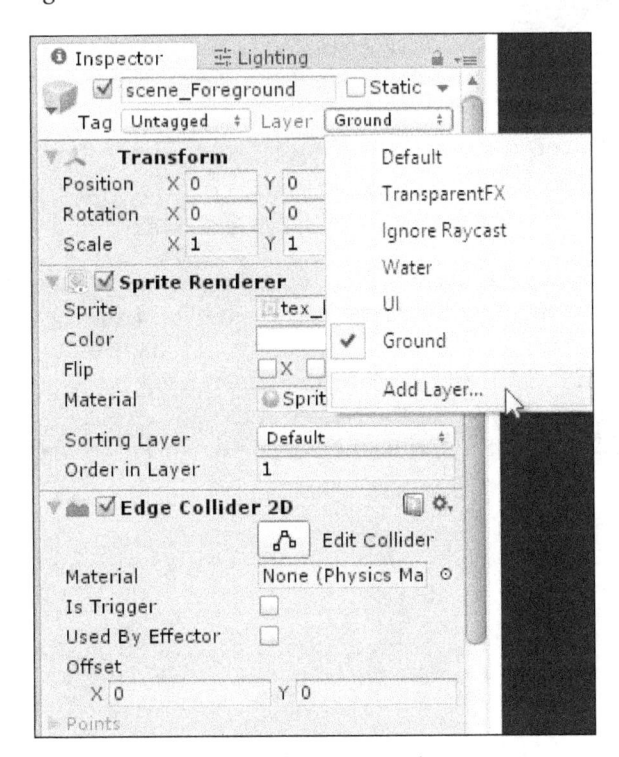

Figure 5.45: Adding a new layer

Then, add a new layer named Ground simply by entering Ground in an available type-in field. See *Figure 5.46*:

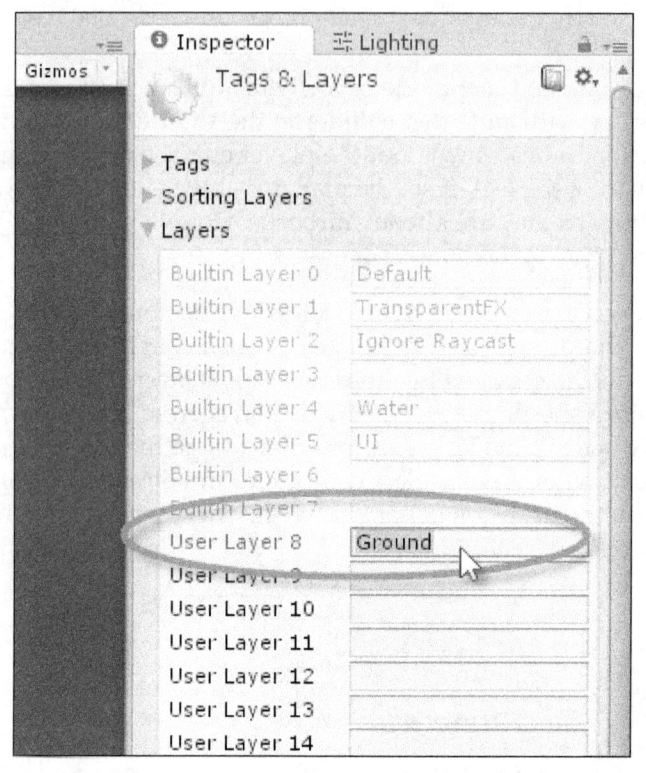

Figure 5.46: Creating a new ground layer

Now, assign the foreground object to the Ground layer. Simply select the foreground object, and then select the **Ground** layer from the **Layer** drop-down in the **Object Inspector**. After the foreground object is assigned to the ground layer, the PlayerControl script requires us to indicate which layer has been designated for the ground. To achieve this, select the **Player** object and, from the **Object Inspector**, select the **Ground** layer for the **Ground Layer** field. See *Figure 5.47*:

Figure 5.47: Selecting the Ground layer for collision detection

In addition, the **Feet Collider** slot needs assignment too in order to indicate which collider object should be used for ground collision detection. For this field, you need to drag and drop the **CircleCollider** component to the **Feet Collider** slot. See *Figure 5.48*:

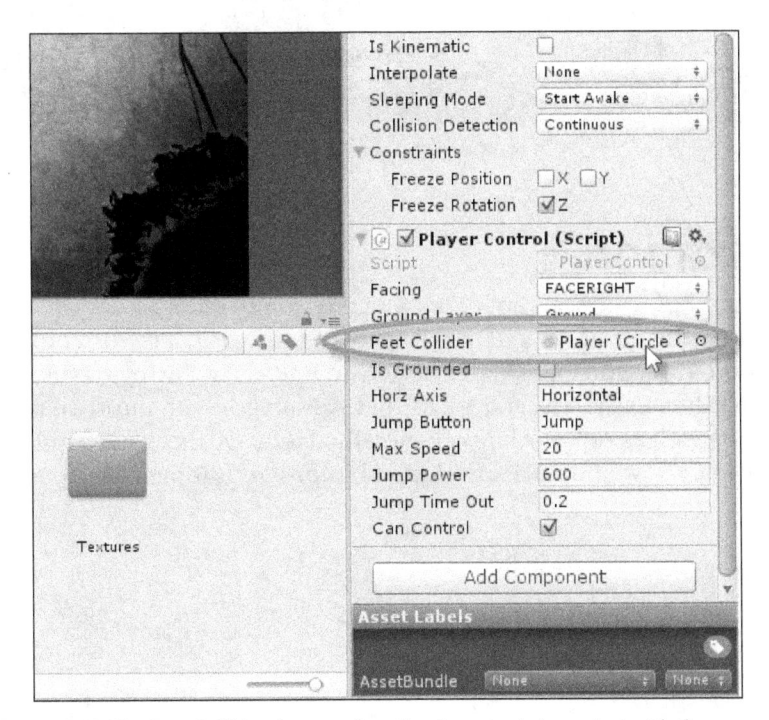

Figure 5.48: The Feet Collider detects when the character is in contact with the ground

Creating a 2D Adventure Game

Now, give the player character a test run. Simply click on the play icon on the toolbar and test out the controls of the player character. *W, A, S, D* (or the arrow keys) will move the player character around. The spacebar makes the character jump. See *Figure 5.49*:

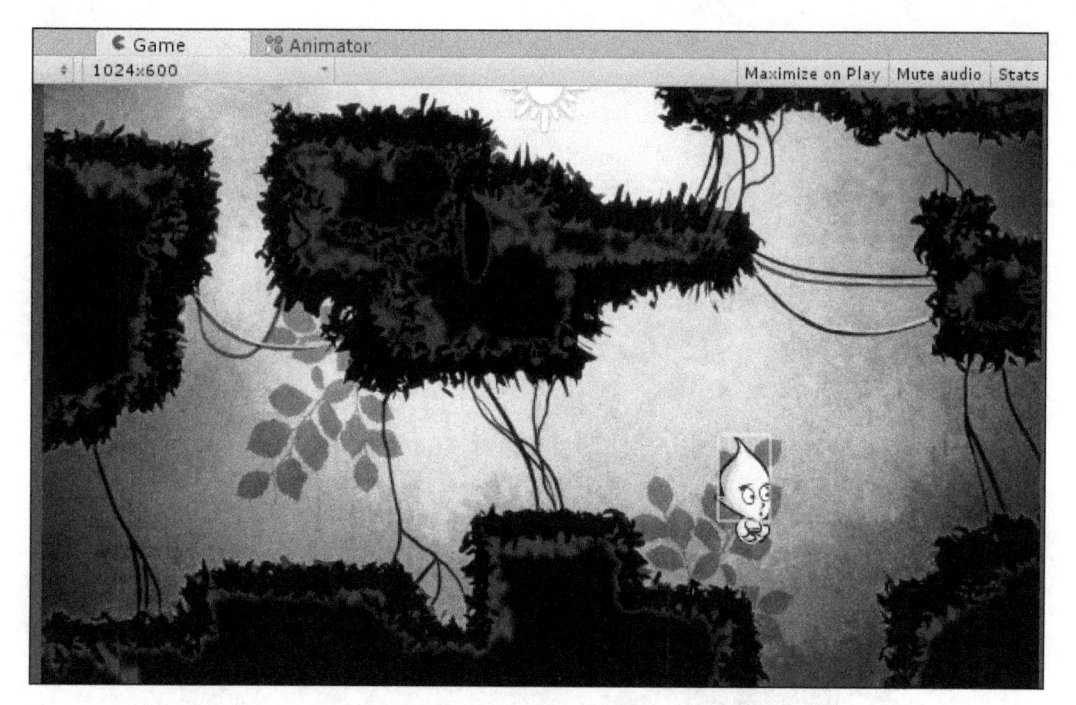

Figure 5.49: Play testing with the player character

Optimization

Our work so far has produced an interesting environment and a controllable character within this environment. Before moving forward, let's turn our attention to optimization – an issue that should be considered early during development. Optimization refers to the tips and tricks that we can apply to improve runtime performance as well as our workflow generally. Here, we'll consider prefabs to improve our workflow and Sprite Packing to improve runtime performance. Let's start with prefabs.

A prefab is a Unity asset that lets you group together many objects in a scene and package them together as a single unit that can be added to the **Project** panel as an asset. From here, the prefab can be added as a complete unit to any other scene or environment as though it were a separate and complete *thing*. The player character is an ideal candidate for a prefab because it must feature in all the other scenes we create. Let's create a prefab from the player. To do this, simply drag and drop the **Player** object to the **Project** panel in a separate folder called `Prefabs`. See *Figure 5.49*:

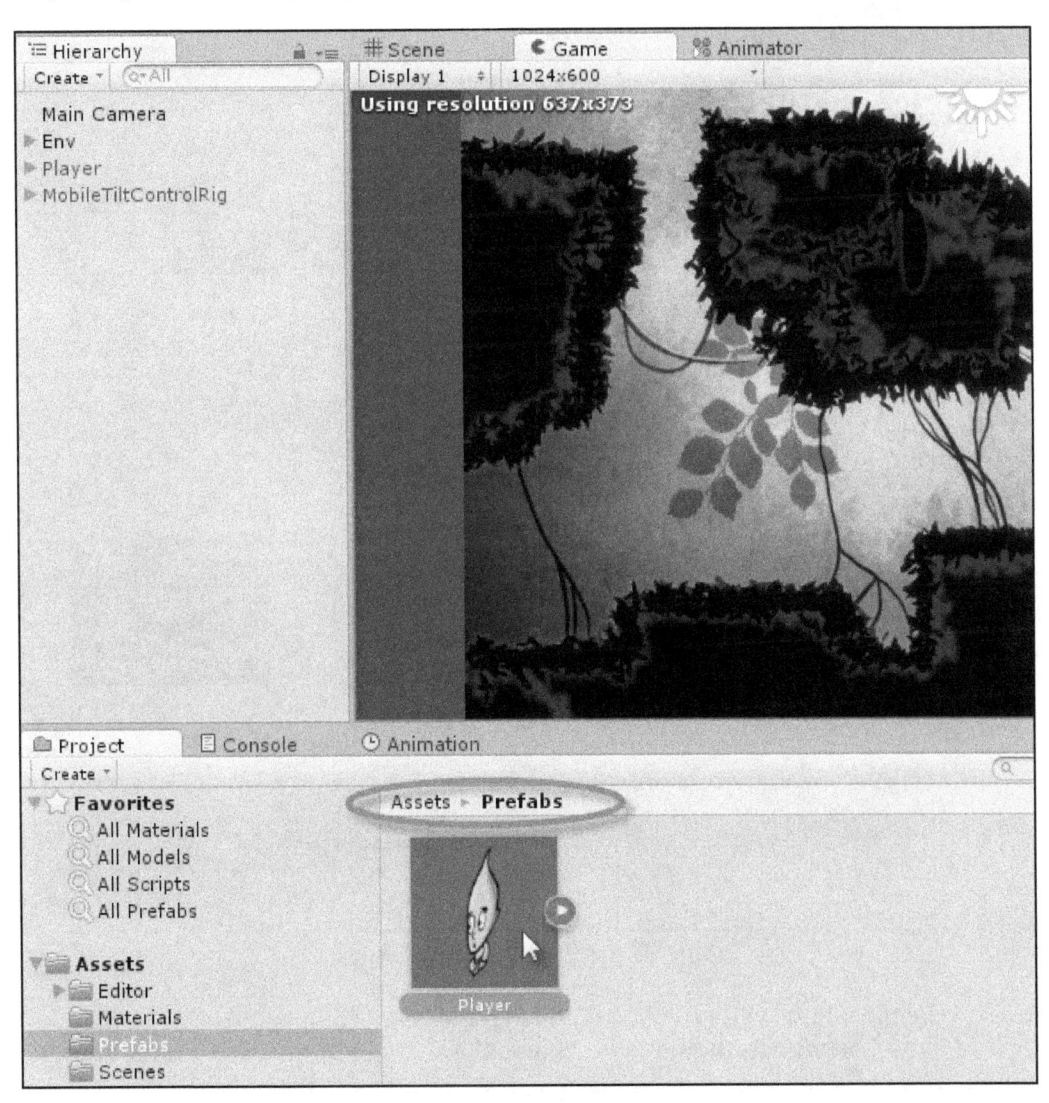

Figure 5.50: Generating a player prefab

Creating a 2D Adventure Game

After the **Prefab** is created, the **Player** object name in the hierarchy panel will turn blue, indicating that it's connected to the Prefab asset. This means that if you select the **Prefab** in the **Project** panel and make changes in the Inspector, then the **Player** object in the scene will change automatically to match these changes. You can, however, break the connection between the **Player** in the scene and **Prefab** by selecting the **Player** object and choosing **GameObject | Break Prefab Instance** from the application menu. This converts the scene object into a separate and independent duplicate of the Prefab. See *Figure 5.51*:

Figure 5.51: Breaking a prefab instance

Most of the time, however, you'll want to keep the connection between objects and their prefabs. Sometimes, though, you may make changes to the object in the scene, and then want these changes to feedback to the **Prefab** asset in the **Project** panel, affecting all other linked instances if there are any. To do this, select the object to which changes have been made, and then select **GameObject | Apply Changes to Prefab** from the application menu. See *Figure 5.52*:

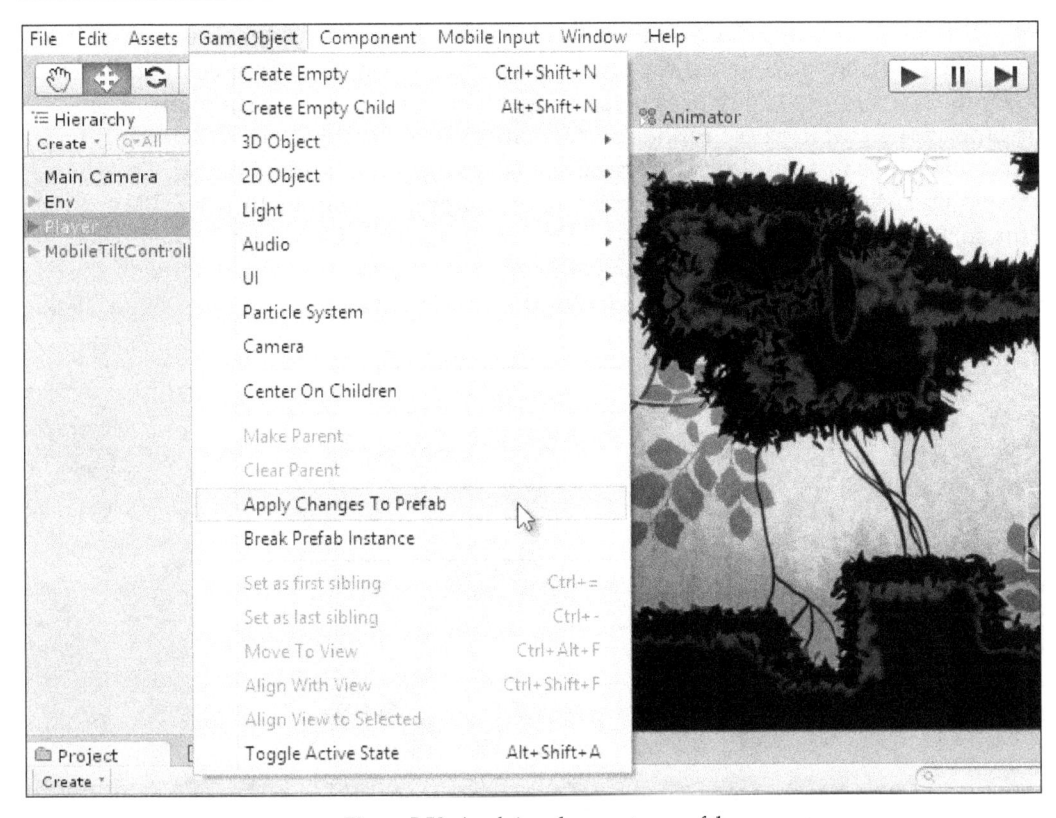

Figure 5.52: Applying changes to a prefab

In addition to making Prefabs, you'll also want to optimize the render performance for your 2D games. Right now, when running the game, Unity will perform a unique and separate draw call for each and every unique texture or sprite onscreen at the time. A draw call simply refers to a step or process cycle that Unity must run through to properly display a graphic onscreen, such as a mesh, material, or texture. Draw calls represent a computational expense, and so it's a good idea to reduce them wherever possible.

Creating a 2D Adventure Game

For 2D games, we can reduce draw calls by batching together related textures, such as all the props for a scene, all the enemies, or all the weapons. That is, by indicating to Unity that a group of textures belong together, Unity can perform internal optimizations that increase render performance. Specifically, Unity will paste all related textures in a single and larger internal texture that it uses instead. To achieve this optimization, select all *prop* textures. For our game, I will include the **Player**, **House**, **Platform**, and **Gem** as props. These textures are all featured in the **Project** panel, though not all are used in the game yet. Select these textures and, from the Inspector, assign them the same name for the **Packing Tag** field (Props). Then, click on **Apply**. See *Figure 5.53*:

Figure 5.53: Assigning multiple textures to the same Packing Tag

Now, repeat this process for the **Backgrounds**, selecting all backgrounds and assigning them to the **Background Packing** tag. Then, click on **Apply**. See *Figure 5.54*:

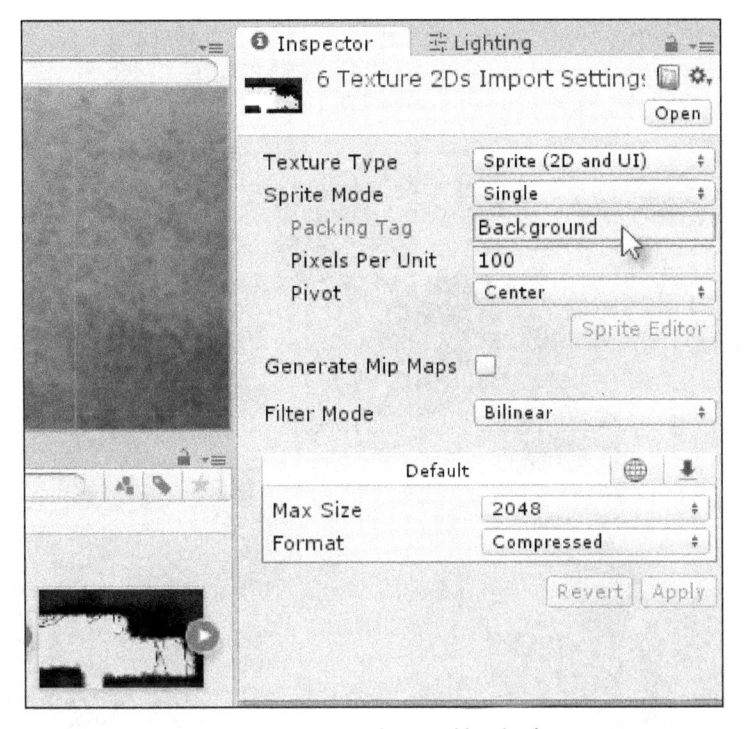

Figure 5.54: Creating a Background batch of textures

Creating a 2D Adventure Game

That's it! Now, when you press on the play icon, Unity will automatically batch and organize the textures for optimal performance based on your groupings. This technique can significantly reduce draw calls. On pressing the play icon, you may see a loading bar or progress bar while Unity internally generates a new texture set. During Play Mode, you can view how Unity has organized the textures through the **Sprite Packer** window. To access this, select **Window | Sprite Packer**. See *Figure 5.55*:

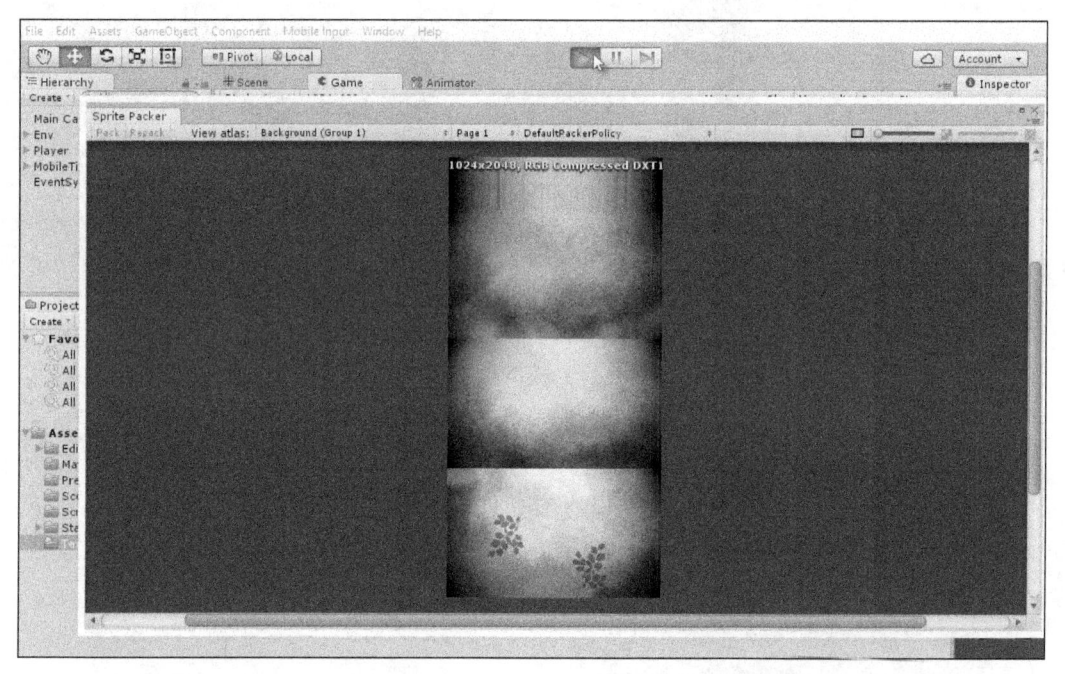

Figure 5.55: Unity organizes all similarly tagged textures into the same texture space as an Atlas

Summary

Superb work! We've come a long way in this chapter, from a blank project to an effective 2D game in which a player character can navigate a complete 2D environment with 2D Physics. The character can move left and right and jump, and the sprite texture will change to match the direction of travel as well. In addition, Sprite Packing has been used to optimize runtime performance, which is ideal for mobile devices. In the next chapter, we'll continue working by adding obstacles, collectable objects, and more!

Test your knowledge

Q1. Edge Colliders lets you...

- A. Create pretty patterns
- B. Draw out collider edges
- C. Create 3D volumes
- D. Create physics animations

Q2. The Sprite Packer is useful for...

- A. Create sprites in rows and columns
- B. Group sprites onto a single atlas texture
- C. Animate sprites
- D. Create multiple color sprites

Q3. Physics Materials can...

- A. Help you define how 2D objects behave
- B. Scale 2D Objects
- C. Rotate Objects
- D. Edit Object Vertices

Q4. The Sprite Editor lets you...

- A. Divide an image into multiple sprites
- B. Animate textures
- C. Create mesh objects
- D. Edit Material Properties

Further reading

Check out the below-mentioned links for more information:

- `https://unity3d.com/learn/tutorials/s/scripting`
- `https://www.packtpub.com/game-development/unity-5-scripting-and-gameplay-mechanics-video`
- `https://www.packtpub.com/game-development/mastering-unity-5x-scripting`

6
Continuing the 2D Adventure

In the previous chapter, we started work on a 2D adventure game. On reaching this point, we've now created a controllable character that can navigate a level using physics and collision detection as well as gravity. This chapter completes the 2D game project by adding the remaining features. Specifically, this chapter will cover the following topics:

- Moving obstacles and features such as an elevator platform
- Gun turrets to attack the player
- An NPC with a quest system

> The starting project and assets can be found in the book companion files in the Chapter06/Start folder. You can start here and follow along with this chapter if you don't have your own project already.

Continuing the 2D Adventure

Moving platforms

Now let's refine the adventure further by adding a moving element to the existing scene; specifically, a moving-platform object. This platform should move up and then down again on a loop, ping-ponging between extremes. The player will be able to jump onto the platform to hitch a ride, and the object will be constructed as a prefab, allowing it to be reused across scenes. See *Figure 6.1* for the result:

Figure 6.1: Create a moving platform

To start, select the platform texture in the **Project** panel, making sure that it's specified as a **Sprite** (2D and UI) texture type in the **Object Inspector**. The **Sprite Mode** should be set to **Single**. Drag and drop the platform texture to the scene and set its **Scale** to (0.7, 0.5, 1). See *Figure 6.2*:

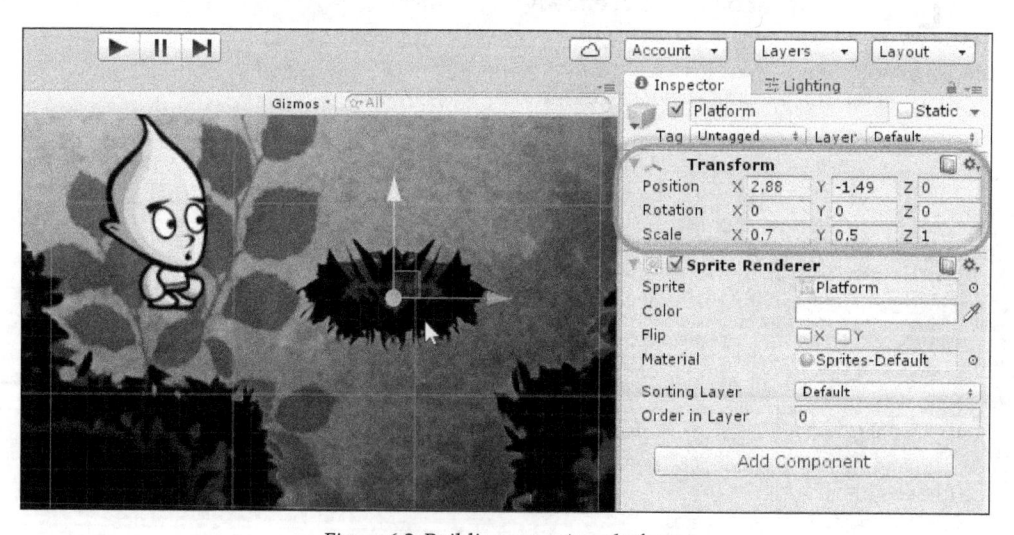

Figure 6.2: Building a moving platform

Next, the platform should be a solid object, the kind of thing with which the player can collide. Remember, the player should be able to stand on the platform. Consequently, a Collider must be added. In this case, a Box Collider 2D is appropriate. To add this, select the platform object in the scene and navigate to **Component | Physics 2D | Box Collider 2D** from the menu. See *Figure 6.3*:

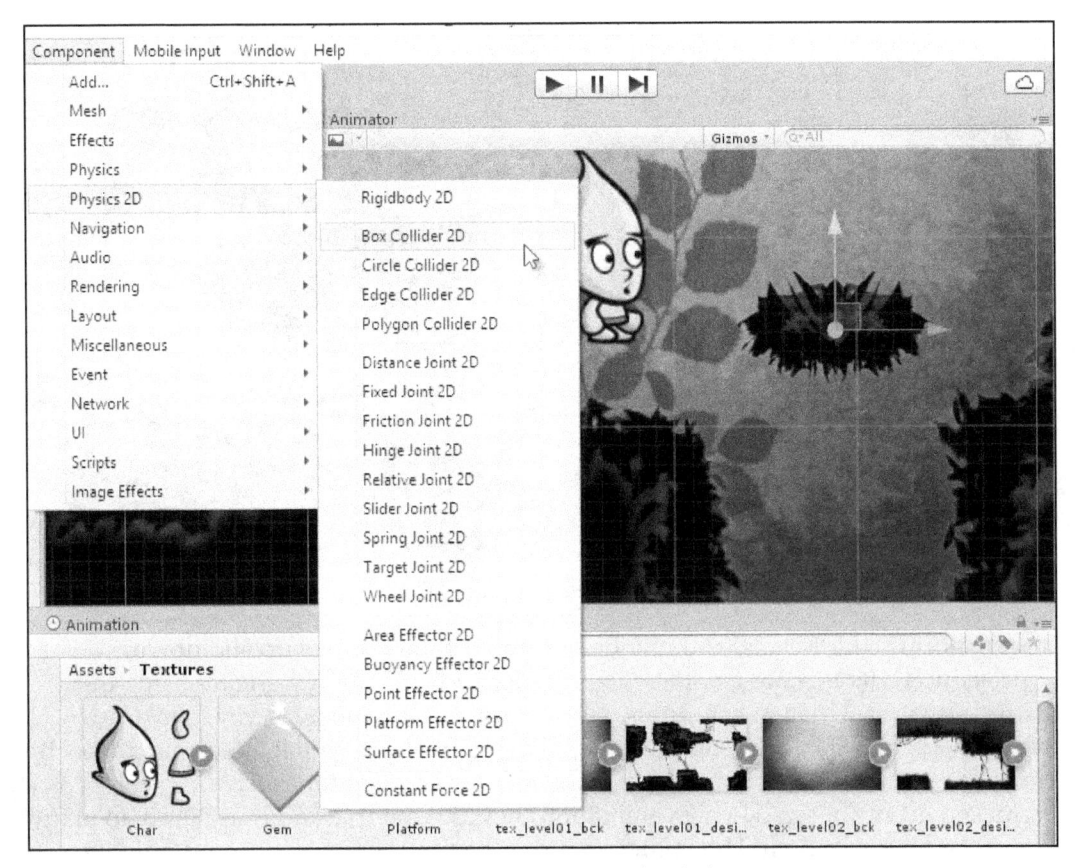

Figure 6.3: Adding a collider to the platform

Continuing the 2D Adventure

After the collider has been added to the platform, you may need to adjust its properties from the **Object Inspector**; specifically, its **Offset** and **Size** fields to make the collider match the size of the platform Sprite closely. Then, finally, test the platform by entering the play mode and standing the player character on the platform. By doing so, the player should not fall through the platform! See *Figure 6.4*:

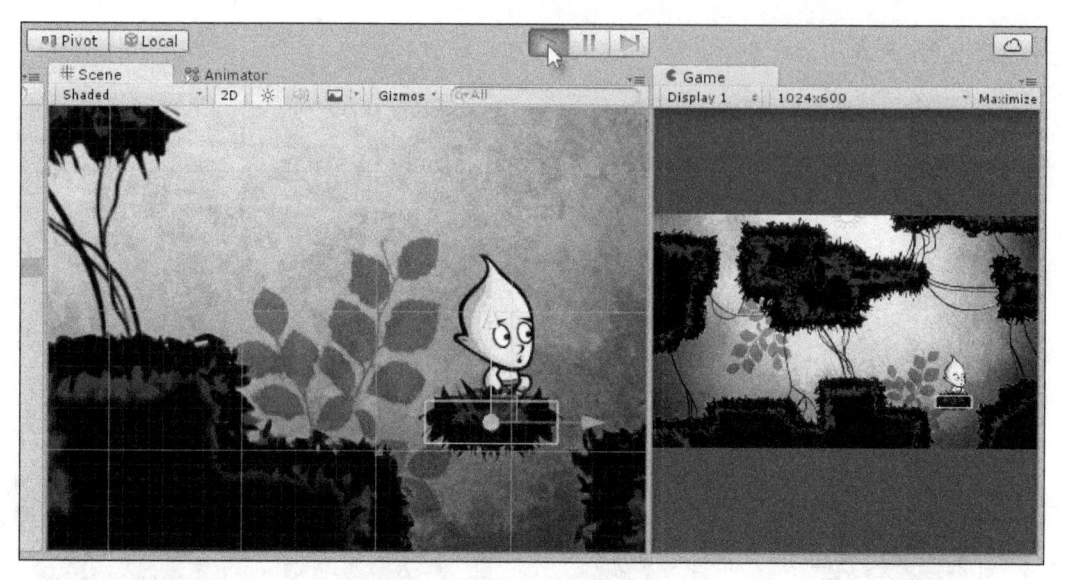

Figure 6.4: Testing platform collisions

The platform so far is static and motionless, and it should move up and down repeatedly. To fix this, we could create a predefined animation sequence using the **Animation Editor** via the **Window | Animation** menu option. However, instead, we'll use a script file. Frequently, when making animations, you'll often need to reach decisions about which option is best: *C# animations* or *Baked animations*. Typically, script should be chosen when an animation should be simple and must apply to many objects and vary for each. The following script file `PingPongMotion.cs` should be created and attached to the platform. See *Code Sample 6.1*, and code comments follow:

```
using UnityEngine;
using System.Collections;
//---------------------------------
public class PingPongMotion : MonoBehaviour
{
    //---------------------------------
    //This transformation
    private Transform ThisTransform = null;

    //Original position
```

```
  private Vector3 OrigPos = Vector3.zero;

  //Axes to move on
  public Vector3 MoveAxes = Vector2.zero;

  //Speed
  public float Distance = 3f;
  //-------------------------------
  // Use this for initialization
  void Awake ()
  {
    //Get transform component
    ThisTransform = GetComponent<Transform>();

    //Copy original position
    OrigPos = ThisTransform.position;
  }
  //-------------------------------
  // Update is called once per frame
  void Update ()
  {
    //Update platform position with ping pong
    ThisTransform.position = OrigPos + MoveAxes * Mathf.PingPong(Time.time, Distance);
  }
  //-------------------------------
}
//-------------------------------
```

Code Sample 6.1

The following points summarize the previous code sample:

- The `PingPongMotion` class is responsible for moving a `GameObject` back and forth from an original starting point.
- The `Awake` function uses the `OrigPos` variable to record the starting position of the `GameObject`.
- The `Update` function relies on the `Mathf.PingPong` function to transition a value smoothly between a minimum and maximum. This function fluctuates a value between minimum and maximum repeatedly and continuously over time, allowing you move objects linearly. For more information, see the Unity online documentation at http://docs.unity3d.com/ScriptReference/Mathf.PingPong.html.

Continuing the 2D Adventure

The completed code should be attached to the platform object in the scene and can be reused easily for any other object that should move up and down regularly (or left and right).

Creating other scenes – levels 2 and 3

Unlike the other games created in the book so far, our adventure game will span multiple scenes. That is, our game features several different screens, which the player may move between by walking off the edge of one screen and entering from the edge of another. Supporting this functionality introduces us to some new and interesting problems in Unity that are well worth exploring, as we'll see later. For now, let's make a second and third scene for the game, using the remaining background and foreground objects, and configuring collisions for each level, allowing the player prefab to work seamlessly with each environment. The details to create a level with collisions (Edge Colliders) are covered in depth in the previous chapter. The final, completed scenes are as follows:

- Level 2 is divided across two vertically arranged ledges with a set of moving platforms on the lower ledge. These are created from the moving-platform prefab created in the previous section. The upper ledge is, for now, non-hazardous but this will be changed later as we add gun turrets that can shoot the player character. This level can be reached from the first original level by walking off the left edge of the screen. See *Figure 6.5*:

Figure 6.5: Scene 2 – dangerous ledges and moving platforms

- Level 3 is reached from the first original level by walking off the right edge of the screen. It consists of one ground-level plane featuring a house. It will be home to an NPC character whom the player can meet and receive a quest to collect an item. This character is created later in the chapter. See *Figure 6.6*:

Figure 6.6: Scene 3 – a lonely house for an NPC

Both Levels 2 and 3 were created entirely with the techniques seen so far. However, to give each scene its own charm and character, some unique elements must be added—some of these are specific to each scene and some are more general. Let's now consider these in turn.

Continuing the 2D Adventure

Kill zones

A common scripted feature required by all scenes, but not yet implemented, is the **Kill Zone**. That is, the functionality to mark out a region of 2D space in the level that, when entered by the player, will kill them or damage them. This is especially useful to kill the player whenever they fall down a hole in the ground. Thus, the Kill Zone will be required in every level because every level created so far contains pits and holes in the ground. To implement this functionality, create a new and empty **GameObject** in any scene. (It doesn't matter which because we'll be making a prefab object that can be reused anywhere.) As previously mentioned, new **GameObjects** are created with the menu option, **GameObject | Create Empty**. Once created, name the object KillZone, then position it at the world origin (0,0,0), and finally, attach a Box Collider 2D component using the menu command, **Component | Physics 2D | Box Collider 2D**. The Box Collider will define the Kill Zone area. Remember to make sure that the **Box Collider 2D** is configured as a Trigger by checking the **Is Trigger** checkbox in the Inspector from the **Box Collider 2D** component. See *Figure 6.7*. A Trigger differs from a Collider; colliders prevent objects from passing through and Triggers detect when objects pass through, allowing you to perform custom behaviors.

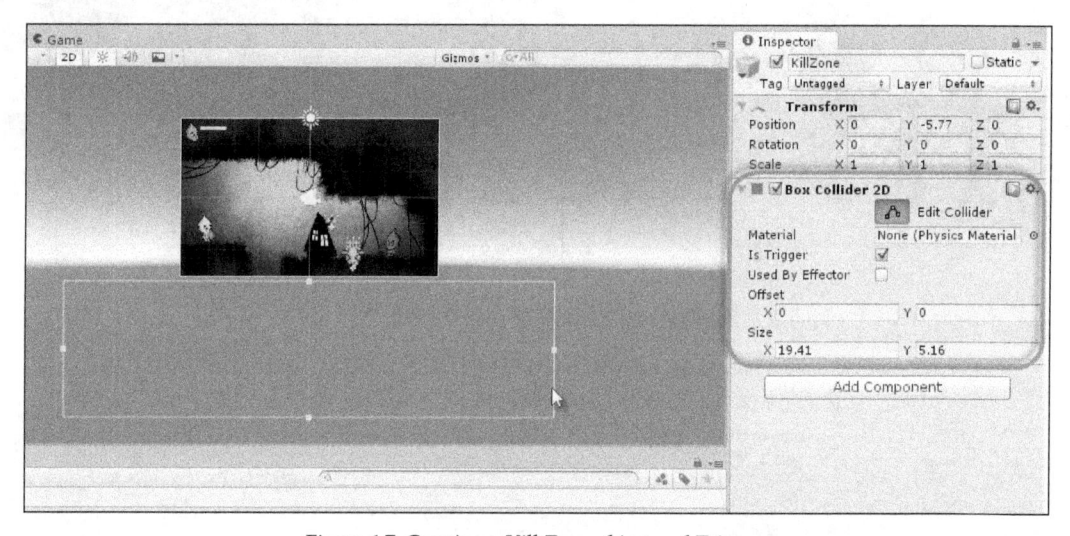

Figure 6.7: Creating a Kill Zone object and Trigger

Next, create a new script file `KillZone.cs`, which should be attached to the Kill Zone object in the scene. This script file is responsible for damaging the player's health for as long as they are in the Kill Zone. At this stage, there are several ways to approach kill zone implementation. One way is to destroy the player as soon as they enter the Kill Zone. The other is to damage the player for as long as they are in the Kill Zone. The second method is preferred here because of its versatility and contribution toward code reuse. Specifically, we get the option to damage the player by reducing their health at a particular speed (if we need to) as well as killing the player instantly simply by reducing their health by an increase in reduction speed. Let's see this at work in the following *Code Sample 6.2*:

```
//--------------------------------
using UnityEngine;
using System.Collections;
//--------------------------------
public class KillZone : MonoBehaviour {
    //--------------------------------
    //Amount to damage player per second
    public float Damage = 100f;
    //--------------------------------
    void OnTriggerStay2D(Collider2D other)
    {
        //If not player then exit
        if(!other.CompareTag("Player"))return;

        //Damage player by rate
        if(PlayerControl.PlayerInstance!=null)
            PlayerControl.Health -= Damage * Time.deltaTime;
    }
    //--------------------------------
}
//--------------------------------
```

Code Sample 6.2

- The `KillZone` class is responsible for continually damaging the player's health when a `GameObject`, tagged as `Player`, enters and remains within a Trigger Volume.

- The `OnTriggerStay2D` function is called automatically by Unity, once per frame, when an object with `RigidBody` enters and remains within a Trigger Volume. Thus, when a physics object enters the Kill Zone Trigger, the `OnTriggerStay2D` function will be called as frequently as the `Update` function. More information on `OnTriggerStay2D` can be found at the online Unity documentation at `http://docs.unity3d.com/ScriptReference/MonoBehaviour.OnTriggerStay2D.html`.

- The `Damage` variable encodes the reduction of health for the player by adjusting the public static property, `Health`, which is part of the `PlayerControl` class. When `Health` reaches 0, the player will be destroyed.

Now, give the game a test run, marking out a Kill Zone in the scene and walking the Player into it during play mode. On entry, the player character should be destroyed or damaged. To ensure that the player is killed instantly, increase the damage to a very high number, such as 9000! After testing, create a prefab from the Kill Zone by dragging and dropping it from the scene **Hierarchy** panel to the **Project** panel in the **Prefab** folder. Then, add the **Kill Zone** prefab to each level, adjusting and sizing the Collider as needed. See *Figure 6.8*:

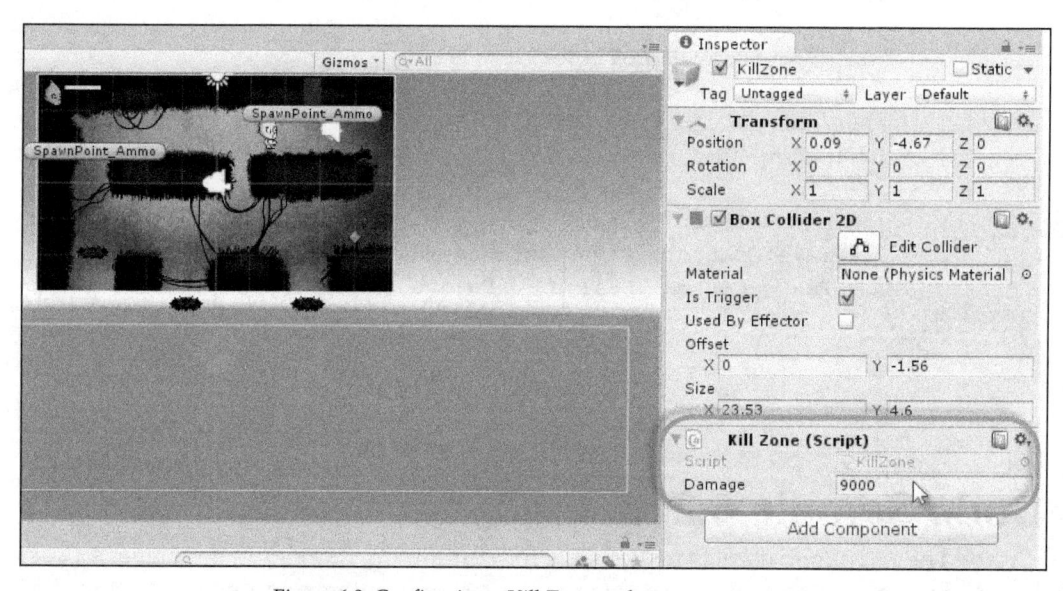

Figure 6.8: Configuring a Kill Zone to destroy on contact

The UI health bar

In the previous section, we introduced the first danger and hazard to the game; namely, a Kill Zone that can damage and potentially kill the player. As a result, their health has the potential to reduce from its starting state. It's therefore useful both to us as developers and gamers to visualize the health status. For this reason, let's focus on rendering player health to the screen as a UI health bar. This configuration of objects will also be made as a prefab, allowing reuse across multiple scenes This will prove a highly useful feature. *Figure 6.9* offers a glimpse of the future, displaying the result of our work to come:

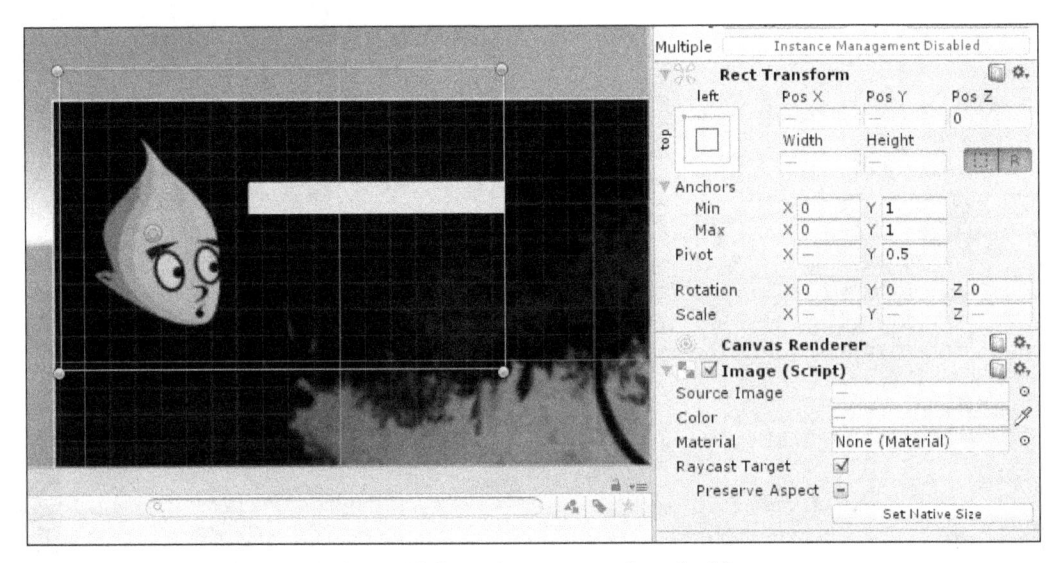

Figure 6.9: Preparing to create player health

Continuing the 2D Adventure

To get started, create a new GUI Canvas in the scene (any scene) by choosing **GameObject | UI | Canvas** from the application menu. Selecting this will automatically create an **EventSystem** object in the scene, if one does not exist already. This object is essential for proper use of the UI system. If you accidentally delete it, **EventSystem** can be recreated by choosing **GameObject | UI | Event System** from the application menu. The newly created Canvas object represents the surface on which the GUI will be drawn. See *Figure 6.10*:

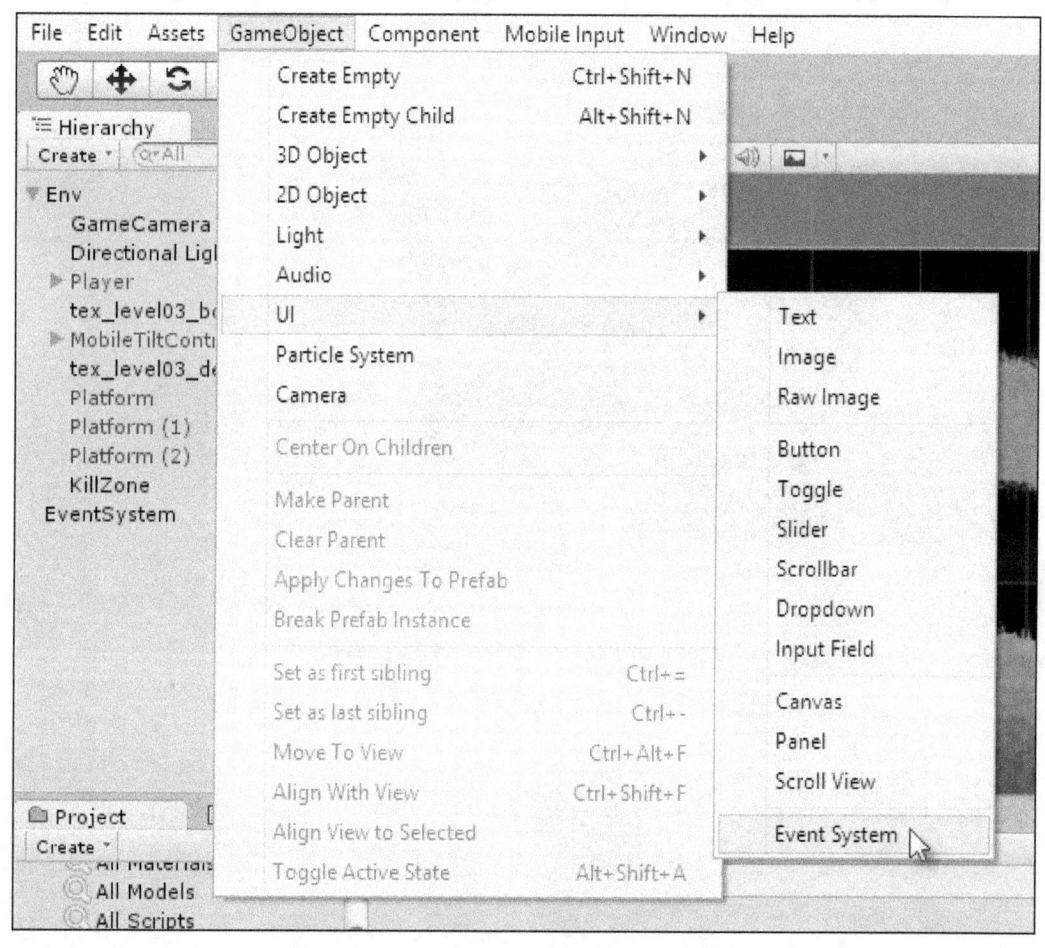

Figure 6.10: Creating a GUI Canvas and Event System

Chapter 6

Next, we'll create a new and separate camera object for the UI, adding it as a child of the newly created Canvas. By creating a separate camera for UI rendering, we can apply camera effects and other image adjustments separately to the UI, if we need to. To create a Camera as a child, right-click on the **Canvas** object in the **Hierarchy** panel and, from the **Context** menu, choose **Camera**. This adds a new camera object to the scene as a child of the selected object. See *Figure 6.11*:

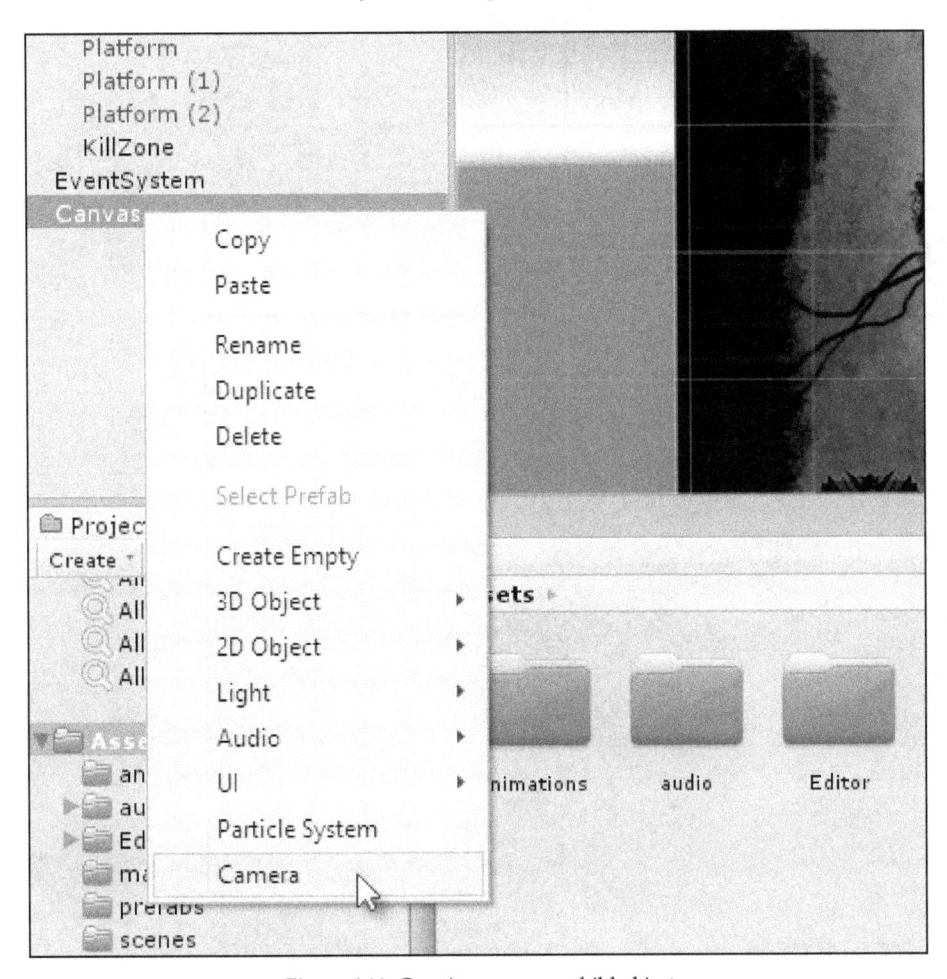

Figure 6.11: Creating a camera child object

Continuing the 2D Adventure

Now, configure the UI camera to be an Orthographic camera. We saw how to do this in the previous chapter, as well as earlier chapters too. *Figure 6.12* displays the camera settings for an orthographic camera. Remember that an Orthographic camera is truly 2D insofar as it removes perspective and foreshortening effects from the render result, which is appropriate for GUIs and other objects that live and work in screen space. In addition, the camera **Depth** field, from the **Object Inspector**, should be higher than the main game camera to ensure that it renders on top of everything else. Otherwise, the GUI could potentially render beneath and be ineffectual in the game.

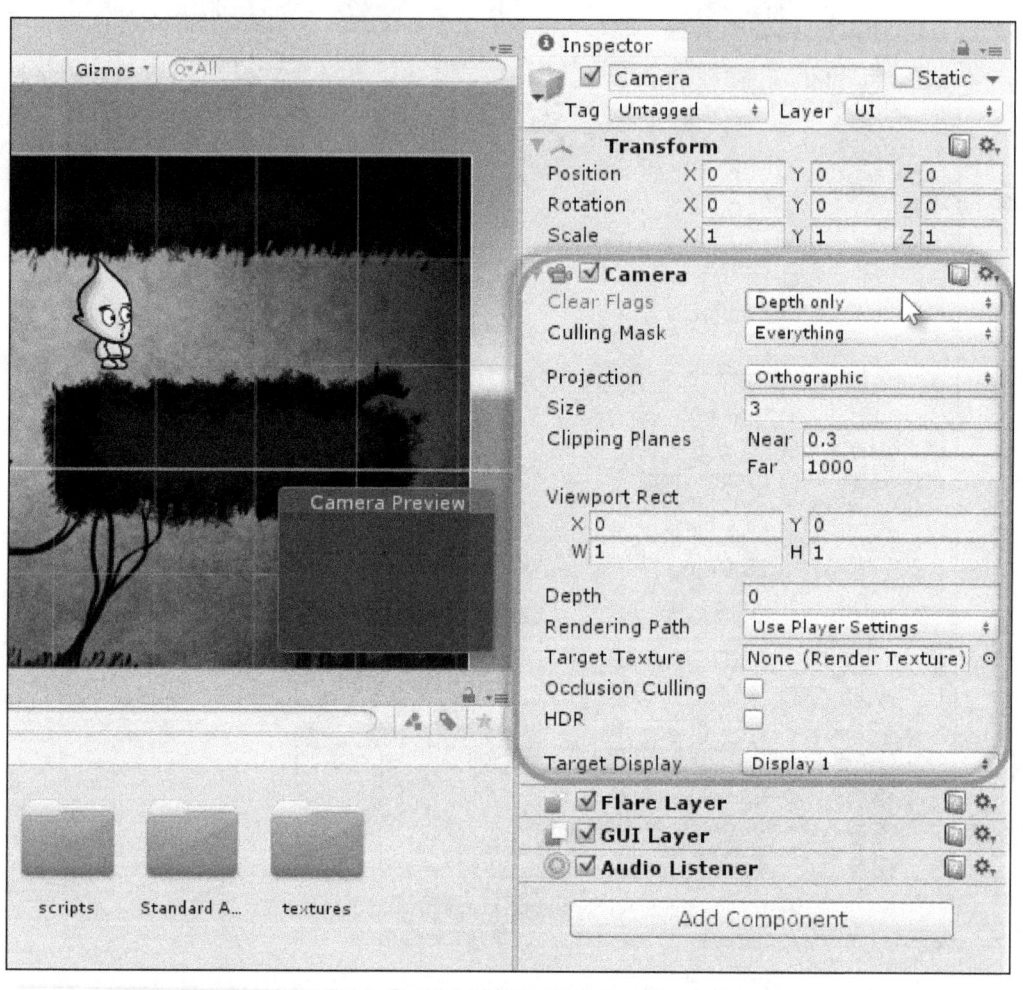

Figure 6.12: Configuring an Orthographic camera for GUI rendering

Chapter 6

The created camera is almost ready to go! However, right now, it's configured to render everything in the scene just like any other camera. This means that the scene is effectively being rendered twice by two separate cameras. This is not only wasteful and poor for performance, but it makes the second camera totally unnecessary. Instead, we want the first and original camera to show everything in the scene, in terms of characters and environments, but to ignore GUI objects, and likewise, the newly created GUI camera should show only GUI objects. To fix this, select the main game camera and, from the **Object Inspector**, click on the **Culling Mask** drop-down list in the **Camera** component. From here, remove the check mark for the UI layer. This drop-down list allows you to select layers to be ignored for the rendering from the selected camera. See *Figure 6.13*:

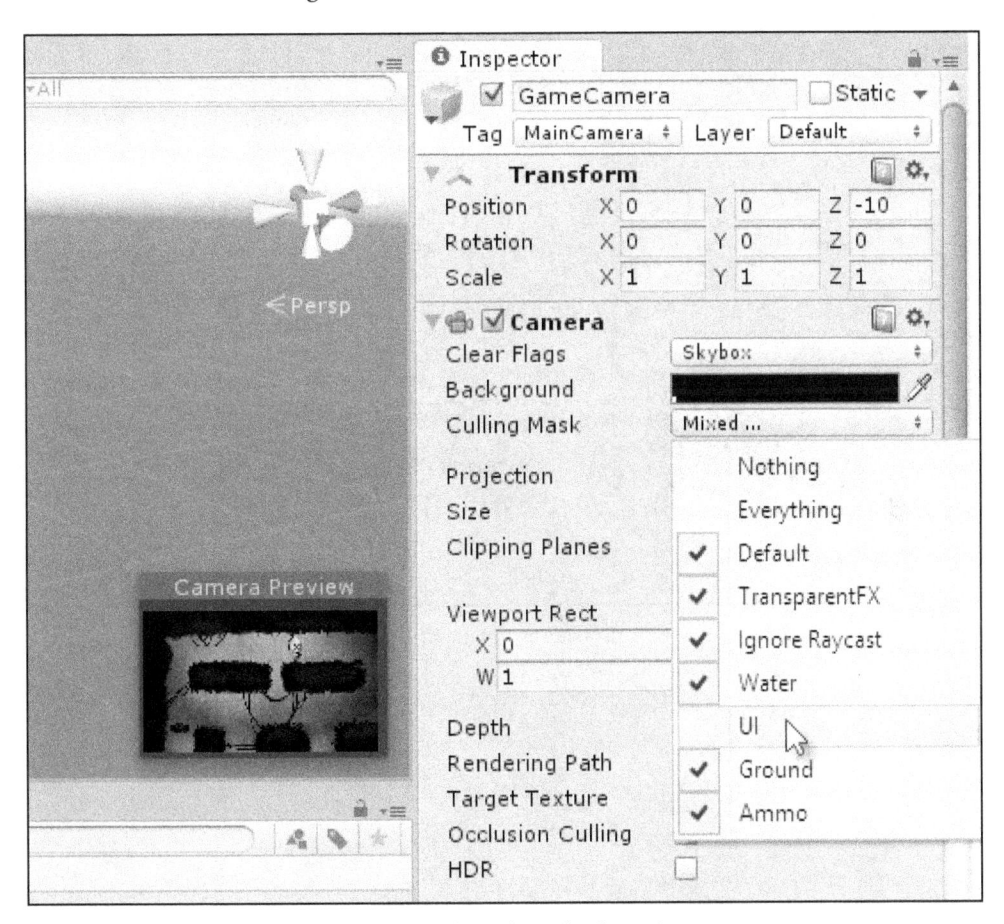

Figure 6.13: Ignore the UI layer for the main camera

[293]

Continuing the 2D Adventure

Now, select the GUI camera object and, for the **Culling Mask** field in the **Camera** component, select the **Nothing** option to deselect all options, and then enable the UI layer to render only UI layer objects. See *Figure 6.14*. Good work!

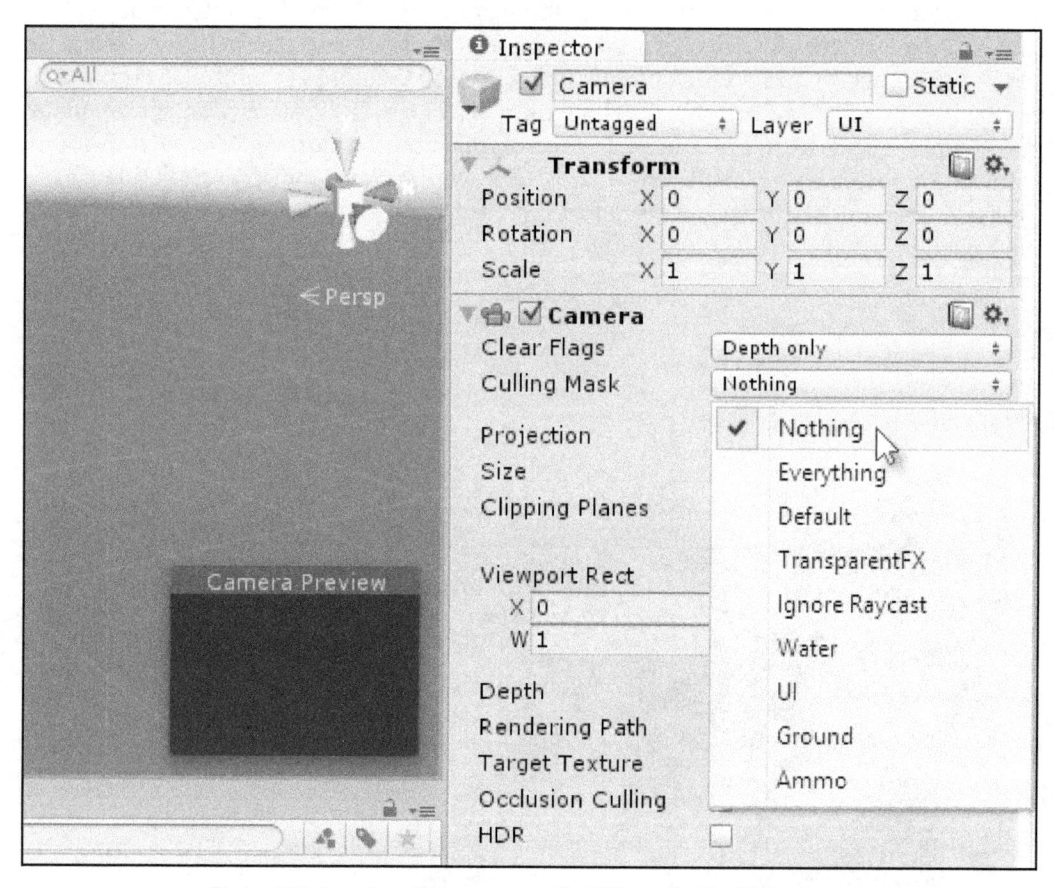

Figure 6.14: Ignoring all layers except the UI layer for the GUI camera

By default, any newly created Canvas is configured to work in the Screen Space Overlay mode, which means it renders on top of everything else in the scene that is not associated with any specific camera. In addition, all GUI elements will be sized and scaled on the basis of this. Consequently, to make our work simpler, let's start creating the GUI by first configuring the **Canvas** object to work with the newly created GUI camera. To do this, select the **Canvas** object and, from the **Canvas** component in the **Object Inspector**, change the **Render Mode** from **Screen Space - Overlay** to **Screen Space - Camera**. Then, drag and drop the GUI camera object to the **Camera** field. See *Figure 6.15*:

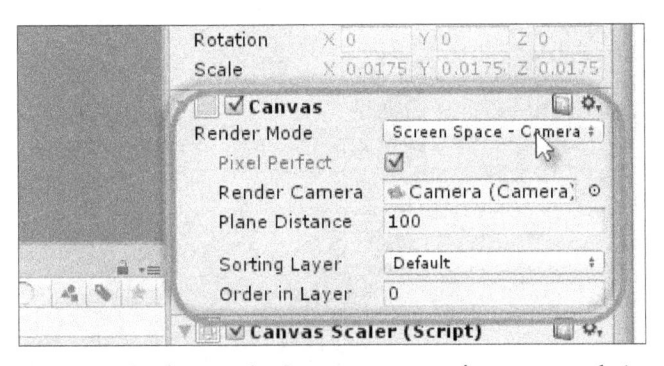

Figure 6.15: Configuring the Canvas component for camera rendering

Next, let's configure the **Canvas Scaler** component, which is attached to the **Canvas** object. This component is responsible for how the GUI appears when the screen size is changed, from either up-scaling or down-scaling. In short, for our game, the GUI should up- and down-scale relatively to the screen size. For this reason, change the **UI Scale Mode** drop-down to **Scale With Screen Size**, and then enter the game resolution of `1024 x 600` in the **Reference Resolution** field. See *Figure 6.16*:

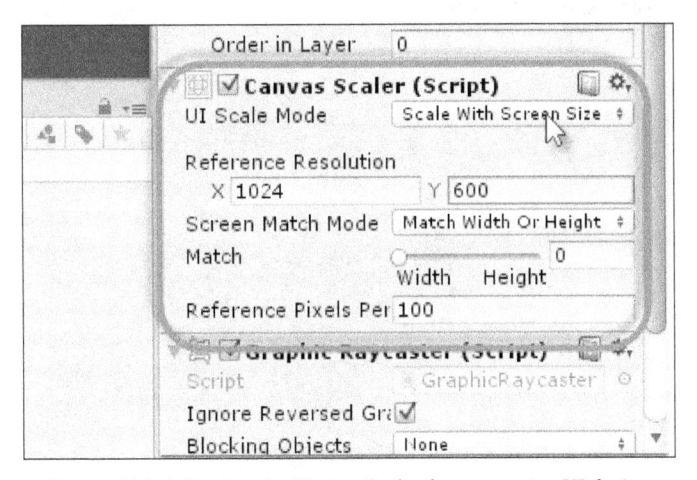

Figure 6.16: Adjusting the Canvas Scaler for responsive UI design

Continuing the 2D Adventure

Now, we can start adding GUI elements to the game, knowing that they will appear correctly when added to the scene. To display health, a representation of the player will be useful. Create a new **Image** object by right-clicking on the **Canvas** object from the **Hierarchy** panel and choosing **UI | Image** from the context menu. Once created, select the **Image** object and, from the **Object Inspector** (in the **Image** component), drag and drop the player head sprite from the **Project** panel to the **Source Image** field. Then, use the **Rect Transform** tool (*T* on the keyboard) to resize the image in place at the top-left corner of the screen. See *Figure 6.17*:

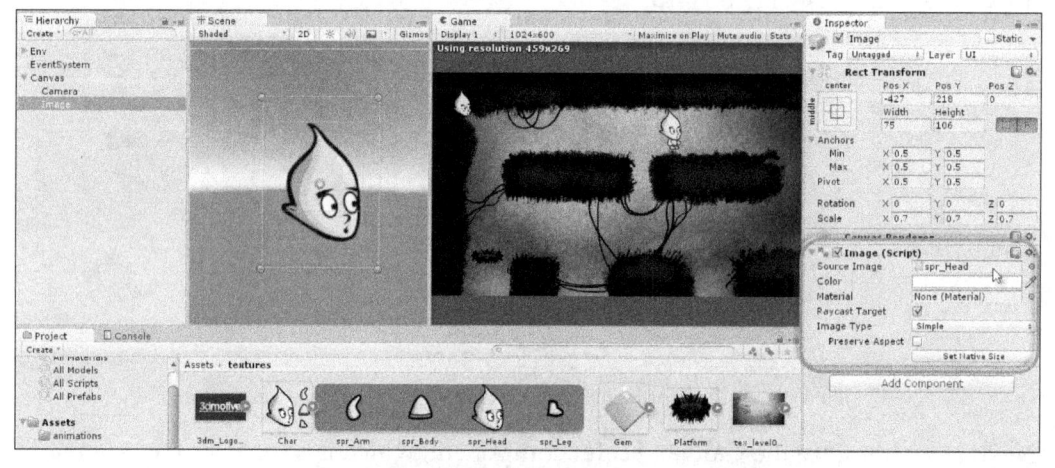

Figure 6.17: Adding a head image to the GUI Canvas

> If you cannot see the added head image, remember to assign the UI layer to render by the UI camera. In addition, you may need to offset the GUI camera back along the Z axis to include the head sprite within the Camera Frustum (Viewing Area).

Chapter 6

Finally, anchor the Head Sprite to the top-left of the screen by clicking on the **Anchor Preset** button in the **Rect Transform** component from the **Object Inspector**. Choose top-left alignment. This locks the head sprite to the screen top-left, ensuring that the interface would look consistent at multiple resolutions. See *Figure 6.18*:

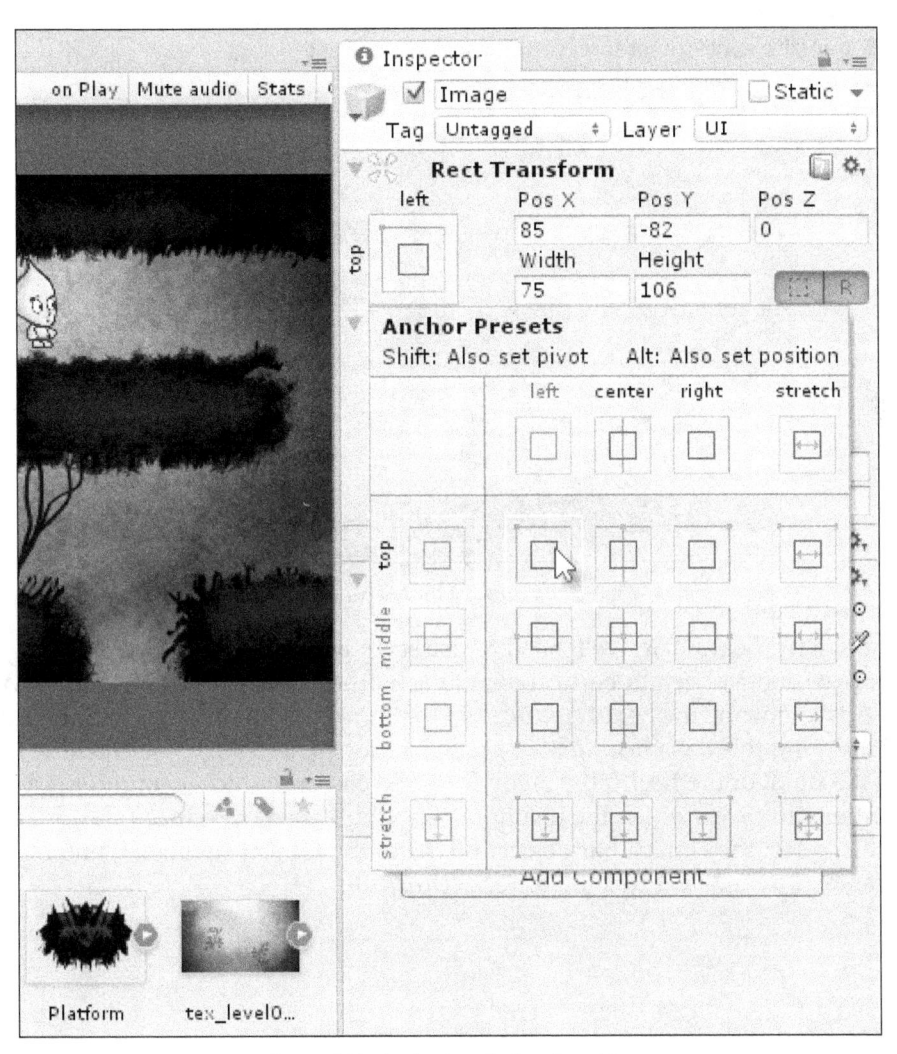

Figure 6.18: Anchoring the head position

Continuing the 2D Adventure

To create the health bar, add a new **Image** object to the GUI Canvas by right-clicking on the **Canvas** and selecting **UI | Image** from the context menu. For this object, leave the **Source Image** field empty and choose red for the **Color** field, **RGB (255,0,0)**. This will represent the background or *red status* for the health bar when it's fully depleted. Then, use the **Rect Transform** tool to resize the bar as needed, anchoring to the top-left screen corner. See *Figure 6.19*:

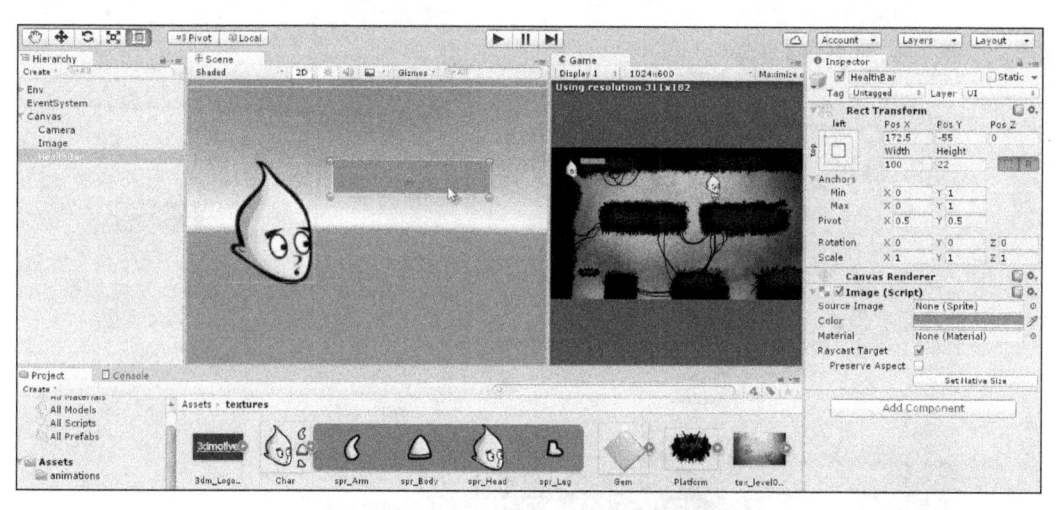

Figure 6.19: Creating the red health status

To complete the health bar, we'll need to use scripting. Specifically, we're going to overlap two identical health bars on top of each other, one red and one green. We'll scale the green bar as the health reduces so that it reveals the red bar underneath. Before scripting this behavior, further configuration is necessary. Specifically, let's change the pivot of the health bar away from the center and to the middle-left point—the point from which the health bar should scale as it reduces and increases. To do this, select the **Health bar** object and, from the **Object Inspector**, enter a new **Pivot** value of 0 for **X** and 0.5 for **Y**. See *Figure 6.20*:

[298]

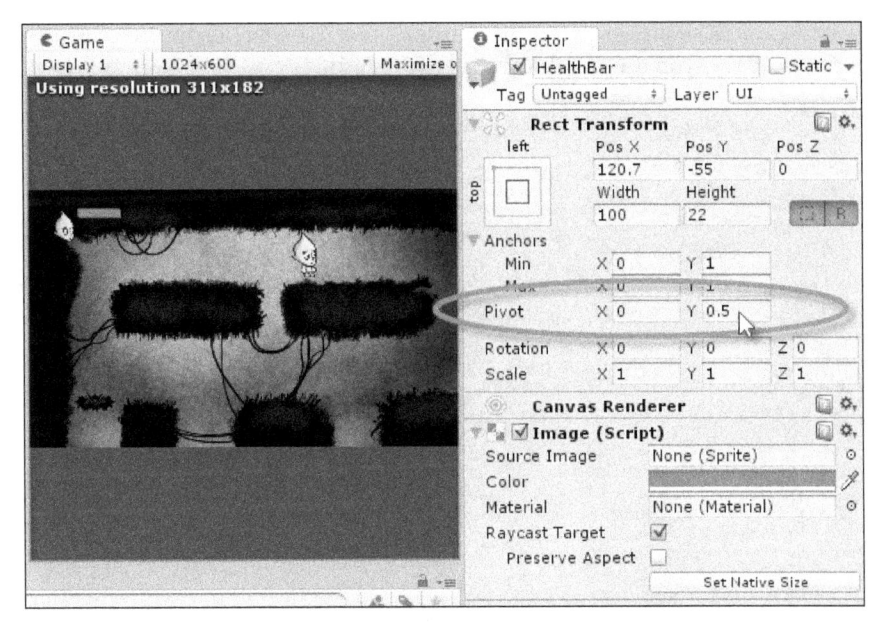

Figure 6.20: Repositioning the Pivot for the health bar

To create the green overlay for the health, select the red health bar and duplicate it. Name the duplicate `Health_Green` and drag and drop it to appear beneath the red version in the **Hierarchy** panel. The ordering of objects in the hierarchy relates to the draw order for GUI elements—lower-order objects are rendered on top of higher-order objects. See *Figure 6.21*:

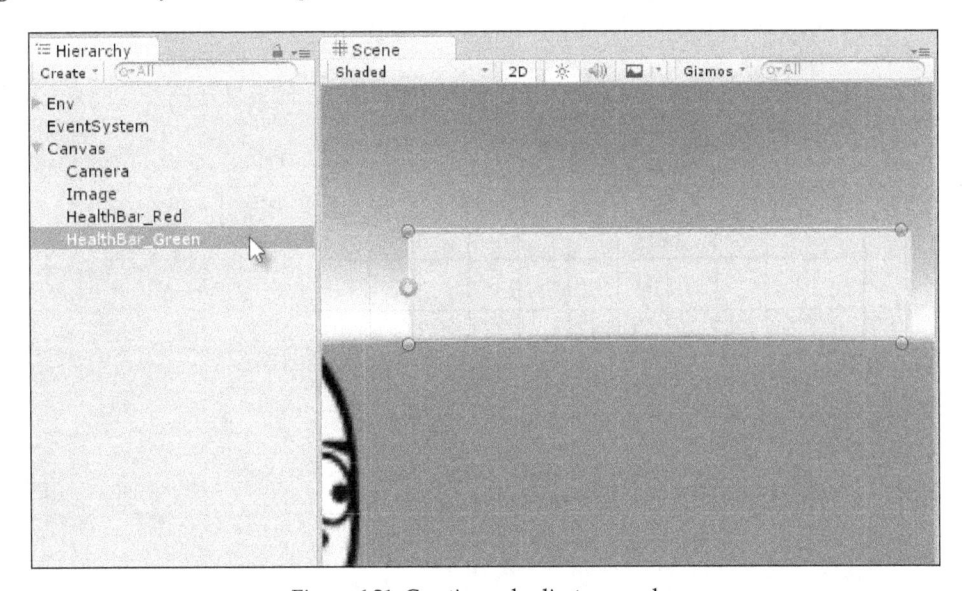

Figure 6.21: Creating a duplicate green bar

Now, we need to make a new script file linking the width of the green bar to the health of the player. This means that reductions in health will reduce the width of the green bar, revealing the red bar beneath. Create a new script file named `HealthBar.cs` and attach it to the green bar. The following is the *Code Sample 6.3* for the `HealthBar` class:

```
using UnityEngine;
using System.Collections;

public class HealthBar : MonoBehaviour
{
  //Reference to this transform component
  private RectTransform ThisTransform = null;

  //Catch up speed
  public float MaxSpeed = 10f;

    void Awake()
    {
      //Get transform component
      ThisTransform = GetComponent<RectTransform>();
    }

    void Start()
    {
      //Set Start Health
      if(PlayerControl.PlayerInstance!=null)
        ThisTransform.sizeDelta = new
          Vector2(Mathf.Clamp(PlayerControl.
Health,0,100),ThisTransform.sizeDelta.y);
    }

    // Update is called once per frame
    void Update ()
    {
      //Update health property
      float HealthUpdate = 0f;

      if(PlayerControl.PlayerInstance!=null)
        HealthUpdate =
          Mathf.MoveTowards(ThisTransform.rect.width,
            PlayerControl.Health, MaxSpeed);
```

```
            ThisTransform.sizeDelta = new 
                Vector2(Mathf.Clamp(HealthUpdate,0,100),ThisTransform.
sizeDelta.y);
    }
}
```

Code Sample 6.3

The following points summarize the code sample:

- The `HealthBar` class is responsible for reducing the width of a green (on the top) health bar, based on the player's health.

- The `SizeDelta` property of `RectTransform` is used to set the width of `RectTransform`. More information on this property can be found at the online Unity documentation at `http://docs.unity3d.com/462/Documentation/ScriptReference/RectTransform-sizeDelta.html`.

- The `Mathf.MoveTowards` function is used to gradually and smoothly transition the health bar width from its existing width to its destination width over time. That is, as and when player health is reduced, the health bar will decrease gradually as opposed to instantly. More information can be found at the online Unity documentation at `http://docs.unity3d.com/ScriptReference/Mathf.MoveTowards.html`.

Finally, make a prefab of the UI objects by dragging and dropping the topmost **Canvas** object from the **Hierarchy** panel to the **Project** panel in the **Prefab** folder. This allows the UI system to be reused across multiple scenes.

Continuing the 2D Adventure

Ammo and hazards

Level 2 is a hazardous place. It should feature not only pits and holes leading to kill zones, but also fixed dangers such as gun turrets that can shoot the player. This section focuses on their creation. To get started, let's make a gun turret. Now, the course companion files don't include a texture or image for the gun turrets, but when using the dark silhouette style as we are here, we can easily make a consistent turret prop from primitives. In particular, create a new cube object (**GameObject | 3D Object | Cube**), rescale it to approximate a gun turret, and then position it to the upper ledge in the scene where it will appear as part of the scenery. See *Figure 6.22*. Note that you can also use the **Rect Transform** tool to resize primitives!

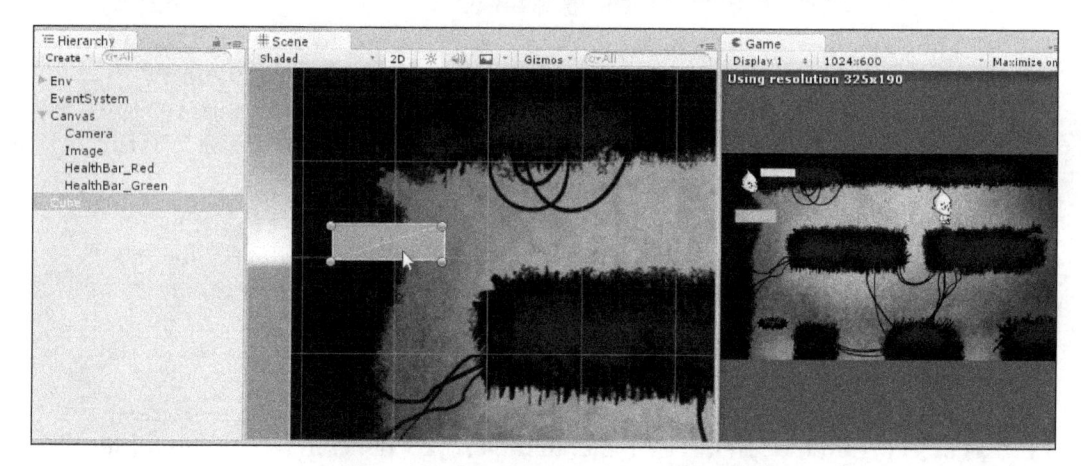

Figure 6.22: Creating a prop for a gun turret

Of course, the gun turret created so far is a conspicuous and obvious gray color. To solve this, create a new black material. Right-click in the **Project** panel and choose **Create | Material** from the context menu. Assign the material a black color from the **Object Inspector** in the **Albedo** field, and then drag and drop the material from the **Project** panel to the **Turret** object in the scene. Make sure that the **Smoothness** field for the black material is reduced to 0 to prevent a shiny or glowing appearance. After the material is assigned, the turret will mix with the scene and its color scheme will be much better! See *Figure 6.23*:

Chapter 6

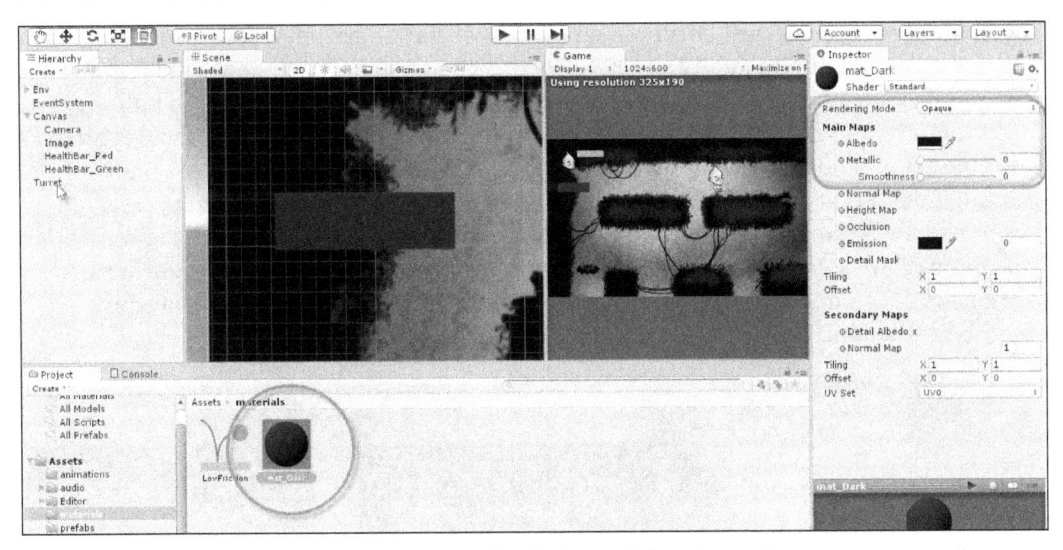

Figure 6.23: Assigning a black material to the turret

Now, the turret must fire ammo. To achieve this, it'll need an empty game object to spawn ammo. Let's create this now by choosing **GameObject | Create Empty** and drag and drop the object in the **Hierarchy** panel to the **Turret Cube** in order to make it a child of the turret. Then, position the empty object to the tip of the cannon. Once positioned, assign an icon representation to the empty to make it visible in the viewport. Ensure that the empty is selected and, from the **Inspector**, click on the cube icon (beside the object name) to assign it a graphical representation. See *Figure 6.24*:

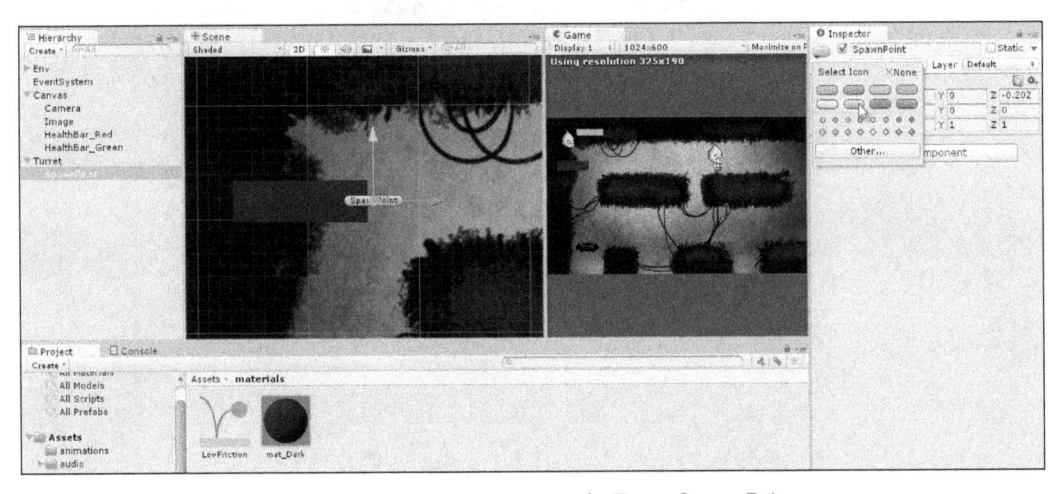

Figure 6.24: Assigning an icon to the Turret Spawn Point

Continuing the 2D Adventure

Before moving further with ammo spawning, we'll actually need some ammo to spawn. That is, the turret must fire something, and now it's time to create this something. The ammo should appear as a glowing and pulsating plasma ball. To build this, create a new particle system by choosing **GameObject | ParticleSystem** from the application menu. Remember that a particle system is useful to create special effects such as rain, fire, dust, smoke, sparkles, and more. When you create a new particle system from the main menu, a new object is created in the scene and is automatically selected. When selected, you can preview how the particle system works and looks in the **Scene** viewport. By default, the system will be spawning small blob-like particles. See *Figure 6.25*:

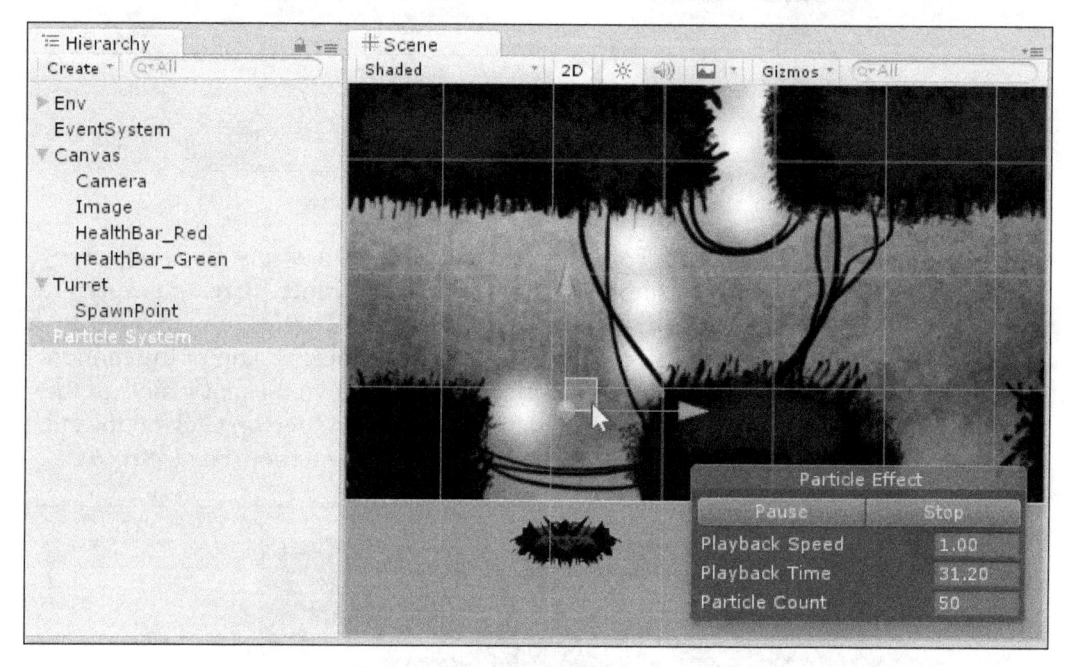

Figure 6.25: Creating a particle system

Sometimes, on creating a particle system for a 2D game, the particles themselves may not be visible because they appear behind other 2D objects in the scene, such as the background and characters. You can control the depth order of the particle system from the **Object Inspector**. Scroll down in the **Object Inspector** and click on the **Renderer** roll-out title to expand more options, bringing them into view. From the **Renderer** group, set the **Order In Layer** field to a higher value, above the order of other objects to render the particles in front. See *Figure 6.26*:

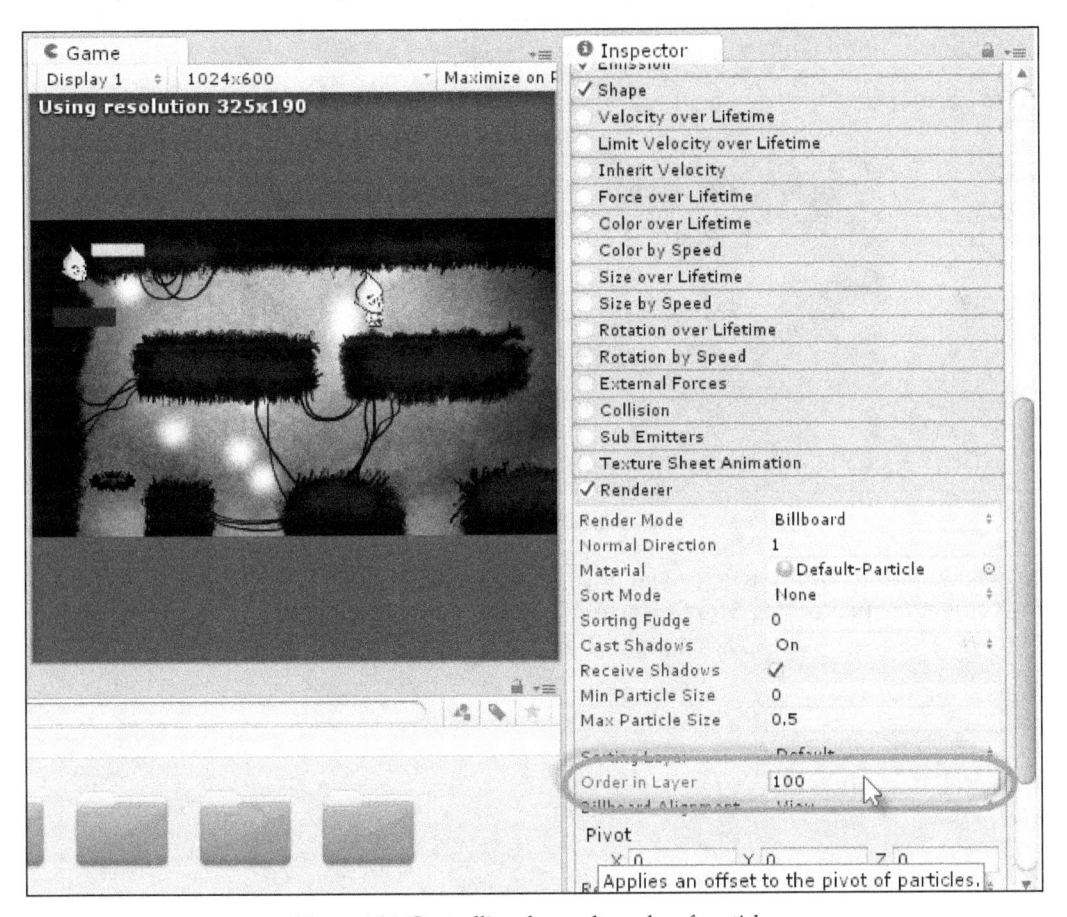

Figure 6.26: Controlling the render order of particles

Continuing the 2D Adventure

Excellent, we should now see particles in the viewport. Getting a particle system to look and behave correctly takes some tweaking and trial and error. It involves testing settings, previewing their effects in the viewport, making judgments about what is needed, and then tweaking and amending as needed. To start creating a more-believable ammo object, I want particles to spawn slowly in multiple directions and not just one direction. To achieve this, expand the **Shape** field from the **Object Inspector** to control the shape of the spawn surface. Change the **Shape** from **Cone** to **Sphere** and set **Radius** to 0.01. On doing this, particles will spawn and travel in all directions emitted from a Sphere's surface. See *Figure 6.27*:

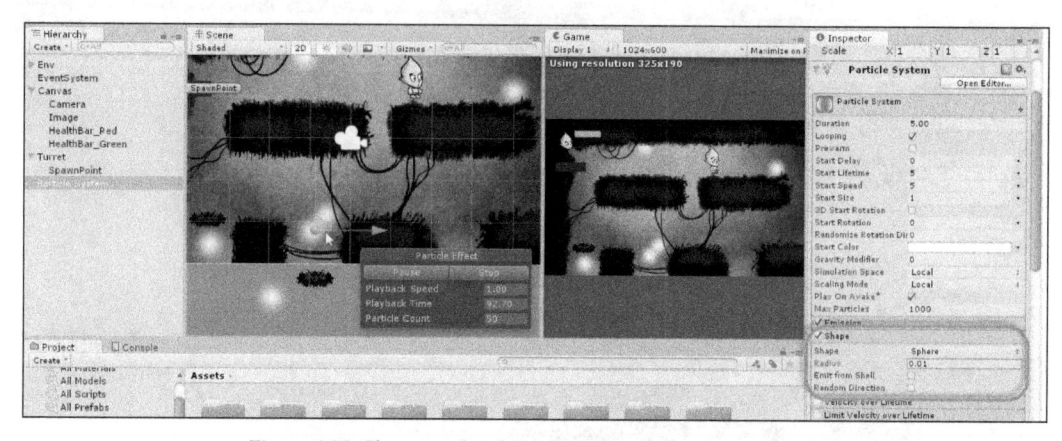

Figure 6.27: Changing the shape of the particle-system emitter

Now, adjust the main particle system properties to create the energy-ball effect. From the **Object Inspector**, set **Start Lifetime** to 0.19, **Start Speed** to 0.88, and **Start Size** to 0.59. Then, set **Start Color** to **teal (light blue)**. See *Figure 6.28*:

[306]

Chapter 6

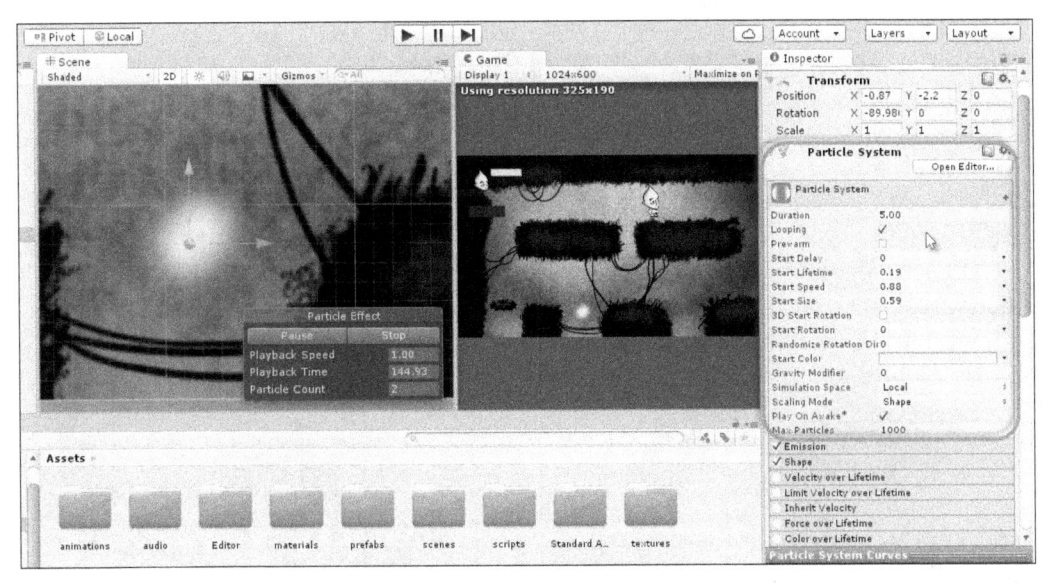

Figure 6.28: Configuring the particle system's main properties

Great! The particle system should now look just as we need it. However, if we press play on the toolbar, it doesn't move. Ammo should, of course, hurtle through the air and collide with its target. So, let's make a Mover script that should be attached to the object. The following is the code:

```
using UnityEngine;
using System.Collections;
//--------------------------------
public class Mover : MonoBehaviour
{
    //--------------------------------
    public float Speed = 10f;
    private Transform ThisTransform = null;
    //--------------------------------
    // Use this for initialization
    void Awake()
    {
        ThisTransform = GetComponent<Transform>();
    }
    //--------------------------------
    // Update is called once per frame
    void Update ()
    {
```

```
        //Update object position
        ThisTransform.position += ThisTransform.forward * Speed *
Time.deltaTime;
    }
    //---------------------------------
}
//---------------------------------
```

The Mover features nothing that we haven't seen before many times already. It moves an object (the ammo) in direction of its forward vector. For this reason, as our game is two-dimensional, the particle system object may need to be rotated in order to turn the forward vector along the X axis. See *Figure 6.29*:

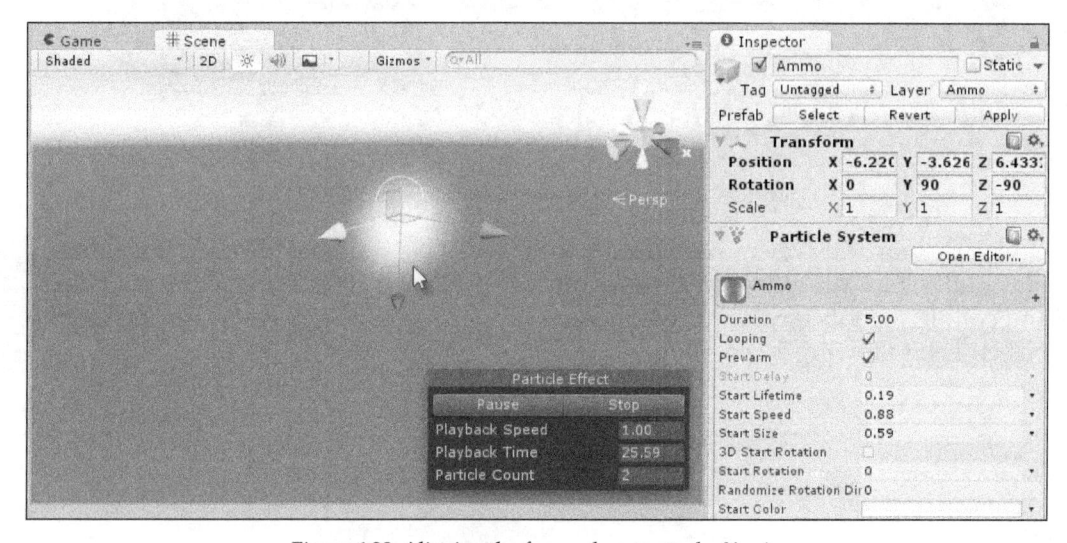

Figure 6.29: Aligning the forward vector to the X axis

Next, in addition to moving through the level, the ammo object must collide with and damage the player character on impact. To achieve this, several steps must be taken. First, a Rigidbody component must be attached to the ammo, allowing it to collide with other objects. To add **Rigidbody**, select the Ammo object in the scene and, from the Application menu, choose **Component | Physics | Rigidbody2D**. Once added, enable the **Is Kinematic** checkbox from the Rigidbody component in the **Object Inspector**. This ensures that the object will travel based on the Mover script and still interact with physical objects without being affected by gravity. See *Figure 6.30*:

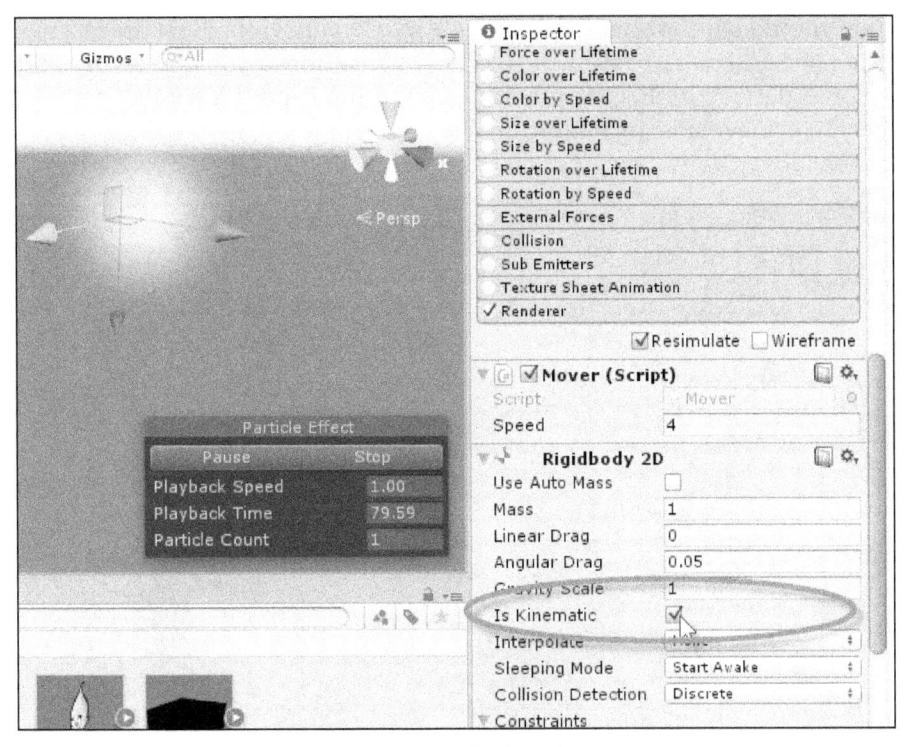

Figure 6.30: Marking Rigidbody with Is Kinematic

Now for a Circle Collider to the ammo object to give the ammo some shape, form, and size in terms of physics, allowing collisions to be detected between the ammo and its target. To do this, choose **Component | Physics 2D CircleCollider** from the application menu. Once added, mark the collider as Trigger and change **Radius** until it approximates the size of the ammo object. See *Figure 6.31*:

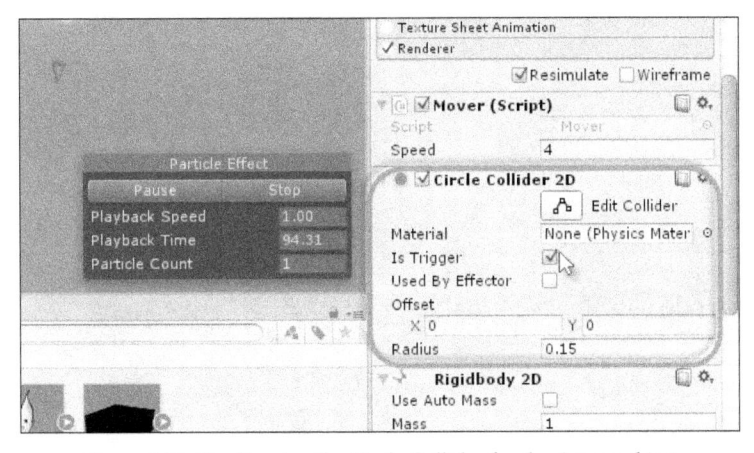

Figure 6.31: Configuring the Circle Collider for the Ammo object

Continuing the 2D Adventure

The ammo should support two final and additional behaviors. First, the ammo should damage and perhaps destroy any target it collides with, and second, the ammo should destroy itself, both after an elapsed time and if it collides with the target. To achieve this, two additional scripts will be created; specifically, CollideDestroy.cs and Ammo.cs. The following code lists the Ammo.cs file:

```csharp
using UnityEngine;
using System.Collections;
//-----------------------------------------
public class Ammo : MonoBehaviour
{
    //-----------------------------------------
    //Damage inflicted on Player
    public float Damage = 100f;

    //Lifetime for ammo
    public float LifeTime = 1f;
    //-----------------------------------------
    void Start()
    {
        Invoke ("Die", LifeTime);
    }//-----------------------------------------

    void OnTriggerEnter2D(Collider2D other)
    {
        //If not player then exit
        if(!other.CompareTag("Player")) return;

        //Inflict damage
        PlayerControl.Health -= Damage;
    }
    //-----------------------------------------
    public void Die()
    {
        Destroy(gameObject);
    }
}
//-----------------------------------------
```

The following code lists the CollideDestroy.cs file:

```csharp
//-----------------------------------
using UnityEngine;
using System.Collections;
//-----------------------------------
```

```csharp
public class CollideDestroy : MonoBehaviour
{
    //---------------------------------
    //When hit objects with associated tag, then destroy
    public string TagCompare = string.Empty;
    //---------------------------------
    void OnTriggerEnter2D(Collider2D other)
    {
        if(!other.CompareTag(TagCompare))return;

        Destroy(gameObject);
    }
    //---------------------------------
}
//---------------------------------
```

The code spanning across these files is functionality that we encountered before when making the Twin-stick Space Shooter. Both the files should be attached to the ammo object in the scene. Once completed, just drag and drop the ammo object from the scene viewport to the **Project** panel in the **Prefabs** folder. This makes an Ammo prefab, ready to add to any scene. See *Figure 6.32*:

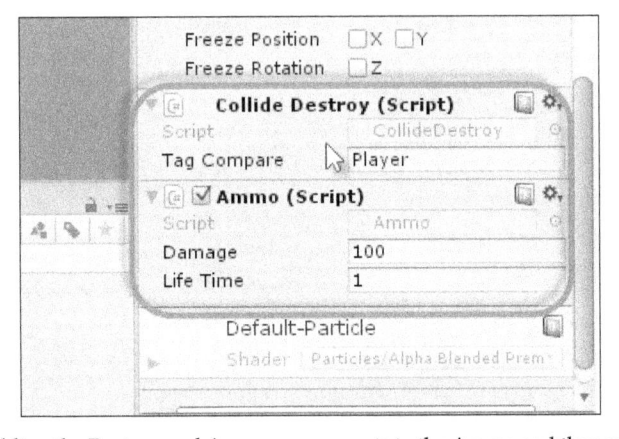

Figure 6.32: Adding the Destroy and Ammo components to the Ammo and then making a prefab

Excellent work! You now have an ammo object that fires, moves, and collides with the player. By setting the **Damage** setting high enough, you will be able to destroy the player on impact. Give this a test now by adding an ammo object to the scene and pressing the play icon. Of course, right now, nothing in the scene actually fires the ammo. We'll explore that next.

Gun turrets and ammo

We've now created an ammo object (a projectile) and we've started to engineer a gun turret object, but it doesn't yet spawn ammo. Let's create this functionality now. We have a spawn point positioned in front of the turret parented to it as a child object. We'll attach a new script file called `AmmoSpawner.cs` to this object. This script is responsible for generating ammo at regular intervals. Refer to the following code:

```csharp
//---------------------------------
using UnityEngine;
using System.Collections;
//---------------------------------
public class AmmoSpawner : MonoBehaviour
{
    //---------------------------------
    //Reference to ammo prefab
    public GameObject AmmoPrefab = null;

    //Reference to transform
    private Transform ThisTransform = null;

    //Vector for time range
    public Vector2 TimeDelayRange = Vector2.zero;

    //Lifetime for ammo spawned
    public float AmmoLifeTime = 2f;

    //Ammo Speed
    public float AmmoSpeed = 4f;

    //Ammo Damage
    public float AmmoDamage = 100f;
    //---------------------------------
    void Awake()
    {
        ThisTransform = GetComponent<Transform>();
    }
    //---------------------------------
    void Start()
    {
        FireAmmo();
    }
    //---------------------------------
    public void FireAmmo()
```

```
    {
        GameObject Obj = Instantiate(AmmoPrefab,
            ThisTransform.position, ThisTransform.rotation) as
                GameObject;
        Ammo AmmoComp = Obj.GetComponent<Ammo>();
        Mover MoveComp = Obj.GetComponent<Mover>();
        AmmoComp.LifeTime = AmmoLifeTime;
        AmmoComp.Damage = AmmoDamage;
        MoveComp.Speed = AmmoSpeed;

        //Wait until next random interval
        Invoke("FireAmmo", Random.Range(TimeDelayRange.x,
            TimeDelayRange.y));
    }
    //---------------------------------
}
//---------------------------------
```

The preceding code relies on the `Invoke` function called at random intervals using `Random.Range` in order to instantiate a new ammo prefab into the scene. This code could be improved using Object Pooling (or Caching), as discussed in the previous chapter with ammo, but in this case, the code performs acceptably. See *Figure 6.33*:

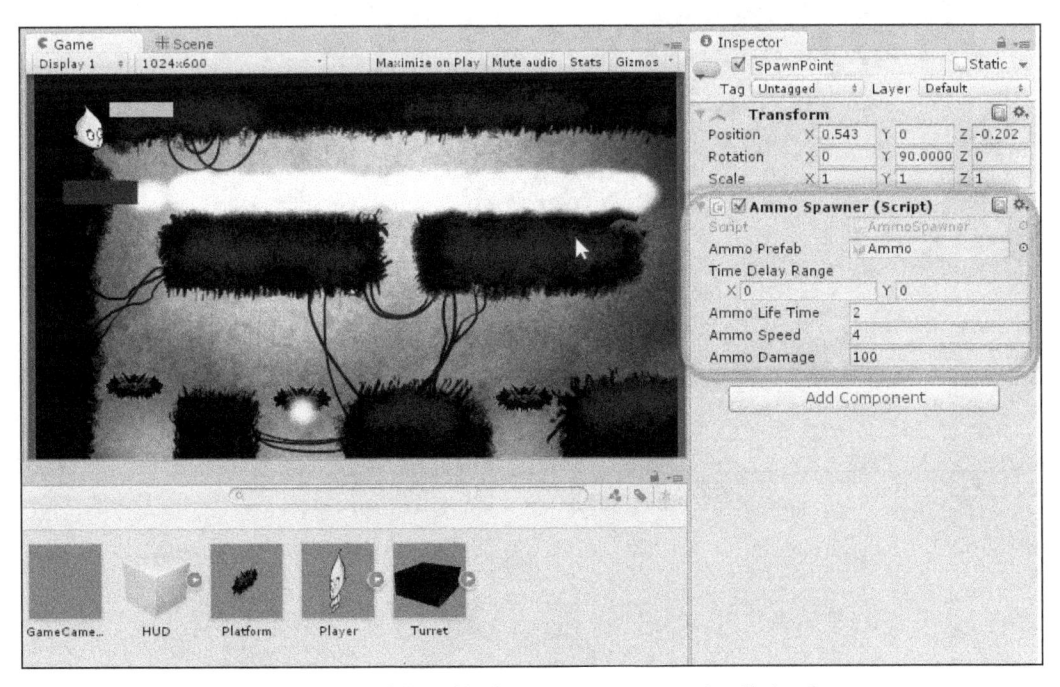

Figure 6.33: A time delay of (0,0) generates ammo continually in a beam.
Increase the value to insert reasonable gaps between ammo spawns

Excellent! We've now created a gun turret that, like the ammo itself, can be turned into a prefab. Make sure that the **Time Delay** range (the time between ammo spawns) is set to a value higher than zero; otherwise, ammo will be continually generated and become practically impossible for the player to avoid. Go ahead and position more turrets, if needed, to balance the difficulty of the scene.

NPCs and quests

NPC stands for **Non-player Character** and typically refers to any friendly or neutral characters other than the player-controlled character. In our adventure, Level 3 should feature an NPC character standing outside their house, and they provide us with a quest; specifically, to collect a gem item from Level 2, which features many hazards, including pits and gun turrets, as we've seen. To create the NPC character, we'll simply duplicate the player and adjust the character color, making them appear distinct. Thus, simply drag and drop the **Player** prefab from the **Project** panel to the Level 2 scene and position it near the house area. Then, remove all additional components (such as the Player Controller and Collider) to return this character back to a standard sprite that is not player-controlled. See *Figure 6.34*:

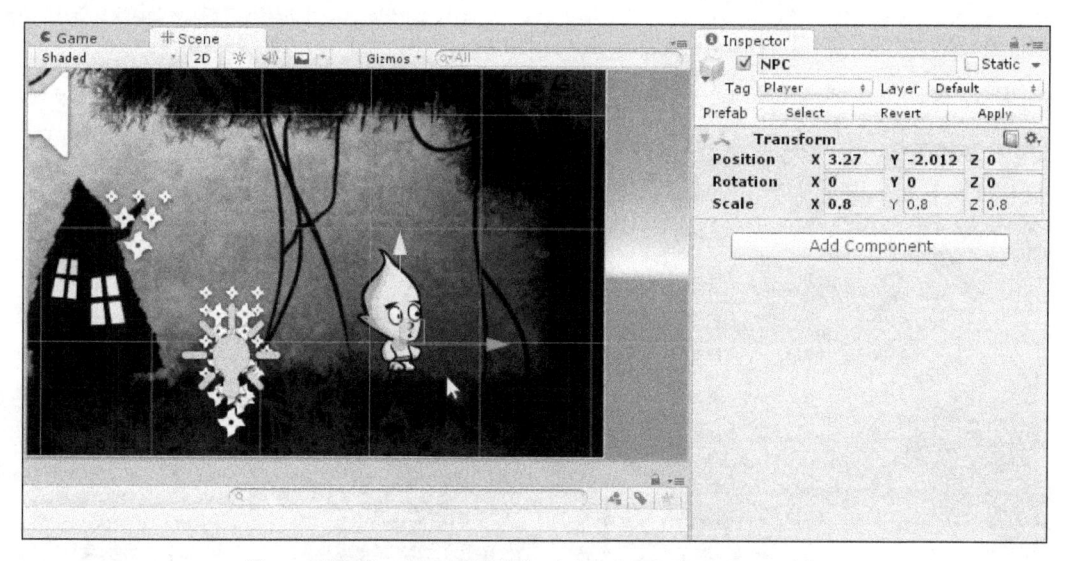

Figure 6.34: Creating an NPC from the player character prefab

Now, let's invert the character's **X** scale to make him or her face left instead of right. Select the parent NPC object as opposed to its constituent limbs, such as hands and arms, and invert its **X** scale. All child objects will flip to face the direction of their parent. See *Figure 6.35*:

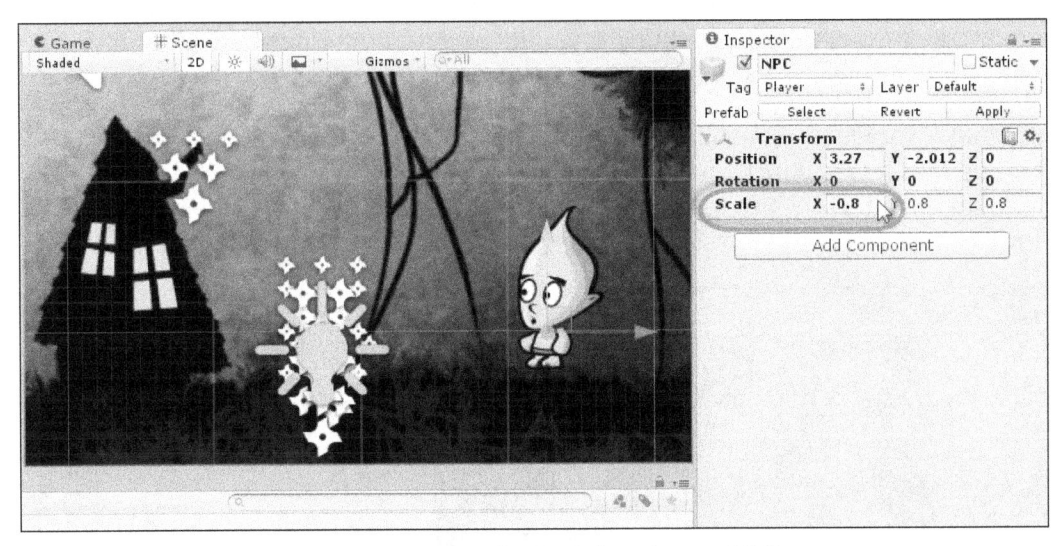

Figure 6.35: Flipping the X scale for a character NPC

We should also change the color of the NPC from green to red to distinguish him from the player. Now, the character is a multipart object composed from several sprite renderers. We could select each object and change its color individually via the **Object Inspector**. However, it's easier to select all the objects and change their color together; Unity 5 supports multi-object editing for common properties. See *Figure 6.36*:

Figure 6.36: Setting the NPC color

Continuing the 2D Adventure

The NPC should talk to the player on approach. This means that when the player approaches the NPC, the NPC should display dialog text. The text to be displayed varies, depending on the status of their quest. On a first visit, the NPC will give the player a quest. On a second visit, the NPC will respond differently, depending on whether the quest has been completed in the meantime. To start creating this functionality, we need to determine when the player approaches the NPC. This is achieved using a Collider. Consequently, select the NPC object in the scene and then choose **Component | Physics 2D | Box Collider 2D** from the application menu. Size the collider not to approximate the NPC specifically, but to approximate the area around the NPC in which the player should enter to have a conversation. Be sure to mark the collider as a Trigger object, allowing the player to enter and pass through. See *Figure 6.37*:

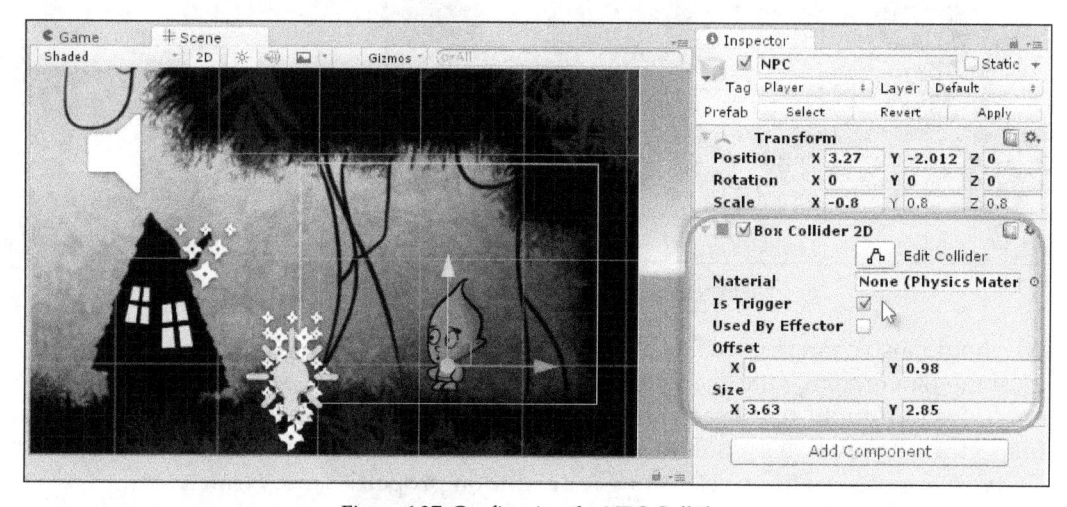

Figure 6.37: Configuring the NPC Collider

At this stage, we need a GUI element to act as the conversation panel to display conversation text when the NPC speaks. This configuration simply consists of a GUI Canvas object with a Text object child. Both of these objects can be created from the application menu with **GameObject | UI | Canvas and GameObject | UI | Text** respectively. The Canvas object should also have a CanvasGroup component attached using the **Component | Layout | CanvasGroup** menu option. This lets you set the alpha transparency for the panel and child objects as one complete unit. The Alpha member can be changed from the **Object Inspector**. A value of 1 means fully visible and value of 0 means fully transparent. See *Figure 6.38*:

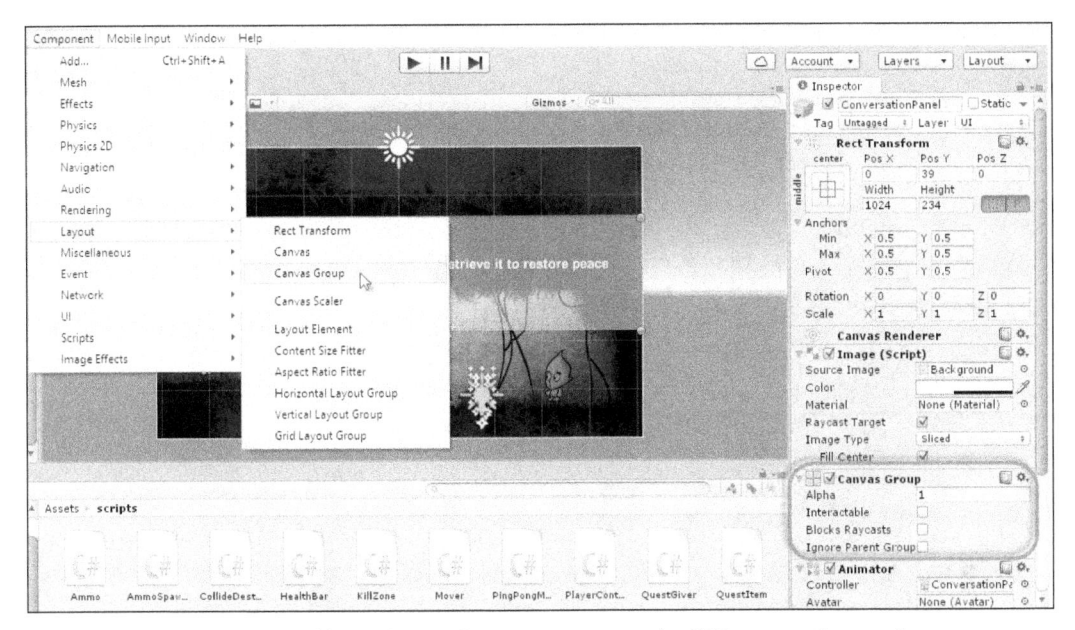

Figure 6.38: Adding a Canvas Group component to the GUI conversation panel

Excellent. We now have the ability, if we need to, to fade the panel in and out simply by animating the Alpha value from 0 to 1 over time. However, we still need functionality to maintain quest information to determine whether a quest has been assigned and to determine which text should be displayed in the conversation, based on the quest completion status. To do this, a new class must be created, QuestManager.cs. This class will allow us to create and maintain quest information. Refer to the *Code Sample 6.8*:

```
//-------------------------------
using UnityEngine;
using System.Collections;
//-------------------------------
[System.Serializable]
public class Quest
{
    //Quest completed status
    public enum QUESTSTATUS {UNASSIGNED=0,ASSIGNED=1,COMPLETE=2};
    public QUESTSTATUS Status = QUESTSTATUS.UNASSIGNED;
    public string QuestName = string.Empty;
}
//-------------------------------
public class QuestManager : MonoBehaviour
{
```

```csharp
    //---------------------------------
    //All quests in game
    public Quest[] Quests;
    private static QuestManager SingletonInstance = null;
    public static QuestManager ThisInstance
    {
        get{
                if(SingletonInstance==null)
                {
                    GameObject QuestObject = new GameObject("Default");
                    SingletonInstance = QuestObject.AddComponent<QuestManager>();
                }
                return SingletonInstance;
            }
    }
    //---------------------------------
    void Awake()
    {
        //If there is an existing instance, then destory
        if(SingletonInstance)
        {
            DestroyImmediate(gameObject);
            return;
        }

        //This is only instance
        SingletonInstance = this;
        DontDestroyOnLoad(gameObject);
    }
    //---------------------------------
    public static Quest.QUESTSTATUS GetQuestStatus(string QuestName)
    {
        foreach(Quest Q in ThisInstance.Quests)
        {
            if(Q.QuestName.Equals(QuestName))
                return Q.Status;
        }

        return Quest.QUESTSTATUS.UNASSIGNED;
    }
    //---------------------------------
    public static void SetQuestStatus(string QuestName, Quest.
```

```
        QUESTSTATUS NewStatus)
        {
            foreach(Quest Q in ThisInstance.Quests)
            {
                if(Q.QuestName.Equals(QuestName))
                {
                    Q.Status = NewStatus;
                    return;
                }
            }
        }
        //-------------------------------
        //Resets quests back to unassigned state
        public static void Reset()
        {
            if(ThisInstance==null)return;

            foreach(Quest Q in ThisInstance.Quests)
                Q.Status = Quest.QUESTSTATUS.UNASSIGNED;

        }
        //-------------------------------
}
//-------------------------------
```

Code Sample 6.8

The following points summarize the code sample:

- QuestManager maintains a list of all quests (Quest). That is, a list of all possible quests within the game and not a list of only assigned or completed quests. The Quest class defines the name and status for a single and specific quest.
- Any single quest can be UNASSIGNED (meaning that the player hasn't collected it), ASSIGNED (the player has collected it but not completed it), and COMPLETE (the player has collected and completed it).
- The GetQuestStatus function retrieves the completed status of the specified quest. The SetQuestStatus function assigns a new status to the specified quest. These are static functions, and so any script can set or get this data from any place.

Continuing the 2D Adventure

To use this object, create an instance in the scene (the first scene of the game), and then define all the quests that can be collected via the **Object Inspector**. In our game, there is only quest available: the quest given by an NPC character to collect a stolen gemstone from Level 2, the hazardous scene protected by gun turrets. See *Figure 6.39* for how I configured quests to work with **Quest Manager**:

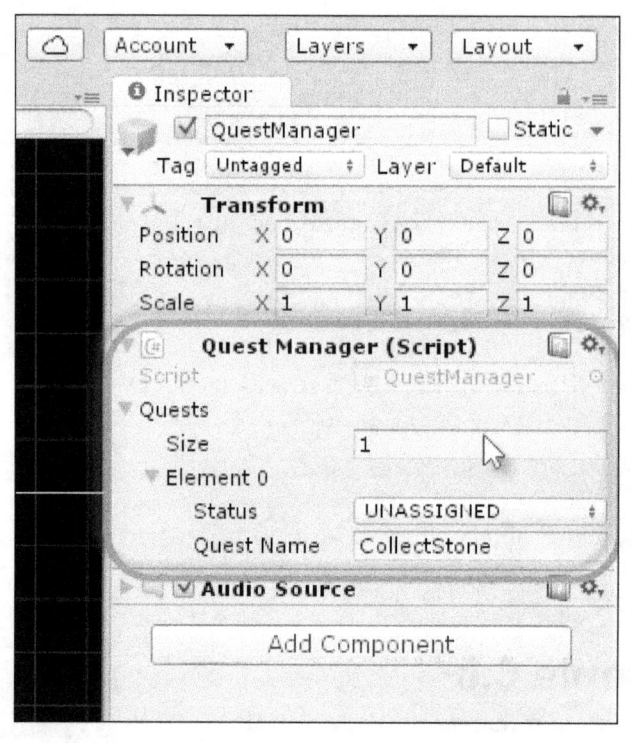

Figure 6.39: Defining in-game quests via QuestManager

`QuestManager` defines all the possible quests in the game, whether or not they're collected by the player. However, the NPC still needs to assign the quest to the player on approach. This can be achieved with the script file, `QuestGiver.cs`. See the following code. This script file should be attached to anything that gives quests, such as the NPC:

```
//---------------------------------
using UnityEngine;
using System.Collections;
using UnityEngine.UI;
//---------------------------------
public class QuestGiver : MonoBehaviour
{
```

```csharp
//-------------------------------
//Human readable quest name
public string QuestName = string.Empty;
//Reference to UI Text Box
public Text Captions = null;
//List of strings to say
public string[] CaptionText;
//-------------------------------
void OnTriggerEnter2D(Collider2D other)
{
    if(!other.CompareTag("Player"))return;

    Quest.QUESTSTATUS Status = QuestManager.GetQuestStatus(QuestName);
    Captions.text = CaptionText[(int) Status]; //Update GUI text
}
//-------------------------------
void OnTriggerExit2D(Collider2D other)
{
    Quest.QUESTSTATUS Status = QuestManager.GetQuestStatus(QuestName);
    if(Status == Quest.QUESTSTATUS.UNASSIGNED)
        QuestManager.SetQuestStatus(QuestName, Quest.QUESTSTATUS.ASSIGNED);

    if(Status == Quest.QUESTSTATUS.COMPLETE)
        Application.LoadLevel(5); //Game completed, go to win screen
}
}
//-------------------------------
```

Continuing the 2D Adventure

After attaching this script to the NPC, give the game a test by pressing the play icon on the toolbar. Approach the NPC, and the GUI text should change to the specified quest as defined for the **QuestName** field for the **QuestGiver** component in the **Object Inspector**. This name should match **QuestName**, as defined in the QuestManager class. See *Figure 6.40*:

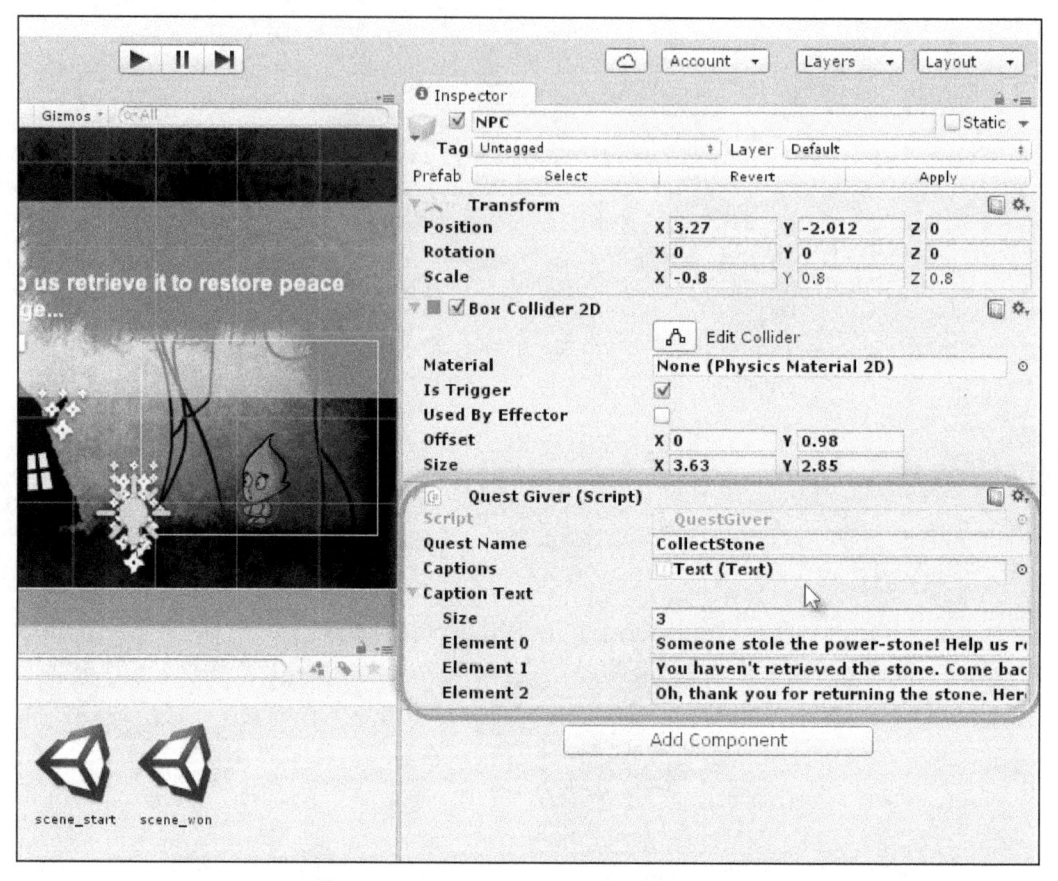

Figure 6.40: Defining the QuestGiver component

The assigned quest is to collect a gemstone, but our levels lack a stone. Let's now add one for the player to collect. To do this, drag and drop the GemStone texture from the project panel (Texture folder) to scene 2 on the topmost ledge so that the player has to climb to reach it (a challenge!). See *Figure 6.41*. Be sure to attach a **Circle Collider** trigger to the object, allowing it to collide with the player.

[322]

Chapter 6

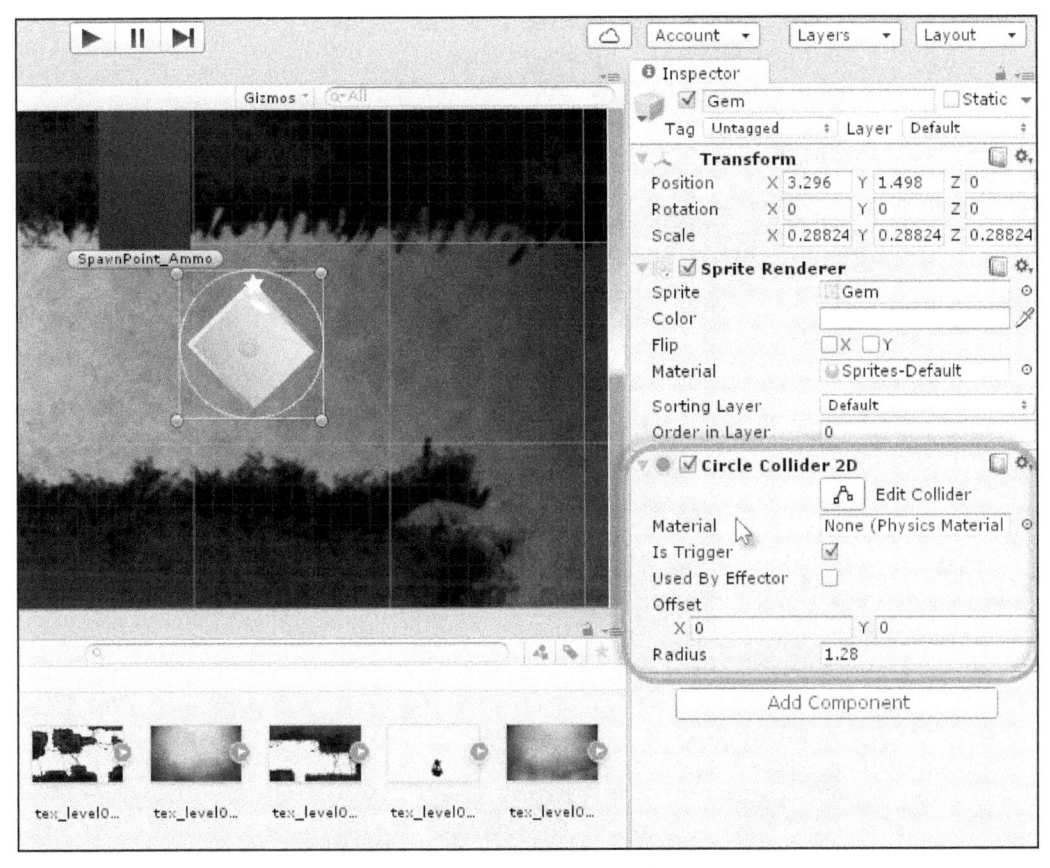

Figure 6.41: Creating a Quest object

Finally, we'll need a `QuestItem` script to set the quest status on the `QuestManager` class when the item is collected, allowing `QuestGiver` to determine whether the gem has been collected the next time the player visits. The `QuestItem` script should be attached to the `Gem` object. Refer to the following code:

```
//---------------------------------
using UnityEngine;
using System.Collections;
//---------------------------------
public class QuestItem : MonoBehaviour
{
    //---------------------------------
    public string QuestName;
```

[323]

```csharp
        private AudioSource ThisAudio = null;
        private SpriteRenderer ThisRenderer = null;
        private Collider2D ThisCollider = null;
        //-------------------------------
        void Awake()
        {
            ThisAudio = GetComponent<AudioSource>();
            ThisRenderer = GetComponent<SpriteRenderer>();
            ThisCollider = GetComponent<Collider2D>();
        }
        //-------------------------------
        // Use this for initialization
        void Start ()
        {
            //Hide object
            gameObject.SetActive(false);

            //Show object if quest is assigned
            if(QuestManager.GetQuestStatus(QuestName) == Quest.QUESTSTATUS.ASSIGNED)
                gameObject.SetActive(true);
        }
        //-------------------------------
        //If item is visible and collected
        void OnTriggerEnter2D(Collider2D other)
        {
            if(!other.CompareTag("Player"))return;

            if(!gameObject.activeSelf)return;

            //We are collected. Now complete quest
            QuestManager.SetQuestStatus(QuestName, Quest.QUESTSTATUS.COMPLETE);

            ThisRenderer.enabled=ThisCollider.enabled=false;

            if(ThisAudio!=null)ThisAudio.Play(); //Play sound if any attached
        }
        //-------------------------------
}
```

The preceding code is responsible for setting the quest status to completed when the gem (quest item) object is collected as the player enters the trigger volume. This happens through the `QuestManager` class.

Excellent work! You now have a completed integrated quest system and an NPC character. The complete files for this project can be found in the `Chapter06/End` folder. I highly recommend checking them out and playing the game. See *Figure 6.42*:

Figure 6.42: The completed game!

Summary

Great work! We've now completed the 2D adventure game. Some minor details were not covered in this chapter for the sake of clarity and conciseness because we've seen the methods or content already in earlier chapters. Hence, it's important to open the course files and check out the completed project, seeing how the code works. Overall, in having reached this far in the book, you have three completed Unity projects to your name. So, in the next chapter, we'll wrap up everything that we've seen so far and get started on the grand finale: the final, fourth project!

Test your knowledge

Q1. `OnTriggerExit2D` is...

- A. A function that runs on repeat
- B. A function that runs when an object leaves a trigger
- C. A function that runs when the player completes the level
- D. A function that runs when the level exits

Q2. A Canvas Group lets you

- A. Play UI Animations
- B. Change the Alpha of multiple UI Objects
- C. Deletes many objects together
- D. Adjust objects for different resolutions

Q3. Enumerations are good for...

- A. Storing lists of values
- B. Counting objects
- C. Searching for objects
- D. Sorting objects by name

Q4. You can pick a random number by using

- A. `Random.Range`
- B. `SelectRandomNumber`
- C. `ChooseRandom`
- D. `GetRandomNumber`

Further Reading

Go through the following links for more information:

- https://unity3d.com/learn/tutorials/s/scripting
- https://www.packtpub.com/game-development/unity-5-scripting-and-gameplay-mechanics-video
- https://www.packtpub.com/game-development/mastering-unity-5x-scripting

7
Creating Artificial Intelligence

In this chapter, we'll start the final project, which will cover extensive ground. This project, unlike the previous three, will not be a fully completed game with a clear win and loss condition but will be a functional prototype and proof of concept style project that highlights a range of important coding techniques and ideas prevalent in games. Specifically, we'll create a world with a terrain, first-person character, and some enemies. The enemies will have Artificial Intelligence (AI), patrol the level searching for the player, and attack the player when found. In this chapter, we will explore the following topics:

- How to build levels and landscapes with the Terrain tools
- How to generate and use navigation meshes
- How to prepare for Artificial Intelligence development

> The starting project and assets can be found in the book companion files in the Chapter07/Start folder. You can start here and follow along with this chapter if you do not have your own project already.

Creating Artificial Intelligence

An overview of the project

The project to be created is a first-person prototype in which the player character can wander and explore a terrain environment. The terrain features hills, valleys, and varied terrain elements. Among the terrain will be scattered several enemy characters (NPCs). Each character features artificial intelligence. Specifically, each character will wander around (Patrol mode) searching for the player. If the player is sighted, the NPC will chase and pursue the player (Chase mode). If, during the chase, the enemy loses sight of the player, they will return to patrolling. On the other hand, if the enemy approaches the player during the chase, the enemy will attack the player (Attack mode). In short, therefore, the AI features three main states: Patrol, Chase, and Attack. This, in short, constitutes the enemy AI and represents the main challenge for the player on this project. See *Figure 7.1* for the completed project:

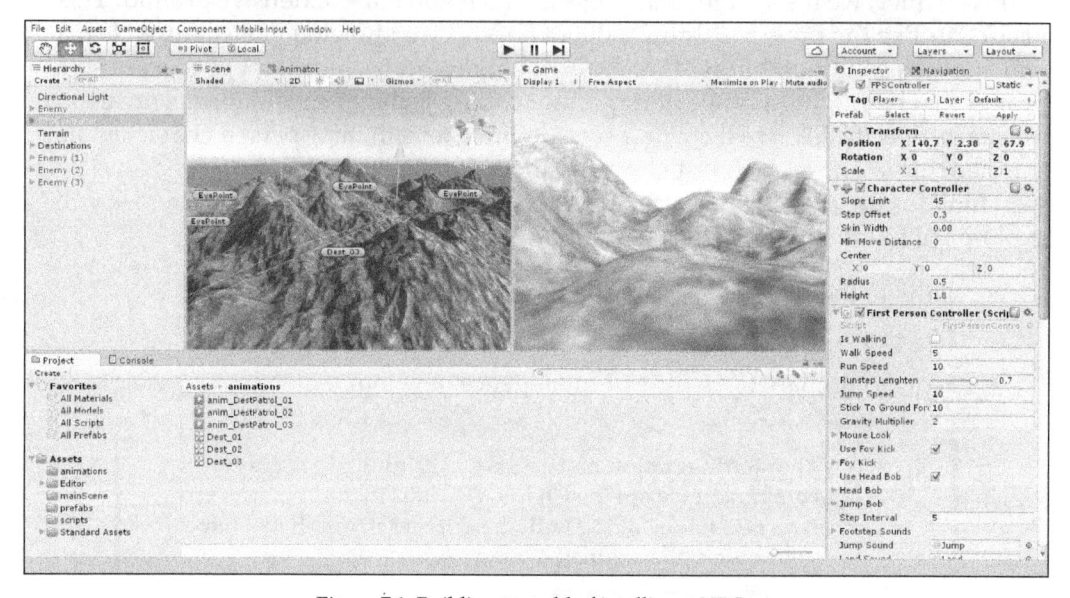

Figure 7.1: Building a world of intelligent NPCs

Getting started

To get started from the beginning, create a new project. The details on this are covered amply in all previous chapters. Throughout this project, we'll be using three main asset packages included with Unity. Specifically, these are **Characters**, **Effects**, and **Environment**. These can be imported via the application menu, through **Assets | Import Packages**. See *Figure 7.2*:

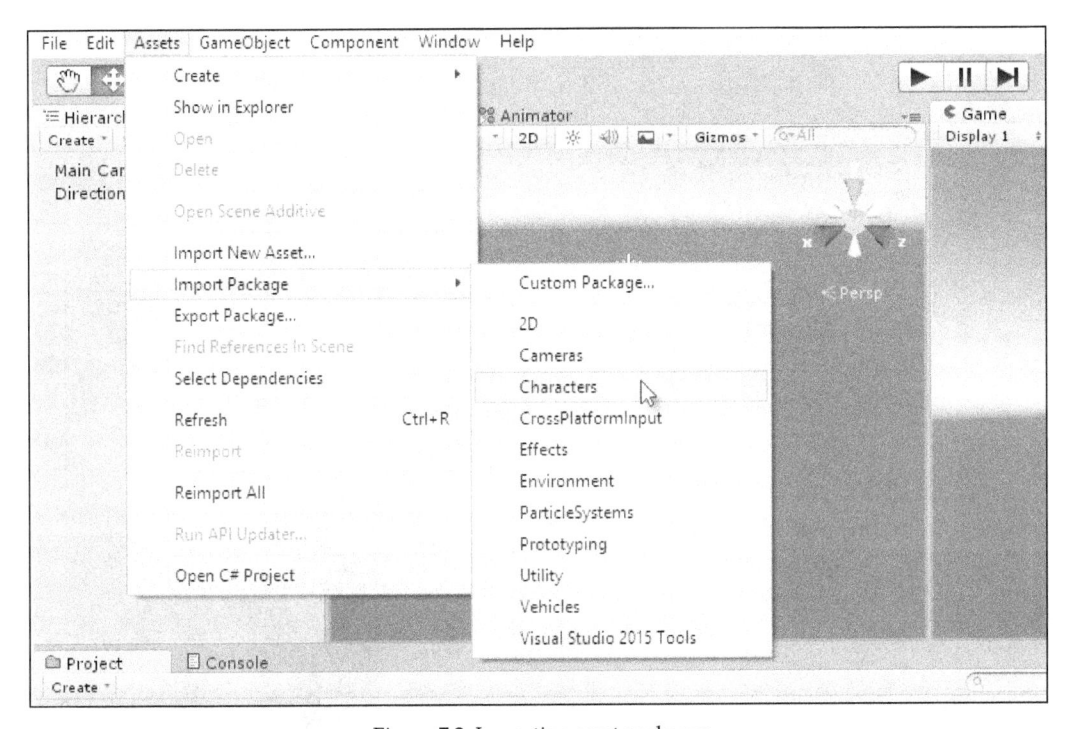

Figure 7.2: Importing asset packages

Creating Artificial Intelligence

To start, we'll need to create the game world itself (the terra firma), which will be an outdoor (exterior) environment. In other words, we'll create a game world with grassy plains, hills, and mountains. Such a landscape can be made in 3D modeling software, such as 3DS Max, Maya, or Blender, and then imported to Unity. However, Unity features native terrain design tools that, though limited in important ways (as we'll see), are still powerful and versatile. To create a new terrain, navigate to **GameObject | 3D Object | Terrain** from the application menu. See *Figure 7.3*:

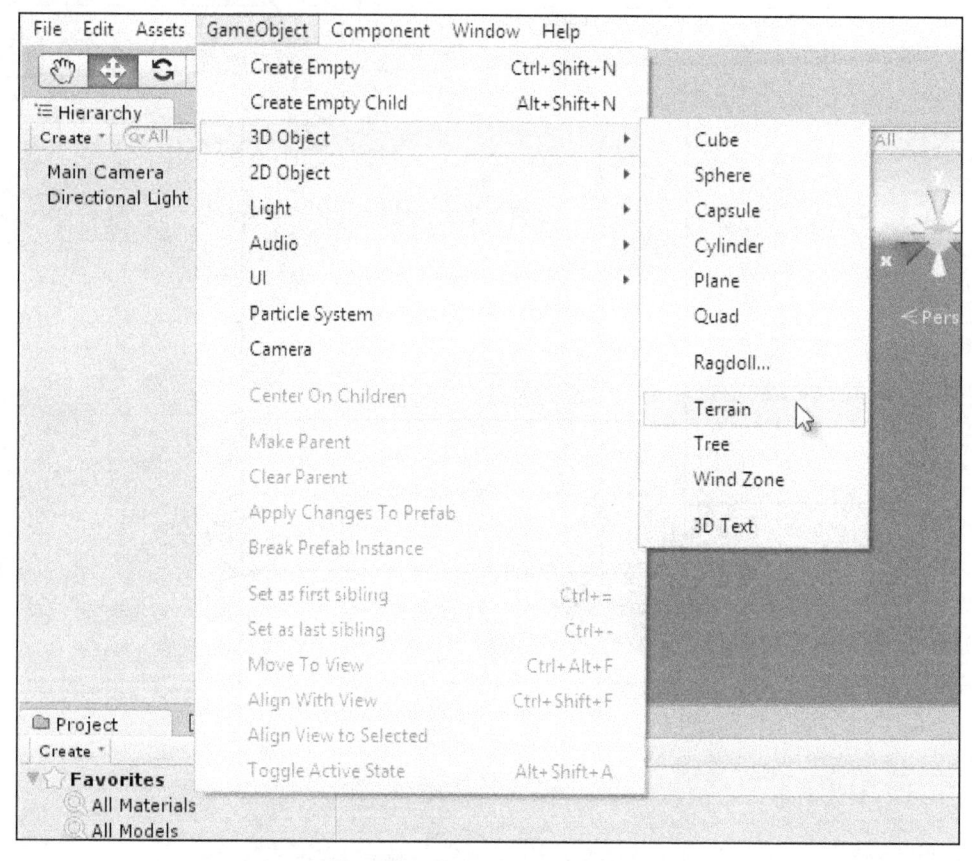

Figure 7.3: Creating a new terrain

Once created, a terrain object is added to the scene at the world origin (0,0,0). It may not immediately appear in the viewport due to its size. To address this, select the terrain in the **Hierarchy** panel and then press *F* on the keyboard to center it in the view. It initially looks like a flat plane object but, unlike planes, it can be reshaped and sculpted, as we'll see soon. See *Figure 7.4*:

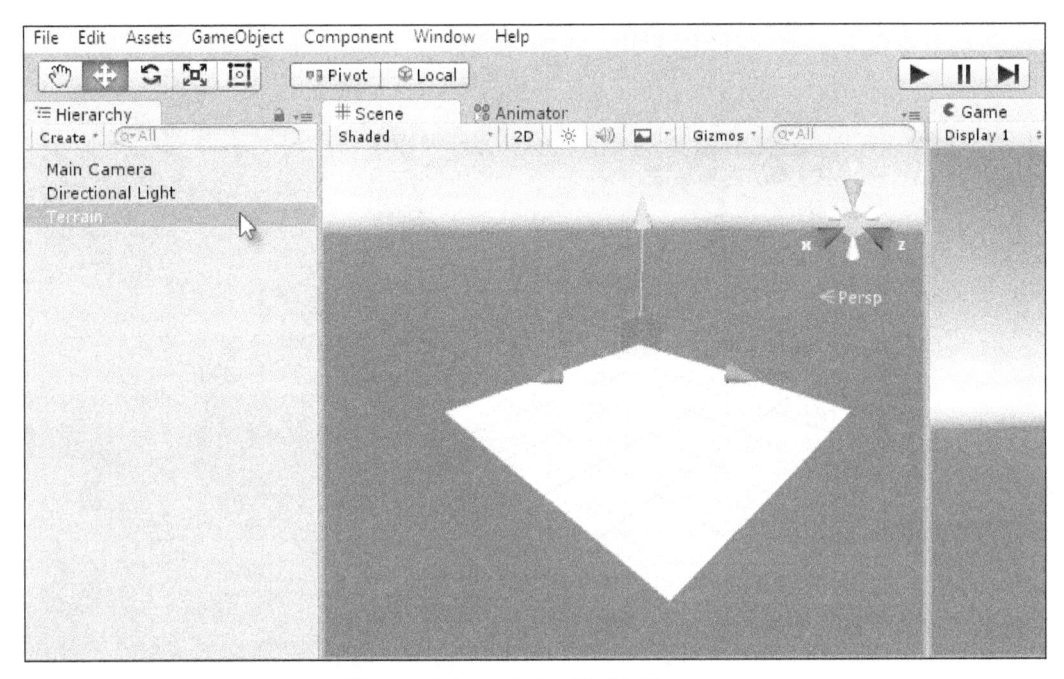

Figure 7.4: A terrain is added to the scene

Creating Artificial Intelligence

Before sculpting and shaping the terrain, you should first set some initial topological settings from the **Object Inspector** in order to ensure that terrain topology is appropriate and sized to support the kind of terrain you need. To do this, select the terrain in the viewport, and then click on the cog icon from the **Object Inspector** to display the terrain settings. See *Figure 7.5*:

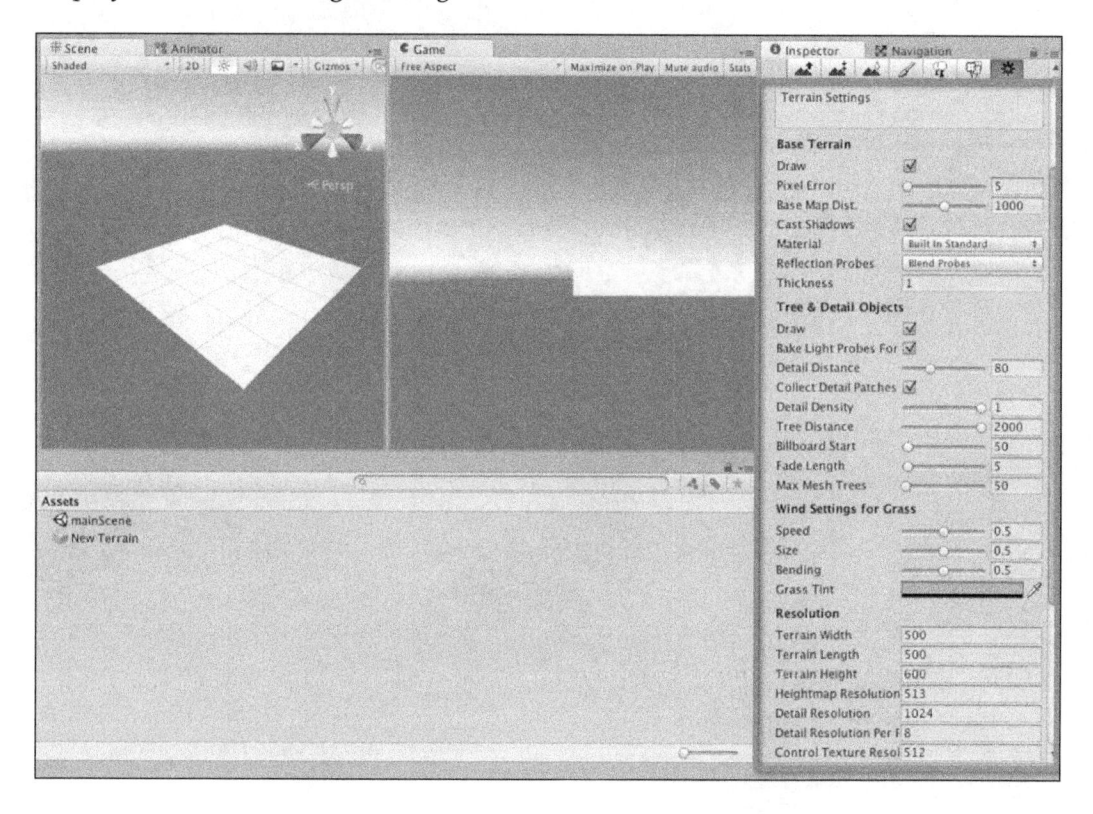

Figure 7.5: Viewing and editing the terrain settings

By default, the terrain is too large for our purposes (500x500 meters). Let's shrink this to 256 x 256, or even smaller, if you prefer! Simply enter 256 in the Width and Length fields. The Height field represents the maximum height that any terrain peak or mountain can possibly reach. For optimization reasons, the terrain should be no larger than needed, as terrain objects are highly tessellated and performance-intensive. See *Figure 7.6*. Be sure to set the terrain dimensions before sculpting as resizing afterward can invalidate or erase sculpting work:

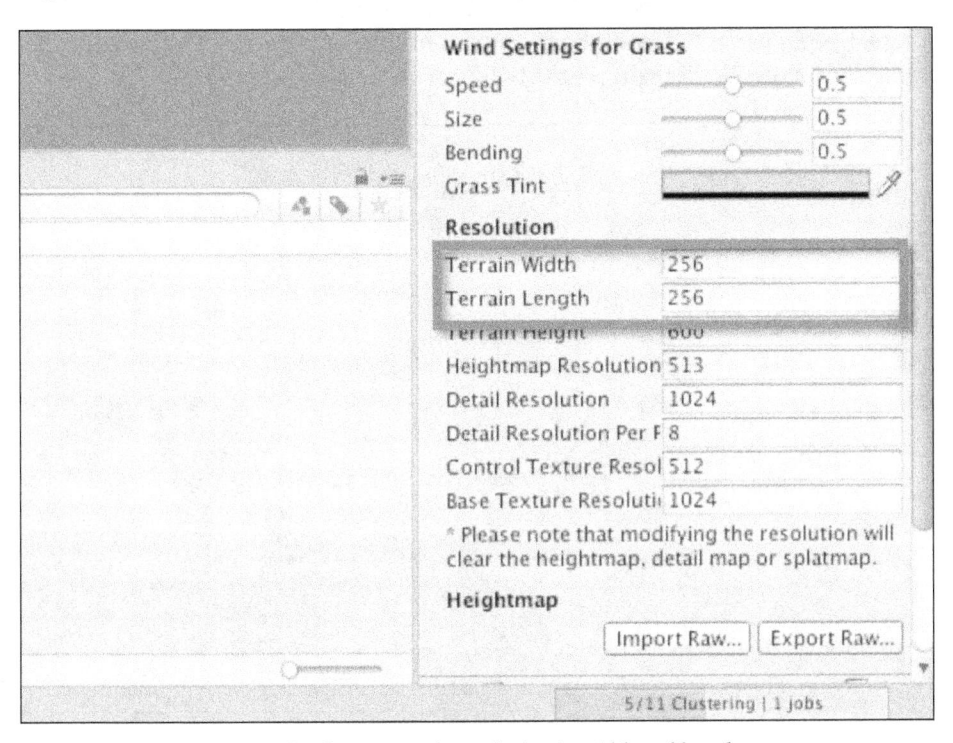

Figure 7.6: Setting terrain resolution in width and length

Creating Artificial Intelligence

Terrain construction

Now let's start sculpting the terrain. With the terrain object selected, click the leftmost palette icon from the Object Inspector (the Raise/Lower terrain tool), available from the Terrain component. This lets you select brush shapes to paint terrain details. Select a soft, round brush and use a large brush size (using the Brush Size slider), along with the Opacity setting to set brush strength. Click and drag over the terrain to paint landscape details. Create some hills and mountains for the landscape. See *Figure 7.7*. Remember, you can hold down the *Shift* key while clicking to reverse (or lower) the terrain painting, if needed:

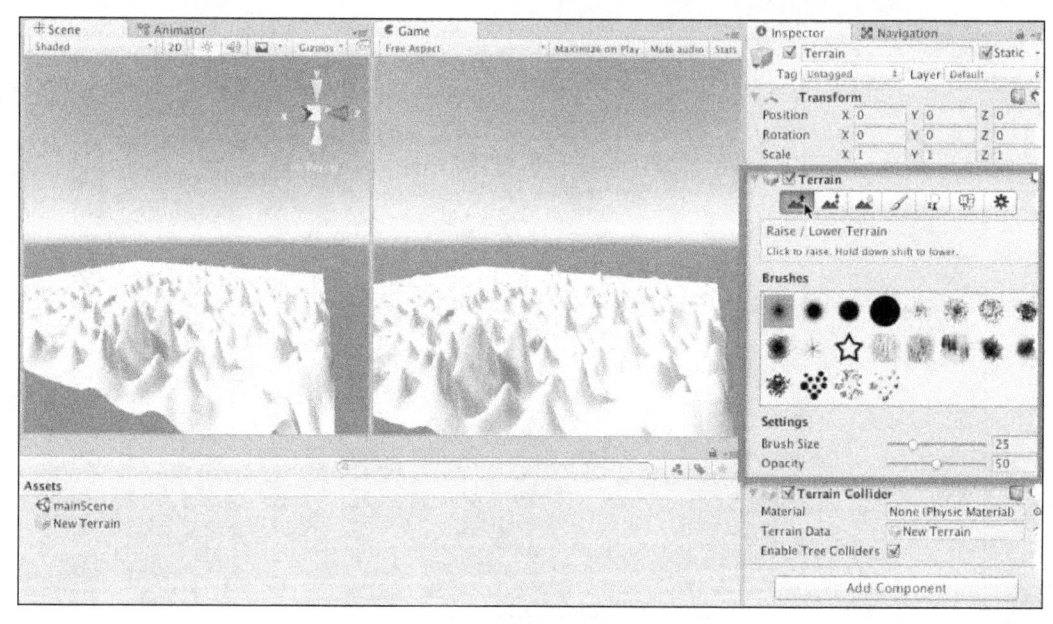

Figure 7.7: Viewing and editing the terrain settings

Chapter 7

If the terrain appears too rough to be natural, you can easily smooth out details by switching to the Smooth Height tool. To do this, click on the third button in the Terrain component. See *Figure 7.8*. When you select this tool, you can choose the Brush Shape, Brush Size, and Opacity as before, but clicking over the terrain will smooth out variations in terrain height:

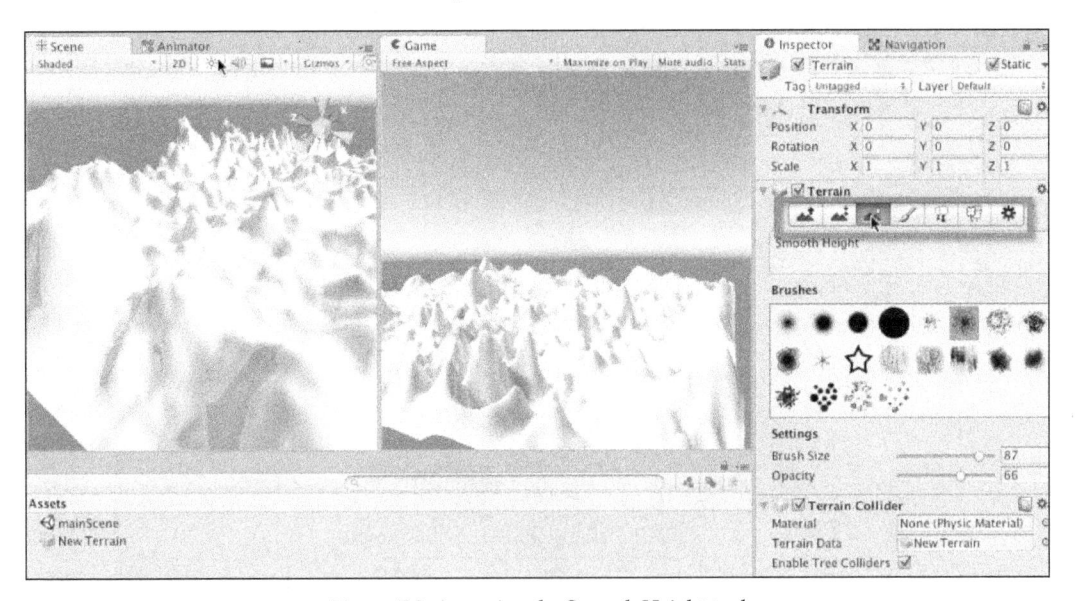

Figure 7.8: Accessing the Smooth Height tool

Creating Artificial Intelligence

Now that the terrain is sculpted, shaped, and smooth as needed, we're ready to start painting it. As it stands, the terrain is grey, dull, and under-defined. It has no clear texture or *look*, such as grass or rock. We'll fix this using the Paint Texture tool. To access this, click on the Paint Texture button (fourth button) in the Terrain component from the Object Inspector. When you do this for the first time, you'll need to load in and prepare a set of textures for the painting. See *Figure 7.9*:

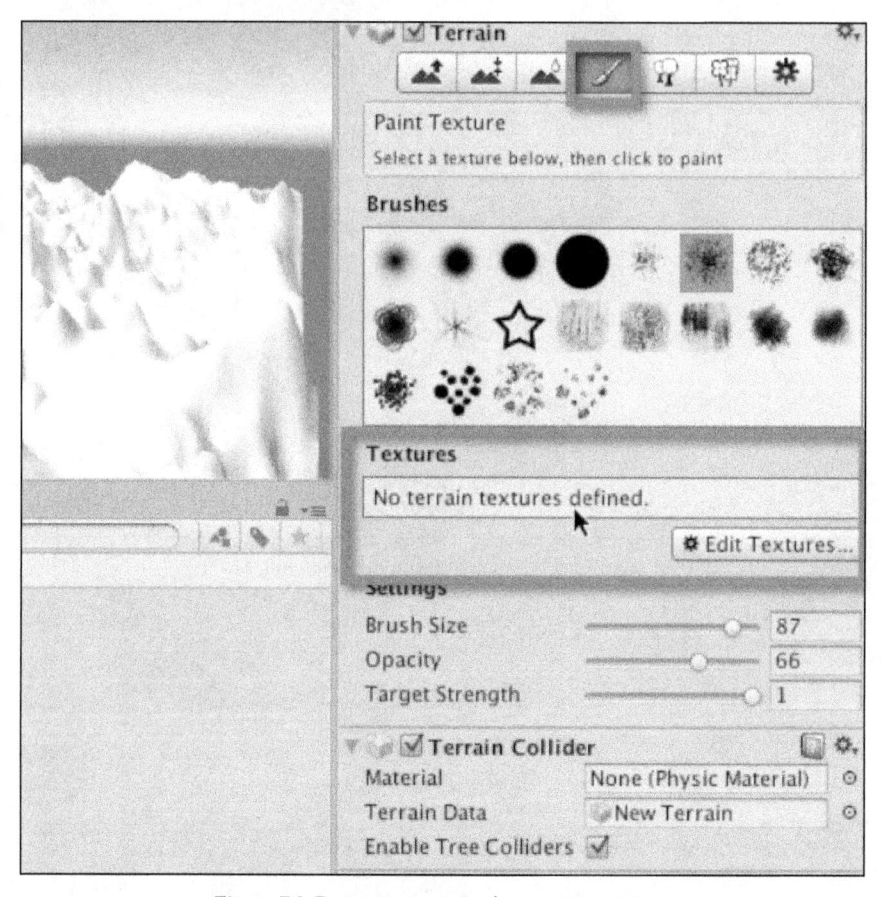

Figure 7.9: Preparing textures for terrain painting

Click on the Edit Textures button, and then select Add Texture... from the context menu that appears. Afterward, a texture configuration dialog appears, allowing you to add new textures to a palette. See *Figure 7.10*:

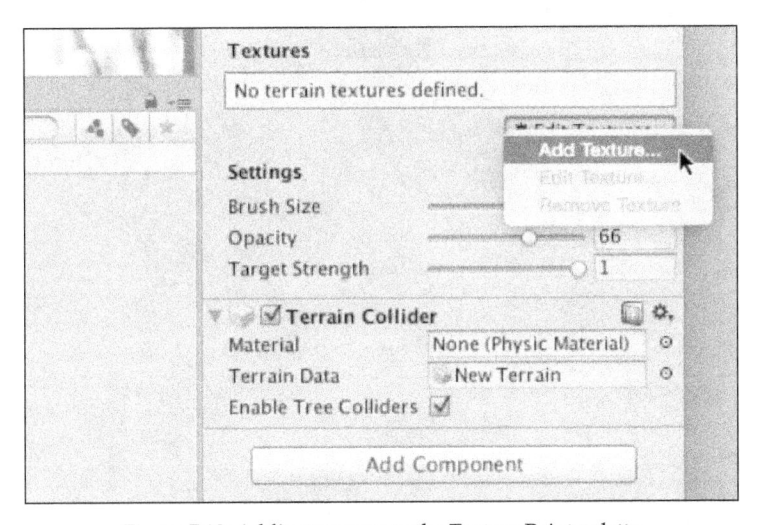

Figure 7.10: Adding textures to the Texture Paint palette

With the Texture Selection dialog open and ready to load our first texture, use the Project panel to find the native terrain textures included with the Unity Environment asset package. These can be found in the **Standard Assets | Environment | TerrainAssets | SurfaceTextures** folder. For this example, I'll select a grassy texture. This texture will be used as a base texture to flood-fill the terrain.

Creating Artificial Intelligence

Click and drag the grass texture from the Project panel to the Albedo slot of the Texture Selection dialog. The normal channel can be left empty. See *Figure 7.11*:

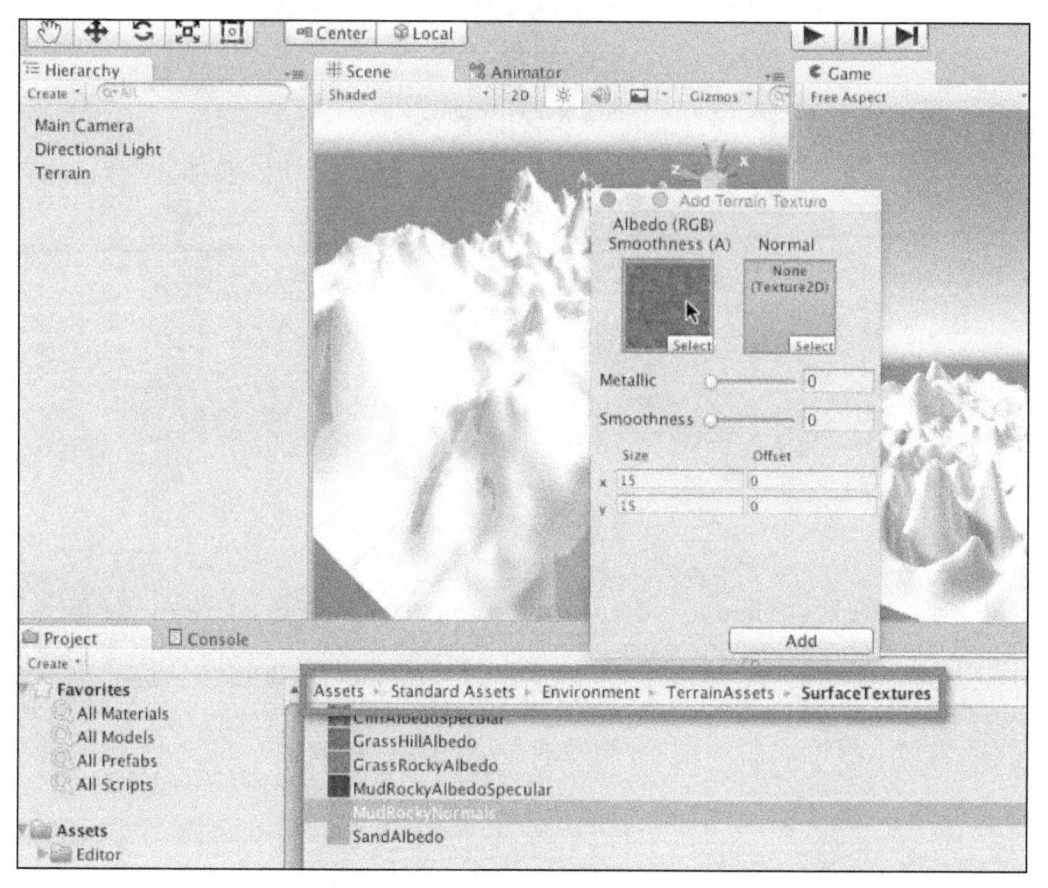

Figure 7.11: Selecting a base texture

After adding the first texture to the Texture Selection dialog, be sure to set the texture size. This refers to the size (in meters) that a single tile of the texture should cover. Smaller values decrease texture tiling but make each tile seem larger. Larger values increase texture tiling but each tile seems smaller. Getting the tiling values correct is a process of trial and error—tweaking values until it looks correct on the terrain. For this example, I've used the values 75 x 75. Then, click on the Add button. See *Figure 7.12*:

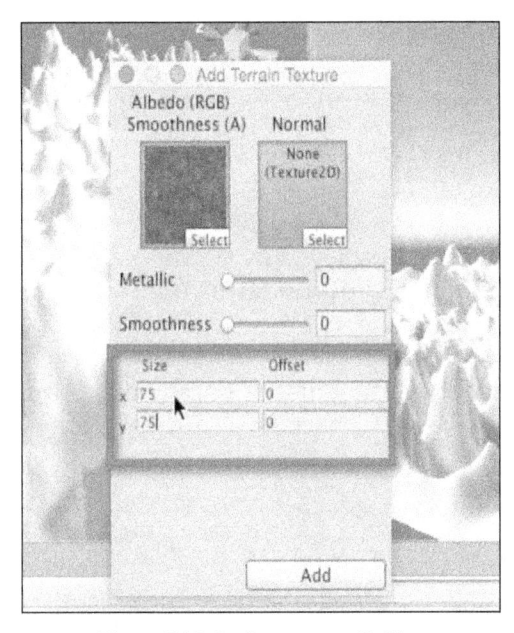

Figure 7.12: Setting texture tile Size

After clicking on the Add button, the base texture will be tiled across the terrain. From a distance, the tiling may look obvious and unpleasant in the scene viewport. You may be tempted, on the basis of this, to adjust the tiling settings. However, from a first-person perspective, the terrain will look very different. For this reason, use a First-person Controller prefab (from the native assets) to preview the terrain in first-person mode, seeing how texture tiling appears at ground-level.

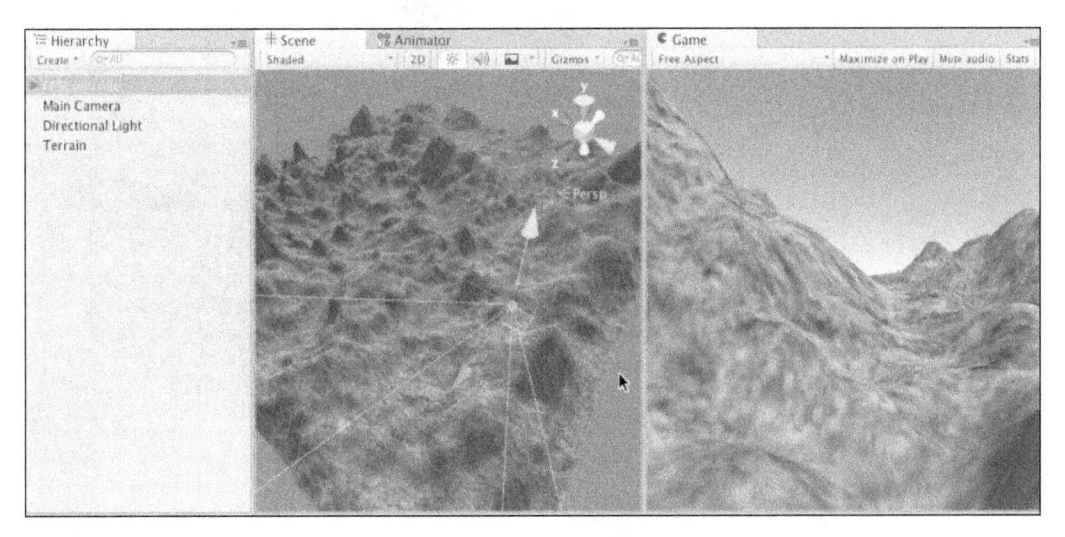

Figure 7.13: Previewing texture tiling on a terrain

Creating Artificial Intelligence

If you need to edit the existing texture tiling, simply select the texture thumbnail from the Textures palette in the Terrain component of the Object Inspector, and then choose the Edit Textures button. Refer to the preceding *Figure 7.10*.

At this stage, the terrain object features a grass texture, tiled seamlessly across the surface, which is the base texture. While this looks acceptable, it'd be great to include greater texture variety in the terrain, including some grassy, rocky, and maybe even desert style terrain. This is achieved by adding more textures via the Terrain Selection dialog. Just click on the Edit Textures button, and then choose Add Texture from the context menu. Then, drag and drop a new and different texture to the Albedo slot of the texture selection dialog, and finally repeat this process to add as many textures as needed. On closing the dialog, all added textures will appear in the Textures Palette from the Object Inspector. See *Figure 7.14*:

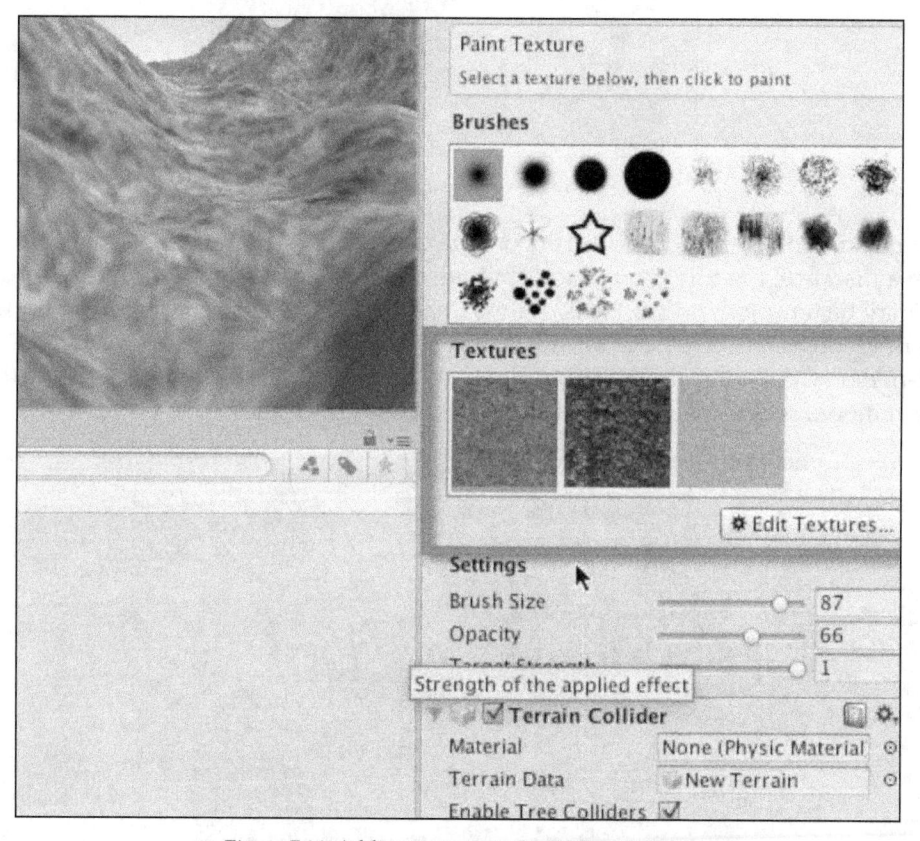

Figure 7.14: Adding textures to the Texture Palette

The active texture assigned to the painter brush is highlighted with a blue border in the Inspector. You can click on a texture thumbnail to select a different texture. When you do this, the selected texture is assigned to the painter brush and can be applied to the terrain just by clicking on it. Clicking and dragging on the terrain will paint the texture to the terrain. You can also use the Brush Shape, Brush Size, Opacity, and Target Strength values to control how strongly the texture is applied and how it is blended into the terrain beneath. See *Figure 7.15*:

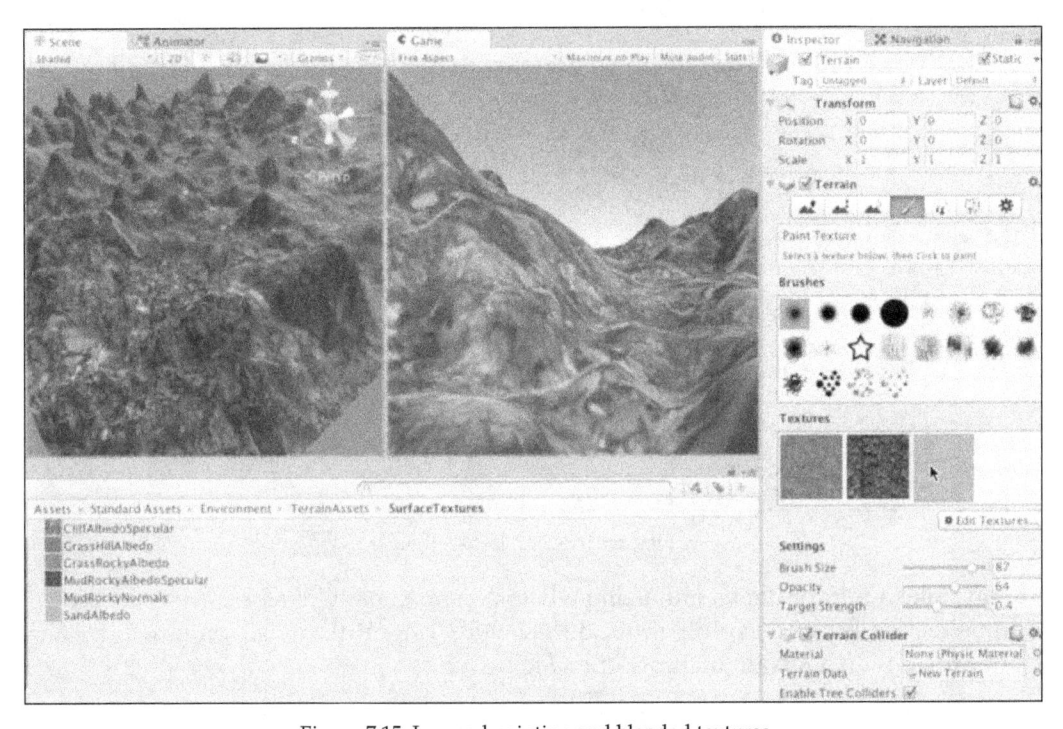

Figure 7.15: Layered painting and blended textures

Now, go ahead and complete terrain painting, creating a look and feel that you like. Once completed, select the scene Directional Light from the Hierarchy panel and change its rotation to position the sun wherever it looks good. As an aside, notice that you can control a complete day and night cycle (in terms of lighting and appearance) by rotating the light a complete 360 degrees.

Creating Artificial Intelligence

Therefore, you can create an easy day and night cycle for games just by animating a directional light using the Animation window, seen in earlier chapters. See *Figure 7.16*:

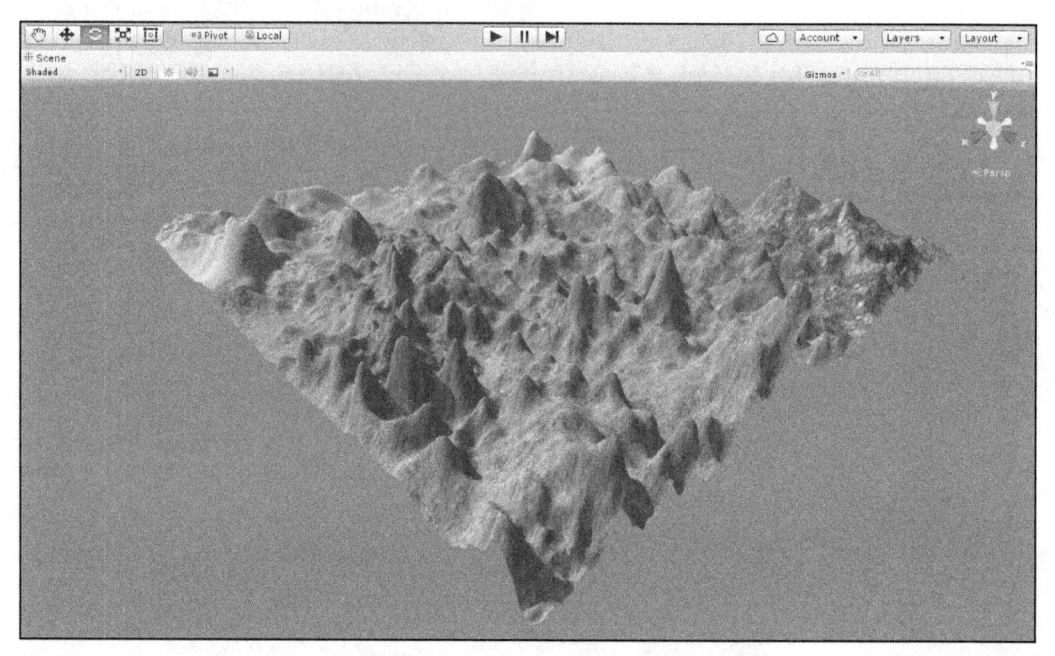

Figure 7.16: Completed terrain

Finally, take a tour of the terrain using a first-person controller asset. Press the play icon on the toolbar and explore around the level! Congratulations, you now have a game world with a terrain included. See *Figure 7.17*:

Figure 7.17: First-person terrain exploration

Before moving forward, let's consider the technical limitations of Unity terrains and the impact that this can potentially have for your games. Specifically, the Unity terrain is height map-based. This means that the elevation (ups and downs) of the terrain are generated internally based on grayscale pixels in an image file (the height map). When painting the terrain using the brushes from the Inspector, you are (under the hood) painting pixels onto the height map, which is used to deform the terrain. This is a clever and fascinating process, but it comes with an important limitation. Namely, a height map is a 2D topographical texture. The result is that Unity terrains are not truly 3D at a procedural level; they cannot contain caves, crevices, caverns, or any inward cutouts. The player cannot *go under* anything. Rather, it consists simply of up and down sections, none of which may have interior spaces. Now, in many cases, this won't be a problem. However, sometimes you'll need these internal spaces, and when you do, you'll want to consider alternatives to the native terrain system. Alternatives include Asset Store plugins, but also manual terrains in 3D modeling software such as 3DS Max, Maya, and Blender.

Navigation and navigation meshes

The world terrain is now fully created. In reaching this stage, we must now start thinking about the main aims of our project. Specifically, the level should be an AI experiment: we want to create enemy NPC characters that can wander freely around the terrain and will chase and attack the player whenever the player enters their field of view. To achieve this, the level must be properly configured for path-finding, which is considered here.

On thinking about NPC AI and NPC movement around the level, it's clear that the terrain is bumpy and features many hills, mountains, dips, and inclines. For an NPC character to navigate this terrain successfully, many complexities are involved. For example, an NPC cannot simply travel in only straight lines from point A to point B because doing so would cause the NPC to pass through solid objects and terrain. The NPC needs to maneuver intelligently around, under, and over appropriate parts of the terrain, just as human intelligence would. This is important to create believable characters. The computational processes involved in calculating appropriate paths for NPCs is called Path-Finding, and the processes to make a character travel those paths is termed Navigation. Unity comes with path-finding and navigation features built-in, making it easy for NPCs to calculate and travel paths.

Creating Artificial Intelligence

To prepare for this, a Navigation Mesh must be generated. This is a special mesh asset included in the scene, which uses non-rendered geometry to approximate the total walkable surface of a scene. This is used by the path-finding and navigation processes to move a character around. To get started with generating a navigation mesh, select **Window | Navigation** from the application menu. See *Figure 7.18*:

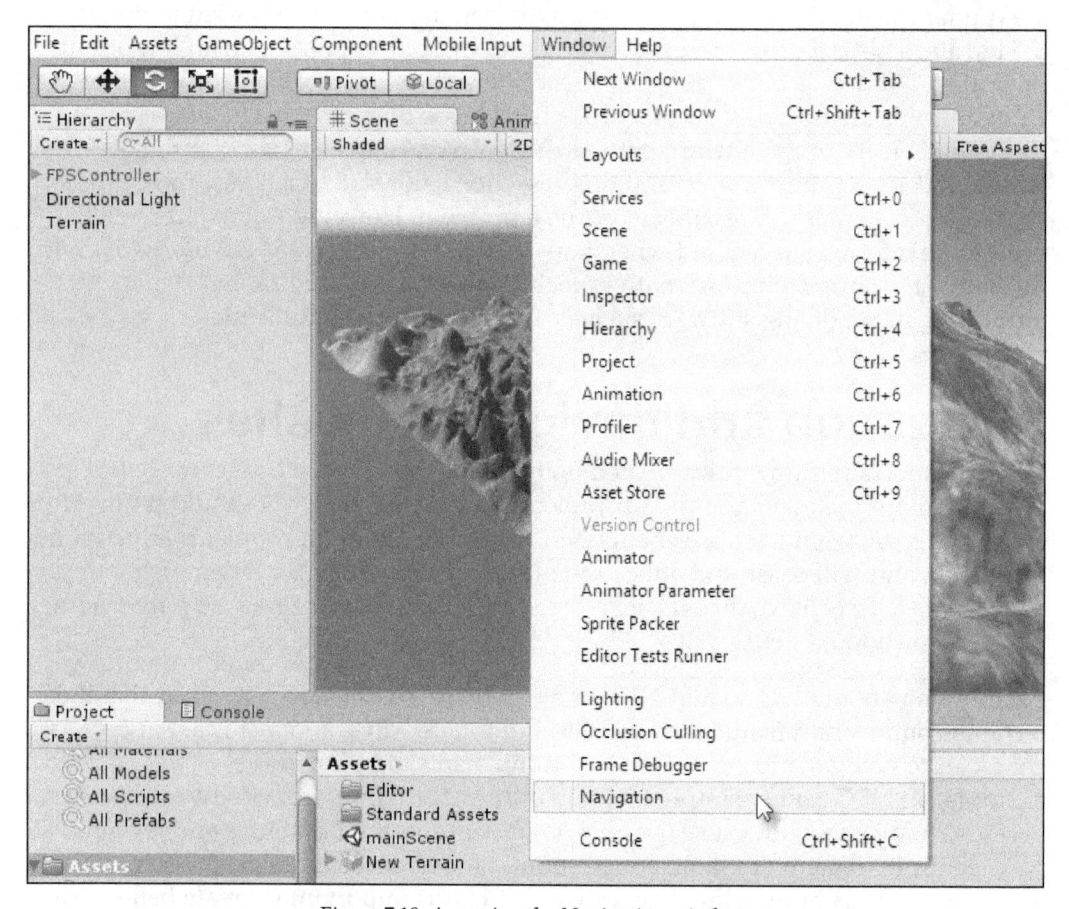

Figure 7.18: Accessing the Navigation window

The purpose of the Navigation window is to generate a low-fidelity terrain mesh that actually approximates the level floor. For this process to work effectively, all non-movable floor meshes in the scene must be marked as Navigation Static. To do this, select the terrain in the Hierarchy panel and, from the Inspector, click on the Static drop-down and enable the Navigation Static option. See *Figure 7.19*:

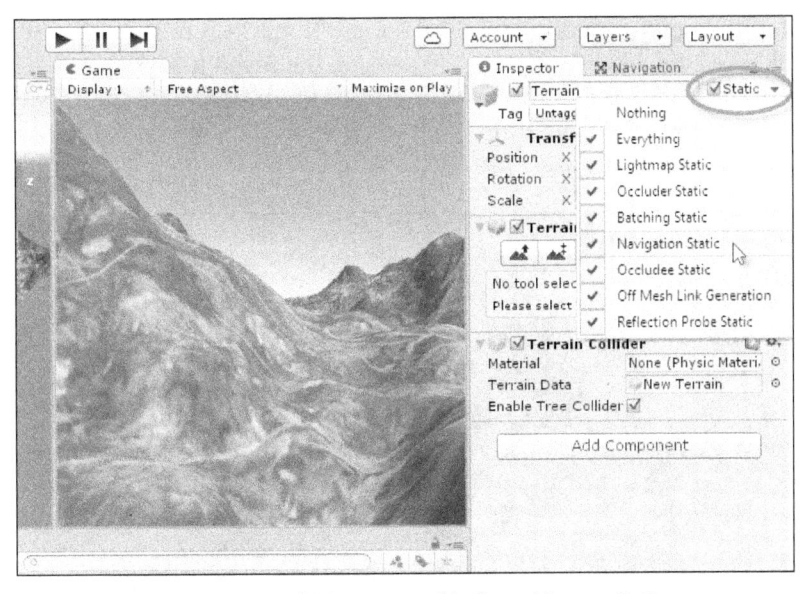

Figure 7.19: Marking non-movable floor objects as Static

Now access the Navigation window (which I typically dock into the Inspector). From here, click on the Bake tab to access the main Navigation settings. From this panel, you can control a range of settings to influence Navigation Mesh (NavMesh) generation. See *Figure 7.20*:

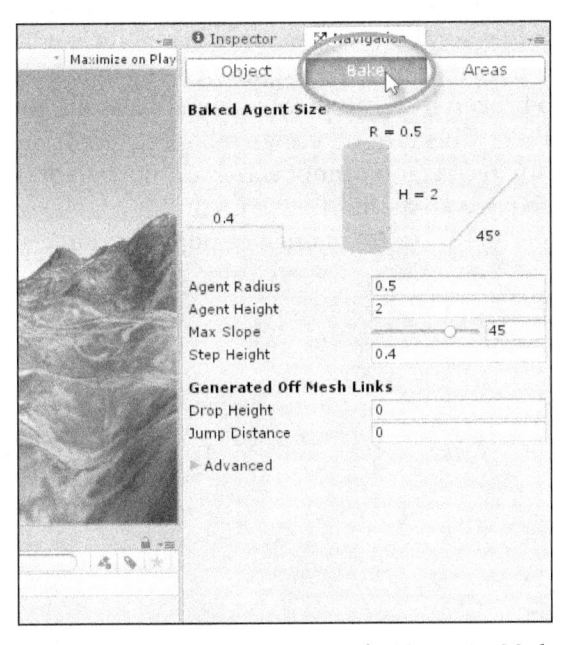

Figure 7.20: The Bake contains the main settings for Navigation Mesh generation

Creating Artificial Intelligence

To get started, let's just generate an initial Navigation Mesh to see how the default settings look. We can easily erase and regenerate the mesh under new settings if needed. To do this, click on the Bake button from the Inspector. When you do this, a default Navigation Mesh is generated and appears in blue above the terrain from the Scene viewport. See *Figure 7.21*:

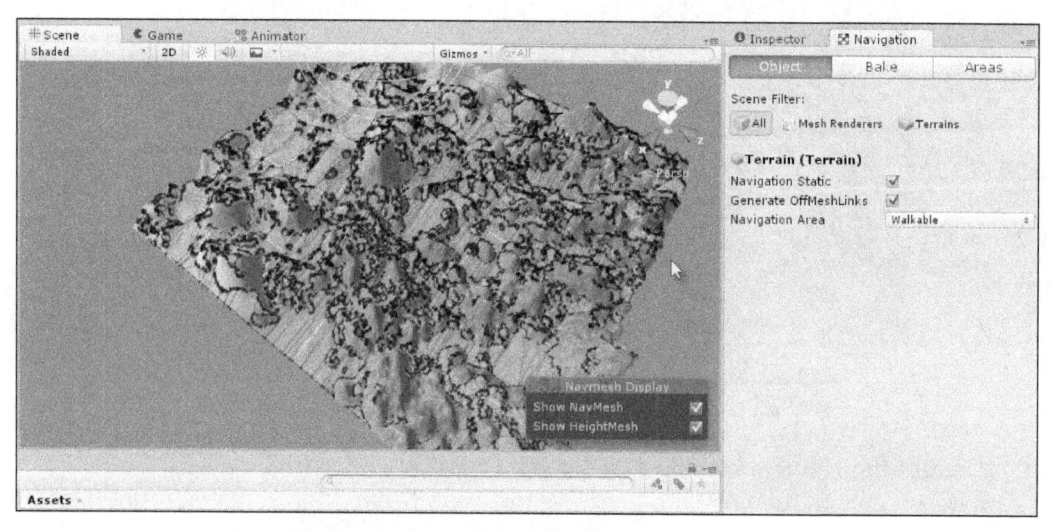

Figure 7.21: A default Navigation Mesh

The default navigation mesh is problematic. It should represent the entire walkable regions of the level. It is, essentially, the area to which NPCs will be restricted when they move around. You'll see from the navigation mesh in the preceding image that it's fractured and broken in many places—some areas are totally isolated and disconnected from others. This is often undesirable because it means that any NPC walking within one isolated region cannot access or move to another as there is no connection between the two areas and the NPC can only move on the navigation mesh. To fix this properly, two settings must be adjusted. First, adjust the Agent Radius setting.

This controls how large an average agent (NPC) is, and it affects how close the Navigation Mesh can expand toward the surrounding mesh floor and its edges. Lower (smaller) settings allow the mesh to encroach nearer to the mesh edges, resulting in an expanded navigation mesh. Try reducing Agent Radius and then clicking on Bake again to observe the result. See *Figure 7.22*:

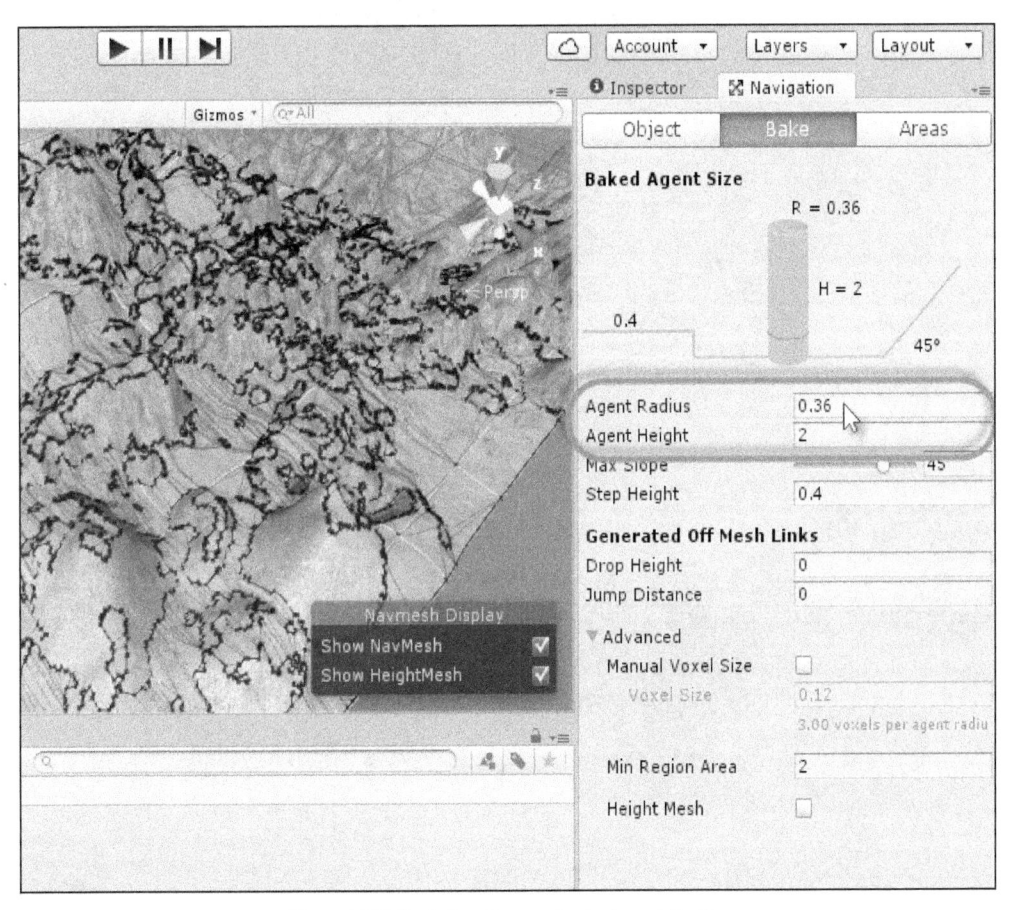

Figure 7.22: Refining the mesh via Agent Radius

Creating Artificial Intelligence

This improves the meshes but we still have broken or fractured areas. This is also because of the Max Slope setting, which controls how steep a surface should be (such as the incline of a mountain) before it becomes unwalkable for an NPC. Increase this setting to expand the navigation mesh further, and click on Bake:

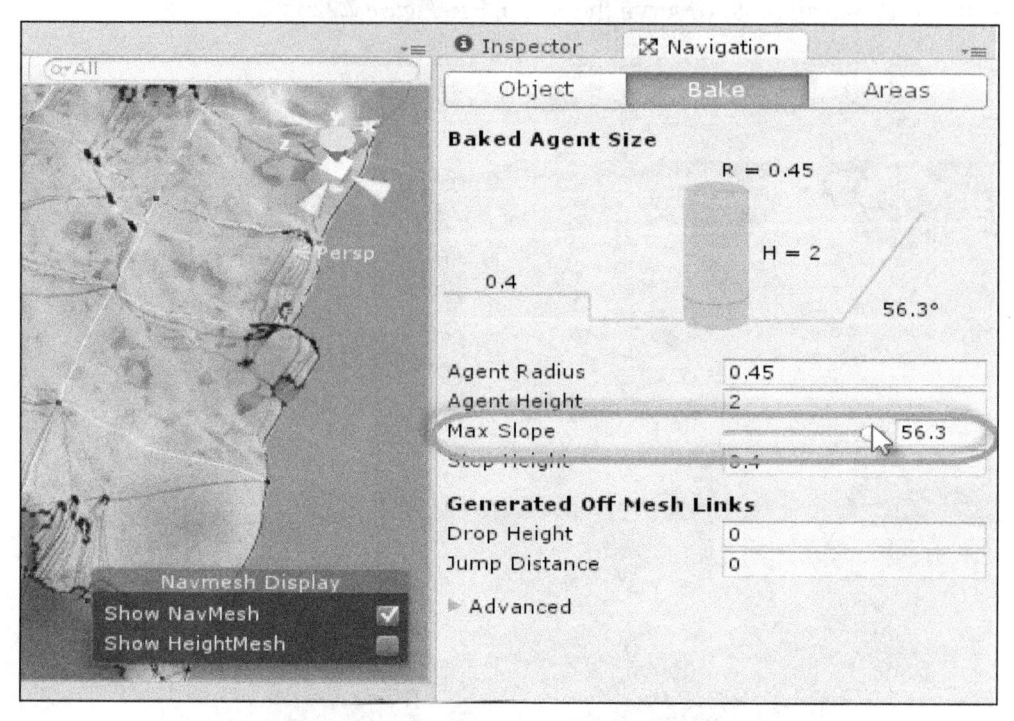

Figure 7.23: Increasing Max Slope to expand the navigation mesh over the terrain

Chapter 7

Congratulations! You have now constructed a Navigation Mesh for the level. The `NavMesh` asset itself is stored in a folder matching the scene name. When selected in the Project panel, you can preview various read-only properties describing the Navigation Mesh, such as Height and Walkable Radius settings. See *Figure 7.24*:

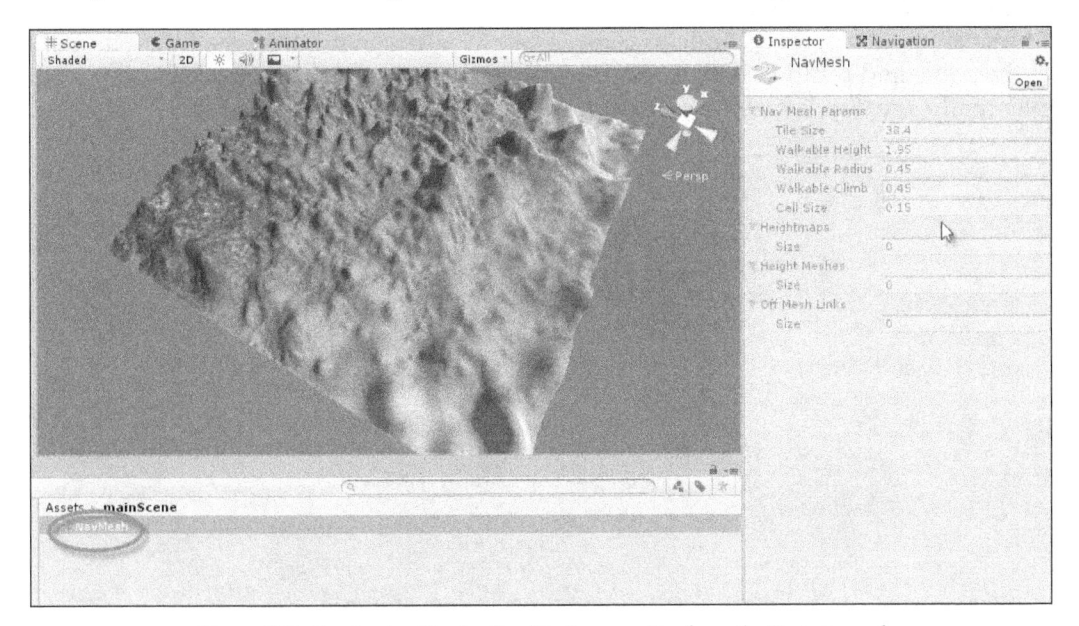

Figure 7.24: Previewing Navigation Mesh properties from the Project panel

Creating Artificial Intelligence

Building an NPC

Now we'll build an NPC character that'll display artificial intelligence. To get started, we'll use the Ethan mesh included in the Unity native companion assets. This can be found in the Project panel under the **Standard Assets | Characters | ThirdPersonCharacter | Models** folder. From here, drag and drop the Ethan model to the scene and position it on the terrain. We'll refine and edit this model and, eventually, create a prefab from it to represent an NPC character. See *Figure 7.25*:

Figure 7.25: Starting an NPC character

When adding the Ethan model to the level, ensure that the blue forward vector of the character is pointing forward, facing the direction in which the character is actually looking. If the forward vector is not front-aligned, then create an empty object and align the character model to that as a child object so that the forward vector of the parent is pointing straight ahead, along the character's line of sight. That is, the blue forward vector should align with the character's eye (be looking in the same direction). This is highly important to make your character move around believably. See *Figure 7.26*:

Figure 7.26: Forward vector (blue arrow) pointing forward at the character's feet

The NPC should navigate and walk around the terrain intelligently using the Navigation Mesh generated for the level. For this, a NavMesh agent component should be attached to the character. Select the Ethan model in the level and, from the application menu, choose **Component | Navigation** NavMesh Agent. The **Nav Mesh Agent** component contains both Path-Finding and Steering (Navigation) behaviors that allow a GameObject to move around a Navigation Mesh. See *Figure 7.27*:

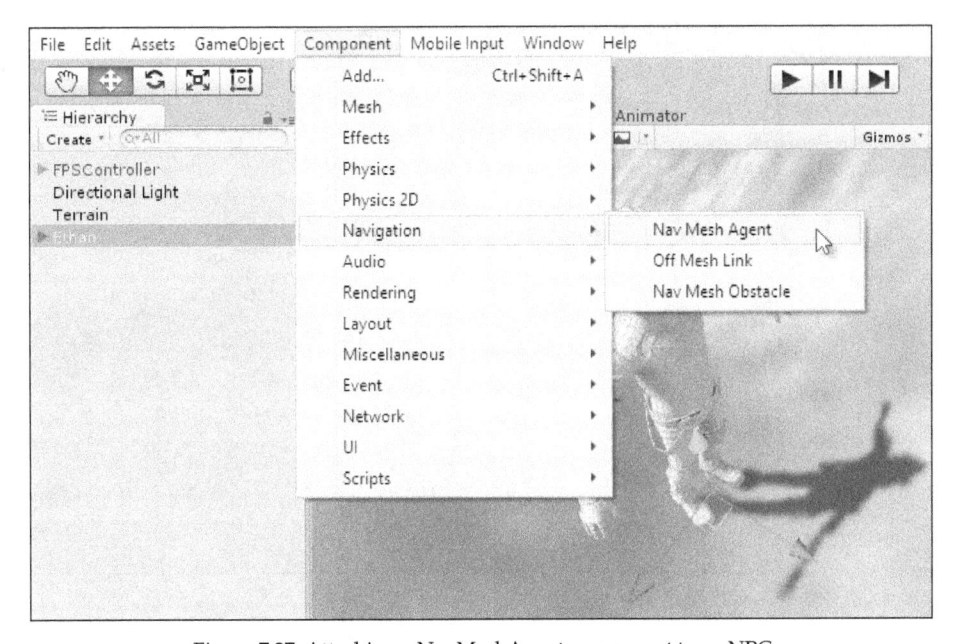

Figure 7.27: Attaching a NavMeshAgent component to an NPC

Creating Artificial Intelligence

By default, the Navigation Mesh assigns a Cylinder Collision volume to the Agent—the object that will navigate and move around. This is not a true collider that acts with the physics system but a pseudo-collider used to determine when the character nears the edge of a navigation mesh. Select the Ethan NPC and, from the Inspector in the NavMesh Agent component, set the Height to 1.66 and Radius to 0.22. This approximates the mesh more closely. See *Figure 7.28*:

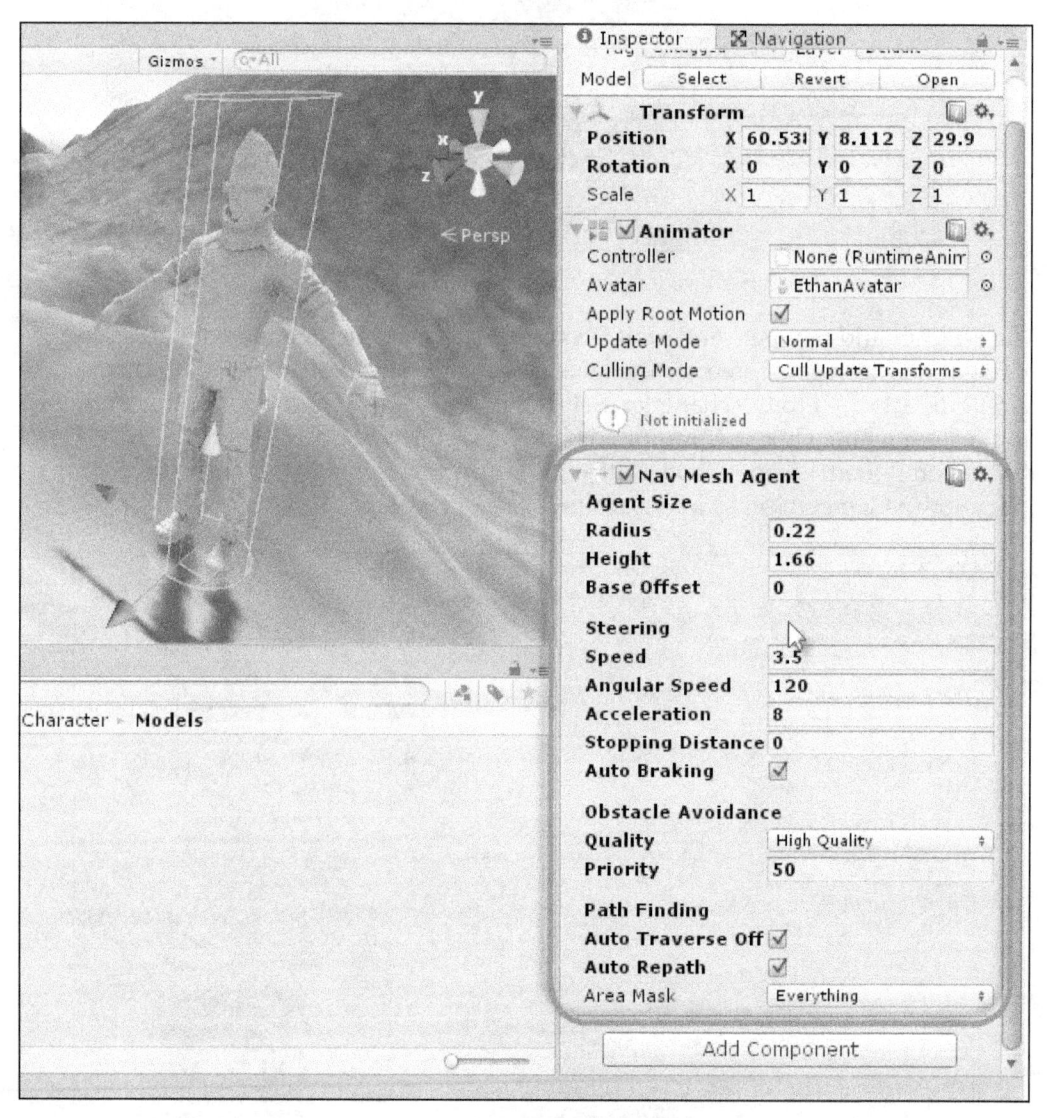

Figure 7.28: Sizing the Agent Collider

For test purposes, let's make the mesh move; just to see that everything is working as it should be. To do this, we'll need to make a new script. First, create a new empty object, which will act as a Destination, that is, a target object that the NPC should reach, wherever it is. Select GameObject | Create Empty from the application menu. Name it Destination, and then assign it a Gizmo icon to make it visible in the viewport. See Figure 7.29. Simply click on the cube icon at the top left of the Object Inspector with the object selected, and then choose an icon representation:

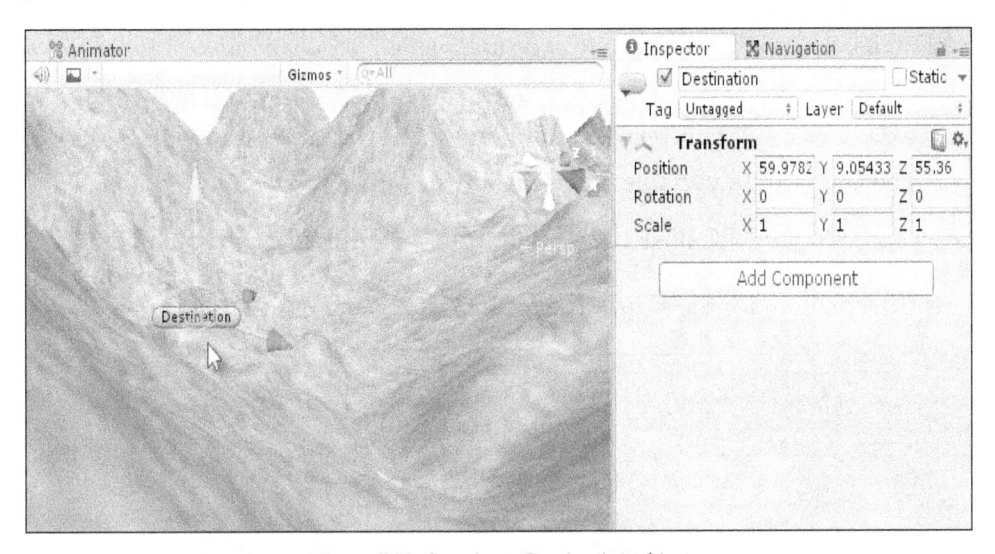

Figure 7.29: Creating a Destination object

Next, create a new C# script file (`FollowDestination.cs`) and attach it to the NPC object in the scene. The code is included in *Code Sample 7.1*, and comments, which is as follows:

```
using UnityEngine;
using System.Collections;

public class FollowDestination : MonoBehaviour
{
  private NavMeshAgent ThisAgent = null;
  public Transform Destination = null;

  // Use this for initialization
  void Awake ()
  {
    ThisAgent = GetComponent<NavMeshAgent>();
  }

  // Update is called once per frame
```

```
void Update ()
{
  ThisAgent.SetDestination(Destination.position);
}
}
```

Code Sample 7.1

The following points summarize the code sample:

- The FollowDestination class can be attached to any object with a `NavMeshAgent`. This object should follow the destination object as it moves.
- The Destination variable maintains the destination object to follow.

Once attached to the NPC object, drag and drop the destination empty object to the Destination slot for the `FollowDestination` component in the Inspector. This assigns a destination for the script. See *Figure 7.30*:

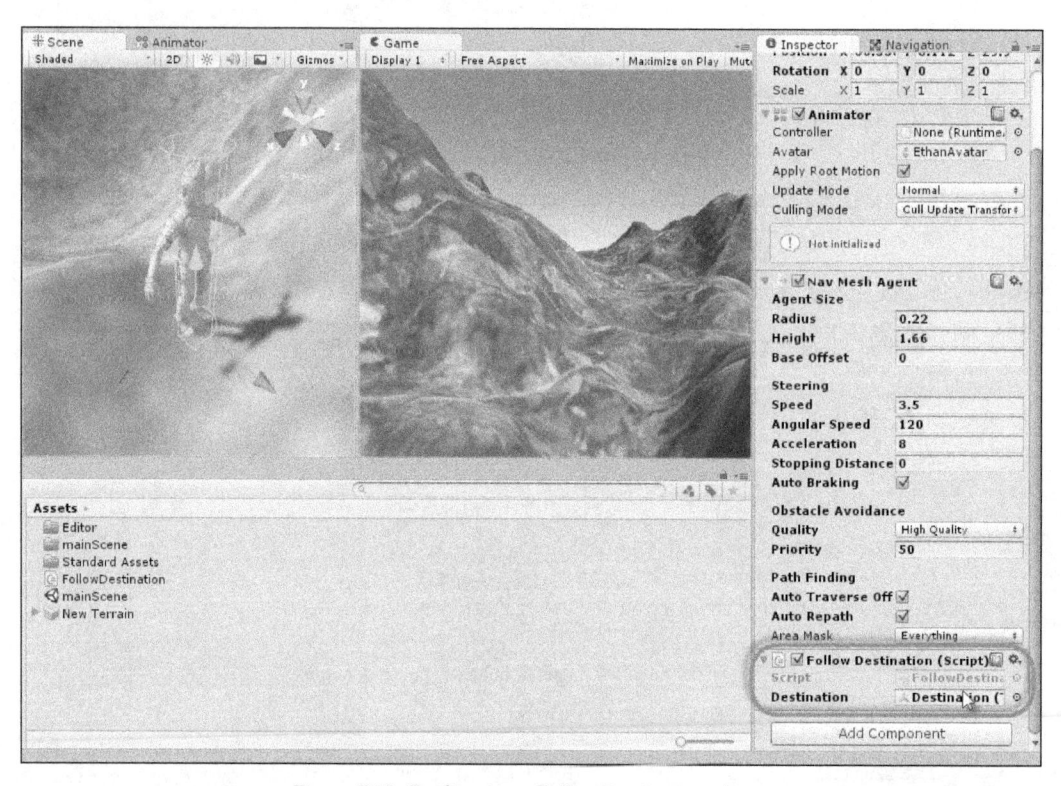

Figure 7.30: Configuring a FollowDestination object

Now give the game a test run. During gameplay, move the destination object around via the Scene tab and see how the NPC responds. The NPC should continually chase the destination object. In addition, if you play the game with the Navigation window open in the Inspector and with the NPC selected in the Hierarchy panel, the Scene view will display diagnostic information and gizmos, allowing you to preview and visualize the route calculated by the NPC. See *Figure 7.31*:

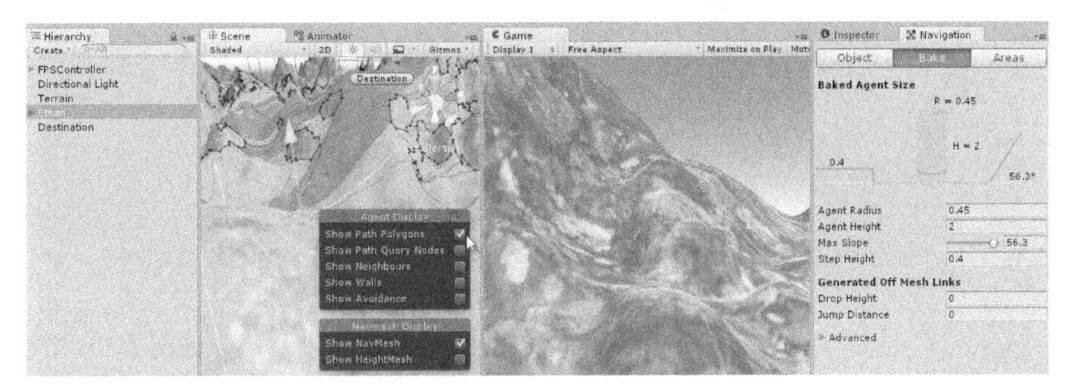

Figure 7.31: Testing NPC Navigation

Creating patrolling NPCs

We now have an NPC that follows a destination object, which is valuable in itself as an exercise, but we'll need more sophisticated behavior than this. Specifically, we'll need the NPC to patrol, that is, move across multiple destinations in order via a waypoint system, moving from one destination to the next in sequence. There are multiple approaches that could be taken to achieve this. One method is through script. Through this method, we'd create an array of different waypoint objects and iterate through them on a loop such that when the NPC reaches one destination, they'll move on to the next one. Now, this approach can be very efficient and effective, but there's another method. Specifically, instead of using script, we can create an animation to move a single destination object to different waypoint locations over time, and because the NPC continually follows the destination wherever it moves, it will continually patrol.

Creating Artificial Intelligence

Let's take this second approach. Start by opening the Animation window by selecting **Window | Animation** from the application menu. See Figure 7.32.

Dock the Animation window into a horizontal view in the Project panel, if you prefer, for ease of viewing:

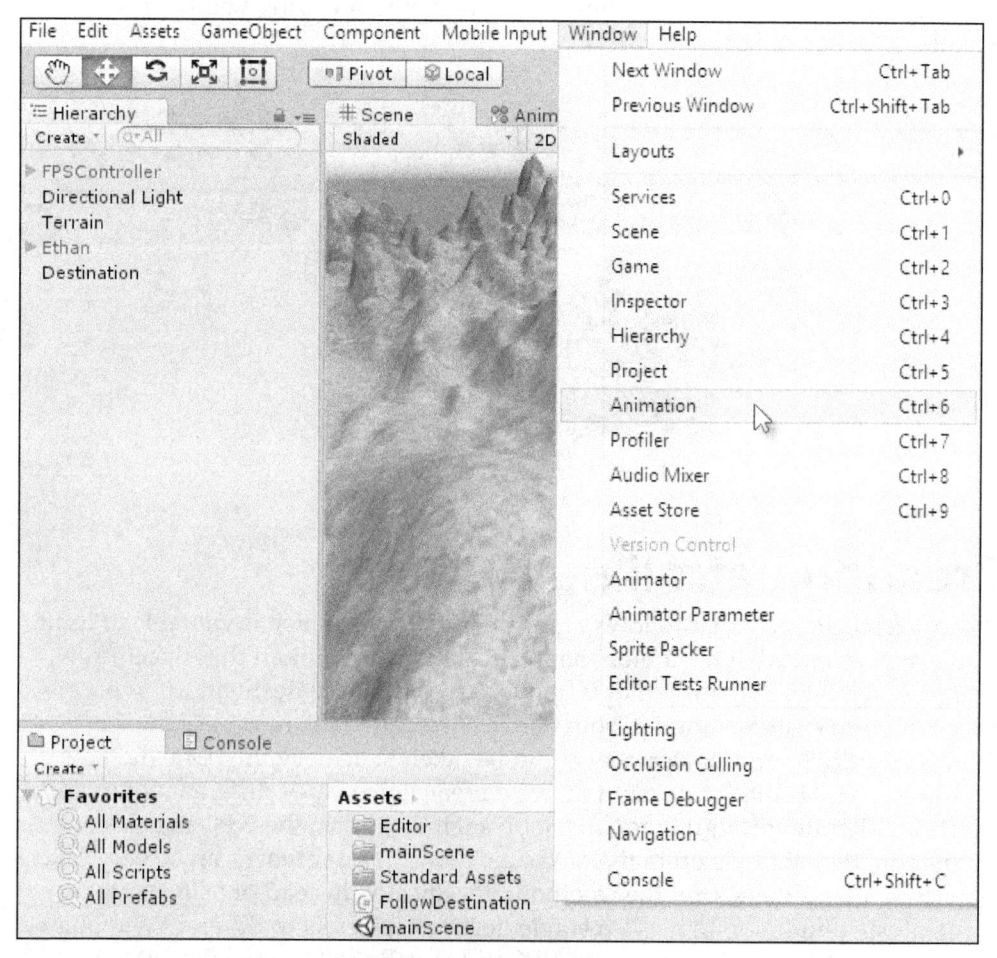

Figure 7.32: Accessing the Animation window

Next, select the object to animate (the destination object) from the Hierarchy panel and, from the Animation window, click on the Create button. From here, you will be asked to name and save the animation. I've called the animation anim_DestPatrol. See *Figure 7.33*:

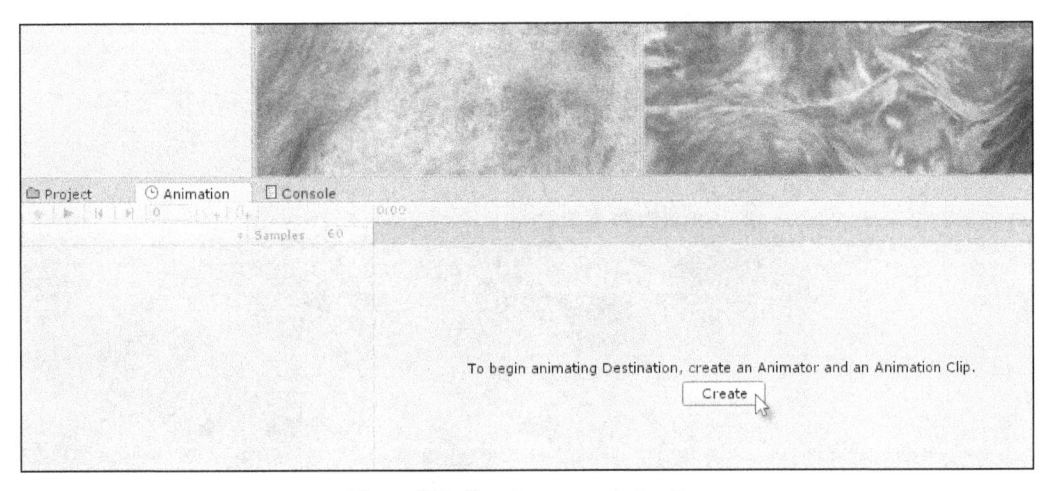

Figure 7.33: Creating a new Animation

Once the animation is created you can proceed to define animation channels. For the destination object, we'll need a channel for the position field as the object should change position around the scene. Click on the Add Property button from the Animation window, and then choose **Transform | Position** to add a new position channel. This will automatically create starting and ending key frames in the timeline, which are identical and hold the object position. See *Figure 7.34*:

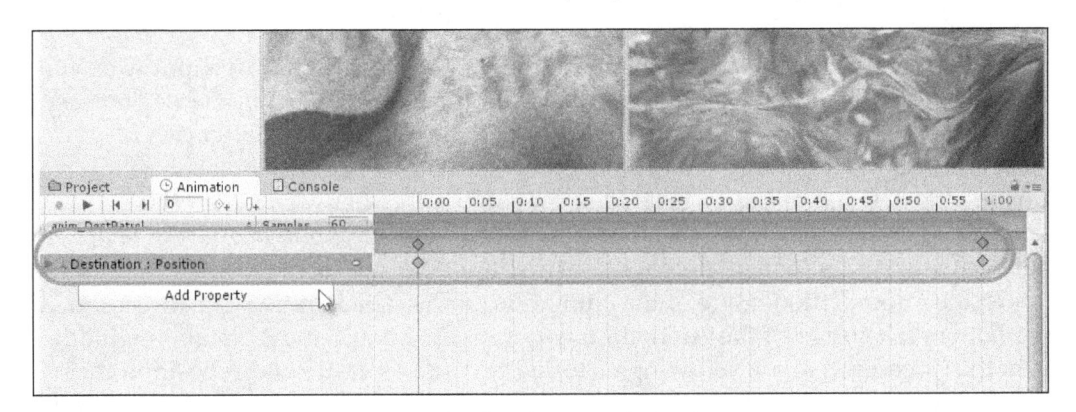

Figure 7.34: Creating a new Animation

Creating Artificial Intelligence

Now, simply click and drag the vertical, red time slider across the timeline in the **Animation** window, between the 0-1 range, and then change the position of the destination object in the **Scene** tab to a new position. When you do this, Unity records the object position for that key frame. Repeat this process across the timeline, moving the destination object to different positions each time, and this creates a complete patrol animation. See *Figure 7.35*:

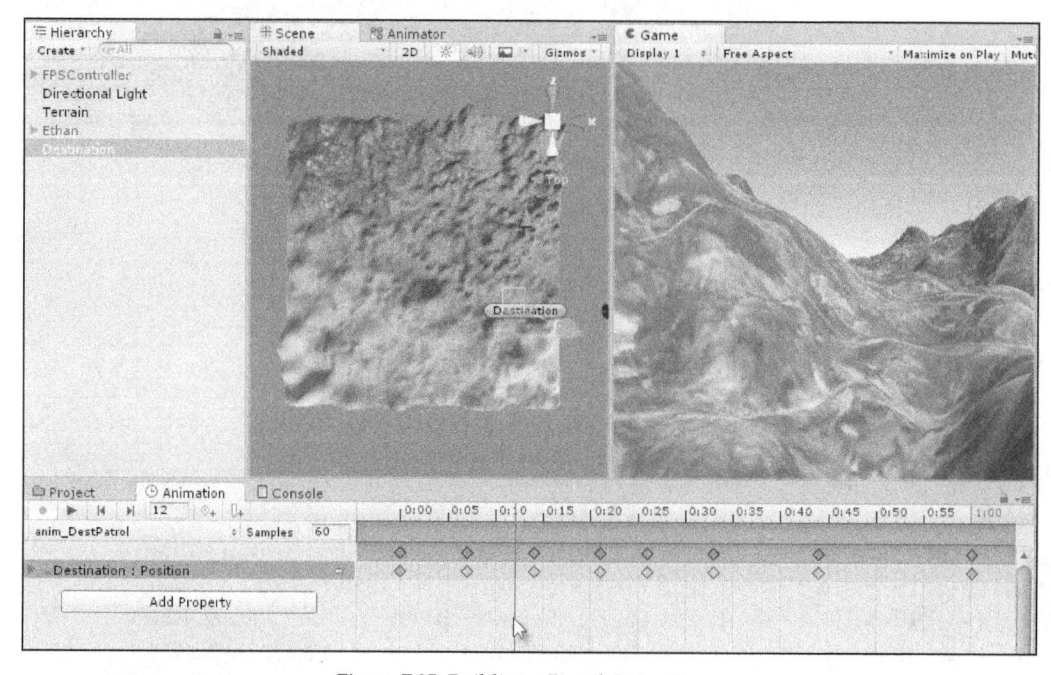

Figure 7.35: Building a Patrol Animation..

Play the animation back by pressing play from either the **Animation** window or via the toolbar. By default, the animation will probably play back too fast (that's an easy fix, as we'll see), but notice also that, as expected, the destination object is *tweened*. That is, the Unity Animation interpolates between the key frames in the timeline, causing the destination object to slide or move smoothly between waypoints.
For animation like this, however, we just want the destination to teleport or snap between waypoints immediately without any transition. To achieve this, we need to adjust the interpolation mode of the animation curves. Click on the Curves button at the bottom left corner of the Animation window. By default, the Animation window is in the DopeSheet mode, allowing us to see key frames easily and reposition them. The Curve mode, however, lets us adjust the interpolation between key frames. See *Figure 7.36*:

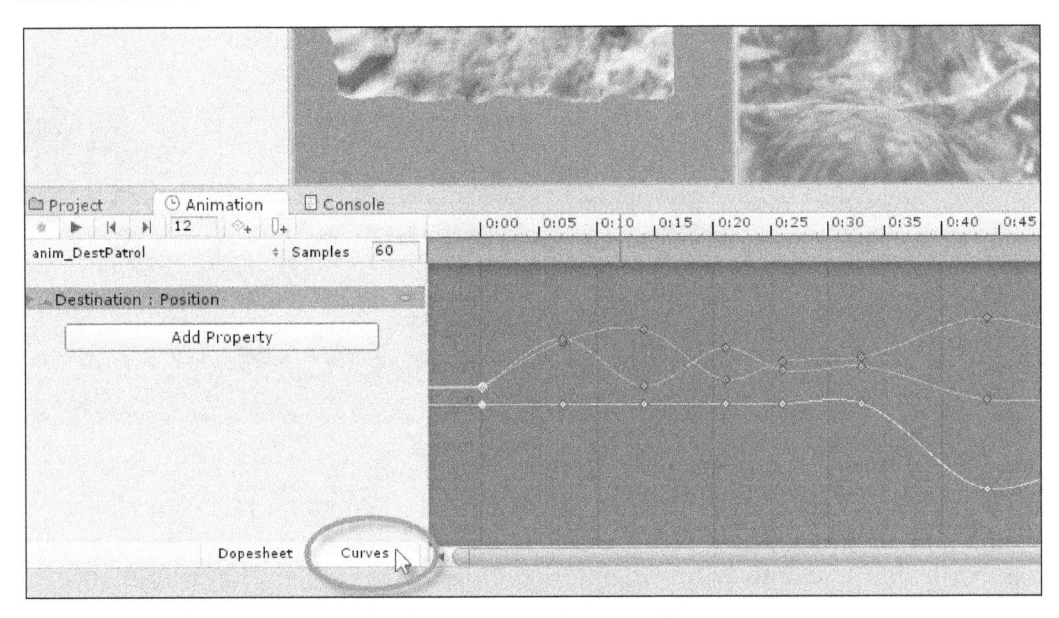

Figure 7.36: Accessing Animation Curves

Now, box-select (click and drag a selection box) across all key frames in the graph view to select them all. Then, right-click to display the key frame context menu and, from the menu, choose Right Tangent | Constant to change all handles to a flat constant shape, meaning all key frames retain their values over the destination object until the next key frame only. See *Figure 7.37*:

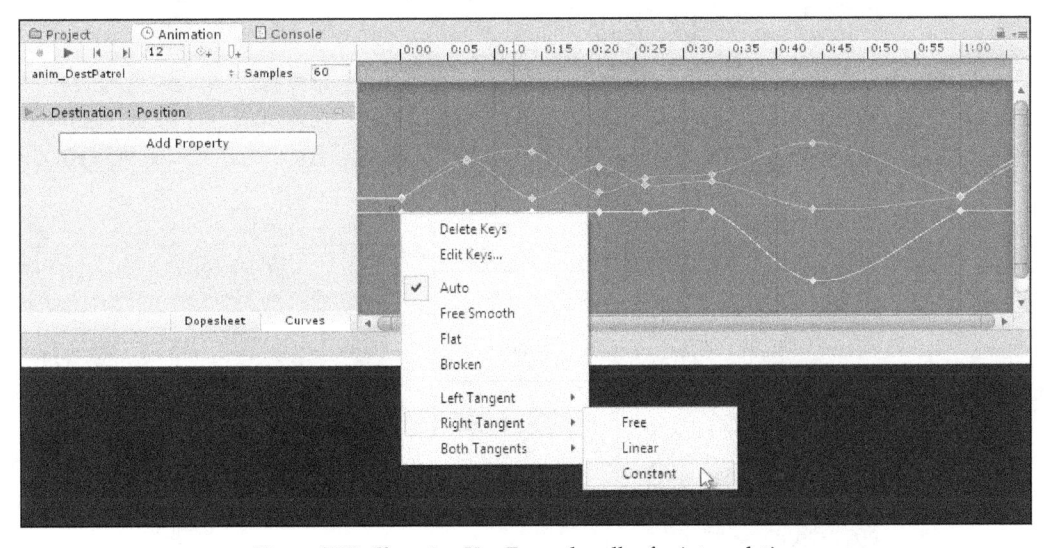

Figure 7.37: Changing Key Frame handles for interpolation

Creating Artificial Intelligence

When the Constant option is chosen from the menu, the curves between key frames will look very different in the graph—a straight line joining them. See *Figure 7.38*:

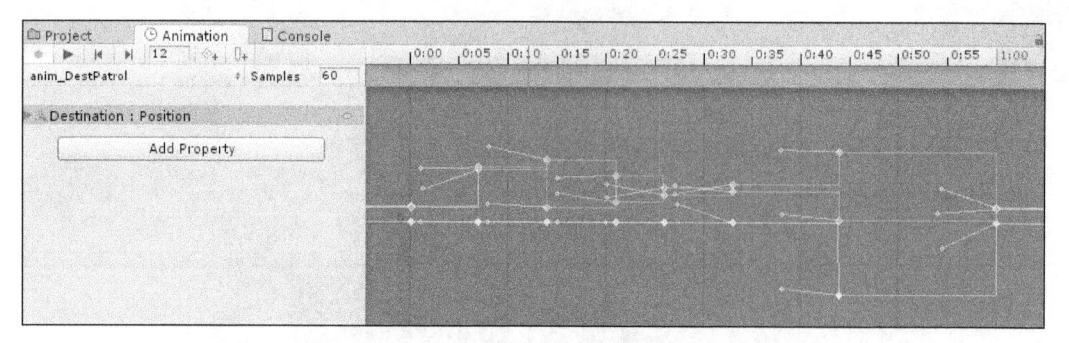

Figure 7.38: Constant interpolation

Now test this by pressing play on the toolbar. When you do this, the Destination should jump between waypoints as the animation progresses, and the NPC will continually move and travel towards the destination. Due to the default speed of the animation, the NPC may seem confused or crazed as he is torn between rapidly changing destinations. To fix this, select the **Destination** object in the Hierarchy panel and, from the Object Inspector, double-click on the Controller field of the Animator component to open the animator graph attached to the object, which controls when specific animations should play. See *Figure 7.39*:

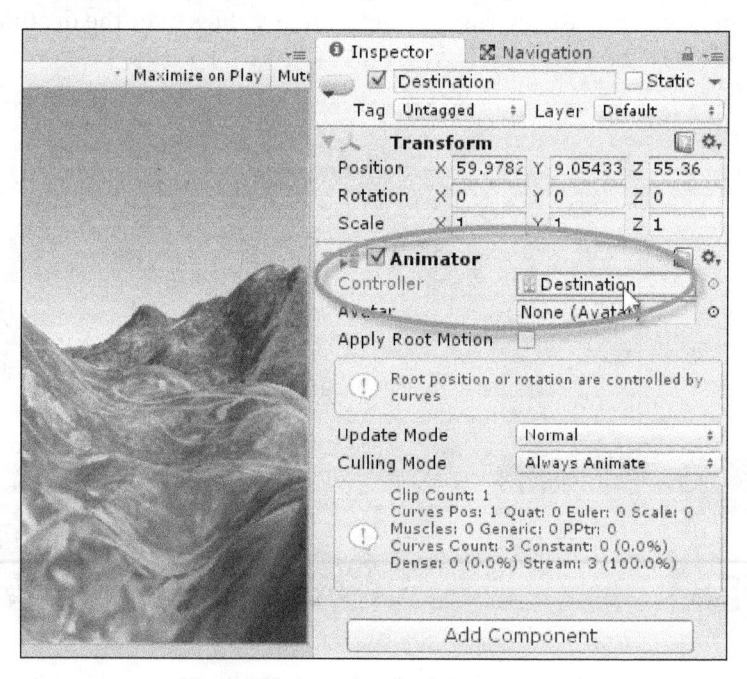

Figure 7.39: Accessing the Animator asset

Chapter 7

You can also show the Animator window manually by choosing **Window | Animator** from the application menu. In the Animator window, the default node is highlighted in orange. This node (animation) will play when the object is first activated in the level, which is normally on level startup. See *Figure 7.40*:

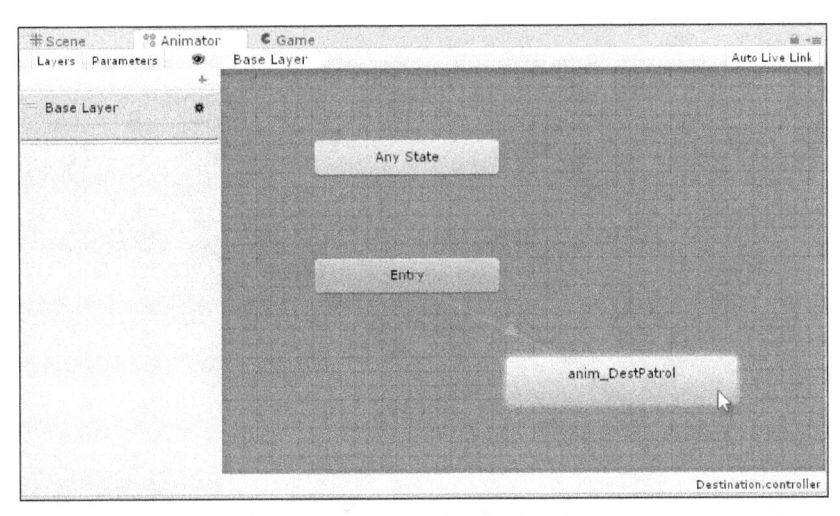

Figure 7.40: The orange DestPatrol animation is the default in the Animator window

Select the DestPatrol node in the graph and reduce its Speed from the Object Inspector. In my case, I've used a value of 0.2, which works well. Once the speed is changed, replay your game to observe the effect. See *Figure 7.41*:

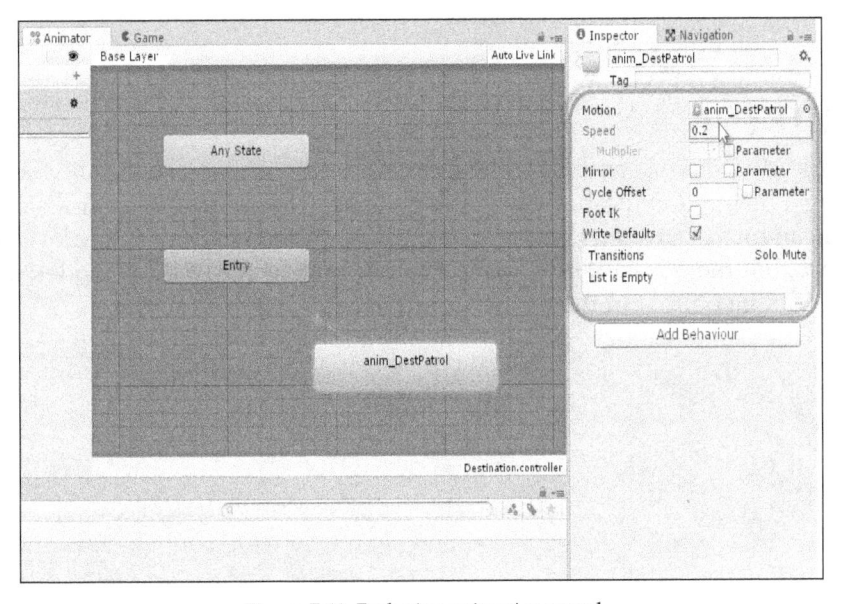

Figure 7.41: Reducing animation speed

Creating Artificial Intelligence

On pressing play, the NPC should now move between destinations at a believable speed, moving from one waypoint to the next. If the NPC moves too fast or too slow between waypoints, increase or decrease the animation speed further to get the result you need. Congratulations! You now have a complete, animated waypoint system. See *Figure 7.42*:

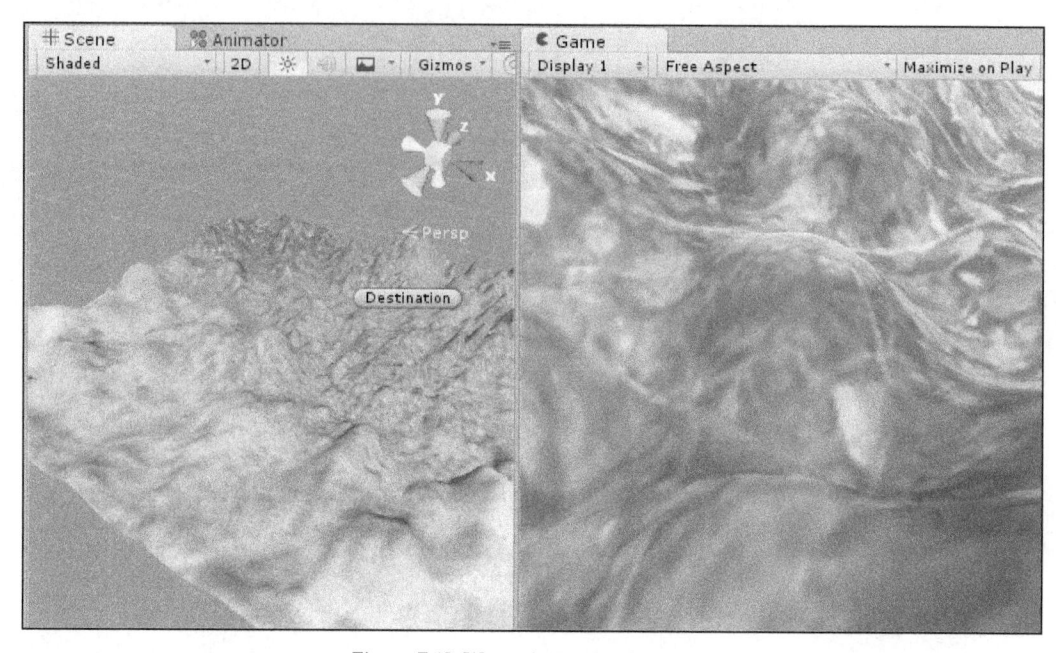

Figure 7.42: Waypoint system in action

Summary

Great work! We've now completed the first part of the AI project: building a terrain, generating a navigation mesh, and creating a basic waypoint system in which the character can move between destinations. This is a good beginning to simulate intelligence, but there is a lot more code to work on to achieve the intended effect. We'll be focusing on that in the next chapter.

Test your knowledge

Q1. You can generate a walkable surface of the level for AI by using...

- A. A* Pathfinding
- B. A Collision Box
- C. Navigation Mesh
- D. A Path Tree

Q2. The Animator Window of Mechanim is useful for...

- A. Controlling when and how animations play
- B. Creating loopable animations
- C. Editing Characters
- D. Applying Inverse Kinematics

Q3. To walk on a Navigation Mesh, an object needs...

- A. A* Pathfinding
- B. A Collision Box
- C. A NavMesh Agent Component
- D. A Collider Component

Q4. You can edit animation interpolation by changing...

- A. High Poly Meshes
- B. Keyframe Curves
- C. Box Colliders
- D. Mesh Renderer Components

Q5. The blue local axis arrow of an object is known as...

- A. Forward Vector
- B. Right Vector
- C. Up Vector
- D. Pitch

Further Reading

Check out the following-mentioned links for more information:

- `https://docs.unity3d.com/Manual/Navigation.html`
- `https://www.packtpub.com/game-development/unity-ai-programming-essentials`
- `https://www.packtpub.com/game-development/advanced-game-mechanics-unity-5-video`

8
Continuing with Intelligent Enemies

This chapter continues with the previous one and completes the AI project by focusing on the theory and related coding underpinning an intelligent enemy. The enemy will demonstrate three main behaviors: patrolling, chasing, and attacking. In this chapter, we will dive into the following topics:

- How to plan and code an AI system for enemy characters
- How to code Finite State Machines (FSMs)
- How to create the line-of-sight functionality

> The starting project and assets can be found in the book companion files in the Chapter08/Start folder. You can start here and follow along with this chapter if you don't have your own project already.

Enemy AI – range of sight

Let's now start developing enemy AI by thinking about our functional requirements. The enemies in the scene will begin in patrol mode, wandering the level from place to place searching for the player character. If the player is spotted, the enemy will change from patrolling and begin chasing the player, attempting to move closer to them for an attack. If the enemy reaches within attacking range of the player, the enemy will change from chasing to attacking. If the player outruns the enemy and successfully loses them, the enemy should stop chasing and return to patrolling again, searching for the player as they were doing initially. This, in sum, describes our needed enemy AI behavior.

Continuing with Intelligent Enemies

To achieve this behavior, we'll need to code the line of sight functionality for the enemy. The enemy relies on being able to see the player character or determining whether the player is visible to the enemy at any one moment. This helps the enemy decide whether they should patrol or chase the player character. To code this, refer to the following code from the source file, `LineSight.cs`. This script file should be attached to the enemy character created so far from the previous chapter:

```
using UnityEngine;
using System.Collections;
//-----------------------------------------
public class LineSight : MonoBehaviour
{
    //-----------------------------------------
    //How sensitive should we be to sight
    public enum SightSensitivity {STRICT, LOOSE};

    //Sight sensitivity
    public SightSensitivity Sensitivity = SightSensitivity.STRICT;

    //Can we see target
    public bool CanSeeTarget = false;

    //FOV
    public float FieldOfView = 45f;

    //Reference to target
    private Transform Target = null;

    //Reference to eyes
    public Transform EyePoint = null;

    //Reference to transform component
    private Transform ThisTransform = null;

    //Reference to sphere collider
    private SphereCollider ThisCollider = null;

    //Reference to last know object sighting, if any
    public Vector3 LastKnowSighting = Vector3.zero;
    //-----------------------------------------
    void Awake()
    {
```

```
    ThisTransform = GetComponent<Transform>();
    ThisCollider = GetComponent<SphereCollider>();
    LastKnowSighting = ThisTransform.position;
    Target = GameObject.FindGameObjectWithTag("Player").
GetComponent<Transform>();
  }
  //-----------------------------------------
  bool InFOV()
  {
    //Get direction to target
    Vector3 DirToTarget = Target.position - EyePoint.position;

    //Get angle between forward and look direction
    float Angle = Vector3.Angle(EyePoint.forward, DirToTarget);

    //Are we within field of view?
    if(Angle <= FieldOfView)
      return true;

    //Not within view
    return false;
  }
  //-----------------------------------------
  bool ClearLineofSight()
  {
    RaycastHit Info;

    if(Physics.Raycast(EyePoint.position, (Target.position - EyePoint.
position).normalized, out Info, ThisCollider.radius))
    {
      //If player, then can see player
      if(Info.transform.CompareTag("Player"))
        return true;
    }

    return false;
  }
  //-----------------------------------------
  void UpdateSight()
  {
    switch(Sensitity)
    {
```

```
      case SightSensitivity.STRICT:
        CanSeeTarget = InFOV() && ClearLineofSight();
      break;

      case SightSensitivity.LOOSE:
        CanSeeTarget = InFOV() || ClearLineofSight();
      break;
    }
  }
  //------------------------------------------
  void OnTriggerStay(Collider Other)
  {
    UpdateSight();

    //Update last known sighting
    if(CanSeeTarget)
      LastKnowSighting = Target.position;
  }
  //------------------------------------------
  void OnTriggerExit(Collider Other)
  {
    if(!Other.CompareTag("Player"))return;

    CanSeeTarget = false;
  }
  //------------------------------------------
}

//------------------------------------------
```

Code Sample 8.1

The following points summarize the code sample:

- The LineSight class should be attached to any enemy character object. Its purpose is to calculate whether a direct line of sight is available between the player and enemy.

- The CanSeeTarget variable is a Boolean (True/False), which is updated on a per frame basis to describe whether the enemy can see the player *right now* (for this frame). True means that the player is in sight of the enemy, and false means that the player is not visible.

- The FieldOfView variable is a floating point value that determines an angular margin on either side of the enemy eye-point, inside which objects (like the player) can be seen. The higher this value, the more chance the enemy has of seeing the player.

- The InFOV function returns true or false to indicate whether the player is within the enemy field of view. This ignores whether the player is occluded behind a wall or solid object (like a pillar). It simply takes the position of the enemy eyes, determines a vector to the player, and measures the angle between the forward vector and player. It compares this to the field of view, and returns true if the angle between enemy and player is less than the FieldOfView variable. In short, this function can tell you whether the enemy would see the player if there were a clear line of sight.

- The ClearLineOfSight function returns true or false to indicate whether there are any physical obstacles (Colliders), such as walls or props, between the enemy eye point and player. This does not consider whether the player is within the enemy field of view. This function, in combination with the InFOV function, can determine whether the enemy has a clear line of sight to the player and is within the field of view, and thus, whether the player is visible.

- The OnTriggerStay and OnTriggerExit functions are called when the player is within a trigger volume surrounding the enemy and when the player leaves this volume respectively. As we'll see, a sphere collider can be attached to the enemy character object to represent its horizon of view. This means the total distance, or radius, inside which the enemy could see the player, provided they were within the field of view and a clear line of sight existed.

Now, attach the `LineSight.cs` script file to the enemy character in the scene as well as a Sphere Collider component (marked as a Trigger) to approximate the viewing horizon of the enemy.

Continuing with Intelligent Enemies

See *Figure 8.1*. Leave the Field of View setting at 45, although this can be increased, if needed, to around 90 to tweak the effectiveness of the enemy viewing range:

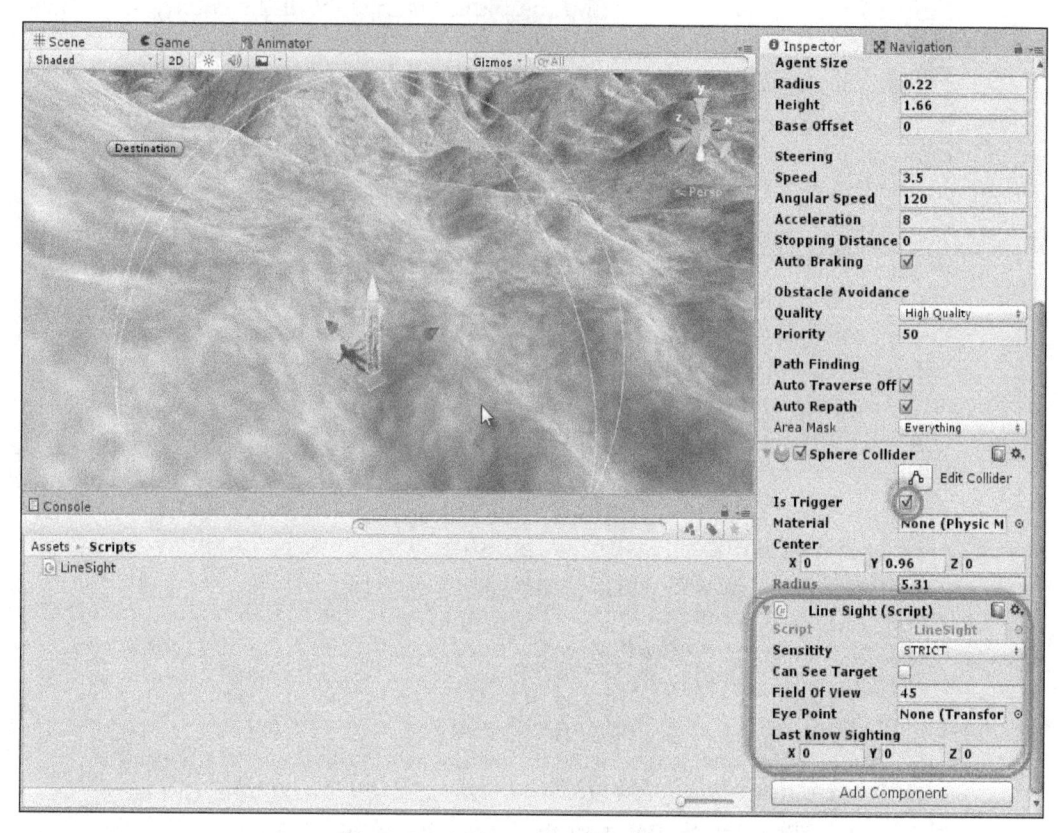

Figure 8.1: Adding a horizon to the NPC

Chapter 8

The Eye Point field is, by default, set to None, which represents a null value. This should refer to a specific location on the enemy character that acts as the eye point—the place from which the character can see. To create this point, add a new and empty game object to the scene using the application menu, **GameObject | Create Empty**. Name the object Eye Point, activate its visibility from the Inspector using a Gizmo icon (so that it can be visible even when deselected), and then add it as a child object to the enemy. Afterward, position the object to the character eye point, making sure that the forward vector is facing in the same direction. See *Figure 8.2*:

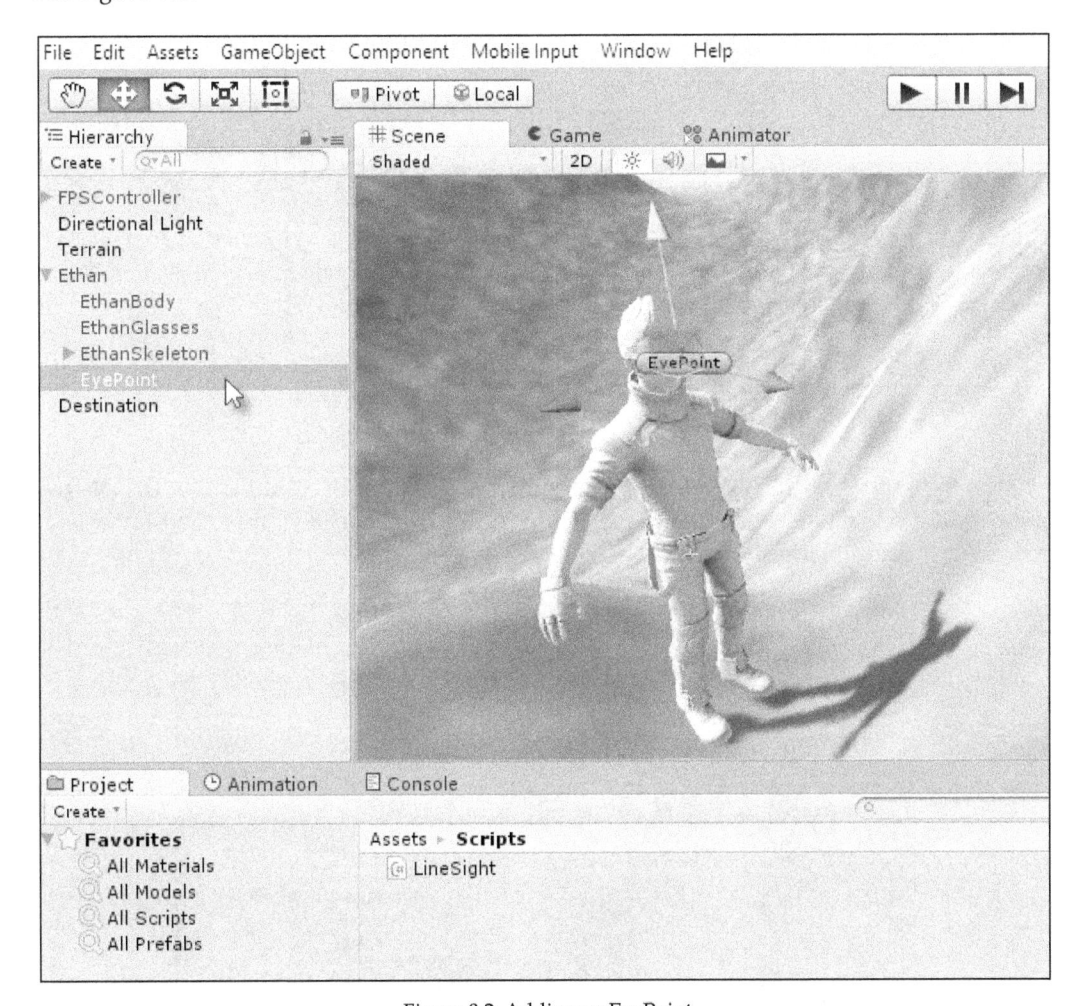

Figure 8.2: Adding an EyePoint

Continuing with Intelligent Enemies

Now, drag and drop the Eye Point object from the Hierarchy panel to the Eye Point field for the LineSight component in the Inspector. This specifies the Eye Point object as the eye point for the enemy character. This will be used in determining whether the enemy can see the player. Having a separate eye point object like this is useful as opposed to using the character position, which is typically at the feet location and not the eye. See *Figure 8.3*:

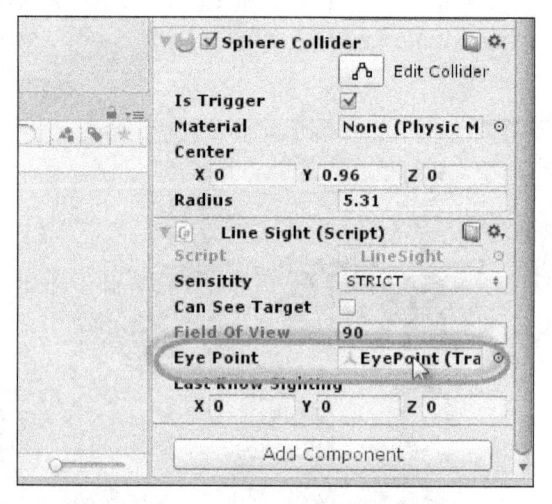

Figure 8.3: Defining the eye point for an NPC

Finally, the LineSight script determines the player location by first finding the player object in the scene using the Player tag. Consequently, make sure that the Player is tagged or labeled using the Player tag. See *Figure 8.4*:

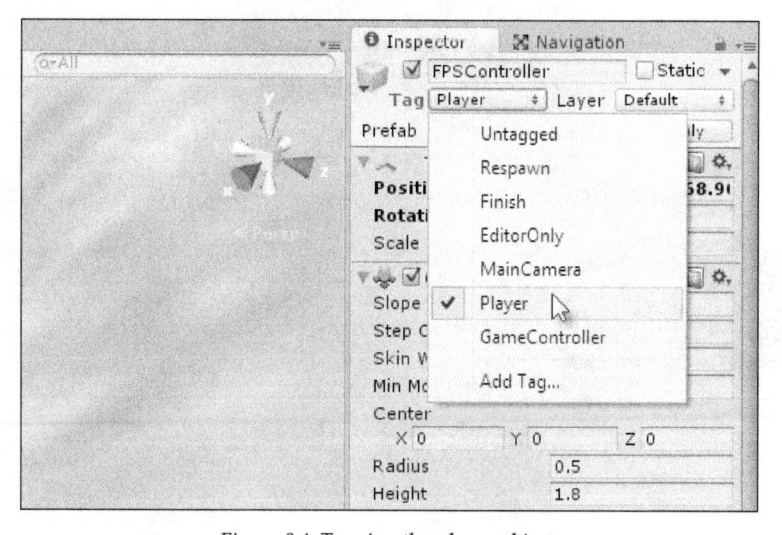

Figure 8.4: Tagging the player object

Now take your game for a test run. When you approach the NPC object, the Can See Target field will be enabled. See *Figure 8.5*. Good work! The line of sight functionality is now completed. Let's move on!

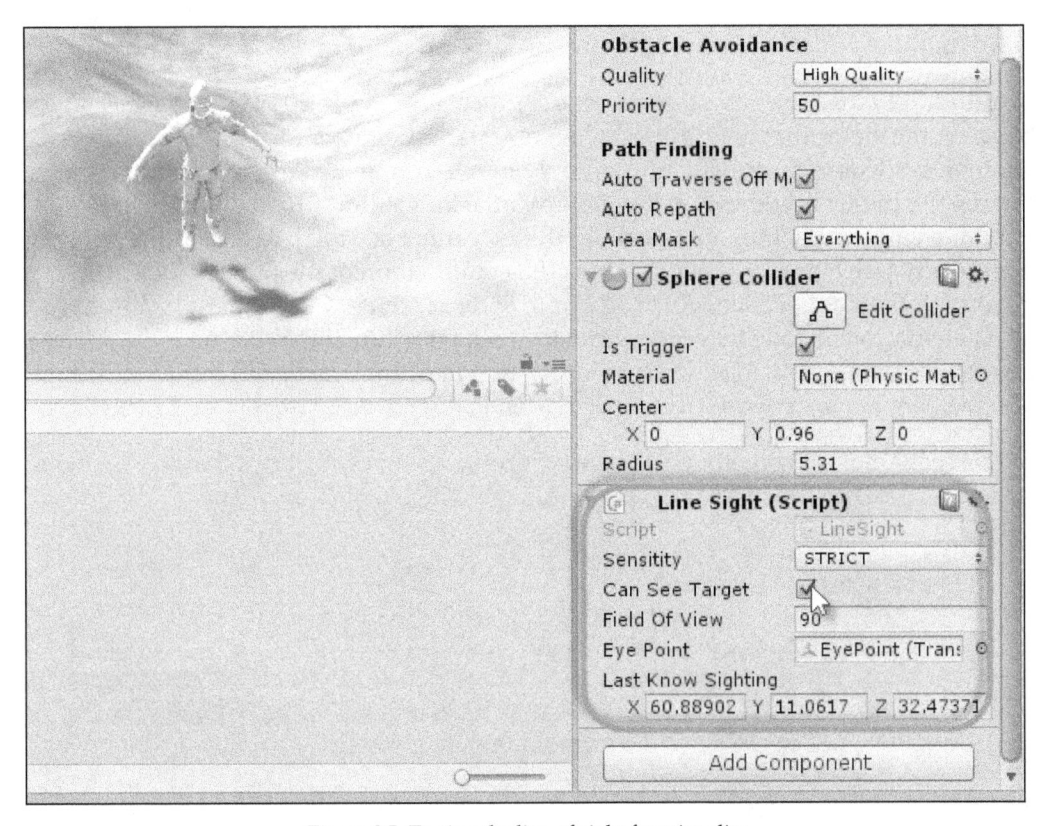

Figure 8.5: Testing the line of sight functionality

An overview of Finite State Machines

To create the AI for an NPC object, in addition to the line of sight code that we already have, we need to use Finite State Machines (FSMs). An FSM is not a thing or feature of Unity, nor is it a tangible aspect of the C# language. Rather, an FSM is a concept, framework, or idea that we can apply in code to achieve specific AI behaviors. It comes from a specific way of thinking about intelligent characters. Specifically, we can summarize the NPC for our level as existing within one of three possible states at any one time. These are patrol (when the enemy is wandering around), chase (when the enemy is running after the player), and attack (when the enemy has reached the player and is attacking). Each of these modes is a State and requires a unique and specific behavior and the enemy can be in only one of these three states at any one time.

The enemy cannot, for example, be patrolling and chasing simultaneously or patrolling and attacking, because this wouldn't make sense within the logic of the world and game. It possible to code alternative systems for different types of AI based on Finite State Machines, such as Hierarchical State Machines and Behaviour Trees, but these alternative systems are not covered here.

In addition to the states themselves, there is a rule set or group of connections between the states that determines when one state should change or move into another. For example, an NPC should only move from patrolling to chasing if they can see the player and they are not already attacking. Similarly, the NPC should only move from attacking to patrolling if they cannot see the player and they are not already patrolling or chasing. Thus, the combination of the States and rules governing their connections form an Finite State Machine. Consequently, any implementation in code that represents this behavior functionally is an FSM. There is no right or wrong way to code an FSM per se. There are simply different ways, some of which are better or worse for particular ends:

In this section, we'll code the FSM using Coroutines. Let's start by creating the main structure. Refer to the following code in the file, `AI_Enemy.cs`:

```
using UnityEngine;
using System.Collections;
//-----------------------------------------
public class AI_Enemy : MonoBehaviour
{
  //-----------------------------------------
  public enum ENEMY_STATE {PATROL, CHASE, ATTACK};
  //-----------------------------------------
  public ENEMY_STATE CurrentState
  {
    get{return currentstate;}

    set
    {
      //Update current state
      currentstate = value;

      //Stop all running coroutines
      StopAllCoroutines();

      switch(currentstate)
      {
```

```csharp
      case ENEMY_STATE.PATROL:
        StartCoroutine(AIPatrol());
      break;

      case ENEMY_STATE.CHASE:
        StartCoroutine(AIChase());
      break;

      case ENEMY_STATE.ATTACK:
        StartCoroutine(AIAttack());
      break;
    }
  }
}
//----------------------------------------
[SerializeField]
private ENEMY_STATE currentstate = ENEMY_STATE.PATROL;

//Reference to line of sight component
private LineSight ThisLineSight = null;

//Reference to nav mesh agent
private NavMeshAgent ThisAgent = null;

//Reference to player transform
private Transform PlayerTransform = null;

//----------------------------------------
void Awake()
{
  ThisLineSight = GetComponent<LineSight>();
  ThisAgent = GetComponent<NavMeshAgent>();
  PlayerTransform = GameObject.FindGameObjectWithTag("Player").GetComponent<Transform>();
}
//----------------------------------------
void Start()
{

  //Configure starting state
  CurrentState = ENEMY_STATE.PATROL;
}
```

Continuing with Intelligent Enemies

```
//-----------------------------------------
public IEnumerator AIPatrol()
{
    yield break;

}
//-----------------------------------------
public IEnumerator AIChase()
{

    yield break;
}
//-----------------------------------------
public IEnumerator AIAttack()
{
  yield break;
}
//-----------------------------------------
}

//-----------------------------------------
```

> More information on Coroutines can be found at the online Unity documentation at http://docs.unity3d.com/Manual/Coroutines.html.

Code Sample 8.2

The following points summarize the code sample:

- The AI_Enemy class created so far does not represent the full and complete FSM but just the skeleton for its beginning. It illustrates the general structure. It features a single coroutine for each state.
- The CurrentState variable defines a property that selects the active state, terminating all existing coroutines and initiating the relevant one.
- Each state coroutine will run on a frame-safe infinite loop for as long as the state is active, allowing the enemy object to update its behavior, as we'll see shortly.

Before proceeding, make sure that the AI_Enemy script is attached to the NPC object. See *Figure 8.6*:

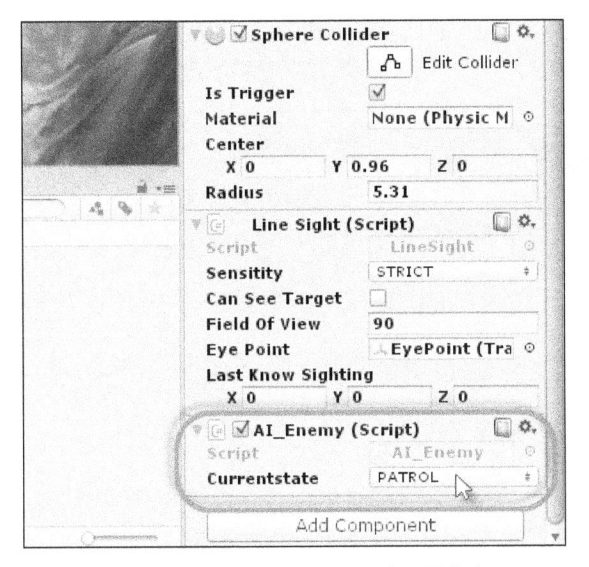

Figure 8.6: Attaching the AI script to the NPC character

The Patrol state

The first of the three states to implement for the NPC AI is the Patrol State. In the previous chapter, we configured an animated patrol object, which the NPC should follow continuously during this state. The patrol object moves around the level from a predefined animation asset, changing from one position to the next. However, previously, the NPC simply followed this object without end, whereas the Patrol State requires the NPC to consider whether the player can be seen on its route. If it can, the state should change. To support this functionality, the Patrol State and Start function of the AI_Enemy class has been coded, as featured in the following code:

```
void Start()
{
  //Get random destination
  GameObject[] Destinations = GameObject.
  FindGameObjectsWithTag("Dest");
  PatrolDestination = Destinations[Random.Range(0, Destinations.
  Length)].GetComponent<Transform>();

  //Configure starting state
  CurrentState = ENEMY_STATE.PATROL;
}
```

```
//-----------------------------------------
public IEnumerator AIPatrol()
{
  //Loop while patrolling
  while(currentstate == ENEMY_STATE.PATROL)
  {
    //Set strict search
    ThisLineSight.Sensitity = LineSight.SightSensitivity.STRICT;

    //Chase to patrol position
    ThisAgent.Resume();
    ThisAgent.SetDestination(PatrolDestination.position);

    //Wait until path is computed
    while(ThisAgent.pathPending)
      yield return null;

    //If we can see the target then start chasing
    if(ThisLineSight.CanSeeTarget)
    {
      ThisAgent.Stop();
      CurrentState = ENEMY_STATE.CHASE;
      yield break;
    }

    //Wait until next frame
    yield return null;
  }
}
```

Code Sample 8.3

The following points summarize the code sample:

- The Start function sets the initial state of the enemy character to Patrol. The coroutine `AIPatrol` handles this state.
- The AIPatrol coroutine loops infinitely for as long as the Patrol state is active. Remember that an infinite loop is not necessarily a bad thing when used in a coroutine and in combination with a yield statement. This allows prolonged behaviors to be coded neatly and easily over time.

- The SetDestination function is called to send NavMeshAgent to the specified destination. This is followed by a pathPending check, which is a variable of the NavMeshAgent. This check waits until the pathPending variable is `false`, indicating that a full traversable path has been calculated from the source to the destination. For short and simple journeys, a path may be calculated almost immediately, but for paths that are more complex, this can take much longer.
- During the Patrol state, we constantly check the LineSight component to determine whether the enemy has a direct line of sight to the player. If so, the enemy changes from the Patrol state to the Chase state.
- Remember that the yield return null statement will pause a coroutine until the next frame.

Now, drag and drop the AIEnemy script to the NPC character in the scene, if you haven't already. The Patrol mode is configured to track a moving object, that is, the enemy will follow a moving destination. A moving destination was created in the previous chapter using the Animation window to move an object around the scene over time, jumping from one place to another. See *Figure 8.7*:

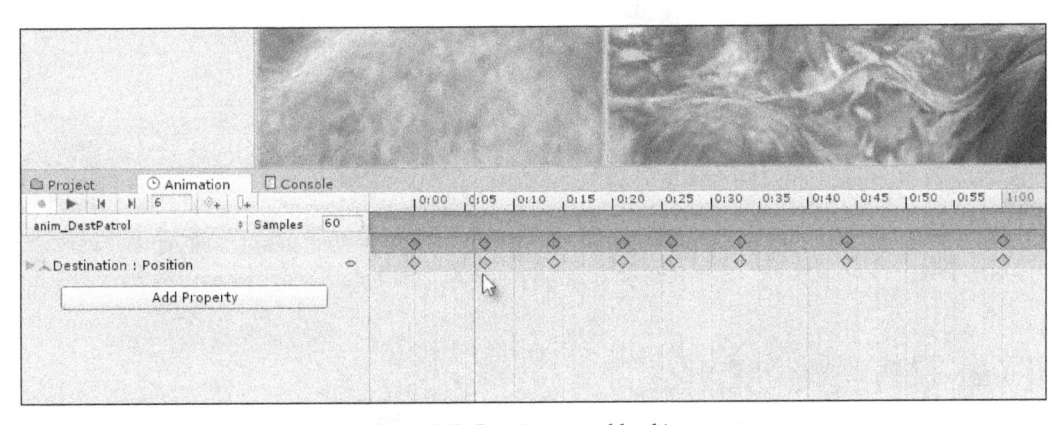

Figure 8.7: Creating movable objects

To achieve movable objects, create one or more destination object in the scene and assign them a Dest tag. Remember that the start function for AIEnemy searches the scene for all objects tagged as Dest and it uses these as destination points.

See *Figure 8.8*:

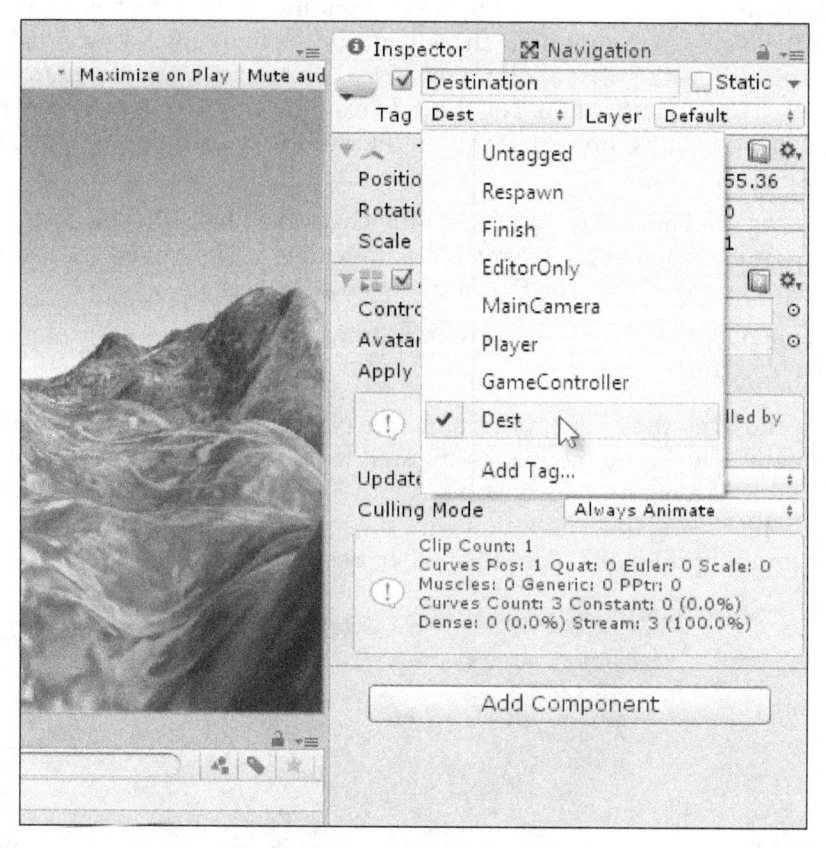

Figure 8.8: Tagging destination objects

The Chase state

The `Chase` state is the second of the three in the enemy FSM. This state connects to both the Patrol and `Attack` states directly. It can be reached in one of two ways. If a patrolling NPC establishes a direct line of sight to the player, then the NPC changes from patrolling to chasing. Conversely, if an attacking NPC falls outside the reach of the player (perhaps because he is running away), the NPC resorts to chasing again. From the chasing state itself, it's possible to move either to the Patrol or Attack state, with the inverse conditions as those, which lead to chase.

That is, if the NPC loses sight of the player, it returns to patrolling and, if the NPC reaches within attacking distance of the player, it switches to attacking. Consider the following code sample, which amends the AIEnemy class to support the chase behavior:

```
public IEnumerator AIChase()
{
  //Loop while chasing
  while(currentstate == ENEMY_STATE.CHASE)
  {
    //Set loose search
    ThisLineSight.Sensity = LineSight.SightSensitivity.LOOSE;

    //Chase to last known position
    ThisAgent.Resume();
    ThisAgent.SetDestination(ThisLineSight.LastKnowSighting);

    //Wait until path is computed
    while(ThisAgent.pathPending)
      yield return null;

    //Have we reached destination?
    if(ThisAgent.remainingDistance <= ThisAgent.stoppingDistance)
    {
      //Stop agent
      ThisAgent.Stop();

      //Reached destination but cannot see player
      if(!ThisLineSight.CanSeeTarget)
        CurrentState = ENEMY_STATE.PATROL;
      else //Reached destination and can see player. Reached attacking distance
        CurrentState = ENEMY_STATE.ATTACK;

      yield break;
    }

    //Wait until next frame
    yield return null;
  }
}
```

Code Sample 8.4

The following points summarize the code sample:

- The AIChase coroutine is started when the Chase state is entered and, like the Patrol state, it repeats on a frame-safe infinite loop for as long as the state is active.
- The remainingDistance member variable of the NavMeshAgent is used to determine whether the NPC has reached within attacking distance of the player.
- The CanSeeTarget Boolean variable of the LineSight class indicates whether the player is visible and is influential in choosing whether the NPC should return to patrolling.

Excellent work! Now give the code a test run in the editor and you have an enemy character than can patrol and chase. Splendid!

The Attack state

The third and final state for the NPC is the Attack state, during which the NPC is continually attacking the player. This state can only be reached from the Chase state. During a chase, the NPC must determine whether they have reached within attacking distance. If so, the NPC must change from chasing to attacking. If, during an attack, the player leaves the attacking distance, then the NPC must change from attacking to chasing. Consider the following code sample, which includes the complete EnemyAI class, with all coded and completed states:

```
using UnityEngine;
using System.Collections;
//-----------------------------------------
public class AI_Enemy : MonoBehaviour
{
    //-----------------------------------------
    public enum ENEMY_STATE {PATROL, CHASE, ATTACK};
    //-----------------------------------------
    public ENEMY_STATE CurrentState
    {
        get{return currentstate;}

        set
        {
```

```
      //Update current state
      currentstate = value;

      //Stop all running coroutines
      StopAllCoroutines();

      switch(currentstate)
      {
        case ENEMY_STATE.PATROL:
          StartCoroutine(AIPatrol());
        break;

        case ENEMY_STATE.CHASE:
          StartCoroutine(AIChase());
        break;

        case ENEMY_STATE.ATTACK:
          StartCoroutine(AIAttack());
        break;
      }
    }
  }
}
//-------------------------------------------
[SerializeField]
private ENEMY_STATE currentstate = ENEMY_STATE.PATROL;

//Reference to line of sight component
private LineSight ThisLineSight = null;

//Reference to nav mesh agent
private NavMeshAgent ThisAgent = null;

//Reference to player health
private Health PlayerHealth = null;

//Reference to player transform
private Transform PlayerTransform = null;

//Reference to patrol destination
private Transform PatrolDestination = null;
```

Continuing with Intelligent Enemies

```csharp
    //Damage amount per second
    public float MaxDamage = 10f;
    //-----------------------------------------
    void Awake()
    {
      ThisLineSight = GetComponent<LineSight>();
      ThisAgent = GetComponent<NavMeshAgent>();
      PlayerHealth = GameObject.FindGameObjectWithTag("Player").
GetComponent<Health>();
      PlayerTransform = PlayerHealth.GetComponent<Transform>();
    }
    //-----------------------------------------
    void Start()
    {
      //Get random destination
      GameObject[] Destinations = GameObject.
FindGameObjectsWithTag("Dest");
      PatrolDestination = Destinations[Random.Range(0, Destinations.
Length)].GetComponent<Transform>();

      //Configure starting state
      CurrentState = ENEMY_STATE.PATROL;
    }
    //-----------------------------------------
    public IEnumerator AIPatrol()
    {
      //Loop while patrolling
      while(currentState == ENEMY_STATE.PATROL)
      {
        //Set strict search
        ThisLineSight.Sensitity = LineSight.SightSensitivity.STRICT;

        //Chase to patrol position
        ThisAgent.Resume();
        ThisAgent.SetDestination(PatrolDestination.position);

        //Wait until path is computed
        while(ThisAgent.pathPending)
          yield return null;

        //If we can see the target then start chasing
        if(ThisLineSight.CanSeeTarget)
        {
          ThisAgent.Stop();
```

```csharp
      CurrentState = ENEMY_STATE.CHASE;
      yield break;
    }

    //Wait until next frame
    yield return null;
  }
}
//-----------------------------------------
public IEnumerator AIChase()
{
  //Loop while chasing
  while(currentstate == ENEMY_STATE.CHASE)
  {
    //Set loose search
    ThisLineSight.Sensitity = LineSight.SightSensitivity.LOOSE;

    //Chase to last known position
    ThisAgent.Resume();
    ThisAgent.SetDestination(ThisLineSight.LastKnowSighting);

    //Wait until path is computed
    while(ThisAgent.pathPending)
      yield return null;

    //Have we reached destination?
    if(ThisAgent.remainingDistance <= ThisAgent.stoppingDistance)
    {
      //Stop agent
      ThisAgent.Stop();

      //Reached destination but cannot see player
      if(!ThisLineSight.CanSeeTarget)
        CurrentState = ENEMY_STATE.PATROL;
      else //Reached destination and can see player. Reached attacking distance
        CurrentState = ENEMY_STATE.ATTACK;

      yield break;
    }

    //Wait until next frame
    yield return null;
  }
```

```csharp
        }
        //------------------------------------------
        public IEnumerator AIAttack()
        {
            //Loop while chasing and attacking
            while(currentstate == ENEMY_STATE.ATTACK)
            {
                //Chase to player position
                ThisAgent.Resume();
                ThisAgent.SetDestination(PlayerTransform.position);

                //Wait until path is computed
                while(ThisAgent.pathPending)
                    yield return null;

                //Has player run away?
                if(ThisAgent.remainingDistance > ThisAgent.stoppingDistance)
                {
                    //Change back to chase
                    CurrentState = ENEMY_STATE.CHASE;
                    yield break;
                }
                else
                {
                    //Attack
                    PlayerHealth.HealthPoints -= MaxDamage * Time.deltaTime;
                }

                //Wait until next frame
                yield return null;
            }

            yield break;
        }
        //------------------------------------------
    }
    //------------------------------------------
```

Code Sample 8.5

The following points summarize the code sample:

- The AIAttack coroutine runs on a frame-safe infinite loop for as long as the Attack state is active (the enemy will be attacking during this state).
- The MaxDamage variable specifies how much damage the enemy deals to the player per second.
- The AIAttack coroutine relies on the Health component to inflict damage. This is an additional custom component that encodes health. Both the player and enemy should have a health component to represent their health.

The Health script (Health.cs) is referenced by the AIEnemy class (the Attack State) to inflict damage on the player. For this reason, the player character needs a Health component attached. The code for this component is included in the following code sample:

```
using UnityEngine;
using System.Collections;

public class Health : MonoBehaviour
{
  public float HealthPoints
  {
    get{return healthPoints;}
    set
    {
      healthPoints = value;

      //If health is < 0 then die
      if(healthPoints <= 0)
        Destroy(gameObject);
    }
  }

  [SerializeField]
  private float healthPoints = 100f;
}
```

Continuing with Intelligent Enemies

The Health script is pretty simple. It maintains a numerical health value that, when reduced to 0 or below, will destroy the host game object. This should at least be attached to the player character, allowing the NPC to inflict damage on approach. It could, however, also be attached to the NPC objects, allowing the player to reciprocate an attack. See *Figure 8.9*:

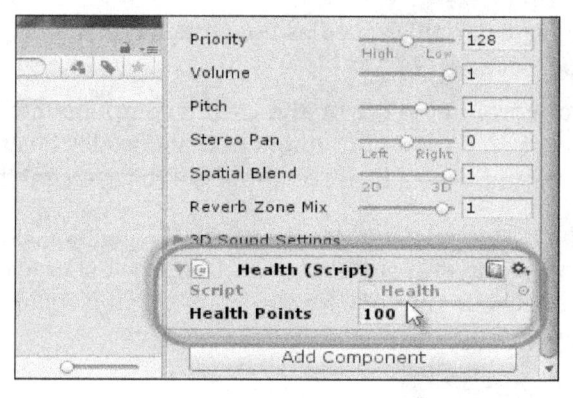

Figure 8.9: Configuring player health

Great, we're almost ready to test this project. First, make a prefab from the enemy object, if you've not already done so, by dragging and dropping the NPC game object from either the Scene view or **Hierarchy** panel to the Project panel. Then, add as many enemies as you want to the level. See *Figure 8.10*:

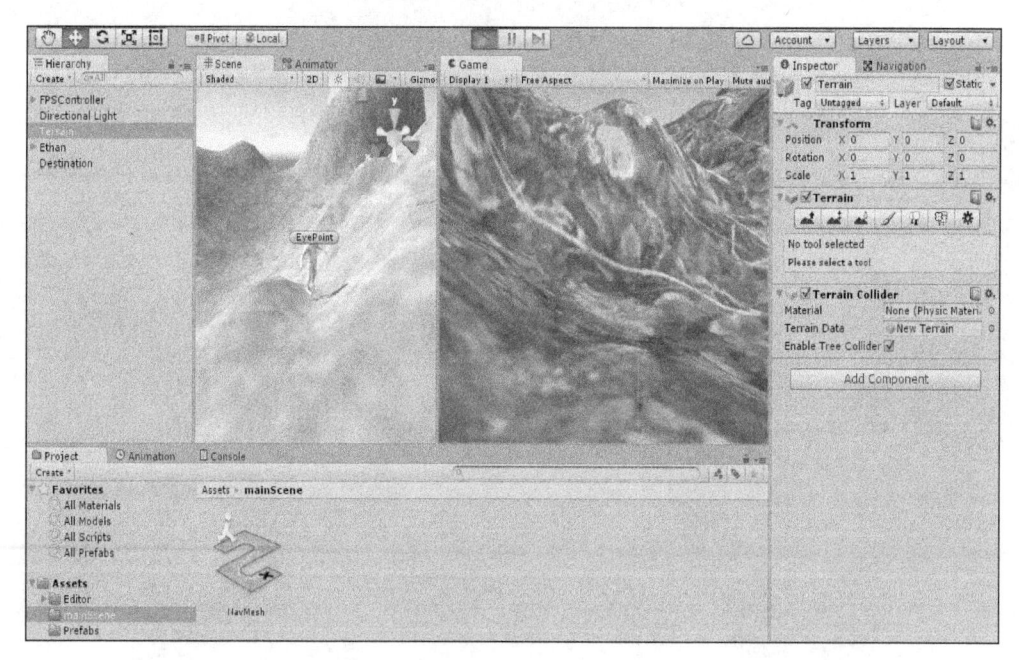

Figure 8.10: Creating an NPC prefab

Now, test the level by pressing the play icon on the toolbar and you should have a complete environment in which intelligent enemies can seek, chase, and attack the player with a significant degree of believability. In some cases, you may need to tweak or refine the enemy FOV to better match your surroundings and character type. Good work! See *Figure 8.11*:

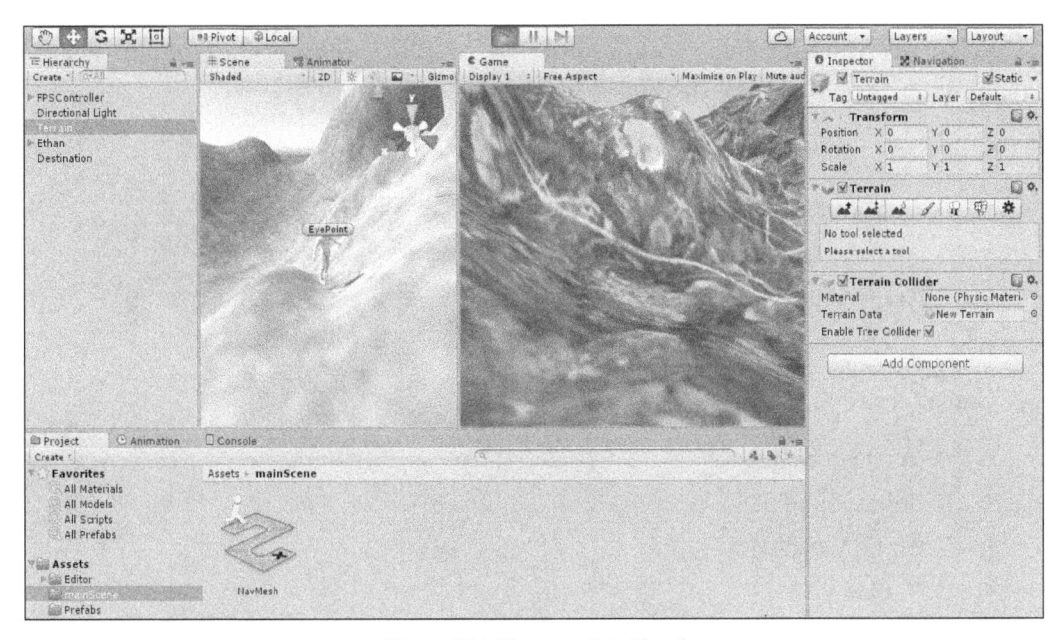

Figure 8.11: The completed level

Summary

Excellent! You've now reached the end of the AI project. In completing this project, you've assembled a complete terrain, an NPC prefab, and a series of scripts that work together strategically to create the appearance of intelligence, and this is *good enough* for AI. For games, AI refers to nothing more than *intelligent-looking* objects and the techniques that create them. Next, we'll enter the world of VR game development!

Test your knowledge

Q1. Many AI behaviours can be encoded using...

- A. Finite State Machine
- B. An if statement
- C. An Animator
- D. A Navigation Mesh

Q2. States can be created using a...

- A. Coroutine
- B. Switch statement
- C. Static Variable
- D. A loop

Q3. One alternative to a State Machine is...

- A. A Mesh Renderer
- B. Behaviour Tree
- C. Static Variable
- D. A Component

Q4. Yield statements are often used to...

- A. Pause and Terminate Coroutines
- B. Rewind Coroutines
- C. Restart Coroutines
- D. Delete Coroutines

Q5. Line of sight determines...

- A. Whether one object can be seen by the camera
- B. Whether one object can see nothing
- C. Whether one object can see another
- D. Whether one object can see anything

Further Reading

Go through following-mentioned links for more information:

- `https://www.packtpub.com/game-development/unity-ai-programming-essentials`
- `https://www.packtpub.com/game-development/advanced-game-mechanics-unity-5-video`

9
Entering Virtual Reality

In this chapter and the next, we'll create a first-person virtual reality (VR) game. The game will be targeted specifically at the powerful *Oculus Rift hardware*, and it's worth declaring this from the outset, as many other VR platforms exist as well. Although development methodologies do differ from device to device, the main principles of VR development within Unity are sufficiently similar that these chapters will still be helpful to any VR development on any of the hardware available today. Specifically, this chapter explores the following topics:

- How to setup VR
- How to use Light Probes
- How to configure input with Touch Controllers

> The starting project and assets can be found in the book's companion files in the Chapter09/Start folder. You can start here and follow along with this chapter if you don't have your own project already.

Project Overview – Getting Started

The project created in this chapter will be a first-person shooter game, which mixes together nearly all the development techniques seen so far, as well as new techniques specific to VR. In this game, the player will be a stationary character that can look around and shoot in any direction, but cannot move around. The player will be standing in a sci-fi interior, and enemy bots will spawn into the level at random intervals. The bots will initially wander around searching for the player and, upon finding them, will run towards them, eventually attacking them. The player will be armed with plasma cannons on each hand, and will have the ability to attack oncoming enemies to avoid being injured. The basic objective is to see how long you can survive!

Entering Virtual Reality

To create this project, we'll begin by creating the core functionality for a standard first-person mode, and then migrate that to VR. To get started, create a new project and import all assets from the Assets_To_Import folder associated with this chapter. This includes two meshes and one texture. One mesh represents the complete sci-fi environment, and the other, a mesh for the enemy bot. To be organized, I recommend storing these meshes in a project folder named Meshes:

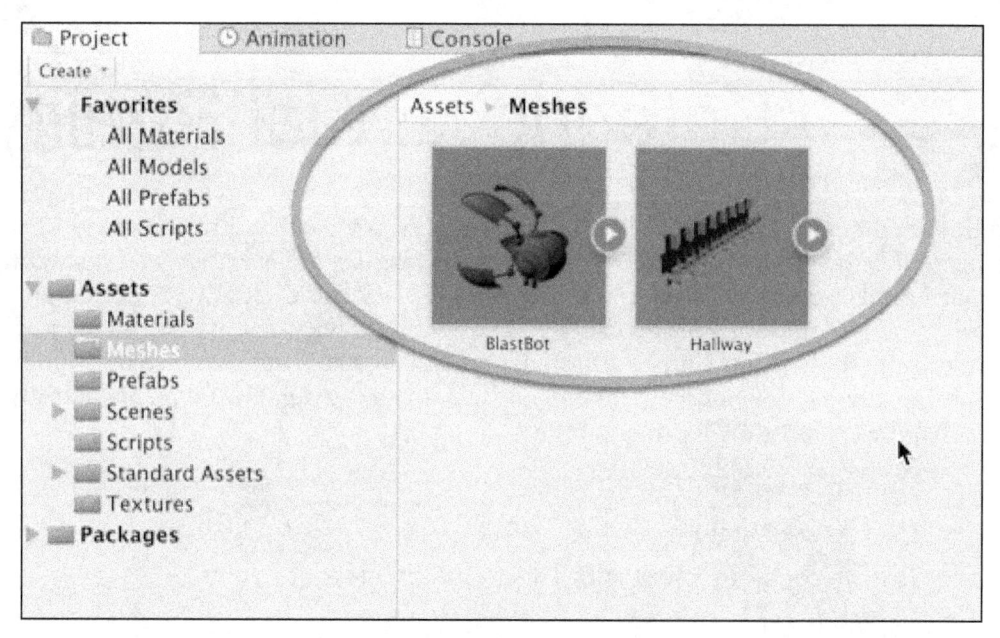

Figure 9.1: Importing game assets

When working with different mesh assets, especially when reusing assets made by others, you'll often find they're made at different sizes and scales. In this case, I've used a Scale Factor of 2 for the environment, and a factor of 0.4 for the enemy bot.

You can change the **Scale Factor** by selecting the mesh asset from the **Project Panel** and assigning a new **Scale Factor** value from the **Model** tab in the **Object Inspector**:

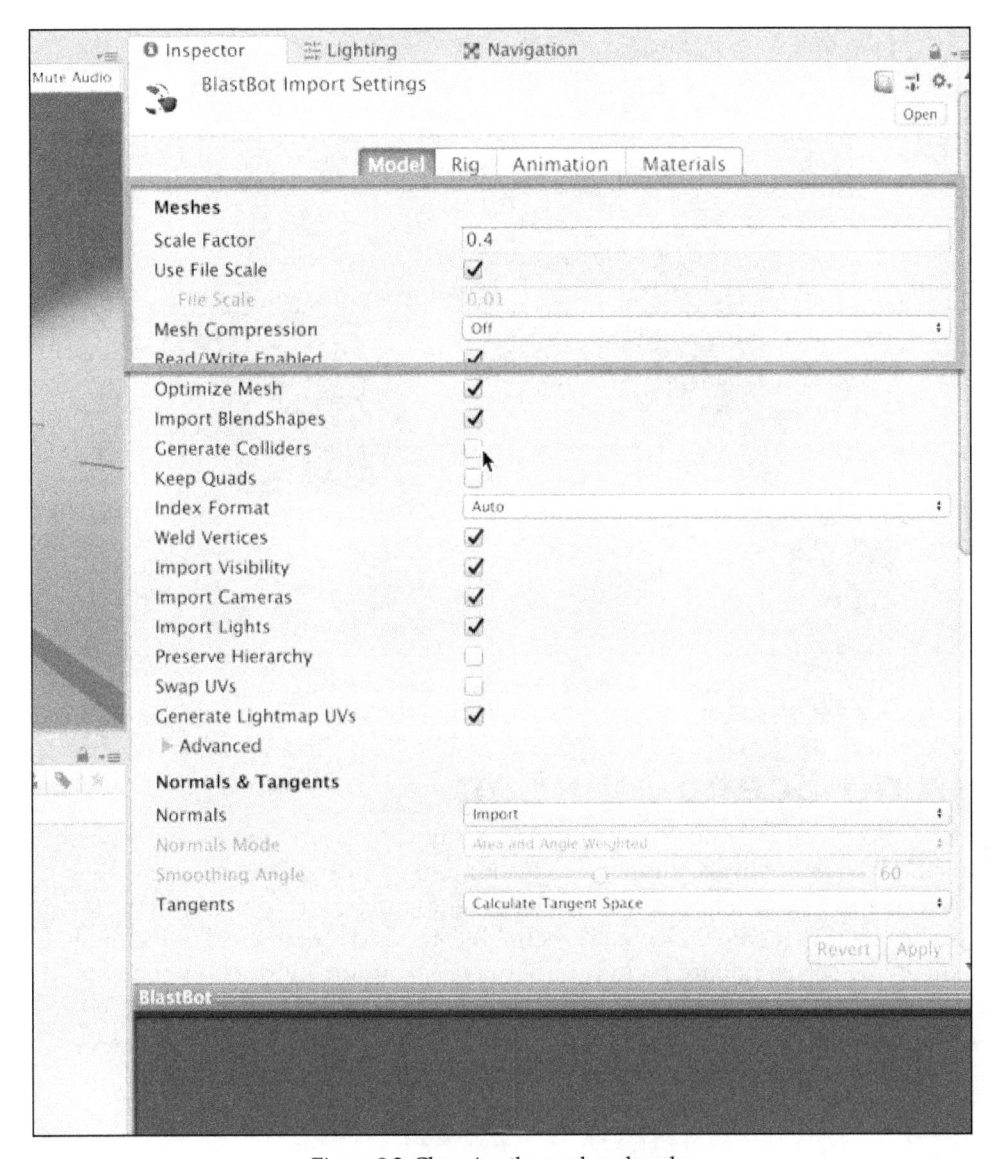

Figure 9.2: Changing the mesh scale value

Entering Virtual Reality

Next, add the hallway environment mesh into a new scene to create the main environment area. To do this, just drag and drop the hallway mesh from the Project Panel into the scene. Afterwards, position the mesh to the world origin and mark it as static in the object inspector. See *Figure 9.3*:

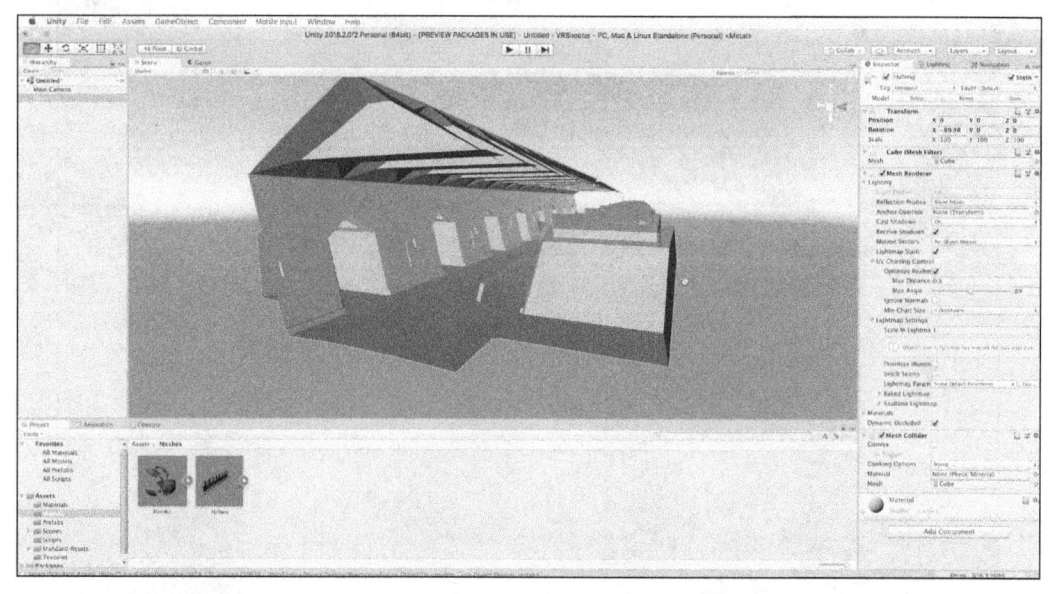

Figure 9.3: Adding the Environment Mesh to the scene

Setting Scene Lighting

Lighting and mood is critically important for any scene, and here we'll create an atmospheric, dystopian sci-fi interior. This kind of environment typically relies on high levels of contrast between lighting; contrasting dark colors with vibrant non-natural lighting colors, such as green, blue and red. Let's start by disabling all lighting in the scene. Ensure all lights are moved from the hierarchy panel, and then access the lighting window by selecting **Window | Rendering | Lighting Settings** from the application menu. See *Figure 9.4*:

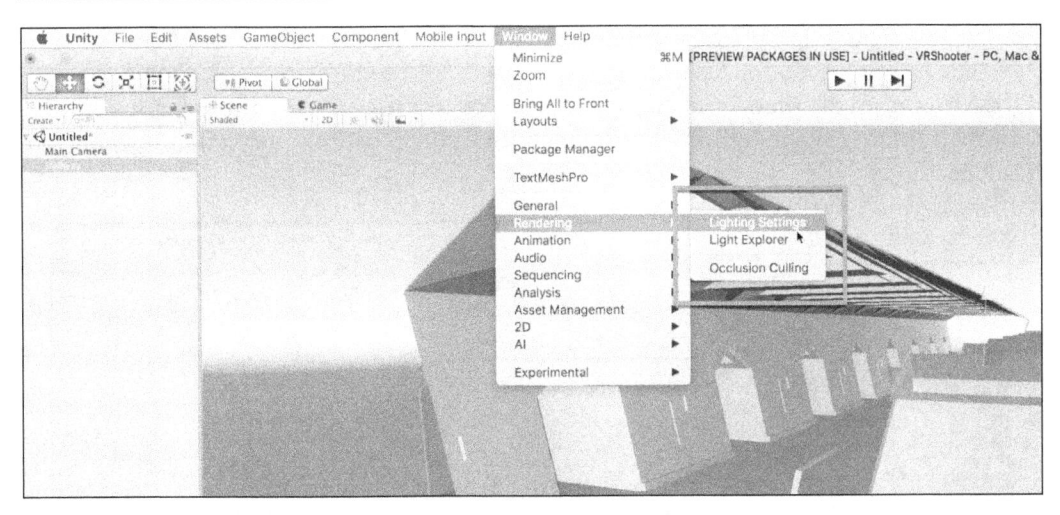

Figure 9.4: Accessing the lighting settings

From the **Lighting** window, remove the day-time skybox from the **Skybox Material** field by choosing **None** via the texture swatch. From the **Environment Lighting** group, set the **Ambient Source** to **Color**, and the **Ambient Color** to **black**. This removes all ambient lighting from the scene, that is, lighting that pervades everywhere and pre-illuminates objects before scene lighting takes effect. See *Figure 9.5*:

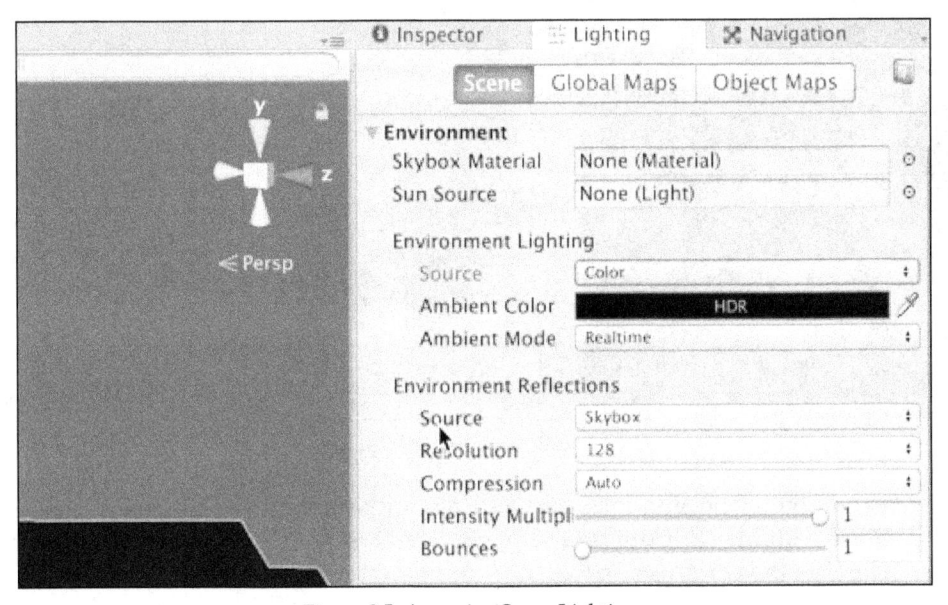

Figure 9.5: Accessing Scene Lighting...

Entering Virtual Reality

Ensure **Realtime Global Illumination** is activated to get the most from Unity's dynamic lighting system. Assuming geometry is held to be static, you can move lights around in the scene and change their color or intensity at runtime, allowing rapidly updating scene lighting complete with indirect illumination, that is, reflected light. See *Figure 9.6*:

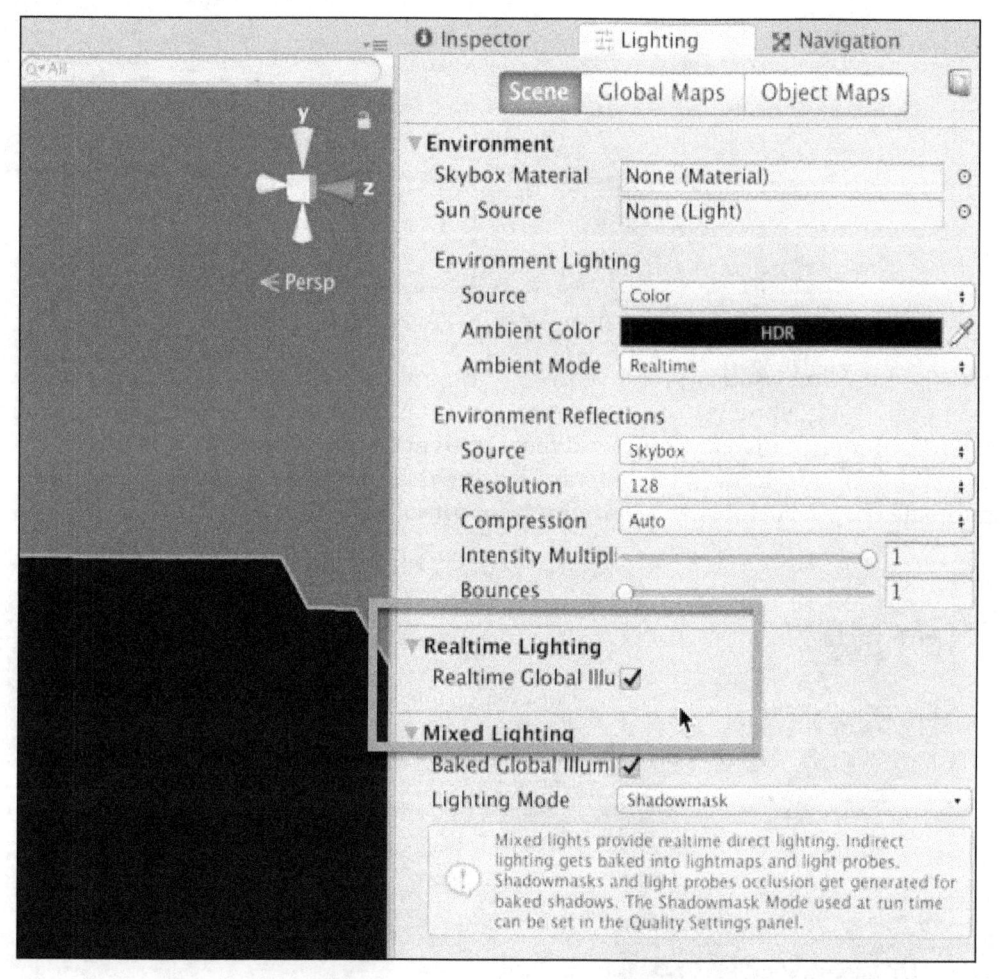

Figure 9.6: Enabling Realtime Lighting

Now return to the scene, and let's start adding our base lighting. Choose **GameObject | Light | Spotlight**, and position it close to the ceiling toward the front of the level. Size the cone, intensity, color, and length from the Object Inspector to match the environment, as shown in *Figure 9.7*:

Chapter 9

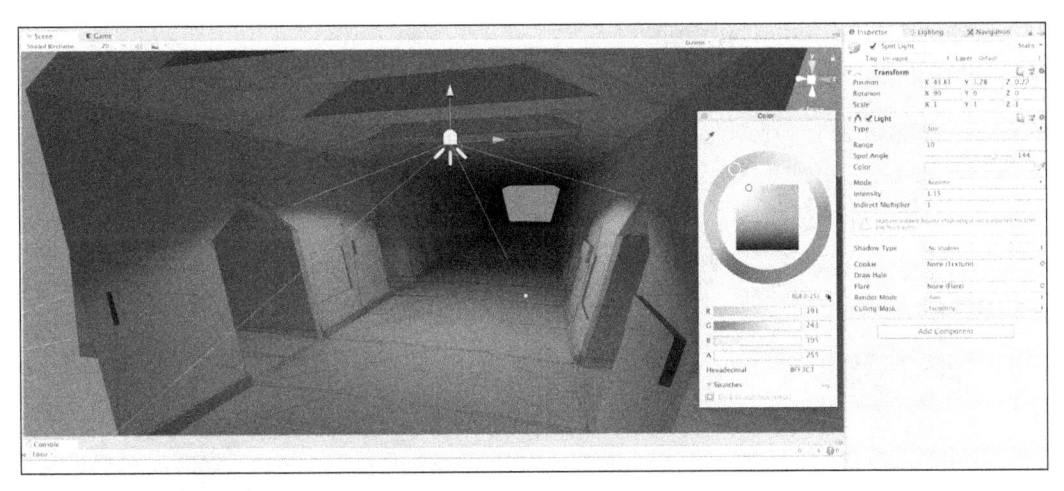

Figure 9.7: Setting the scene's base lighting

Duplicate the lighting along the corridor, and then duplicate the corridor mesh itself for a further stretch of the level. This allows a significant area of the corridor to disappear into the distance, into darkness outside of the reach of lighting. See *Figure 9.8*:

Figure 9.8: Duplicating scene lights

Entering Virtual Reality

Let's add some emissive lighting from the wall panels. **Emissive lighting** lets you use a material, and its maps, as a light source. This can be emitted from a mesh. To do this, first create a new material. From the Project Panel, right-click and choose **Create | Material** to create a new material asset. Simple. See *Figure 9.09*:

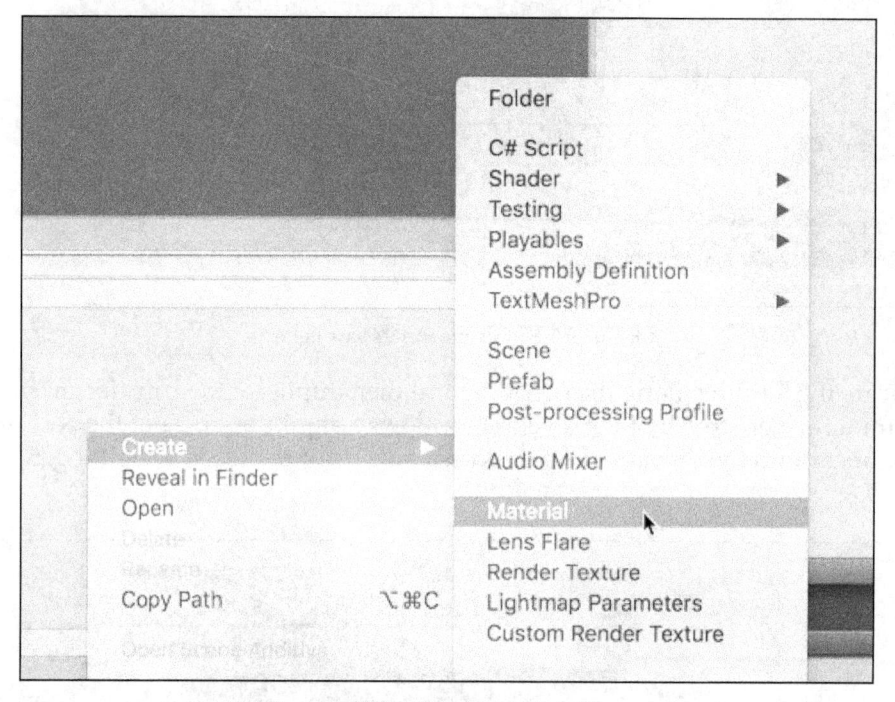

Figure 9.09: Creating a new Material…

Next, select the material in the **Object Inspector**, and then enable the **Emission** check box. Click the **Emission** color swatch and, from the color selector, specify both a color and intensity for the emission.

This will be the color and intensity of the emissive light when assigned as a material to a mesh. See *Figure 9.10*:

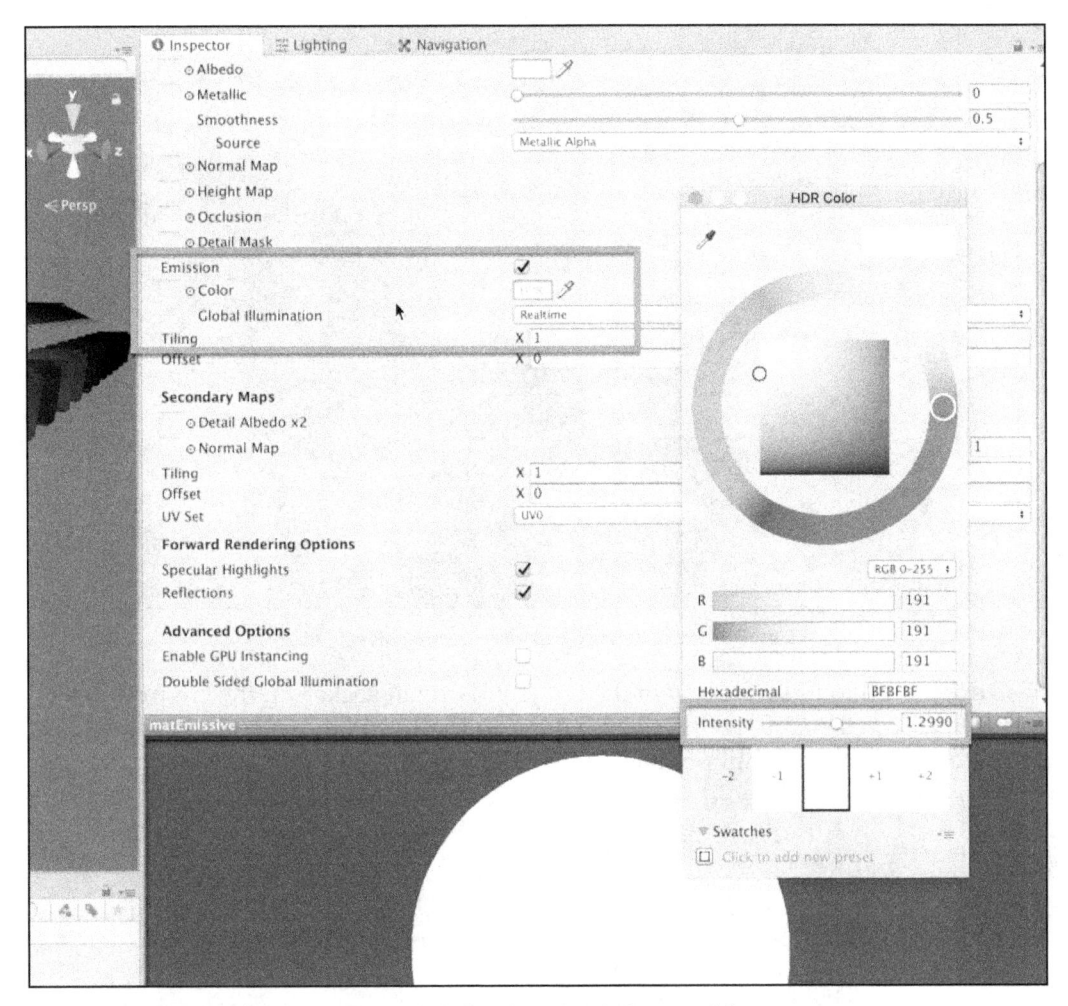

Figure 9.10: Creating an emissive material

Entering Virtual Reality

Great! You've just created an emissive material. Now let's assign it to a mesh to illuminate the scene. Create a Quad object by selecting **GameObject | 3D Object | Quad** from the application menu. See *Figure 9.11*:

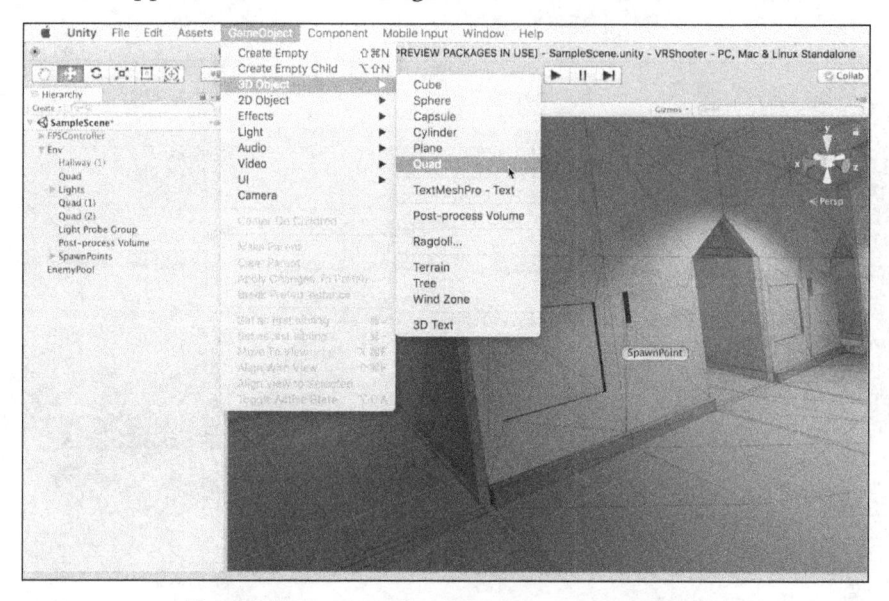

Figure 9.11: Creating a Quad object for emissive lighting

Resize the quad to fit inside any of the rectangular wall sockets in the environment, and then assign the emissive material onto it. Mark the quad as static from the Object Inspector, and let the lighting rebuild to see the results. See *Figure 9.12*:

Figure 9.12: Adding Emissive Quads

Excellent. Duplicate the quad several times, adding a duplicate into each vacant wall socket in the environment. Then add a red-colored point light into each recessed alcove. The presence of an off-screen red light adds ambiance and an other-worldly feel:

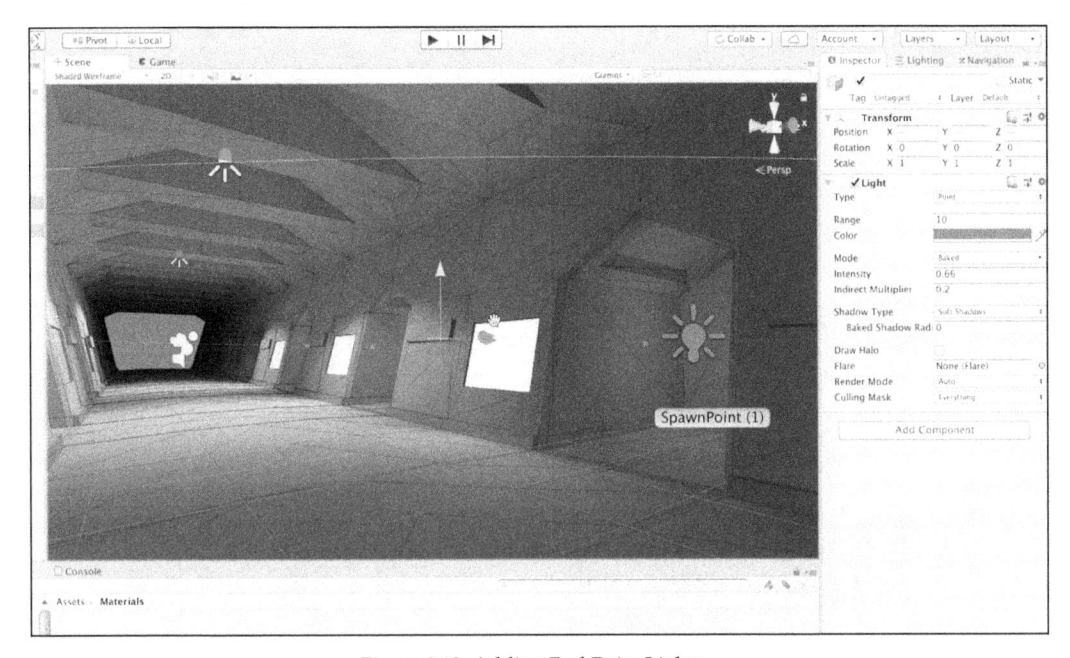

Figure 9.13: Adding Red Point Lights…

Let's complete the lighting by adding Light Probes. **Light Probes** are useful for adding indirect illumination to real-time (dynamic) objects, such as the player character and enemies. Light Probes refer to a connected network of empty-style objects, each object (a Node) records the averaged color and intensity of neighboring lights in the scene within a specified radius. These values are stored in each node and are blended onto moving objects.

Entering Virtual Reality

To start with Light Probes, create a new Light Probe Group by choosing **GameObject | Light | Light Probe Group** from the application menu:

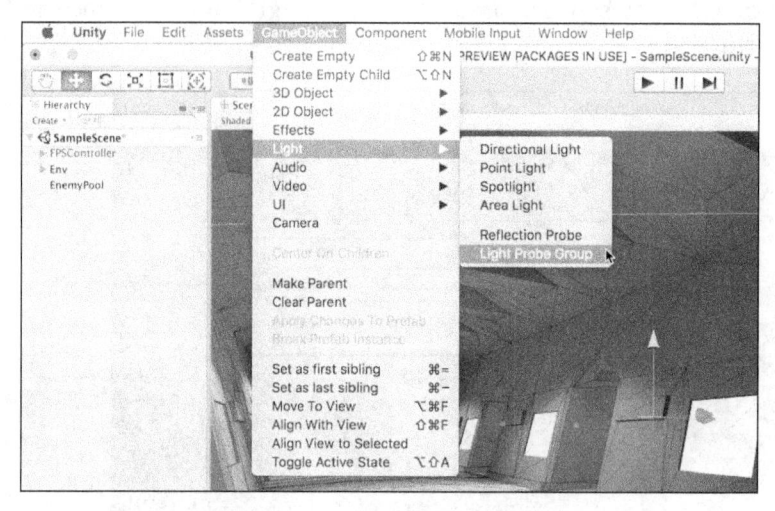

Figure 9.14: Creating a Light Probe Group

Move the Light Probe Group to the center of the scene. You will see a network of yellow spheres neatly arranged in a grid pattern. Each sphere represents a node (Probe) in the group, and it records the color and intensity of light in surrounding areas:

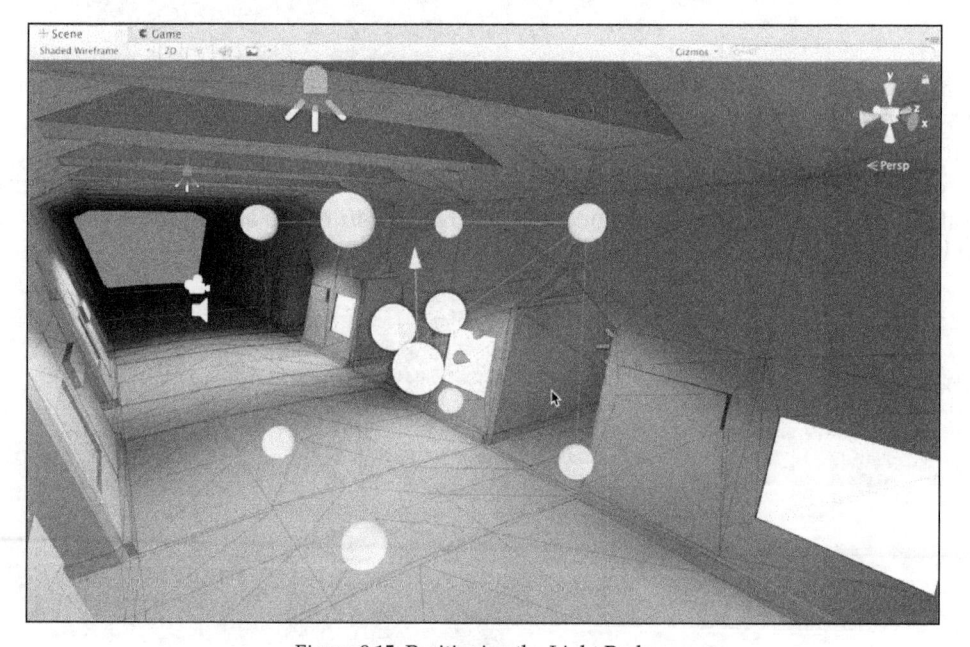

Figure 9.15: Positioning the Light Probes

The main idea is to add or duplicate more probes within the network, and to position them strategically around the level in areas where the light changes significantly, in either color or intensity, or both. The probe network should capture the distribution of light in the scene. To get started with this, select the **Light Probe**, and from the **Light Probe** component in the Object Inspector, click the **Edit Light Probes** button. When activated, you can select, duplicate, and move around individual probes within the group:

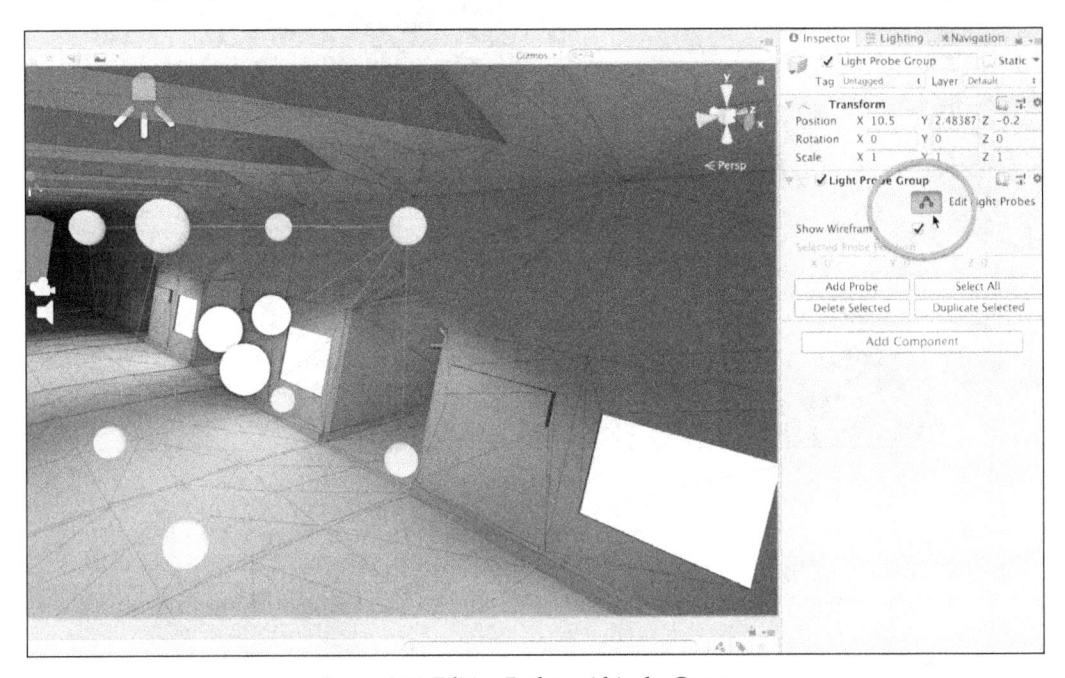

Figure 9.16: Editing Probes within the Group...

Entering Virtual Reality

Select a probe, click the **Duplicate Selected** button, and then move the duplicate to a new location in the scene, capturing the surrounding light. Next, duplicate another and move that further along still. Try keeping the probes regularly spaced and tidy. See *Figure 9.17*:

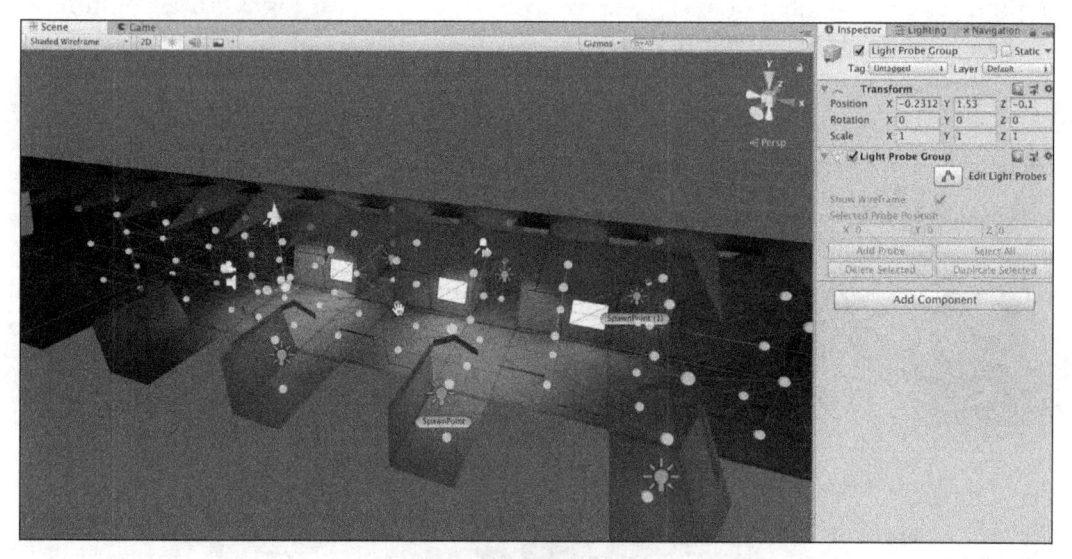

Figure 9.17: Spacing Light Probes...

Excellent, we've now completed the lighting for the environment: we've added both spot and point lights, emissive lights, and Light Probes. These components are working to ensure objects are illuminated correctly. Things are looking good! See *Figure 9.18*:

Figure 9.18: Complete lighting

Post-Processing Stack 2

Unity 2018 and above ships with a newer version of the post-processing stack for adding volume-based post-process effects to your project. Let's use these post-processing camera effects to enhance the appeal of the scene. As mentioned in earlier chapters, post-process effects are filters and adjustments applied to the pixels of the scene camera to stylize or improve the aesthetics of the rendered frame.

Entering Virtual Reality

To add the newest version of the Post-Processing Stack, choose **Window | Package Manager** from the application menu. See *Figure 9.19*:

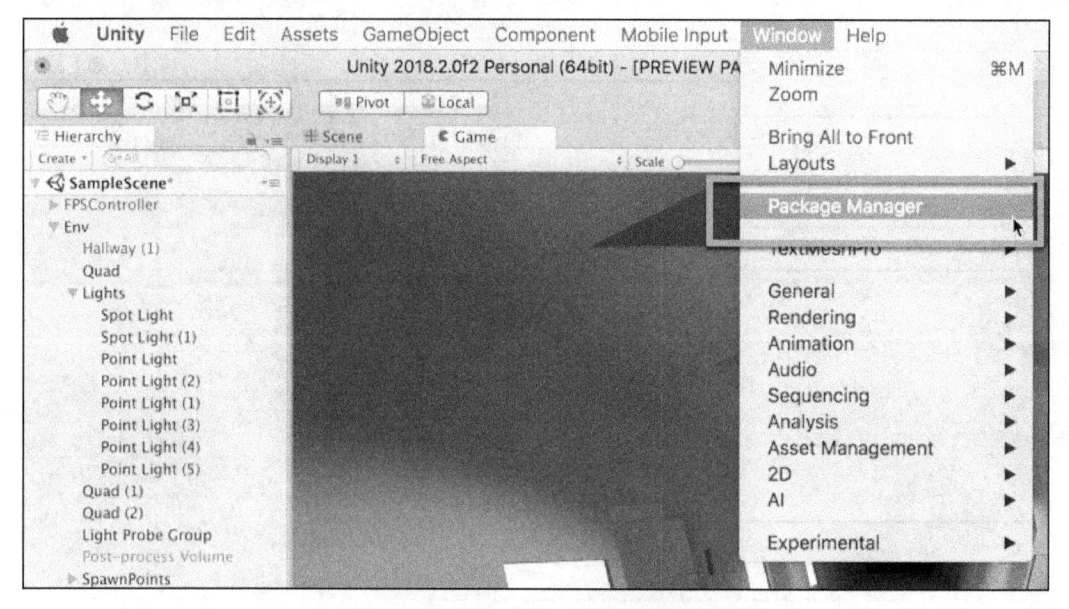

Figure 9.19: Displaying the Package Manager...

From the Packages List, click the **All** button to filter the list and view all available or installed packages. Select the **Post-Processing** package by clicking on it from the list. Once selected, click the **install** button to add the package to your project. If the project is already added, you may have the option of updating to the latest version by clicking the **Update** button. See *Figure 9.20*:

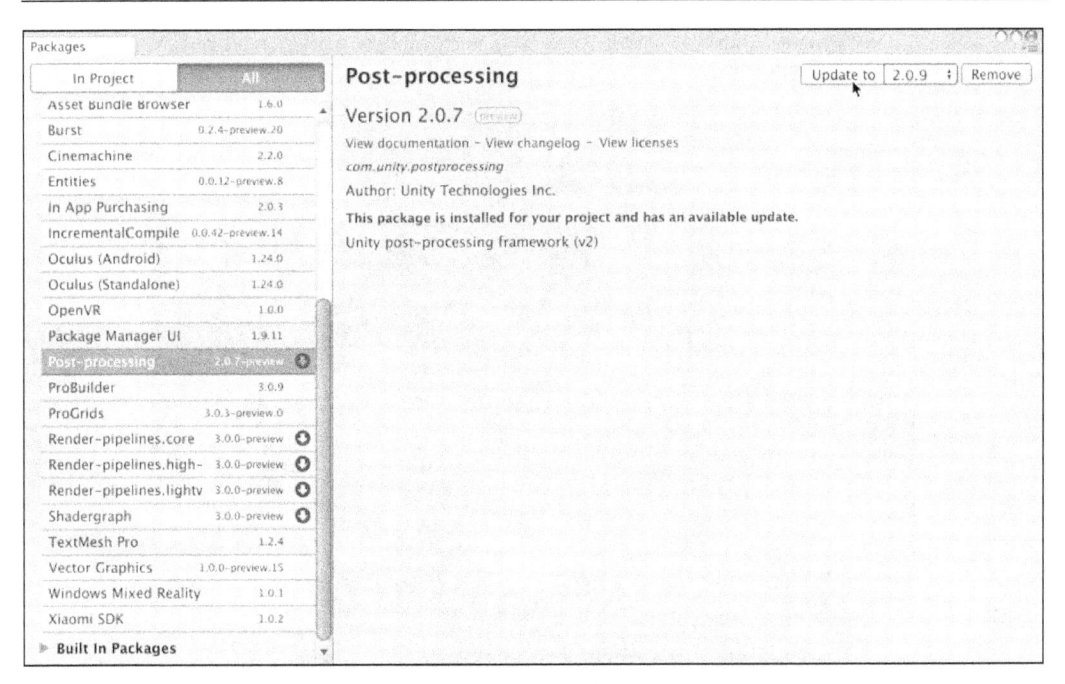

Figure 9.20: Installing the Post-Processing Package

After installation, the complete post-processing functionality has been added to your project. This workflow depends on two main concepts or steps. First, we need to mark out volumes in the level which, when entered by the camera, effects will be applied to it. Second, we must specify which cameras are to be affected by the volumes. Let's start by creating a single post-processing volume in the level. To do this, choose **GameObject | 3D Object | Post-Process Volume** from the application menu.

Entering Virtual Reality

This adds a new game object, complete with a trigger box and post-processing settings. See *Figure 9.21*:

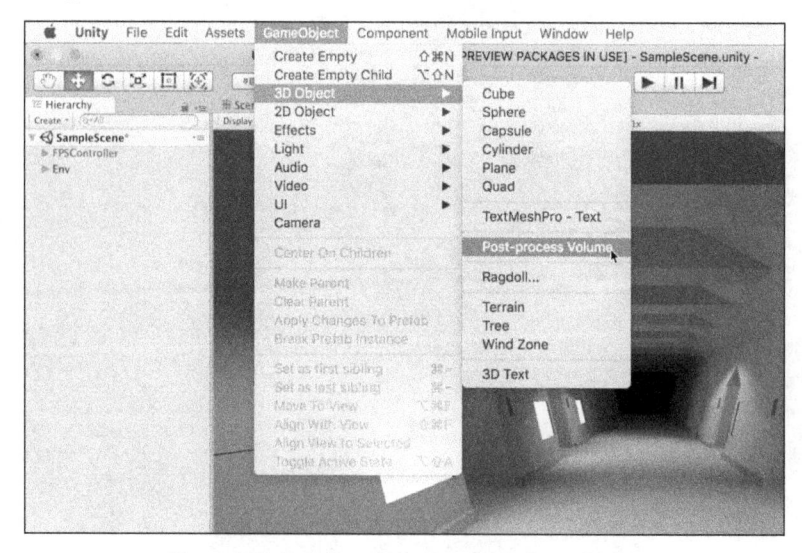

Figure 9.21: Creating a Post-Process Volume Object

After creating a post-process object, you'll need to position and resize it. The idea is to enclose the area inside which camera effects should occur. For our game, we'll enclose the complete level, as we'll make only one set of effects that should always apply. Use the Box Collider component fields for **Size** to resize the bounding volume. You can also use the **IsGlobal** checkbox on the Post-Process Volume component. See *Figure 9.22*:

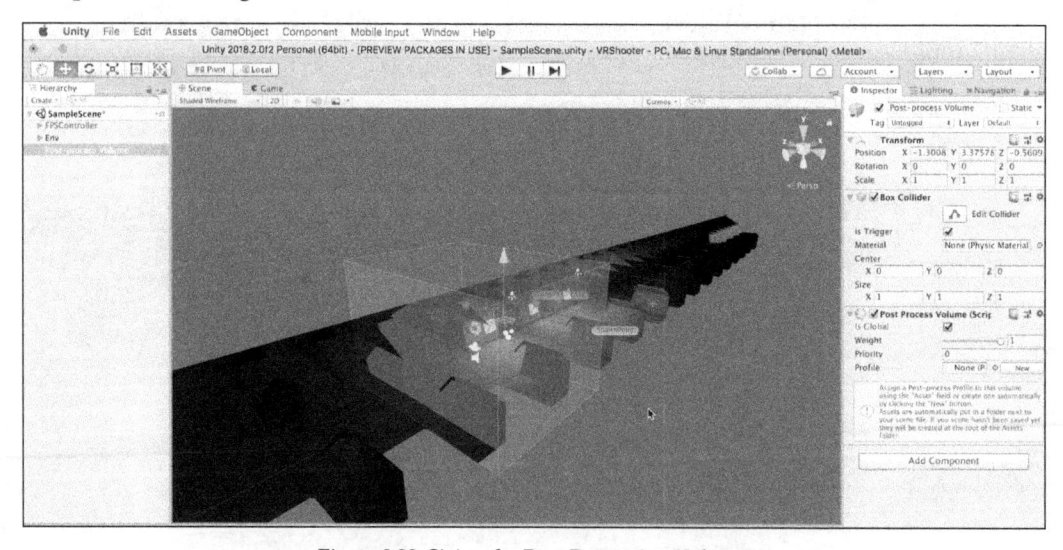

Figure 9.22: Sizing the Post-Processing Volume

Now let's configure our camera to respond to post-process volumes. To do this, I'll add a first-person controller to the scene, from the **Characters** package, and then select the camera of the controller. You can import the FPS controller by importing the characters package via **Assets | Import Packages | Character**. To do configure our camera, expand the first-person controller object in the scene hierarchy, and select the camera object. Then add a Post-Process Layer component by selecting **Component | Rendering | Post Process Layer** from the application menu:

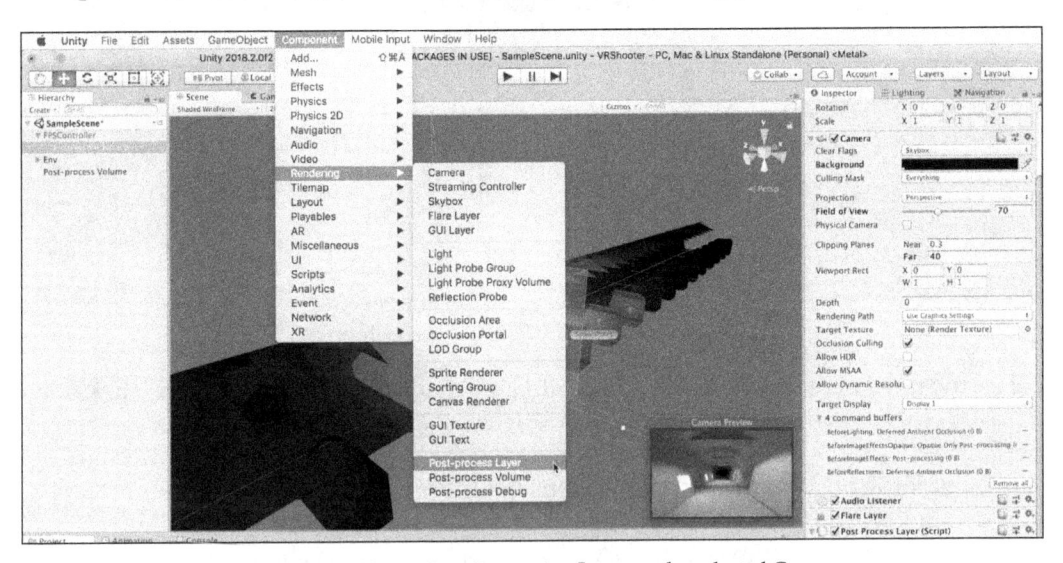

Figure 9.23: Adding a Post-Processing Layer to the selected Camera

We've added a Post-Process Volume **to the scene** and a Post-Process Layer **to the camera**, and now we need to associate some post-process effects with the volume, which will be rendered to the camera when it enters the volume. To do this, we need to associate a **Post-Processing Profile** with the volume.

Entering Virtual Reality

Create a profile by right-clicking inside the Project Panel and choosing **Create | Post-Processing Profile** from the context menu. See *Figure 9.24*:

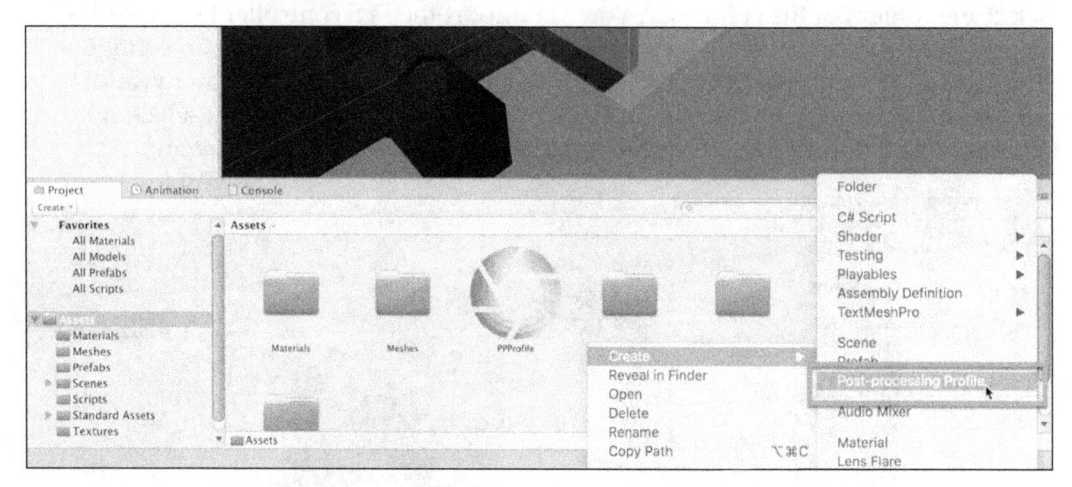

Figure 9.24: Creating a Post-Processing Profile

Select the newly created Post-Process Profile asset, and from the Inspector, click the **Add Effect** button. You can add as many effects as desired, but each effect carries a performance implication. Consequently, you should add as few effects as needed, while retaining your central artistic vision. To this profile I've added two effects: namely, Bloom and Ambient Occlusion. Bloom blurs and intensifies highlights, adding a dreamy or whimsical feel. Ambient Occlusion adds shadows to areas where adjacent geometry meets, such as the wall meeting the floor and the walls meeting the ceiling. See *Figure 9.25*:

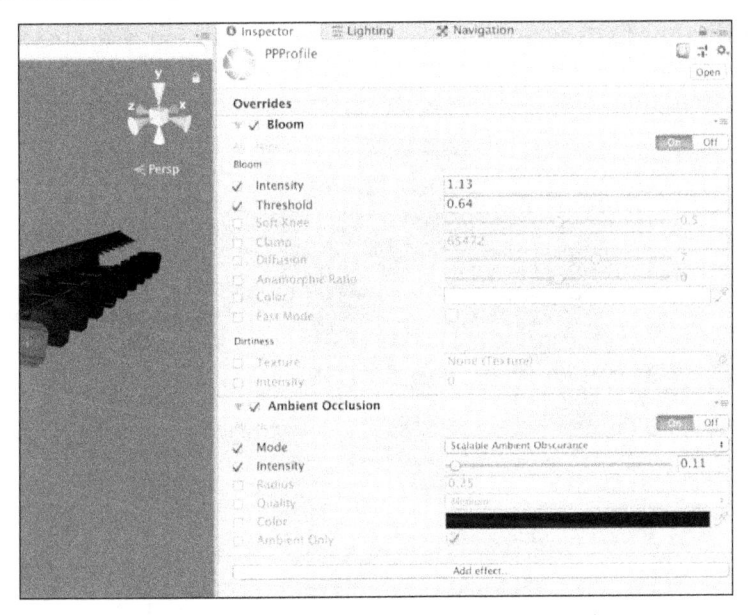

Figure 9.25: Adding Post-Processing Effects

Drag and drop the Post-Processing profile into the Post-Processing Volume component, in the **Profile Field**. This associates the profile with the volume. See *Figure 9.26*:

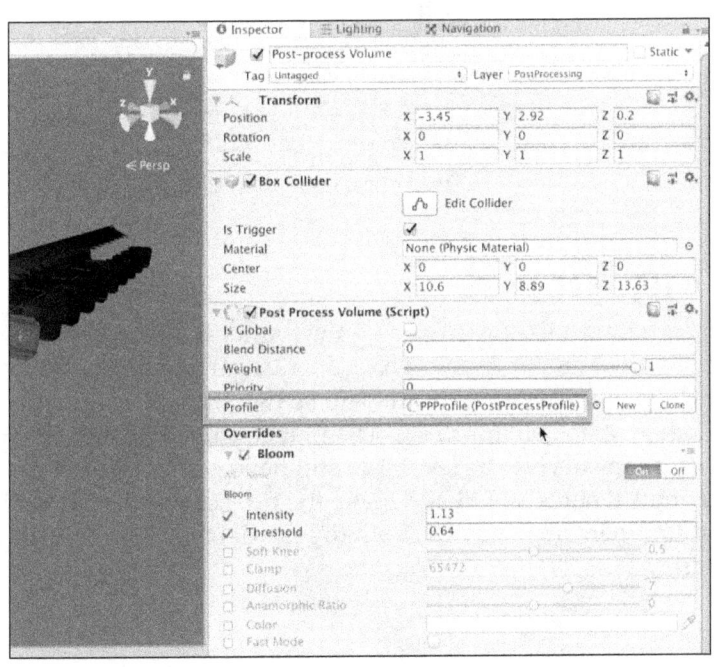

Figure 9.26: Associating a Profile to a Volume

Finally, ensuring the first-person camera is inside the volume, you should immediately see the result in the Game tab. Excellent work. Our scene is looking great, with both lighting and post-processing combined. See *Figure 9.27*:

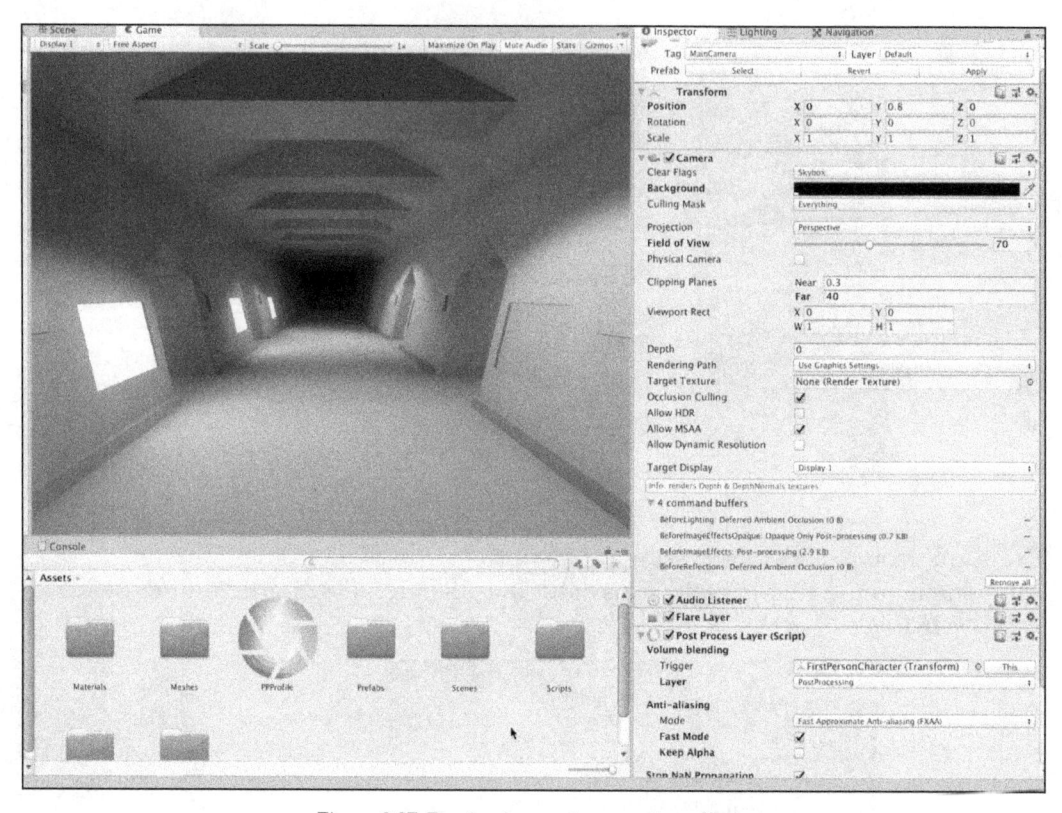

Figure 9.27: Previewing post-processing effects

Preparing for VR

In this chapter so far, we've been preparing the foundations for a scene, ready to add core functionality and gameplay. To recap, our game will be a first-person VR shooter, in which waves of enemy droids will spawn into the level, move towards the player, and then attack on approach. The player must dispatch all enemies and see how long they can survive the level. We still have gameplay to implement, and whenever creating VR content, I like to make the project compatible with both VR and a standard first-person controller, both to help debugging and to aid testing without a headset.

But, before moving forwards with development, let's prepare for VR development generally. This section uses the Oculus Rift device, although the development workflow is similar for Oculus Go too. To get started, you'll need to connect and install your Oculus Rift device. Instructions for doing this can be found online at https://support.oculus.com/guides/rift/latest/concepts/rgsg-2-hw-hardware-setup/:

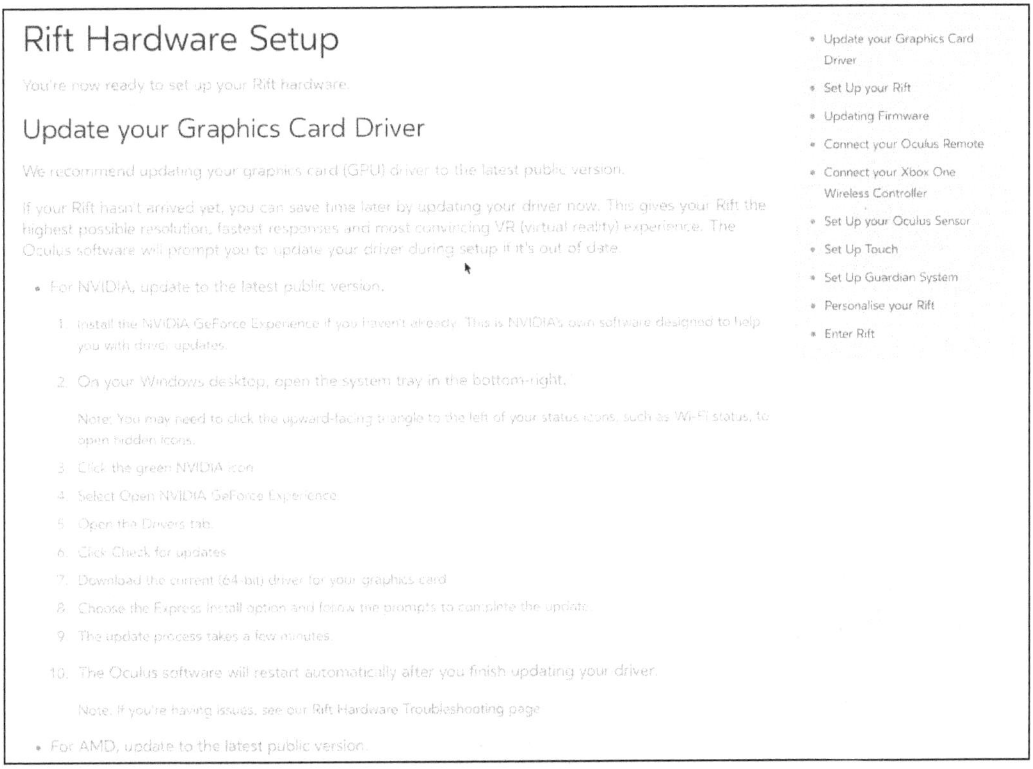

Figure 9.28: Connecting the Oculus Rift

With the Oculus hardware connected, open Unity and navigate to the **Player Settings** window by choosing **Edit | Project Settings Player** from the application menu. From here, expand the XR (Extended Reality) group and enable the checkbox, which says **Virtual Reality Supported**.

Entering Virtual Reality

This configures the project to utilize any connected VR hardware. See *Figure 9.29*:

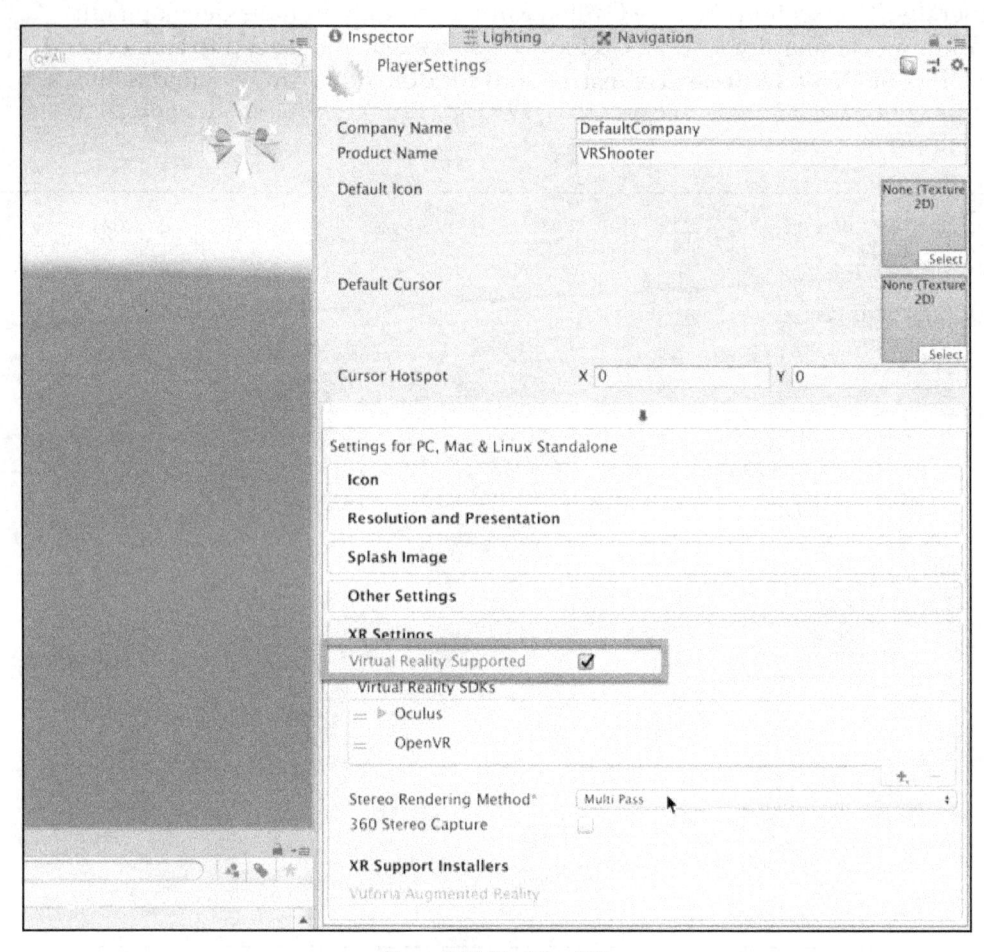

Figure 9.29: Enabling VR

Excellent. Once it's activated, we'll need to specify the Software Development Kit (SDK) preference order for the connected VR device. This means we need to steer Unity towards using the right libraries, commands, interface protocols, and functions that apply to the connected device. Doing this is easy. View the Virtual Reality SDKs list from the PlayerSettings window in the Object Inspector. Ensure **Oculus** is listed at the top.

You can click and drag items in the list to rearrange them if needed. See *Figure 9.30*:

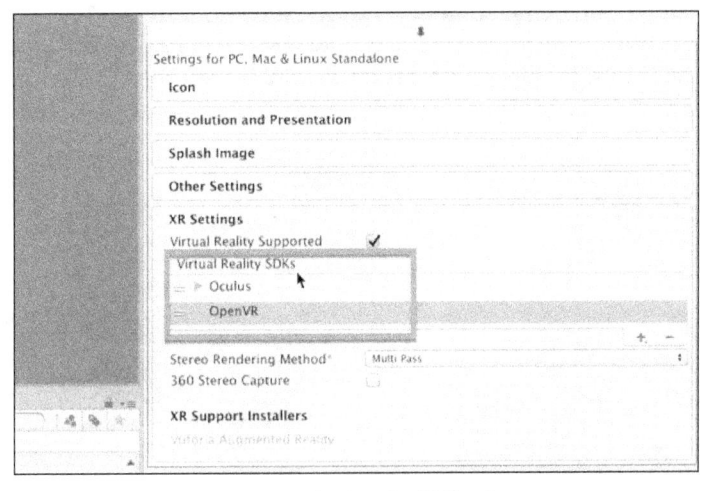

Figure 9.30: Setting the SDK order

You can test whether this configuration has found and worked with your device, simply by pressing play on the toolbar. The orientation of the **Head Mounted Display (HMD)** will automatically control the scene camera, so you'll be able to look around in VR. If this doesn't work, ensure the Oculus Device is connected and installed, and can play VR content normally. See *Figure 9.31*:

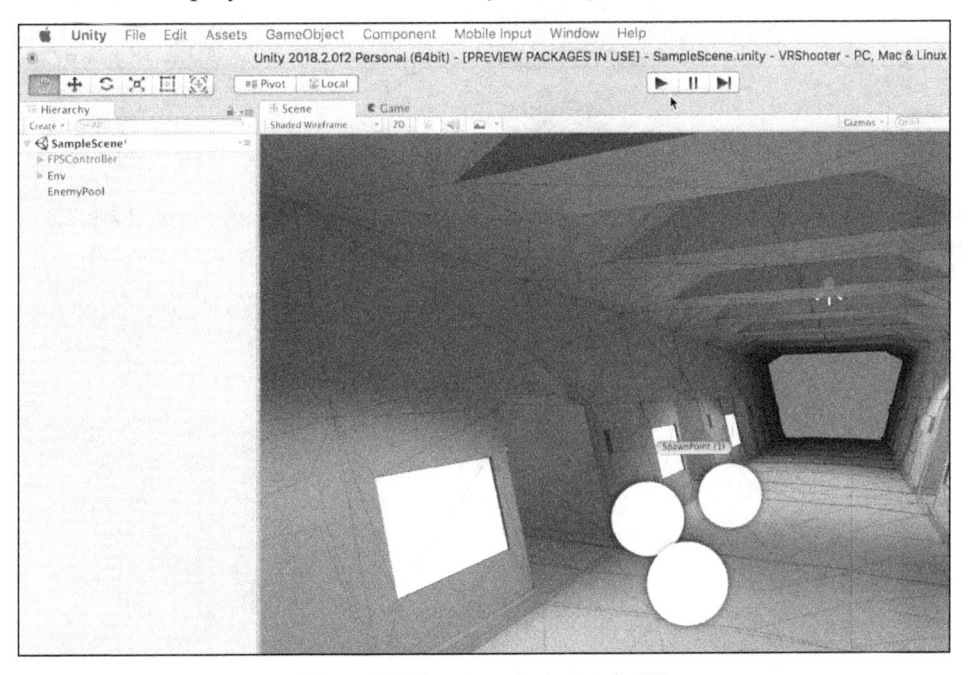

Figure 9.31: Pressing play to test the VR

Entering Virtual Reality

If all you wanted to do was look around in VR wearing the HMD, then you'd be done already! But we need VR interactivity. To achieve more complex behaviors with Oculus Rift, we'll import some additional Asset Packages made freely available to us on the Asset Store from Oculus Technologies. Open the Asset Store by choosing **Window | General | Asset Store** from the application menu. See *Figure 9.32*:

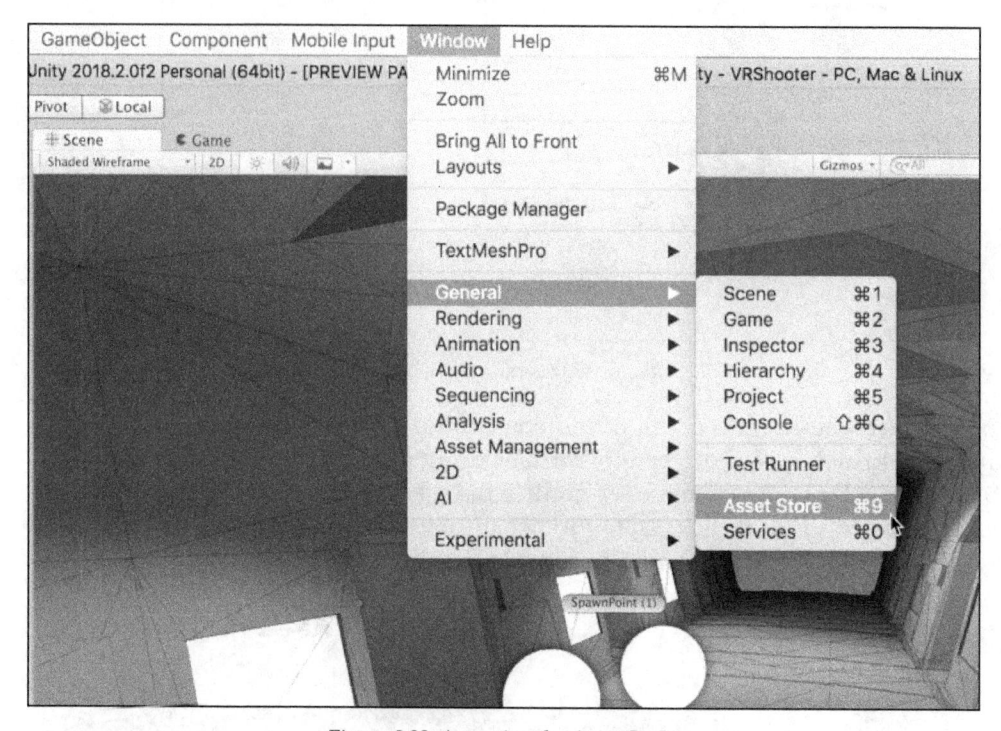

Figure 9.32: Accessing the Asset Store

You'll need to download the *Oculus Integration package*, which contains the basic libraries needed to quickly create Oculus-compatible content. Search for and import the Oculus Integration Package. See *Figure 9.33*:

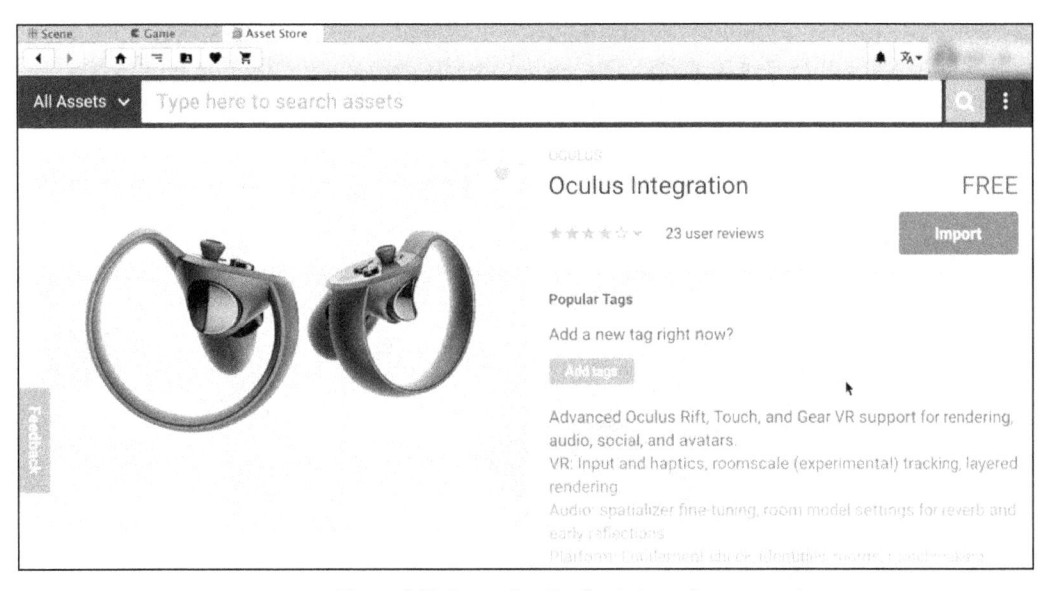

Figure 9.33: Importing Oculus integration

Once imported, you'll see a range of folders added to the Project Panel in the Oculus folder. Many of these were previously separate asset packages, but have since been integrated into one for ease of use:

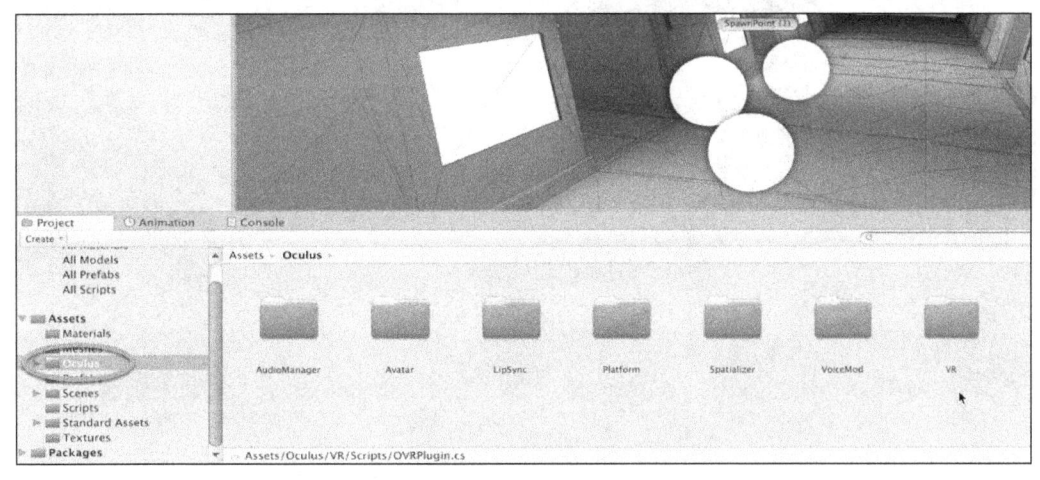

Figure 9.34: Reviewing the Oculus Integration Package

Critically important is the **Oculus | VR | Prefabs** folder, which contains an Oculus Player Character, namely the **OVRPlayerController**.

Entering Virtual Reality

This works much like the FPSController, but dedicated to VR. Drag and drop this prefab into the scene, positioning it at the end of the hallway, which is where the player will stand as they face the oncoming enemies:

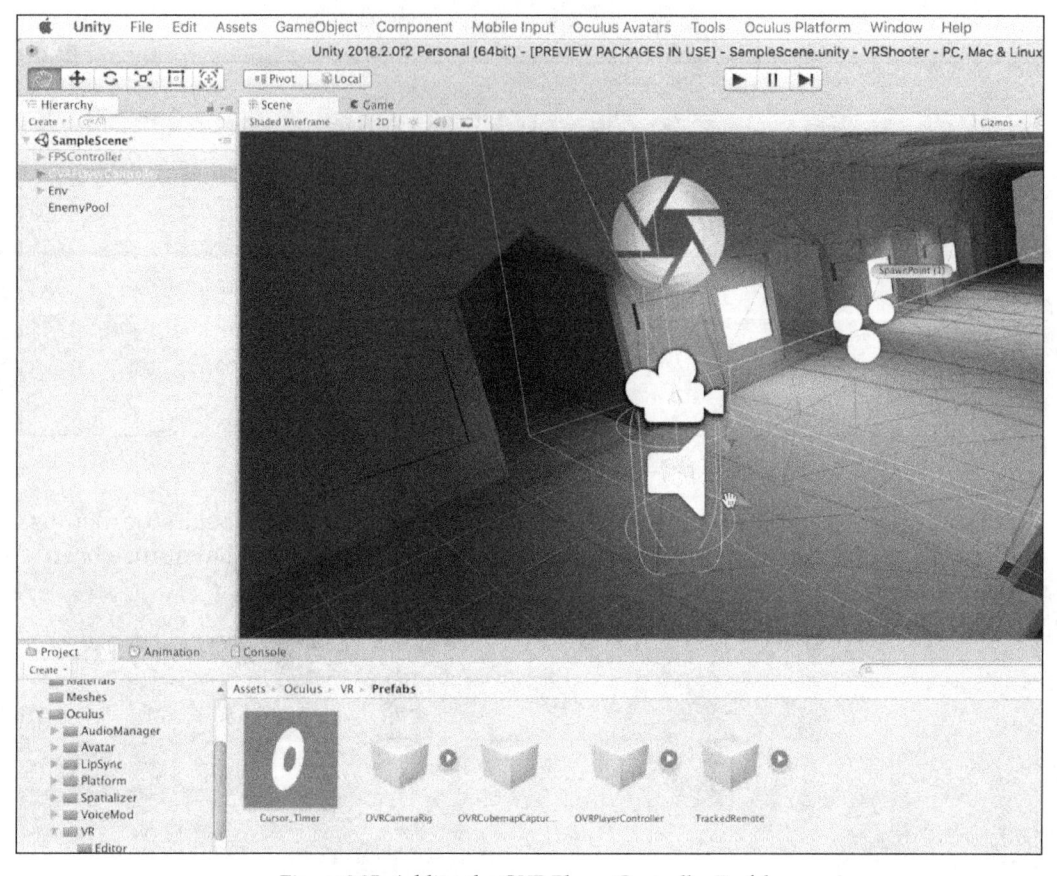

Figure 9.35: Adding the OVR Player Controller Prefab

After adding the OVR Player Controller, new cameras will be added to the scene; one for the left and one for the right eye. Your post-processing effects won't work by default. To make them work, add a Post Processing Layer component to the central eye anchor, which is part of the OVR Player Controller hierarchy of objects. See *Figure 9.36*:

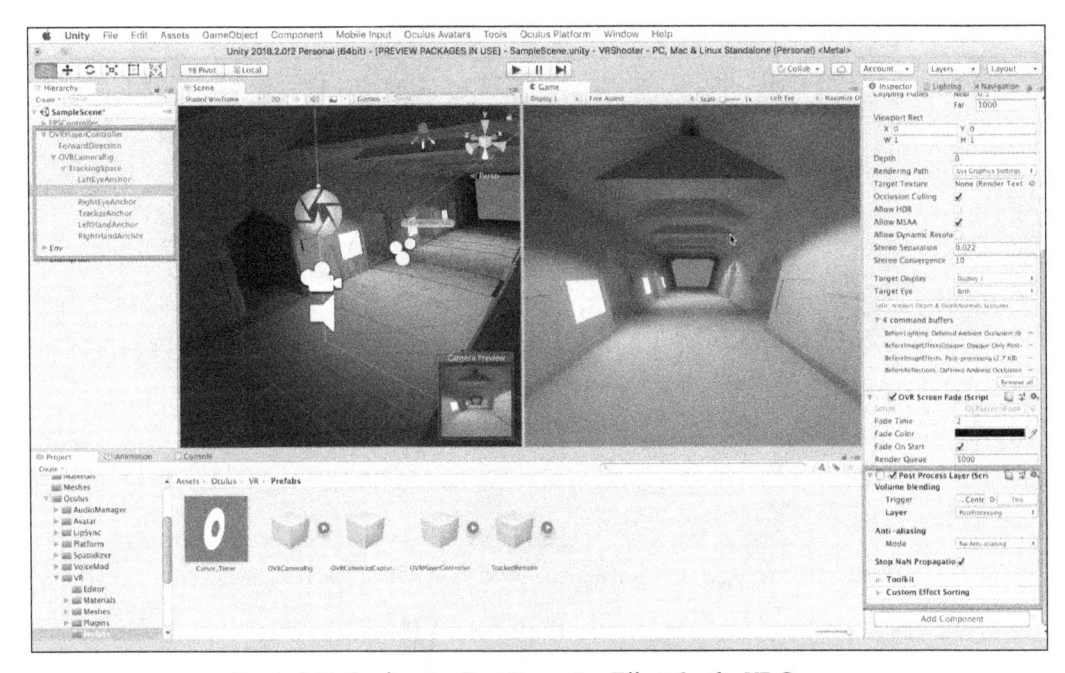

Figure 9.36: Configuring Post Processing Effects for the VR Camera

Let's give the player character some hands using the Oculus Avatar prefab, which integrates directly into the Player controller and is based on input from the Oculus Touch Controllers. This asset provides a mesh representation of the location and the status of the hands, as understood from player input within the tracking space (the play area).

Entering Virtual Reality

Find the **LocalAvatar** prefab in the **Oculus | Avatar | Content | Prefabs** folder. Drag and drop this into the **TrackingSpace** child object, part of the OVR **PlayerController** object in the scene. See *Figure 9.37*:

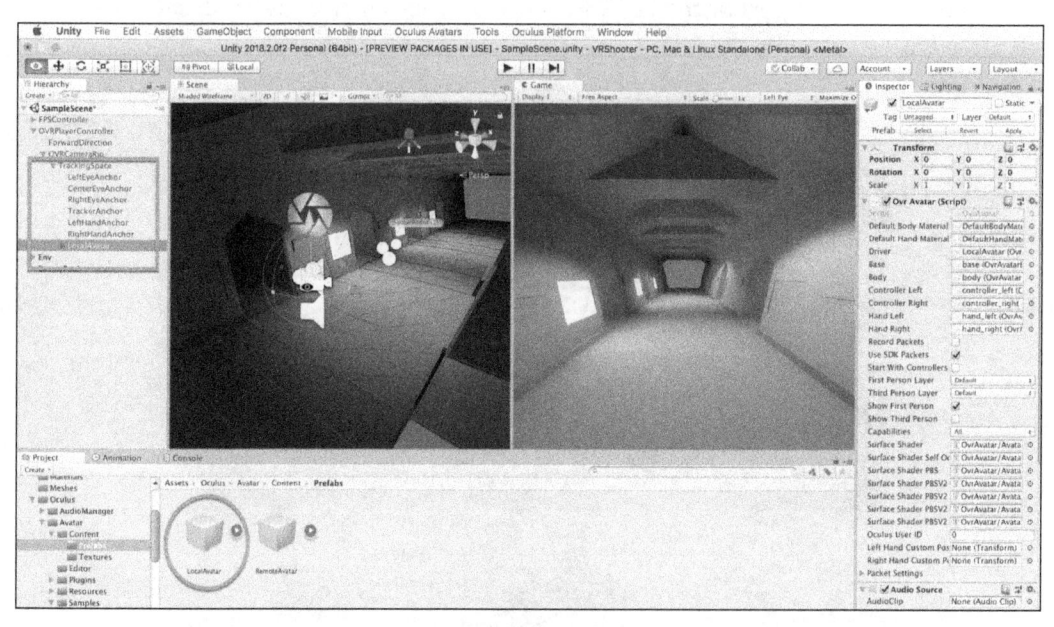

Figure 9.37: Adding a local avatar to the OVR Player Controller Tracking Space

Excellent. We're now up and running with Oculus VR, ready to implement core functionality for the first-person shooter game. We'll do that in the next chapter.

Summary

Great work. So far we've imported all project assets, configured those assets, set up the environment, and calibrated the lighting. In addition, we've got started on the path to VR development. This is splendid, but there's more to do. In the next chapter, we'll complete our first-person shooter game.

Test your knowledge

Q1. XR stands for…

- A. Extended Realities
- B. Extensible Realism
- C. X Rated
- D. Expansive Reality

Q2. Light Probes are useful for…

- A. Adding Indirect Illumination to Moving Objects
- B. Light-mapping non-UV'd objects
- C. Unwrapping UV sets
- D. Adding soft shadows on static objects

Q3. Emissive lighting can…

- A. Break easily
- B. Cast light from mesh surfaces via materials
- C. Hide static objects
- D. Customize the Object Inspector

Q4. The Post Processing Stack 2 includes…

- A. Post-Processing Volumes
- B. Particle systems
- C. Terrain tools
- D. Cameras

10
Completing the VR Game

This chapter continues from the previous one and completes the VR first-person shooter project by focusing on the underpinning code and functionality for creating gameplay, both in VR and normally. Specifically, we'll see how to do the following:

- Create intelligent AI characters
- Create Object Pools
- Work with collisions and particles
- Create a first-person shooter

> The starting project and assets can be found in the book's companion files in the Chapter10/Start folder. You can start here and follow along with this chapter if you don't have your own project already.

Completing the VR Game

Object Pool and Spawning

This chapter is based on the assets and project completed in the previous chapter. See *Figure 10.1*. Here, we'll add gameplay elements to our project and make it come alive:

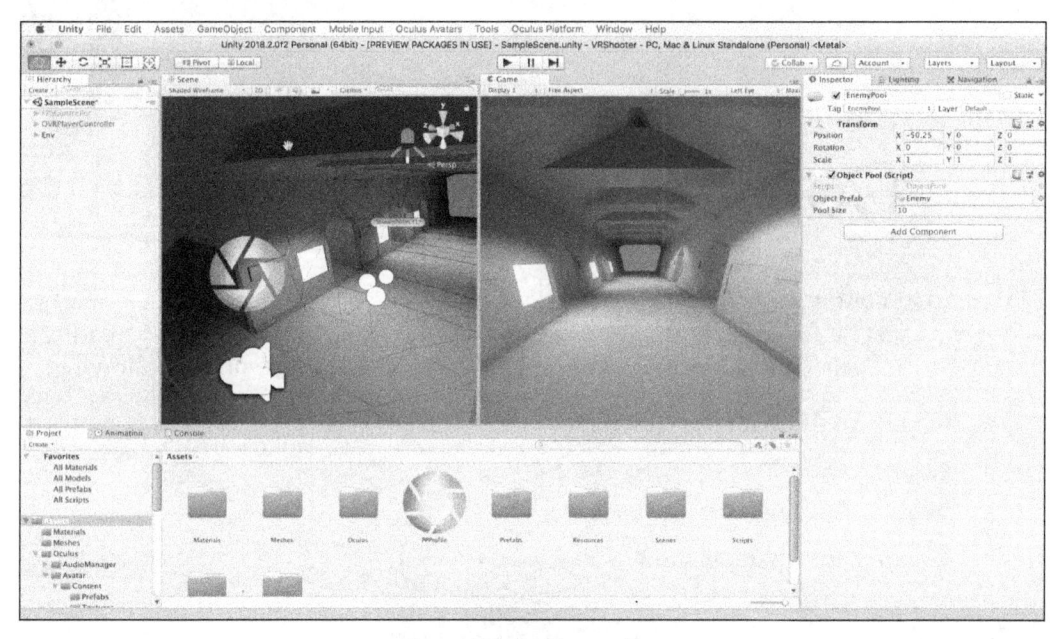

Figure 10.1: Starting project

Let's start by creating a pooling system. Our game will feature enemy prefabs (yet to be made). At regular intervals, enemy droids spawn into the level at specific spawn points. Once spawned, each enemy will wander the level searching for the player, and then attack. This functionality immediately depends on a spawning system, as enemies need to be *generated* in the scene at a specific *location* and at a specific *interval*. The spawning behavior could be achieved using the paired Instantiate and Destroy functions, for creating and removing objects respectively. These functions are slow, however, and should be avoided. It is better to generate a batch of enemies when the level starts up, hide them away, and then simply recycle the enemies when needed to appear as though they've been generated in the scene at the moment they're needed. To do this, we'll need two elements: an object pool (the collection of pre-generated objects) and a spawner (to select from the pool at a specified interval and to configure the spawned object). Let's first create the pool. Consider the following code for a new script file, `ObjectPool.cs`:

```
using System.Collections;
using System.Collections.Generic;
using UnityEngine;
//---------------------------------
```

```csharp
public class ObjectPool : MonoBehaviour
{
private Transform ThisTransform = null;
public GameObject ObjectPrefab = null;
public int PoolSize = 10;
//---------------------------------
private void Awake()
{
ThisTransform = GetComponent<Transform>();
}
//---------------------------------
private void Start()
{
GeneratePool();
}
//---------------------------------
//Generates initial object pool
public void GeneratePool()
{
for (int i = 0; i < PoolSize; i++)
{
//Generate child object
GameObject Obj = Instantiate(ObjectPrefab, Vector3.zero, Quaternion.identity, ThisTransform);
Obj.SetActive(false);
}
}
//---------------------------------
//Function to spawn a new object in the level at the specified
position, rotation and scale
public Transform Spawn(Transform Parent,
Vector3 Position = new Vector3(),
Quaternion Rotation = new Quaternion(),
Vector3 Scale = new Vector3())
{
//No object available
if (ThisTransform.childCount <= 0) return null;

//Get first child
Transform Child = ThisTransform.GetChild(0);

//Activate
Child.SetParent(Parent);
Child.position = Position;
```

```
        Child.rotation = Rotation;
        Child.localScale = Scale;
        Child.gameObject.SetActive(true);
        return Child;
}
//--------------------------------
public void DeSpawn(Transform ObjectToDespawn)
{
//Deactivate
ObjectToDespawn.gameObject.SetActive(false);
ObjectToDespawn.SetParent(ThisTransform);
ObjectToDespawn.position = Vector3.zero;
}
//--------------------------------
}
```

Code Sample 10.1

The following points summarize the code sample:

- The PoolSize defines how many instances of ObjectPrefab should be spawned at level start-up. These will normally be instances of our enemy droids, but could apply to any objects suitable for pooling. These instances will be added as child objects and hidden away in the scene until needed.
- The GeneratePool function is called once at level start-up to create the object pool, and all generated objects are children of the GameObject.
- The Spawn function is public, and can be called to generate or select an object from the pool to be added to the scene as an active object.
- The Despawn function removes an object from the scene, or rather, returns an object back to the pool.

Great. This code creates a multi-purpose pooling object effectively. Now we'll need a Spawn object to make use of the pool. For our enemies, we'll need to time the spawning behavior. Consider the following script, `SpawnTimer.cs`:

```
using System.Collections;
using System.Collections.Generic;
using UnityEngine;
```

```
public class SpawnTimer : MonoBehaviour
{
public string SpawnPoolTag = "EnemyPool";
private ObjectPool Pool = null;
public float SpawnInterval = 5f;
private Transform ThisTransform = null;

private void Awake()
{
Pool = GameObject.FindWithTag(SpawnPoolTag).
GetComponent<ObjectPool>();
ThisTransform = GetComponent<Transform>();
}

private void Start()
{
InvokeRepeating("Spawn", SpawnInterval, SpawnInterval);
}

public void Spawn()
{
Pool.Spawn(null, ThisTransform.position, ThisTransform.rotation,
Vector3.one);
}
}
```

Code Sample 10.2

The following points summarize the code sample:

- The Awake function searches the scene for a pool object with a specified tag, assuming this is the only such pool object, and then caches a reference to it.
- The Start function initiates an InvokeRepeating cycle to repeatedly spawn objects from the associated pool.

To complete the spawn functionality, let's add our scripts to objects in the scene. First, create an empty object for the pool and position it outside the main level area. Attach the ObjectPool component onto to it, and specify a size for the pool. I've used 20.

Completing the VR Game

We don't yet have an enemy prefab to become part of the pool yet, and this will be created in the next section. See *Figure 10.2*:

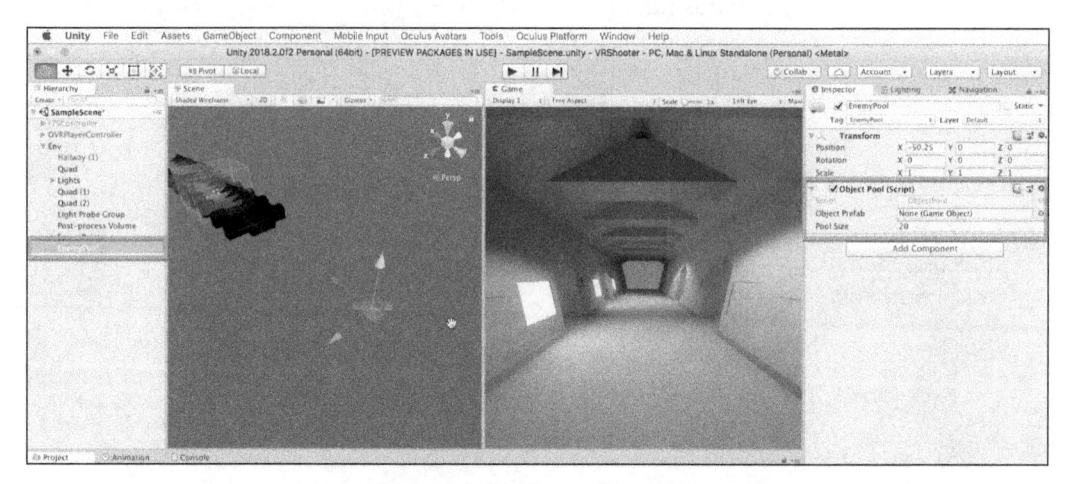

Figure 10.2: Creating an Object Pool

Next, let's make spawn points. Initially, I'll make two. For the first, make an empty object in the scene and attach the **SpawnTimer** script to it. Then specify the tag for the ObjectPool object, and the interval in seconds for spawning from the pool. Remember to tag your object pool with a matching tag, to ensure the spawner finds the pool. See *Figure 10.3*:

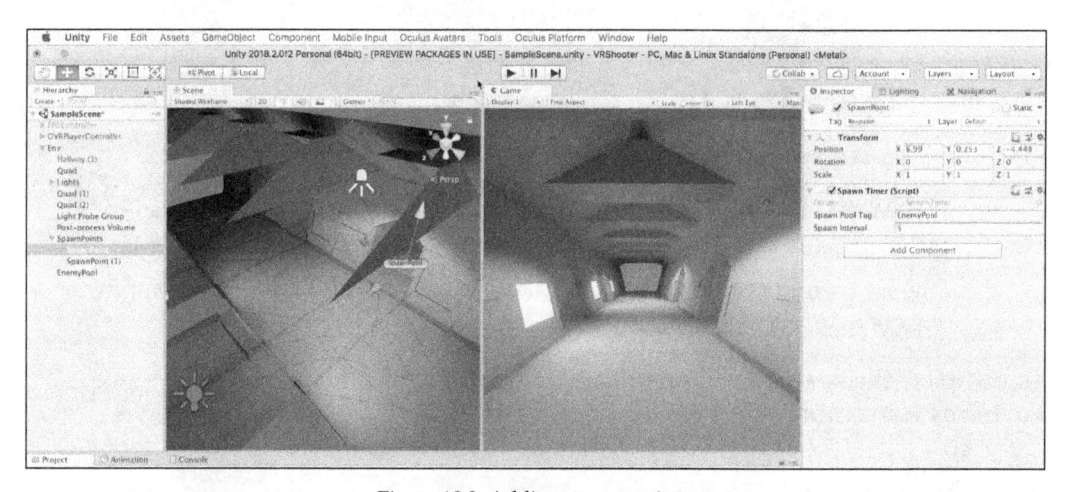

Figure 10.3: Adding spawn points

You can make the second object through duplication. But we still have the following problem: we have no enemy to spawn yet. So, we'll need to make that.

[430]

Creating Intelligent Enemies – Navigation

In *Chapters 7, Creating Artificial Intelligence* and *Chapter 8, Continuing with Intelligent Enemies* we saw how to create enemy AI, and we'll apply that knowledge again here to create droids using a simple **Finite State Machine** (**FSM**). The droid will be constructed as a Prefab. To start, drag and drop a Droid mesh into the scene. See *Figure 10.4*:

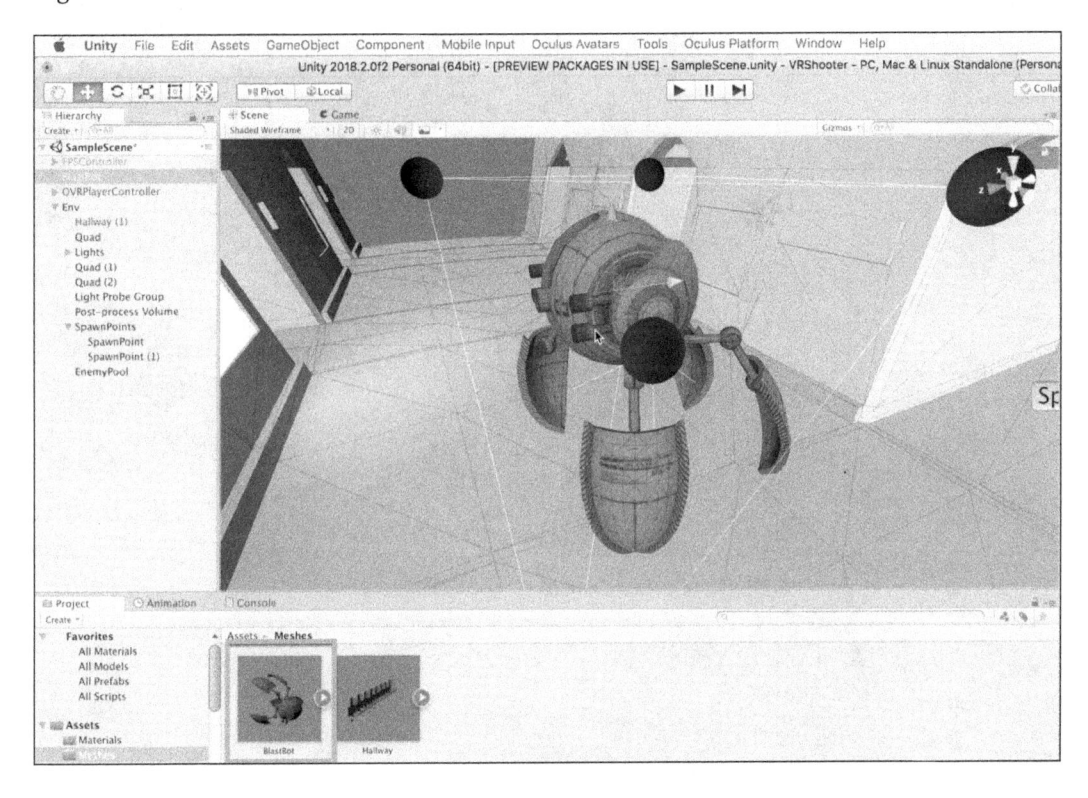

Figure 10.4: Creating an Enemy Droid

The enemy droid mesh will form part of a more complex object. The mesh itself is a fraction of the whole. To start building the droid enemy, create an empty object, named Enemy, and make the droid mesh a child of it.

Ensure the empty parent has a blue forward axis representing the direction in which the droid is looking. See Figure 10.5:

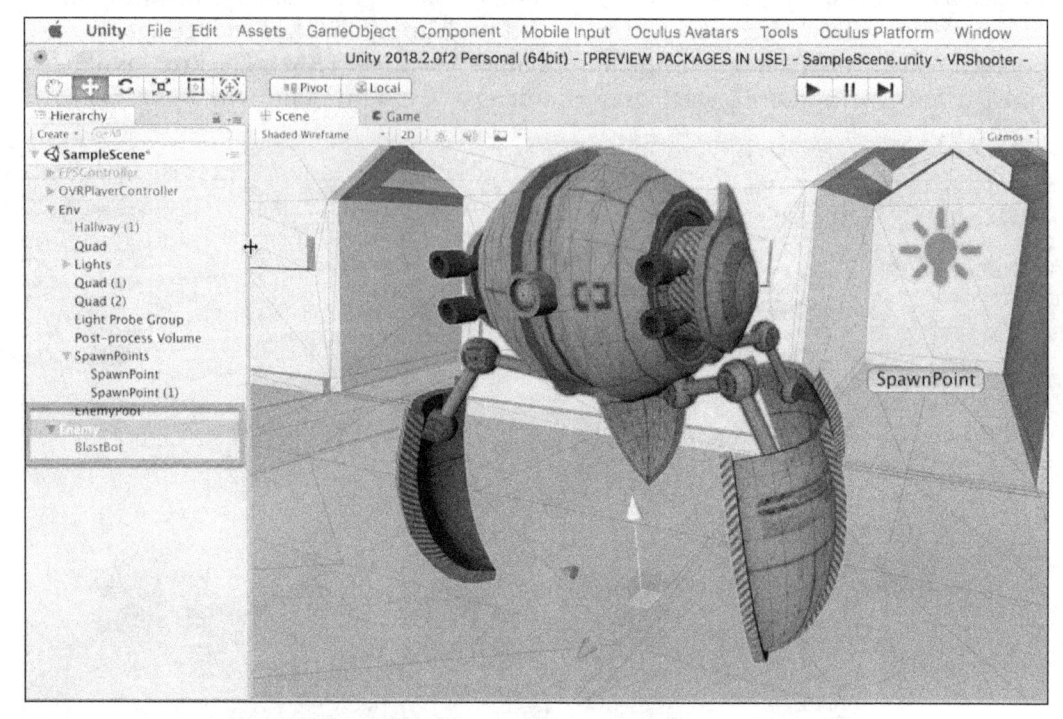

Figure 10.5: Configuring the Droid Object Hierarchy

Let's add collision and physics data to the object. Add both a **RigidBody** component and a Box Collider, which roughly approximates the mesh. Ensure the **Rigidbody** is marked as **isKinematic**. See *Figure 10.6*:

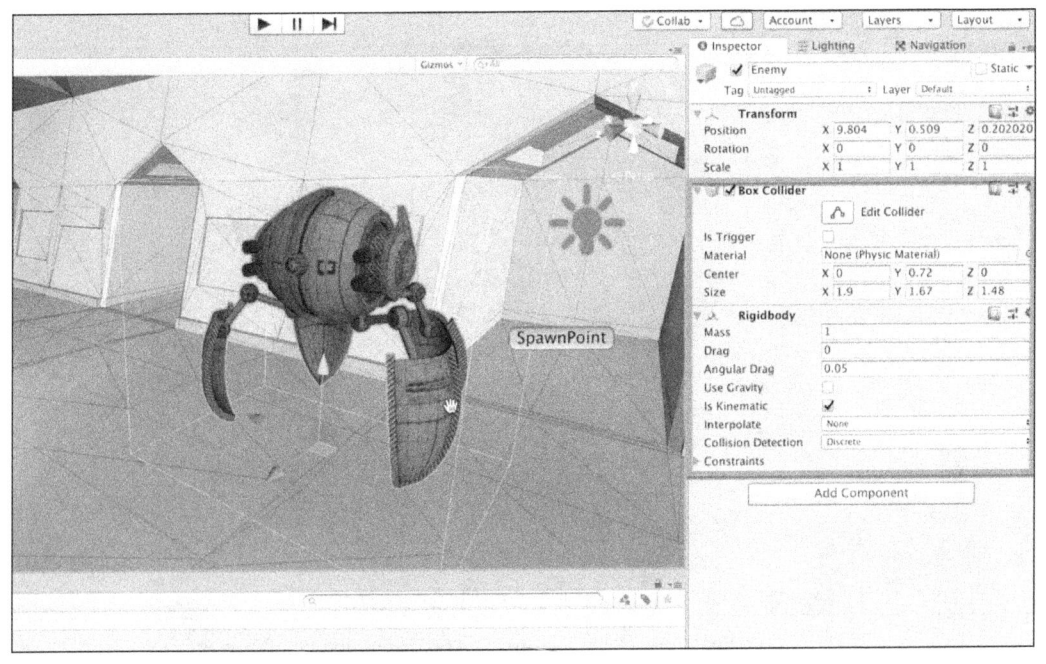

Figure 10.6: Adding physics components to the Droid

Completing the VR Game

The droid will need to navigate around the scene intelligently, avoiding obstacles. To achieve this, a NavMesh can be generated for the environment. First, ensure all environment meshes are marked as **Navigation Static** from the Object Inspector. See *Figure 10.7*:

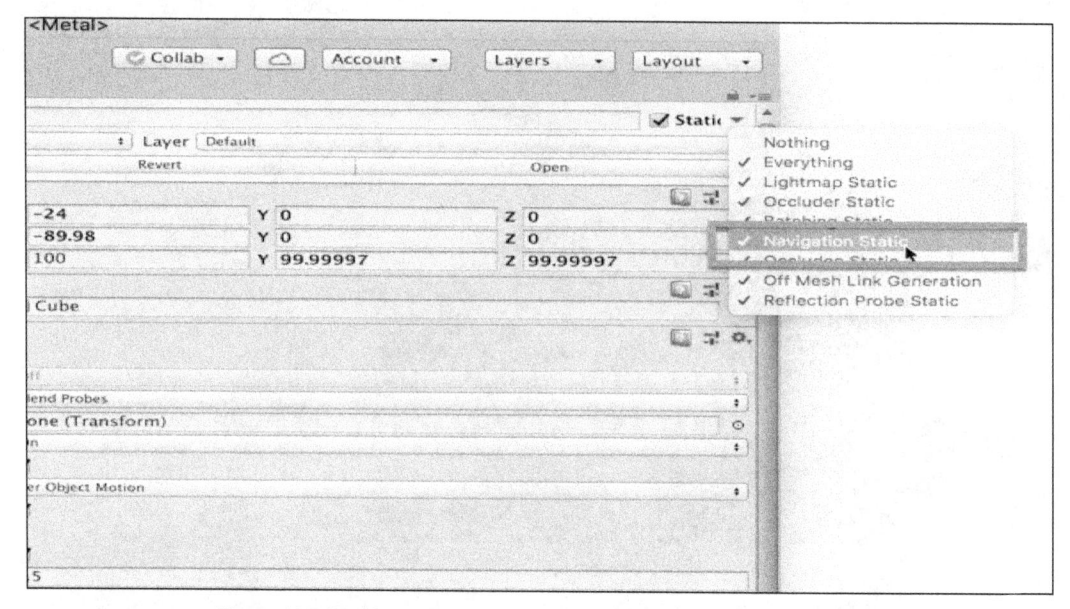

Figure 10.7: Enabling Navigation Static for Static Environment Meshes

Open the Navigation Window by choosing **Window | AI | Navigation** from the application menu. This displays the Navigation Mesh Window. From here, open the Bake tab and click the **Bake** button to generate a mesh representing the walkable area of the floor. The blue region illustrates the complete surface area inside which an enemy droid can walk.

If the mesh doesn't look right, tweak the **Agent Radius** and **Agent Height** settings (and hit Bake again!) until you get a navigation mesh allowing the droid to move successfully around the environment. See *Figure 10.8*:

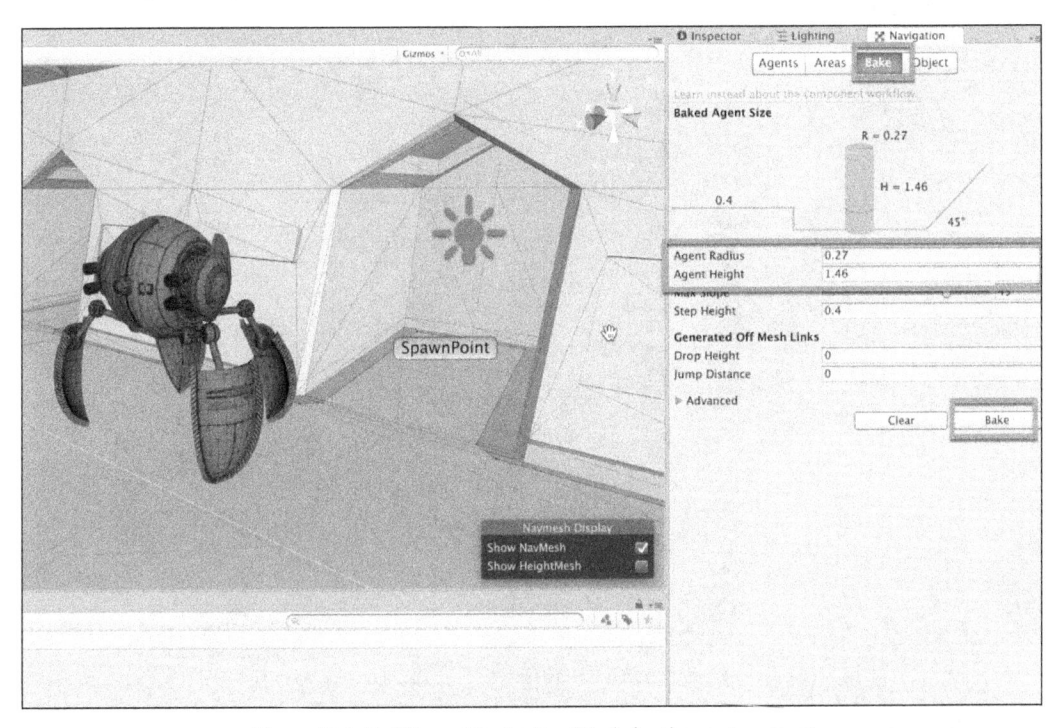

Figure 10.8: Building a Navigation Mesh for the environment

Completing the VR Game

Now add a NavMeshAgent to the droid object (the parent). Select the parent, and choose **Component | Navigation | NavMeshAgent** from the application menu. Once added, set the Agent Radius and Height to match the droid mesh. Simple. See *Figure 10.9*:

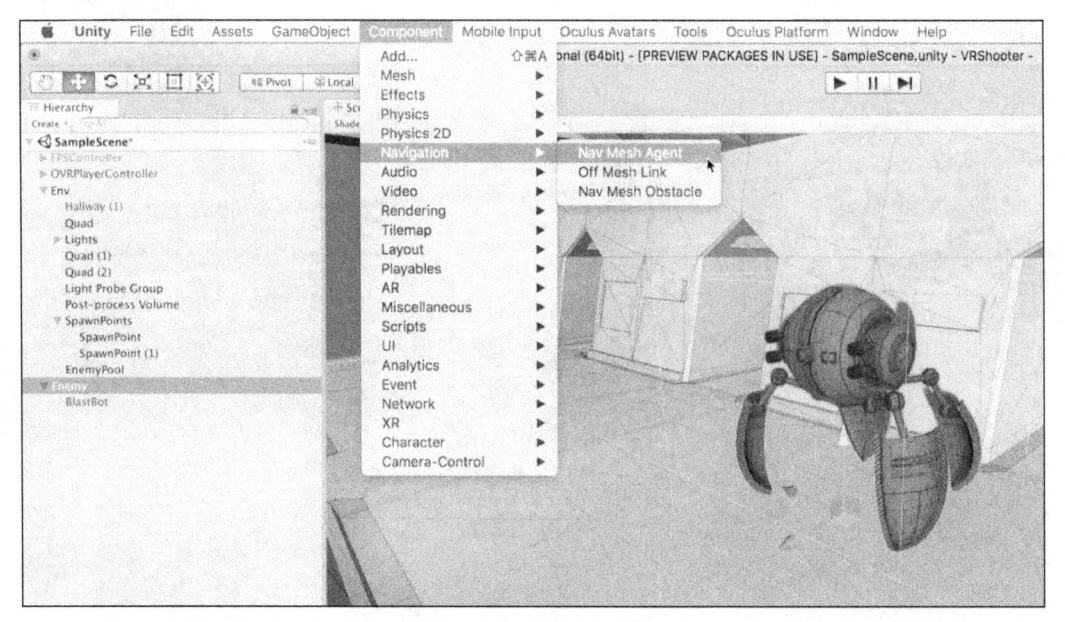

Figure 10.9: Configuring a NavMeshAgent

Great. We've now set up the enemy's movement around the level. Let's create a Prefab for him now; and we can always amend later if needed. Just drag and drop the parent object from the hierarchy panel into the project panel, and then a Prefab is created from the selection.

We now have an enemy prefab, as shown in *Figure 10.10*. Go ahead and add this prefab to the ObjectPool too:

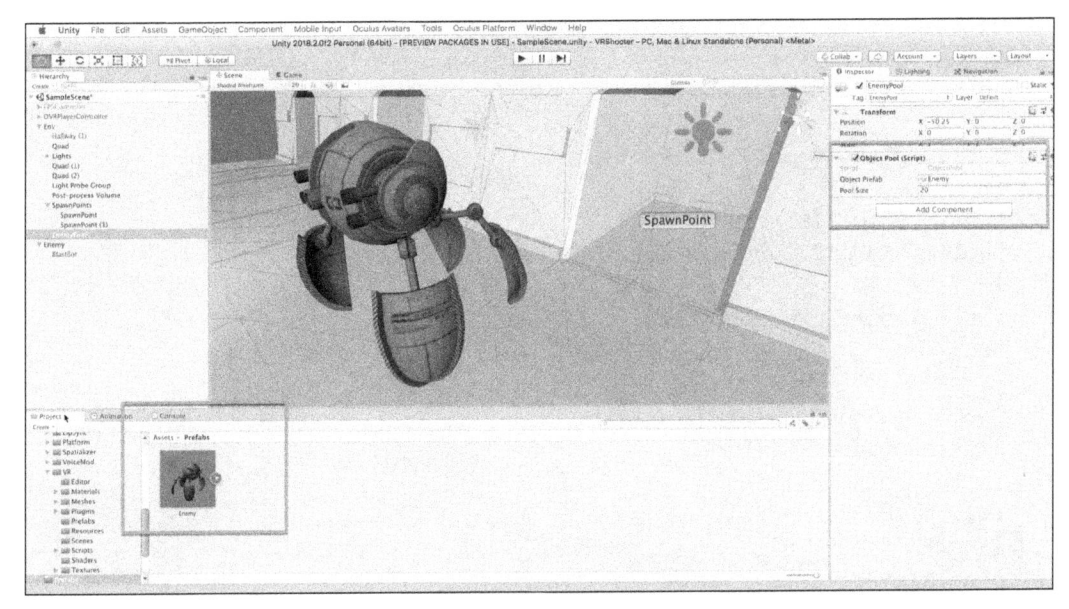

Figure 10.10: Creating a Prefab from the Enemy Object

Creating Intelligent Enemies – FSMs

In this section, we'll define the code to work with the enemy prefab; specifically, the FSM defining its core behavior. The enemy, once spawned in the level, will enter chase mode, causing it to follow the player, wherever they may be. On reaching the player, the enemy will attack and cause damage.

Completing the VR Game

The enemy AI is encoded in the `BotAI.cs` script file. See the following code sample:

```
using System.Collections;
using System.Collections.Generic;
using UnityEngine;
using UnityEngine.AI;

public class BotAI : MonoBehaviour
{
public enum AISTATE { CHASE = 0, ATTACK = 1 };
public AISTATE CurrentState
{
get { return _CurrentState; }
set
{
StopAllCoroutines();
_CurrentState = value;

switch(_CurrentState)
{
case AISTATE.CHASE:
StartCoroutine(StateChase());
break;

case AISTATE.ATTACK:
StartCoroutine(StateAttack());
break;
}
}
}

[SerializeField]
private AISTATE _CurrentState = AISTATE.CHASE;
private NavMeshAgent ThisAgent = null;
private Transform ThisPlayer = null;
private Transform ThisTransform = null;
public ParticleSystem WeaponPS = null;

private void Awake()
{
ThisAgent = GetComponent<NavMeshAgent>();
ThisPlayer = GameObject.FindWithTag("Player").
GetComponent<Transform>();
ThisTransform = GetComponent<Transform>();
```

```csharp
}

private void Start()
{
CurrentState = _CurrentState;
}

private void OnEnable()
{
CurrentState = AISTATE.CHASE;
}

private void OnDisable()
{
StopAllCoroutines();
WeaponPS.Stop();
}

public IEnumerator StateChase()
{
WeaponPS.Stop();
ThisAgent.SetDestination(ThisPlayer.position);

while (CurrentState == AISTATE.CHASE)
{
//Check distance
float DistancetoDest = Vector3.Distance(ThisTransform.position,
ThisPlayer.position);

if (Mathf.Approximately(DistancetoDest, ThisAgent.stoppingDistance) ||
DistancetoDest <= ThisAgent.stoppingDistance)
{
CurrentState = AISTATE.ATTACK;
yield break;
}

yield return null;
}
}

public IEnumerator StateAttack()
{
WeaponPS.Play();
```

Completing the VR Game

```
while (CurrentState == AISTATE.ATTACK)
{
Vector3 Dir = (ThisPlayer.position - ThisTransform.position).
normalized;
Dir.y = 0;
ThisTransform.rotation = Quaternion.LookRotation(Dir, Vector3.up);
yield return null;
}
}
}
```

Code Sample 10.3

The following points summarize the code sample:

- The CurrentState property defines which state is currently active with the FSM, either Chase or Attack.
- The WeaponPS variable refers to a particle system object, which will be a gun for the enemy droid. Collision can be enabled for the particles to hit the player.
- The Chase state uses the SetDestination function of the Navigation Mesh to continually follow the player.

In addition to the FSM, enemy objects (and also the player) must be able to take damage when hit by weapons. Therefore, both the player and enemies require health. A health script is also given here, Health.cs:

```
using System.Collections;
using System.Collections.Generic;
using UnityEngine;
using UnityEngine.Events;
using UnityEngine.EventSystems;

public class Health : MonoBehaviour
{
public UnityEvent OnHealthChanged;
public string SpawnPoolTag = string.Empty;
private ObjectPool Pool = null;
private Transform ThisTransform = null;
```

```
public float HealthPoints
{
get { return _HealthPoints; }
set
{
_HealthPoints = value;
OnHealthChanged.Invoke();

if (_HealthPoints <= 0f) Die();
}
}

[SerializeField]
private float _HealthPoints = 100f;

private void Awake()
{
ThisTransform = GetComponent<Transform>();

if(SpawnPoolTag.Length > 0)
Pool = GameObject.FindWithTag(SpawnPoolTag).
GetComponent<ObjectPool>();
}

private void Die()
{
if (Pool != null)
{
Pool.DeSpawn(ThisTransform);
HealthPoints = 100f;
}
}

void Update()
{
if (Input.GetKeyDown(KeyCode.Space))
{
HealthPoints = 0;
}
}
}
```

Completing the VR Game

Code Sample 10.4

The following points summarize the code sample:

- The `HealthPoints` property is used to change object health, and potentially to notify other objects and processes about the event.
- The `Update` function features test code that reduces health points to 0 on a space bar press
- The `Pool` variable allows the Health component to link with Object Pooling so that, if the object is dying, it can be returned to the Object Pool rather than remove entirely from the scene.
- You can now update the enemy prefab with both scripts by selecting it from the Project Panel, and add the BotAI and Health script to it. Easy! See *Figure 10.11*:

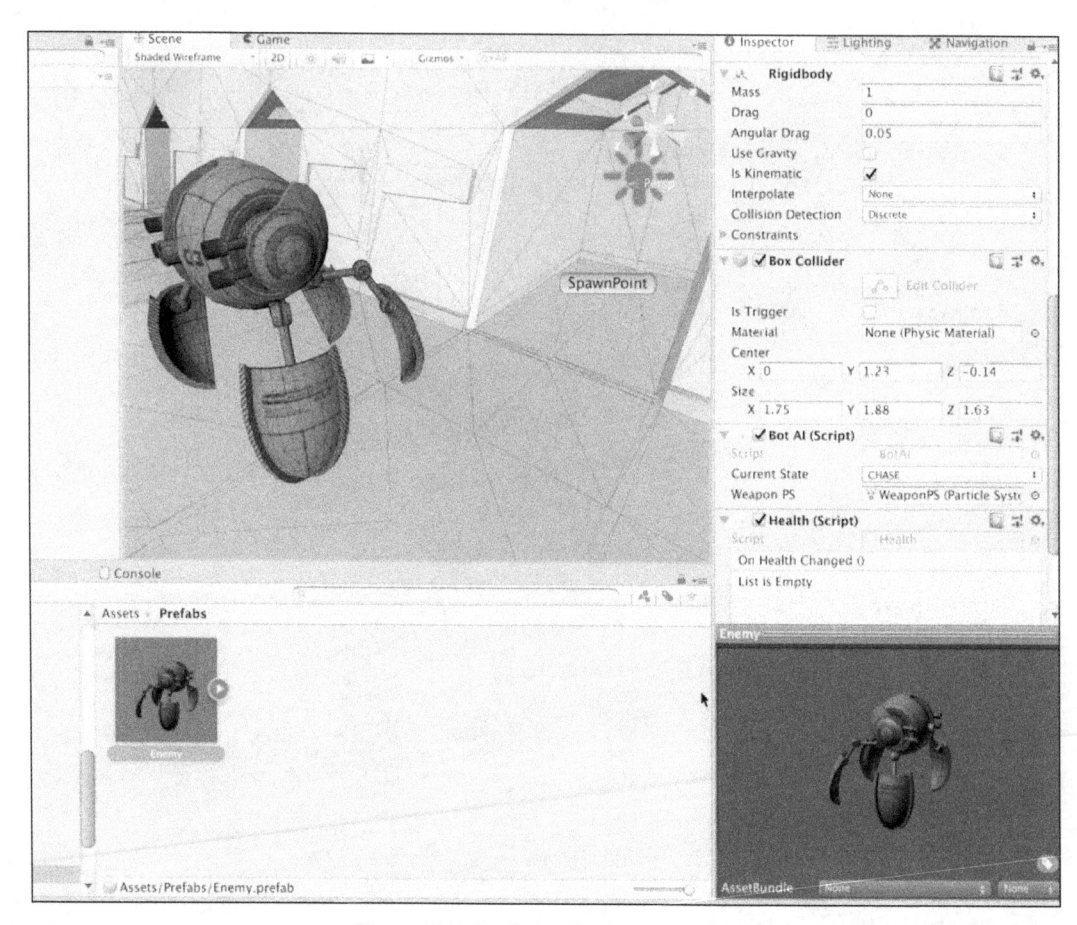

Figure 10.11: Updating the Enemy Prefab

Excellent! Our enemy is ready. It can't attack yet, but neither can the player. We can create both attack and damage mechanics for the player and enemy at the same time. In the next section, we'll see how...

Attack and Damage

Enemies should attack the player, and the player should attack the enemies. Both depend on the concept of attacking and taking damage. In this section, we'll use particle systems for inflicting damage, and we'll create script to take damage. First, let's create a player weapon by generating a new particle system. In VR, this object can be made a child of the hand controllers; each hand can have one weapon. In standard first-person mode, the particle system will be a single-fire weapon. To get started for the player attack, create a new particle system in the scene by choosing **GameObject | Effects | Particle System**. See *Figure 10.12*:

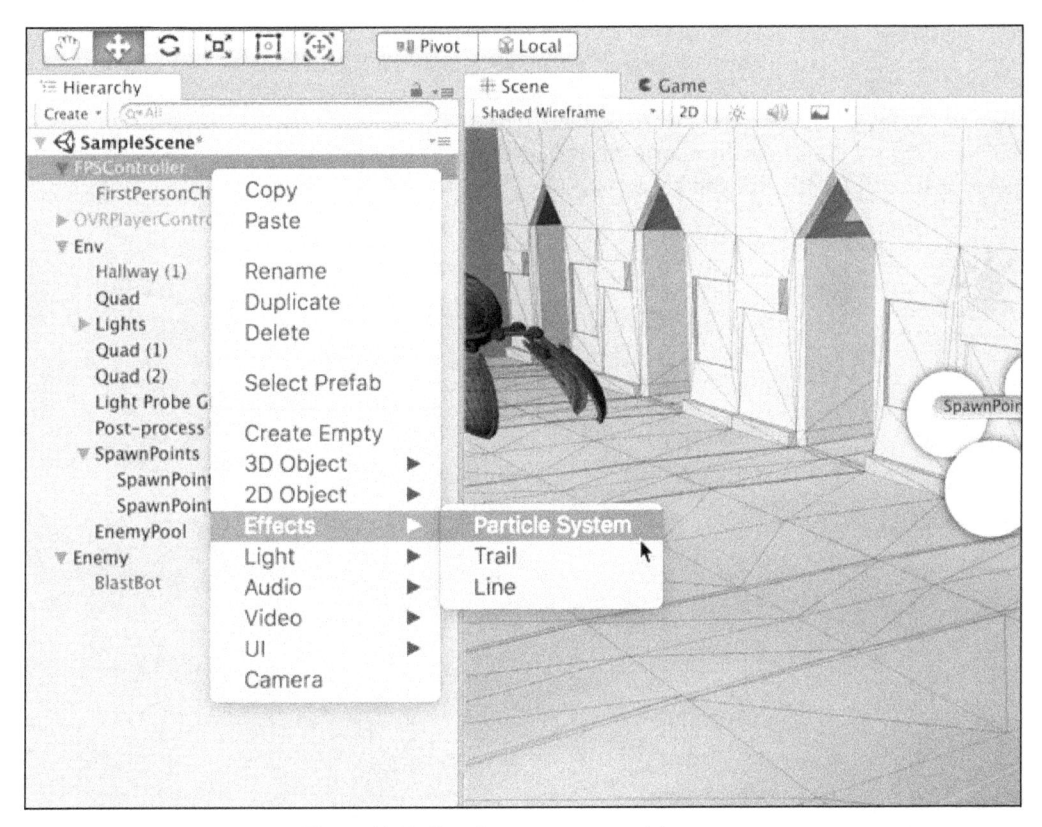

Figure 10.12: Creating a weapon particle system

Completing the VR Game

Once added, we'll need to tweak a lot of settings to make it look like a plasma beam, or a laser cannon. Expand the Shape and Emission settings from the Object Inspector to reveal those particle system properties. See *Figure 10.13*:

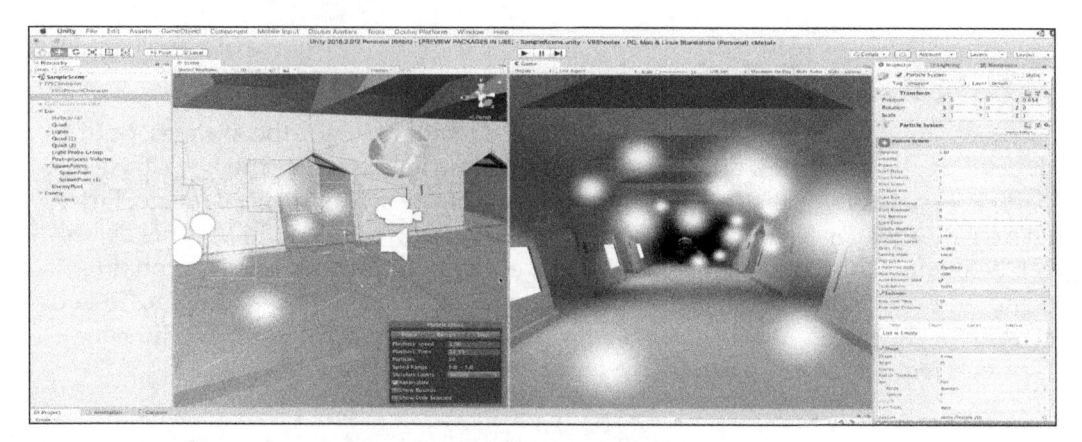

Figure 10.13: Tweaking the Particle System for a plasma cannon

Change the **Start Speed** and **Start Lifetime** to affect the speed and range of the projectiles. Then change the **Cone Shape** and **Radius** to narrow the profile trajectory; and finally, adjust the spawn **rate**.

Higher values will produce a beam, and lower values will produce bolts or balls instead. See *Figure 10.14*:

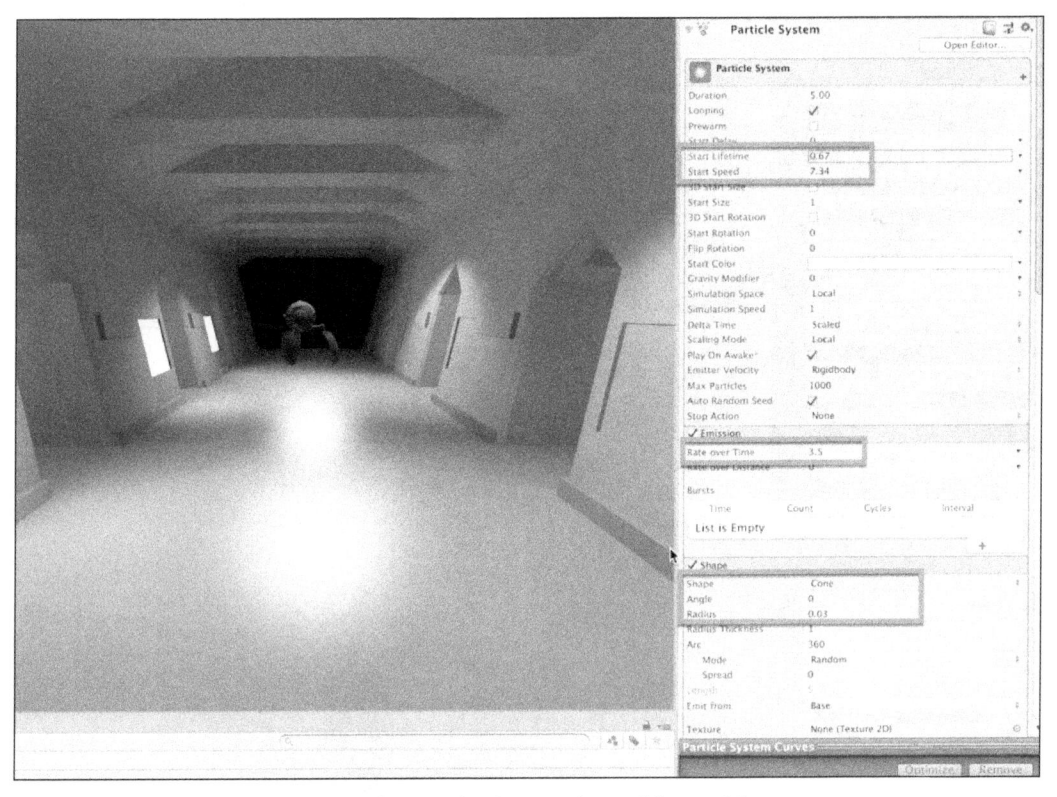

Figure 10.14: Adjusting the shape and rate of the particle system

Completing the VR Game

Now let's change the particle appearance using the **Renderer** section. Click the **Material** field and pick a style for the particles. See *Figure 10.15*:

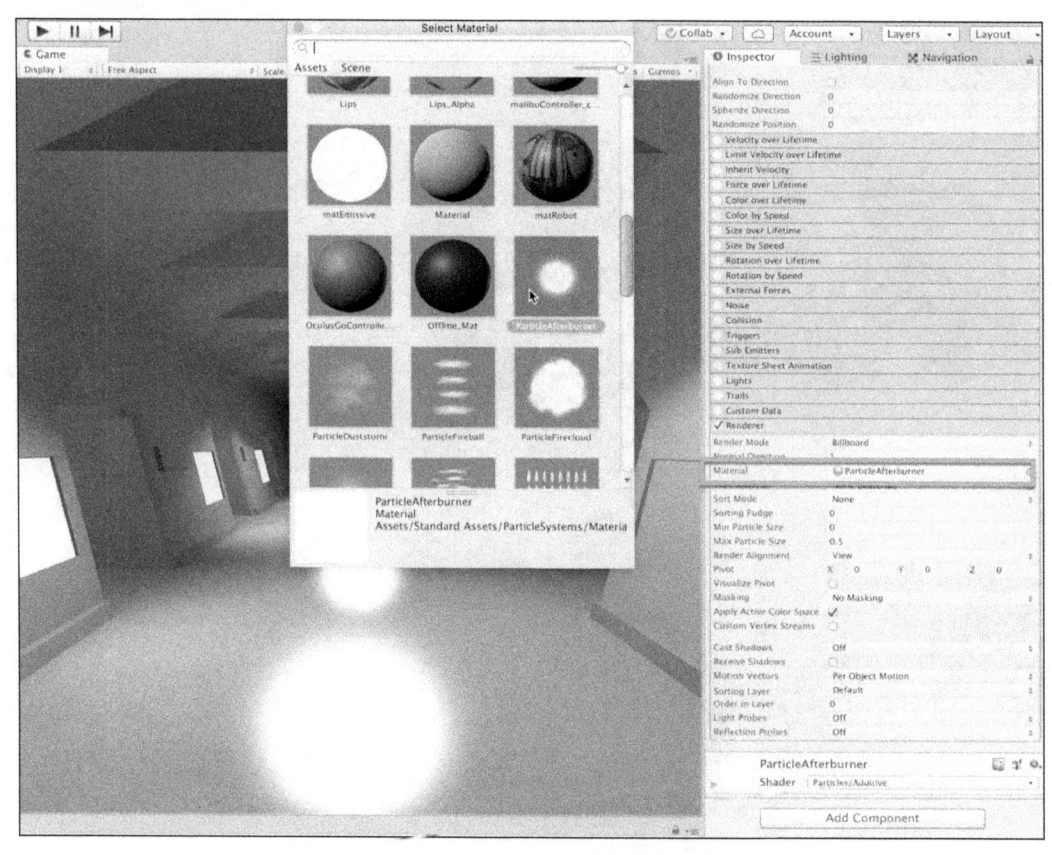

Figure 10.15: Controlling particle appearance

Next, we'll add collision data to the particles so they can collide with other objects, such as enemies, allowing enemies to respond and take damage from collision. To do this, expand and enable the **Collision** group from the Object Inspector, and then enable the **Send Collision Messages** option.

Further, set the **Collision Type to World**. This ensures an **OnParticleCollision** event is invoked when an object collides with the particles. See *Figure 10.16*:

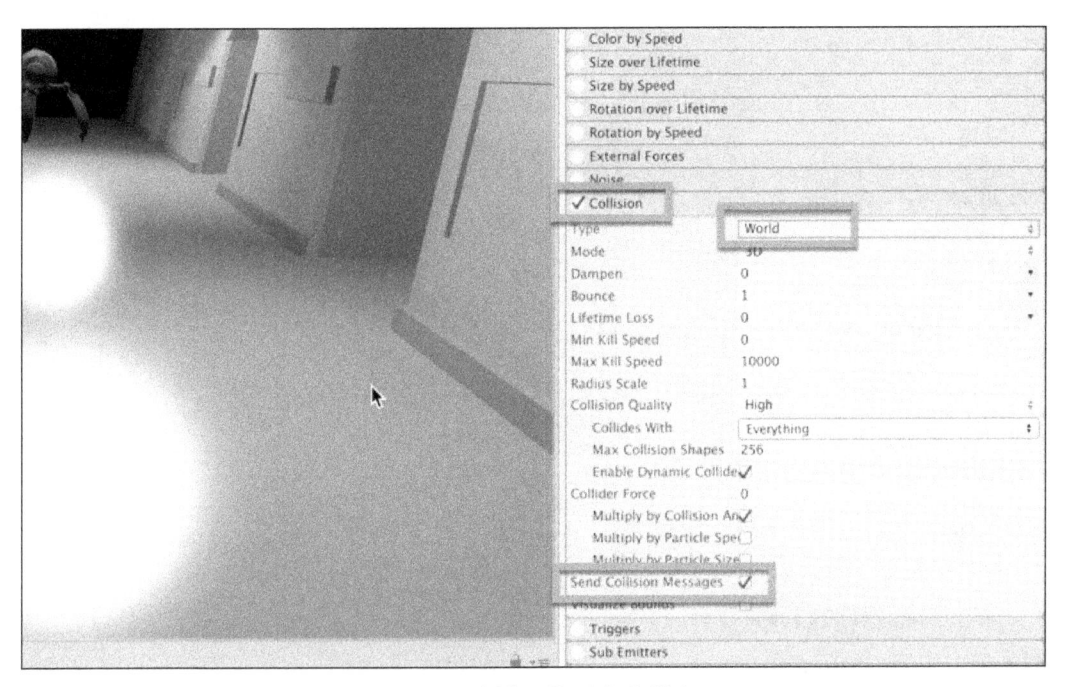

Figure 10.16: Adding Particle Collisions

Now we need only two scripts: one for firing the player weapon, and another that causes an object to take damage when hit by ammo. Let's create the weapon script, Weapon.cs:

```
using System.Collections;
using System.Collections.Generic;
using UnityEngine;

public class Weapon : MonoBehaviour
{
private ParticleSystem PS;

    // Use this for initialization
    void Awake ()
{
PS = GetComponent<ParticleSystem>();
```

Completing the VR Game

```
    }

    // Update is called once per frame
    void Update ()
{
if(Input.GetButtonDown("Fire1") || OVRInput.GetDown(OVRInput.Button.One))
{
PS.Play();
return;
}

if (Input.GetButtonUp("Fire1") || OVRInput.GetUp(OVRInput.Button.One))
{
PS.Stop();
return;
}
    }
}
```

Code Sample 10.5

The following points summarize the code sample:

- The PS variable references the attached particle system to be started or stopped when a trigger is pressed.
- The OVRInput class is used to detect when a button is pressed on the Touch Controllers. This means the code can be linked both to desktop PC input, as well as VR controller input.

OK. So, let's make the damage script. This should be attached to both the player and the enemies, and it's used to respond to damage from a particle system:

```
using System.Collections;
using System.Collections.Generic;
using UnityEngine;

public class DamageAffectorParticles : MonoBehaviour
{
public string TagDamage = "Enemy";
```

```
private Health ThisHealth = null;
public float DamageAmount = 2f;

private void Awake()
{
ThisHealth = GetComponent<Health>();
}

private void OnParticleCollision(GameObject other)
{
if (!other.CompareTag(TagDamage)) return;
ThisHealth.HealthPoints -= DamageAmount;
}
}
```

Attach **DamageAffectorParticles** to the enemy and the player, and add a particle weapon to the enemy. When you've done this, both the player and enemies can deal and take damage. Great work! See *Figure 10.17*:

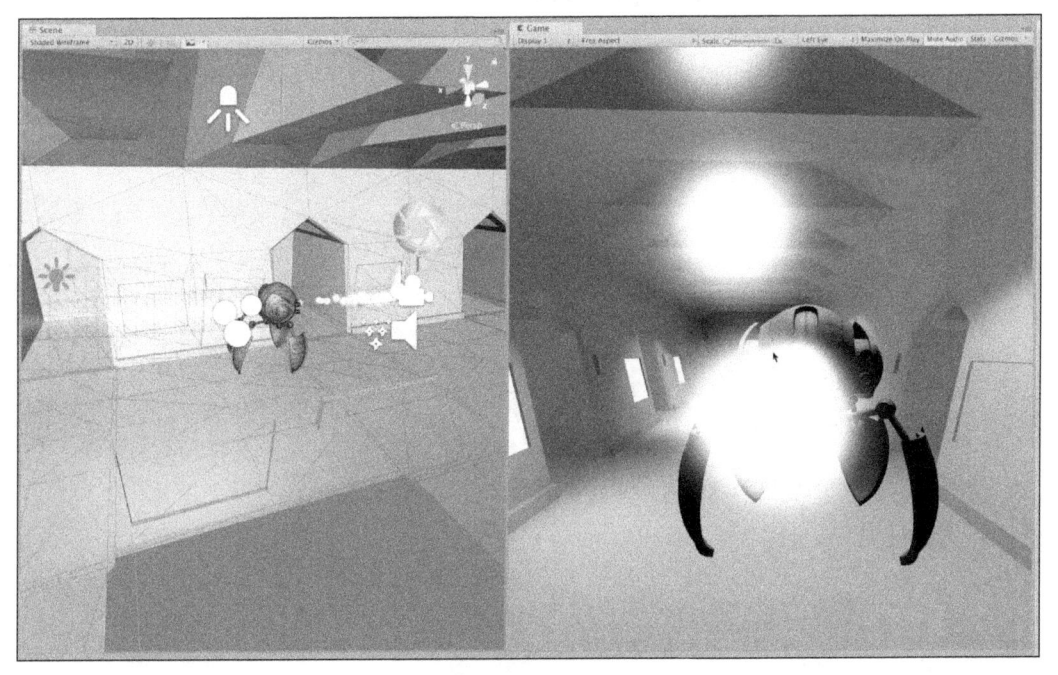

Figure 10.17: Completed VR game

Congratulations! You completed the VR game. We now have a game that works with a VR headset, allows you to look around, and prevents movement. You can shoot oncoming enemies, which spawn into the level, using the touch controllers. This relies on a collision-based particle system. In reaching this far, you've not only seen how to build a VR game, but also a few neat optimization tricks: object pools and script reuse.

Summary

Great work. You've completed this chapter, the VR game, and the book too. By this point, you've put together five different Unity projects, each with different requirements and specifications, each relying on different techniques and tricks. Of course, these solutions are not limited to just these projects, but can be countlessly reused in many projects!

Test your knowledge

Q1. Particle Systems do NOT support object collisions.

- A. FALSE
- B. TRUE

Q2. FSM stands for...

- A. Finite State Machine
- B. Full Static Method
- C. Fast Linear Mode
- D. Fetch Sort Master

Q3. Oculus Rift is supported on Mac computers.

- A. True
- B. False

Q4. `OVRInput` is primarily used to...

- A. Read input from Oculus Touch Controllers
- B. Read the orientation of the HMD
- C. Read the player position in the tracking space
- D. Reset the player position

Test Your Knowledge Answers

This appendix contains answers to all the Test Your Knowledge quizzes that appear in the chapters.

Chapter 1- Unity Fundamentals

Q1. Assets are imported directly into the…

- D. **Project Panel**

Q2. You can quickly create first person controls using

- C. **First Person Controllers**

Q3. The Prototyping Package is most useful for…

- A. **Building Levels**

Q4. When pressed in the scene tab, the F key will…

- A. **Center the view on the selected object**

Q5. You can access the Snapping Feature by pressing…

- B. **V**

Test Your Knowledge Answers

Chapter 2- Creating a Collection Game

Q1. You can easily find `GameObjects` in code by using...

- B. **Tags**

Q2. You can search the hierarchy for objects that contain specific component types by using a prefix of...

- B. **T**

Q3. Static variables are always...

- A. **Shared across all instances of a class**

Q4. The main color for a material is defined by the...

- C. **Albedo Channel**

Q5. By default, when you run a Unity game, you will first see...

- D. **The Resolution Config Dialog**

Chapter 3- Creating a Space Shooter

Q1. `SerializableField` makes...

- B. **Private variables visible in the inspector**

Q2. Importing audio with the Streaming Load Type means...

- B. **The Audio will be loaded in segments**

Q3. Orthographic Cameras Remove...

- A. **Perspective effects**

Q4. The `Input.GetAxis` function lets you read input from...

- A. **Horizontal and Vertical Axes**

Chapter 4- Continuing the Space Shooter

Q1. Static Variables are...

- B. **Shared variables across all instances of a class**

Q2. The profiler is useful for...

- B. **Identifying performance issues**

Q3. UI Objects are useful for...

- A. **Creating interface elements**

Q4. The Collision Matrix lets you

- A. **Prevent groups of objects colliding**

Chapter 5- Creating a 2D Adventure

Q1. Edge Colliders lets you...

- B. **Draw out collider edges**

Q2. The Sprite Packer is useful for...

- B. **Group sprites onto a single atlas texture**

Q3. Physics Materials can...

- A. **Help you define how 2D objects behave**

Q4. The Sprite Editor lets you...

- A. **Divide an image into multiple sprites**

Test Your Knowledge Answers

Chapter 6- Continuing the 2D Adventure

Q1. `OnTriggerExit2D` is...

- **B. A function that runs when an object leaves a trigger**

Q2. A Canvas Group lets you

- **B. Change the Alpha of multiple UI Objects**

Q3. Enumerations are good for...

- **A. Storing lists of values**

Q4. You can pick a random number by using

- **A. Random.Range**

Chapter 7- Creating Artificial Intelligence

Q1. You can generate a walkable surface of the level for AI by using...

- **C. Navigation Mesh**

Q2. The Animator Window of Mechanim is useful for...

- **A. Controlling when and how animations play**

Q3. To walk on a Navigation Mesh, an object needs...

- **C. A NavMesh Agent Component**

Q4. You can edit animation interpolation by changing...

- **B. Keyframe Curves**

Q5. The blue local axis arrow of an object is known as...

- **A. Forward Vector**

Chapter 8- Continuing with Intelligent Enemies

Q1. Many AI behaviours can be encoded using...

- A. **Finite State Machine**

Q2. States can be created using a...

- A. **Coroutine**

Q3. One alternative to a State Machine is...

- B. **Behaviour Tree**

Q4. Yield Statements are often used to...

- A. **Pause and Terminate Coroutines**

Q5. Line of Sight determines...

- C. **Whether one object can see another**

Chapter 9- Entering Virtual Reality

Q1. XR stands for...

- A. **Extended Realities**

Q2. Light Probes are useful for...

- A. **Adding Indirect Illumination to Moving Objects**

Q3. Emissive lighting can

- B. **Cast light from mesh surfaces via materials**

Q4. The Post Processing Stack 2 includes

- **Post Processing Volumes**

Chapter 10- Completing the VR Game

Q1. Particle Systems do NOT support object collisions

- A. **FALSE**

Q2. FSM stands for

- A. **Finite State Machine**

Q3. Oculus Rift is supported on Mac computers

- B. **False**

Q4. `OVRInput` is primarily used to

- A. **Read input from Oculus Touch Controllers**

Other Books You May Enjoy

If you enjoyed this book, you may be interested in these other books by Packt:

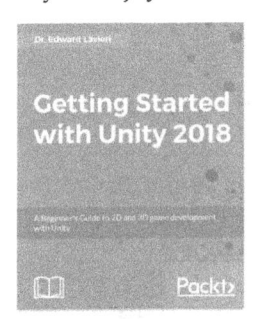

Getting Started with Unity 2018 - Third Edition

Dr. Edward Lavieri

ISBN: 978-1-78883-010-2

- Set up your Unity development environment and navigate its tools
- Import and use custom assets and asset packages to add characters to your game
- Build a 3D game world with a custom terrain, water, sky, mountains, and trees
- Animate game characters, using animation controllers, and scripting
- Apply audio and particle effects to the game
- Create intuitive game menus and interface elements
- Customize your game with sound effects, shadows, lighting effects, and rendering options
- Debug code and provide smooth error handling

Unity Virtual Reality Projects - Second Edition
Jonathan Linowes

ISBN: 978-1-78847-880-9

- Create 3D scenes with Unity and other 3D tools while learning about world space and scale
- Build and run VR applications for specific headsets, including Oculus, Vive, and Daydream
- Interact with virtual objects using eye gaze, hand controllers, and user input events
- Move around your VR scenes using locomotion and teleportation
- Implement an audio fireball game using physics and particle systems
- Implement an art gallery tour with teleportation and data info
- Design and build a VR storytelling animation with a soundtrack and timelines
- Create social VR experiences with Unity networking

Leave a review - let other readers know what you think

Please share your thoughts on this book with others by leaving a review on the site that you bought it from. If you purchased the book from Amazon, please leave us an honest review on this book's Amazon page. This is vital so that other potential readers can see and use your unbiased opinion to make purchasing decisions, we can understand what our customers think about our products, and our authors can see your feedback on the title that they have worked with Packt to create. It will only take a few minutes of your time, but is valuable to other potential customers, our authors, and Packt. Thank you!

Index

Symbols

2D Adventure game
 about 228, 279
 ammo and hazards 302-311
 camera orthographic size, configuring 234
 Capsule Collider component, removing 243, 244
 Edge Collider 245-249
 environment, creating 234-242
 gun turrets and ammo 312-324
 imported textures, configuring 231
 kill zones 286, 287
 Non-player Character (NPCs) 314-317
 optimization 270-276
 Physics and Colliders, using 242
 platforms, moving 280-283
 player, creating 249-261
 player movement, scripting 262-270
 resolutions, adding 232, 233
 Rigidbody 2D component, adding 244
 scenes, creating 284, 285
 starting 229
 texture assets, importing 230
 UI health bar 289-300
2D texture settings and Mip Maps
 reference 123
3DS Max 9

A

AddForce
 reference 136
Ammo prefabs, space shooter game
 about 178
 ammo object, building 182
 ammo sprite, aligning 180, 181
 creating 178
 gravity, removing from ammo object 182
 multiple sprites, separating 179
Ammo spawning, space shooter game 185-198
Artificial Intelligence (AI)
 about 327
 creating 329-333
 navigation 343-349
 navigation meshes 343-346, 349
 overview 328
 terrain, constructing 334-342
assets
 importing 9-13
Atlas Texture 250
Attack state 382, 387, 388
Audacity 9

B

Blender 9

C

canvas object
 adding, to scene 202
 canvas scalar component, adjusting 204, 205
 in viewport, examining 202, 203
Chase state 380-382
coin collection game
 about 1, 2
 assets, importing 10-13
 building 104-115

camera, finding on first-person controller 48
coin, adding to collect 57-59
coins, collecting 79,-87
coins, counting 78, 79
console window output 47
first-person controls, using 29
FPSController, adding to scene 43
Game tab 41, 42
level, starting 15-19
lighting 35-39
lighting, enabling 38-40
object, centering to world origin 22, 23
object translating, translate Gizmo used 24
play, testing 41-46
prefabs 87-90
rotate and scale tools, accessing 24
scene, building 30-34
scene, saving 42
sky, enabling 35-37
testing 101-104
timer countdown, creating 91
transformations and navigation 20
water plane, adding 50-56
win condition, handling 96-101
zooming in and out 26-29

coin material
  creating 64-73

Coroutines
  reference 376

C# scripting
  features 74
  in Unity 74-77

D

death and particles
  reference 148
deltaTime
  reference 95, 161

E

emissive lighting 400
enemies 156
enemy AI
  developing 365-373

F

Finite State Machines (FSMs)
  about 431
  Attack state 382
  Chase state 380
  creating 437-443
  overview 373-376
  Patrol state 377
First-In-First-Out (FIFO) object 188
first-person shooter game
  enemies, attacking 443-450
  enemy AI, creating 431-436
  object pool 426-430
  spawning 426-430
  starting with 393-396
FixedUpdate
  reference 266

G

GetAxis function
  reference 135
GI Cache 40
GIMP 9
Gizmo 22
guns
  about 176, 177
  and gun turrets 177

H

Head Mounted Display (HMD) 417

K

kill zones, 2D Adventure game 286, 287

L

LateUpdate
  reference 144
level
  starting 15-19
Light Probes 403
Light Propagation Paths 40
LookRotation
  reference 164

M

material 65
Mathf.MoveTowards function
  reference 301
Maya 9

N

Non-player Character (NPCs) 314-316
NPC character
  building 350-354

O

object caching 186
object pooling 186
OnTriggerEnter function
  reference 84
OnTriggerStay2D
  reference 288
optimizing rendering performance
  reference 73

P

Particle System packages 96
patrolling NPCs
  creating 355-362
Patrol state 377-379
Photoshop 9
platforms, 2D Adventure game
  moving 280-282
pooling 186
post-processing stack
  using 407-414
project 4-8
project folders 4-8

R

RectTransform
  reference 301
Rect Transform tool
  selecting 207
RigidBody2D.Velocity variable
  reference 266

S

scene
  building 30-34
scene lighting
  setting 396-406
scores, space shooter game
  Code Sample 4.4 213
  working with 210-213
ScreenToWorldPoint
  reference 136
SendMessage
  reference 147
space shooter game
  about 121-126
  Ammo prefabs 178
  Ammo spawning 185
  bounds locking 143, 145
  building 223
  camera, configuring 136-142
  completed project 120
  death and particles 148-150
  diagnosis 219-222
  enemies 156-160
  enemy spawning 168
  final touches 214-219
  guns and gun turrets 176, 177
  health 145
  player input 133, 135
  player input, URL 201
  player object, creating 127-132
  scores 202, 210
  testing 219-222
  UI and text objects 202
  user controls 198-201
Sprite Sheet 250
Stats panel
  reference 220

T

text object
  aligning, to screen 210
  creating, for UI 205-208
  text, aligning within boundary 209
timer countdown
  creating 91-96

U

UI health bar, 2D Adventure game
  about 289-300
  Code Sample 6.3, comments 301
Unity
  and projects 2, 3
  documentation, reference 94, 283
Unity Editor 2
Unity Standard Asset packages 15

V

virtual reality (VR) game
  about 393
  preparing for 414-422

CPSIA information can be obtained
at www.ICGtesting.com
Printed in the USA
LVHW061256100722
723139LV00007B/364